Modern Macroeconomics

This comprehensive textbook deals with multidimensional aspects of macroeconomics through lucid presentation of concepts and critical comparison of different schools of thought.

The book explains how the incomes of a country, prices of goods and services, level of employment, interest rates, and so on are determined and how an economy progresses. It attempts to re-establish the existing theories behind the determination of macro variables and the growth process of an economy. In the process, it captures the significance of the debate between the classical orthodox theories and Keynesian modernism and its implications.

Besides adhering to traditional aspects, the volume also focuses on recent developments such as green macroeconomics. Undergraduate and postgraduate students of economics and business economics will find this book immensely helpful.

Dibyendu Banerjee is currently Associate Professor of Economics at Serampore College, West Bengal, India; with 21 years of teaching and research experience in various fields of the subject. He completed his bachelor (Hons.) of economics at R. K. Mission, Narendrapur, West Bengal; and his master's degree at University of Calcutta. He obtained his doctorate from the same university, working under the supervision of Professor Sarbajit Chaudhuri. He started his career as a lecturer in economics at A. K. P. C. Mahavidyalaya, Hooghly. Dr. Banerjee, with his specialisation in advanced economic theory, has contributed several research papers to many renowned national and international journals such as *Research in Economics*, *Economic Modelling*, *International Review of Economics*, and *Finance*. He has coauthored a textbook titled *Macroeconomics: From Short Run to Long Run*. His current research interests include labour economics, development economics, competitive general equilibrium models, and applied microeconomics.

Ramesh Chandra Das is currently Professor at the Department of Economics of Vidyasagar University in the state of West Bengal, India. He has obtained his master's, M. Phil, and PhD in economics from the University of Calcutta. Prof. Das has the teaching and research experience of about 25 years to his credit. His main areas of research lie in theoretical and applied macroeconomics, financial economics, environmental economics and political economics. He has contributed more than 100 research papers to national and international journals and books along with more than a dozen of edited volumes in different areas of the subject. Besides, he has written text and reference books on microeconomics, macroeconomics, and banking economics with internationally reputed publishers for different fields of readers and academicians and has been acting as the editor-in-chief of a couple of refereed journals.

Modern Macroeconomics

Theory, Application, and Sustainability

Dibyendu Banerjee and Ramesh Chandra Das

Routledge
Taylor & Francis Group
LONDON AND NEW YORK

Designed cover image: © Getty Images

First published 2025
by Routledge
4 Park Square, Milton Park, Abingdon, Oxon OX14 4RN

and by Routledge
605 Third Avenue, New York, NY 10158

Routledge is an imprint of the Taylor & Francis Group, an informa business

British Library Cataloguing-in-Publication Data
A catalogue record for this book is available from the British Library

ISBN: 978-1-032-69591-4 (hbk)
ISBN: 978-1-032-81736-1 (pbk)
ISBN: 978-1-003-50113-8 (ebk)

DOI: 10.4324/9781003501138

Typeset in Sabon
by Apex CoVantage, LLC

To our sweet daughters
Aishani
Anureema

Contents

Figures

Tables

Preface

It was indeed a challenging task to write a text cum reference book on macroeconomics for the assortment of students belonging to different curriculums in a position where a collection of good quality books by renowned writers were available in the market. We, as the authors, took the challenge and submitted a book proposal to Routledge, United Kingdom. After a round of review and repeated scrutiny, the publisher decided to move forward with us and the title of the book was agreed on as *Modern Macroeconomics: Theories, Applications, and Sustainability*. It is really an inexplicable pleasure now that said title has now been unveiled before the readers. But the decisive pleasure will only be there when the ultimate deciders, the readers, will be able to grasp the best of the book.

Opening with the Adam Smith's classical thinking about how the capitalistic economies in the world operate in a free market economy up to the fall of this thought until the great Depression of the 1920s and 1930s, the entire economic system was conceptualised around a myth of full employment that corresponds to system in the long run. Whatever was produced was thought to be automatically demanded; there was no necessity on the demand side or analysis of the parts of households, firms, and government sectors in the classical thought. Always the economy produced real sectors with full employment output; there were no monetary effects. Money, according to them, was just a variable outside the purview of the economic modelling, and the role of money was to determine only the price level. The idea about the automatic full employment equilibrium was a noble thought but it broke down during the early 1920s when leading capitalist countries like the USA and UK faced severe unemployment problems with no sufficient demand for the goods sector output to be absorbed. As a way to manage the crisis, in a conference in New Hampshire, J. M. Keynes proposed the active role of demand in the economy which the classical economists drastically discarded in their modelling. Additionally, Keynes argued for the intervention of the government sector into the economic system in an active manner to boost up the volume of aggregate demand which was in a stagnant position. According to him, we are all dead in the long run and stressed in the short run problem related to the depression. His book on general theory started a revolution in the macroeconomic thoughts and showed how a rise in the private or public investment levels led to aggregate output in a multiplier process and solved the persistent unemployment problem. Keynesian economics considers both the real and monetary sectors to play a role in economic activity. After this critical differences of opinion between the classical economists and the Keynesian, there arose the monetarists counterargument by Milton Friedman who argued that the fluctuation in the business cycle was due to fluctuations in the money supply. Next was the New Classical thought which considered how expectations about the economic variables by the economic agents make the policies effective or ineffective. The real business cycle model, after that, which believed in real factors in the business cycle, explains the fluctuation. In the longer run, solving all sorts of problems, an economy will grow on the basis of its accumulated capital stocks, technological progress and endogenous factors, etc. and try to converge into its own steady-state level of output to catch up with the so-called developed economies.

The purpose of the present book is to construct the existing macroeconomic thoughts in a new format so that they can be easily accessible to the students of under graduate and post graduate levels of economics in the country and abroad. The scope of the present book is to analyse the macroeconomic events from the short run to the long run which correspondingly cover the Keynesian simple economics to the growth of analysis of different aspects. The book includes a thorough discussion of different macroeconomic schools of thoughts in very lucid manner suitable to all categories of readers. It also highlights the incorporations of environmental factors into the study of macroeconomics and reorients the traditional tools in line with the environmental pollution factors which will show a route towards sustainable development. The readers will have additional benefits in reading the book since it provides empirical sample results on different theories, applications, illustrations, and multiple-choice questions and answers in each of the chapters.

Though it now sounds good that the title has been unveiled, its credit not only goes to the authors but to the persons and organisations whose active support and cooperation definitely added values to this academic venture. We do not want to miss this opportunity to acknowledge their efforts. First, we must be thankful to the publisher and its editorial portfolio holders for accepting our proposal and accordingly smoothening the process towards publication. We really appreciate the active support and encouragement given by Professor (Retd) Soumyen Sikdar, Indian Institute of Management, Kolkata; (Late) Professor Sarbajit Choudhury, Calcutta University; Professor Asis Kumar Banerjee, formerly of Calcutta University; Professor Sarmila Banerjee, formerly of Calcutta University; Professor Manas Ranjan Gupta, Indian Statistical Institute, Kolkata; (Late) Professor Amaresh Das, Southern University at New Orleans, USA; Dr. Hasan Dincer, Istanbul Medipol University, Turkey; Dr. Enrico Ivaldi, University of Genoa, Italy; Professor Jose Vargas Hernandez, University of Guadalajara, Mexico; Professor Sudhakar Patra, Berhampur University, India; and more. Our colleagues in the department of economics at Serampore College and Vidyasagar University have been supportive and never failed to ask how the book was coming along. We are grateful to all of them.

Last but not least, we must say that we would not have reached the present positions without the blessings of our parents. We also express our gratitude to our spouses Sanchita and Amrita and our sweet daughters, Aishani and Anureema, for enduring the boring period of preparation of the manuscripts. Without their support and encouragement, it would not have been possible to bring such a herculean task to completion.

Dibyendu Banerjee
Ramesh Chandra Das

Part I

Macroeconomics – objectives, instruments, concepts, and phases of developments

1 Why study macroeconomics and what are its objectives?

1.1 Introduction to macroeconomics

Macroeconomics is the study of the behaviour of the economy as a whole as opposed to microeconomics which mainly deals with the individual decision-making process. In the 1930s, Ragnar Frisch classified economics into these two branches – *micro* and *macro*. Although any economy consists of millions of economic agents interacting with each other in the market on the basis of their own preference, macroeconomics concentrates on those macro relationships which are important from the perspective of the functioning of the entire economy. According to Paul Samuelson, "Macroeconomics is the study of the behaviour of the economy as a whole. It examines the forces that affect many firms, consumers, and workers at the same tine". Thus, as the definition indicates, it studies the determination of broad aggregates of an economy, like aggregate production, employment, aggregate price level, and the unemployment situation of a country rather than what goes on at the individual level. It is also concerned with interest rates, foreign exchange rates, financial markets, and the overall effects of government policies. It seeks to explain how the economy grows and fluctuates over time and studies various policy measures that can be adopted to ensure short run stability and long run growth of the economy. Macroeconomics is of crucial importance because macroeconomic events have an important influence on the lives and welfare of all of us. Macroeconomics as a distinct branch of economics emerged after the publication of the revolutionary book *The General Theory of Employment, Interest and Money* by English economist John Maynard Keynes in 1936. To understand how different social and political issues are continuously affecting our lives, we need to have a clear understanding of macroeconomics. An economy that has successful macroeconomic management should experience high employment, low inflation, and sustained economic growth. Let us first concentrate on the evolution of macroeconomics.

1.1.1 Evolution of macroeconomic schools of thought

Evolution of the subject of "macroeconomics" is based on the developments of different schools of thought arguing in favour of their own paradigms. The earliest paradigm originates from the mercantilist approach which originated from the rise of the nation-state in Europe during the sixteenth and seventeenth centuries. It believes in the myth that a country's progress is dependent upon the stock of precious metals like gold and silver, and the stock of these metals can be achieved by state endorsed favourable international trade. This approach is called *bullionism*. Till the age of mercantilism, there

DOI: 10.4324/9781003501138-2

was no formal theory on economics. The first theoretical model on macroeconomics was developed by the physiocrats in France. They criticised the mercantilists on the grounds that the trade sector was unproductive and could not produce surplus. The concept of circular flow of output among different sectors was established in the *Tableau economique* of Francois Quesnay in the mid of the eighteenth century. The physiocrats believed that the growth of an economy depended upon the growth of the agricultural sector and that agriculture is the only sector that can generate surplus.

In the late 1880s, a new group of economists, called classical economists, claimed that entire wealth of the nation could be managed and controlled by the free market mechanism; no state control was required (laissez faire). The proponents of the classical school of thought are Adam Smith, David Ricardo, J. S. Mill, R. Malthus, etc. In 1776, Adam Smith's *An Inquiry into the Nature and Causes of the Wealth of Nations* was published, in which he set forth the invisible hand theorem and denied the possibility of general overproduction or underproduction. The pursuit of self-interest and laissez faire policy is at the heart of the philosophy of classical macroeconomics. The invisible hand and free-market principles failed during the great depression of the 1930s and orthodox classical economists could not find a suitable answer to the causes of such a deep and prolonged depression. The Keynesian Revolution emerged as a possible solution to the classical failure. The Keynesian approach was that of a short run system and there were the conditions of sticky prices and slumps in aggregate demand that were identified as the cause of depression, and thus he opined for the active intervention of the government sector into economic activities. Keynesian postulates achieved remarkable success in combating depression and it continued until the 1970s. It is popularly known in the macroeconomic literature as the "era of stabilisation optimism".

The defect of the Keynesian system was observed in the 1970s when the US economy suffered from the long-term stagflation. The new school, called "monetarists", was founded by Milton Friedman who strongly criticised the Keynesian orthodoxy and opined that economic agents' expectations of inflation should be given importance. They maintained that most fluctuations in real output were caused by fluctuations in the money supply, rather than by fluctuations in consumption or investment spending like that of Keynes. In addition, they proposed that a stable and consistent money supply policy could control price instability and that no government intervention was desirable.

The classical followers, motivated by the monetarists and challenging the Keynesian orthodoxy, formed a new school of thought called "new classical" which heavily depended upon the roles of rational behaviours of the economic agents in deciding their personal objectives. A popular theory, rational expectation, was developed by three well-known economists, Robert Lucas, Thomas Sargent, and Robert Barro. Policy ineffectiveness was established by the theory because of rational behaviour of the economic agents on the basis of microeconomic tools and thus it justified the central proposition of the classical economists. The economic fluctuations during the 1980s pinpointed the failure of the rational expectation hypothesis. The proponents of real business cycle (RBC) theory like Edward Prescott and Finn Kydland agreed to the rational expectation hypothesis of the new classicists but did not agree to why there were fluctuations in real GDP. According to them, it was the temporary shocks to productivity that explained fluctuations in real GDP. The RBC model focuses on real factors like decline in the availability of oil or other raw materials or technological progress that creates productivity shocks rather than changes in the quantity of money. Real business cycle theory categorically rejects Keynesian economics.

The new classical school and their followers, the RBC theoreticians, tried to establish that Keynesian doctrine was dead and there was nothing to justify their positions regarding the economic fluctuations. James Tobin, an old follower of Keynes, reacted sharply to the claim of the new classicists and RBC theoreticians and established that the Keynesian economics was not dead, rather it had lot to offer. A new Keynesian school known as New Keynesian economics emerged through Robin Bade and Michael Parkin, Gregory Mankiw, and others. They paid respect to the rational expectation hypothesis but assumed a variety of market failures like the presence of market imperfections or monopolistic structure in price and wage setting to explain why prices and wages can become sticky. That means, on the basis of microeconomic arguments, their claim of involuntary unemployment persisted and thus the New Keynesians argued that macroeconomic stabilisation by the government using fiscal policy or by the central bank of the country using monetary policy could lead to a more efficient macroeconomic outcome than the classicists' laissez faire policy would. The economic events of the late twentieth century and to date show the applicability of the combinations of new classical and new Keynesian schools.

1.2 Goals of macroeconomics

Before studying macroeconomic theory, we must discuss the major goals and instruments of macroeconomic policy. There are three major macroeconomic goals:

i) High and rapid growth of national output
ii) High level of employment with low involuntary unemployment
iii Stable prices

We discuss these goals one by one.

1.2.1 Growth of national output

Let us first discuss the first issue – that is the issue of output growth. The ultimate objective of economic activity is to provide the goods and services that the population desires. A country's wellbeing depends mainly on the availability of goods and services for consumption. With higher output growth, society will have more goods and services at its disposal and a correspondingly better standard of living. The most comprehensive measure of the total output of an economy is gross domestic product (GDP). GDP is the measure of the market value of all final goods and services produced within the geographical territory of a country during the year. Figure 1.1 shows how India's GDP has been changing during 1991–2021, as per World Bank data source. The vertical axis measures GDP in USD and the horizontal axis shows different years. Overall the trend demonstrates that, except the pandemic years, there is no substantial fluctuation in GDP from 1991–2021.

The fact that GDP includes only current production means that we need not count raw materials and the intermediate products while calculating it. In this respect we should make a distinction between *final and intermediate products*. Products that come out at the ultimate stage of the production process are known as the final product. On the other hand, the products which are being used up in the production of other goods during the same period in which they were produced are known as intermediate products. In GDP calculation intermediate products like wheat should not be double counted when final

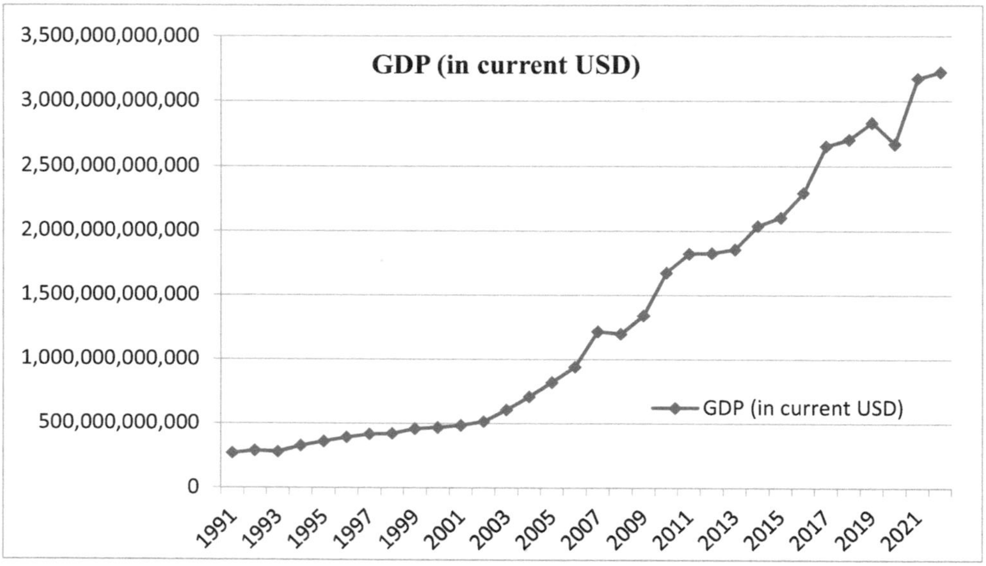

Figure 1.1 GDP in India from 1991–2021

Source: World Development Indicators

output, like flour, is produced. There are two approaches to avoid this error of double counting: to consider only the sales of final goods or to consider value added by all the economic entities. An economic agent's value added is calculated by subtracting costs from his revenue.

There are two different concepts of GDP. *Nominal GDP* is measured in terms of current market prices whereas real GDP is calculated in terms of constant or base year prices. To explain, the economic progress of a country, the concept of real GDP, is more useful, as it is free from the effect of inflation. Hence, growth of *real GDP* reflects the nature of economic growth of a country. Advanced economies generally exhibit a steady long-term growth in real GDP and an improvement in living standards. One thing should be pointed out in this respect. Real GDP or the aggregate output of the economy is either sold or added to stocks. The proceeds of sales of goods must cover the costs of production and allow for profit.

So total value of output produced or nominal GDP must equal the total value of income generated in producing the output. Concepts of nominal and real GDP and the associated problem with its measurement and the idea of the value-added method will be discussed in detail in Chapter 2.

Now we make another important distinction between *actual and potential GDP*. Actual GDP represents what the economy actually produces. It is affected largely by business cycles. A related concept is potential GDP, which measures what the economy could produce if all its resources where fully employed at their normal rates of utilisation. In other words, the market value of all final goods and services within a country in a year represents actual GDP and the maximum sustainable level of output that a country can produce in a given year is known as potential GDP. This is sometimes referred to as potential income or full employment income. Potential GDP is determined by economy's productive capacity which in turn depends upon the available resources as well as on the economy's technical efficiency. Potential GDP tends to grow steadily over time because the economy's resource allocation and technological improvement take place quite slowly overtime. When an economy is operating at its potential, there are high rates of utilisation of an economy's resources. Government, by changing its policy instruments, can increase the growth rate of potential output. When output rises above the potential level, inflation rises, while a below-potential level of output leads to high unemployment. During *business downturns or recession*, when demand is sluggish, actual GDP falls below its potential level and unemployment rises. So, a recession occurs when real GDP is unusually low relative to its trend value which might last for six months to a year. The end of each recession is called a *trough*. A severe downturn in the business cycle is called a *depression*. Output can be temporarily above potential levels during *booms* or high economic activity. In this situation capacity limits are strained but the high utilisation rates bring rising inflation. It can be controlled by suitable monetary and fiscal policies.

After getting the concepts of actual and potential GDP, now we are in a position to clarify another related concept known as output gap. *Output gap* or *GDP gap* measures the difference between what could have been produced if potential or fully employed GDP had been achieved and what is actually produced. The gap is calculated by subtracting actual GDP (Y) from Potential GDP (Y^*). This GDP gap is positive, i.e., $(Y^* - Y) > 0$, when $Y^* > Y$. The goods and services that are not produced when the economy is operating below Y^* are permanently lost to the economy. As these losses occur when employable resources are unused, they are often called dead-weight loss of unemployment. When the economy is operating below its potential level, the output gap is called *recessionary gap*.

During booms or periods of optimism, actual GDP may exceed potential GDP, i.e., $Y > Y^*$, causing the output gap to become negative i.e., $(Y^* - Y) < 0$. Actual output can exceed potential output because potential GDP is defined as a normal rate of utilisation of the economy's resources or factors of production. But this normal rate can be

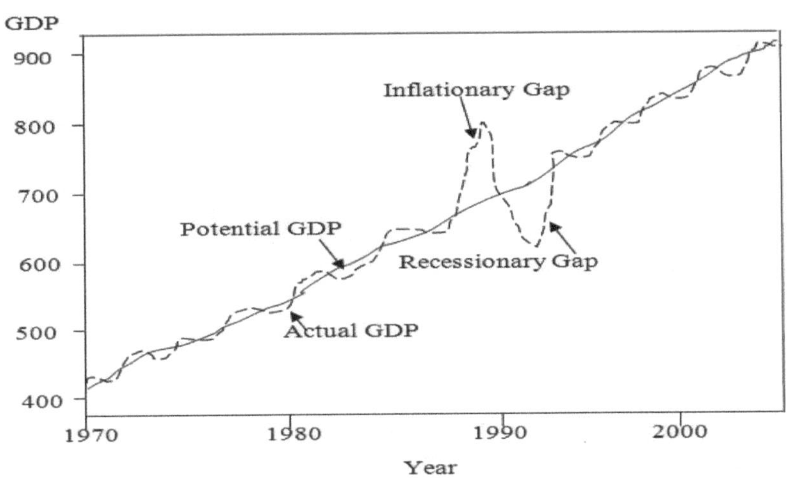

Figure 1.2 Potential GDP, actual GDP, and GDP gap

increased temporarily. Workers may work longer hours; factories can operate an extra shift or not close for routine maintenance. When actual GDP exceeds the potential level then there is generally upward pressure on prices. For this reason, when $Y > Y^*$ the output gap is called *inflationary gap*. Diagram 1.2 is used to visualise the concepts explained earlier, taking hypothetical data on GDP on the vertical axis and years on the horizontal axis. The upward rising curve, shown by a solid line, represents potential GDP, and that with the dashed line represents actual GDP. Despite short term fluctuations, the country concerned exhibits a steady long-term growth in GDP from 1970 onwards. This will definitely improve the living standard of the countrymen. Recessionary and inflationary gaps are also depicted in the same diagram. Policymakers may try to reduce this output gap through suitable stabilisation policies. Expansionary fiscal and monetary policies like reduction in taxes, increase in government expenditure, monetary relaxation, etc. can raise effective demand and control the recessionary gap. Contractionary fiscal and monetary policies, on the other hand, might be effective in reducing the inflationary gap. One point should be mentioned in this connection –GDP is a measure of value of production of final goods sold on markets; it does not measure pollution, crime, health, leisure time, qualities of goods, or quality of life. These points are elaborated on in the next chapter of the book.

1.2.2 *Employment and unemployment issues*

The greater the level of employment, the greater will be the amount of goods and services available to the society. People always want to get high-paying, secure jobs without searching too long. High employment or low unemployment is thus another important macroeconomic objective of every economy. Unemployment is perhaps the most worrisome macroeconomic problem in any country. Voluntary unemployment may be okay but forced or involuntary unemployment is extremely bad, leading to loss of income or output and feelings of desperation.

Conceptually, a person is *employed* if he is working for a paid job or temporarily absent from the job because of illness, vacation, etc. Similarly, a person is *unemployed* if he is not employed and has been looking for a job during the prior four weeks. It also includes those waiting to be recalled to a job from which they have been laid off. The government classifies people who do not have jobs but have given up hope of finding them and stopped looking as *discouraged workers*; they are considered as *not in the labour force*. Examples of this category are home makers, retirees, chronically sick people, full-time students, etc. The *labour force* includes all employed persons and those unemployed individuals who are seeking jobs. It excludes those without work or those who are not looking for jobs. Level of unemployment is usually measured by unemployment rate. *Unemployment rate* is defined as the ratio of the number of those unemployed and the total work force multiplied by 100.

$$\text{Unemployment rate} = \frac{\text{Number of Unemployed}}{\text{Total Labour Force}} \times 100$$

When output is falling, the demand for labour falls and the unemployment rate rises. Higher unemployment rate indicates a greater level of divergence between actual and potential GDPs. On the other hand, the lower unemployment rate indicates a smaller divergence.

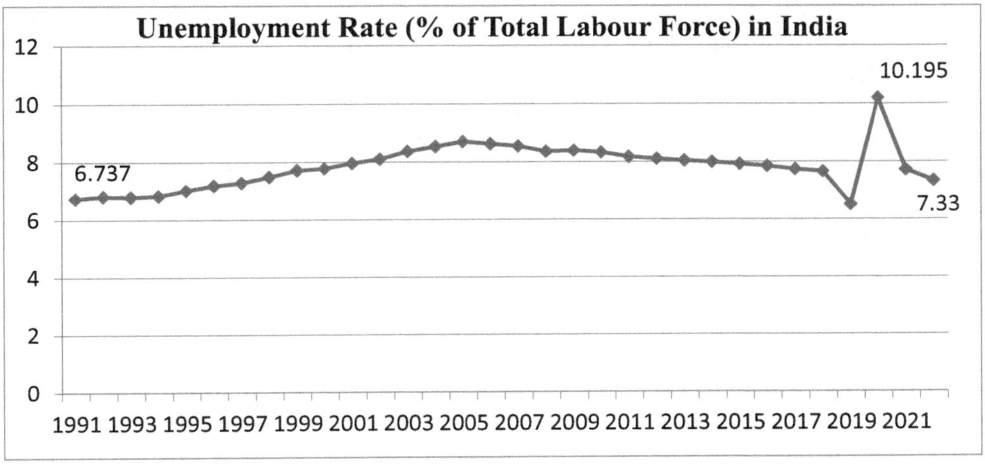

Figure 1.3 Unemployment rate in India, 1991–2021

Source: World Development Indicators

Figure 1.3 shows how the unemployment rate is changing in India for the time period 1991–2021. The vertical axis measures unemployment rate and the horizontal axis shows different years. The overall trend shows that there is no substantial fluctuation in unemployment rate during 1991–2019, reaching a maximum value of 8.7% in 2005 and a minimum of 6.51% in 2019. From 2008 onwards, the unemployment rate declined steadily up to 2019. It shoots up to the highest value of 10.19 % in 2020 because of lockdown as a result of the COVID-19 pandemic.

Let us now discuss the classification of unemployment. There are many ways of classifying unemployment among which the following are the most common.

Frictional or turnover unemployment arises while transitioning between different jobs or just entering the labour market. Though the labour market serves to match available jobs with available workers, this can be a time-consuming process as both workers and jobs are heterogeneous. This type of unemployment is known as *equilibrium unemployment*, because the market is clearing properly in the sense that those who desire jobs at the going wages and working conditions can find it. People are unemployed because they prefer that state over other labour market states, hence it is *voluntary* in nature. Such unemployment is quite prevalent in developed countries where jobs are very demanding and available in plenty. Workers take off from their current jobs to be available full time to find more suitable jobs at higher wages. Though short in duration, this unemployment is always present in a market economy as the economy is always changing. It is a healthy phenomenon of a dynamic growing economy and creates no serious burden.

Structural unemployment is a longer term and chronic form of unemployment as compared to frictional unemployment. This often occurs in the period of economic change when new jobs are being created having requirements of different skills. It is thus caused by the mismatch of vacancies and skills of unemployed people. This type of mismatch between supply of and demand for labour can occur because the demand for one kind of labour is rising and that of another kind is falling and markets do not quickly adjust.

Speaking differently, the unemployment that arises when changes in technology or international competition change the skills needed to perform jobs is called structural unemployment. With the booming of information technology, sophistication in production of goods and services, and the changing structure of economies away from the primary sector and towards the secondary and tertiary sectors, traditional jobs are disappearing. However traditional workers lack the education and training that is a prerequisite for working in the new emerging jobs. This leads to structural unemployment until traditional workers are retained and reemployed. This type of unemployment also arises when there exist labour market barriers to employment, such as downward inflexibility of wages caused by minimum wage law imposed by government or a union's collective bargaining or efficiency wages. So structural unemployment that arises from wage rigidity is different from frictional unemployment that arises from the process of the job search. In the case of a job search, workers are searching for jobs that best suit their taste and skill. On the other hand, wage is fixed above equilibrium level, labour supply exceeds labour demand, and workers are waiting for jobs to open up.

Cyclical unemployment refers to the year-to-year fluctuations in unemployment around its natural rate. Natural rate of unemployment (NRU) is the steady-state rate of unemployment around which the actual rate of unemployment fluctuates in the long run. It refers to a situation when all the unemployment is frictional and structural (and seasonal but no cyclical unemployment). Cyclical unemployment is caused by business cycles and economic fluctuations. This type of unemployment increases when there is a slowdown in economic activity and overall decline in labour demand during business cycle downturn. When there is an expansion in economic activity and real output, the actual unemployment rate is lower than the natural rate, and cyclical unemployment is negative. Thus,

Cyclical unemployment = Total unemployment – Natural rate of unemployment

A worker who is laid off because the economy is in a recession and who gets rehired some months later when the expansion begins has experienced cyclical unemployment. This type of *demand-deficient unemployment* occurs when aggregate spending in the economy is insufficient to purchase the output that would be supplied when the economy is at potential GDP. Structural and cyclical unemployment are known as *disequilibrium unemployment* as the macroeconomy is not functioning properly in this situation. Qualified workers who are willing to work at the going wage cannot find jobs, so it is *involuntary* in nature. In macroeconomics *full employment* occurs when there is no cyclical unemployment but there will exist frictional, structural, and some seasonal unemployment.

We may now turn to another type of unemployment, prevalent in most countries. Some occupations are seasonal, for example agriculture, tourism, etc. Unemployment that varies with the seasons is called *seasonal unemployment*. For example, farmers are occupied a lot during the Kharif (June–October) and Rabi (December–March) seasons and have little work during the lean periods. Unless these farmers diversify and take up some other activities during the off seasons they will be seasonally unemployed. Such off seasons arise even in agro-based industries e.g., sugar, tea, food processing, etc.

The focus of macroeconomics is to reduce cyclical unemployment such that full employment or natural rate of unemployment can be achieved.

1.2.3 Price stability

The third macroeconomic objective is to maintain price stability, which means that the overall price level is either unchanged or is rising very slowly. To measure the overall price level statisticians often construct price indices. An important price index is the *consumer price index (CPI)* which measures the average price of goods and services bought by consumers.

Price stability can be checked by looking at inflation rates. *Inflation* refers to a sustained rise in price level. It can be of different types depending on its severity. Inflation beyond a certain mild level is harmful for the economy, because it affects the standard of living of the common people. But a mild inflation is beneficial for the economic progress as it acts as an incentive to producers. When the inflationary situation reaches an alarming level, the concerned government can take appropriate fiscal and monetary measures. To gauge the nature and trend of an inflationary situation, the concept of *inflation rate* is also used which is the percentage change in the overall level of prices from one year to the next. *Deflation* occurs when prices decline. It may be viewed as negative inflation. *Hyperinflation* is a situation where price level rises a thousand or million percent per year. Such a situation occurred in Germany in 1920 where prices virtually became meaningless and the price system broke-down. Price stability or stable inflation is important because a smooth functioning market system requires that prices accurately and easily convey information about relative scarcity. With high inflation, taxes become highly variable, the real values of people's fixed income like pensions are eroded, and people are forced to spend real resources. But declining prices or deflation is also costly. Hence most nations want to achieve slowly rising prices as the best way of encouraging the price system. Details regarding types, causes, and effects of inflation and the nature and costs of hyperinflation are discussed in Chapter 13 of the book.

The *GDP deflator* is the measure of inflation that takes into account the inflation in all the goods and services produced in the economy. Other measures of inflation are the wholesale price index (WPI) and the consumer price index (CPI). These are calculated by selecting a fixed set of goods rather than all goods available in an economy. The bundle of goods used in calculating the WPI is different from that incorporated into the calculation of the CPI.

The *consumer price index (CPI)* is the weighted sum of prices of the set of goods and services that consumers purchase each year. It can be constructed using the following formula

$$\text{CPI} = \frac{\text{Total cost of the goods in the current year}}{\text{Total cost of the goods in the base year}} \times 100$$

Normally the government conducts a survey to determine the importance of different expenditures by the average household. Weights are assigned to the different expenditure categories to reflect the importance of each in household spending. Unlike the CPI, the *wholesale price index (WPI)* measures price change from the perspective of the seller. WPI measures the average level of price of goods sold by producer. If producers are receiving higher prices from their sales to wholesalers, we could expect that sooner or later the retailer would have to charge higher prices. This will then be reflected in a higher CPI. Both the WPI and the CPI are measured using base year quantities as weights. Both the WPI and the CPI represent only a subset of all the goods and services produced by

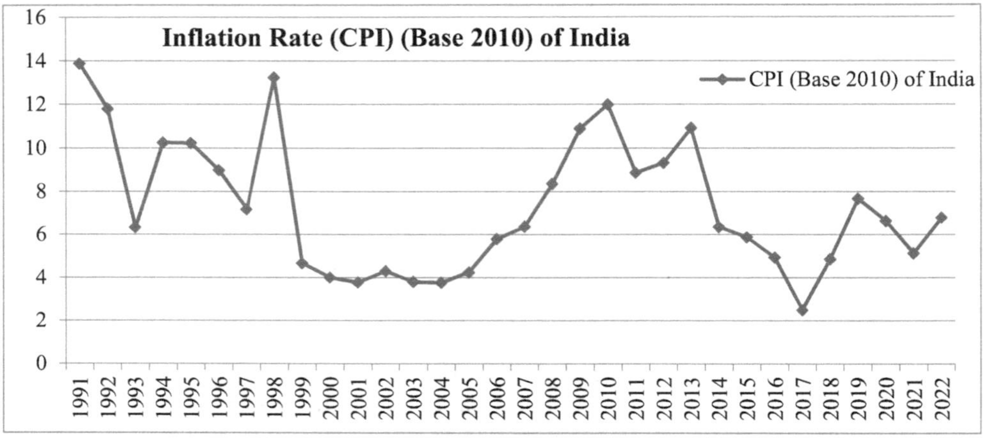

Figure 1.4 Inflation rate in India based on the CPI

Source: World Development Indicators

the entire economy and so may not reflect all changes in price levels. Hence the GDP deflator – CPI and WPI measure average prices only imperfectly and each has limitations.

Figure 1.4 shows the trend of inflation rates in India from 1991–2022 based on the CPI. In the horizontal axis we have considered different years and the vertical axis measures the inflation rate in percentage terms. The graph demonstrates that inflation was much higher and more volatile during 1990s in India. It started declining from 13.23% in 1998 and reached its lowest figure of 3.77% in 2001, then again started rising more or less steadily and reached around 12% in 2010. During 2017 inflation rate declined to 2.49%. In fact, a sudden jump in CPI from 1998–1999 was due to excessive increase in food prices, mainly potato and onion, during that year mainly because of inadequate production. During 2019–2021 it took a downturn mainly because of lack of aggregate demand due to pandemic crisis all over the world. More detailed analysis including a comparison between CPI and GDP deflators is done in Chapter 2.

1.2.4 *Okun's law*

After discussing the objectives of output growth and unemployment reduction we need to mention an important relationship relating to these two goals. Arthur Okun first pointed out that in the short run, unemployment and output are pretty tightly linked. As an economy gets out of a recession, output increases by a greater percentage than the rise in employment. Similarly, when the economy moves into a recession, output decreases by a greater percentage than the reduction in employment. Okun's law allows us to link fluctuation in the unemployment rate with the fluctuations in the output gap. The relationship between actual and potential output and between actual and benchmark unemployment can be formally expressed as follows:

$$\frac{Y - Y^*}{Y^*} = -\omega(u - u^*);$$

Where ω is known as Okun's coefficient and its estimated value is around 2.

Y^* and Y, as before, represent potential and actual output; u and u^* are actual and benchmark unemployment rate. The left-hand side of the expression represents the output gap expressed as percentage of actual output. Taking USA data of 1930 to 1980, Okun estimated that

Rate of change in real GDP = 3.0 – 2 Rate of change in unemployment rate.

According to this law, a rise in one percentage point in the unemployment rate causes the economy to lose 2% of its output. This also indicates that the growth rate in real GDP would be 3% if the unemployment rate remained the same. This normal growth in the production of goods and services is a result of growth in the labour force, capital accumulation, and technological progress. The growth rate in real GDP would fall to nil if the unemployment rate increased by 1.5%. It should be mentioned here that this estimate constitutes no iron law, as it is an average result. This could vary over space as well as time. Though for India, we do not have such estimate.

1.3 Instruments of macroeconomic analysis

Macroeconomics is also concerned with the effect of various governmental activities that can be used to achieve the targeted goals mentioned in previous section. Governments have certain policy instruments which they can use to raise potential GDP or to raise employment or to contain inflation within a limit.

Fiscal policy, which is the prime instrument of macroeconomic policy, refers to government actions that affect total *government spending*, tax rates, and revenues. It is primarily employed today to affect long term economic growth through its national saving and the incentive to work and save. Government expenditure comes in two distinct forms. The first component of government expenditure is government purchases. These comprise spending on goods and services, for example, construction of roads, salaries of judges, and expenditure on health and education and on other administrative expenses. The effect of increase in government purchase on the economy depends on how productive the spending is and how the government pays for its spending. Another component is *government transfer payment*. Social security payments and unemployment compensation payments are examples of this category. It boosts the incomes of targeted groups, such as the unemployed, the elderly, pensioners, etc. Transfer payments can affect demand and supply for various goods and services. It raises demand for goods purchased by individuals who receive transfers and decreases the demand of individuals who pay the taxes to finance this transfer payment. Aggregate demand rises if the government transfers money from people who save most to people who spend most of each rupee.

Another tool of fiscal policy is *taxation*. It affects the economy in two ways. Primarily taxes affect an individual's income level. In leading households with more or less disposable income, taxes tend to affect the amount people spend on goods and services as well as the amount of private saving. Private saving has an important effect on equilibrium investment, the country's capital stock, and thereby the aggregate output of the country. We know advances in technology result from investment in research and development. Increase in taxes that reduce this investment may slow down the growth of technology. In addition, indirect taxes affect the prices of goods and factors of production and thereby affect incentives and behaviour of people, which in turns affect the resource allocation process in an economy. Taxes are also considered an important instrument to combat inequality and poverty in an economy.

The second major instrument of macroeconomic policy is the *monetary policy*, which is conducted through managing the nation's money, credit, and banking system. Monetary policy refers to changes in the nominal money supply through open market operations or other actions by a central bank. Monetary policy has an important effect on both actual and potential GDP. By changing the money supply, the central bank of a country can influence different economic variables like interest rate, foreign exchange rates, etc. In times of inflation, tight monetary policy or contractionary monetary policy is undertaken. It causes a reduction in money supply in an economy, leading to an increase in interest rate. This increased rate of interest reduces investment as well as GDP. Consequently, inflation is controlled to some extent. On the other hand, in times of high unemployment, expansionary or cheap monetary policy is adopted by the government. It increases the money supply in the economy and decreases interest rate. Investment increases as a result, leading to an increase in aggregate demand and national income. Accordingly, the unemployment is reduced to some extent.

Friedman opined that economists' knowledge of the state of the economy is not adequate to stabilise output. Policymakers could not be trusted to do the right thing. So, he suggested the use of steady growth in money supply. This may not imply perfect stability but it would prevent output fluctuations over time, though there are serious limitations to the use of discretionary monetary policy and it may sometimes make the situation worse.

1.4 Tools used to achieve the targets

In this section we will apply two important tools of macroeconomics and see how these two opposite forces can be used to explain some important macroeconomic activities including economic fluctuations. These two tools are aggregate supply (AS) and aggregate demand (AD) curves. *Aggregate supply* shows the total amount of output that production units or firms are willing to produce in a given period. AS curve, in price quantity plane, will be upward sloping in the short run, as firms want to sell more at a higher price. Upward slope of the short run aggregate supply curve is derived and explained in Chapter 11, using the micro foundation of macroeconomics. It has also been shown there that the AS curve will be vertical at the potential level of output in long run. Position and shape of the AS curve depends on overall price level, productive capacity of the economy or potential output, and costs or technology.

Aggregate demand (AD), on the other hand, refers to the total amount that different sectors in the economy are willing to spend in the given period. Aggregate demand is thus the sum of spending by the firms, consumers, and government (assuming a temporarily closed economy). It is determined by the aggregate price level and influenced by investment, government spending, consumption function, and money supply. It is also influenced by exogenous forces like weather condition, war, etc. As aggregate price level increases, total spending by all the economic units decreases (with other factors affecting aggregate demand remaining constant). Thus, the AD curve will be downward sloping. Its position and shift depend on the fiscal and monetary policy of the government. Detail derivation of the AD curve is carried out in Chapter 11.

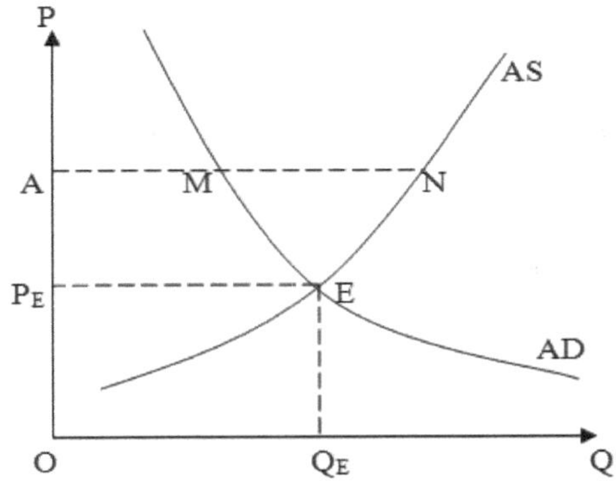

Figure 1.5 Macroeconomic equilibrium

1.4.1 *Aggregate demand supply analysis and macroeconomic equilibrium*

Using both the tools, AD and AS, we can demonstrate the *macroeconomic equilibrium* position. National output and price level are determined where AD and AS curves intersect each other. In the diagram AD and AS curves of an economy are drawn, measuring national output on the horizontal axis and price level on the vertical axis.

Macroeconomic equilibrium is a combination of overall price and quantity at which all buyers and sellers are satisfied with their purchases, sales, and prices. In Figure 1.5, *E* represents equilibrium position where *AD* and *AS* intersect each other. P_E and Q_E are the equilibrium price and output respectively. If $P > P_E$, then firms would like to sell more than the purchasers would want. According to this diagram at price *OA*, sellers would desire to sell quantity *AN*, where buyers would want to purchase quantity *AM*. Hence, inventory accumulation takes place. In other words, goods would pile up on the shelves of firms. But once the equilibrium is reached, neither buyer nor seller wishes to change the quantity demanded and supplied. There is no pressure on the price level to change either.

1.4.2 *Effects on macroeconomic equilibrium*

In this section we will examine the impacts of certain policy changes and changes in economic fundamentals on the equilibrium using the AD–AS apparatus.

First consider the impact of a *large cut in personal and business taxes* on the economy. A large cut in personal and business taxes will increase the disposable income of the individuals, which will increase the aggregate consumption expenditures. We know the consumption is an important item of AD or aggregate spending. As consumption increases due to tax cuts, AD will also increase. Diagrammatically, the AD curve will shift rightward, with the AS curve remaining unchanged. Both equilibrium price and quantity will increase.

In times of recession this type of expansionary fiscal policy will help to reduce unemployment and make price stable. Initially the equilibrium point was E_0, but after the tax cut it becomes E_1, as shown in Figure 1.6. So, price rises from P_E to P_1 and output rises from Q_E to Q_1.

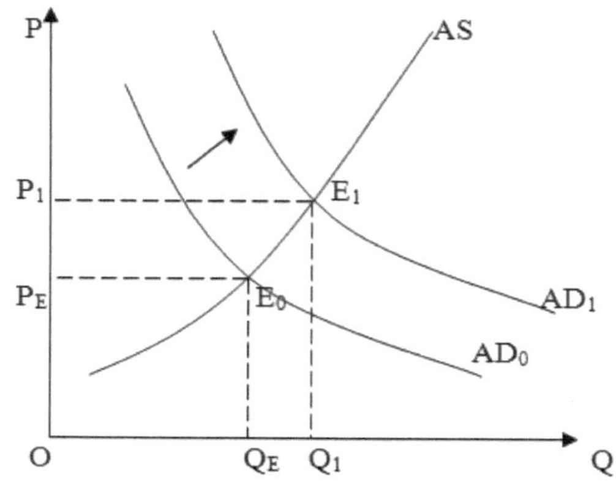

Figure 1.6 Impact of tax cut on the economy

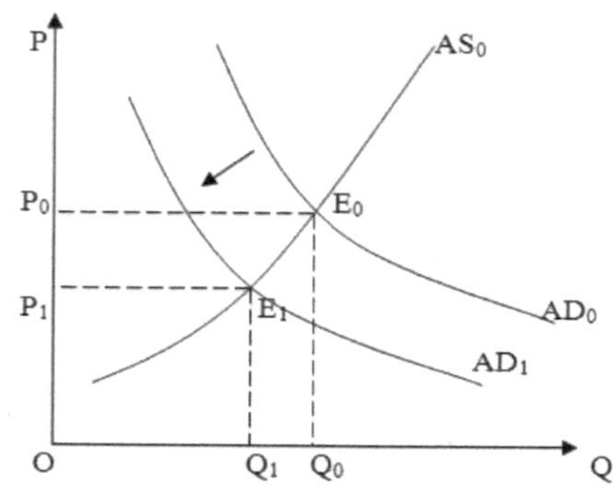

Figure 1.7 Impact of reduction in defence expenditure

Next, we consider the impact of adoption of *an arms reduction agreement* which reduces defence spending, an example of contractionary fiscal policy.

Arms reduction agreement is a part of government spending on defence which, in turn, is a part of government expenditure on goods and services. So, in this particular situation government expenditure will fall, leading to a leftward shift of the AD curve, which will reduce price and output and increase unemployment, as shown in Figure 1.7.

Now, we analyse the impact of an *increase in a potential output* on the macroeconomic equilibrium. Potential output is determined by an economy's resource endowment and the managerial and technical efficiency of the production units. An increase in potential output (may be due to an increase in productivity) will increase aggregate supply in the economy, leading to a rightward shift of the AS curve.

Figure 1.8 demonstrates this impact on price and employment level of the economy. Clearly, price level falls from its initial position P_0 to P_1, while increase in output leads to a reduction in economy's unemployment level.

Let us now see what happens to the economy as a result of a *monetary relaxation* by the government. Monetary relaxation is an example of expansionary monetary policy

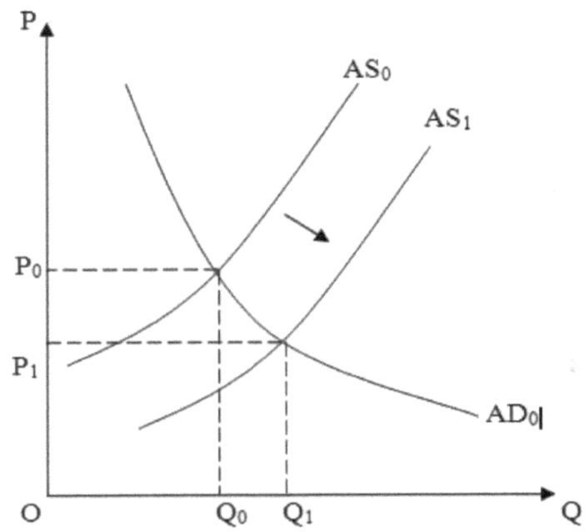

Figure 1.8 Impact of increase in potential output

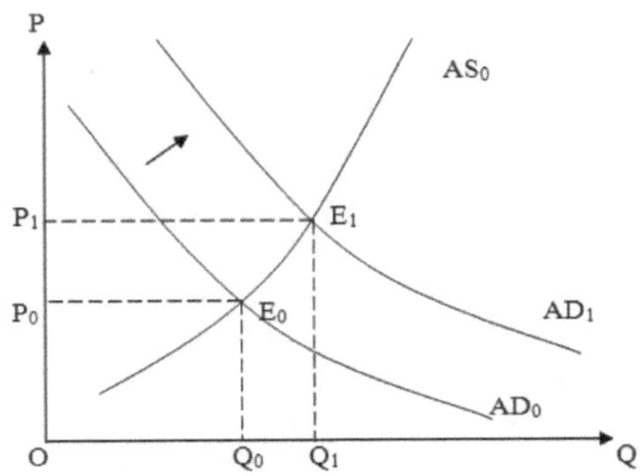

Figure 1.9 Impact of monetary relaxation

which will reduce the rate of interest. This in turn will increase the investment as interest rate and investment are inversely related. We know that investment is a major component of aggregate demand; hence the AD curve will shift upward to the right from AD_0 to AD_1 (see Figure 1.9) leading to an increase in both P and Q.

Last, we examine the effect of a contractionary monetary policy or *tight monetary policy* adopted by the monetary authority or government. This reduction in money supply by the government will increase the rate of interest and reduce investment. As the fall in investment spending reduces aggregate demand directly, it will produce a leftward shift of AD curve. Ultimately the output level would reduce from Q_0 to Q_1 (as shown in Figure 1.10), leading to an increase in unemployment.

The tight monetary policy may succeed in bringing down inflation as price level decreases, but for this achievement, the nation has to pay in terms of higher unemployment and lower output.

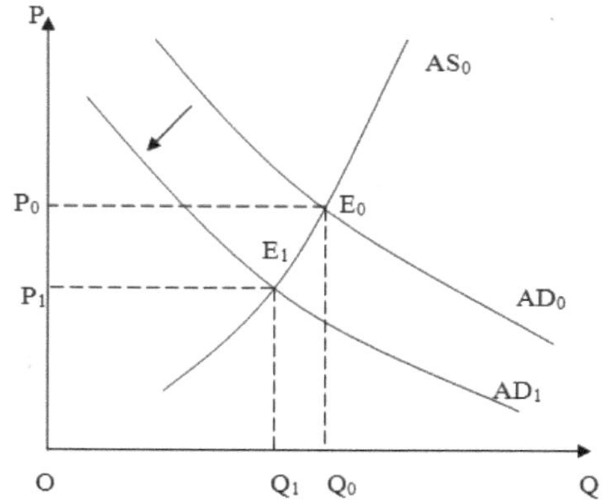

Figure 1.10 Impact of tight monetary policy

1.5 Preview of the book

It is time to introduce the coverage of the remaining part of the book to the potential readers. Chapter 2 deals with the issues related to national income accounting. Different concepts of national income, various national income aggregates, and different approaches of estimation of national income are discussed in Chapter 2. The circular flow of income explanation depicts how different sectors of the economic system are interrelated. Some important aspects of computing GDP and limitations of considering GDP as an indicator of economic wellbeing have been addressed in this chapter.

In Chapter 3 the classical model is introduced which captures a number of broad aspects of the macroeconomic performance, like neutrality of money and classical dichotomy. Classical structure always ensures automatic full employment via the market mechanism, hence it has ruled out the role of interventionist policies in affecting real output. The supply-determined nature of output and employment generates a vertical aggregate supply curve in this model. The model demonstrates that money is nothing but a veil; changes in money supply no way affect the real variables of the model as the system is dichotomised. Only in determination of nominal variables of the model does the role of money come in. Wage price flexibility and perfect information about the market are two essential features of the classical model. The classical model does not face the demand problem. It is based on Say's law which states that supply creates its own demand leading to no overproduction.

How money supply changes can affect the rate of growth of price level is the main focus of Chapter 4. Here we look at the different measures of money supply and simplified format of the balance sheet of the central bank to estimate money supply, following which we derive the money multiplier. Using the quantity theory of money, this chapter also establishes a link between quantity of money supply in the economy and the rate of inflation.

The important phenomenon of inflation is addressed in Chapter 5. There are mainly two types of inflation, but in reality, there may arise difficulty in making a clear-cut distinction between different types of inflation. Cost of inflation includes shoe leather costs, menu costs, confusion and inconvenience, arbitrary redistribution of wealth, etc. Causes, determinants, and consequences of inflation on the economy are analysed in this chapter. Different policies designed to control inflation or to maintain price stability have also been described in this chapter. Different fiscal and monetary measures that can be adopted by the government of a country to combat inflationary pressure have also been discussed here.

Chapters 6 and 7 focus on the determination of equilibrium output with the help of the simple Keynesian model. A simple framework of Chapter 6 is broadened in Chapter 7 to include government activities. How equilibrium income is determined in the product market with government in the context of a closed economy is shown in Chapter 6. Impacts of different fiscal policies of the government on the level of aggregate demand and hence on income are explained using the concept of expenditure multiplier.

Chapters 8, 9, and 10 present the famous IS-LM framework which assumes that there exist unutilised resources in the economy, a basis of post-depression Keynesian economics. The IS-LM model presents a theory of short-term fluctuation in output where real output is governed purely by effective demand. Interactions of product and money markets generate equilibrium income and interest rate, though price level does not vary in this analysis because of excess supply condition. Short run impacts of demand management policies, like fiscal and monetary policies, are analysed in this chapter.

The IS-LM model concentrates only on the demand side of the macro model. It ignores the supply side of the economy completely. The AD–AS model, discussed in Chapters 11 and 12, integrates aggregate supply with the aggregate demand and determines price level and output simultaneously. Chapter 11 depicts a general view of the economy and shows how any exogenous shock or policy effect can shift AD and AS curves, leading to change in the aggregate output and overall price level. The inverse relationship between inflation and unemployment, popularly known as the Phillips curve, will be discussed in detail in Chapter 12.

Chapter 13 concentrates on developing the **complete Keynesian model** by taking into account both the aggregate demand and supply factors required to explain the fluctuations in the business cycle. The chapter is based on the counterarguments against the classical supply-side model. It explains why government intervention is still required even under variable money wage and price levels.

Chapters 14, 15, and 16 discuss the aggregate consumption behaviour of the households, aggregate investment behaviour of the firms, and the aggregate demand for money theory purely on the microeconomic foundations, respectively. These are the chapters where rational decisions of the individual consumers, firms, and economic agents are aggregated to explain the consumption, investment and money demand patterns in the whole economy.

In Chapter 17 we cover details of the money supply system of an economy in general and the Indian economy in particular. The exogenous money supply assumptions of classical and Keynesian models are dropped and the money supply determination in an endogenous system is explained. The money market equilibrium is accordingly reoriented and the fiscal and monetary policy effects are revisited.

Chapter 18 includes discussions about all schools of thoughts developed in the history of macroeconomics. It starts with the ancient phase to the new Keynesian phase and all the schools are briefly discussed as part of their own paradigms.

Open economy macroeconomics is covered in Chapter 19, 20m and 21. Chapter 19 presents the conceptual notes on the international transactions with their empirical presentations. Chapter 20 covers the accounting of the international transactions in a double-entry book-keeping system and cites appropriate policies to correct the deficit in the balance of payments. Finally, Chapter 21 emphasises the interactions among the product market, money market, and external transactions and analyses the effectiveness of different policies in the presence of perfect and imperfect capital mobility conditions.

We present the economic events of the countries in the long run or even in the longer run in Chapters 22, 23, and 24 by means of different theories of economic growth. Chapter 22 focuses on the classical and Keynesian version of growth models. The Keynesian version is followed and established by the Harrod-Domar model. In Chapter 23, we present the neoclassical theory of growth where exogenous technological progress is put forward as the way of combating diminishing returns to restore the steady-state growth rate of an economy. The cross-country convergence analysis based on empirical data is also covered. Finally, in Chapter 24, we cover some popular models of endogenous growth theory. The models explain how perpetual growth solution is possible if the economies endogenise technologies by means of human capital formation, experience gathering, public spending on social and economic infrastructures, etc.

The final couple of chapters of the book, Chapters 25 and 26, focus respectively on sustainable development and remodelling of the entire economic system by the incorporation of environmental factors into it. The traditional theories did not account for the loss of natural and environmental resources by the performance of economic activities and thus the system was unsustainable as has been explained in detail in Chapter 26. The chapter highlights the reorientation of the national income accounting system – named *green accounting* – and remodels the product and money market interactions by the inclusion of the environmental sustainability factors to understand how the national output is sustainable.

1.6 Conclusion

The introductory chapter portrays principal objectives of studying macroeconomics. It opens up the opportunity to the readers to make themselves acquainted with the prime variables of the subject. It also covers the brief descriptions on all the remaining chapters to end up with successful debates among different macroeconomic models developed to date to determine the policy variables.

Summary

- Macroeconomics as a separate branch developed after the emergence of new macroeconomic theories developed by Keynes. The classical school emphasised the market mechanism for solving the basic economic problems of an economy, whereas the Keynesian school emphasised the fiscal and monetary policy of the government
- Macroeconomics is the study of the economy as a whole – aggregate output, aggregate employment, average price level, interest rate, foreign exchange rate, economic growth, overall impacts of governments' policies
- Output and employment fluctuate in the short run in an irregular manner. Interest rates and inflation also track fluctuations
- The goal of macroeconomics is to give a clear understanding of short-term fluctuations and long-term economic growth
- These fluctuations prompt governments to devise appropriate fiscal, monetary, and other policies to improve economic performance
- AD and AS tools can be used to understand different economic fluctuations

Keywords

Employment	Unemployment rate
Recessionary gap	Inflationary gap
Deflation	Consumer price index (CPI)
GDP deflator	AD curve
Potential	GDP Hyperinflation

Multiple choice questions and answers

1. AD shifts to the left when
   (a) Government purchases are decreased.
   (b) Government taxes are increased.
   (c) Government transfers are decreased.
   (d) All of the above.
2. The use of government taxes and spending to alter economic outcomes is known as
   (a) Fiscal policy.
   (b) Monetary policy.
   (c) Foreign trade policy.
   (d) Income policy.
3. In stagflation
   (a) Potential output of the economy declines.
   (b) The inflation rate is increasing because of rising demand.
   (c) The output gap is negative.
4. When national output rises, the economy is said to be in
   (a) An expansion.
   (b) A deflation.
   (c) An inflation.
   (d) A recession.
5. The number of unemployed divided by the labour force equals
   (a) The inflation rate.
   (b) The labour force participation rate.
   (c) The unemployment rate.
   (d) The misery index.
6. The inflation rate is the
   (a) Percent increase in the average level of prices over a year.
   (b) Percent increase in output over a year.
   (c) Percent increase in the unemployment rate over a year.
   (d) Price level divided by the level of output.
7. The difference between microeconomics and macroeconomics is that
   (a) Microeconomics looks at supply and demand for goods, macroeconomics looks at supply and demand for services.

(b) Microeconomics looks at prices, macroeconomics looks at inflation.
(c) Microeconomics looks at individual consumers, macroeconomics looks at national totals.
(d) Microeconomics looks at national issues, macroeconomics looks at global issues.

Answers

1. (d); 2. (a); 3. (a); 4. (a); 5. (c); 6. (a); 7. (c)

Descriptive questions

1. What are the major objectives of macroeconomics? Explain carefully why each objective is important.
2. Discuss in brief major schools of macroeconomic thoughts.
3. How do economists evaluate the success of an economy's overall performance? What are the policy instruments by which the goals can be achieved?
4. Using an AD and AS diagram, show the effect of an explosion in oil refinery.

   a. In the market for crude oil.
   b. In the market for refined oil.

5. What would be the effect of each of the following on AS (assuming other things constant)?

   a. A large cut in personal and business taxes (on AD).
   b. An arms-reduction agreement reducing defence spending (on AD).
   c. An increase in potential output (on AS).
   d. A monetary loosing that lowers interest rates (on AD).

6. Write short notes on:

   a. GDP Gap.
   b. Okun's law.
   c. Structural Unemployment.
   d. Cyclical Unemployment.
   e. Frictional Unemployment

Additional readings

Keynes, J. M. (1936). *The General Theory of Employment, Interest, and Money*, Chapter 8–10. London: Palgrave Macmillan.

Samuelson, P. A. & Nordhaus, W. D. (2009). *Economics*, 19th ed., Chapter 19. Mc Graw Hill Education, New York, Original from Pennsylvania State University, USA.

2 National income accounting

2.1 Usefulness of national income accounting

A country's economic performance is frequently assessed by its national income (NI) growth, which serves as an indicator of the nation's capacity to acquire goods and services. As a result, it serves as a valuable tool for economic planning and predicting future trends.

The performance of a country is frequently assessed by its growth of *national income* (NI). This provides a measure of the nation's capacity to acquire goods and services. Hence it serves as a valuable tool for economic planning and forecasting. Every country prepares statistics on national income each year. The method through which national income statistics is prepared and compiled is called *national income accounting*. All types of transactions conducted in a year are recorded and systematically classified in national income accounts by statisticians. Statisticians from the Indian Statistical Institute and the Central Statistical Organization have played a pivotal role in advancing and shaping this methodology. National income accounts reflect how millions of transactions that are conducted are interrelated. These figures are also of importance for making international comparisons. Success and failure of policymakers is often judged by the rate of growth of real national income during their regime. National income divided by the total population of the nation is called *per capita income* (PCI). PCI helps in measuring changes in the standard of living of the residents of the country over time. Thus, a clear understanding of the meaning and measurement of national income is essential. We begin this chapter by explaining several brief concepts related to national income and discuss various national income aggregates and estimation of national income. We take up the circular flow of income to show how different sectors of the economic system are interrelated. Three different approaches of measuring national incomes are also discussed in detail.

2.2 Some important concepts related to national income aggregates

2.2.1 Concepts of GDP, GNP, NNP, and NDP

Gross Domestic Product (GDP) is the market value of all final goods and services produced within the geographical territory of a country within a given period of time, normally a year, regardless of who owns the productive resources. It is a flow concept as it refers to flow of output during a time period and not stock of goods and services. GDP is thus obtained by valuing all final goods and services produced domestically during a particular year at market prices. Contribution of both nationals and non-nationals

DOI: 10.4324/9781003501138-3

in production is captured in this concept. Market values are calculated by multiplying quantities of goods and services produced by their market prices. Market prices always include indirect taxes and subsidies above cost of production of the commodities. Indirect tax, which is taxes on goods and services, raises the market price. Similarly, subsidies, financial help to the producers from the government, will lower the market price. To get the true figure of production, taxes are to be excluded and subsidies are to be included from market value. If we deduct net indirect taxes (equal to indirect taxes – subsidies) from GDP at market prices (GDP_{MP}) then we get GDP at factor cost (GDP_{FC}). Thus:

$$GDP_{FC} = GDP_{MP} - Net\ indirect\ taxes. \tag{2.1}$$

This GDP_{FC} reflects true incomes of productive inputs.

Gross National Product (GNP) of a country, which is the most commonly used measure of national income, is the market value of all final goods and services produced by the domestically owned factors of production in a particular year regardless of whether the factors are located within the country or abroad. Hence GNP is also expressed in terms of money because physical quantities of goods and services are not additive due to differences in the units of measurement. GNP at market price (GNP_{MP}) differs from GNP at factor cost (GNP_{FC}) to the extent of net indirect tax in the same way as described earlier. Thus

$$GNP_{FC} = GNP_{MP} - Net\ indirect\ taxes. \tag{2.2}$$

While GNP consists of income produced by a nation's owned resources, irrespective of the place of production, GDP refers to the income produced within the national territory irrespective of the owners of the resources who produced it. In Indian context, i.e., GDP is the output of all Indian enterprises located in India and GNP is the output of all Indian enterprises, whether located in India or abroad. The difference between GNP and GDP is accounted for by the net factor income earned abroad (NFIA). Factor income earned abroad is a part of factor income earned by nationals of a country but not a part of the domestic production. This part should be added to GDP to get GNP. Similarly, some part of domestic product may have been generated by nationals of other countries working in our country. This part should be deducted from GDP to get GNP. So, NFIA stands for the incomes earned in the forms of wages, interests and dividends (factor incomes) by the resident factors abroad minus the income earned by the non-resident factors in the home country. Thus,

$$GNP = GDP + NFIA \tag{2.3}$$

NFIA may be positive or negative. If NFIA > 0, then GNP > GDP. If NFIA < 0, then GNP < GDP; and if NFIA = 0, then GNP = GDP.

From the point of employment generation in any country GDP is more relevant than GNP.

Net National Product (NNP) refers to the sum total of the value of the final goods and services produced in an economy in a particular year that is devoid of depreciation of capital (D) or capital consumption allowance (CCA). It measures the total market value of the economy's net output of final goods and services. Depreciation of capital is the consumed part of fixed capital in the production process. It measures the amount of economy's stock of fixed capital equipment and residential structures that wears out during the year and hence represents the cost of producing output in the economy. Thus, to measure NNP we must take into account depreciation which also represents the difference between *gross investment* (I_G) and *net investment* (I_N).

Gross investment is the total market value of purchases of newly produced structures, durable business equipment, plus the value of change in the volume of inventories held by a business. It also includes the construction of residential housing. Hence the purchase of a newly constructed house is considered as investment rather than consumption. A portion of gross investment is used to replace structures and equipment that have worn out during the year. Net investment is obtained by subtracting depreciation of capital or capital consumption allowance (CCA) from gross investment. Net investment is important as a measure of the net increase in the nation's capital stock. Hence, we can write,

$$D = I_G - I_N, \text{ and } NNP = GNP - D. \tag{2.4}$$

Subtraction of depreciation shows the net result of economic activity. In practice, GNP is considered as a more commonly used indicator than NNP as it gives a better indication of economic performance. Similarly, we can measure *Net Domestic Product (NDP)* as follows:

$$NDP = GDP - D. \tag{2.5}$$

2.2.2 *Concepts of NI, PI, and PDI*

National income (NI) can be defined as the sum of all the incomes accruing to the inhabitants, or normal residents, of a country from their contribution to current production. In essence, NI encompasses the combined earnings of the factors of production which arise from the current production of goods and services in the economy. After making the following adjustments we can obtain NI from NNP.

One *major* difference between NNP measured at market price and NI is the *net indirect tax* (or net indirect business tax). Net indirect tax, which includes indirect taxes (like sales, excise, and business property taxes) and subsidies, represents the difference in what buyers pay for the final product and what sellers receive. *Net indirect tax* = (*IBT* – *subsidies*). National income is measured in terms of the prices firms receive for the product they sell. On the other hand, GDP or GNP is measured in terms of the prices paid by buyers i.e., at market prices. Indirect tax or IBT pushes market price above cost of production and subsidies do the opposite. To obtain the value of output at factor cost, net indirect tax should be deducted from NNP at market price.

Second, *minor* adjustment requires subtraction of *Business transfer payment (BTP)* from NNP. Business transfer payments are payments by business to individuals and non-profit organisations including universities. This must be subtracted because they are a part of business receipt from the sale that is not passed on as factor incomes. Business transfer payments thus represent a drain on the resources of business which are not available for payments to the factors of production. This item will be added back when we go from NI to PI.

The third *minor* item of adjustment is *net subsidies made by government-to-government enterprises*. These enterprises are the business sectors, hence on the product side their output is measured as sales value. But if they incur loss, their payments to factor income for current production exceed the value of their output by the amount of loss which in turn is made up by a net subsidy by the government. So, the net subsidies must be added with NNP to get NI. Hence, we can write,

$$NNP_{MP} - Net\ Indirect\ Tax\ -\ BTP\ + \\ Net\ Subsidy\ to\ Government\ Enterprises\ =\ NI \tag{2.6}$$

As the sum of the last two minor entries in the above relation are very negligible, we can write, $NNP_{MP} - Net\ Indirect\ Tax = NNP_{FC} = NI.$

Personal income (PI) can be defined as the sum total of all current incomes received by households from all sources. It includes income earned by individuals as factor owners and certain transfer payments from the government and businesses. To calculate PI from NI we need to subtract factor incomes that do not pass on to persons as pretax income and add items that enter PI but are not part of NI. A series of adjustments are required to arrive at personal income (PI) from NI.

First, we need to reduce NI by the amount that a corporation earns but doesn't pay out. We know corporate profit (CP) is composed of three components: dividend, undistributed corporate profit, and corporate profit tax. All the profits of corporations are included in NI but only dividends are included in PI. The company has to pay corporate profit tax (CPT) to the government out of its earned income and keep a portion of their profit, maybe for production expansion, known as undistributed corporate profit (UCP) or corporate retained earnings (CRI) or net business saving. Thus, the first adjustment is made by subtracting corporate profit and adding back dividend, which is equivalent to subtraction of UCP and CPT from NI.

$$CP = Dividend + UCP + CPT.$$

Therefore, $(-\ CP + Dividend) = -\ (UCP + CPT)$

Next, we increase NI by the net amount the government pays out as transfer payments. This adjustment equals government transfer to individuals minus social insurance contribution (SIC) paid to the government. Government transfer payments to individuals (e.g., social security payments like pensions, gratuity; unemployment benefits and welfare benefits like medical and health benefits, etc.) do not represent current earning, hence they are not a part of NI though it raises personal income and thus should be added to obtain PI. Similarly, both employer and employee need to pay social security taxes, like social insurance taxes, unemployment compensation taxes, etc., which are earned but not available to households for spending. SIC is thus taken out of NI while calculating PI.

Last, we adjust NI to include the interest that a household earns rather than the interest that the firms pay. This adjustment is made by adding all personal interest income, mostly interest payments by the government to individuals, and subtracting net interest. Net interest consists of interest paid by a business minus interest received by a business plus net interest received from abroad. These are payments for factor services and are already included in NI. Personal interest incomes do not include the net interest payments by business or corporations. Thus, while calculating PI, net interest payments by business should be deducted from NI. But interest paid by consumers and government

Table 2.1 From GDP to disposable personal income

Step 1: Gross Domestic Product	
Plus:	net factor income from abroad
Equals:	gross national product
Step 2: Gross National Product	
Less:	depreciation
Equals:	net national product at market price
Step 3: Net National Product	
Less:	net indirect business tax
	Business transfer payment
Plus:	net subsidy to government enterprises
Equals:	national income
Step 4: National Income	
Less:	corporate profit
	Social insurance contribution
	Net interest
Plus:	dividend
	Government transfer payments to individuals
	Personal interest income
Equals:	personal income
Step 5: Personal Income	
Less:	personal direct and indirect tax payment
Equals:	disposable personal income

to individuals are not part of NI, as they do not represent income arising from current economic production, hence should be added to earned income to get PI. Thus, we have

$$PI = NI + (Dividend - Corporate\ Profit) + (Government\ Transfer\ to\ individuals - SIC) + (Personal\ Interest\ Income\ of\ Individuals - Net\ Interest) \quad (2.7)$$

Disposable personal income (DPI), often termed as personal disposable income (PDI), is the level of income available to the household for spending and saving. It is an important determinant of an individual's ability to spend. The term "disposable" implies that individuals can dispose of it as they wish. DPI is obtained by subtracting personal tax payments (income tax, property tax, etc.) and certain non-tax payments from PI. This disposable personal income is used for consumption and savings. So,

$$DPI = PI - Personal\ Tax\ and\ Non\text{-}Tax\ Payments \quad (2.8)$$
$$DPI = Consumption\ (C) + savings\ (S). \quad (2.9)$$

This is how we can find out personal savings from national income. Derivation of DPI from GDP is shown in Table 2.1.

2.3 Circular flow of income

The fundamental concept of the *circular flow model* gives insight into the mechanism of the macro-economy and can be used to enhance our understanding of GDP. The circular flow of income model offers a comprehensive depiction of how diverse sectors within the economy are interconnected. It shows how goods, services, and money flow to and from various sectors in the economy. Let us start with a hypothetical economy with only two types of economic agents: households and firms. Households' own factors of production (land, labour, capital, and entrepreneurship) and firms use these factors of production for production purposes. One point should be remembered in this connection. Though these two concepts are not mutually exclusive (because the owners of the firms are the members of the households also) the distinction we made between households and firms is only a distinction from the viewpoint of taking decisions and not otherwise. When individuals take decisions about production of output, then it is the decision of firms. Again, when individuals take decisions regarding supply of factors of production, it is decisions of the households.

There is a continuous flow of goods and services from firms to households, to satisfy their demand, in every economy. This flow of goods, services, and factor services is called *real flow*. Firms sell these produced goods and services to households for money and households make payments from the factor incomes (rent for land, wages for labour, interest for capital, and profit for entrepreneurship) they receive from firms. This flow of money income from firms to households for factor services and from households to firms for purchase of produced goods and services is known as *money flow*. These two flows are in opposite directions of each other. This flow of goods and services and factor services among firms and households in the economy is known as *circular flow of income*. Income flows from firms in the form of factor payments to households and then from households to firms in the form of expenditure on goods and services. Goods and services flow in one direction and money payments to acquire this flow in the opposite direction, leading to a circular flow. We have shown this circular flow in a *two-sector model*, consisting of households and firms, in Figure 2.1.

In Figure 2.1 we assume that there are only two groups in the economy: households and firms. Households take consumption and savings decisions and firms are the productive enterprise. Interaction between them takes place in two sets of markets: factor markets and product markets. The households are supplying factor services to the firms (flow 1 in the upper loop). Using them, firms are producing goods and services. These produced goods and services go to the households (flow 2 in lower loop). These are two

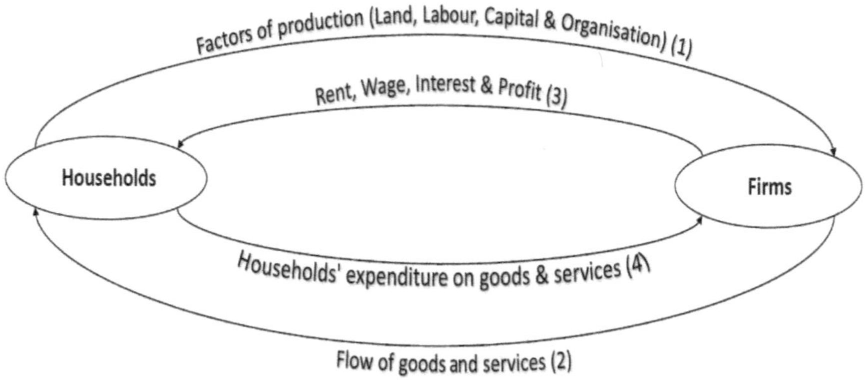

Figure 2.1 Two sector circular flow diagram

real flows. Any of them may be regarded as national income. However, we cannot measure national income in terms of goods and services. We have to express those goods and services in monetary terms.

As households' sale factor services, they get factor income in return from firms. This is a money flow shown by flow 3 in the diagram. This flow gives us the value of national income as sum of factor payments. This again goes back to the firms as their revenues when households purchase those goods and services (flow 4). This gives us the national income as a value of final products total. These two flows (3 and 4) are in monetary terms. Thus, the money payments go around in a circular manner from firms to household and from households to firms. In the same way, we obtained the circular flow of goods combining both types of real flows. As households spend all their income in purchasing goods and services from firms, total money receipts of the firms will be equal to the total income of the households. Similarly, total income of the households is equal to the expenditure of the firms on the purchase of factor services. Hence, there would be equilibrium in the circular flow and it will continue to operate at unchanged level. This is a macroeconomic equilibrium, since demand for goods and services is exactly met by the supply and there will be a tendency to perpetuate itself.

Let us move to *three sector model* by incorporating government into the economy. As government performs a wide variety of economic functions in a modern economy, there is need to include activities of the government. To keep the analysis simple, we consider two major activities of the government: collecting taxes and expenditure on goods and factor services. So, we consider that we are living in a market-oriented economy or capitalist economy, where there are three decision makers: firms, households, and government. Firms, who are the employer of resources, undertake production decision; households, who are the owner of factors, undertake consumption decision; and government imposes taxes on firms and households and spends money to purchase output and factor services. Figure 2.2 presents a closed economic circular flow among the households, firms, and government sectors.

In the upper loop individuals are paid for factor services and government receives indirect taxes which it imposes upon the output of goods and services produced by firms. Individuals use their income payments to consume, to save, and also to pay income taxes (direct tax) to the government. Government spends its tax receipts for making government

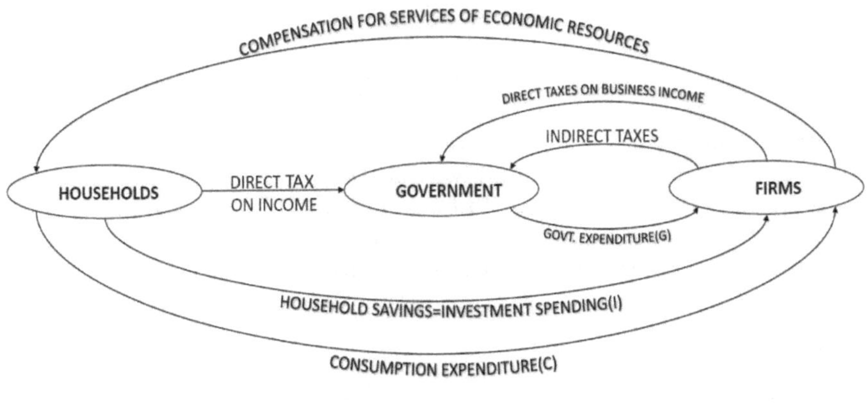

Figure 2.2 Three sector circular flow diagram

expenditures (G). Government may also purchase factor services from households and pay them wages and salaries in return (though this has not been depicted in the diagram). Individuals are assumed to save a fraction of their income which reduces their consumption expenditure. This savings may be used for undertaking investment expenditure by firms (in new plants and equipment). This creates additional income for the firms which do not arise from expenditure of households and government. It is thus an addition to the circular flow of income. In the lower loop the spending flow includes consumption (C), investment (I), and government expenditure (G). As we know the sum of the factor payments represent GDP, comparing upper and lower loops we get,

$$Y = C + I + G \qquad (2.10)$$

This is the national income identity in the context of a closed economy.

Tax revenue causes disposable income of the individuals to fall. As a result, effective demand falls. So, tax can be considered as withdrawal from the system, hence constituting *leakage*. It is not passed on to the circular flow of income and hence is not available for expenditure. It causes income and hence expenditure of firms and households to fall. Government expenditure acts as *injection* in the flow that causes effective demand to rise. It is an exogenous addition. Thus, the government may influence the level of circular flow through its activities of imposing taxes and incurring expenditure. Savings also acts as withdrawal because it causes demand to fall. But when savings is converted into investment, it acts as injection and causes income to rise.

However, if the government spends its entire tax revenue in the form of expenditure, there would be equilibrium in the circular flow. Total leakage in this three-sector model is ($S + T$) and total injection is ($I + G$). So, the system will be in equilibrium if

$$S + T = I + G \qquad (2.11)$$

In this way circular flows of income point out the condition of macroeconomic equilibrium. When the foreign sector is introduced in this economy then we have savings, taxes, and imports (goods purchased from abroad) as leakages and investment and government expenditure and exports (foreigners purchase goods from this country) as injections. Circular flow of income for four sector economy (considering open economy) will be discussed in Chapter 19 of the book.

Equation (2.10) links spending and output, taking into account the mutual feedback between the two. Spending determines the output, which provides income for spending. Clearly if government increases spending, output will increase, which in turn raises income and consumer expenditure, leading to further increase in output and income. This provides rationale for stimulating government spending during recession. In fact, this was the policy prescription of John Maynard Keynes, who argued that the proper response to economic slowdowns was to boost demand through government spending. His idea was widely accepted and became the cornerstone of government policy. We will present the *Keynesian macro model* in detail in Chapter 7 of the book.

2.4 Estimation of national income

From the circular flow diagram, we observed that production gives rise to income, income gives rise to expenditure, and expenditure gives rise to income again. Following

Table 2.2 Different approaches of measuring national income

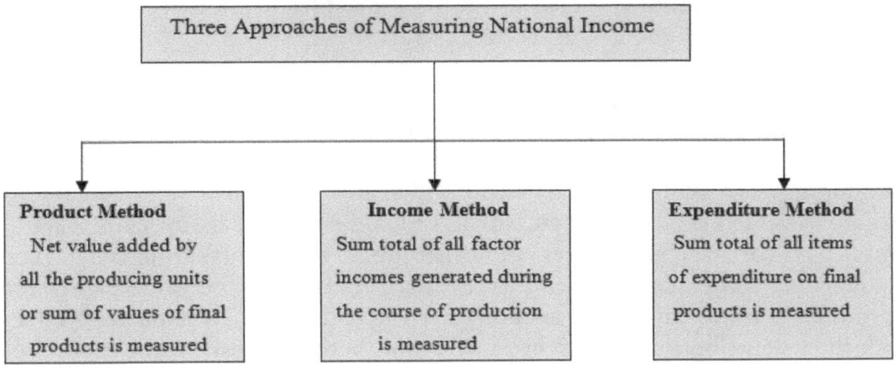

the same logic national income of a country can be viewed from three different angles. Accordingly, there are three alternative ways of measuring national income, as shown in Table 2.2. One way to measure NI is to calculate the value of the goods and services produced in the economy. This is the product method of calculating NI. During production households supply factor services in return for which they receive factor income. If all income received by households is added then we can have an estimate of NI from the income side. From circular flow it is also clear that whatever is produced is sold. Thus, the sum total of expenditure on currently produced final goods and services yields NI from the expenditure side. Thus, there are three ways of measuring NI:

i) product census method
ii) income census method
iii) expenditure census method.

We consider them one by one and show that each method produces the same result; i.e., Total Product = Total Income = Total Expenditure.

In fact, three methods provide different ways of looking at the same thing: national income.

2.4.1 *Product census method*

National income (NI) of a country is the money value of all final goods and services produced in a year. In order to estimate the national income of a country through the product census method, we must have a clear idea about the measurement of "value of output" produced in an economy. If we take the values of each and every final product separately, some products will be counted twice or more. Hence there will be a problem of double or multiple counting. To avoid this problem two methods are available: i) final product method, ii) value added method. Both the methods give the same estimate of NI.

In the *final product method*, all products are divided into two categories: intermediate and final products. If a product produced in a year is employed and used in the production process in the same year as an input, then it is called an intermediate product. These intermediate products are not included in NI accounting. This will enable us to avoid double or multiple counting. Thus, in the final product method we add up the total money value of all final goods and services produced.

The *value-added method* measures national income as the sum total of net final output produced or net value added by all the production units during a year. The concept of value added was developed to prevent double counting. Value added (*VA*) of each production unit is the value of its output (revenue that firms earn) minus the cost of intermediate inputs (*CII*) that it purchases from other firms. For firm "*i*", $VA_i = TR_i - CII_i$. For example, value added of Maruti Udyog Ltd is the revenue from selling cars less the amount it pays for steel, glass, tyres, and other inputs that it buys from other intermediate input selling companies. Value added is thus a measure of the value that is added to each product by production units at each stage of production. To calculate NI using this method, thus, contribution of each producing unit in the domestic territory of the country is calculated and then sum them up to get the aggregative figure. This can be shown as follows:

Profit of the *i*th firm (π_i) = $TR_i - TC_i$; where TC_i and TR_i represent the total cost and total revenue of the ith firm respectively.

$$\begin{aligned} \pi_i &= TR_i - (CIIi + PC_i) \\ &= (TR_i - CIIi) - PC_i \\ &= VA_i - [W_i + K_i + R_i] \\ \text{or } & W_i + K_i + R_i + \pi_i = VA_i \\ \text{or } & \Sigma\, \mathrm{W_i} + \Sigma\, \mathrm{K_i} + \Sigma\, \mathrm{T_i} + \Sigma\, \pi_i = \Sigma\, \mathrm{VA_i} \end{aligned} \tag{2.12}$$

Here, PC_i, W_i, K_i, *and* R_i represent primary cost, wage bill, capital bill and rental bill of firm *i* respectively. Equation (2.12) demonstrates NNP at factor cost or total factor income or NI equal to total (sum of) value added.

Let us clarify the concept of value added with the help of the following example.

Suppose a firm sells goods worth Rs. 80,000/- in 2022 added to a stock of goods worth Rs. 5,000/-, such that the value of output of the firm is Rs. 85,000/- i.e. (Rs. 80,000 + Rs. 5,000). Now for producing this, the firm purchases raw materials and other required services of Rs. 19,000/- from other producing units within the country. Hence, in this case, the value added of the producing units is the value of output minus the value of raw materials and other services.

Value Added = Value of output minus the Value of raw materials
= Rs. 85,000/- – Rs. 19,000/-
= Rs. 66,000/-.

Adding up all the value added we can determine the NI of a country. The value-added method counts the flow of output through each production process whereas the final product method counts the flow of the output at the end of the production process. We can easily show that the value-added method and the final product method give us the same estimate of GNP total.

Let us clarify this with the following example: suppose, in an economy, wheat worth of Rs. 23/- is produced during a year. The entire wheat is transformed into flour in the same year. Its value then becomes Rs. 53/-. The flour is again transformed into bread in the same year and its value is raised to Rs. 110/-. Finally sandwich of Rs. 190/- is produced using the flour. If we add up the values of wheat, flour, bread, and sandwich, we face the problem of multiple counting. In the *final product method*, we shall take the value of sandwich only, that is Rs. 190/-, as the estimate of NI. Alternatively in the *value-added method*, value added at each stage of the production process can be estimated by taking the value of the product leaving the production process and the value of the product entering the production process. In this particular example, value added in wheat production is Rs. 23/-, value added in the production of flour is Rs. 30/-, value added in the production of bread is Rs. 57/-, and ultimately value added in sandwich production is Rs. 80/-. So, the total value added becomes Rs. (23 + 30 + 57 + 80)/- = 190/-. Sum of value added and final sales proceeds lead to the same figure. In practice there might be some measurement errors that cause a slight discrepancy, called *statistical discrepancy*, between actual and estimated value.

More elaborately, to find out the value of NI of an economy by this method we have to first calculate sum of net value added at factor cost by each production unit and then add net factor income from abroad.

Net value added at factor cost = (*Value of gross output* – *Intermediate consumption*) – *Depreciation* – *Net indirect tax.*

Value of gross output minus intermediate consumption gives gross value added (GVA). Here intermediate consumption refers to use of inputs or intermediate products in the production process. GVA minus depreciation represents net value added (*NVA*) at market price. Deducting net indirect tax from net value added at market price we arrive at net value added at factor cost. Summing net value added at factor cost of all production units we get net domestic product at factor cost (NDP_{FC}). *NI* or NNP_{FC} is obtained by adding *NFIA* to the NDP_{FC}.

$$NI = NNP_{FC} = NDP_{FC} + NFIA$$

To clarify the concept let us consider an example of calculating NI using this method. Suppose following information is given.

i)	Gross value of output at market prices	Rs. 15,000/- crore
ii)	Value of intermediate consumption	Rs. 4,900/- crore
iii)	Consumption of fixed capital	Rs. 1,650/- crore
iv)	Net indirect taxes	Rs. 850/- crore
v)	Net factor income from abroad	Rs. 400/- crore

National income (*NI*) = *Gross value of output at market prices* – *Value of intermediate consumption* – *Consumption of fixed capital* – *Net indirect taxes* + *Net factor income from abroad*
= 15,000 – 4,900 – 1,650 – 850 + 400
= Rs. 8,000/- crore.

The value-added method can help us to find out the share of different sectors in national income. Now we come to the second method of calculating national income, which is the income method.

2.4.2 Income census method

In *Income Census Method* of calculating NI, we need to identify the income of all the earning units of an economy. An earning unit may be an individual or an institution. Incomes of all earning units who participate in the production process are added up to find out the NI of the economy. As it is already assumed that production takes place only in firms, households supply different factors of production as in land, labour, capital, and organisation. Firms earn revenue which is utilised for factor payments. Households get factor income in the form of rent, wages, interest and profit. Hence NI, which is the sum total of all net incomes accruing to the owners of primary factors of production, equals the sum of all rents, wages, interests, and profits.

Thus,

$$NI = Rent + Wages + Interest + Profit \tag{2.13}$$

This method is also known as *Factor Payment method.*

2.4.2.1 Steps involved in income census method

While computing national income by income census method, the following steps are to be involved:

Step 1: all producing enterprises are identified and classified broadly into three categories: primary sector, secondary sector, and tertiary sector.

Step 2: factor incomes are grouped into the following heads: (a) compensation of employees (wages, salaries, etc.) (b) rent (c) interest (d) profits. Traditionally factors are grouped into four categories: land, labour, capital, and organisation. Accordingly, factor incomes are classified into the previous four categories. But in national income accounting factors are broadly grouped into two primary factors: labour and capital, and accordingly factor income is classified into three broad categories: labour income or compensation of employees, capital income or operating surplus, and mixed income.

i) *Compensation of employees* includes *wages and salaries* paid by producers to employees including dearness allowance (DA), house rent allowance (HRA), leave travel concession (LTC), bonus, sick leave allowance, etc.; *supplementary labour income* paid by employer (employers' social security contribution), i.e., pension, provident fund, gratuity, group insurance; and *payments to employee in kind*, like free medical facilities, subsidised food, free educational, accommodation and transportation facilities, etc.
ii) *Capital income* includes rent (from building as well as from land), royalties (from patents, copyrights), interest (except interest paid by consumers on their borrowings and that from government debt), dividends, undistributed corporate profits, etc.
iii) *Mixed income* incorporates income of those persons who provide both labour and capital in the production. This category also includes income of self-employed workers and unincorporated enterprises. Income from agriculture, transport, trading, legal and medical professions, and own account workers (carpenter, plumber, electricians, mechanics) etc. are counted in this category.

Step 3: By summing up all factor payments as mentioned earlier, we get domestic factor income. National income is finally measured by adding net factor income from abroad (NFIA, discussed earlier) to domestic factor income. Hence, we can write,

$$NI = Compensation\, of\, employees + Capital\, income + Mixed\, income + NFIA \quad (2.14)$$

Let us now estimate NI for a hypothetical economy following income method considering the following data: wages and salaries Rs. 1,500 crore, rent Rs. 110 crore, interest paid by production unit Rs. 150 crore, national debt interest Rs. 20 crore, corporation tax Rs. 70 crore, contribution to provident fund by employers Rs. 150 crore, contribution to provident fund by employees Rs. 200 crore, dividends Rs. 130 crore, undistributed profits Rs. 25 crore, net factor income from abroad Rs. 30. We can find out NI using the income method in the following manner.

NDP_{FC} = Wages and salaries + Rent + Interest paid by production unit + Corporation tax + Contribution to provident fund by employers + Dividends + Undistributed profits
= 1,500 + 110 + 150 + 70 + 150 + 130 +25
= Rs. 2,135 crore

National Income = NDP_{FC} + Net factor income from abroad
= 2,135 + 30
= Rs. 2,165 crore

Data on national debt and contributions to provident fund by employees are not required here. National debt interest is not included because it is treated as transfer payments. Contribution to a provident fund by employees is not included as it is paid out of wages and salaries.

While computing the NI from the income census method the following points should be considered:

i) *Transfer payments*, such as unemployment benefits, pension etc., should not be included in NI. Such payments are made without receiving any services in return.
ii) Estimation of mixed incomes, earned by unincorporated sector, is difficult due to lack of reliable information from unorganised sector. In India also a significant portion of residents are *self-employed*, so the *mixed income* category is a dominant component here.
iii) Incomes received are normally calculated from income tax returns. In underdeveloped countries only a small part of income earners file income tax return. This is another limitation with this approach. There are other problems also which will be summarised in the next chapter.

2.4.3 *Expenditure census method*

Third approach of calculating NI is to add up all expenditures on final goods and services in a particular year, known as expenditure census method. In this method total expenditure on goods and services produced by a country during any period can be broken down as follows:

2.4.3.1 *Consumption (C)*

Final consumption is defined as spending by households. It includes purchase of *durable goods*, such as washing machines, cars etc., which could be used for a longer period of time; *non-durable goods* such as food and clothing; and *services* such as education, transport, etc. which are used within a short span of time. Spending on new houses is the only type of household spending that is *not included* in consumption. It is included in *fixed investment*.

Expenditure on old goods should not be included as these goods do not represent current production. But production for self-consumption is a part of current final production and income and hence should be included here.

2.4.3.2 *Investment (I)*

Investment is the sum of spending by firms on plants, equipment, and inventories and spending by households on residential houses. We separate total investment into *fixed investment* and *inventory investment*. Gross fixed investment is the total amount of investment in fixed capital, like purchase of new factories, machines, and houses. Inventory investment is the change in inventory at the business firms.

2.4.3.2.1 FIXED INVESTMENT

Fixed investment can be broken down into *non-residential fixed investment* and *residential fixed investment*. Non-residential fixed investment is spending on structures, machinery, and equipment for use in business. Office buildings, power plants, and steel plants are examples of *structures*. Computers, printers, laptops, etc. are examples of *equipment*. Residential fixed investment is spending on the construction of new houses and apartment buildings. However, as the capital stock is continuously wearing out, a part of the investment (depreciation; defined earlier in this chapter) reported in each year's GDP is actually used to replace worn out capital, not for increasing the capital stock.

2.4.3.2.2 INVENTORY INVESTMENT

This is the change in the stock of inventories held at business. Inventory investment this year equals the stock of inventory at the end of this year (closing stock) minus the stock of inventory at the end of last year (opening stock). For example, when a publisher produces and stores 7,000 copies of a newly produced book in his warehouse, the books are counted in GDP as inventory investment. Even though no one has yet purchased the books, they have been produced during the year, therefore they are added to the year's output. If someone purchases a book directly from the publisher, consumption increases by one book and inventory investment decreases by one book. If the publisher sells a book to a bookstore, the publisher's inventory investment decreases by one book and book store's inventory investment increases by one. Hence, total inventory investment does not change and neither does GDP.

2.4.3.3 *Governments' purchase (G)*

Government expenditure refers to the sum of expenditure incurred by various governmental units, like, local, state, central etc., to protect and maintain the welfare of the countrymen. Defence expenditure, like military arms purchase; expenditure on maintenance of law and order; expenditure on social welfare services, like education, sanitation, etc.; and expenditure on administration are examples of governments' purchases. Governments' transfer payments, like unemployment benefits, social security, and welfare payments are excluded from NI as they do not generate any current output.

The distinction among *C*, *I*, and *G* is based primarily on the type of the purchaser, rather than on the type of the product that is being purchased. For example, if a car is purchased by a household, then it will go into consumption as a consumer durable. If it is purchased for use by a businessman then it goes into investment as business fixed investment. If it is purchased by the government then it goes into government purchase.

2.4.3.4 *Export (X) and import (M)*

In the context of open economy exports are deliveries of goods and services from a country to the foreigners. On the other hand, imports are deliveries of goods and services from foreigners to the home country. Exports represent expenditure made by foreigners on domestic goods, and imports are expenditure by the residents on foreign goods. Thus, only net export ($NX = X - M$) is added to the total volume of spending when computing GDP. The net export, the difference between value of goods and services exported and the value of goods and services imported, is referred to as *trade balance*. When net export (NX) is positive then there is *trade surplus* and when it is negative there is *trade deficit*.

The sum of four expenditures give us GDP at market price (GDP_{MP}).

$$GDP = C + I + G + (X - M) \tag{2.15}$$

Deducting depreciation from there we get NDP_{MP}. Again, deducting net indirect taxes from NDP_{MP} we have the NDP_{FC} figure. Adding $NFIA$ to this we can arrive at NNP_{FC} or NI. Thus,

$$NI = C + I + G + (X - M) - D - net\ indirect\ tax - NFIA \tag{2.15.1}$$

For conceptual clarity regarding calculation of NI using the expenditure method consider the example of a hypothetical economy with the following data: private final consumption expenditure Rs. 1,000 crore, net domestic capital formation Rs. 200 crore, government final consumption expenditure Rs. 500 crore, consumption of fixed capital Rs. 60 crore, net factor income from abroad Rs. (-) 10 crore, indirect taxes Rs. 100 crore, net export Rs. (-) 20 crore, subsidies Rs. 20 crore.

To find out NI using the expenditure method let us first estimate GDP_{MP}.

GDP_{MP} = Private final consumption expenditure + Net domestic capital formation + Government final consumption expenditure + Consumption of fixed capital + Net export
= 1,000 + 200 + 500 + 60 + (–20)
= Rs. 1,740 crore.

The next step is to find out NI from GDP_{MP}.

National Income = GDP_{MP} – Consumption of fixed capital + Net factor income from abroad – Indirect taxes + Subsidies
= 1,740 – 60 + (–10) – 100 + 20
= Rs. 1,590 crore

If there is depreciation, *NFIA* and net indirect taxes are negligible amounts; then we can write

$$NI = Y = GDP = C + I + G + (X - M) \tag{2.15.2}$$

2.5 Use of accounting formulae with numerical examples

i) One day Niladri collects Rs. 400 from a haircut. Over this day his equipment depreciates in value by Rs. 50; of the remaining 350, he sends Rs. 30 to the government as sales tax, takes home Rs. 220 in wages and retains Rs. 100 in his business to add new equipment in the future. From Rs. 220 that Niladri takes home he pays Rs. 70 in income tax. Based on this information compute Niladri's contribution to the following measure of income –

a) *GNP*
b) *NNP*
c) *NI*
d) *DPI*

Ans: *NNP* = *GNP* – *D* [Since *NIA* = 0, so, *GNP* = *GDP* = 400]
NNP = 400–50
= 350
NI = *NNP* – *IBT*
= 350–30
= 320
PI = *NI* – Retained earning
= 320 – 100
= 220
DPI = 220 – 70 = 150

ii) Consider the following information:

Government business transfer = Rs. 15
IBT = Rs. 30
GNP = Rs. 630
SIC = Rs. 20
Personal taxes = Rs. 25
Depreciation = Rs. 80
Residential consumption = Rs. 40
Rental earning = Rs. 0
Consumption = Rs. 390
CPT = Rs. 40
Find out *NNP, NI, PI, DPI*.

Ans: *NNP* = *GNP* – *D*
= 630–80
= 550
NI = NNP_{MP} – *IBT*
= 550–30
= 520

$PI = NI - SIC - UCP - CPT +$ Transfer payment from govt. to individual
$= 520 - 20 - 0 - 40 + 15$
$= 475$
$DPI = PI -$ Personal tax
$= 475 - 25$
$= 450$

iii) Suppose for a hypothetical economy

$GDP = 10{,}000$
Gross investment = 2,000
Net investment = 1,500
$SIC = 350$
$CPT = 500$
$CP = 1{,}000$
$UCP = 200$
$IBT = 100$
Total taxes = 700
Subsidy = 50
Government and business transfer = 225
Personal interest income = 25
Obtain *NDP, PI, DPI.*

Ans: NDP_{MP} = xi – (Gross investment – net investment)
$= 10{,}000 - (2{,}000 - 1{,}500)$
$= 9{,}500$
$NI = NDP_{MP} - IBT +$ Subsidy
$= 9{,}500 - 100 + 50$
$= 9{,}450$
$PI = NI +$ (dividend – CP) + Government transfer to individual – SIC + Personal interest income
$= 9{,}450 + 300 - 1{,}000 + 225 - 350 + 25$ (Since dividend = $CP - CPT - UCP$ So, dividend = 1,000 – 500 – 200 = 300)
$= 8{,}650$
DPI = PI – tax
$= 8{,}650 - 700$
$= 7{,}950$

2.6 Revisiting the concept of disposable income

As already discussed, disposable personal income is that part of personal income which the household spends on consumption or can save as they desire. Out of the GDP personal taxes (like income tax, wealth tax, etc.) and some other miscellaneous receipts (fees, fines) are collected by the government which is not available to the household. But the same government also makes transfer payments like pensions and unemployment compensation, which adds to the households' ability to spend and save. Households are also the owners of firms and hence are therefore entitled to receive the profit of business. However, most corporations keep a part of their profit undistributed, also called business savings or undistributed corporate profit (UCP) or corporate retained earnings (CRI). The undistributed profit lowers disposable income related to GDP. Net earnings from abroad (NFIA) represent an addition to disposable income. Incorporating these facts, DPI can be directly approximated from GDP as follows:

$$DPI = GDP + TR - T + NFIA - UCP - D$$

If NFIA and UCP are neglected, D is assumed to be zero, and all taxes are direct tax in nature (though $D = NFIA = IBT$ are already assumed to be zero at the beginning of the analysis for analytical convenience), then $GNP = NNP_M = NNP_F = NI = Y$. With this modification we can write

$$DPI = Y + (TR - T) \qquad (2.16)$$

2.7 Saving investment identity and equality

We know that the national product of the country can be divided into two parts. One part is production of consumer goods, and the other part is the production of capital goods. The value of the production of consumer goods is known as consumption expenditure and the value of the production of capital goods is known as investment expenditure. Thus, national product is equal to the sum of consumption expenditure and investment expenditure for instance $Y = C + I$. Again, we know that one part of national income is consumed, and the other part is saved. Thus, national income is equal to the sum of consumption expenditure and saving. Thus, $Y = C + S$. Now from these two relations we get $C + I = C + S$ because national product and national income are identically equal. We then get $I = S$; private investment equals private saving. This is known as the *identity* between saving and investment.

It should be noted that the identity between savings and investment follows from the definitions of savings and investment. Investment refers to the purchase of new capital such as equipment, buildings etc. In the context of a *closed economy without government* it represents that part of output which is not consumed. If Aishani borrows from the bank to purchase a new house, she adds to the nation's investment. Again, savings is also that part of income is not spent on consumption expenditure. Thus, saving and investment are so defined that they always refer to the same thing. However, when we say saving and investment are *identically equal*, we refer to *ex post or realised* magnitudes. But if by saving we mean planned saving or intended saving and by investment we mean planned investment or intended investment, then we may not get the equality of saving and investment. This is so because in a modern economy the decisions to save and decisions to invest are taken by two separate groups of people. The people who save may not invest. The savers save their savings in banks or other financial institutions. Hence planned saving and planned investment may not always be equal. It is only when the national income of the economy is in equilibrium that *planned or ex ante* saving will be equal to *planned or ex ante* investment. But whether the national income is in equilibrium or not, realised aggregate saving is always identically equal to realised aggregate investment for the economy as a whole. One point should be remembered in this connection; even if realised saving and realised investments are equal for the entire economy, this may not be true for each and every individual in the economy. Aishani's investment can be greater than her saving; she can borrow (taking a loan) the extra amount from a bank. The bank in this situation balances this loan amount from other individuals' saving.

If we consider a closed economy with a government which does not participate in foreign trade, GDP is the sum of consumption, investment, and government expenditure. Referring to Equation (2.10) we can write $Y = C + I + G$ or $Y - C - G = I$.

The left-hand side of this equation, showing the economy's total income that remains after paying for consumption and government purchase, represents national saving (S). We know by definition $DPI = Y + TR - T$. As DPI is spent for consumption and saving purpose, it can be rewritten as $DPI = C + S$. Equating the two we get,

$$Y = C + S + T - TR \tag{2.17}$$

Equation (2.10) and (2.17) together give

$$C + I + G = C + S + T - TR$$
$$Or, I = S + (T - G - TR) \tag{2.18}$$

Hence the previous equation states that in a closed economy with a government, the sum of private and public saving (which is equal to national saving) is equal to aggregate private investment. The concept of national saving has also been explained in Chapter 11 of this book.

If we now extend our analysis to incorporate the open economy which participates in foreign trade then Equation (2.10) can be modified as follows

$$Y = C + I + G + NX \tag{2.19}$$

Again, as already discussed, disposable personal income can be estimated as:

$$DPI = GDP + (TR - T) + NFIA - UCP - D;$$

Out of GDP personal taxes (T) are collected by the government, which also makes transfer payments (TR) like pension, unemployment compensation, etc. Business saving or UCP partly lowers disposable income relative to GDP. Net earnings from abroad (NFIA) are additional to disposable income. Assuming UCP, D, and $NFIA$ to be insignificant (as already pointed out),

$$DPI = Y + (TR - T) \tag{2.20}$$

This DPI is either used for consumption or for saving, so

$$DPI = C + S \tag{2.21}$$

Combining (2.20) and (2.21) we have

$$C + S = Y + (TR - T)$$
$$Or, Y = (C + S) + (T - TR) \tag{2.22}$$

Equations (2.19) and (2.22) together give

$$C + I + G + NX = C + S + (T - TR)$$
$$\text{Or } S = I + (G+TR-T) + NX$$
$$Or,\ S - I = BD + NX \tag{2.23}$$

BD in Equation (2.23) represents a budget deficit. This is also called public dissaving. $BD > 0$ means government expenditure exceeds its revenue $[(G + TR) > T]$. $NX > 0$, on the other hand, represents surplus in our trade balance and also represents the current account surplus in this context. A *current account surplus* usually implies that the nation is a net exporter having a positive trade balance. Equation (2.23) depicts the relationship between excess of private saving over private investment with a budget deficit and balance of trade. If, for example, $S = I$, then the government's budget deficit is reflected in an equal external deficit.

The inverse of BD is called budget surplus (BS) which represents public saving, as the government earns excess revenue in this situation. Likewise, NX < 0 is called trade deficit or current account deficit (CAD) in this context, in which situation we are indebted to foreigners. Our exports are not sufficient to meet our expenditure for imports in this situation. From (2.23) one can write $CAD = (I - S) + BD$. Current account deficit is, thus, excess of government expenditure $(G + TR)$ over its income (T) and excess of I over S. So even if I exceeds S, CAD will widen if the governments' budget deficit rises.

Equation (2.23) can alternatively be interpreted as follows,

$$I + NX = S + BS \tag{2.24}$$

The right-hand side of Equation (2.24) represents the sum of private and public savings; the left-hand side is often interpreted as the sum of private and foreign investments. It can also be interpreted differently by rewriting Equation (2.24) in an alternative manner:

$$I = S + BS - NX \tag{2.25}$$

The total value of all exports to the rest of the world is denoted by X, while the total value of all imports from the rest of the world is denoted by M. Thus, the negative of net export (i.e., $M - X$) represents the *rest of the world savings* of a country. The rest of the world savings in India, for example, is the payment received from India less payment made to India, which is nothing but our import minus our export (i.e. –NX). This is also the amount that we borrow from the rest of the world. So, Equation (2.25) shows that investments are financed by private, public, and the rest of the world savings (or borrowing from the rest of the world).

2.8 GDP at current and constant price

Nominal GDP or GDP at current price measures the value of an output in a given period in the prices of that period. This measure does not accurately reflect how well the economy can satisfy the demand of households, firms, and governments. Nominal GDP can change partly because of change in quantity of output produced and partly because of change in the market prices. Hence, an inflationary trend in an economy may cause a rise in the value of GDP between the concerned periods. Suppose output produced remains exactly same between two consecutive years but price level has been doubled. This doubles the nominal GDP, with the volume of output remaining unchanged. So, nominal

GDP doesn't reflect the true picture of economic performance and hence wellbeing. To remove the impact of price change and to get a better measure of economic wellbeing, the concept of *real GDP or GDP at constant price* is introduced. Real GDP measures changes in the physical output in the economy between different time periods by valuing all goods and services using a constant set of prices (base year prices). Hence, it is often called inflation adjusted GDP. For example, if we consider 2010–2011 as the base year and express GDP of 2016–2017 at 2010–2011 prices then it is known as GDP at constant prices. An increase in real GDP indicates a real increase in the physical quantity of production. Thus, real GDP more accurately reflects the performance of an economy. There is no unique measure of real GDP, as it depends on the choice of the base year. Nominal GDP can be converted into real GDP by eliminating the effect of price change with the help of a suitable price index called an implicit price deflator.

2.9 GDP deflator and CPI

2.9.1 *The concept of GDP deflator*

Usually consumer price index (CPI), discussed in Chapter 1, is not used as a suitable price index in the construction of real GDP. The problem with CPI is that it considers only consumer goods, whereas GDP includes investment goods as well. Thus, to calculate real GDP we use GDP deflator as an implicit price index, which gives a useful measure of inflation. The GDP deflator is the ratio of nominal GDP in a year to real GDP of that year. The GDP deflator is based on a calculation involving all goods and services produced in an economy. The deflator measures the change in prices that has occurred between the base year and the current year.

$$GDP\ deflator = Nominal\ GDP\ /\ Real\ GDP = P_tQ_t\ /\ P_0Q_t.$$

Q_i represents output in period i and P_i represents price level in period i.

Often it is expressed in percentage terms. As an example, if the value of deflator is 190, then it implies that in the current year, the value of GDP rose from 100 (in base year) to 190 in the current year. Alternatively, we can say that the price level increased by 90%.

The GDP deflator reflects what is happening to the overall level of prices of final goods and services in the economy. It is also known as the *implicit price index* because we first construct real GDP which is a quantity measure, then we compare the movement in GDP to measure the change in prices. We do not try to directly or explicitly measure the change in prices by taking the weighted average of the price indexes for various components of GDP. It ignores the prices of the *imported goods* which enter our consumption basket and *list of inputs* in production.

Now we estimate the GDP deflator (for all the years) with the help of *an example* of a hypothetical economy which produces only wheat and textiles.

Year	*Price of wheat*	*Quantity of wheat produced*	*Price of Textile*	*Quantity of textile produced*
2005	2	200	4	750
2006	3	300	6	800
2007	5	350	7	900
2008	8	500	8	100

Solution: calculation of values of nominal, real GDP, and the GDP deflator is shown in tabular form. 2005 has been considered as the base year here. GDP deflator can also be expressed in terms of percentages (not done here).

Year	*Wheat*		*Textile*		*Nominal GDP*	*Real GDP*	*GDP Deflator*
	Price	*Quantity*	*Price*	*Quantity*			
2005	2	200	4	750	400 + 3,000 = 3,400	3,400	1
2006	3	300	6	800	900 + 4,800 = 5,700	600 + 3,200 = 3,800	5,700 / 3,800 = 1.5
2007	5	350	7	900	1,750 + 3,600 = 8,050	700+ 3,600 = 4,300	8,050 / 4,300 = 1.87
2008	8	500	8	100	4,000 + 800 = 4,800	1,000 + 400 = 1,400	4,800 / 1,400 = 3.42

2.9.2 *CPI and inflation rate*

The GDP deflator, as mentioned in the previous section, is the ratio of nominal GDP to real GDP, frequently used as a measure of inflation. As nominal GDP is the value of current output valued at current prices and real GDP measures current output valued at constant or base year prices, the GDP deflator reflects the current level of prices relative to the level of prices in the base year. It is an index of the prices of the items in consumption, investment, government expenditure, and net export. The concept of CPI, the most widely used price index, is introduced in Chapter 1 of this book. Each month Bureau of Labour Statistics computes CPI. Economic policymakers monitor both the GDP deflator and the consumer price index (CPI) closely to understand how quickly prices are rising. Similarly, CPI compresses the prices of numerous goods and services into a single index for measuring the general price level. CPI is a weighted average of all the prices of a fixed basket of consumer goods and services. This index indicates the cost of buying a fixed basket of goods today to compare to how much it cost to buy the same basket in a base year. It is a measure of the prices paid by the typical urban working-class family for a fixed basket of goods and services. Thus, it talks about the value of money in the consumer's pocket. Using CPI, we can calculate inflation rate between two consecutive years. Detailed analysis on inflation is done in Chapter 5 of this book. Using the following formula, inflation rate between two consecutive years can be calculated.

$$\text{Inflation rate} = \frac{CPI \text{ in current year} - CPI \text{ in previous year}}{CPI \text{ in previous year}} \times 100$$

Let us consider the following example to see how inflation rate, which is the percentage change in the CPI from the preceding period, is computed.

Let the consumers in country have a fixed basket of goods containing 4 units of commodity X and 2 units of commodity Y. The prices of X are Rs. 1, Rs. 2, and Rs. 3 respectively and the per unit prices of Y are Rs. 2, Rs. 3, and Rs. 4 respectively for the same years. We want to compute CPI for each year considering 2015 as the base year first and then using CPI to determine the inflation rate over the years.

The given data is summarised here for computing the cost of the basket of goods in each year.

Year	*Price of A*	*Price of B*	*Cost of the basket*
2015	1	2	$1\times4+2\times2=8$
2016	2	3	$2\times4+3\times2=14$
2017	3	4	$3\times4+4\times2=20$

CPI for base year 2015 is always 100.

$$\text{CPI for 2016} = \frac{\text{Cost of busket in 2016}}{\text{Cost of busket in 2015}}\times100 = \frac{14}{8}\times100=175$$

$$\text{CPI for 2017} = \frac{\text{Cost of busket in 2017}}{\text{Cost of busket in 2015}}\times100\ \frac{20}{8}\times100=250$$

$$\text{Inflation rate in 2016} = \frac{CPI\text{ in }2016-CPI\text{ in }2015}{CPI\text{ in }2015}\times100$$

$$=\frac{175-100}{100}\times100=75\%$$

$$\text{Similarly, inflation rate in 2017} = \frac{CPI\text{ in }2017-CPI\text{ in }2016}{CPI\text{ in }2016}\times100$$

$$=\frac{250-175}{175}\times100=\frac{300}{7}=42.85\%$$

2.9.3 *Comparison between GDP deflator and CPI*

Usually both the statistics, CPI and GDP deflator, tell a similar story. Yet there are *some important differences* that can cause them to diverge. The differences between the two measures can be summarised as follows:

i) The GDP deflator measures the prices of all goods and services *produced domestically*, whereas CPI measures the prices of only the goods and services bought by the consumers. Thus, an increase in the price of goods bought by firms or the government will show up in the GDP deflator but not in the CPI.
ii) CPI measures the cost of a *given basket of goods* which is fixed from year to year but in the case of the GDP deflator the basket of good is not fixed; it changes over time if composition of GDP changes. Thus, the group of goods and services used to compute the GDP deflator changes automatically from one period to another. When vegetable production is large, vegetables receive a relatively large weight in the computation of GDP deflator. A price index with a fixed basket of goods is called a Laspeyres index and a price index with a changing basket of goods is called Paasche index. So, CPI is a Laspeyres index and GDP deflator is a Paasche index. When prices of different goods are changing by different amounts, the Laspeyres index tends to overstate the increase in the cost of living, whereas a Paasche index tends to understate it. Thus, CPI tends to overstate inflation whereas the GDP deflator understates it. CPI hence cannot account for price change in newly invented goods as it is calculated on a fixed

bundle of goods. If prices of new laptops, for example, start falling rapidly from a high level as production expands, then CPI in the initial years would overstate inflation.

iii) The GDP deflator includes only those goods produced domestically. Imported goods are not a part of GDP and do not show up in the GDP deflator. Hence, an increase in the price of products produced in foreign countries and sold in domestic country affects CPI, but it does not affect the GDP deflator. For example, when the price of imported oil rises sharply CPI is likely to rise faster than GDP deflator as oil products constitute a much larger share of consumer spending than that of GDP. In this situation GDP deflator underestimates inflation.

2.9.4 Limitations of CPI

CPI is not a perfect measure of cost of living; it suffers from certain limitations. Three major limitations of CPI are substitution bias, new good bias, and quality change bias.

The first problem is *substitution bias*. The CPI measures the prices of baskets of commodities with weights given to each category fixed in the base year. Weights are changed approximately after 10 years based on a consumer expenditure survey. But during this period when prices of the products change, consumers may shift away from some items whose relative prices have risen by a large amount to items whose relative prices fall. Assumption of a fixed basket of goods ignores this substitution possibility. Using the base year's weights will overstate inflation by overweighting the items whose prices have risen substantially. Suppose, for example, in the base year people buy a large amount of rice and a lower amount of wheat. Now suppose that price of wheat falls 15%. This will encourage people to buy more wheat and less rice than before. As CPI assumes that consumers will continue to buy the same basket even after price change, it overstates the increase in cost of living by ignoring the consumer's substitution to wheat.

Introduction of new goods offers greater variety to the consumers. Prices of the newly introduced goods usually decline sharply after some time. For example, when mobile phones were first introduced, they were very costly. But the price came down after few years. So, for any given amount of money, this availability of a new product made people better off. This in fact reduces the cost of maintaining the same level of standard of living. But this reduction in cost of living associated with the introduction of mobile phones didn't show up in the index immediately. The government normally puts these new goods into the CPI with a delay, several years after their introduction. Thus, their price decline does not get reflected in CPI, overstating the rate of inflation for that intermediate period. In this way CPI has *new good bias*.

CPI also suffers from *quality change bias*. Due to rapid technological progress quality of products are continuously changing. If the quality of the product improves, the value of money rises because, price remaining same, consumers are getting more of better-quality goods spending the same amount of money. Recently Apple introduced the iPhone X with a much higher price and improved quality. But how much has price really increased? Is the price increase adequate compensation for better quality and facilities in this situation? CPI underestimates this change in quality as it is hard to measure. Despite different efforts to incorporate quality change in CPI it remains a problem and consumers must use their subjective judgements here.

2.10 Issues to be remembered while measuring NI

2.10.1 *Treatment of inventories*

In GDP estimation of a country, we should consider the situation of the inventory. The treatment of inventories in NI accounting depends on the fate of inventory, that is whether it is spoiled or not. If it is *spoiled* then we find that wages are increased by the amount of the value of inventories, as it is currently produced. But simultaneously profits of firms get reduced by the same amount, as it cannot be sold anymore. So, total income has not changed in this situation as additional wages cancel out negative profit. Total expenditure has not changed either, because no one buys the product. So, from the income side, $NI =$ Wage + rent + interest + profit and from the expenditure side $NI = C + I + G$, which remain unaltered. So, the spoiled inventory cannot influence the GDP of an economy.

But if the inventories are *not spoiled* then both wages (as workers are paid extra wages to produce the inventory) from the income side and investment (as firms are assumed to have to purchase it for stock holding) from the expenditure side are increased by the amount of inventory. The firm's profits are not reduced by the additional wages it has paid because the higher wages raised total income and greater spending raises total expenditure, leading to an increase in GDP. If some *inventory is lost* in the current period due to theft, fire, or such other reasons, it reduces profit by the loss amount. Such lost inventory is not a part of the GDP.

However, *sell out inventory* is like a used good which involves dual transaction. It does not influence GDP because it is a combination of positive spending by the consumer and negative spending by the firms (C increases and I falls by same the amount).

For *valuation of inventory* two methods are available: the market price method and the cost price method. In market price method valuation is done on the basis of current market price which incorporates an imputed profit which may or may not be realised in the future. In the cost price method valuation is imputed on the basis of cost of production which includes depreciation cost and cost of materials.

2.10.2 *Treatment of used goods*

GDP measures the value of currently produced goods and services; the sale of used or second-hand goods are *excluded from* GDP. For example, sale of an old house will not influence the GDP of an economy in a particular year; only the broker's fee will be considered. Likewise, the trade of second-hand cars, old houses, and old bonds *are not part of GDP*. However, the sales commissions on used cars or on any second-hand sale etc. are counted in current GDP because the salesperson performed a service during the current year. Expenditure on repair of used goods, for example refrigerators, AC machines, and cars, are parts of final expenditure, hence they will be included in NI.

2.10.3 *Imputation*

The concept of imputation is quite common in NI accounting. Here we try to obtain the value of some products and services which are not within the purview of market relation. Although most of the goods and services are valued at their market prices while computing GDP, some are not sold in the marketplace and therefore do not have the market prices. If GDP is to include the value of these goods and services, we must use an estimate of their values. Such an estimate is called *imputed value*. For example, in the case of the value of housing, imputation is very important. A person who rents a flat or house is buying housing services and providing income for the landlord. The rent is a part of GDP both as the expenditure by the renters and as income for the landlord. Many people, however, live in their own houses. Though they do not pay rent, they are enjoying housing services similar to those that renters purchase. To take account of the housing services enjoyed by home owners, GDP includes notional rent that these home owners pay to themselves. An *estimate of the market rent for the house should be included* as part of the GDP. This imputed rent is included both in the home owner's expenditure and in the home owner's income. Even if an individual keeps his house vacant, he has to pay tax on notional rent. In this situation the value of the services rendered by the house also has to be imputed.

Imputation also arises in the case of valuing government services. Government provides various services to the public without any payment. For example – general administration, police, and fire fighters provide services to the public free of cost. Finding a value of these services is difficult because they are not sold in the marketplace and do not have the market price. NI account includes these services in GDP by valuing them at the cost which is incurred in providing them. For example – wages of public servants are used as a measure of the value of their output.

2.10.4 Treatment of intermediate goods

Final goods mean the good is ready for its designated ultimate use. But there are some goods which are used in the production of other goods, known as intermediate goods. If we include both the value of intermediate and final goods while computing GDP then we face the problem of double counting. This is because the value of final goods includes all intermediate transactions. To avoid double counting we must calculate only the value added at each stage of production or the value of final products only. As the sum of all value added must equal the value of all final goods and services (as described in the product method of NI estimation), GDP is also the total value added of all firms in the economy.

However, in practice, many goods can be considered as intermediate as well as final depending upon their use. For example, when flour is used by a household it is a final good but when the same is used by a bakery for bread production it is an intermediate good. So, often it becomes difficult to make a clear-cut distinction between final and intermediate goods.

2.10.5 Treatment of transfer payment

There are some market transactions which are very much official for which no quid pro quo relationship exists. One important example of such transactions is transfer payment. These are *not included in GDP* because such transactions do not constitute current production. We normally have two types of transfer payments – public and private. Public transfers are subsidies to producers, social security payments, relief payments, retirement and pension benefits, and interest on public debts (which the government makes to firms and household). In these transactions the residents make no contribution to current production in return for these benefits. Hence, they are *excluded from GDP*. Private transfer payments like a son paying father for his old age expenditure, a father's gifts to a son, and rich household gifts to a poor person do not entail production but simply the transfer of funds from one household to another. If a student receives a scholarship for higher studies sponsored by any private company, then it is an example of a business transfer.

A surprise omission from NI accounting is *interest on government bonds*. It is an example of government transfer. It is excluded from NI because the government pays interest on bonds not from profit of public sectors but by imposing taxes on people. So, there is a transfer of income from taxpayers to bond holders but there is no net increase in society's output of goods and services in the process.

However, the treatment of *interest on private (corporate) bonds* is something different. It is not a transfer of income thus will be *included* in NI. The reason is that a company pays interest on its bond from its current sales revenue for receiving a useful productive input – financial services. Any *transfer payment from abroad* will be counted as a part of country's NI. If an individual receives Rs. 8,000/- from his father who is a non-residential Indian, it will be a part of India's NI.

Capital gains (buying and selling of stocks and bonds) are also a form of transfer income, as this money just gets transferred from the buyer to the seller and is therefore *excluded from NI*, because, in case of capital gains, money just gets transferred from the buyers to sellers with no change in society's output.

2.10.6 *Treatment of underground economy*

Underground or parallel economy is that part of economy which people hide from the government, either because they want to avoid taxation or because the activity is inherently illegal. The underground economy includes transactions involving illegal goods and services such as trading harmful drugs, gambling, smuggling, black marketing, etc. These illegal goods and services are final products but *not included* in GDP. The transactions of the underground economy also include activities by people who do not comply with tax laws, government regulations, and immigration laws and who do not report their income to tax authorities. Businesspeople, for example, often overstate their expenses and understate reported incomes in order to avoid tax. Although an underground economy has always existed in India, its volume is now becoming much larger, maybe due to increased burden of government regulation. Given the shadowy nature, we cannot be optimistic about reducing its size by devoting more resources to law enforcement.

2.10.7 *Treatment of non-marketed activity*

GDP accounts only for goods and services that are traded through formal markets. This is a limitation of the measure, but this is accepted internationally owing to the difficulties in measuring non-marketed or non-officially marketed production. This *ignores "do-it-yourself" activities* (which are not paid for) as well as under-reported production. For example, the household work including whitewashing of one's own house, tutoring of one's own children, cooking for consumption for the family members, and other do-it-yourself activities are excluded while payments to maids, private tuition, and so on are included in GDP. Also, activities like painting, drawing, photography, etc. which are carried out for self-consumption (or even for sale but not in the current year) are left out of the GDP. Similarly, unreported production, for example, agricultural production for self-consumption, is not included in the GDP. In less-developed countries like India, subsistence farmers produce a substantial portion of output for their self-consumption. As this portion of output does not get traded in markets, it is excluded from GDP.

2.11 GDP as an index of social welfare

GDP is often regarded as an index of the wellbeing or welfare of the residents of a country. But we will see that GDP data is an imperfect measure, as it shows a loose correlation between GDP (even real GDP) and society's welfare because of the following reasons.

i) GDP says nothing about *distribution of income*. Equitable distribution of income should have a much higher priority than high rate of output growth. Suppose a society in which 100 people have annual incomes of Rs. 1,50,000 has a GDP of Rs. 15 million. So, GDP per person is Rs. 1,50,000. The same will be the case with a society in which ten people earn Rs. 1,500,000 and 90 suffer with nothing at all. So, if incomes of fewer people become very high and that of most of the others falls, GDP remaining the same, that in no way it implies greater wellbeing for the entire society.
ii) GDP excludes *non-market transactions*. Important productive services left out of the account include the services of women working at home and self-employed persons. GDP omits value of goods and services produced at home, i.e., unpaid services rendered by the family members. But welfare depends on non-marketed transactions also. Volunteers' work also contributes to the wellbeing of those in society but GDP does not reflect these contributions. In underdeveloped countries like India where non marketed activities contribute substantially, GDP fails to represents a true indication of the nation's welfare.
iii) GDP ignores *environmental cost of production* which affects the quality of life of the residents. Increase in GDP, hence more production, is often associated with more depletion of natural resources and more environmental degradation. Social cost of production, as a result, becomes higher than private cost (due to negative externality). The deterioration in the environmental quality would more than offset the gain from higher production. This is a matter of concern to almost all countries, particularly to developing countries like India. Even if some abatement expenditures are made to mitigate environmental damage (e.g., expenditure on installation of air and water purification systems etc.), in no way does it contribute to production and hence GDP. Likewise, depletion of non-renewable natural resources also stands in the way of GDP becoming a sustainable measure of the economy's welfare. Overextraction of coal, for example, reduces the availability of this resource for future. This issue of conservation of natural resources is not reflected in GDP.
iv) GDP fails to take into account the changes in the *quality of goods and services*. This is a serious limitation because qualitative improvement is always a major source of improvement in the general standard of living. In case of electronics goods, for example, qualitative improvement has taken place dramatically over time, often accompanied by a substantial reduction in prices. But GDP is not concerned with quality changes of goods and services.
v) GDP ignores *importance of leisure* which helps in improving individuals' wellbeing and standard of living. Other things remaining the same, the more leisure we have, the better off we are. Suppose, for instance, everyone in the economy started working overtime every day. This would definitely increase the production of goods and services and hence GDP. But this would reduce the health and happiness of everyone

in the society. Welfare is a psychological concept linked with happiness. An increase in GDP does not always bring about increased welfare for the individuals of the society.

Given these limitations we can say that GDP *should not be considered as a good index of social welfare or even of material wellbeing*, though it can be used as a useful measure of the level of economic activity. Two points should be mentioned in this connection. First, as NFIA figures are often very small, GDP and GNP reflect the same estimate, hence the previous discussion is equally applicable to GNP. For this reason, in the starting point of Chapter 26, while revisiting the same concept, we have discussed whether GNP is a suitable indicator of development. Second, we have extended this analysis by introducing a relatively new idea of macroeconomics called "green macroeconomics" through accommodation of environmental costs into determination of principal variable, national income, in Chapter 26. The analysis there shows how inclusion of different natural resource factored into the economic activities gives rise to the concept of *green macroeconomics or sustainable macroeconomics.*

2.12 Growth of NI of India in different plan periods at a glance

Plan-wise study of growth of real national income was relatively low at 3.8% per year during the first three plan periods as is evident from the Table 2.3, constructed on the basis of CSO data. From the fifth plan onwards, it rose continuously (except in the ninth plan). During the ninth plan (1997 to 2002) growth of NI dropped to 5.6%. This disastrous performance of the economy was due to the failure of industrial production. In 2001–2002, the growth rate of industrial production was only 2.7% per year, which was the poorest during the last 10 years. The growth rate for the thirteenth FYP (2018–2022) is 3.76% because of a negative (–7%) growth due to worldwide lockdown during the COVID-19 period,

Table 2.3 Growth of NI of India in different Five-Year Plans

Five Year Plan	*Annual average growth rates of gross national income at constant Prices (% per annum)*
First Plan (1951 to 1956)	4.0
Second Plan (1956 to 1961)	4.1
Third Plan (1961 to 1966)	3.4
Fourth Plan (1969 to 1974)	3.2
Fifth Plan (1974 to 1979)	5.1
Sixth Plan (1980 to 1985)	5.4
Seventh Plan (1985 to 1990)	5.8
Eighth Plan (1992 to 1997)	6.5
Ninth Plan (1997 to 2002)	5.6
Tenth Plan (2002 to 2007)	7.6
Eleventh Plan (2007 to 2012)	7.8
Twelfth Plan (2012 to 2017)	6.8
Thirteenth Plan (2018 to 2022)	3.76

Source: CSO, Economic Survey Report 2022.

2.13 Conclusion

This chapter introduces different concepts related to national income. Three methods of measuring national income have been demonstrated one by one, resulting in same estimate of NI. Circular flow models, both two and three sectors, clearly depicted the national income identity in the context of closed economy. Open economy extension of circular flow model is carried out in Chapter 19. In reality, most of the developing countries face the problem of an inadequate and unreliable data set; hence they are not able to estimate NI by each method separately. Production units in underdeveloped countries remain scattered and in distant interiors of the country, so collected data for estimation of NI is neither complete nor reliable. Most of the people who are self-employed in such countries do not keep records of production and costs. Data regarding part of goods used in self-consumption is also not available. Classification of labour income is also very difficult due to lack of categorisation of occupation. Agriculture, e.g., in underdeveloped countries, is overburdened with the surplus labour, also seasonal in nature. During the lean season farmers are engaged themselves in non-farming activities. Therefore, data related to their incomes from different occupations are not satisfactory. Therefore, underdeveloped countries often combine two or more methods to get the estimate of NI. In India, for example, contribution of agriculture is estimated by output method and that of small-scale unregistered manufacturing units by income method. The chapter also introduced three key statistics, real GDP, GDP deflator, and consumer price index (CPI), which are relevant to measure an economy's performance. Comparison between CPI and GDP deflator, movement of which are indicators of price change, has been addressed here. Traditionally, economic welfare was measured in terms of GDP. Different limitations of considering GDP as an indicator of economic wellbeing has also been addressed in this chapter, which shows that perfect manifestation of welfare experience is not possible with the concept of GDP. Now we are in a position to discuss formal models of income determination in subsequent chapters of the book.

Applications

1. Consider the following information:

   GNP = 5,000, Consumption = 3,800, DPI = 4,100, Trade deficit $(M - X) = 100$, Governmental budget deficit = 200.

   Find out the values of government spending and gross investment expenditure and saving.

   Solution: Saving $= DPI - C$
   $= 4{,}100 - 3{,}800$
   $= 300$
   $DPI = GNP + TR - T$
   $4{,}100 = 5{,}000 + (TR - T) = -900$
   $BD = G + (TR - T)$
   $200 = G - 900$
   $G = 1{,}100$
   $Y = C + I + G + (X - M)$
   $5{,}000 = 3{,}800 + I + 1{,}100 - 100$ (substituting the given values)
   I (gross) $= 200$

2. In the following table are some data for a hypothetical economy

Year	*Price per good X (Rs.)*	*Quantity of good X*	*Price per good Y (Rs.)*	*Quantity of good Y*
2015	10	200	8	75
2016	14	200	10	75
2017	14	350	10	125

a. Compute nominal GDP, real GDP, and the GDP deflator, using 2015 as the base year.
b. Compute the percentage change in nominal GDP, real GDP, and the GDP deflator in 2016 and 2017, from the preceding year 2015. For each year, which variable changes? Why?
c. Did economic wellbeing rise more in 2016 or 2017? Why?

Solution

Year	*Price per good X (Rs.)*	*Quantity of good X*	*Price per good Y (Rs.)*	*Quantity of good Y*
2015	10	200	8	75
2016	14	200	10	75
2017	14	350	10	125

a. In 2015, Nominal GDP = Real GDP = $10\times200+8\times75$ = 2,600 $\Rightarrow$ GDP Deflator = 1.

In 2016, Nominal GDP = $14\times200+10\times75=2{,}800+750=3{,}550$

Real GDP = $10\times200+8\times75=2{,}600$ [Base = 2015]

$\therefore$ GDP deflator = $\dfrac{3{,}550}{2{,}600}=1.365$

In 2017, Nominal GDP = $14\times350+10\times125=4{,}900+1{,}250=6{,}150$

Real GDP = $10\times350+8\times125=3{,}500+1{,}000=4{,}500$ [base = 2015]

GDP deflator = $\dfrac{6{,}150}{4{,}500}=1.365$

b. Percentage change in Nominal GDP: from 2015 to 2016 = $\dfrac{3{,}550-2{,}600}{3{,}550}\times100=36.5\%$

& from 2016 to 2017 = $\dfrac{6{,}150-3{,}550}{3{,}550}\times100$ = 73.2%

Percentage change in real GDP: from 2015 to 2016 = 0

from 2016 to 2017 = $\dfrac{4{,}500-2{,}600}{2{,}600}\times100=73.2\%$

Percentage change in GDP deflator: from 2015 to 2016 = 36.5% from 2016 to 2017 = 0%
From 2015 to 2016, real GDP does not change, as outputs are unchanged.
From 2016 to 2017, GDP deflator, which measures the inflation rate, does not change, as prices are unchanged.

c. Economic wellbeing rose from 2016 to 2017 as more goods were produced. Economic wellbeing did not change at all from 2015 to 2016, as prices are unchanged.

Summary

- Gross domestic product, GDP, is a measure of aggregate income and output in an economy. It is the total value of the current production of final goods and services at current prices within the national territory during a given period of time.
- In macroeconomics, aggregate output equals aggregate income, which, in turn, equals aggregate expenditure. Using product, income, or expenditure methods we can calculate GDP.
- As some residents work for foreign-owned business organisations and some foreigners work for domestically owned organisations, gross national product (GNP) measures aggregate output by the domestically owned factor of production regardless of where in the world they work.
- National income is the sum of aggregate domestic income and net factor incomes from abroad, though it is not a good measure of social welfare.
- Depreciation is the loss of capital from wear and tear and net investment is gross investment less depreciation.
- Two important identities of NI accounting are $Y = C + I + G + X - M$ and $S - I = BD + NX$.
- An important implication of the equality of income and product is the equality of saving and investment. Excess of the private sector's saving over investment is equal to the sum of budget deficit and net export.
- Measures of aggregate income are incomplete due to underreported income and participation in underground and non-market activities.
- In order to understand whether income increases represent an increase in command over goods and services we differentiate between real income (income measured in constant prices) and nominal income. The rate of change in prices of goods and services produced is measured by GDP deflator.
- The consumer price index CPI measures the price of a fixed basket of goods and services purchased by the typical urban working-class family. Thus, an increase in the price of products produced in a foreign country and sold in a domestic country affects CPI.
- GDP, though is a useful measure of economic activities, fails to represent a true indication of economic wellbeing or a nation's welfare.

Keywords

Gross domestic product
Personal income
Depreciation
Net national product
National saving
Implicit price index
National income
Real GDP
GDP deflator
Consumer price index
Value added
Budget deficit

Multiple choice questions

1. To what extent are homemaking and child-rearing accounted for in the GDP accounts?

   (a) Not at all.
   (b) Only to the extent that they are provided for pay.

(c) Only to the extent that taxes are paid on them.
(d) All homemaking and childrearing are accounted for.

2. GDP differs from GNP because

(a) GDP = GNP – net factor payments from abroad.
(b) GNP = GDP – net factor payments from abroad.
(c) GDP = GNP – capital consumption allowances.
(d) GNP = GDP – capital consumption allowances.

3. Which of the following is *not* a category of consumption spending in the national income accounts?

(a) Consumer durables.
(b) Nondurable goods.
(c) Services.
(d) Housing purchases.

4. Intermediate goods are not included to calculate the final output because:

(a) They do not have value.
(b) They have unknown value.
(c) Their value is included in final goods so they are not added to avoid the problem of double counting.
(d) None of the above.

5. Which of the following is included in India's GDP?

(a) The sale of a new car from a manufacturer's inventory.
(b) The purchase of a watch from a Swiss company.
(c) The sale of a used car.
(d) A newly constructed house.

6. Because government services are not sold in markets,

(a) They are excluded from measurements of GDP.
(b) The government tries to estimate their market value and uses this to measure the government's contribution to GDP.
(c) They are valued at their cost of production.
(d) Taxes are used to value their contribution.

7. The government budget surplus equals

(a) Government purchases plus transfers.
(b) Net government receipts minus government purchases.
(c) Government purchases minus net receipts.
(d) Government purchases minus transfers.

8. In 2015, national saving was Rs. 1,456 billion, investment was Rs. 1,945 billion, and private saving was Rs. 1,590 billion. How much was the current account balance?

(a) Rs. 489 billion.
(b) Rs. 221 billion.
(c) –Rs. 221 billion.
(d) –Rs. 489 billion.

9. The uses of saving identity says that an economy's private saving is used for

   (a) Investment, interest expenses, and the government budget deficit.
   (b) Investment, the government budget deficit, and the current account.
   (c) Investment, interest expenses, the government budget deficit, and the current account.
   (d) Investment, interest expenses, the government budget deficit, transfer payments, and the current account.

10. In 2015, private saving was Rs. 1,590 million, investment was Rs. 1,945 million, and the current account balance was – $489 million. From the uses-of-saving identity, how much was government saving?

    (a) –Rs. 134 million.
    (b) –Rs. 844 million.
    (c) Rs. 844 million.
    (d) Rs. 134 million.

Answers

1 (b); 2 (a); 3 (d); 4 (c); 5 (d); 6 (c); 7 (b); 8 (d); 9 (b); 10 (c).

Descriptive questions

1. Gross national product, net national product, and national income are measures of the nation's output. Yet, from a conceptual standpoint, they differ. Briefly explain what each attempts to measure.
2. Indicate whether each of the following is included or excluded from GDP and the reasons for its inclusion or exclusion:

   a. Government transfer payment.
   b. Changes in inventories.
   c. Services of homemakers.
   d. Indirect business taxes.
   e. Exports of goods and services.
   f. Imports of goods and services.
   g. Business transfer payments.

3. What would happen to national income in each of the following cases?

   a. Introduction of cash assistance scheme by the state government for agricultural labourers.
   b. Abolition of subsidy on cooking gas.
   c. Replacement of unemployment assistance scheme for part-time employment without any change in expenditure.
   d. Purchase of foreign submarines by the defence department.

4. State whether the following statements are true or false and give reasons for your answers:

   a. For a country where GNP exceeds GDP, we find that the residents of that country are earning less abroad than the foreigners are earning in that country.
   b. For a particular firm, wages and salaries paid to the employees are always a part of its value added.
   c. In computing GDP by the value-added method, firms producing intermediate goods should be disregarded.

d. In order to measure national income, we consider income from various types of employment except income from self-employment.

5. What is the difference in the national income accounts between:

   a. A firm's buying an auto for an executive and the firm's paying the executive additional income to buy the automobile himself?
   b. You hiring your spouse rather than having him or her do the work without pay?

6. Suppose GDP = 5,000

   a. Domestic residents receive factor payments from abroad of Rs. 150. Foreigners receive Rs. 90 as factor payment from this country. What is the value of GNP?
   b. If women work more hours in a paid job and fewer in unpaid household work, how will the GDP be affected? Explain.

7. Consider the following data for an economy

	(in crores)
The value added of all producing units	900
The tax revenue of the government	100
Direct taxes	70
Gross fixed capital formation changes in stocks	50
Gross domestic product at all market prices	950

   Determine consumption expenditure and net investment.

8. From the following data find out NI, PI, DPI, and S.

   Compensation of employees = Rs. 1,866.3
   Business interest payment = Rs. 264.9
   Rental income of persons = Rs. 34.1
   Corporate profit = Rs. 164.8
   Proprietors' income = Rs. 120.3
   Corporate dividend = Rs. 66.4
   SIC = Rs. 253.0
   Personal taxes = Rs. 402.1
   Interest paid by consumers = Rs. 64.4
   Interest paid by government = Rs. 105.1
   Government and business transfer = Rs. 374.5
   Personal consumption expenditure = Rs. 1,991.9

9. Find value added of the two firms from the given data

   Closing stock of firm A = 30
   Closing stock of firm B = 20
   Opening stock of firm A = 5
   Opening stock of firm B = 10
   Domestic sales of firm A = 250
   Purchase of A from B = 100
   Purchase of B from A = 80
   Domestic sales of firm B = 250
   Export by firm B = 30
   Import of raw materials by firm A = 65

10. Can exports exceed GDP?
11. Consider the following data on GDP of a country.

Year	*National GDP (Rs. in billion)*	*GDP Deflator (Base year 2005)*
2010	9,873	118
2009	9,269	113

   a. What was the growth rate of nominal GDP between 2009 and 2010?
   b. What was the growth rate of the GDP deflator between 2009 and 2010?
   c. What was the real GDP in 2009 measured in 2005 prices?
   d. What was the real GDP in 2010 measured in 2005 prices?
   e. What was the growth rate of GDP between 2009 and 2010?
   f. Was the growth rate of nominal higher or lower than the growth rate of real GDP? Explain.

12. Which of the following activities/transactions are included in the national income and why?

   a. A father teaching his son.
   b. A maid's work in her employer's house.
   c. Direct sale of an old car by Suresh to Sanchita.
   d. Depreciation of machines due to wear, tear, and obsolescence.
   e. Profits of a foreign company.
   f. Pension payments to retired employees.
   g. Earnings a share broker.
   h. Monthly allowance that a child gets from his parents.

13. National income neither includes all the market transactions nor excludes all the non-market transactions in goods and services. Explain.
14. In what sense is saving always equal to investment?
15. Increases in real GDP are often interpreted as increase in welfare. What are some problems with this interpretation? Which do you think is the biggest problem with it, and why?
16. What, if anything, is wrong with the following data?
    In an economy investment exceeds saving by Rs. 12,000. Budget deficit is Rs. 7,000 and net export is Rs. 5,000.
17. a. The CPI of a country was 177.1 in 2021 and 179.9 in 2022 (with base year 2011)

    Calculate the inflation rate for 2022

    b. The following table shows how much a family spends on pizzas, ice-cream, and two bottles of antacid every month for the year 2010 and the current year.

    How much has the average price level of prices increased?

Goods	*Price in 2010*	*Current price*	*Quantity purchased*
Pizzas	Rs. 80 per piece	Rs. 100 per piece	10
Ice-cream	Rs. 30 per piece	Rs. 40 per piece	8
Antacid	Rs. 30 per piece	Rs. 30 per piece	2

18. Consider the following information:

    GNP = Rs. 4,800, Gross investment = Rs. 800, Net investment = Rs. 300,
    C = Rs. 3,000, G = Rs. 960, Budget surplus = Rs. 30.
    Find out NNP, Net Export, Tax – Transfer, DPI, S.

19. Consider the following information:

    Consumption = Rs. 4,500
    Government expenditure = Rs. 1,100
    Gross investment = Rs. 800
    Net investment = Rs. 550
    GDP = Rs. 7,000
    Budget surplus = Rs. 30
    Find out net export, DPI, personal saving.

20. Consider the following information:

    NI = 3,850
    G = 930
    C = 3,000
    Net investment = 300
    Gross investment = 800
    Personal tax and non-tax payment = 600
    Transfer Payment = 510
    Net interest = 120
    Govt budget surplus = 30
    Dividend = 100
    Proprietor's and rental income = 320
    Wages and salaries = 2,920
    GNP = 4,800
    Compute (T – TR), PI, NX, Net indirect tax.

Additional readings

Ackley, G. (1987). *Macroeconomics: Theory and Policy*, Chapters 1–3. New York: Macmillan.
Minhas, B. S. (ed) (2002). *National Income Accounts and data Systems*. New Delhi: Oxford University Press.
Samuelson P. A. (1970). *Economics*, 8th ed., Chapter 10. New York: McGraw-Hill.
Stone, R. & Stone, G. S. (1958). *National Income and Expenditure*. Oxford: Oxford University Press.

Part II

Classical school of thought – the long run supply side model

3 Classical model

3.1 Introduction

Macroeconomic analysis essentially tries to explain cyclical fluctuations of different macro aggregates of an economy or business cycles. To study business cycles we should start with the long run equilibrium values of macroeconomic aggregates like national income, employment, price level, real wage level, real interest rate, etc. The classical macro model is considered as a benchmark model for this analysis. John Maynard Keynes first used the term "classical" to refer to that body of thought which existed before the publication of Keynes's (1936) general theory. That's why we will discuss classical theory prior to Keynesian. In fact, no single formalised theory of aggregate employment existed before the publication of general theory. The term "classical economics" was first used by Karl Marx, who used it to cover the theories of Adam Smith, David Ricardo, John Stuart Mill, J. B. Say, and Robert Malthus among others. Keynes extended the period to include the works of the followers of Ricardo, who believe in Say's law of markets, namely, Alfred Marshall, A. C. Pigou, F. Y. Edgeworth, Leon Walras, and Irving Fisher. Say's law, one of the pillars of the classical system, states that the supply creates its own demand and there is no possibility of general overproduction. The classical economists believe that in a competitive capitalist economy there exists an automatic mechanism, known as the invisible hand, which brings about full employment. For the classical economists, thus, full employment was the normal state of affairs. Classical idea emerged as a revolution against mercantilist thoughts.

Mercantilists focus on two things:

i) Accumulation of precious metal to make a country prosperous.
ii) In this process, government should take a positive role.

Mercantilists considered accumulation of precious metals as the over-riding goal of every economy. Favourable international trade can ensure the greatest possible holdings of precious metals. So government should promote foreign trade. Classical ideas depart significantly from those thoughts and are thus considered the first revolution in macroeconomic theory and policy.

Unlike mercantilists, classicalists believe in i) laissez faire; ii) the optimisation theory; iii) Say's law. They believed that people are rational and act optimally. Classical economists had faith in the free-market mechanism and self-adjusting tendencies of the economy, with the least government intervention. Government only looks after the defence, law and order, provision of public works, promotion of free trade, etc. According to the

DOI: 10.4324/9781003501138-5

famous Say's law, "supply creates its own demand". The demand was given no role in income determination and was considered purely supply determined. Classical economists were aware that a market economy could deviate from its equilibrium level of output and employment. However, they believed that such disturbances would be temporary and very short lived. The market mechanism would operate quickly and efficiently to restore full employment equilibrium. Thus, government intervention, in the form of stabilisation policies, would be neither necessary nor desirable. Indeed, such policies were likely to create greater instability. Hence fiscal policy was considered to be totally ineffective with respect to output and employment. The classical writers gave little attention to either the factors which determine aggregate demand or the policies which could be used to stabilise aggregate demand in order to promote full employment.

Classical theory was founded on two basic postulate: i) Wage-price flexibility and ii) perfect information about the market. The assumption of wage price flexibility ensures full employment equilibrium and below-full employment was regarded as abnormal. The model tries to show that through the market mechanism, the market always clears (i.e. demand equals supply). If there is excess supply the price falls and demand supply ultimately matches. Similarly in the labour market the flexibility of real wage will ensure full employment. In this model saving and investment depend on interest rate. People save in order to earn interest, hence saving is considered to be a rising function of interest rate. Investment, on the other hand, depends negatively on the interest rate. Accordingly, interest rate is determined by saving and investment in the capital market. Variation in the interest rate would thus ensure the equilibrium in the capital market. The sum total of the private consumption, investment, and government expenditure would always equal the level of output governed by the full employment of all resources.

The other important feature of the classical model is that the model is segmented or *dichotomised*, for instance it is made of parts, each of which is independent. This refers to the division of the economy into the real and monetary sectors and considerations that they are working separately. Classical economists feel that on account of predominance of monetary transaction, people look at the monetary side without looking at the real income or actual production. This creates what is known as money illusion. The classical economists have tried to remove the monetary veil underlying the working of the real economy, thus the role of money is very insignificant in this model. Let us now concentrate on the structure of the model.

3.2 The model

The classical model happens to be the first full-fledged macroeconomic model and its implications were well accepted as the reality until the outburst of the great depression of the 1930s. The experience of the Great Depression (1929–1933) had left serious doubts regarding the classical theory. This inspired Keynes to give a new twist to macroeconomic theory and policy.

Let us first concentrate on the description of the model constructed by classical economists. As already mentioned, in this dichotomised structure, real variables are determined in the real sector of the economy whereas nominal variables are determined in the monetary sector. The production function and factor market independently determine the full employment level of output; product market determines the equilibrium rate of interest but price level is determined in the money market.

3.2.1 *Output and employment relationship*

Production function provides the relation between a quantity of factor inputs and maximum quantity of outputs that can be produced given the production technology. To present the classical model we start with the two-input production technology; $Y = f(L, K)$. Assuming capital to be constant $(\bar{K})$, in the short run it can be written as

$$Y = f(L, \bar{K}) \tag{3.1}$$

Here Y represents real output and L is the quantity of homogeneous labour input. Technology and population are assumed to be constant over the period considered. Marginal productivity of labour is positive but follows a diminishing marginal product of labour, for instance, $f' > 0, f'' < 0$. This property implies that although more capital always leads to more output, it does so at a decreasing rate. Successive increases in the amount of labour employed yield less and less additional output. Thus, total product curve (TP) is upward rising and concave from below as drawn in Figure 3.1. The production function will shift upwards if the fixed input capital is increased and/or there is an increase in the productivity (technological improvement). This production function is assumed to obey constant returns to scale in the long run.

Classical economists assume that the quantity of labour employed would be determined by the forces of demand and supply in the labour market.

3.2.2 *Labour market*

Analysis of labour market involves two concepts; labour demand (L^D) and labour supply (L^S).

3.2.2.1 *Labour demand: (L^D)*

The demand for the labour comes from the employer. From Say's law it follows that whatever be the aggregate level of output produced, it will create an equal amount of demand. In this scenario the employer or the producer takes the decision of labour employment and hence produces the level of output on the basis of his profit-maximising behaviour. So, we shall derive the profit maximising level of output of the firms, when they can sell whatever they produce. In the classical model all markets are perfectly competitive. However, we focus here only on the short run such that stock of capital

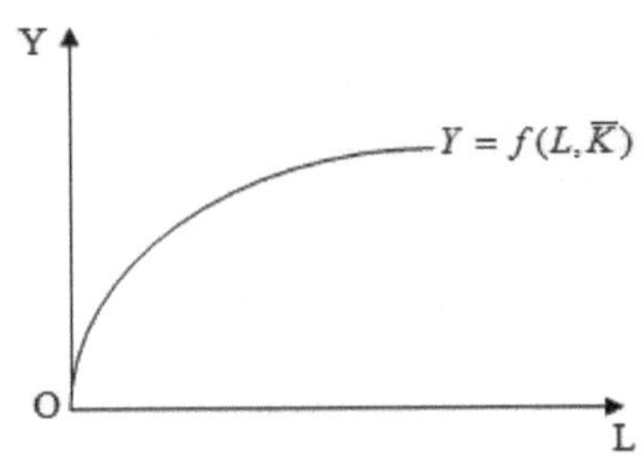

Figure 3.1 Classical production function

is given. Profit of a particular price taker firm operating under a perfectly competitive market is given by

$$\begin{aligned}\pi &= R - C \\ &= PY - C \\ &= Pf(L,\bar{K}) - (wL + r\bar{K})\end{aligned}$$

FOC for maximisation implies:

$$\frac{d\pi}{dL} = 0 \Rightarrow P.f'(L) - w = 0 \Rightarrow f'(L) = \frac{w}{P}.$$

SOC for maximisation implies:

$$\frac{d^2\pi}{dL^2} < 0 \Rightarrow Pf''(L) < 0.$$

The perfectly competitive firm will thus increase output until the marginal cost of producing a unit is equal to the marginal revenue received from its sale. The marginal cost of each additional unit of output is equal to the marginal labour cost. Marginal labour cost equals the money wage divided by the no. of units of output produced by the additional unit of labour, for instance $MC = \frac{w}{f'(L)}$. Also under perfectly competitive equilibrium, $P = MC$. Hence, we get $P = \frac{w}{f'(L)} \Rightarrow \frac{w}{P} = f'(L)$. Hence, we can write $L^D = g(\frac{w}{P})$. If we plot the level of employment on the horizontal axis and real wage on the vertical axis, the marginal product of labour curve will represent the firm's demand curve for labour. It gives us the amount of labour demanded at different real wage rates.

We can derive the slope of labour demand curve mathematically also. Substituting profit maximising level of employment by L^D and putting it into first order condition (FOC) we get $f'(L^D) = \frac{w}{P}$. Taking total differential, we have $f''dL^D = d(\frac{w}{P})$

$$\text{Or, } \frac{dL^D}{d(\frac{w}{P})} = \frac{1}{f''} < 0.$$

Thus, we get an inverse relationship between the real wage rate and the demand for labour. Because the MP_L and labour demand curves are identical, a beneficial supply shock that raises the MP_L at every level of labour shifts the MP_L curve and hence labour demand curves upward and to the right.

In the prior analysis we considered the behaviour of an individual firm. The same reasoning can be applied to the economy as a whole. Aggregate labour demand curve is the horizontal summation of an individual firm's labour demand curve which will also be negatively sloped, i.e., an increase in real wage lowers labour demand. The aggregate labour demand function is expressed in Equation (3.2)

$$L^D = L^D(\frac{w}{P}), L^{D'} < 0 \tag{3.2}$$

Because the aggregate demand for labour is the sum of firms' labour demands, the factors that determine the aggregate demand for labour are the same as those for an individual firm.

3.2.2.2 *Labour supply (L^s)*

We now concentrate on the supply side of the labour market. It is assumed in the classical model that households aim to maximise their utility.The utility maximisation exercise of an individual with regard to the work establishes a direct relation between real wage and labour supply. How much labour will be supplied depends on household preferences for consumption and leisure, both of which yield positive utility. A rise in the real wage makes leisure more expensive in terms of forgone income and will tend to increase the supply of labour. This is known as the substitution effect. On the other hand, a rise in the real wage makes workers better off, so they can afford to choose more leisure. This is known as the income effect. The classical model assumes that the substitution effect dominates the income effect so that the labour supply responds positively to an increase in the real wage. Hence, we get positively sloped classical labour supply function as

$$L^s = L^s(\frac{w}{P}) \; ; L^{s'} > 0 \tag{3.3}$$

The aggregate supply of labour is the total amount of labour supplied by everyone in the economy. An increase in the real wage raises the aggregate quantity of labour supplied for two reasons. First, when the real wage rises, workers already employed may supply more hours. Second, a higher real wage may induce some voluntarily unemployed persons to join the labour force. Thus, a higher real wage induces people to want to work more. Thus, the aggregate labour supply curve slopes upward.

We are now in a position to examine the determination of the competitive equilibrium output, employment, and real wage in the classical model. The labour market is in equilibrium when labour demand and labour supply are equal; this requires

$$L^s(\frac{w}{P}) = L^D(\frac{w}{P}) \tag{3.4}$$

Solving (3.4) we get the full employment real wage rate $(\frac{w}{P})_f$. The level of employment in equilibrium represents "full employment", in that all those members of the labour force who desire to work at the equilibrium real wage can do so. Putting this value of the market clearing real wage rate either in the labour demand function or in the labour supply function, we get an equilibrium level of employment, which is also full employment level of employment (L_f). Graphically at the intersection of downward sloping labour demand and the upward rising labour supply curve, equilibrium real wage rate $(\frac{w}{P})_f$ and equilibrium level of employment L_f are determined. According to classicalists, any unemployment that exists at real wage rate $(\frac{w}{P})_f$ must be voluntary in nature.

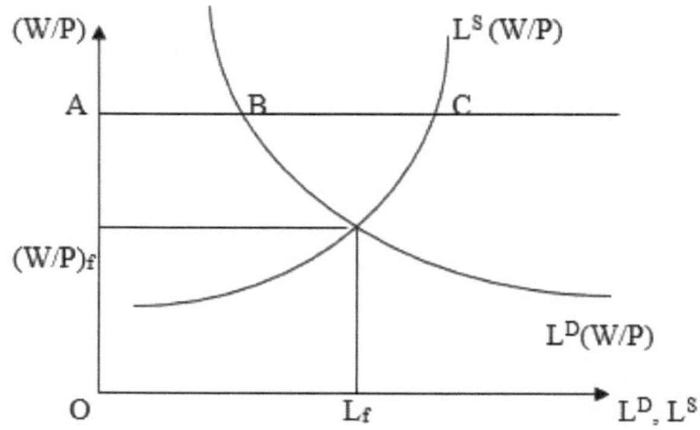

Figure 3.2 Labour market equilibrium

The classical model assumes wage price flexibility both in upward and downward directions which automatically ensures full employment. If the real wage rate rises above $(\frac{w}{P})_f$, labour supply exceeds labour demand and unemployment will prevail. As shown in the previous diagram, there exist excess supply of labour by an amount BC, if real wage rate is OA. Employment and output will fall below full employment level and will be determined by the amount of labour demand. In this situation money wages will fall because of competition among workers. More workers will be demanded and more employment will be created. Supply of output will increase as a result until full employment is reached. Here wage rate falls and ultimately full employment is restored. This result is guaranteed in the classical model because the classical economists assumed perfectly competitive markets, flexible prices, and full information. So, there cannot be any question of underemployment equilibrium, as competition in the labour market ensures full employment. One point should be remembered in this connection: classical full employment equilibrium is perfectly compatible with the existence of frictional and voluntary unemployment, but it does not admit the possibility of involuntary unemployment. At the equilibrium real wage, no person who wishes to work at that real wage is without employment. Substituting the value of L_f in the production function we get full employment level of output (Y_f). As production simultaneously creates income and purchasing power, there could be no obstacle to the full employment due to deficiency of aggregate demand. Thus, in the classical model *output and employment are determined solely by supply factors*. Keynes, however, regarded the full employment equilibrium of the classical model as a special case because it corresponded to a situation where aggregate demand was just sufficient to absorb the level of output produced. He objected that there was no guarantee that aggregate demand would be at such a level.

3.3 Capital market and the interest rate determination in the classical model

The simplified version of the classical model has not shown the way in which output would be allocated between consumption and investment. It was Knut Wicksell who first addressed this issue. According to him, since households do not automatically spend all of their income, they will hold some percentage of it in the form of saving. Instead of keeping it in idle form, income devoted to saving would be used to purchase interest-bearing assets. Purchasing of these assets would facilitate investment by the seller of these assets. As a result, the sum of consumption and investment would necessarily be equal to the actual level of income. Thus, the amount of income saved by an individual depends upon the rate of interest. As rate of interest could be considered as a reward for saving, the higher the rate of interest the more willing the savers would be to replace present consumption with future consumption.

Thus,

$$S = S(r), S' > 0. \tag{3.5}$$

Wicksell also presumed investment to be negatively related to interest rate. The higher the rate of interest, the higher the explicit (and implicit) cost of the funds used to purchase the capital goods. Investment expenditure on capital goods is thus negatively related to the rate of interest and also represents a demand for loanable funds in the capital market.

$$I = I(r), I' < 0 \tag{3.6}$$

Equilibrium in the capital market would occur at that interest rate where

$$S(r) = I(r) \tag{3.7}$$

$$C = Y - S \tag{3.8}$$

In Figure 3.3, r_f, S_f, I_f represent equilibrium values of interest rate, saving, and investment. Thus, in the classical model *interest rate itself is determined in the capital market.*

In Figure 3.3 the vertical income schedule reflects the constancy of full employment income level. Corresponding to equilibrium interest rate, r_f, saving and investment take on the values S_f and I_f respectively; as $C = Y - S$, the level consumption at r_f is measured as

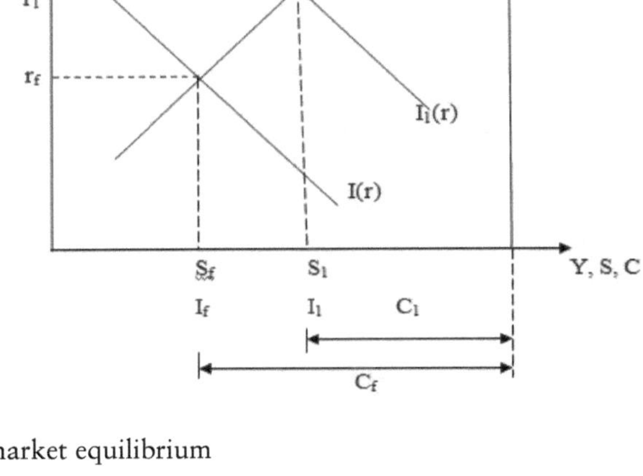

Figure 3.3 Capital market equilibrium

the distance from S_f to Y_f. If *investment function takes another value* $I_1(r)$, the resultant equilibrium interest rate will be r_1 and the equilibrium level of saving (S_1) will be higher.

Thus, again the sum of component of income $(C_1 + S_1)$ would be equal to the sum of value of expenditure $(C_1 + I_1)$. Even though in the classical model the decisions to save and invest can be carried out by different sets of people, the rate of interest will change so as to reconcile the desires to save and invest.

Similarly, if *households suddenly decided to save more*, consuming less, there will be a rightward shift of the saving function. The initial excess supply of loanable funds would lead to a fall in the rate of interest that would encourage an increase in investment expenditure. Aggregate expenditure $(C + I)$ would remain the same, although its composition would change (shown in Figure 3.4). In the case of an increase in saving, the Keynesian model predicts a decline in aggregate spending, output, and employment resulting in paradox of thrift. But in the classical model there will be a change in the composition of final demand though no prolonged demand deficiency and involuntary unemployment will appear.

The Wicksellian capital market is an extremely important building block in the classical model. It presumed that the interest rate would be flexible enough to bring saving–investment equality. As long as this flexibility is maintained, full employment income level would also be an equilibrium level. The capital market has a completely different function in the Wicksellian model than it had in the SKM. In SKM, the equality of saving and investment determine the equilibrium level of income whereas in the Wicksellian model income is determined from outside the capital market. Capital market simply generates the value of saving and investment which will accommodate that predetermined level of income.

3.4 Money market in the classical system

A model is not complete unless it shows how nominal variables like money, wage rate, and money prices are determined. In the classical model these nominal variables are determined in the monetary sector. Like any other market, the money market has two sides – the demand side and the supply side. Equilibrium in the money market is achieved when the supply of money is equal to demand for money. The quantity of money includes the sum of outstanding paper money and coins, for instance currency held by the public, and

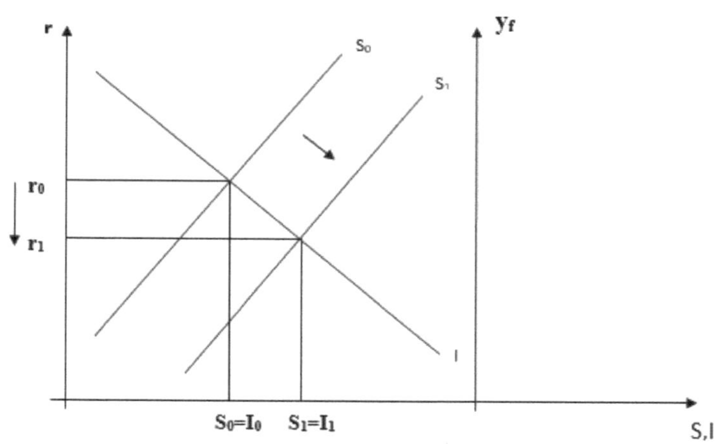

Figure 3.4 Change in aggregate expenditure

the demand deposit in the commercial banking system. Supply of money in the classical model is exogenously determined by the central bank of the concerned economy; we have

$$M^S = \overline{M} \tag{3.9}$$

The motive for money holding in the classical model is to carry out day-to-day transactions. The demand for money is therefore dependent on the level of income only and not on the rate of interest. Money demand is assumed to be proportional to nominal GDP. If P denotes price level and Y denotes real output or GDP, then

$$M^D = kPY \tag{3.10}$$

Parameter k in the previous equation is the reciprocal of the income velocity of circulation of money (discussed later under quantity theory of money). Money market equilibrium condition is thus given by

$$\overline{M} = kPY \tag{3.11}$$

As equilibrium value of Y is determined in the real sector, given $Y = Y_f$, we can solve for equilibrium value of P from Equation (3.11). This equation is also known as quantity theory of money. Therefore, $P = \dfrac{\overline{M}}{kY_f}$. Since Y_f and k are constant, the price level (P) depends only on nominal money supply ($\overline{M}$). Determination of equilibrium value of price level in the money market can be shown graphically with the help of Figure 3.5.

Equation $\dfrac{\overline{M}}{k} = PY$, similar to that of Equation (3.11), can be represented by a rectangular hyperbola in the P, Y plane. The equilibrium value of P, labelled P_f, corresponds to the equilibrium (also full employment) value of Y, determined in the real sector of the economy. Given that the equilibrium value of real wage, $(\frac{w}{P})_f$, is determined in the labour market and price level in the money market, nominal wage rate can be obtained from the relation $W = (\frac{w}{P})_f P$. Since $(\frac{w}{P})_f$ is a constant, the equation represents a straight line through the origin. Given the equilibrium value of P, determination of equilibrium nominal wage is shown in Figure 3.6.

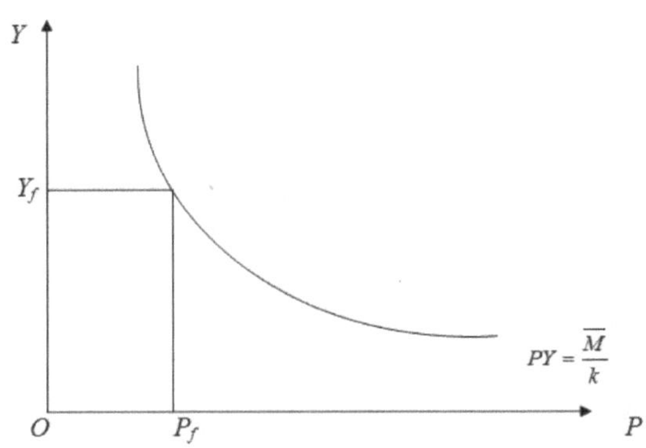

Figure 3.5 Determination of price level in classical model

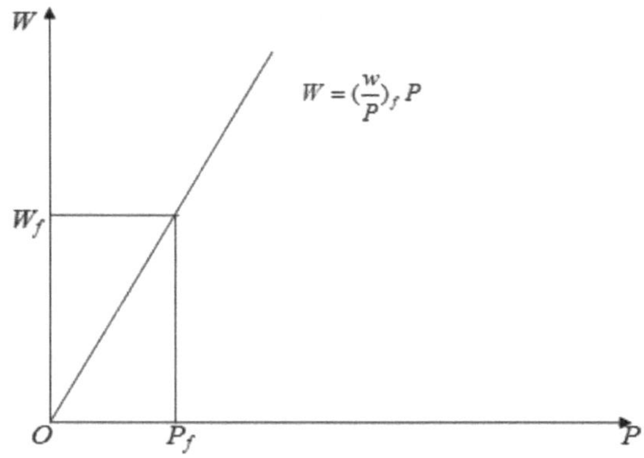

Figure 3.6 Determination of money wage

3.5 Complete picture of the classical model and classical dichotomy

In order to demonstrate the complete picture of the stylised classical model we have drawn the six panels in diagram (3.7). In panel I of the figure, the labour market determines the equilibrium real wage $((\frac{w}{P})_f)$ and the level of employment (L_f). The labour market equilibrium is one in which the market is cleared; that is, full employment of labour is attained at the point of equilibrium. Given employment (L_f), total output (Y_f) can be derived from the production function represented in panel (II). Panel (III) is used as a mechanical device to aid in the presentation in the model where we have sketched a 45-degree line in order to cast the full employment level of output (L_f) from the vertical axis of panel (II) to the horizontal axis of panel (IV).

Given this full employment level of income, the decomposition of income into consumption and saving and the corresponding decomposition of aggregate expenditures into consumption and investment are accomplished in the capital market. This is shown in panel (IV). In the classical model, the interest rate is assumed to adjust to that value (r_f) at which saving (S_f) and investment (I_f) are equal. The determination of the level of income and the assumption of a given nominal money supply $(\bar{M})$ allow a solution for the corresponding price level (P_f) through the quantity-theory equation depicted in panel (V). Then, given the price level, the value of the money wage (W_f) is found through the real-wage identity shown in panel (VI). It is evident that the determination of the equilibrium real rate of interest is independent of the determination of equilibrium values of other variables.

The goods market, production function, and capital market constitute the *real sector* of the economy. All real endogenous variables of the system $(Y,\ r,\ L^D,\ L^s,\ S, C,\ I, (\frac{w}{P}))$ are determined in this real segment without any reference to the monetary sector. The real sector of the classical model is therefore a self-contained independent system. Endogenous nominal variables like price level and money wage are determined from the monetary sector of the economy. But the determination of the absolute prices depends on the values of the real variables obtained from the real sector. Any change in the real sector, thus, affects the monetary sector, but changes occurring in the monetary sector do not affect the real sector. This separation of the two sectors is known as *classical dichotomy*. It can be further illustrated with the help of the following flow chart, incorporating the equations of the classical model.

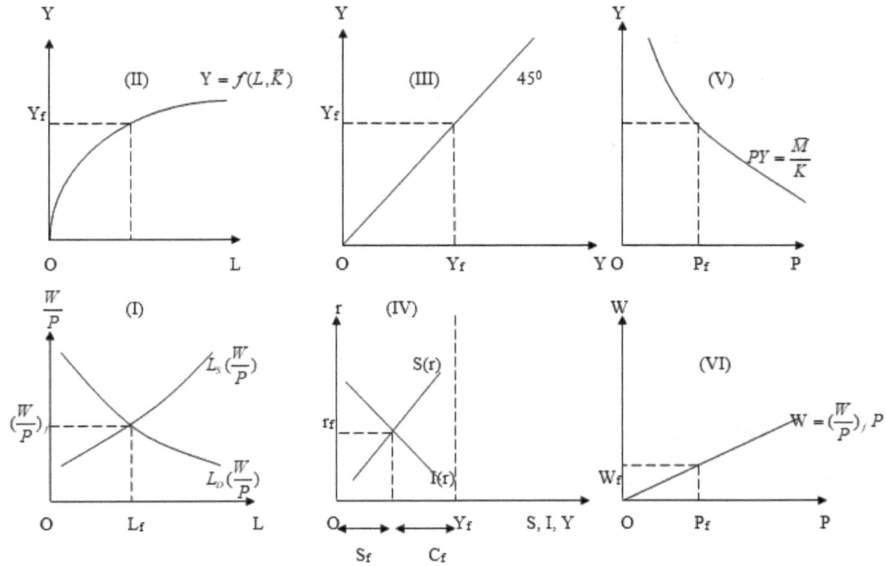

Figure 3.7 Complete picture of classical model

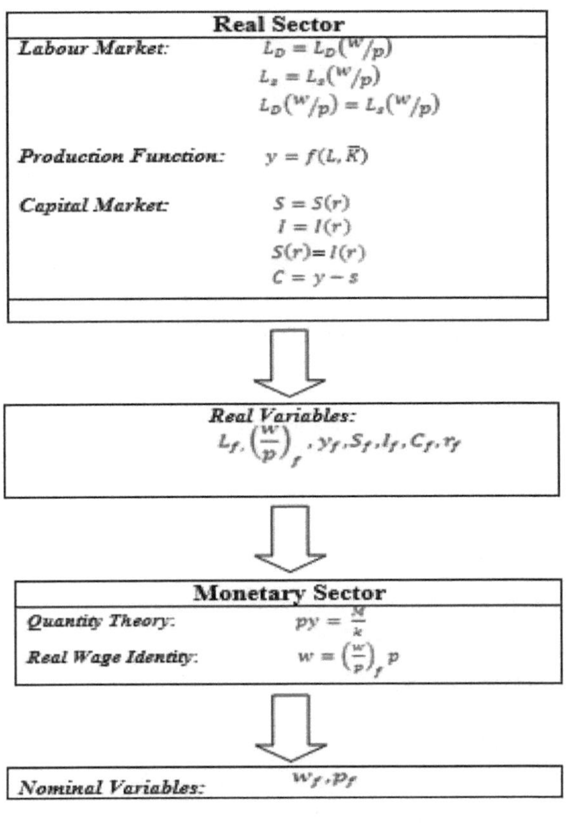

Figure 3.8 Flow chart showing determination of variables

3.6 Effect of change in money supply

An important feature of classical model, as already discussed, is that the real wage rate, employment, real income, and real interest rate are independent of the quantity of money. Any change in money supply by monetary authority will create disequilibrium in the money market. So, if money supply changes, income, employment, real wage, interest rate, etc. will not be affected. Only Equation (3.11) will be affected. If $\overline{M}$ increases, then the right-hand side of the equation $\overline{M} = kPY$ has to increase to maintain money market equilibrium. As k and Y are constant in the classical model, P must increase in the same proportion to maintain equilibrium. Since the real wage is unaffected, money wage must also increase in the same proportion in which the price level increases. If money supply is doubled from $\overline{M}$ to $2\overline{M}$ then the rectangular hyperbola curve will shift upward as shown in Figure 3.9. As Y_f is unchanged, P_f has to be doubled to maintain money market equilibrium.

Figure 3.10 explains the impact on money wage graphically. Real wage $(\frac{w}{P})$ is determined in the real sector of the economy, hence it will not be affected as a result of money

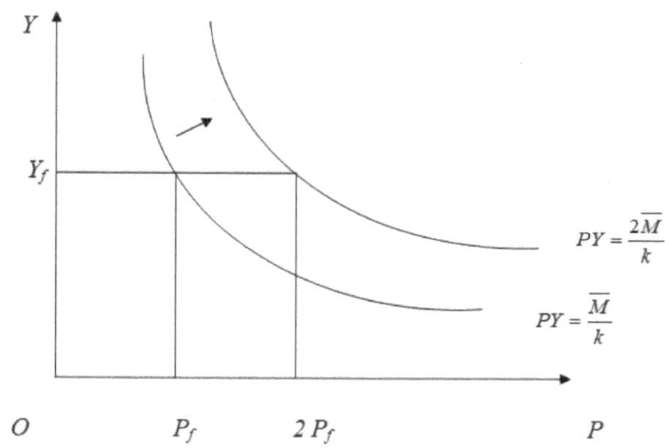

Figure 3.9 Impact of money supply change on price level

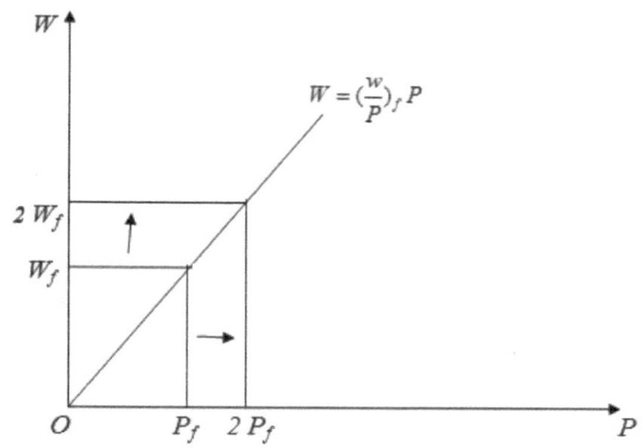

Figure 3.10 Impact of money supply change on nominal wage

supply change. So as price increases from P_f to $2P_f$, nominal wage must increase from W_f to $2W_f$, to keep real wage unchanged. Thus, like fiscal policy, monetary policy has no stabilisation role. Rather *money is a veil* which leaves real variables of the system unaffected while monetary variables will change proportionately.

3.7 Neutrality of money and AD-AS curve

We have pointed out earlier that the equilibrium values of the real variables are independent of money supply. The competitive labour market generates equilibrium employment of labour and real wage. The equilibrium value of Y, determined at Y_f, is derived from production function. It therefore follows from (3.11) that the increase in money supply will only lead to a change in the price level, P. The money wage rate (another nominal variable) will also increase in the same proportion as the price level and the money supply, to keep real wage unchanged. A change in the money supply in classical model, as is evident from the previous analysis, does not produce any real effect. It only brings about equi-proportionate changes in the nominal variables, namely the money price and the money wage rate. This result is referred to as the *neutrality of money*.

This result can be explained graphically using AD and AS curves. For a given money supply, the AD schedule can be derived using Equation (3.11). The money market equilibrium condition $\frac{\overline{M}}{k} = PY$ clearly represents a rectangular hyperbola in (Y, P) plane, for given values of $\overline{M}$ and k. Hence, the *classical AD curve is negatively sloped* reflecting the fact that, for given values of $\overline{M}$ and k, a higher price level is associated with a lower level of real output. With higher prices, each transaction requires more money. Therefore, the quantity of goods and services that can be bought will fall. This rectangular hyperbola or AD curve is consistent with a given money stock. An increase in money stock, at a given price level, shifts the AD curve rightward.

Let us start from the full-employment situation. Suppose price level increases, then at the given money wage rate (W), real wage rate ($\frac{W}{P}$) falls. This obviously leads to rise in labour demand (L^D) and fall in labour supply (L^S). Thus, there arises excess demand, ($L^D - L^S$) in the labour market and money wage will rise as a result. Actually, firms responding to higher prices attempt to expand employment and production. To expand employment, they raise money wage. The process of raising money wage will stop only when it has increased sufficiently to re-equilibrate the supply and demand in the labour market with real wage maintaining the full employment level. Thus, whatever be the price level, output always remains at the full-employment level. Hence, *the classical aggregate supply curve is vertical.*

Vertical AS curve corresponding to full employment level of output is then superimposed on the downward sloping AD schedule in the following figure such that the point of intersection gives equilibrium value of P.

Following an increase in $\overline{M}$ (from $\overline{M}_0$ to $\overline{M}_1$), the money market equilibrium condition $\frac{\overline{M}}{P} = kY$ will be satisfied, given Y, if P rises in the same proportion as $\overline{M}$ so that $(\frac{\overline{M}}{P})$ remains unchanged. The AD schedule in Figure 3.11 therefore shifts upward (from AD_0 to AD_1) in the same proportion as money supply. But the vertical AS schedule remains

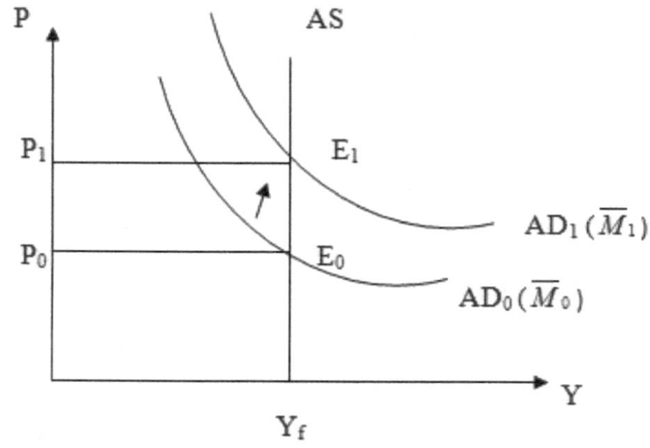

Figure 3.11 Neutrality of money

unchanged at full employment level. Hence, the equilibrium P, given by the point of intersection of the AD and AS, rises from P_0 to P_1 in the same proportion as nominal money supply.

Following an increase in money supply, people find that they have more money in their hands. They will use this excess money balance to purchase goods and services creating excess demand in the goods market. This will start raising the price level. The rise in the price level will lower the real wage rate below its market clearing level generating excess demand for labour. The money wage rate will rise instantaneously to keep the labour market in equilibrium. Thus, with the rise in the price level, the money wage rate will also start increasing in the same proportion, keeping the real wage rate at the market clearing level. Hence, producers will continue to produce the full employment level of output. This process of increase in the price level and the money wage rate will continue until the rise in the price level transaction demand for money goes up and becomes equal to the new higher money supply. When this happens excess demand for goods and services also disappears as people cease to have any excess money to spend on goods and services. This justifies the neutrality of money proposition and explains why a change in money supply brings about an equi-proportionate increase in the price level and the money wage rate, leaving all the real variables unaffected.

3.8 Effect of a shift of the production function

We can see the effect of an upward shift of the production function in the classical model. The upward shift implies an increase in productivity or marginal product of labour. As the marginal product of labour increases, the labour demand curve shifts to the right. In the "b" part of Figure 3.12, the production function shifts from Y to Y_2; accordingly we get a new marginal product curve or labour demand curve L_d^2 in part "a" of the following figure. The equilibrium real wage rate increases from $(\frac{W}{P})_f$ to $(\frac{W}{P})_2$ and the equilibrium employment increases from L_f to L_2. Output increases from Y_f to Y_2 both because of

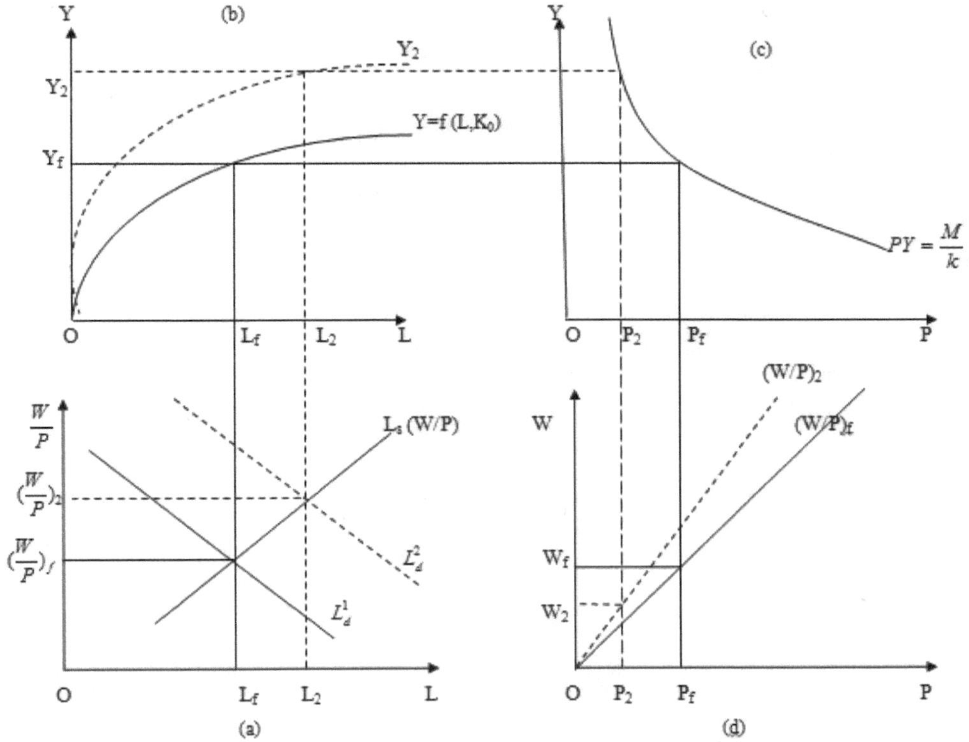

Figure 3.12 Shift of production function

higher productivity and larger employment. Money supply remaining unchanged, price level falls from P_f to P_2 in part "c" of the diagram. Since the real wage rises, the real wage line rotates from $(\frac{W}{P})_f$ to $(\frac{W}{P})_2$. As can be seen from part "d" of the figure, when the price level falls, money wage rate also falls from W_f to W_2. However, depending on the slopes of the various functions, the new money wage might also be higher than the old. The real wage rate will definitely be higher as well.

3.9 Effect of shift of supply of labour

We can see the effects of a rightward shift of the labour supply curve (money supply remaining unchanged) in the classical model. The effects can be analysed with help of Figure 3.13. In the diagram, the labour supply curve has shifted from $L_1(\frac{W}{P})$ to $L_2(\frac{W}{P})$. This has the effect of increase in the equilibrium level of employment from L_1 to L_2 and reducing the equilibrium real wage rate from $(\frac{W}{P})_1$ to $(\frac{W}{P})_2$. From the diagram, we can also see that when the level of employment has increased from L_1 to L_2, the level of output has also increased from Y_1 to Y_2. Now, as the level of output increases from Y_1 to Y_2,

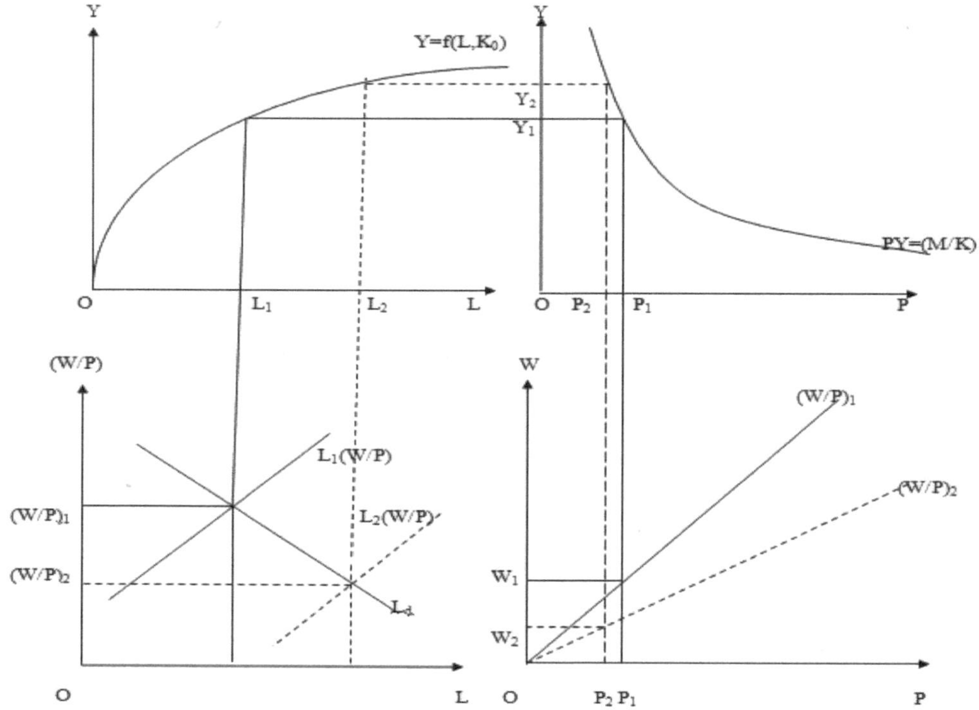

Figure 3.13 Shift of labour supply

the equilibrium price level decreases from P_1 to P_2, given the money supply. As the real wage rate has decreased from $(\frac{W}{P})_1$ to $(\frac{W}{P})_2$, the real wage line $(\frac{W}{P})_2$ has a lower slope than the real wage line $(\frac{W}{P})_1$. From the real wage line $(\frac{W}{P})_2$ it can be seen that the money wage rate is lower at W_2, when the price level has come down to P_2. Thus, the effect of increase in the supply of labour can be summarised as follows: a lower real wage, a larger employment, a larger output, a lower money wage rate and the lower price level. The rate of interest will remain unaffected. It is interesting to note that a change in the real variable affects the money variable as well.

One interesting situation is when both labour supply and productivity increase together, as is evident in a growing economy. Output will grow in this situation as a result of both the reasons. Whether real wage increases or decreases depends on whether labour supply grows faster or less rapidly than labour productivity. But in either case price level must fall. The impact of deflation as a result of this has been described as a source of populist political movement in the American economy during the nineteenth century.

3.10 Long run equilibrium using loanable fund approach

It should be noted in this connection that classical economists did not explicitly explain the capital market. Equilibrium interest rate can thus alternatively be determined in terms of the *loanable fund approach*, also discussed in Chapter 6 while discussing the derivation of the IS curve. The two approaches are two sides of the same coin. From the GDP equation, as resources are fully employed in the classical model, we can write $\bar{Y} = C(\bar{Y} - \bar{T}) + I(r) + \bar{G}$

$$\text{or, } \bar{Y} - C(\bar{Y} - \bar{T}) - \bar{G} = I(r)$$

$$\text{or, } [\bar{Y} - \bar{T} - C(\bar{Y} - \bar{T})] + (\bar{T} - \bar{G}) = I(r) \quad (3.12)$$

The first term on the left-hand side represents disposable income minus consumption, which is known as *private saving*. The second term in the left-hand side, for instance government revenue-government spending, represents government or *public savings*. Hence, the left-hand side of the equation represents *national savings* which is the sum total of two components. It depends on income and fiscal policy variables. This saving also represents *aggregate supply of loanable funds* because households lend their savings to investors or deposit it in a bank that loans out the fund. For fixed values of $\underline{Y}$, $\underline{G}$, and $\underline{T}$, supply of loanable funds is fixed. So, we can write $[\bar{Y} - \bar{T} - C(\bar{Y} - \bar{T})] + (\bar{T} - \bar{G}) = \bar{S}$. The right-hand side of Equation (3.12) represents investment or the *demand for loanable fund* as investors borrow funds from the public directly or indirectly. As investment depends on interest rate, demand for loanable funds also depends on the interest rate. In this equation r is the only variable yet not determined. It must adjust to ensure equilibrium. If we measure investment and saving on the horizontal axis and real interest rate on the vertical axis then savings – or the supply of loanable funds – being independent of rate of interest, will be a vertical line whereas investment or demand for loanable funds will be a downward sloping curve. One might think of a "good" as loanable fund and its price as interest rate. Equilibrium interest rate, r^*, is determined at the intersection point of demand for and supply of the loanable fund schedule.

Any kind of disequilibrium in the system will be taken care of by the variation in the rate of interest. Thus, in the classical model, though the decisions to save and invest are taken by different sets of people, interest rate will change to reconcile the desires to save and invest.

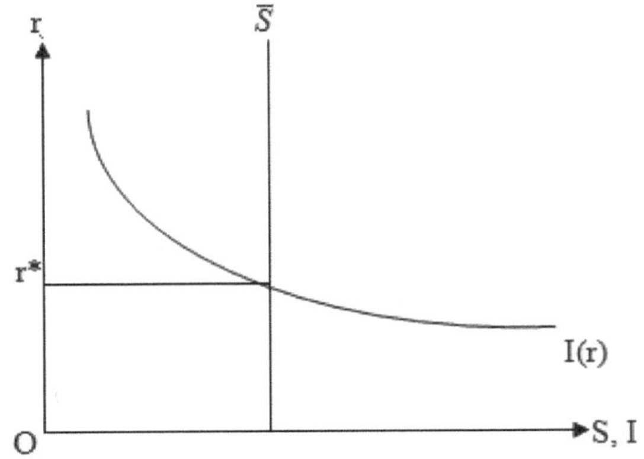

Figure 3.14 Determination of real interest rate

3.10.1 *Fiscal policy and loanable fund approach*

3.10.1.1 *Impact of change in* G

Let us first consider the impact of change in G. Suppose G increases from the previous level $\bar{G}$. From loan market equilibrium condition, we know that $\bar{Y} - C(\bar{Y} - \bar{T}) - \bar{G} = I(r)$ or, alternatively, $[\bar{Y} - \bar{T} - C(\bar{Y} - \bar{T})] + (\bar{T} - \bar{G}) = I(r)$.

An increase in G will cause a reduction in public saving $(\bar{T} - \bar{G})$ but private saving will remain unchanged since Y, C, and T are unchanged. Y is fixed at $\bar{Y}$, due to the assumption of full employment of resources. T is an exogenously fixed policy parameter. Again, consumption remains unchanged as disposable income is unchanged. So, government finances this additional spending by borrowing, thereby reducing public savings. Therefore, national savings or aggregate supply of loanable fund decreases. As shown in the figure, the saving schedule will shift leftward from S_0 to S_1. At the initial interest rate, demand for loanable funds exceeds the supply. Interest rate increases from r_0 to r_1 as a result and investment decreases accordingly.

3.10.1.2 *Impact of change in* T

Let us consider a reduction in taxes by an amount ΔT. This will cause increase in disposable income by ΔT and thereby increase in consumption expenditure by an amount $MPC \times \Delta T$. We know national saving $= [\bar{Y} - \bar{T} - C(\bar{Y} - \bar{T})] + (\bar{T} - \bar{G}) = [\bar{Y} - C(\bar{Y} - \bar{T}) - \bar{G}]$. As consumption expenditure increases, Y and G remaining unchanged, national savings or national supply of loanable funds will be reduced. The supply of loanable funds curve shifts leftward leading to a rise in interest rate and reduction in investment expenditure. Alternatively, we can say that increase in consumption expenditure must be met by a decrease in investment to satisfy $[\bar{Y} - C(\bar{Y} - \bar{T}) - \bar{G}] = I(r)$. For investment to fall, interest rate must rise. Thus, reduction in taxes crowds out investment and raises interest rate.

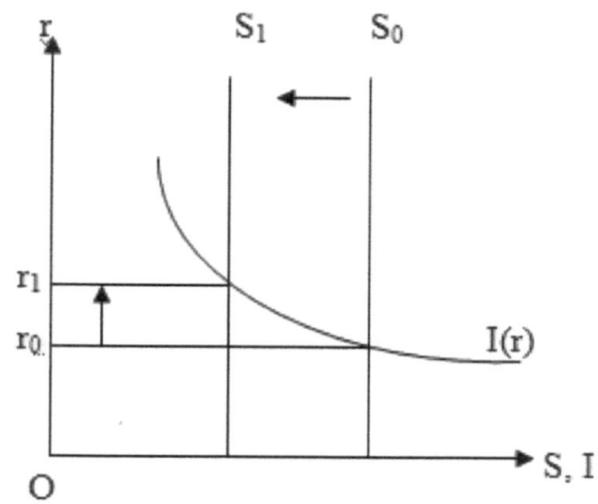

Figure 3.15 Impact of increase in G

3.10.1.3 Change in investment demand for technological innovation

Due to technological innovation, for example, railroads, computers, etc., investment demand may increase which will cause an upward shift of the investment schedule because corresponding to any given interest rate the demand for investment goods is higher. As a result, the interest rate will rise. This can be shown with the help of Figure 3.17. But surprisingly, the equilibrium amount of investment is unchanged as it is determined by the fixed level of saving, by assumption. So, increase in investment will only raise the equilibrium interest rate.

But if the supply of loanable funds and savings become sensitive to interest rate, as in $S = S(r)$, $S' > 0$, where interest rate is the return to savings, then the curve will be positively sloped as shown in Figure 3.18. As a result, any kind of technological innovation leading to an increase in investment demand will cause not only increase in r but also an increase in the level of savings. Increase in r causes households to consume less and save more. The decrease in consumption releases resources for investment.

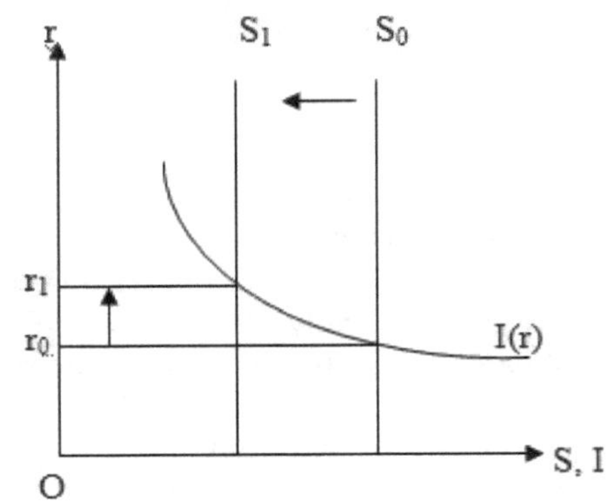

Figure 3.16 Impact of a tax cut

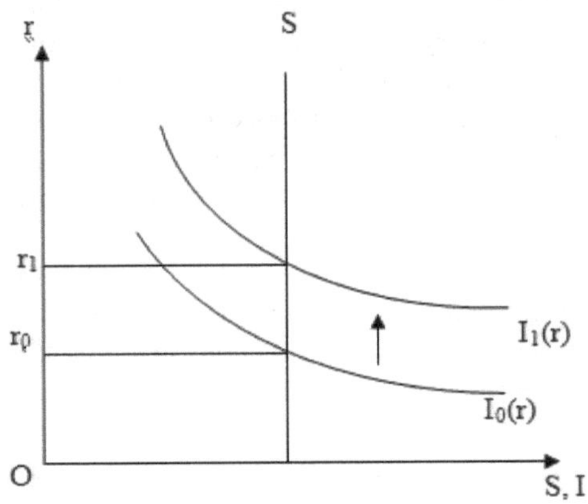

Figure 3.17 Impact of increase in investment demand

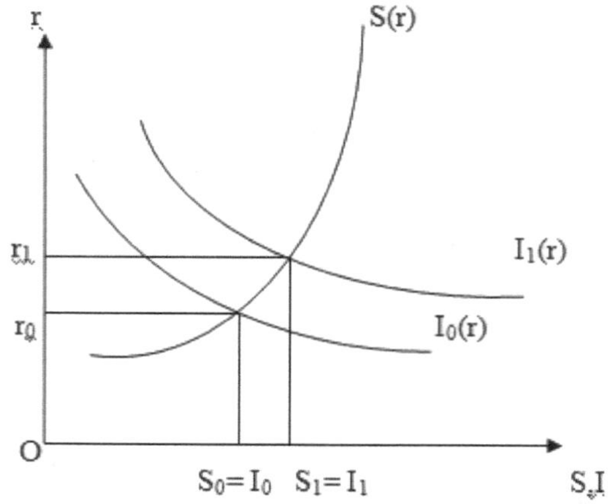

Figure 3.18 Impact of increase in investment demand when saving depends on *r*

3.11 Say's law revisited

One major result of the classical model is Say's law of market, named after J. B. Say, the French economist (1767–1832), which is summarised as "supply creates its own demand". It implies that, whatever be the level of aggregate production, a market economy contains a mechanism that automatically generates a level of aggregate demand that equals the given level of aggregate supply. In other words, because the act of production simultaneously creates income and purchasing power, there could be no impediment to full employment caused by a deficiency of aggregate demand. In a barter economy, Say's law always holds. In a barter economy people exchange goods against another commodity or service. Whenever the individual demands a particular commodity, he at the same time supplies another commodity. Thus, demand is always associated with a supply. But does it hold for a money economy? Money is nothing more than a convenient medium of exchange which enabled market participants to avoid the inconvenience of barter. Classical economists opined that money is a veil, only a medium of exchange, behind which transaction occurs. No rational individual will have any desire to hold it for its own sake. So the law will be equally applicable for a money economy. Say's law does not deny the possibility that a misallocation of resources can occur and that a glut of certain commodities can develop, but this problem would be temporary and no such excess supply could occur for goods as a whole.

The motivation for Say's law is something like this. If production increases (net value) by one crore, the national income will also increase by one crore. This means that individuals will have exactly one more crore for spending. Demand will thus increase by one crore. Hence an increase in supply by one crore has increased demand by the same amount. So, whatever be the amount of output produced, it creates an equal amount of income which in turn create its own demand. There can be no such thing as deficiency of aggregate demand. For example, if at any time overproduction takes place, the market price begins to reduce and demand increases; as a result, the problem of over-production will be removed. Similarly, so long there is unemployment in the labour market, money wages will fall and employment and output will increase. Underemployment equilibrium due to deficiency of effective demand is not possible if Say's law is valid. Full employment must automatically be achieved. If this is the case then there is no need to model aggregate demand. This is also the conclusion of the classical model of income and employment.

An important significance of Say's law is that there is no need for government intervention; the economic system will be controlled automatically without the regulation of regulatory authority. If anywhere equilibrium does not exist, it must be a short run issue; there would be a tendency to correct it through the activities of market force. But there is an important challenge to the correctness of Say's law when individuals save some part of their income. Saved income is derived from the value of final output but doesn't constitute any demand for a final product. Say's law, thus, holds good for a market of consumer goods only, where each participant is spending his entire real income for consumer goods. Classicalists also argued that in money economy, when one sells something one gets money. The money will be used either in buying goods or lending. Since lending gives positive interest, no one will hold idle money. So if one sells goods, either he or the borrower of the money will spend it on goods and hence supply will always be matched by demand. There cannot be mismatch between lending and borrowing, since the interest mechanism equalises demand and supply of loanable fund.

3.12 Criticism of the classical theory

Though the classical model captures a number of broad aspects of macroeconomic performance, the predictions of the model are sometimes imperfect. *Unemployment* is one such aspect. A significant drawback of this basic model is that it cannot be used to study unemployment, because it assumes that any worker who wants to work at the equilibrium real wage can find a job. Keynes argued that, because of monopoly power and many other reasons, in both the goods and labour markets wages and prices will tend to be inflexible downward. This means that in a situation where savings exceeds investment so that aggregate demand is less than the total value of production, firms will reduce output and lay off workers. In this way that demand-deficient unemployment is created. Again, even if wages and prices are flexible, aggregate demand may not be sufficient to ensure full employment. The equilibrium level of income in the Keynesian model is not necessarily the same as the full employment level of income. For this reason, Keynesian theory is called a general theory; the classical theory is no more than the "special case" whose equilibrium and full employment level of income coincided. The general situation in a capitalist economy is one of underemployment. This is because the capitalist society does not function according to Say's law. Keynes rejected the classical quantity theory of money on the grounds that increase in money supply will not necessarily lead to a rise in prices. It is not essential that people spend all their extra money. They may deposit it in the bank or save. So, the velocity of circulation of money may slow down. The classical economists assumed that money is demanded for transactional purposes and did not recognise the speculative demand. Keynes did not agree with this view, instead emphasising the importance of speculative demand for money. Investment often depends on business expectations. So, it is unlikely that the rate of interest would ensure equality between planned savings and planned investment. Also, he rejected wage and price flexibility as reliable methods of restoring equilibrium on theoretical grounds. Classical economists had their eyes fixed firmly on the long run, whereas Keynes was more concerned with the short run.

3.13 Conclusion

The classical model no doubt captures a number of broad aspects of the macroeconomic performance. But many predictions of the model are imperfect (e.g., attainment of full employment) in the real world. We often observe, for example, mild to severe recessions with large inventory unemployment to occur regularly in many economies. Booms with spiralling inflation also occur frequently. So, in the face of hard reality, the description of classical theory seems like a fairy tale. Defenders of classical macroeconomics argue that predictions of the classical system would be fulfilled if many artificial obstacles to free competition (e.g., monopoly power, trade unions, minimum wage law) were removed. But the world in which we live is full of such obstacles, many of which are inherent and durable in nature. The very existence of governments, as well as some almost unavoidable aspects of their performance, also invalidate certain results of classical theory. Thus, a macroeconomic theory was needed to develop which can capture all of these elements of real world. A massive blow to the belief of classical theory came from the Great Depression of the 30s which incentivised Keynes to develop a theory which can explain involuntary unemployment of resources as well as short run cyclical fluctuations in market economies.

Applications

1. Suppose that a country experiences a reduction in productivity – that is adverse shock to the production function.

   a. What happens to the labour demand curve?
   b. Would this change in productivity affect the labour market – that is, employment and real wages – if the labour market was always in equilibrium?
   c. How would this change in productivity affect the labour market if unions prevented real wages from falling?

2. The labour demand curve is given by the marginal product of labour schedule faced by firms. If a country experiences a reduction in productivity, then both the production function and the labour demand curve shift downward. If labour becomes less productive, then at any given real wage, firms demand less labour. Suppose production function shifts from TP_1 to TP_2 as a result of fall in productivity (see Figure 3.19 (a)). Marginal productivity and hence labour demand curve shift inward (see Figure 3.19 (b)) as well from L_1^D, to L_2^D.

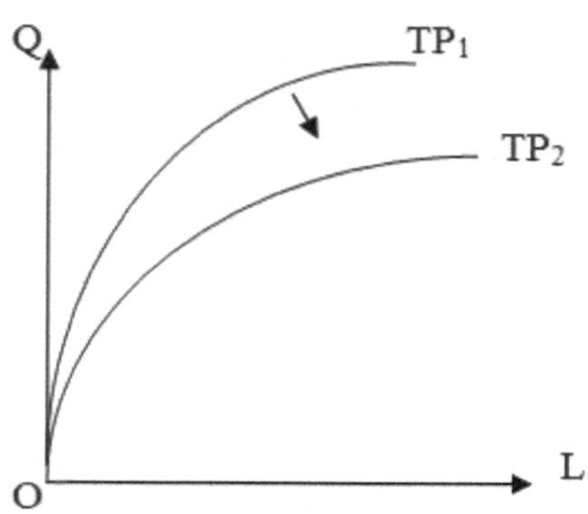

Figure 3.19(a) Downward shift of TP curve

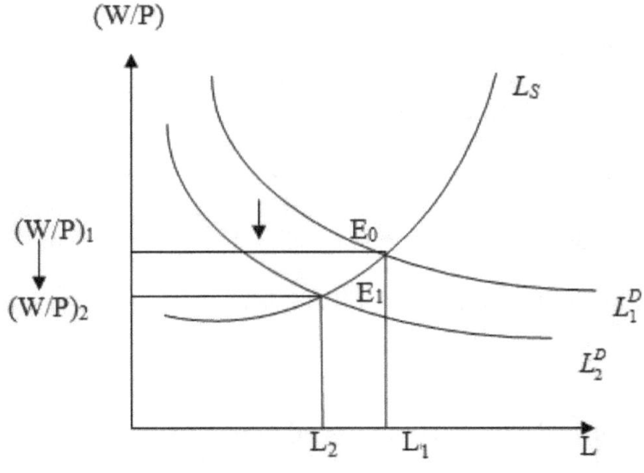

Figure 3.19(b) Downward shift of labour demand curve

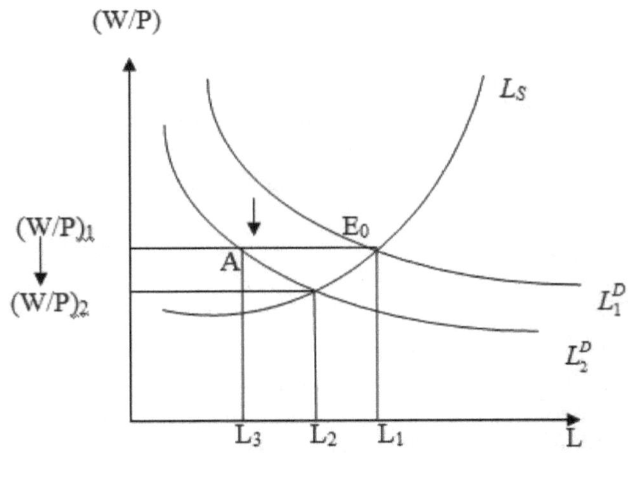

Figure 3.19(c) Downward shift of labour demand curve and downward rigid real wages

3. If the labour market is always in equilibrium, then an adverse productivity shock causes a decrease in the real wage as well as employment as shown in the previous figure. Real wage falls from $(W/P)_1$ to $(W/P)_2$ and employment falls from L_1 to L_2.
4. If unions constrain real wages to remain unaltered at $(W/P)_1$, then as illustrated in Figure (3.19(c)) employment falls to L_3 and unemployment equals $(L_1 - L_3)$. At the initial real wage AE_0 is the measure of unemployment. If real wage continues to be rigid downward, then unemployment will persist. This example shows that the effect of a productivity shock on an economy depends on the strength of union bargaining power.

Summary

- The classical model is sequentially decomposable. The capital market determines the rate of interest and the labour market and production function determine real wage and output. The money market alone determines the absolute price and money wage, given the values of full employment output and real wage respectively.
- In the classical model, the self-stabilising market mechanism always ensures full employment of output. There is no role of fiscal and monetary policies in affecting real output. It thus ruled out interventionist policies. If unemployment somehow occurs, it will be extremely short lived.
- Supply determined nature of output and employment leads to vertical aggregate supply curve.
- Wage price flexibility and perfect information about the market are two essential features of the classical model.
- Money is a veil; it helps in determining only the nominal variables of the model. It cannot influence the quantities of real variables of the system. This feature is known as the neutrality of money.
- The classical model does not face the demand problem. It holds Say's law that supply creates its own demand to be true and there can be no overproduction. Say's law implies that the demand for goods is equal to the supply of goods.

Keywords

Production function
Classical dichotomy
Real wage
Loanable fund approach
Full employment
Neutrality of money
Say's law
Wage price flexibility

Multiple Choice Questions

1. The two cornerstones of classical economics are – .

   (a) The Phillips Curve and Say's law.
   (b) Say's law and the quantity theory of money.
   (c) The quantity theory of money and the liquidity preference theory.
   (d) Say's law and the liquidity preference theory.

2. Which of the following statements is *inconsistent* with Say's law?

   (a) The economy has flexible wages and prices.
   (b) The economy's level of investment spending depends solely on the level of income.
   (c) The economy will produce at the full-employment level of output.
   (d) The economy has an environment of "laissez faire".

3. In classical theory, interest rates are determined – .

   (a) By the price level and unemployment.
   (b) Strictly by the money supply.
   (c) By the supply and demand for money.
   (d) By saving and investment.

4. In the classical view, the price level is determined by – .

   (a) Aggregate supply.
   (b) Aggregate demand and supply.
   (c) Supply of money.
   (d) Aggregate demand.

5. In the classical model, the aggregate supply curve determines the – .

   (a) Money supply.
   (b) Inflation rate.
   (c) Level of output.
   (d) Price level.

6. Which of the following ensures full employment in the classical model?

   (a) The equation of exchange.
   (b) Wage and price flexibility.
   (c) A constant velocity.
   (d) Inventory adjustment.

Answers

1. (b); 2. (b); 3. (d); 4. (d); 5. (c); 6. (b)

Descriptive questions

1. What are the major factors that determine the output and employment in the classical system? What role does aggregate demand have in determining unemployment level?
2. Point out the main features of the classical model.
3. What is the nature of AD curve in classical theory? What do you mean by neutrality of money?
4. "Inflation is always a monetary phenomenon in the long run". Explain this position of the monetarist.
5. Explain the impact of the following on output, employment, and real wage in the classical model:

   a. Shift in the supply schedule of labour.
   b. Upward shift of the production function.

6. "An increase in labour productivity would have the same effect on output, employment, real wage, price level, and money wage as an increase in supply of labour under the classical model". Do you agree? Why or why not?
7. Examine the effect of technological progress on output, employment, and price level in the classical model.
8. Suppose people become thrifty. How does it affect the endogenous variables of the system?
9. How will the equilibrium values of the variables be affected if wages are rigid in the classical economy?

10. Explain the loanable funds theory and its significance in the context of classical model.
11. Why is the classical model of the labour market not very useful for studying unemployment?

Additional readings

Ackley, G. (1987). *Macroeconomics: Theory and Policy*, Chapters 4–5. New York: Macmillan.
Keynes, J. M. (1936). *The General Theory of Employment, Interest, and Money*, Chapter 2. London: Palgrave Macmillan.
Patinkin, D. (1965). *Money, Interest and Price*. New York: The MIT Press.

4 Money, quantity theory, and price level

4.1 Introduction

We have discussed, so far, how different economic forces determine output and price level in an economy. Chapter 2 of the book captures the concepts of nominal GDP, national income, personal income, etc., all measured in monetary units. Nominal GDP, for example, may rise due to increase in production of real output or due to increase in price level. Increase in nominal GDP, thus, may not always be a sign of good health of an economy if it is only due to a rise in the price level. Hence without having a clear-cut idea about price level and its determinants we cannot measure the real impact of different variables on the economy. The overall continuous increase in the general price level is known as inflation. But before analysing inflation, which is a source of anxiety to politicians also, we should have some idea regarding various facets of money, because change in money supply plays a major role in determination of movement in price level. In Chapter 9, in the context of the IS-LM model, we will introduce the money market and observe thereafter, in Chapter 10, how the money market plays an important role in determination of overall economic output and employment. In this chapter we will discuss different concepts of money, its function, and its influence on price level. Discussion in the previous chapter of the classical model shows that money is nothing but a veil. Changes in money supply no way affect the real variables of the model as the system is dichotomised. This implies long run neutrality of money. Only in determination of nominal variables of the model does the role of money come in. In this theory prices, instead of being sticky, are fully flexible. How money supply changes can affect the rate of growth of price level is the main focus of this chapter, which will be discussed with the help of the quantity theory of money. Hence, this chapter establishes a link between quantity of money supply in the economy and rate of inflation. After doing this, our next objective will be to focus on the important phenomenon, inflation, which may even unseat a government through elections as voters dislike it. That discussion will be carried out in Chapter 5.

4.2 What is money?

Money is one of the greatest inventions of modern society. Milton Friedman emphasised the paramount significance of the quantity of money within the system. It is impossible to imagine a modern economy operating without the use of money. It acts as the lubricant that enables the smooth functioning of the economy across its diverse facets. Therefore, the key attribute defining money is its liquidity. In a barter economy, where there is no money, goods are exchanged against goods. The actor in need of a dress would have to

DOI: 10.4324/9781003501138-6

locate a tailor who is interested in attending a performance. Barter economy permits only simple transactions requiring *double coincidence of want* – two people each having a good that the other wants at the right time and place. Money eliminates the need for a double coincidence of wants, making transactions possible without this requirement. Initially money was deemed of anything which is generally accepted in exchange. So, money was the means of payment or medium of exchange. In the past, precious metals like silver, copper, and gold served as money. Designated amounts of precious metals were used as units of account as well as means of payment. For example, in England when silver was the universally accepted means of payment, a pound of silver became the unit of account. But metallic money had some inherent defects. Ascertainment of quality of metal and divisibility of metals for smaller transactions was highly inconvenient. It also suffers from the disadvantages of being stolen easily. Because of these inherent difficulties of metallic money, paper money evolved. The government's paper money and coins are called *currency*. Until the nineteenth century, currency was virtually the only means of payment. As monetary system evolved during the nineteenth and twentieth centuries, currency began to be replaced by other means of payment. With the introduction of banking system, chequable bank accounts also served as a medium of exchange (as a means of settling debts). A cheque is an instruction to the banking system to make accounting entries to transfer wealth from one person to another person. Economic transactions have become easier and smoother with the use of credit money or bank money (cheques, drafts, promissory notes, etc.). Nowadays, as we are heading towards a near cashless society, the importance of electronic money has received substantial priority. Its important forms are debit cards, credit cards, internet banking, etc. Net banking permits its users to pay their payments directly over the internet without sending a paper cheque. Credit and debit cards are another way to issue instructions to the banking system to transfer funds from one person to another, often called plastic money.

However, recognising the other roles, money is considered a "matter of functions four: A medium, a measure, a standard and a store".

4.3 Functions of money

In the modern economy, money is the most liquid financial asset which does not need to be converted into something else before transaction. There are four traditional functions of money, of which medium of exchange is the first. The other three are store of value, unit of account, and standard of deferred payment. Medium of exchange and unit of account are the primary functions of money; the other two are secondary functions.

Money acts as a *medium of exchange* for all kinds of goods and services. It facilitates transactions by removing the main difficulties of the barter system where all individuals are required to find someone who has a good that they want and who want to get the good that they offer. A modern economy cannot be imagined in the absence of a generally acceptable medium of exchange. Money is accepted in payment only because of the belief that it will later also be accepted in payment by others. Hence money made the transaction system easy and simple by removing the main problem of inconsistency of demand in the barter system of exchange. To act as an ideal medium of exchange, money should have the following attributes: general acceptability, portability, divisibility, durability, homogeneity, etc.

A *store of value* is an asset that maintains value over time. Thus, an individual holding a store of value can use that asset to make purchases at a future date. Because of perfect liquidity, money serves as a store of value and/or a means of saving. The value of produced commodities of the society can be preserved at the hands of the people in terms of money. As liquid assets facilitate transactions, people prefer to keep their assets or wealth in the form of money. There are other stores of value, like government bonds, but they are not money as they do not perform other functions of money.

The *unit of account* is the unit in which prices are quoted and debts are recorded. Money acts as a unit of account, a sort of common denominator, through which the exchange value of all goods and services can be expressed without any difficulty. In hiring resources or buying goods and services, money facilitates economic decision making by serving as a common expression of value. Suppose there are n commodities in an economy, one of which is a unit of account; there will be $(n - 1)$ rates of exchange then. In the barter system we will get separate exchange rates. Acting as a unit of account, money has greatly reduced the number of exchange rates. Numerous prices are quoted in rupees and paise, hence rupees and paise are the units in which the money stock is measured in our country. In United States prices are measured in terms of dollars, in Britain the pound, in Japan the Yen, in the Soviet Union the soviet ruble, in the European Union the euro.

Money allows individuals to save and lend their saving to borrowers. Credit is normally accepted on the basis of future or deferred payment. Money is used in long-term transactions, such as loans. The amount that has to be paid back in 5 or 10 years is specified in monetary units. With the expansion of trade and commerce based on credit, money has become a *standard of deferred payments*. This function of money is very important in modern economy. But the value of money should remain constant so that money may act as an accurate unit of standard of deferred payments. So the stability of the value of money is essential for this function of money. The last two of the four functions of money are functions that money usually performs but not functions that it necessarily performs. According to the Keynesian view, the first two functions are the main functions of money, whereas classical economists admit medium of exchange as the principal function.

4.4 Types of money

There are different types of money. Money that has no intrinsic value but is established as money by government decree or fiat (in the form of paper or any other form) is known as *fiat money*. Alternatively, the issue of purchasing power of the central bank of a country on behalf of government decree is called fiat money. As mentioned in the previous section, most of the societies in the past used commodities with some intrinsic value. Such money is called *commodity money*. It has intrinsic value in the sense that this commodity can generate utility from its use other than purchasing power. The most common example of commodity money is gold. Gold as commodity money also has intrinsic value since, other than purchasing power, it can be used for various other purposes like making jewellery, dental fillings, etc. When people use gold as money the economy is said to be on a *gold standard*. The gold standard existed in many countries during the late nineteenth century. But at present metallic coins are not made of precious metals like gold; instead they are made of low-value metals. In India metallic coins of Rs. 1, Rs. 2, Rs. 5, Rs. 10, etc are circulated. Paper is also used to make *paper money*. It is widely accepted compared to metallic money due to its ability to perform large transactions and its low cost of production. In the modern era deposit money is also used along with metallic and paper money. The deposits with the bank which are used for transaction purposes are termed deposit money. The current deposit and some part of savings deposit for which a cheque can be written are called deposit money.

Another important distinction between *legal tender* and *non-legal tender* should be considered in this connection. Coins and notes are legal tender as they cannot be refused in settlement of payments of any type. Legal actions can be taken against the persons who are not willing to accept legal tender This is not true for non-legal tender money like demand deposits of banks. A payee may not accept a cheque drawn on a demand deposit in a commercial bank. Legal action cannot be taken against the persons who are not willing to take it. For this reason, it is also termed optional money.

In this context we should point out the notion of *near money*. Near monies are financial assets which cannot be used as a medium of exchange but are close substitutes for a transaction balance. Savings deposits, money market mutual funds balances, money market deposits accounts, time deposits, etc. are examples of near money. These are transferable into more liquid form (M_1 balance) with no loss of nominal value and are therefore a liquid store of value.

4.5 Gresham's law

Gresham's law is a historical statement about the debasement of money. Sir Thomas Gresham was a member of the Elizabethan court who stated that "Bad Money (debased coins) drives out good money (undebased coins)", which came to be known as Gresham's law. During the reign of Queen Elizabeth (I), there were coins in England made of relatively inferior metals whose asset values were lower than face values. The queen decided to melt all the coins and make them new with complete value like the face value in gold. But it was soon observed that even if coins of superior quality were issued by the government, only the coins of inferior quality were circulating – newly made coins vanished. Sir Thomas Gresham was appointed by the Queen to enquire into this phenomenon. In his report, Gresham pointed out the causes of disappearance of superior quality coins. Operation of Gresham's law can be explained as follows. To a certain extent, this phenomenon is influenced by human psychological instincts. It is frequently noted that individuals tend to hoard good coins while using inferior ones for spending. Consequently, new coins disappear, leaving only the older ones in circulation. Sometimes the good coins are melted and used for other purposes, leading to scarcity of good coins. Since good or undebased coins have greater intrinsic value, only the good coins are melted. Additionally, as precious metals find easy acceptance among foreigners, the melted coins are frequently exported as metal. Gresham's law holds less relevance in a paper money system, as paper currency cannot be melted down or sent abroad. Therefore, this law is of very limited acceptability in modern times. However, Gresham's law will not be applicable if the total supply of money (including good money and bad money) is less than the total amount of money required for making transactions (i.e. demand for money). People will be forced to spend good money along with bad money in this situation.

4.6 Measurement of quantity of money

The amount of money that rotates in the economy at a particular time is the quantity of supply of money. Being a stock variable, money supply can be measured at a particular point in time. Central banks usually define four kinds of monetary aggregates, M_1,

M_2, M_3, and M_4, though the definition may vary across countries. Usually, two basic measures of money supply, M_1 and M_3, are most commonly used. M_3 is referred to as broad and M_1 as narrow money. Narrow money supply (M_1) consists of currency with the public, (net) demand deposits of commercial banks, and other deposits with the Central Bank. The term "public" refers to all economic agents other than the government, commercial banks, and the central bank. Demand deposit consists of all current deposits and the part of the saving deposits withdrawable by cheque. Deposit in a current account can be withdrawn through cheque at any time according to the will of the depositors. "Net demand deposit" is obtained by subtracting inter-bank claims from gross demand deposits. Since interbank claims do not enter into the demand deposits of the public with the commercial banks, this portion is subtracted from gross demand deposits. "Other deposits" with the central bank refer to deposits by economic units other than the government and commercial bank of the concerned country, and it consists of demand deposits held by some foreign central banks, foreign governments, international financial institutions (say, World Bank, IMF, Asian Development Bank, etc.), and by some development financial institutions (say, Industrial Finance Corporation of India, Industrial Development Bank of India, etc.). This M_1 measure of money has the attribute of greatest liquidity.

M_2 measure of money includes, in addition to M_1, post office saving bank deposits. These deposits are liquid but not quite as liquid as demand deposits included in M_1, in the sense that they are not instantly available for transaction. These deposits could be utilised for transaction only after a certain time lag. But the share of post office saving deposits is a small component and has also declined over time. Thus, the distinction between M_1 and M_2 is becoming narrower over time. Another (broad) measure M_3 includes M_1 and time deposits of commercial banks net of interbank deposits. Time deposits are included in the definition of broad money because they can be converted into demand deposits or currency whenever the depositors want at a very low cost. Banks allow premature withdrawal of time deposits against the payment of a fine by a small amount. People can also take a loan from the commercial banks against such term deposits. Finally, adding all the deposits of post offices (except National Savings Certificates) with M_3, we get M_4 definition of money. It is difficult to say which measure of money supply is the best. From the point of view of liquidity, M_1 is supposed to be most liquid and M_4 is supposed to be the least liquid asset. Thus, we can write;

M_1 = Currency with the public (C) + (net) net demand deposits of commercial banks (DD) + other deposits of the central bank (OD).
M_2 = M_1 + saving deposit with post office savings bank.
M_3 = M_1 + (net) time deposits of commercial banks.
M_4 = M_3 + total deposits under post office saving schemes.

Indeed, supply of money is nothing but the *monetary liability* of the banking system to the public. Currency with the public along with "other deposits" of the central bank is the liability of the central bank while bank deposits constitute the liability of the commercial banks. Since the "other deposit" component in M_1 is very small, no harm will be done if we ignore this item for future discussion. Hence, for our theoretical analysis we define ordinary money as

$$M = C + DD \quad (4.1)$$

4.7 The balance sheet of the central bank

A balance sheet of the of the central bank is its statement of assets and liabilities. Let us present the simplified format of the balance sheet of the central bank as follows.

Liabilities	*Assets*
IV. Monetary liability of central bank. V. Net non-monetary liability of central bank.	I. Net central bank's credit to the government. II. Net central bank's credit to commercial banks and commercial sectors. III. Net foreign exchange assets of central bank.

From the *accounting point of view*, total assets must be equal to total liabilities. Thus,

Monetary Liability of Central Bank = (Net Central Bank's Credit to the Government + Net Central Bank's Credit to Commercial Banks and Commercial Sectors + Net Foreign Exchange Assets of Central Bank) – Net Non-Monetary Liability of Central Bank. The *net non-monetary liability* of the central bank consists mostly of its capital and reserves and compulsory deposits of the public. The monetary liability of the central bank represents money supplied by the central bank.

High-powered money (H) is the central bank's currency along with government money. High-powered money serves as the reserve for the generation of bank deposits and hence is also called *reserve money*. The aggregate amount of H, which also forms the monetary base, is held partly by the public and partly by commercial banks.

Monetary liabilities of the central bank consist of: i) currency issued by the central bank; ii) reserves held with the central bank by commercial banks; iii) other deposits with the central bank. Data from India's central bank depicts that the other deposit part (OD) holds very low share compared to the total H-money and therefore we can avoid this head to deal with a simplistic formulation of high-powered money.

$$
\begin{aligned}
H &= \text{Monetary liabilities of the central bank} + \text{Government's monetary liability} \\
&= \text{Currency with the public } (C) + \text{Reserves of banks } (R) + \text{Other Deposits } (OD) \\
&= C + R \text{ (ignoring other deposits)}
\end{aligned}
$$

$$\text{Or, } H = C + R \tag{4.2}$$

This empirical definition is viewed from its holder's side, not from its producer's side. Most of the high-powered money consists of the central bank's monetary liabilities as the government's monetary liability is negligible.

We see that the difference between Equations (4.1) and (4.2) arises due to DD and R since "C" is the common term to both the forms of money. The difference between the two arises since demand deposits are produced by the banks which are counted as money. Again, to produce DD, banks have to maintain R, which is a part of H, which is the part and parcel of only the monetary authority and not of banks themselves. In a fractional reserve banking system, DD is a certain multiple of R and hence it lends to H, the quality of high-poweredness over the ordinary money, M. It is the power of serving as the base for the multiple creation of DD. For this reason, it is known as base money.

4.8 Determinants of money supply

According to Friedman, money supply is a function of three exogenous variables. They are high-powered money (*H*) or the monetary base, which is directly controlled by the central bank of the country; reserve to deposit ratio (*rd*), and currency to deposit ratio (*c*). From the definitions of *H* money, we know that $H = C + R$. Again, $rd = R / D$ which is determined by the business policies and the laws of banks. Finally, $c = C / D$ which is the amount of currency held by people (C) as a fraction of their holdings of demand deposits (*D*). Again, the ordinary money as stated earlier is $M = C + D$. Now,

$$M / H = (C + D) / (C + R) \tag{4.3}$$

By some manipulations, the previous relation is converted into –

$$M / H = [C / D + 1] / [C / D + R / D]$$

$$Or,\ M / H = (c + 1) / (c + rd) = m \tag{4.4}$$

$$Or,\ \mathrm{M} = mH \tag{4.5}$$

"*m*" is known as the *money multiplier* (the concept of a multiplier will be discussed in detail in Chapter 6 of the book). From Equation (4.5) it is clear that money supply depends on three exogenous variables: *H*, *rd*, and *c*. Money supply is directly proportional to the monetary base or high-powered money, for instance ($\delta M / \delta B > 0$). Again, money supply is inversely related with "*rd*". Lower "*rd*" enables the bank to extend a greater number of loans and thus the money supply will be greater ($\delta M / \delta rd < 0$). Finally, money supply is inversely related with "*c*". The lower the value of "*c*", the greater the credit creation and thus money supply. Low value of "*c*" means less currency will be held by the public and more currency will be held by the banks. Therefore, banks will be able to create more money ($\delta M / \delta c < 0$).

4.8.1 *Money supply and interest rate cohesion*

The linking of money supply with the interest rates can be made using the concept of s money multiplier. From the previous analysis, we have $m = (1 + c) / (c + rd)$, where, c = currency–deposit ratio and rd = reserve–deposit ratio. It can be shown that both currency–deposit ratio and reserve–deposit ratio are inversely related to rate of interest (*r*). If "*r*" increases, "*c*" falls since the bank deposit now becomes more attractive compared to keeping currency in hand. Banks can now lend more, leading to a secondary expansion of deposits. Again, an increase in "*r*" makes reserves relatively costly to hold, leading to a fall in "*rd*". Lending capacity of the commercial banks expands as a consequence.

Thus, both $c(r)$ *and* $rd(r)$ get reduced with an increase in "*r*" leading to a secondary expansion of deposits. The money multiplier becomes a positive function of "*r*". Thus, Equation (4.5) can be rewritten as:

$$M = m(r)H,\ m' > 0 \tag{4.6}$$

$$Or,\ M = M(r, H),\ \frac{\partial M}{\partial r} > 0\ and\ \frac{\partial M}{\partial H} > 0 \tag{4.7}$$

The money supply function is vertical when it is interest insensitive but becomes upward sloping in the (r, M) plane when it is interest sensitive, as given in Equation (4.7).

4.9 Deposit creation by banking system

The commercial banking system of a country supplies money that is held by the common people in the form of currency and demand deposits. But we did not discuss how such a process works. Here we highlight this issue. Banks create deposits in two ways – the direct way, which is known as primary deposit and the indirect way, which is known as derivative deposit. Primary deposit is the amount of money deposited by any individual into a bank and the derivative deposit is the money which is created by the bank when it gives loan to any person. The important difference between these two types of deposits is that in case of primary deposit total money supply remains the same whereas in the case of derivative deposit the money supply in the economy increases. Every loan or credit creates a deposit. Banks create deposits out of the excess reserves which they have. Excess reserve is the balance of funds held by the banks after deducting the minimum cash ratio (which is the reserve ratio required for dealing with regular transactions) from the total deposits made by the public with the banking system.

Let us explain the mechanism of deposit creation. Before explaining the mechanism, we need to assume some necessary conditions about the banking system. There are several banks with a standard reserve ratio fixed statutorily. Also, individuals do not hold any amount of money as cash; that is, all money should be deposited into the banking system either by households or firms or both in any way. Suppose there are two banks, I and II, and for the sake of simplicity they each maintain the reserve ratio (that is reserve–deposit ratio) of "*rd*". Each bank provides a loan on the basis of excess reserves it holds statutorily to meet the regular demands of the depositors. The balance sheets of the two banks will together show the method of money supply creation. Suppose Bank I has excess reserve of ΔR equal to Rs. 1,000 and reserve–deposit ratio, *rd*, equal to 20%. Bank I will create loan of Rs. 1,000 (which is the derivative deposit). If the borrowers put this money in Bank II, then Bank II will have Rs. 800 (= 1,000 – 20% of 1,000) as excess reserve which it can give as loans to the public. Similarly, the borrower, say, deposits this Rs. 800 in Bank I again. Bank I will then have Rs. 640 (= 800 – 20% of 800) as excess reserve that it can give as loans to the public. Individuals will then withdraw the loan amount and deposit it in, say, Bank II which will have excess reserve of Rs. 512 (= 640 – 20% of 640) which again will be given as loans. The process continues for an indefinite period and the total deposit or credit created by the banking system (ΔM) from the initial excess reserve of Rs. 1,000 is given as follows –

$$\Delta M = 1{,}000 + 800 + 640 + 512 + \ldots\ldots\ldots\ldots\ldots\ldots \tag{4.8}$$

The previous relation is an infinite GP Series. It can be expanded into the following expression as –

$$\Delta M = 1{,}000 + 800 + 640 + 512 + \ldots\ldots\ldots\ldots\ldots\ldots$$

$$Or,\ \Delta M = 1{,}000 + 1{,}000 \times \left[1 - 20/100\right] + 1{,}000 \times \left[1 - (20/100)^2\right] + 1{,}000 \times \left[1 - (20/100)^3\right] + \ldots\ldots$$

$$Or,\ \Delta M = \Delta R\left[1+(1-rd)+(1-rd)^2+(1-rd)^3+..............\right]$$

$$Or, \Delta M = 1{,}000[1+[1-(20/100)]+\left[1-(20/100)^2\right]+[1-(20/100)^3]+......$$

The bracketed term represents an infinite G. P. series, which can be reduced to

$$\Delta M = \Delta R\left[1/(1-rd)\right] \quad (4.9)$$

$$Or,\ \Delta M = (1/rd)\times \Delta R \quad (4.10)$$

The previous expression is a reserve multiplier or *deposit creation multiplier* or *credit multiplier*. It shows that the amount of created money, ΔM, will be a multiple (= 1/rd) of the excess reserve, ΔR. This shows that as excess reserve in a bank is more, then its created money will be more with a given reserve ratio. That is, the credit or deposit multiplier is –

$$\Delta M/\Delta R = 1/rd > 1 \quad (4.11)$$

since $0 < rd < 1$.

On the other hand, if "*rd*" increases, that is, the commercial banks are required statutorily to hold more money as reserve, then created money will be less since the amount of the loan (or deposit) created will be less than that in the situations with relatively lower values of "*rd*".

Now suppose people do not deposit all their borrowed money in the banking system, rather they hold *b*% of the borrowed money. Then the capacity of the banks to create deposit will be less. Further, the deposit creation series will be as follows:

$$\Delta M = \Delta R\left[1+(1-rd)(1-b)+(1-rd)^2(1-b)^2+(1-rd)^3(1-b)^3+........\right] \quad (4.12)$$

$$Or, \Delta M = \Delta R\left[1/(1-(1-rd)(1-b)\right] \quad (4.13)$$

$$Or, \Delta M = \Delta R\left[1/(rd+b(1-rd)\right] \quad (4.14)$$

That is the credit multiplier is

$$\Delta M/\Delta R = 1/(rd+b(1-rd) > 1 \quad (4.15)$$

The magnitude of the multiplier is less than the earlier multiplier. As excess reserve increases, the created money will be less now. If we assume "*b*" equals zero then the credit multiplier turns down to the earlier one. Hence, there are three factors responsible for credit or deposit creation. They are excess reserve with $\delta M/\delta R > 0$, reserve to deposit ratio with $\delta M/\delta rd < 0$ and cash held with $\delta M/\delta b < 0$.

4.10 The quantity theory of money — Fisherian approach

In the classical model we have observed that the price level is determined by money supply. So, money supply plays an important role in aggregate price level determination. The main tenet of the quantity theory of money (QTM) is that price level changes in the same direction and in the same proportion as the change in quantity of money such that if the quantity of money is doubled price level will also be doubled. The relation between money supply and aggregate price level was first studied in a systematic way by American economist Irving Fisher in 1911. Later an alternative approach was given by a group of Cambridge economists though both approaches lead to the same conclusion. Fisher explained this with a simple identity referred to as *Fisher's equation of exchange*. It is an identity relating the volume of transaction at current prices to the supply of money times the turnover rate of money (known as velocity of money in circulation). It measures the average number of times each rupee is used in transactions during the period. This identity is expressed as

$$MV_T \equiv P_T T \tag{4.16}$$

Where M is the quantity of money in circulation.
V_T is the transaction velocity of money.
P_T is the price index for all the traded items.
T is the volume of transaction.

At first sight this version of quantity theory is a *tautology*; it is true by definition.

To turn this identity into a theory of price determination, Fisher made the following assumptions:

i) Money is used only as a *medium of exchange*. People hold money only for transaction purposes. Money is not used as a store of value.
ii) *Say's law* of market holds such that total supply of good and services is always equal to total demand for goods and services.
iii) The economy is always in *full employment* level. The supply of goods and services is completely inelastic.

The right-hand side of Equation (4.16) represents the total money value of a transaction in a fixed period of time which is also equal to the demand for money. The left-hand side, on the other hand, is the amount of money in circulation times the transaction velocity of money. The average number of times a unit of money is used for transaction during the period is called transaction velocity of money (V_T). Thus, MV_T gives the total supply of money used for transaction of goods and services.

Therefore $\frac{V_T M}{T} \equiv P_T$ shows that price level varies directly with the quantity of money in circulation and transaction velocity of money and inversely with the volume of trade done by it.

Volume of transaction (T) includes not only purchase and sales of newly produced goods but also that of previously produced goods. It is difficult to measure also. If we replace T with the transaction involving currently produced goods and services, Y (real income), then we get

$$MV \equiv PY \tag{4.17}$$

Here P = price index for currently produced output and V = the income velocity of money, as in the average number of times a rupee is used in a transaction involving current output. Equation (4.17) is known as the income version of QTM.

According to Fisher, in the short run, due to institutional characteristics, velocity of circulation of money remains constant as it is determined by such factors as spending habits of the people, the method of payments in society (whether cash or cheques or credit cards are used), etc. Again, in the classical model aggregate real output (and hence transactions) remains constant in the short run as it is supply determined. If V is a predetermined constant, then equation of exchange is no longer an identity, rather it represents a relationship of proportionality between the price level and exogenously given money supply (determined by monetary authority of the concerned country). We can now write

$$P = \left(\frac{\bar{V}}{\bar{Y}}\right) M \tag{4.18}$$

This equation shows the direct and proportional relationship between P and M. Doubling of M doubles P. The direction and rate of increase of quantity of money and price level is same. This is the main result of *QTM*; a change in money supply will cause an equal proportionate change in the general price level. This also justifies the "Neutrality of money" proposition; money supply cannot affect real variables of the economy. Hence inflation can be viewed as a purely monetary phenomenon.

As money supply increases, people hold more money than their need for transaction purpose. They spend this useless excess amount of money to purchase more goods and services which puts upward pressure on price level. This process will in turn raise demand for money until the equality between supply of and demand for money is re-established.

QTM can be explained with the help of a hypothetical numerical example. Suppose in an economy nominal money supply (M) is Rs. 500; the general price level (P) is 2 and real output produced (T) is 1,000 kg (of rice, say). Therefore, PT = Rs. 2,000. From equation of exchange, we get $\frac{PT}{M} = V$.

$V = 2{,}000 / 500 = 4$. If, now, nominal money supply increases to Rs. 1,000, given V and T, then general price level increases to 4 $[P = \left(\frac{\bar{V}}{\bar{T}}\right) M = \frac{4 \times 1{,}000}{1{,}000} = 4]$.

Thus, price level increases with the nominal money supply in the same proportion.

4.10.1 *Criticism of Fisher's quantity theory*

There are several criticisms against the QTM. The main criticisms are:

i) Professor Halon criticises Fisher for multiplying M and V because M relates to a point of time, whereas V relates to a period of time. The former is a static concept and the latter dynamic. It is therefore technically inconsistent to multiply two non-comparable factors. Also, this theory does not explain how the changes in price level take place as a result of change in quantity of money in the short run.

ii) According to Keynes, Fisher's theory is based on unrealistic assumptions. This theory is inoperative below full employment level. Only under full employment is T constant. In reality, the full employment condition is a rare possibility. The general situation is one of the under-employment equilibrium. Keynes also argued that increased money supply raises effective demand, which will raise price level after full employment level, though not proportionately.

iii) Also, short run changes in price level cannot be analysed with this theory. Quantity of money cannot analyse upswing and downswing of a business cycle.
iv) There is no clear explanation regarding the concept of price level, whether it refers to price level of consumer goods or price level of capital goods or both.
v) It is assumed that money does not work as store of value. The entire amount of money is spent to purchase goods and services. But if the quantity of money increases and the additional amount is saved by the people, not used to purchase commodities, the price level will not increase.

In spite of all the aforementioned limitations, Fisher's theory has some element of truth, though the relationship is not as simple as it is expressed here.

4.11 Cambridge approach to the quantity theory

The Cambridge approach, named after Cambridge University, the academic home of its originator Alfred Marshall, also demonstrated a proportional relationship between the quantity of money and the aggregate price level. This version, also known as *cash balance approach*, was later modified by A. C. Pigou and D. H. Robertson. The foundation of this relationship was, however, less mechanistic than the transactions or Fisherian version of quantity theory. Marshall began by focusing on the individual's decision on the optimal amount of money to hold. Some money will be held because of the convenience that money provides in transactions compared with other stores of value. Money also helps to meet up unexpected necessities in the future. Cambridge economists assumed that people hold a part of their real income as cash balance. Demand for money can thus be written as

$$M^d = kPY \tag{4.19}$$

Money demand (M^d) is assumed to be a proportion (k) of nominal income, the price level (P) times the level of real income (Y). The primary desirable property of money is its usefulness for transactions, so it follows that the demand for money depends on the level of transactions, which may be supposed to vary closely with the level of income. The proportion of income that would be optimal to hold in the form of money (k) is assumed to be relatively inelastic in the short run, depending, as in the Fisherian formulation, on the payment habits of the society.

In equilibrium, the exogenous stock of money (M) must equal the quantity of money demanded as in

$$M = kPY \tag{4.20}$$

With k treated as fixed in the short run and real output (Y) determined, as before, by supply conditions (full employment condition), the *Cambridge equation* also reduces to a proportional relationship between the price level and money stock. As in the Fisherian approach, the quantity of money determines the price level. Direct and proportional relation exists among the quantity of money and price level. Price level increases along with the increase in quantity of money, and the rate of increase in price level is the same as the rate of increase in the quantity of money.

However, we may mention some *limitations* of the Cambridge equation also. The unrealistic assumptions of Fisher's equation are also present in the Cambridge equation.

Demand for money, according to Keynes, depends both on the level of income and rate of interest. Hence many economists argued that "*K*" should not be considered as a constant. It depends on rate of interest and on some other factors such that the demand for money becomes a function of rate of interest also.

There is no time consistency between demand for and supply of money in the Cambridge approach. National income and hence demand for money is a flow concept, measured per year. Supply of money, on the other hand, is a stock concept, measured at a point of time. Thus, there is an inconsistency.

4.11.1 *Comparison between Cambridge and Fisher's approach*

Comparing the Cambridge equation and Fisher's equation, one can see that the two formulations are equivalent, with V equal to $1 / k$. So, k and V are the two sides of the same coin. Alternatively, we can say that these approaches differ in their focus on the use of money. As the amount of k (fixed ratio of real income which people want to keep at hand as cash balance) increases, people will keep a larger amount of money on hand as cash balance; as a result the amount of velocity of circulation of money will reduce. If, for example, individuals wish to hold an amount equal to one-fourth of the nominal income in the form of money, the number of times the average unit of money is used in income transactions will be four.

Real income (Y) used in the Cambridge cash balance approach is more important than the total volume of transaction of goods and services (T) used in Fisher's approach because real income can easily be calculated. The total part of the volume of transaction in a period of time is not included into the real national income; only transactions involving final products are included. In this respect it can be said that in the Cambridge equation Y is more important compared to T in Fisher's quantity equation.

The transaction approach emphasises the medium of exchange function of money. On the other hand, the cash balance approach stresses equally the store of value function of money. In the Cambridge equation it is assumed that individuals keep a part of their real income in liquid form on hand, for example in the Cambridge equation money is demanded not only for transaction but also to be stored up or reserved.

Although the two formulations of the quantity theory are formally equivalent, the Cambridge version represents a step towards more modern monetary theories. The Cambridge focus was on the quantity theory as a theory of the demand for money. The proportion of nominal income people wished to hold in the form of money (k) was constant and the level of output was fixed by supply conditions. Monetarists also take the Cambridge form of the quantity theory as the starting point for their theory of money demand.

In addition, the Cambridge focus on the quantity theory as a theory of money demand leads naturally to an answer to the question raised about the mechanism by which money affects price level. If money supply is increased, initially, there will be an excess of money supply over the amount demanded. Individuals try to reduce their money holdings to the optimal proportion of their income by putting this excess into alternative uses of consumption and investment in production activities. They increase their demand for goods for both consumption and investment. This increased demand for commodities puts upward pressure on prices. In the language of the classical economists, there is too much money chasing too few goods. If output is unchanged, as it would be in the classical model, and k is constant, a new equilibrium will be reached only after the price level is doubled. At that point nominal income and hence money demand will have doubled. Judged from this angle it can be said that the Cambridge approach is more developed compared to Fisher's cash balance approach.

Though there exist some differences between Fisher's equation and the Cambridge equation, the basic interpretation of both the versions are the same. From both the equations it is proved that price level increases along with the increase in quantity of money, and rate of increase in price level is the same as the rate of increase in quantity of money. Direct and proportional relation exist among the quantity of money and price level.

4.11.1.1 *Numerical example*

Suppose the public wants to hold money balances equal to 20% of their real income. If real output is 1,000 and money supply is Rs. 400, then price level must be 2, since $\frac{M}{kY} = P$. Now suppose money supply increases from Rs. 400 to Rs. 800. With no change in k and Y, price level must be 4 to maintain equilibrium in demand for and supply of real balances.

4.11.2 *The role of demand for money in the QTM equation*

A money demand function is an equation that shows what determines the quantity of real money balance that people used to hold. A single money demand function can be written as $(\frac{M}{P})^d = kY$ where k is constant. It tells us how much money people want to hold for every rupee of income. This equation states that the quantity of real money balances demanded is proportional to real income. This money demand function offers another way to view the quantity equation. Let us now consider the equilibrium condition that demand for real money balances $(\frac{M}{P})^d$ must equal the real money supply $(\frac{M}{P})$. Hence, substituting this, we can write $(\frac{M}{P}) = kY$ or $M \times \frac{1}{k} = PY$ or $MV = PY$ where $V = \frac{1}{k}$. This simple mathematics shows the link between the demand for money and the velocity of money. When people want to hold a lot of money for each rupee of income (i.e. when k is large), money changes hands infrequently, that is, V is small.

4.11.3 *Impact of a decline in the velocity of circulation of money*

We know that the equation of exchange in QTM can be written as $MV = PY$ where V is income velocity of circulation of money. It is the number of times, in a fixed period, that the money stock M turns over to finance transaction. Monetarists believe that V is a stable constant determined by the degree of financial development of an economy and the payment habits of its citisens. In long run, if Y attains the full employment value Y_f so that both V and Y are given, then the previous equation yields a proportional relation between M and P. So from the above equation we can write

% change in M + % change in V = % change in P + % change in Y.

Due to full employment and constancy of V assumptions, we can write % change in M = % change in P such that if M increases by 5%, price level will also increase by 5%. But if V decreases by 2% (say) then price level will increase by (5% – 2%), which is 3%, as a result of an increase in money supply by 5%. Hence monetary expansion will have less inflationary effect in the situation when V decreases than in the situation when V is constant.

4.12 Compatibility between Say's law and quantity theory of money

Oskar Lange took a fresh look at Say's law of markets and highlighted its incompatibility with the QTM. In his restatement, Lange asserted that the overall value of supplied commodities, incorporating money as a medium of exchange, is precisely equivalent to the total value of demanded commodities incorporating money. Lange emphasises the integral role of money as a medium of exchange within the framework of Say's law. This is known as *Walras law*. If there are "k" commodities including money, then Walras law can be stated as

$$\sum_{1}^{k} p_i q_i^d \equiv \sum_{1}^{k} p_i q_i^S \tag{4.21}$$

This relation has nothing to do with equilibrium; it's a fundamental truth embedded in its definition.

Contrastingly, *Say's law* posits that the aggregate demand for goods, excluding money, is identical to the overall supply of all goods, excluding money.

Considering kth good as money, Say's identity can be stated as

$$\sum_{1}^{k-1} p_i q_i^d \equiv \sum_{1}^{k-1} p_i q_i^S \tag{4.22}$$

Combining (4.21) and (4.22), Walras' law and Say's law together imply that

$$q_k^d \equiv q_k^S \tag{4.23}$$

Money demand is identical to money supply.

As an identity inherently lacks the capacity to determine unknown variables, the previous identity cannot establish the absolute or nominal price level. Thus, if Say's law holds, absolute price level will remain indeterminate.

Quantity theory, on the other hand, explains that given the velocity of circulation and real output (determined at full employment level), quantity of money determines the absolute price level. Thus, according to QTM,

$$M^S = kPY_f \tag{4.24}$$

Where M^S = money supply, $v = \frac{1}{k}$ = velocity of circulation, P = absolute price level, Y_f = full employment output.

∴ given k *and* Y_f; P is determined by M^S.

Thus, Say's law and quantity theory given by Equation (4.24) are logically inconsistent. If Say's law holds, the absolute price level remains indeterminate and so quantity theory cannot hold and vice versa. Thus, the classical model is said to suffer from an internal contradiction. In addressing these issues, classical economists divided the pricing process into two parts: the determination of relative prices in the real sector (commodity market) and the determination of money or absolute prices in the monetary sector (money market).

4.13 Reestablishing the quantity theory of money by Friedman

Friedman's version of the quantity theory is closest to the Cambridge version that focused on the demand for money. From Equation (4.19) we observed that $M^d = kPY$; that is, money demand is proportional to the nominal income, as "k" is constant in the short run. Friedman accepted Keynes's emphasis on the role of money as an asset and rewritten money demand function as

$$M^d = L(P, Y, r_B, r_E, r_D) \tag{4.25}$$

where, r_B, r_E, r_D represent, respectively, nominal interest rate on bonds, equities, and durable goods. Thus, following Keynes, Equation (4.25) assumes that the amount of money demanded depends on the rate of return offered on alternative assets like bonds, equities, and durable goods such as consumer durables, land, and houses. Durable goods do not pay any explicit interest rate. Their return is the expected increase in the price of the good over the period. An increase in the rate of return on any of these alternative assets causes the demand for money to decline. This money demand theory of Friedman can be used to restate the Cambridge equation as follows:

$$M^d = k(r_B, r_E, r_D)PY \tag{4.26}$$

In Equation (4.26), k is not a constant but a function of rate of return (r_i) from different alternative assets. Thus, Friedman did not believe that money demand is completely independent of these rates of return. Any change in "r_i" will affect k and hence M^d. Incorporating this modified money demand function, the money market equilibrium condition can now be rewritten as

$$M = k(r_B, r_E, r_D)PY \tag{4.27}$$

Equation (4.27) states that any exogenous change in M will be balanced either through change in PY or through alteration in k, caused by changes in the rates of return of different assets.

4.14 Conclusion

We now conclude the entire chapter on money supply determination with the following points. Ordinary money or narrow money is defined as the sum of currency and demand deposits of commercial and central banks held by the public. On the other hand, high-powered money or reserve money is the money produced by the central bank and the government of the country and held by the public and banks.

Economic activity in one way or the other involves use of money. Prices of different goods are quoted in terms of monetary units. Price level and hence the inflation rate are influenced greatly by the quantity of money in the economy. In this chapter, after defining different functions and measures of money, we introduced quantity theory of money (QTM). QTM shows how money supply plays an important role in aggregate price level determination in the classical model. The discussion ignores the short run stickiness of prices and focus on the price behaviour in the long run. Two different versions of QTM have been analysed here, though the basic result of both approaches is the same: the quantity of money determines the price level. In this sense this analysis depicts an important approach of examining the classical theory of inflation. After presenting the link between increase in money supply and inflation we move to the next chapter to discuss the theory of inflation in detail.

Summary

- Money supply not only includes currency and notes in circulation but also the demand deposit with the commercial banks. There are various definitions of money supply; denoted by M_1, M_2, M_3, and M_4.
- The quantity theory of money shows that any change in the quantity of money would cause a change in the price level of the economy.
- The money supply, M_1, is made up of currency and chequeable deposits. A broader measure, M_2, also includes savings and time deposits at depositary institutions as well as some other interest-bearing assets.
- The deposit creation multiplier in general is defined as the inverse of the reserve–deposit ratio. As the banks hold more money as reserve, the value of the money multiplier will be smaller in the sense that the economy will get less money for productive purposes.
- The cash transaction version of this theory has been popularised by Irving Fisher. The Fisher's Equation of Exchange is expressed as $MV = PT$. This theory assumes that money is demanded only for transaction purposes.
- The cash balance version or the Cambridge version of the quantity theory was popularised by the economists like Marshall, Pigou, etc. The Cambridge equation of the quantity theory is expressed as $M = kPY$.

Keywords

Seigniorage
Transaction velocity of money
Unit of account
Standard of deferred payment
Commodity money
Income velocity of money
Quantity theory of money
Medium of exchange
Store of value
Fiat money

Multiple choice questions

1. The quantity theory of money tells that
   (a) The velocity of money times the money multiplier equals the total spending in the economy.
   (b) The price level equals the money supply times the money multiplier.

(c) The quantity of money in the economy multiplied by velocity will be equal to total spending.
(d) The quantity of money in the economy has little effect on total spending and income.

2. The quantity theory of money is a theory of how

(a) The nominal value of aggregate income is determined.
(b) The money supply is determined.
(c) The real value of aggregate income is determined.
(d) The interest rates are determined.

3. The equation of exchange is

(a) $M + V = P + Y$.
(b) $M + Y = V + P$.
(c) $M * P = U * Y$.
(d) $M * V = P * Y$.

4. In the famous equation $M = PkY$; k stands for

(a) Fraction of real output held for transaction.
(b) Fraction of money supply held by persons.
(c) Fraction of money value of output (transactions) held by the public.
(d) None of the above.

5. The quantity theory of money implies that a given percentage change in the money supply will cause

(a) A larger percentage change in nominal GDP.
(b) An equal percentage change in nominal GDP.
(c) A smaller percentage change in nominal GDP.
(d) An equal percentage change in real GDP.

6. The velocity of money is

(a) The number of times per year a rupee is used to buy goods and services produced in India.
(b) The rate at which new rupee note is printed.
(c) The number of times per year a rupee is used to pay wages.
(d) The same as the inflation rate.

7. Which one of the following is not a function of money?

(a) Medium of exchange.
(b) Means of barter.
(c) Standard of deferred payment.
(d) Store of value.

8. Which of the following would (other things equal) result in a rise in prices under the "equation of exchange" in the quantity theory of money?

(a) Fall in amount of money in circulation.
(b) Fall in the rate at which a given amount of money in circulation is passed from one person to another.

(c) Rise in the rate at which a given amount of money in circulation is passed from one person to another.
(d) Greater the fraction of a given amount of money in circulation which is held as an asset.

9. If the money supply is Rs. 500 and nominal income is Rs. 4,000, the velocity of money is

   (a) 1 / 20.
   (b) 1 / 8.
   (c) 8.
   (d) 20.

10. In the terminology of economics and money demand, the terms *M1* and *M2* are also known as:

    (a) Short money.
    (b) Long money.
    (c) Broad money.
    (d) Narrow money.

11. In an economy operating at full employment with constant velocity of 6, an increase in the money supply of 4% will cause ___.

    (a) The price level to rise by 24%.
    (b) Output to rise by 4%.
    (c) Output to rise by 24%.
    (d) The price level to rise by 4%.

12. High-powered money is defined as the

    (a) Money produced by the central bank and the government of the country and held by the public and banks.
    (b) Currency and demand deposits of commercial and central banks held by the public.
    (c) Demand deposits of commercial and central banks held by the public.
    (d) Currency of commercial and central banks held by the public.

13. Commercial banks create deposit through a particular process. The derived deposit creation multiplier gives the

    (a) Direct relation between the extra money created and the reserve-deposit ratio.
    (b) Inverse relation between the extra money created and the reserve-deposit ratio.
    (c) Neither direct nor inverse relation with the reserve-deposit ratio.
    (d) Any one of the above.

Answers

1. (c); 2. (a); 3. (d); 4. (c); 5. (b); 6. (a); 7. (b); 8. (c); 9. (c) 10. (d); 11. (d), 12. (a); 13. (b)

Review questions

1. "The quantity theory of money operates under condition of full employment". Analyse the statement.

2. Explain the quantity theory of money with the help of the equation of Fisher. Mention the limitations of the quantity theory of Fisher.
3. Briefly state the Cambridge equation. What is the difference between the equation of Fisher and the Cambridge equation?
4. Distinguish ordinary money from high-powered money. Explain how commercial banks create deposit with the help of excess reserves and reserve-deposit ratio. What happens if people hold a part of money in their hand without depositing them to the bank? Explain.
5. Define M_1, M_2, M_3, and M_4 money. What happens to money supply of an economy if M_1 money increases? Explain.

Short answer:

1. Write down the equation of exchange and the Cambridge equation.
2. What is velocity of money?

Additional readings

Reddy, Y. V. (2000). *Monetary and Financial Sector Reform in India*. New Delhi: UBS.

5 Theory of inflation

5.1 Introduction

Chapter 1 of the book analysed that maintaining price stability is one of the major objectives of policymakers of a country. The previous chapter also establishes a link between growth of money supply and growth of price level or inflation. During inflation, prices of some products may rise and some prices may even fall but there must be an upward trend of general price level. Inflation doesn't imply a once-and-for-all increase in the price level for which no policy action is required to halt the upward trend; rather prices rise indefinitely in this situation. Though during inflation nominal variables change, real variables, such as relative prices, may remain unaltered. The price level, which is the average level of nominal prices of goods and services, is measured by taking the weighted average of a large number of commodities at a particular moment of time. The weight attached to the price of each commodity is the proportion of total expenditure devoted to that good. Price indices can cover a group of commodities such as food, housing, etc. Price indices that give an idea of general price level are WPI, retail price index, CPI, and an implicit deflator. The concepts of WPI, CPI, and the GDP deflator are discussed in previous chapters. Inflation can be measured by the percentage increase in CPI or GDP deflator or WPI. Inflation reduces the purchasing power of money. The loss that people suffer when inflation reduces the purchasing power of their assets is called the inflation tax, as inflation acts like a tax on holding money. In this chapter we discuss causes, consequences, and impacts of inflation on the economy in detail. Different policies designed to control inflation or to maintain price stability have also been addressed.

5.2 Types and causes of inflation

Inflation, as already defined earlier, is a state of rising prices and is indicated by increase in the index number of prices over time. So, inflation means *rising price level* and not merely the rise in price level. So, rise in prices must be sustained, as in prices must be continuously rising. From the definition it is clear that inflation reflects disequilibrium condition in the economy. Hence it should be analysed dynamically. Static analysis only gives us the condition of price stability. Sometimes an inflationary situation may not exhibit itself by an increase in the price index because of the government's policies, like price control and rationing, etc. In order to distinguish between the two situations, two terms can be used, "open inflation" and "suppressed inflation". In case of open inflation the government does not adopt any measure to control the rise in price level whereas in

DOI: 10.4324/9781003501138-7

case of suppressed inflation the government adopts price controlling measures. Deflation is slowing down of the rate of inflation, a state of falling prices.

The neoclassical economists used to believe that inflation is created by the increase in the supply of money. The speed of inflation is determined by the rate of increase of money supply. This approach of linking the quantity of money with the price level, *quantity theory approach*, has already been addressed in a previous chapter. This approach assumed that there was always full employment in the economy. If there is an increase in money supply in the economy, there will be an expansion of aggregate demand. The inevitable result is an increase in price level as the supply of output is fixed at the full employment level. Thus, the cause of excess demand is the rise in the money supply, which has produced an inflationary situation. However, Keynesian economists denied the rigid link between the quantity of money and the price level. They pointed out that even if the quantity of money remains the same, an inflationary situation may emerge if aggregate demand is greater than aggregate supply. Keynes regards that the change in the stock of money is of minor importance in times of unemployment and may exercise a significant influence only when there is full employment.

Excess demand in the output market will raise the price level. But this type of an inflationary situation is also generated by an autonomous fall in the aggregate supply, which means a leftward shift in the supply curve. We know that the supply curve is derived from the marginal cost curve. Thus, an autonomous increase in the cost of production leads to a leftward shift in the supply curve. When the rise in the cost of production affects almost all of the producers in the economy, the aggregate supply falls. This type of inflation is known as "cost-push inflation". It is called this because the rise in the cost of production pushes the price up. Cost of production may rise due to increase in the price of raw materials. If labour unions, for example, raise the wage rate through collective bargaining but the productivity of the labour does not increase, then the cost of production also increases. Hence trade union activity may become a source of inflation if wage rate is not market determined. Again, say, if the price of imported oil increases in the international market, then the cost of production in the oil importing country will also increase. As a result of its influence, price level will increase. Here the source of cost-push inflation is the rise in the price of oil in the international market. At the same time, producers are also responsible as they raise prices to enhance their profit margins. Thus, there are two sources of cost inflation: wage cost-push and profit cost-push. Whatever may be the reason, aggregate supply curve will shift leftward.

Also, given the aggregate supply, there may be an autonomous rise in the aggregate demand, when an excess demand appears in the economy to raise the price level. Whenever the autonomous rise in the aggregate demand is associated with an inelastic aggregate supply, an excess demand must arise in the market, and this leads to a rise in the price level. The ultimate responsibility for the price rise, then, lies in the autonomous increase in the aggregate demand, and for this reason it is called the "demand-pull inflation". The essence of this type of inflation is "too much spending chasing too few goods". From the demand side, inflation can arise in two ways: excess demand in the commodity market or in the factor market (say in the labour market).

5.3 Inflation in Indian scenario

Inflation is one of the serious threats in most of the economy and India is also not an exception. Except for the First Five Year Plan, the inflation trend in India has been gradually mounting during the other Five-Year Plans. The average annual growth rate of prices in terms of percentage during the First Five-Year Plan to the Thirteenth Five-Year Plan is shown in the following table:

Table 5.1 Inflation rate in India in different plan periods

Five-Year Plans	*Inflation Rate (%)*
First Five-Year Plan	(–)3.6
Second Five-Year Plan	6.3
Third Five-Year Plan	5.8
Fourth Five-Year Plan	9.0
Fifth Five-Year Plan	6.3
Sixth Five-Year Plan	9.7
Seventh Five-Year Plan	6.7
Eighth Five-Year plan	6.6
Ninth Five-Year Plan	3.9
Tenth Five-Year Plan	5.04
Eleventh Five-Year Plan	7.4
Twelfth Five-Year Plan	6.5
Thirteenth Five-Year Plan	6.7

Source: Ministry of Statistics and Programme implementation (MOSPI)

According to this table, the inflation rate of India during the First Five-Year Plan was (–)3.6%. However, during the Second and Third Five-Year Plans, it was 6.3% and 5.8% respectively. In the Fourth and Sixth Five-Year Plans it was 9% and 9.7% respectively. Thereafter it declines more or less steadily, reaching the lowest value in the Ninth Plan (3.9%). In the Thirteenth Plan the average annual growth rate of prices reaches a value 6.7%. The presence of a high inflation rate in several plan periods had a negative effect on the economic growth of India.

5.4 Consequences of inflation

When inflation takes place in an economy, it will have different effects on different situations and on different classes of people, such that inflation creates different types of effects on the economy. Some are benefited as a result of inflation while some are adversely affected as a result of inflation. The economic effects of inflation can be divided in three categories.

i) Effects on production;
ii) Effects on distribution of income and wealth;
iii) Other effects

We shall discuss all three of these effects one by one.

5.4.1 Effects of inflation on production

How production is affected by inflation depends on the economic condition of the country. If full employment exists in the country and if inflation arises due to excess demand, then production will not increase as a result of this inflation, because under condition of full employment it is not possible to increase the production of a commodity as a result of inflation, only the price level of the country tends to increase, total product or real national income remaining constant. On the other hand, if inflation takes place even before full employment is reached, then production may increase during a period of inflation. Rising price and rising profit encourage firms to make larger investments. The multiplier effect will then lead to higher output. Thus, if inflation rises until the economy reaches the full employment stage, then it is possible to increase production, income, and employment by employing factors that are not engaged in economic activities. However, it should be noted that only mild inflation has an encouraging effect on aggregate output.

But, if the rate of inflation is very high, then it acts as a disincentive to long run economic growth. If the speed of inflation is very rapid then producers are motivated to hoard instead of increase production as this will provide them a higher return. In this situation unrest is created in the society, and as a result production, employment, income, etc. cannot increase though price level rises regularly.

Sometimes, under the condition of full employment due to rapid increase in price level, hyperinflation is created in the country. Hyperinflation discourages savings and thereby reduces capital formation, hindering economic growth. In this situation, production and the economic, political, and social structure of the country may break down.

5.4.2 *Effects of inflation on distribution of income and wealth*

Let us now consider the effect of inflation on different classes of people. Different classes of people are differently affected during the process of inflation. A group of people gain at the expense of others. Thus, inflation redistributes income and wealth.

i) *Debtors and creditors:* during the period of inflation, the creditors lose because when the creditors get back the money that they lent they receive less in real terms because the purchasing power of money falls as a result of inflation. On the other hand, the borrowers welcome inflation because they take credit at the nominal rate of interest which is fixed by a contract. Even if the price level increases, the nominal rate of interest remains the same. Therefore, the real value of the interest burden also decreases. So, from both sides, the debtors are benefited, whereas the creditors are adversely affected during the period of inflation.
ii) *Producers and labourers:* during the period of inflation producers are benefited because the amount of profit of the producers continuously rises along with the price level. But the prices of factors of production do not increase in the same proportion. Sometimes the prices of factors of production are fixed by contract, and unless the contract period ends, the prices do not increase even if the prices of final products go up. As a result, the profits of the producers increase. On the other hand, the workers are adversely affected because during the period of inflation the wages do not increase in proportion to prices. The real wages then fall. As a result, the workers are adversely affected.
iii) *Fixed Income Group and Variable Income Group:* during the period of inflation, individuals of fixed income, for example, government employees, pensioners, interest earners, etc. are damaged by inflation; though their incomes remain the same, price level increases. Real purchasing power of those individuals decreases, as a result. On the other hand, the variable income group, for example businessmen, are not so

seriously affected because nominal incomes of such people outstrip the general price rise. By increasing the prices of the commodities sold by them, they can increase their income during the period of inflation and thereby gain.

iv) *Investors of Share and Debenture:* different investors are differently affected during the period of inflation. Investors investing in shares are expected to gain during the period of inflation because the possibility of earning more dividends brightens. On the other hand, investors investing in fixed interest-bearing bonds or debenture are adversely affected because they get only fixed interest rate according to the agreement while the purchasing power of money and hence real income is falling during inflation. Similarly, beneficiaries from life insurance programmes are also hit badly since the real value of savings deteriorates.

v) *Speculators, Hoarders, Black Marketeers, and Consumers Group:* during the period of inflation, speculators and hoarders are benefited because they get the chance to earn supernormal profit. Black marketeers are also benefitted by inflation. On the other hand, consumer groups are adversely affected because they are exploited by the speculators and holders.

vi) *Self-Employed Persons:* the self-employed persons can increase their incomes by raising the fees charged for the services rendered by them. For example, the lawyers or the doctors can increase their fees during the period of inflation and, in this way, they can increase their incomes. Therefore, they are not very much adversely affected as a result of inflation. Thus, it is seen that structure of income and wealth distribution are changed significantly; someone wins and someone loses from inflation.

5.4.3 Other effects

Other effects of inflation are discussed in this section.

Domestic prices are increased during inflation. If the domestic price becomes higher than the international price, the price of export goods is increased but the foreigner gets a higher price for imported goods. Due to this, the amount of export is decreased and the amount of import is increased. As a result, deficit arises in balance of payment.

Revenues of the government increase during inflation as the government gets more revenue from different sources. But government expenditures also increase due to rising cost of government projects and increase administrative expenses due to inflation. As a result, deficit in government budget generally increases.

During inflation people want to hold a smaller amount of money at hand as the value of money decreases. They want stock in commodity form. Further, people like to hold gold, jewellery, real estate, etc. instead of keeping saved money in bank on the expectation of higher return. This hampers the process of capital formation.

During the period of inflation, prices of consumer goods go up and ordinary people cannot purchase commodities. As a result, fewer resources are devoted to the production of consumer goods and more resources can be diverted to the production of capital goods. People are forced to save more and, in this way, inflation helps in forced saving.

In conclusion, it can be said that, though inflation may have some good effects, on the whole inflation is not desirable. Rising inflation is a sign of failure on the part of the government as people's harassment increases.

5.5 Demand-pull theory of inflation — inflationary and deflationary gaps

The earliest attempt to explain inflation was made by classical economists with the help of the QTM. According to this theory, already discussed before, the price level depends directly and proportionately on the quantity of money. The rate of inflation depends on the rate of growth of money supply. The quantity theory in this form could not explain the mechanism through which price level will rise as a result of the rise in money supply. It was Wicksell who analysed the mechanism by which an increase in money would lead to an increase in the price level. Wicksell's theory states that, when money supply increases, the market rate of interest falls below the natural rate and this will induce investors and consumers to spend more in the economy. As a result, the aggregate demand will increase, which will increase the price level, assuming that aggregate supply will remain constant at full employment level. When money supply stops increasing, the market rate of interest will rise and will become equal to the natural rate and the inflationary pressure will be halted with it. That is why monetarists or classical economists argue that inflation is always and everywhere a monetary phenomenon.

Keynesians, in contrast, argued that aggregate demand may rise due to a rise in consumer or investment demand or due to government expenditure (or net export in case of open economy) or a combination of all of these factors. Thus, Keynes broke the close tie between the quantity of money and the level of aggregate demand emphasised by classical economists. According to Keynes, there may be some inflation in the economy even with a constant money supply. In a situation of constant money supply, an increased price level would raise the transaction demand for money and, thus, push up interest rate, which would reduce investment demand. The decreased investment demand will moderate the inflationary pressure, but is unlikely to eliminate it. There is, thus, a significant difference between Wicksell's and Keynes' theory of inflation. For the former any increase in the supply of money is inflationary. For the latter, inflation originates in the non-monetary sector or real sector of the economy. Despite these differences, both the theories explain inflation as arising from an excess of aggregate demand over the full employment aggregate supply.

The Keynesian theory of inflation is normally explained with the help of the "inflationary gap" which is defined as an excess of aggregate demand over aggregate supply at full employment. The concept of inflationary gap can be analysed with the help of the following Keynesian cross diagram. In the vertical axis of Figure 5.1, we measure the aggregate expenditure ($E = C + I + G$) and in the horizontal axis we measure real national income or aggregate output. Let curve $E_0 = (C + I + G)_0$ represents aggregate demand (for the time being we are considering a closed economy) and Y_f represents the value of the full employment output. At point A the price level is in equilibrium. There will not be any price rise since aggregate demand is equal to aggregate supply. If for some reason the aggregate demand or aggregate expenditure curve shifts to E_1, an inflationary gap of size AB appears in the output market.

Because full employment output cannot increase beyond Y_f, AB measures the excess of aggregate demand over aggregate supply at full employment level which pulls up prices. So long as the inflationary gap persists, the price level will continue to increase. The inflationary gap thus describes a *disequilibrium situation*. Inflation goes on without limit unless the inflationary gap is eliminated by some governmental initiative.

If, on the other hand, aggregate demand is less than aggregate supply at full employment, then we have the *deflationary gap*. The vertical distance between the 45-degree line

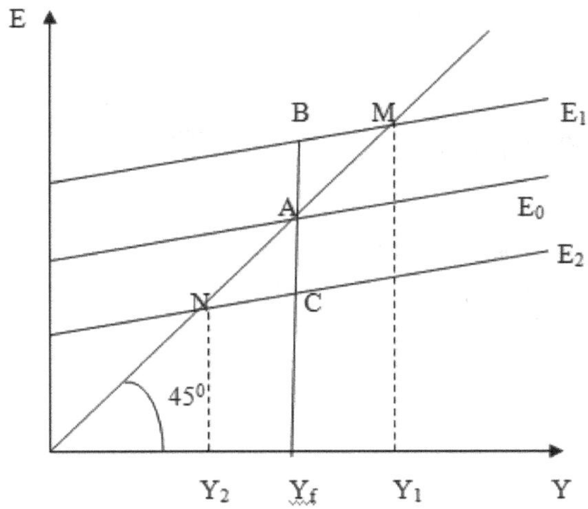

Figure 5.1 Demand-pull inflation

and aggregate demand line at full employment output situation measures this gap. Relevant aggregate demand curve is given by E_2 in the diagram, and AC represents deflationary gap. The economy faces unemployment in this situation. The deficiency in aggregate demand thus causes price level to fall. When there is a deflationary gap, the economy will settle at a less than full employment situation where income level is Y_2, but when there is an inflationary gap income level cannot increase to Y_1 as it is not physically possible to increase output beyond Y_f.

5.5.1 *How to remove an inflationary gap?*

An inflationary gap can be removed in two ways. One was is the *direct method* and the other is the *indirect method.*

The government should initiate policies to reduce the rate of growth of the money supply or slow the rate of increase in its spending or increase taxes to remove the inflationary gap ***directly***. If these policies or some combination of them are pursued, aggregate demand will increase less rapidly and the upward pressure on prices will be alleviated. For example, the bank of the country may reduce the inflationary gap by *reducing the amount of credit* through its different methods of credit control, for example, increase in bank rate or variable reserve ratio. Again, the government of the country may reduce the inflationary gap by reducing consumption expenditure and investment expenditure of the country by increasing the tax rate through fiscal policy. As the tax collection rises faster than prices (especially in the case of income tax), disposable income will fall, which will also reduce consumption expenditure. Further government may reduce its own expenditure.

The inflationary gap may also be reduced or eliminated *indirectly* in the following way.

Real value of the asset (house, land, liquid cash) in the hands of the people tends to be reduced as a result of increase in price level. In this situation people want to increase the quantity of assets through increase in the amount of saving. As a result, total real consumption expenditure of the country is reduced and total demand is also reduced.

The inflationary gap is also reduced due to it. This is known as the real balance effect or *Pigou effect* according to the name of the professor Pigou.

Domestic price level increases due to inflationary gap in the country, but if the rate of increase in domestic price level is greater than the rate of increase in international price then price of the exportable item is high but the foreigner gets the high price for importable items. As a result, the amount of export decreases and the amount of import increases and net income from abroad tends to reduce. This reduces the total demand in an open economy (though not considered in Figure 5.1), narrowing down the inflationary gap. However, Prof. Keynes was of the opinion that inflationary gap cannot be completely removed automatically through indirect effect. For this he is of the view that to remove inflationary gap, the government of the country or the central bank should take the necessary action using the direct method.

5.5.2 Criticisms against this demand-pull theory of inflation

Keynesian theory of inflation suffers from the several *limitations*.

This theory is *static* in the sense that it does not determine the rate of inflation. Inflation is a dynamic process, but the concept of inflationary gap is a static one. As a result, it is not possible to explain the dynamic process of inflation with the help of inflationary gap. This limitation may be removed by dynamising it by assuming that the rate of inflation is proportional to the length of the inflationary gap.

This theory has considered *excess demand in the commodity market only*. If there is excess demand in the factor, market inflation may develop from that market. This possibility was not considered by Keynes at all. This limitation has been removed by Bent Hansen, who introduced both goods and factor gaps in the analysis of inflation.

The Keynesian theory assumed that inflation arises only *after full employment is reached*. So long as full employment is not reached, there is no possibility of price increases. But when full employment is reached, the supply of commodity remains stationary and only the price level can increase. But, in reality, the inflation can begin even in a period of unemployment as we have observed in reality in the 1970s and 1980s.

Keynes also ignored cost-push inflation. Even when there is unemployment in the labour market, the wage rate may increase due to trade union pressure. If the productivity of labour does not increase with wage increases, unit cost of production will increase. This will push up prices.

5.6 Cost-push inflation

Cost-push inflation arises when there is an increase in the cost of production due to increase in the prices of the factors of production. It is the cost factors that push the prices upward here. A rise in cost of production may come from various factors, such as labour cost, raw materials, etc. Often firms may exercise market power by pushing up prices independent of consumer demand to expand their profit margin. Cost-push inflation caused by monopolistic practices of firms may be referred to as profit cost-push, whereas cost-push inflation caused by unions may be referred to as wage cost-push. We start by considering wage cost-push inflation.

According to the modern economists, labour cost is the most important factor among other factor costs. So, the cost of production will increase substantially, fuelling cost inflation if the wage rate rises. Wage rate may increase due to several factors, like collective bargaining or trade union pressure, increase in demand for labour, etc. One point should be noted here: if the wage rate increases due to excess demand for labour it should not be considered cost inflation, because it is a case of demand inflation where inflationary forces originated in the factor market. A theory of cost inflation can be developed under the assumption that the wage rate is not market-determined, which means that the forces of demand and supply in the labour market do not play any role in wage determination.

For true cost inflation to take place, wage rate increase should be due to trade union pressure even when there is no excess demand for labour. Suppose the trade union asks for a higher wage rate in the absence of excess demand for labour and that compels the employers to accept the higher wage demands. It may so happen that the higher wage rate is followed by a rise in productivity, but if the rise in the wage rate exceeds the rise in productivity, this amounts to an autonomous rise in the wage rate. The wage cost per unit of output is raised as a consequence. Employers will be willing to produce less at the prevailing product price. A reduction of supply would not be accompanied by an equivalent reduction of demand leading to an increase in the price level. Unless and until prices rose in the same proportion as wage rates there would exist a tendency for the output to fall short of demand, thus causing the price rise to continue.

Wage-price spiral through the cost-of-living adjustment will further accentuate the price trend. The autonomous rise in the wage rate will be followed by an increase in the price level and this increases the cost of living of the workers. The price rise leads to a fall in the real wage rate. The trade unions will then demand a higher wage increase. Once this higher wage claim is granted by the employer, there is a second round of price inflation caused by the cost factor. This process may continue indefinitely if it is not checked by other factors.

We now turn to the cost-push inflation caused by firms. It is alleged that firms cause inflation through monopolistic pricing policies. The wage profit margins in some oligopolistic or monopolistic industries may encourage inflation. If the economy is becoming more monopolistic, prices will rise.

We can explain the cost-push inflation with the help of the following diagram.

In Figure 5.2, amount of commodity and price level are plotted on the horizontal axis and vertical axes respectively. In the diagram OY_f represents the amount of full

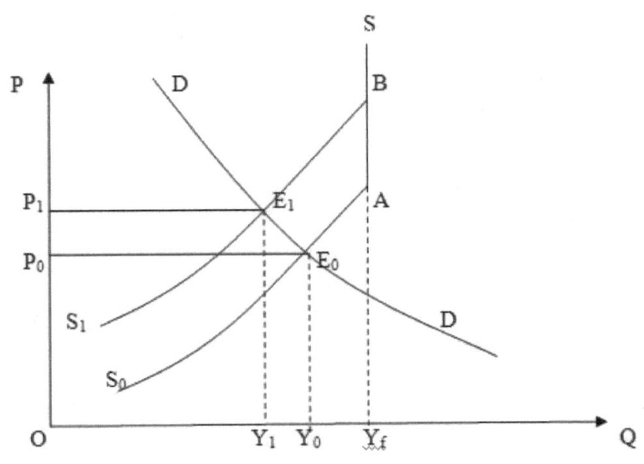

Figure 5.2 Cost-push inflation

employment level of production. Here S_0AS is the primary supply curve. The S_0A portion of this supply curve is rising; this is because before full employment, supply of commodity increases as price level increases. Further, the portion AS of the supply curve is parallel to vertical axis; this is because at full employment the level of production supply of commodity remains fixed (OY_f). As a result, production remains constant even though the price level increases after full employment. From the diagram it is seen that aggregate demand curve of the society *DD* and aggregate supply curve S_0AS intersect each other at point E_0 which is the equilibrium point. Here the equilibrium price is OP_0 and the equilibrium amount of commodity is OY_0, which is less than that corresponding to full employment level.

If the wage rate increases due to trade union pressure but the productivity of labour remains the same, then cost of production rises and the production unit claims a higher price than before for the same amount of commodity. As a result, the supply curve shifts to the left. From the diagram it is seen that a new supply curve S_1BS intersects the fixed demand curve *DD* at point E_1. Here E_1 is the new equilibrium point and the equilibrium price level is OP_1 and the equilibrium amount of commodity is OY_1. So here equilibrium price level increases from OP_0 to OP_1 and the equilibrium amount of supply decreases from OY_0 to OY_1. Cost of production tends to increase as the wage rate increases due to trade union pressure. As a result the total supply curve continues to shift leftward, pushing price level upward. This continuous rise in price level results in cost-push inflation. So, it is seen that before full employment level, demand remains constant; due to wage increases, cost of production rises and as a result price level increases leading to cost-push inflation.

Restrictive monetary or fiscal policies may be used to combat cost-push inflation but at the cost of higher unemployment. To avoid cost inflation, aggregate demand must be kept low enough and sufficient unemployment is to be created so that unions will not seek wage increase in excess of productivity increase. The government could also impose price and wage controls. But if the controls are effective, they are likely to be discriminatory and distort the allocation of resources. Cost-push inflation can also be controlled by making the economy more competitive. In this case firms and unions would have little power to raise wages and prices. But to do so the government has to adopt vigorous anti-trust policies like breaking up some firms or weakening labour unions. But such actions are unlikely for political reasons.

5.6.1 *Criticisms against the cost-push theory*

This analysis presupposes the non-market clearing assumption in the labour market due to trade union pressure. It assumes that trade unions should increase wage rate, which also presupposes the nonexistence of perfect competition in the labour market. If perfect competition exists in the labour market, then only one type of inflation can exist, that is, demand pool inflation and not cost-push inflation.

It should be noted that if the amount of money supply and government expenditure remain constant, the price level which has increased as a result of increase in cost of production due to wage increase through trade unions pressure cannot continue for a long time. If the amount of money supply and government expenditure remain constant, the demand for commodity decreases along with the increase in the price level. As a result, the amount of production and supply tend to reduce, aggravating the unemployment problem in the economy. Increase in wage rate and increase in price level will stop as a result.

5.6.2 Distinction between demand-pull and cost-push inflation

It is difficult to make the distinction between demand inflation and cost inflation in practice. The wage-price spiral is a normal feature of both types of inflation. In the case of demand inflation, the rise in the price level leads to the rise in the wage rate. In the case of cost inflation, the causal sequence is reversed, i.e. rise in the wage rate leads to a rise in the price level. If we could identify what had risen first, we could then say whether it was demand inflation or cost inflation. In practice, both prices and wages are unstable over time. This instability can be created either from the demand side or from the cost side. Thus, in a period of time when both wages and prices are rising, it is difficult to say whether it is a demand inflation or cost inflation as the time gap between a price rise and a wage rise is much shorter. Also, in a modern economy, wages and many commodity prices are determined administratively, not determined by market forces. Under these circumstances it is not possible to distinguish between demand-pull and cost-push inflation.

It may further be argued that if increases in the wage rate are caused by rises in labour productivity, it would not be a cause of inflation. Thus, when the rise in the wage rate exceeds the rise in labour productivity it may be regarded as the case of cost inflation. However, demand inflation does not leave the wage rate unchanged; the rise in the wage rate produced by the increase in demand for labour may be so high that it exceeds the rise in labour productivity. Thus, the comparison between the rises in the labour productivity and the wage rate is inconclusive with regard to the distinction between a demand and cost inflation.

The theoretical model of the two types of inflation discussed earlier suggests a method of distinction which should be examined in detail. There is an excess demand for labour in the case of demand inflation and, thus, we can expect that demand inflation should be associated with a condition of full employment in the economy or at least a falling unemployment, whereas cost inflation should be associated with a rise in the level of unemployment. Thus, we need to examine the percentage of labour force unemployed to make a distinction between demand inflation and cost inflation. A rising percentage of unemployment indicates cost inflation, whereas a falling percentage indicates demand inflation. In case of demand-pull inflation, monetary and fiscal policy measures are recommended while for cost-push inflation certain nonmonetary and non-fiscal measures are recommended. So, it is practically very difficult to distinguish between demand-pull and cost-push inflation.

5.7 Mark-up inflation

In the case of mark-up pricing, firms set their price by incorporating a margin or standard mark-up over the production cost per unit. This mark-up pricing tends to facilitate the inflationary potential of a cost-push. The mark up is expressed as a percentage of the average direct cost. This type of price determination is very common in an imperfectly competitive market structure. For simplicity, we prioritise labour as the predominant factor of production. Firms set P to account for the unit labour cost and incorporate a mark-up on it to accommodate additional expenses related to non-labour inputs and other complementary factors.

The cost of labour for each unit of output can be expressed as the product of the labour hours required to produce one unit (denoted as h) and the wage per hour (denoted as W). The labour requirement coefficient, h, is the reciprocal of average labour productivity, which is defined as the output per unit of labour. An enhancement in labour productivity corresponds to a decrease in the value of h. The pricing formula in case of mark-up pricing asserts that the selling price is equivalent to the unit cost, with an additional mark-up applied to it.

$$P = (1+\alpha)hW, \qquad \alpha > 0. \tag{5.1}$$

Where (hW) is the unit labour cost and α represents the constant mark-up chosen by the firm. Here labour productivity can be defined as $\rho\ (=\frac{1}{h})$.

The pricing Equation (5.1) posits that P rises under three conditions: i) when wage is elevated, ii) when non-labour costs experience an increase, and (iii) when labour productivity is lower (h is higher), signifying an inverse relationship between P and productivity.

By establishing a direct connection between rises in production costs and the subsequent elevation of P, mark-up pricing offers a cost-push rationale for inflation. This phenomenon occurs even when the markup factor α remains consistent.

Equation (5.1) can be rewritten as $P = (1+\alpha)\frac{W}{\rho}$.

Assuming α to be constant, this gives

$$\hat{P} = \hat{W} - \hat{\rho} \tag{5.2}$$

That is, the proportionate change in P equals the rate of wage inflation minus the rate of growth of labour productivity. Prices rise when money wages rise in excess of the rise in productivity. Thus, mark-up inflation signifies that labour is not solely responsible for cost inflation.

5.8 The social cost of inflation

Inflation hampers output only indirectly, though it has some significant benefit as well. Due to this fact, there is lack of consensus among economists as to whether inflation is necessarily bad. Economists like J. Tobin argued that some inflation is good for the economy as it keeps the real wage rate low and thereby the employment and output level higher than otherwise. According to Arthur Okun, however, inflation is as bad as unemployment. We will analyse the social costs of inflation in two steps.

i) Analysing the cost of anticipated inflation
ii) Analysing the cost of unanticipated inflation

5.8.1 The costs of anticipated inflation

When the inflation is exactly as per expectation, without any surprise, it is called anticipated inflation. This type is less costly to the society because all future receipts and payments could then be fully adjusted in advance for inflation. Even in this situation, there are some costs to the society, which could be explained as follows:

People hold cash in hand to use in their day-to-day transactions, asset demands, and precautionary needs. So, demand varies inversely with nominal interest rate (the Baumol and Tobin model demonstrates how transaction demand for money also depends on nominal rate of interest). As nominal interest rate goes up (explained with the help of Fisher's equation), people wish to hold less cash at their disposal. If, on average, people hold lower money balances, they are required to visit to banks more frequently than otherwise. These efforts reduce the time available for leisure or productive work. It consumes time and reduces the life of shoes due to their increased wear and tear. The inconvenience of reducing money holding is known as *shoe-leather cost* of inflation. Shoes are very costly in Western countries. There is no market for repairing shoes. So as people go to the bank more and more frequently, they have to replace their shoes again and again at a high cost. This cost varies directly with the rate of inflation.

High inflation induces firms to change their printed prices (on menu cards of restaurants, catalogues, etc.) every now and then. These costs are known as *menu costs*. But frequent price changes create confusion among buyers and adversely affect consumer psychology and emotion. Retailers, who meet the people (the actual buyers) at the grassroots level, have to face the trouble. The truth is that the higher the rate of inflation, the more often restaurants have to print new menus. There is the need to print new prices, announce price changes through newspapers and T.V. commercials, distribute catalogues to dealers and customers, and even the cost of dealing with customer annoyance over price changes. Menu cost is independent of the rate of inflation and symmetric with regard to increase or decrease in price. It occurs, also, irrespective of whether the inflation is as per expectations or not.

Inflation also adds to the plight of firms facing menu costs. Due to such costs they cannot change prices frequently. So the higher the rate of inflation, the greater will be the *variability in relative prices*. Since market economies rely on relative prices to allocate resources efficiently, resources are inefficiently allocated.

Some, particularly the less educated, act on the basis of the nominal values rather than the real values of their incomes and wealth. Economists call this the money illusion. Inflation or deflation can cause poor decisions by otherwise rational people. For example, if someone's salary goes up, say, by 15% when the inflation rate was also 15%, a person not subject to the money illusion, would then consider this as no change in his purchasing power and, hence, would make no change in his purchases. However, persons subject to money illusion might take the previous scenario as an increase in their incomes and enhance their consumption spending, which is, obviously, the wrong thing for them as well as for society. Society, therefore, is worse-off now than before inflation and, accordingly, inflation is associated with a cost called the *money illusion cost*. This cost varies with the rate of inflation and it is symmetric to inflation as well as deflation.

The inconvenience of living in a world with a changing price level often imposes costs on the individuals. Money is the measuring rod of everything. During inflation it fails to perform this function because the unit of account itself changes. For example, during inflation, *people cannot do proper financial planning*. They do not know how much to consume and how much to save. Another significant cost of inflation is created by the interaction between *inflation and the tax system*. This problem arises because the income levels corresponding to different income tax rates are not revised systematically with inflation. Many provisions of tax code do not take into account the effects of inflation. A person moves into a higher tax bracket and pays more tax just because his money income, not real income, is higher due to inflation. However in the case of low to moderate inflation, the costs of fully anticipated inflation are small.

5.8.2 *The costs of unanticipated inflation*

Unanticipated inflation refers to price increases which are not expected or are larger than expected. The main costs of unexpected or unanticipated inflation are redistribution of income and wealth in undesirable ways and generation of uncertainties. The following points may be discussed in this context:

Unexpected inflation arbitrarily redistributes wealth among individuals. Since most loan agreements are denominated in nominal terms and there is no inflation clause (adjustment of nominal interest rate against actual rate of inflation), debtors gain and creditors lose if the actual rate of inflation turns out to be higher than the expected rate. If the rate of inflation falls below the expected level (unexpected deflation), the shoe is on the other foot. It is because the repayment is greater than what was expected by both the parties. Either way, someone wins and someone loses. People having fixed income such as most wage-earners, pensioners, rentier class, and holders of government bonds suffer loss of real income (purchasing power) during inflation. They are robbed by such forces which they cannot see or identify. The redistribution effect operates with respect to all assets fixed in nominal terms, like, money, bonds, saving accounts, insurance contracts, etc. Realised real interest rates are lower than nominal interest rates and may even become negative. This effect is extremely important as it can erode the purchasing power of a lifetime's saving which is supposed to finance retirement consumption. The amount of gain or loss due to the surprise inflation is proportional to the degree of that inflation.

In general, the business sector gains as their assets are mostly in the form of real assets like equipment, structures, and inventories; their liabilities are mostly in nominal assets like equity and debt. Since the government is normally the net debtor to the private sector, this is another source of gain to the government through inflation. The government might also lose due to inflation. The debt servicing charge will increase due to increase in nominal interest rate (via Fisher's equation) and tax collection will decrease due to the time lag between the increase in the tax base and the payment of taxes. Hence some might argue that fiscal deficit tends to increase during inflation. Thus the possibility of unanticipated inflation introduces an extra element of risk. This is a clear cost associated with unanticipated inflation, though it is quite hard to measure.

The gains and losses from the *redistributions of wealth and income* among sectors and individuals that take place as a result of unanticipated inflation basically cancel out over the economy as a whole. Though the government gains from inflation, the private sector pays lower taxes. When the corporate sector gains from inflation, owners of corporations benefit at the expense of others. If we ignore the redistribution of wealth among individuals, the costs of unanticipated inflation would be negligible.

The greater the variability of the rate of inflation, the greater the *uncertainty* faced by the individuals. The unpredictable nature of a highly volatile rate of inflation hurts most risk-averse people who do not want to learn to live with inflation. They never develop any taste for uncertainty which traders and speculators often love to cherish. In short, volatile inflation is something which most people find unpalatable. Some rational risk-lovers will, on the other hand, try to hedge against such inflation. Managing such uncertainty calls for speculations and unproductive investments.

Finally high inflation, being highly *volatile* and variable in nature, increases uncertainty of both lenders and borrowers by subjecting them to arbitrary and potentially large redistributions of wealth.

In an environment of high average rate of inflation, the rate itself changes greatly from one year to the next. In a particular year it is unexpectedly high; in another it is unbelievably low. High rates of inflation are better than highly volatile inflation just as some inflation is better than no inflation.

5.8.3 Social benefits of inflation

Inflation brings some social benefits as well. From the Phillips curve relationship, discussed in Chapter 10, it is clear that there exists a negative relationship between inflation and unemployment. The existence of short run trade off will be appealing to the governments and the voters as high inflation lowers unemployment and increases output.

Tobin argued that sometimes firms find it difficult to reduce the nominal wage rate. Nominal pay cuts have been relatively rare. Workers are extraordinarily reluctant to cuts in nominal pay. Such cuts are therefore very costly to firms. A mild inflation reduces real wage slightly without lowering nominal wage. It is not possible to make such automatic reductions in real wages in a situation of stable prices. On such occasions inflation helps in *reducing real wage*. A fall in real wage leads to an increase in employment, which is good for the economy. Thus mild inflation is good for the economy because it lubricates the economic machine and gives firms the necessary encouragement to produce more output by hiring more labour and adding to their capital stock.

Printing money to raise revenue is like imposing inflation tax, a tax on holding money which reduces real balances of the individual. Another possible benefit of inflation is that the inflation tax is a less costly way of raising tax revenue than other forms of taxation. This is likely to be more relevant for less developed economies.

5.9 Hyperinflation

Hyperinflation is a period when the price level explodes, with inflation rate reaching astronomical levels. In Hungary, for example, monthly inflation rate was as high as 19,800% in 1945–1946 supported by an extremely high growth rate of money supply (12,200% during the same period). During hyperinflation money supply always explodes which illustrates an implication of the quantity theory that sustained high inflation requires accommodating high money growth rates.

Relative prices fail to give a clear picture of true scarcity of commodities and factors of production in this situation. In the face of large and frequent price changes, consumers cannot find out or search out the best possible prices of the product they want to buy. Menu costs also keep on increasing during hyperinflation. Firms remain so busy with constantly changing prices that their normal business activities are hampered. They find it virtually impossible to print and distribute catalogues with fixed prices. Thus, highly volatile and rapidly rising prices can alter the behaviour of both producers and consumers in unpredictable and undesirable ways. The shoe-leather costs associated with reduced money holding are much higher during hyperinflation. Business people have to devote more time and energy to managing their cash which itself loses its value every day. So, they cannot pay attention to more socially desirable activities such as investment and production. The end result is inefficient functioning of the economy.

During hyperinflation the real tax burden of people falls. Due to time lag between levying taxes by the government and paying taxes by individuals and companies, the real tax revenue of the government falls, leading to deficit in the budget. This is often met by resorting to printing money. As new money is printed and put into circulation, the rate of inflation is accelerated. This virtually painless method of financing government expenditure has ruined many governments in the past. Deficit financing adds fuel to the inflationary fire and generates a cumulative spiral of rising inflation, growing deficit, and more reliance on the method of deficit financing which itself is inflationary in its outcome. The velocity of circulation approaches infinity and the value of money tends to fall to zero. People refuse to accept the legal tender money as a medium of exchange. Commodities are demanded against commodities. Finally, the monetary system gradually becomes less and less competent to perform its main function: to supply the economy with the much-needed medium of exchange, unit of account and store of value, with money economy yielding place to barter economy. So people have to learn to live with hyperinflation.

History demonstrates that rapid monetary growth causes hyperinflation. Most hyperinflation occurs due to financing budgetary deficits by printing new currency notes. This becomes a necessity rather than a deliberate act of choice. As growth rate of money supply accelerates, even mild inflation is converted into hyperinflation in the absence of monetary discipline on the part the central bank and its loss of credibility. Although inflation is caused by monetary expansion, it comes to a halt only with fiscal reform, that is to say, reduced government spending and increased tax revenue, thereby reducing the need for inflation tax (seigniorage), and allowing a reduction in money growth. Thus, even if inflation begins as a monetary phenomenon, it ends in fiscal reforms.

5.10 Stagflation

After studying the concepts of inflation and unemployment and observing their trend in the context of the Indian economy we focus our attention on one burning issue of the 1970s – *stagflation*. Most of the oil importing countries in the world experienced surges in inflation along with a rise in unemployment during the 70s. In fact, in the 1960s petroleum and oil exporting countries formed a cartel, the organisation of petroleum exporting countries (OPEC). During the 1970s, OPEC raised the prices of petroleum and petroleum products. As oil constituted an extremely important intermediate input, this leads to huge increase in cost of production and stagflation. The term stagflation refers to combination of inflation and economic stagflation; it is a result of co-existence of slow growth with rising prices. Since stagflation is a situation in which price level increases without increasing output, this results in high unemployment rate. Such a situation may also arise due to *adverse supply shocks* that affect the production side of the economy. Natural disasters, climatic change, and innovation in technical knowledge are examples of supply shocks. Inflationary expectation may also lead to stagflation. If an economy experiences inflation for some time, people may expect such a situation to continue in the future also. Such expectations are called entrenched inflation. This might cause the aggregate supply curve to shift left ward, leading to stagflation. The term was first used in 1970 when the US economy experienced inflation in spite of depression in their economic activities. We can explain this economic phenomenon and its possible remedies using an AD – AS diagram.

Any kind of adverse supply shock (e.g., increase in world oil price, rise in cost of production of many firms) which will shift aggregate supply curve left-ward leads to lower equilibrium output (stagnation) and higher price level (inflation). In Figure 5.3, the AS curve shifts left from AS_0 to AS_1 as a result of adverse supply shock. The economy

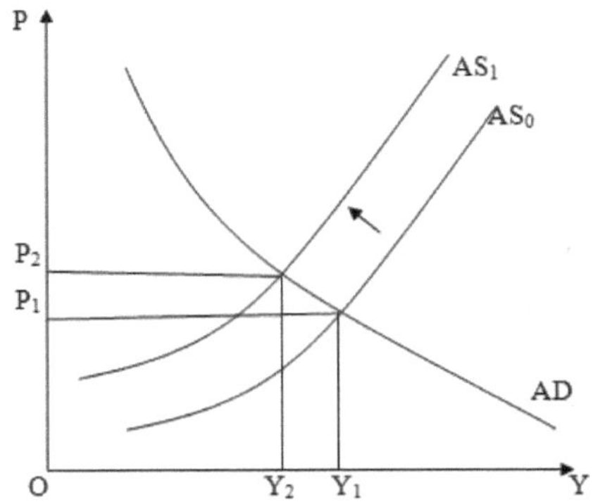

Figure 5.3 Showing stagflation due to adverse supply shock

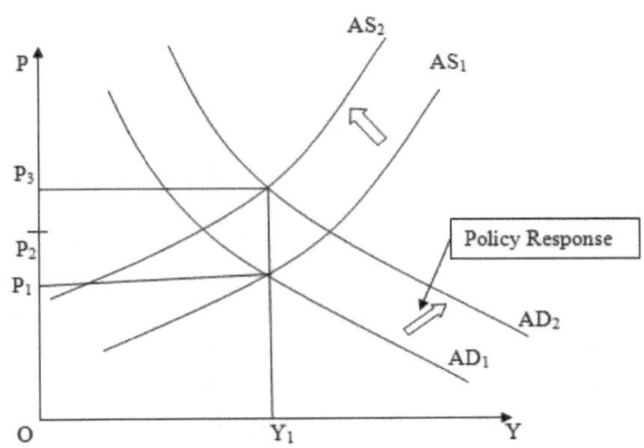

Figure 5.4 Stagflation and expansionary policy

suffers a double setback, falling output from Y_1 to Y_2 as well as higher prices from P_1 to P_2.

Confronted with stagflation, policymakers face a difficult choice between fighting inflation and fighting unemployment. Policymakers who control monetary and fiscal policy might offset some of the effects of the shift in the short run aggregate supply curve by expanding AD. This is described with the help of Figure 5.4. AD curve shifts from AD_1 to AD_2 as a result of expansionary policy taken by the government – exactly enough to prevent the shifts in aggregate supply from affecting output. Price level rises from P_1 to P_3 though output remains unchanged as a result of this policy change. In this case policymakers are said to accommodate the shift in AS. This accommodative policy accepts a permanently higher level of prices to maintain a higher-level output and employment.

Alternatively, if contractionary policies are undertaken by the government, price will be reduced but output falls further. Inflation can be controlled in this situation but at the cost of higher unemployment.

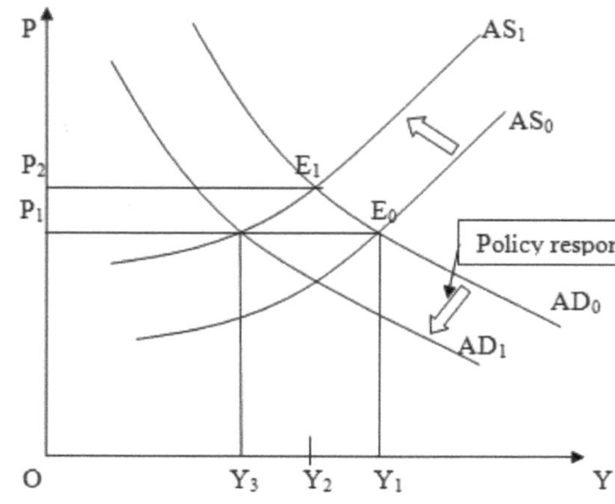

Figure 5.5 Stagflation and contractionary policy

As shown in Figure 5.5, the economy initially moves from E_0 to E_1 as an impact of adverse supply shock. Contractionary demand management policy undertaken to curb this stagflationary situation will lead to a downward movement of AD curve from AD_0 to AD_1 in such a way that price level comes back to the initial level P_1 from where it rose to P_2 after supply shock. The economy has to suffer a lot in accepting huge unemployment to get out of stagflation.

However, in no way can both price stability and full employment be attained. This is the limitation of stabilisation policies in dealing with these twin evils of unemployment and inflation simultaneously. Rather, a relatively better remedy for an adverse supply shock lies in reversing it through favourable supply shock of the same amount. This might be done through incentives given by cut in income tax rate of workers, cut in corporate profit tax rate of firms, etc. In this situation as a policy response AS will come back to its original position AS_0 (in Figure 5.3), eliminating both the problems.

5.11 Inflation and interest rates

The *nominal rate of interest* is the amount charged for a loan by a bank or other lenders per year expressed as a percentage. For instance, if an individual borrows Rs. 100 and repays Rs. 120 after one year the interest rate is 20%. Interest rates usually rise with inflation to compensate lenders for the following purchasing power of the rupee. The *real interest rate* is obtained by subtracting the rate of inflation from the nominal rate of interest. If i denotes the nominal interest rate, r the real interest rate, and π the rate of inflation, then the relationship among these three variables can be written as $r = i - \pi$. In other words, the real interest rate is the difference between the nominal interest rate and the rate of inflation. In a period of low inflation the distinction between the two rates gets blurred. The real rate of interest corrects nominal rate for expected change in the price level. If, for instance, a bank pays 9% on deposit for a year and a depositor expects inflation to be 5% for the year, then the real rate of interest is 4%. The real rate of interest measures how much a depositor will earn on his deposit after taking account for the fact that inflation will increase the prices of products that the depositor might purchase in a year.

From the previous analysis we can write the nominal interest rate as the sum of the real interest rate and the inflation rate, such as

$$i = r + \pi. \tag{5.3}$$

Equation (5.3) is known as *Fisher's equation* after the name of economist Irving Fisher. It shows that nominal interest rate can change for two reasons: i) if real interest rate changes and ii) if inflation rate changes.

The link can be explained as follows. In the presence of inflation, lenders try to protect the real value of their interest income. So nominal interest charged by them tends to incorporate a premium equal to the expected rate of inflation. As inflation persists in long run, its actual value is anticipated more or less correctly and we get $i = r + \pi$. Hence in long run, a change in inflation will be translated into an equal change in the nominal rate of interest, leaving real interest unchanged. This one-to-one relation between the inflation rate and nominal interest rate is called the Fisher effect. The Fisher effect does not hold in the short run to the extent that inflation is unanticipated. To be precise, the Fisher effect states that the nominal interest rate adjusts to expected inflation. Expected inflation moves with actual inflation in the long run but not necessarily in the short run.

Real interest rate (r) is determined in the real sector of the economy and it adjusts to equilibrate savings and investment. QTM shows that rate of growth of money supply determines the rate of inflation. The quantity theory and Fisher's eq. together tell us how money growth affects the nominal interest rate. According to quantity theory, if money supply grows by 1% this will lead to 1% rate of inflation. According to Fisher's eq., 1% increase in inflation rate in turn causes 1% increase in nominal interest rate (i).

In this respect we should make a distinction between ex ante and ex post real interest rates. Lender and borrower cannot predict the future rate of inflation with certainty, but they do have some expectation of the inflation rate. The real interest rate that borrowers and lenders expect when the loan agreement is made is called the ex-ante real interest rate and that actually realised is called ex post real interest rate. If π and π^e denote actual and expected future inflation rates respectively then $(i - \pi)$ is the ex post real interest rate and $(i - \pi^e)$ represents ex-ante real interest rate. Nominal interest rate cannot adjust to actual inflation; it can adjust to expected inflation only because actual inflation is not known when the nominal interest rate is set. Incorporating this Fisher equation can be rewritten as $i = r + \pi^e$.

5.12 Anti-inflationary policies

Anti-inflation policies may be grouped into three categories: i) monetary policy, ii) fiscal policy and iii) non-monetary policy or direct control. Let us discuss these policies one by one. Monetary and fiscal policies are called demand management policies, whereas non-monetary policy includes income and pricing policies.

5.12.1 Monetary policy

Monetary policy refers to the credit control policy of the monetary authority or central bank of the country. During inflation the central bank tries to reduce the total expenditure of the country by reducing the amount of commercial bank credit. It is thus also known as credit control policy. The central bank can take the following measures to control the volume of credit.

i) *Bank Rate:* the commercial banks may face cash or fund crunch if the demand for credit or loan is high or the minimum cash reserve falls short of the statutory level. To manage the situation, the commercial banks have to take additional funds from the central bank by means of discounting their securities. The rate of discount in this case is called *bank rate*. Hence, bank rate is the interest rate charged by the central banks upon the additional fund demanded by them. The logic of bank rate working as one of the credit control instruments is that as bank rate increases, the cost of loans from the central banks will increase and the commercial banks will be forced to increase the rate of interest which they charge upon their loan customers. Hence, the commercial banks will take a smaller loan from the central bank and as a result the capacity of the commercial banks to give loans to the general public (households, firms, etc.) will decrease. As amount of loan in the hands of the general public falls, the demand for goods and services will also fall which will pull down the general price level and reduce the inflationary pressure. On the other hand, as bank rate falls during the slump phase of the business cycle, the commercial banks will be eager to take additional funds at the cheaper rate from the central bank and their capacity to provide loans to the general public will increase, which will further lead to increase in aggregate demand for goods and services. The general price level will then increase which will have beneficial effects on the producers.
ii) *Open Market Operations:* sometimes, the central bank of the country deliberately and directly buys and sells bills and securities in the money market to control money supply. This process is called *open market operations*. During the period of inflation or boom in the economy, the amount of money supply should be reduced, and during the slump phase the amount of money supply should be increased to incentivise the goods and service sectors of the economy. In the USA, the Federal Reserve, the central bank of the country, calls the first situation *quantitative restrictions* (QR) and the second situation *quantitative easing* (QE). During the global financial crisis of 2007–2009, the Federal Reserve applied the QE policy to provide additional funds to the banking system to fight against the crisis and the time now has come to them to apply the QR as the economy has recovered significantly from the crisis.

During the inflationary period, the central bank may sell government securities to the commercial banks and others. Once the commercial banks purchase the securities, they have to pay for them out of their loanable funds. As a result of that, the credit opportunity of the commercial banks falls and hence the aggregate demand falls which ultimately pulls down the general price level. The reverse, that is, buying of securities by the central bank, works when there is a deflationary situation in the economy. The general price level boosts after the commercial banks get additional funds from selling securities to the central bank.

Which one is better? Strategically the open market operation is more effective than the bank rate policy to control money supply and inflationary pressure since it is done exclusively by the central bank and no association or consultation with the commercial banks is required. But the process of discounting in the case of bank rate policy needs the cooperation of the commercial banks to execute. It can also be said that open market operations are used to make the bank rate policy effective. How? Suppose in the slump phase of the business cycle the Central Bank will lower the bank rate to increase money supply. At the same time, the central bank will go for buying securities from the market and make available additional funds for the commercial banks to increase their loanable capacity so that money supply ultimately increases.

iii) *Variable Reserve Ratio*: the central bank frames the guidelines as to which proportion of the commercial banks will be held as cash account or loanable account. The ratio is variable depending on the market conditions as well as the preference of the account holders in cash or savings. The variable reserve ratio is two-fold – cash reserve ratio (CRR) and statutory liquidity ratio (SLR).

5.12.1.1 CRR

The commercial bank cannot use all of its deposits in lending to different sectors of the economy since the depositors may require cash for withdrawal for meeting transaction needs. Therefore, a part of the deposit is kept with the central bank in the form of reserves or balances. This proportion of cash is called CRR. It is thus clear that the higher the CRR with the central bank, the lower will be the supply of money in the system and vice versa. In India the central bank of India (RBI) has been empowered to vary CRR between 15%and 3%. But as per the suggestion by the Narsimhan Committee Report on the banking sector reforms in 1990–1991, the CRR was reduced from 15% in 1990 to 5% in 2002. After repeated sliding of the rates, it reached 3% in 2022 (refer to Figure 5.6).

5.12.1.2 SLR

Besides CRR, all the financial institutions will have to maintain a certain quantity of liquid assets with themselves at any point in time of their total time and demand liabilities.

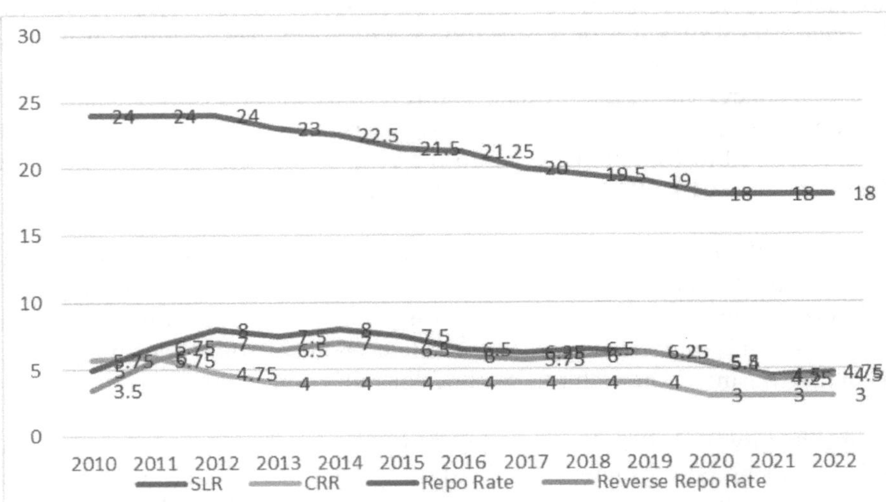

Figure 5.6 CRR, SLR, repo rate, and reverse repo rate in India

Source: RBI.

Further, these assets have to be kept in non-cash form such as approved government (central and state governments) securities like bonds, etc. This particular ratio of the liquid assets to time and demand assets is called SLR. It is forced investment of the commercial banks upon government securities. Governments use this fund in their developmental projects. As the rate of SLR falls, more funds are available for private investors through loan and aggregate demand raises, which further leads to increase in rate of inflation. The opposite logic works in the case of increase in SLR. In India there was the recommendation by the Narsimhan Committee to reduce of SLR from 38.5% to 25% during the early 1990s to improve the balance sheet of the commercial banks. Since investment in government securities provides the commercial banks returns with certainty, although with a relatively lower rate compared to the rate earned from the private investors, banks sometimes prefer to go for approved securities. In India the current SLR is around 18% (refer to Figure 5.6).

All three measures make bank credit more costly and thereby reduce the credit creating potential of commercial banks. Aggregate spending is reduced as a result.

5.12.1.3 Repo rate and reverse repo rate

The central bank of India (RBI) has introduced two new instruments for the last couple of years to control monetary system. They are repo rate and reverse repo rate. *Repo rate* is the rate at which RBI lends to commercial banks generally against government securities. Reduction in Repo rate helps the commercial banks to get money at a cheaper rate and thus the rate of interest charged on their lending falls and, as a result, the aggregate demand as well as price level increase, creating a favourable business environment. On the other hand, increase in Repo rate discourages the commercial banks from getting money as the rate increases and becomes expensive. On the other hand, *reverse repo rate* is the rate at which RBI borrows money from the commercial banks. The increase in the repo rate will increase the cost of borrowing and lending of the banks which will discourage the public to borrow money and will encourage them to deposit. As the rates become high, the availability of credit and demand decreases resulting in decrease in inflation. This increase in repo rate and reverse repo rate is a symbol of tightening of the monetary policy. The easing of repo and reverse repo rates create expansion in the money supply. Figure 5.6 highlights the trends of repo rate and reverse repo rates for the period March 2010 to March 2022. Up to the year 2012, both the rates increased and then fluctuated for 2013–2014 and thereafter decreased gradually.

iv) *Selective Methods of Credit Control*: to control credit in some selective or particular sectors of the economy the selective methods of credit control like regulation of margin requirements or regulation of consumer credit may be used. During inflation the central bank might reduce the amount of credit in some selective sectors (say, speculative business) through this method for reduction in total expenditure.

The main difficulty with the monetary policy is that it affects aggregate demand only indirectly by raising rates of interest and reducing money supply. Hence, its efficacy can be obtained only after a time lag. Moreover, the extent to which the monetary policy will be successful depends on the sensitivity of different economic variables to changes in the supply of money and the rate of interest. Monetary policy can combat demand-pull inflation more or less successfully compared to cost-push inflation. In Indian context an imperfect money and credit market poses an additional obstacle in the way of success of monetary policy to control inflation.

5.12.2 Fiscal policy

As a result of the previously mentioned difficulties with the monetary policy, fiscal policy may also be used to control inflation. The fiscal policy refers to taxation, borrowing, and expenditure policies of the government which influence aggregate spending. Different fiscal parameters such as the changes in the government expenditure including transfer payments, changes in taxes, or changes in government borrowing can directly affect aggregate demand. Contractionary fiscal policy should be used such that total expenditure of the society is reduced. During the period of inflation, it can take the following steps:

i) Government can reduce its expenditure which will reduce aggregate demand, as *government expenditure* is a major component of aggregate demand. Sometimes governments undertake unproductive expenditure to please the voters without caring about its impact on inflation. Such unproductive government expenditure must be reduced.
ii) *Taxes* should be increased during inflation to wipe out excess aggregate demand. An increase in rate of existing taxes or imposition of new taxes will reduce the disposable income, thereby reducing consumption expenditure. But, often, the government is reluctant to do so since taxpayers may vote out a government from power. It should be mentioned that, as anti-inflationary measures, direct taxes are superior to indirect taxes. Since the impact of indirect taxes can be shifted, imposition of indirect taxes will lead to an increase in the price level.
iii) The government may *borrow from the public* during a period of inflation by selling bonds. When people buy bonds, they surrender purchasing power which may, otherwise, have been spent on consumption or investment. As a result, total expenditure of the country is also reduced. In this way it is possible to reduce the price level of the country by reducing the total amount of expenditure through *public debt*.

Fiscal policies are also subject to certain limitations. A cut in tax rates will reduce saving rates and hence capital formation. Expenditures on subsidy programs like food subsidy to the poor, unemployment benefits, etc are desirable and seem to be unwise to curb even in the face of inflation. Political compulsions also greatly reduce the effectiveness of fiscal policy.

5.12.3 Non-monetary policy

Apart from the monetary and fiscal measures, the non-monetary policies may also be adopted to control the inflationary situation. The most commonly used anti-inflationary measure is *income policies*. It refers to a wide range of policies, from the government's setting of guidelines for wages and price increase, to consultation on wage and price norm between unions' management and government, to compulsory controls on wage, price, and profit increases. By controlling wages and other allowances, inflation of cost-push variety can be checked.

The non-monetary measure may also include output adjustment and rationing; inflation may rise because of shortage of output. Thus, to control inflation the level of output should be increased in real terms. By shifting resources from the unproductive to the productive sectors, output can be increased. The measures to control price and rationing are actually short run measures. However, if demand cannot be controlled, mere price control may lead to the creation of the black market. Rationing, however, functions as a device of stabilising consumer price and assuring distributive justice. However, rationing by weak administration may lead to black market and corruption.

Introduction of new currency by cancelling the old one is called demonetisation. This process can also be used to control inflation temporarily. India demonetised its currency last time in 2016, though with a different objective (the main objective was control of black money and not inflation). The government can also control this demon through the management of government administration in a proper path against tax evaders, speculators, hoarders, black marketeers, etc., as their activities provoke inflation.

Different anti-inflationary policies should not be regarded as competitive. All of them should be undertaken concurrently to get the desired result.

5.13 Additional teaching notes

5.13.1 Seigniorage

A government can finance its spending in three ways: by raising revenue through taxes, by borrowing from the public through selling government bonds, or by printing money.

The revenue raised by printing money is called seigniorage. The term comes from "Seigneur", the French word for feudal lord. Historically the feudal lord had the exclusive right in his possession to coin money. Seigniorage was a levy on metals brought to a mint for coining to cover the cost of mining and providing revenue to the ruler. Today this right belongs to the note-issuing authority like the central government or central bank and it is one source of revenue. So, now, the term refers to the amount of real resources brought by the government with newly created money.

5.13.2 Inflation tax

When the government prints money to finance expenditure it in fact increases the money supply which increases money inflation. Printing money to raise revenue is like imposing inflation tax. The holders of money pay the tax in the sense that money in the wallet becomes less valuable as prices rise. The inflation tax is not like other taxes, because no one receives a bill from the government for this tax. When the government prints new money for its use it makes the old money in the hands of the public less valuable. Thus, inflation is like a tax on holding money which reduces real balances of the individual. The importance of this tax varies from country to country and over time.

5.13.3 Demonetisation in India — a recent bombshell of monetary policy

The Indian Prime Minister Mr. Narendra Modi made a remarkable and bold announcement on the evening of November 8, 2016 before the 125-crore people of the country as well as of the world communities that, from that day, the running 500 and 1,000 denominations of notes would not remain legal tender because these two denominations bore the most black and counterfeit currencies in the country. In this sense, the pro BJP people are saying it is another surgical strike against the Pakistanis since it is widely believed by them that this country is the prime source of production of Indian counterfeit currencies of these two denominations. But what happened after that decision the people of India and the RBI and most of the growth forecasters all around the world would witness – that India would face a drop of growth in GDP of at least 1% by March 2017. That means about one and a half lacs crores rupees of GDP would go out of the Indian economy that would create disasters mostly in the unorganised sectors' employment and output.

Before going on to discuss on the impacts of the sudden policy announcements on different aspects of the Indian economy, we need to highlight how a monetary system of our country works. As an easy solution to the problems faced in the barter system of exchange some years ago, the concept of exchange through monetary standard was introduced and to date the system has been well accepted by all sorts of exchange makers in the world. But there was a natural question of how much money would be required to make smooth exchanges of goods and services in an economy. The classical economists had proposed that quantity of money required for exchange would be the exact value of goods and services in an economy in a given time period where quantity of money is the product of quantity of money in circulation and the velocity of money in circulation. Hence, withdrawal of money in 500- and 1,000-rupee denominations from the public and kept with the banking system means there is increase in money supply in the monetary system that will lead to fall in rate of interest, price levels, and overall GDP of the country. Besides, there are some unaccounted for incomes in the hands of people in the form of black money and some fake currencies in circulation, both of which hamper the government's revenue collection as well as inflation levels. According to the RBI data and statement by the prime minister, as of October, 2016 there were about 17 lacs crore of money in all denominations in circulation to exchange 135 lacs crore of GDP, out of which 86% was of 500 and 1,000 notes, and 6% of this 86% was black, that is, about 14.6 lacs crore of banned 500 and 1,000 notes and Rs. 88 thousand crores as black money (Table 5.2).

In addition to that, the prime minister announced that total fake and black currency would be around 3–4 lacs crore out of 14.6 lacs crore which they thought would not be returned to the formal banking system to avoid conviction and punishments. Hence, we need to identify some pros and cons of the demonetisation policy that intuitively follows from the macroeconomic theory.

Table 5.2 Data on money supply, GDP, velocity of money, and black money

Money SS (Rs. crore) as of Oct 2016	*GDP 2015–2016 in Rs crore*	*Velocity of all cash money (M1)*	*Velocity of 500 and 1,000 notes*	*86% on M1 is of 500 (45%) and 1,000 (41%) notes*	*6% of 86% is black in Rs crore*
1701380	13576086	7.979455501	9.278435361	1463186.8	87791.208

5.13.3.1 *Pros*

i) It will help the government to fight black money, corruption, terrorism, and counterfeit currency with one single decision. Arms smuggling, espionage, and terrorist related activities will be choked due to lack of funding.
ii) Heavy deflation that benefits the consumers in short term. Commodity price and gold price will fall.
iii) Rate of interest will go down as there is excess supply of money. Investment demand will rise that will raise inflation but not overnight. Deflation and inflation will balance each other out in the future.
iv) This decision will help institutionalise the real estate sector, bringing more transparency in the Indian real estate industry. This step would give the Indian real estate sector more credibility, making it more attractive to the foreign as well as domestic investors.
v) Housing prices could experience downward pressure, helping revive demand in the sluggish housing segment (this will give much needed life to the sector).
vi) The traditional benami transactions have already received a big blow as the new legislation has a provision for seven-year imprisonment and fine, replacing the three-year jail term, or fine, or both.
vii) A cashless way to fight against black money and corruption and fake currency.
viii) More financial inclusion.
ix) Reducing terrorist funding, arms smuggling, etc.

5.13.3.2 *Cons*

i) Deflation will hurt the producers.
ii) Inconvenience to common people who will start running to the nearby bank to exchange the 500 and 1,000 currency notes. If we add the death of 100 persons standing in the ATM queue, the cost will be huge. That is loss of workdays + cost of death = total social cost since it is unrecoverable.
iii) Cost of replacing the 500 and 1,000 Rs. notes will be about 12,000 crore in terms of 100 Rs. notes production. Hence, it is a costly idea to scrap 500 and 1,000 notes.
iv) Very difficult for more than half the population who are not well versed with card transactions.
v) Employment will fall as an immediate effect. This move deeply impacts the working sections of society: drivers, maids, cooks, electricians, plumbers. Anybody who provides services in the informal sector and depends on monthly or bi-monthly cash payments.
vi) The small businesses will be affected, at least in the shorter run.
vii) The Jan Dhan scheme, UPI/digital payment stack, and payment banks are still in the nascent stage. It will be a long time before rural India moves to completely cashless transactions. In the short term, people in rural India who have a significant amount of Rs. 500 and Rs. 1,000 notes but no official form of identification will have a tough time in exchanging their notes.
viii) Recession in agricultural and industrial activity, particularly of small and medium enterprises, will appear, which will further boost the inflation in the next season.
ix) The big fish will be left out whose black money is in the form of foreign currency and gold and stashed away in tax havens.

x) Duplicity in the Jan Dhan A/Cs where the black money are deposited. If detected, the case will be settled after a long duration because of poor governance. Hence, what is the utility of this move?

What the reality is today after the end of about 100 days from the declaration is that most of the currencies held by the public, as reported in some of the leading newspapers and channels in India, have been deposited into the banking system. The Income Tax Department has raided the sum of around Rs. 5,000 crores of money as they thought it had the possibility of being black. And interestingly, the central bank and even the finance ministry have not clearly unveiled the truth to date, which made the common people more skeptical about the feasibility of such a policy announcement. Besides, if we make a cost–benefit analysis of such policy announcements, we can find in the immediate term that the magnitudes of cost (the cons items), including the costs of popular policies and imputed costs of deaths due to standing in long queues before the ATMs and bank offices, will definitely supersede the benefits at all to date received by the common people. Although, theoretically it is possible to get the positive benefits from recovery of black money in the long run, the existing judiciary system can take it up to the next generation at the cost of the current generation. That means the elderly get worse treatment than the young. Different institutions like the World Bank, the IMF, and even the RBI have reduced the growth forecasts of up to 1.5%. It is the long-term effects which will answer to the effectiveness of the demonetisation policy.

5.14 Conclusion

This chapter examines types, causes, and costs of inflation. Demand-pull and cost-push theories of inflation are discussed in detail. If demand-pull inflation occurs, price level and output increase, with unemployment rate constant or falling. Consequently, demand-pull inflation does not explain the movements in prices, output, and unemployment rate that we sometimes observe. Cost of inflation includes shoe leather costs, menu costs, confusion and inconvenience, arbitrary redistribution of wealth, etc. These costs become huge during hyperinflation. Usefulness of different anti-inflationary policies in controlling inflation are also examined. It can be concluded from that discussion that the anti-inflationary measures must be used simultaneously so as to obtain the best result. These policy measures should not be viewed as competitive; rather they are complementary. All of them should be used together.

Summary

- High inflation is bad because it causes people to hold too little money. It is also difficult to adjust the tax system to be neutral to inflation. Inflation also sometimes brings higher uncertainty. Deflation is undesirable for similar reasons.
- There are mainly two types of inflation, namely, demand-pull inflation and cost-push inflation. In case of demand-pull inflation, price level rises due to the excess demand condition in the product market. However, in case of cost-push inflation, price level rises due to some cost-push factors such as the demand for a wage hike by the trade unions.

- An inflationary gap is created in the economy when the aggregate demand for goods and services becomes more than the full-employment level of income. Both fiscal and monetary measures can be adopted by the government of a country to combat the inflationary pressure.
- Some of the basic objectives of the monetary policy are: price-stability, economic growth, stability in the foreign exchange rate, full-employment, etc.
- The costs of expected inflation include shoe leather costs, menu costs, the cost of relative price variability, tax distortions, and the inconvenience of making inflation corrections. One possible benefit of inflation is that it improves the functioning of labour markets by allowing real wages to reach equilibrium levels without cuts in nominal wages.
- Seigniorage is the revenue that the government raises by printing money. It is a tax on money holding.
- During hyperinflation, most of the costs of inflation become severe. Hyper inflations typically begin when governments finance large budget deficits by printing money. They end when fiscal reforms eliminate the need for seigniorage.

Keywords

Fisher effect	Hyperinflation
Seigniorage	Money illusion
Menu costs	Inflation tax
Shoe leather costs	Cost-push inflation

Multiple choice questions

1. If the economy is operating at potential GDP, an increase in money supply will lead to
   (a) Stagflation.
   (b) Structural inflation.
   (c) Demand-pull inflation.
   (d) Cost-push inflation.
2. Which of the following conditions is most likely to benefit a debtor under new classical economic framework?
   (a) Anticipated deflation.
   (b) Anticipated inflation.
   (c) Unanticipated deflation.
   (d) Unanticipated inflation.
3. A recessionary gap measures the
   (a) Amount by which autonomous spending is below that needed to achieve a full employment equilibrium.
   (b) Amount by which aggregate spending exceeds that needed to achieve full employment.
   (c) Difference in real output between the classical model and the Keynesian depression model.
   (d) Extent of paradox of thrift.

4. Match the following

List 1	*List 2*
A. Stagnation with inflation	1. Stagflation
B. Continuous fall in prices	2. Deflation
C. Vertical AS	3. Full employment
D. Continuous increase in price level	4. Inflation

Codes

	A	B	C	D
(a)	1	2	3	4
(b)	4	3	2	1
(c)	2	4	1	3
(d)	4	1	3	2

5. The economy is in inflationary equilibrium. A reduction in
   (a) Government spending permanently lowers the economy's rate of inflation.
   (b) Nominal money supply growth lowers the inflation rate with no effect on output in the short run.
   (c) Nominal money supply growth lowers the inflation rate and the level of output in the short run.
   (d) Government spending lowers the rate of inflation with no effect on output in the short run.

6. The inflation rate
   (a) Is positive during stagflation.
   (b) Is negative during stagflation.
   (c) Is always negative during recession.

7. Demonetisation is a part of monetary policy of a country which means
   (a) Increase in supply of money to the public.
   (b) Decrease in supply of money to the public.
   (c) Control of inflation.
   (d) All of the above.

Answers

1. (c); 2. (d); 3. (a); 4. (a); 5. (c); 6. (a); 7. (b)

Descriptive questions

1. A redistribution of income and wealth occurs when inflation is unanticipated. Little or no distribution occurs when inflation is anticipated. Are these statements correct?
2. If inflation is less than expected, who benefits – debtors or creditors? Explain.

3. Hyperinflations are extremely rare in countries whose central banks are independent of the rest of the government. Why might this be so?
4. What is credit control policy of a central bank of a country? What are the major instruments to control money supply of a country?
5. Define cost-push inflation. What policies might be used to stop this type of inflation? Describe how each policy works to stop the inflation.
6. How does inflation occur due to rise in wage rate?
7. Describe the effect of inflation on production.
8. Show how investors are affected by inflation.
9. What is demonetisation? Explain the possible advantages and disadvantages of recently announced demonetisation policy of India's government from a theoretical background.

Short-answer questions

1. What is inflationary gap?
2. What is cost inflation?
3. What is hyperinflation?
4. What is demand inflation?
5. What does one mean by stagflation?

Additional Readings

Ackley, G. (1978). "The cost of Inflation". *American Economic Review*, 68, 149–154.

Balakrishnan, P., Surekha, K. & Vani, B. (1994). "The determinants of inflation in India". *Journal of Quantitative Economics*, 10.

Fisher, S. & Modigliani, F. (1979). "Towards an understanding of the real effects and costs of inflation". *Weltwirtschaftliches Archiv*, 114.

Friedman, M. (1977). "Nobel lecture: Inflation and unemployment". *Journal of Political Economy*, 85, 3.

Kahn, R. (1976). "Inflation: A Keynesian view". *Scottish Journal of Political Economy*, 23, 1.

Laider, D. E. W. & Patinkin, M. J. (1975). "Inflation: A survey". *Economic Journal*, 85, 741–809.

Rowthorn, R. E. (1977). "Conflict, inflation and money". *Cambridge Journal of Economics*, 1.

Part III

Modern macroeconomics – the Keynesian short run demand side models

6 The simple two sector economy

Simple Keynesian model without government (model I)

6.1 Introduction to the simple Keynesian model

In 1936 the British economist John Maynard Keynes revolutionised economics with his book *The General Theory of Employment, Interest, and Money*. In this book he not only criticised the classical macro-economics but also presented a new theory of income and employment. Keynes wrote this book with the objective to analyse the causes of economic downturn (1929–1933) and to suggest some measures to reduce the economic hardship. Keynes pointed out that Say's law of market does not operate during the Great Depression of 1929. Rather, a lack of aggregate demand (AD) is responsible for low income and high unemployment that characterised economic downturn. AD was too low because of inadequate investment demand. Keynes' theory thus favoured the use of economic policies (fiscal and monetary) to regulate AD and to combat unemployment. Policies should be aimed at stimulating AD.

The simple Keynesian model (SKM) captures the fundamental ideas developed by Keynes to explain short run year-to-year fluctuations in the aggregate output and employment in a developed market economy. It should be kept in mind that Keynes' theory is a "short run theory" when population, labour force, stock of capital, etc. do not change. The maximum level of output that can be produced utilising all its productive resources fully is referred to as its full employment output in the given time period. This model assumes that actual output of the economy is less than its full employment level. Thus, this theory of employment determination is a demand-deficient theory where the volume of employment in an economy depends on the level of effective demand and unemployment is attributed to the deficiency of effective demand. The model considers only a commodity market where prices remain fixed and producers simply adjust their output to the demand at the given price. However, the assumption of constant price level will be relaxed in Chapter 11. In order to concentrate on the basic model, we are omitting the government sector and foreign trade sector for the time being. The government sector will be introduced in the next chapter. The theory of income determination in this chapter and a few subsequent chapters are short run theory also because we are temporarily ignoring the effect of technological progress on the economy's productive capacity. However, in the long run, these effects are very important. We deal with long run classical model and growth theories later in this book.

DOI: 10.4324/9781003501138-9

6.2 Assumptions of two-sector simple Keynesian model without government

This model makes the following assumptions:

i) The economy we are considering is *closed* (having no foreign transaction) *and without government*. The economy is a pure laissez faire economy where government does not interfere in economic activities.
ii) Only the *goods market* of the economy is considered in the model. For simplicity we assume that only *one commodity* is produced which is used for consumption as well as for investment. The same commodity works as a consumer good as well as a capital good.
iii) Real national income is an important determinant of aggregate real *consumption expenditure*. Consumption function can be written as $C = C(Y)$.
iv) Aggregate real *investment expenditure* is autonomously given and is independent of level of income and interest rate. Hence investment function becomes $I = I_0$
v) Rate of interest, money, wages, and prices are assumed to be fixed.
vi) There exist *unutilised and underutilised resources* in the economy (excess capacity). Thus, this model assumes that actual GDP is less than its full employment or potential level at every period. If demand for output increases, supply of output will automatically increase, price level remaining constant. For this reason, SKM is said to be a demand determined model where equilibrium is achieved through quantity adjustment.
vii) Producers are rational and guided by a motive of short run profit maximisation. Producers understand the change in demand by observing their *existing inventory level.* Behavioural pattern of the producer is that if they face excess demand then they will increase output.

6.3 Equilibrium analysis under the SKM

Equilibrium is a state of rest of an economic system where no change-creating force is generated from within the system to affect the equilibrium values of the variables. In equilibrium the plans of different decision makers are mutually consistent. The equilibrium level of income (or output) in this model requires that output to be equal to planned expenditure (PE) which is the amount that household, firm, and government would like to spend on goods and services. On the other hand, the economy's GDP is equal to its actual expenditure, which is the amount that household, firm, and government spend on goods and services. So, in equilibrium actual expenditure or GDP $(Y) = PE$. In this model *inventory* plays an important role in restoring equilibrium. Whenever an economy is not in equilibrium, firms observe unplanned inventory changes which induce them to alter their production level. This change in production in turn influences total income and expenditure. When firms sell less of their product than they planned, their stock of inventory rises. On the other hand, if there exists excess demand in the economy then volume of inventory will fall which will induce them to increase output. These unplanned changes in inventory are counted as investment spending by firms, thus actual expenditure can be either above or below PE.

6.3.1 *The aggregative structure of the economy — the Keynesian cross*

Aggregate demand (AD) or planned expenditure (PE), the amount of goods that people want to buy, in this model consists of the amount of consumption that households plans to carry out and the amount of investment planned by firms, as we have excluded the government sector and foreign sector from our analysis temporarily.

Let us focus on aggregate planned consumption expenditure in real terms. Aggregate planned consumption expenditure denoted by C in a closed economy without government may be considered as a function of real GDP (Y).

The consumption function can be written as

$$C = C(Y);\ 0 < C' < 1$$

Where C' = marginal propensity to consume (MPC). MPC gives the amount of increase in planned consumption expenditure due to a unit increase in Y. Keynes assumed that an increase in Y usually induces individuals to spend more on consumption, but the increase in consumption expenditure is generally less than that in Y. Keynes also assumed that MPC is less than APC (defined as $\frac{C}{Y}$). Writing the consumption function in linear form we have

$$C = a + bY;\ a > 0;\ 0 < b < 1 \tag{6.1}$$

where "a" and "b" are constants or parameters of the consumption function. "a" is autonomous consumption expenditure which is independent of Y and "b" is the induced component that depends on Y. "b" is called MPC which also represents the slope of consumption function. Dividing both sides of the previous equation by Y, we get $APC = \frac{C}{Y} = \frac{a}{Y} + b$. It is clear that APC falls with an increase in Y. From Equation (6.1) it can be said that as Y increases C will increase but the growth rate of Y will be greater than that in C.

According to Keynes, investors' investment decisions are driven by some kind of optimism which he referred to as animal spirit and did not try to explain. Thus, in SKM real planned investment (I) is simply regarded as exogenously given which can be represented as $I = I_0$. Aggregate demand (AD) for goods and services or PE is therefore given by

$$PE = AD = a + bY + I_0 \tag{6.2}$$

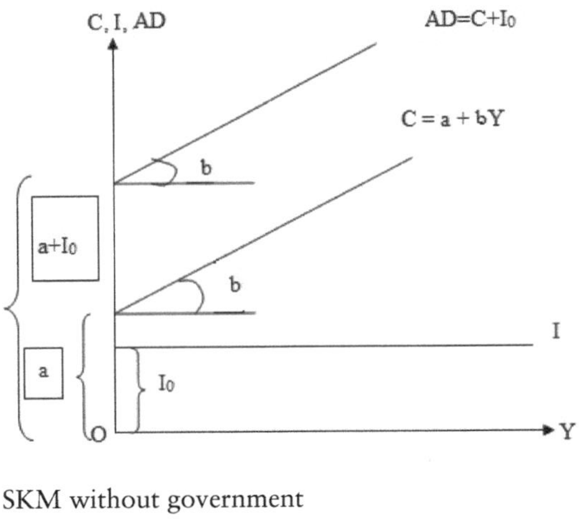

Figure 6.1 AD curve in SKM without government

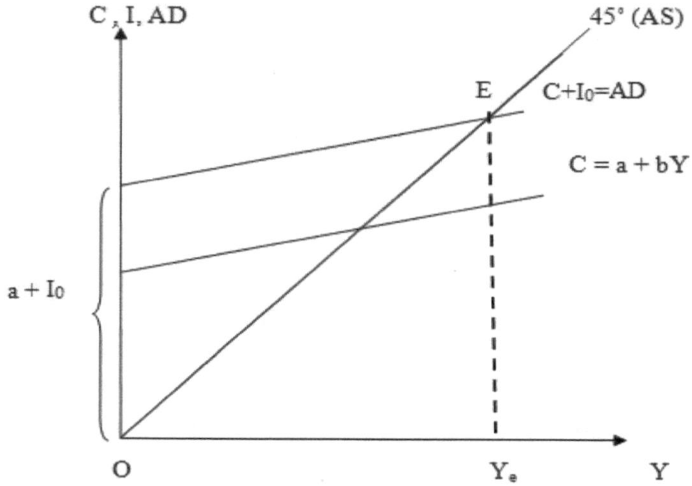

Figure 6.2 Equilibrium under SKM without government

On the other hand, output produced represents the level of supply, so $Y_S = Y$. At the equilibrium level, planned AD is equal to AS.

Hence

$$Y = (a + I_0) + bY, \quad \text{or} \quad Y_e = \frac{(a + I_0)}{(1 - b)}. \tag{6.3}$$

In the following figure we draw a 45-degree line, and at any point on it vertical distance is equal to horizontal distance. So along the 45-degree line AD equals output or aggregate supply. The AD curve intersects the 45-degree line at point E, corresponding to which Y_e is obtained.

Y_e represents the equilibrium level of income which depends on subsistence level of consumption expenditure (a), MPC (b) and autonomous investment expenditure (I_0). If "a" or "I_0" changes, the equilibrium income will change as the AD curve will shift parallel, but if "b" changes, keeping "a" and "I_0" unchanged, the slope of AD will change. In both these situations equilibrium income will be affected. Other things being equal, the greater the value of autonomous consumption and investment expenditure, the higher will be the value of equilibrium output. Again, given the value of autonomous expenditure, higher MPC will lead to higher output.

6.3.2 *The planned savings and planned investment version*

SKM for a closed economy without government equilibrium can also be presented in terms of a saving investment diagram. The saving function can be derived from consumption function as $S(Y) = Y - C(Y)$. This $S(Y)$ gives aggregate planned saving. The equilibrium condition can now be rewritten as

$$Y = C(Y) + I, \text{ or } Y - C(Y) = I, \text{ or } S(Y) = I \tag{6.4}$$

Let us take linear form of saving and investment function as follows:

Equation of saving function:

$$S = Y - a - bY = -a + sY \tag{6.5}$$

" $-a$ " is the negative intercept and $s = 1 - b$ is the slope of the upward sloping straight line saving curve. As $0 < s < 1$, the saving function will be flatter than the 45-degree line.

The equation of investment function is $I = I_0$, which is a horizontal straight line. The equilibrium condition of SKM with linear saving and investment function can be expressed as

$$-a + sY = I_0 \tag{6.6}$$

Equation (6.6) can be represented in terms of Figure 6.3.

Equilibrium is attained where planned saving is equal to planned investment. As shown in the lower part of the diagram, this happens at point E, where an upward rising straight line saving curve and linear investment curve intersect each other. Y_e represent macroeconomic equilibrium income in SKM. From the equilibrium condition (6.6) we have $Y_e = \frac{I_0 - a}{s}$. If $I_0 > a$, then unique positive value of equilibrium income will exist.

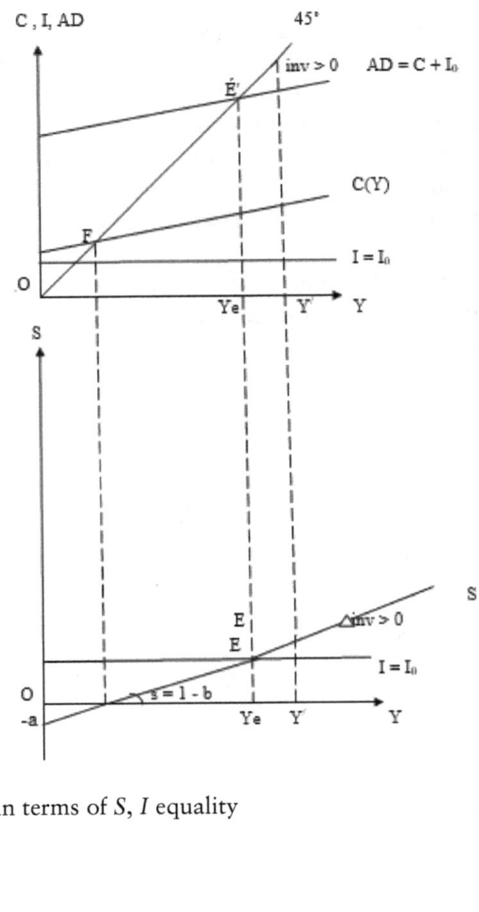

Figure 6.3 Equilibrium in terms of *S*, *I* equality

This means excess of planned investment over planned saving at zero income should be positive. In response to this excess demand pressure, producers will raise output to eliminate it and achieve equilibrium at a unique positive Y.

Example: Suppose consumption function is given by $C = 40 + 0.8Y$. *Find out the saving function.*

We know $S = Y - C$. Thus,

$$S = Y - 40 - 0.8Y$$

$$\text{Or } S = -40 + 0.2Y.$$

This is the equation of the saving function having slope 0.2 – also known as marginal propensity to save (MPS) – and negative intercept 40.

6.3.3. Saving and investment: planned and actual concepts

From national income identity, $C + S + T \equiv C + I + G$ or $S + T \equiv I + G$, we cannot determine any variable. It is an expost concept which is always true. So, to determine NI of a country, this identity has to be converted into equality. Equilibrium condition in the goods market implies that planned demand must be equal to planned supply; alternatively, planned saving must be equal to planned investment. In a closed economy without government, as we already know, planned aggregate demand or planned expenditure consists of two components: planned consumption and planned investment. From Figure 6.4 it is clear that aggregate planned expenditure (AY′) = planned consumption expenditure (BY′) + planned investment expenditure (AB). But actual income, DY′ (= OY′), is different from planned expenditure or aggregate demand (AY′). Again, we know that the sum of planned investment (AB) and change in inventory (–AD) represents actual or realised investment (–BD). As consumption and saving plans are always realised, we have planned consumption = actual consumption = BY'.

Clearly, realised consumption (BY') + realised investment ($-BD$) = realised income (DY').

Thus, realised or actual investment (–BD) is always equal to realised or actual saving ($DY' - BY'$); though planned saving (–BD) is not equal to planned investment (AB). These two are equal only at equilibrium, where the ($C + I$) curve intersects a 45-degree line.

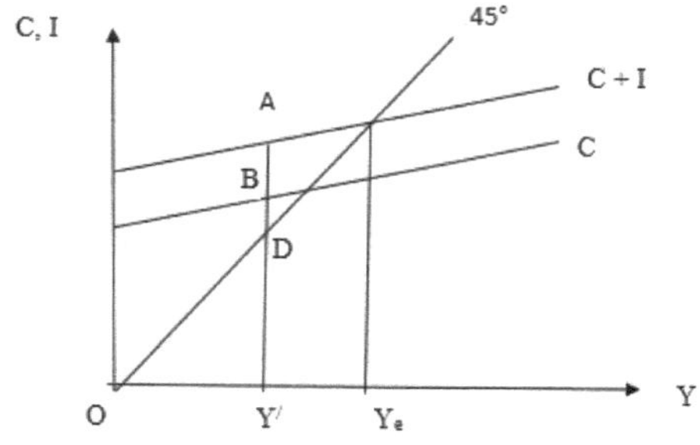

Figure 6.4 Planned and realised *S*, *I* equality

6.4 Stability of equilibrium

In order to be stable, we have to check whether the system has any tendency to come back to its original equilibrium position if disturbed from Y_e. Unplanned changes in inventory play a crucial role in achieving equilibrium. Unplanned inventory changes alter output, income, and hence expenditure, leading the economy to move towards equilibrium.

Suppose we disturb the economy by an external force from Y_e to Y_1, such that $Y_1 < Y_e$. At Y_1, aggregate demand or planned expenditure is greater than actual output. So, there will be excess demand pressure in the economy. Firms meet this excess demand by running down their inventories. This means that unplanned changes in inventory will be negative. So, the firms hire extra workers and increase production. Hence, output or income will rise and the system will move towards Y_e. So, inventories play a balancing role because they bring actual output back to the equilibrium level. If, alternatively, the actual output is increased to Y_2 such that $Y_2 > Y_e$, then aggregate supply corresponding to Y_2 will be greater than aggregate demand leading to unplanned inventory accumulation. The firm will react by producing less. Income and output fall from Y_2 to Y_e. Hence, if, at a given output level firms are accumulating unplanned inventories or are observing their inventories being depleted, there is a tendency for output to change. But when aggregate demand equals output there is neither an unintended inventory accumulation nor a shortfall. Firms will be satisfied with their current output level and there will be no tendency for output to change. As the system reflects a tendency to come back to its original equilibrium position if it is disturbed from there, *E* represents a stable equilibrium. Clearly inventories act as the balance wheel of the economy.

We can find out the ***stability condition*** by using the Walrasian stability approach which states that any equilibrium is stable if excess demand varies inversely with the

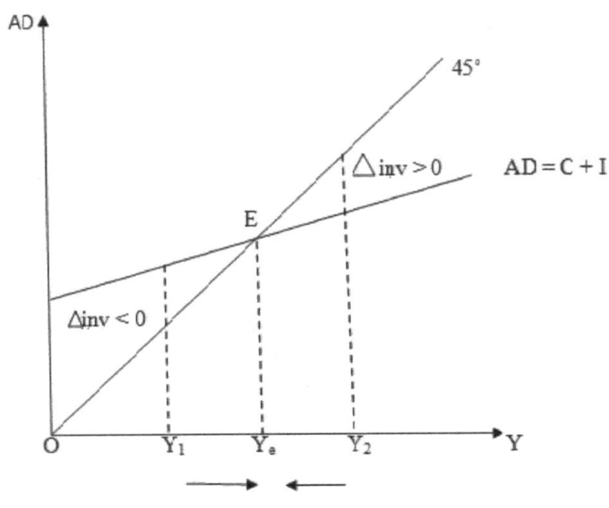

Figure 6.5 Output adjustment process

decision variable. In this closed economy model output or income is the decision variable. So, for stability, excess demand should vary inversely to the income.

$$\text{i.e., } \frac{d(ED)}{dY} < 0$$

$$\text{or } \frac{d(C + I_0 - Y)}{dY} < 0$$

$$\text{or } \frac{d[(a + I_0) + (b - 1)Y]}{dY} < 0$$

$$\text{or } (b - 1) < 0$$

$$\text{or } b < 1 \tag{6.7}$$

We know that $MPC = b$ = slope of AD curve. So, stability requires that the AD or planned expenditure curve cut the 45-degree line from above. This is the condition for stability in this fixed price model with only output adjustment.

In terms of a saving investment diagram also we can explain stability. As shown in the lower part of Figure 6.3, $Y > Y_e, S > I$, representing positive excess supply. Inventory accumulation takes place and Y will tend to fall as a result of this movement. On the other hand, if Y falls from equilibrium value, then excess demand will appear, leading to a rundown of inventory. Here Y will show a tendency to rise back to its original value. Thus, again the equilibrium presented in the figure in terms of a saving investment diagram is stable. For stability, excess demand should vary inversely to the income,

$$\text{such that } \frac{d(ED)}{dY} < 0$$

$$\text{or } \frac{d(I_0 + a - sY)}{dY} < 0$$

$$\text{or } -s < 0; \text{ or } s > 0. \tag{6.8}$$

Condition (6.8) says that marginal propensity to save (s) has to be positive, which is the same as saying MPC < 1 because we have the result $MPC + MPS = 1$.

6.5 Effect of increase in autonomous expenditure and the concept of the multiplier

After discussing the stability of the model, our objective is to examine how equilibrium Y gets affected following a change in the exogenous variable, like I_0. The concept of a multiplier is generally used to measure the effect on some endogenous variable of a unit change in an exogenous value. In our SKM the endogenous variable is real income. On the other hand, the exogenous variable is a variable whose level is not determined from within the system. These variables are taken as parameters in the model. Government expenditure, autonomous investment expenditure, etc. are examples of exogenous variables. A multiplier, in other words, represents a factor by which change in autonomous expenditure is to be multiplied to get the resulting change in equilibrium level of income. Therefore, in SKM the *autonomous expenditure*

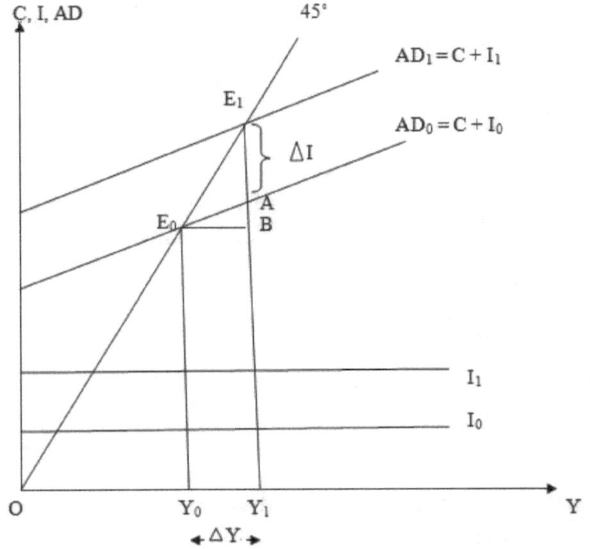

Figure 6.6 Effect of increase in *I* on Y

multiplier is defined as the rate of change in the equilibrium level of income caused by a unit change in the autonomous spending in the economy. In this present version of the model where there are no governmental activities, the only exogenous variable is autonomous investment expenditure.

Since investment in this model is independent of Y, any change in I_0 represents change in autonomous expenditure. So, an increase in I_0 raises aggregate demand for each Y leading to an upward shift of the AD curve. Corresponding to higher investment, I_1, higher aggregate demand is reflected by the AD_1 curve in the following diagram where Y and *AD* are measured on the horizontal and vertical axes respectively. Equilibrium position shifts from E_0 to E_1 and equilibrium Y rises from Y_0 to Y_1. It is evident from the diagram that $\Delta I < \Delta Y$, because $\Delta Y = \mathrm{E}_0 B$, $\Delta I = \mathrm{E}_1\mathrm{A}$, and $E_0B = E_1B = AB + E_1A$ (as both E_0 and E_1 lie on the 45-degree line). So, we have $\frac{\Delta Y}{\Delta I} > 1$. Expression $\frac{\Delta Y}{\Delta I}$ represents autonomous investment (expenditure) multiplier, showing the amount by which Y rises following a rise in autonomous investment (expenditure). The result that an exogenous increase in the autonomous expenditure by a given amount raises equilibrium Y by a larger amount can also be shown mathematically.

In equilibrium the condition $Y = (a + I_0) + bY$ will be satisfied. Differentiating both sides, we can write $\Delta Y = \Delta I_0 + b\Delta Y (\text{as } \Delta a = 0)$ $\frac{\Delta Y}{\Delta I_0} = \frac{1}{1-b}$. This is the value of an SKM multiplier in a simple model without government. The multiplier is equal to the reciprocal of the marginal propensity to save.

Stability condition of the system will be satisfied if $b < 1$. Thus, in a stable system $\frac{\Delta Y}{\Delta I_0} > 1$ or $\Delta Y > \Delta I_0$. Hence a given increase in the autonomous component of aggregate demand or expenditure raises Y by a multiple of it. More precisely an increase in I has a multiplied effect on the economy.

If b (MPC) = 0.6, for example, then $\frac{\Delta Y}{\Delta I_0} = 2.5 > 1$.

It can easily be checked that the value of the multiplier is an increasing function of MPC. Suppose MPC rises from 0.6 to 0.8. Clearly, value of multiplier rises from 5 / 2 to 5. If, on the other hand, $b = 0$, then the multiplier becomes unity, so effectively there will be no multiplier.

6.5.1 *Logic of static multiplier*

The process of adjustment is not instantaneous; it requires involvement of different groups of people in an economy and also takes some time to materialise. Let us explain the process of multiplication intuitively in terms of the following example in the Keynesian cross model. Consider an economy where there are different groups of people with the same MPC (b). Also assume that there is an increase in autonomous investment expenditure by an amount ΔI by group I. Consequently, the income of another group (say, group II) and hence the entire economy goes up by ΔI because total expenditure which determines income has gone up by that amount such that $\Delta I = \Delta Y$ in first round. In an interdependent economy one person's (group's) consumption expenditure is another person's (group's) income. A change in income induces further change in consumption because of the dependency of consumption upon disposable income. Suppose the group II people whose income has risen consume $b\Delta I$ (b = MPC) out of their additional income which adds to the income of group III. Hence, we get $\Delta Y = \Delta I + b\Delta I$ increase in income at the end of second round for the economy. In a similar way group III will spend $b(b\Delta I) = b^2\Delta I$ amount in consumption and therefore the income of people belonging to group IV increases by the same amount. Group IV people will spend $b(b^2\Delta I) = b^3\Delta I$ and so on. The process would continue until the stimulus exhausts. The total increase in income would thus be given by

$$\Delta Y = \Delta I + b\Delta I + b^2\Delta I + b^3\Delta I + \ldots. = \Delta I\{1 + b + b^2 + b^3 + \ldots.\}$$

$$\text{or } \frac{\Delta Y}{\Delta I} = \frac{1}{1-b} \geq 1$$

An increase in autonomous investment, other factors remaining unchanged, causes output to change more because a change in personal disposable income induces a change in consumption. Ultimately change in income is equal to the initial change in investment plus an induced change in consumption (secondary effect). When MPC = 0, the entire increase in income is saved, and value of the multiplier becomes unity. In this situation secondary effects will be absent. The higher the value of MPC, higher will be the value of multiplier. High MPC implies a rise in demand in each round and hence the rise in output will be high. The value of the multiplier will be slightly complicated when we introduce the government sector in the next chapter. Modification in the value of the multiplier by incorporating foreign transaction has been done in Chapter 18.

6.5.2 *Illustrative examples*

i) Suppose $C = 60 + 0.8Y$ and investment is 40. In the absence of a government sector find out equilibrium output.

We know in equilibrium $Y = C + I$

$$= 60 + 0.8Y + 40$$

$$\text{or } Y(1 - 0.8) = 100$$

$$Y = 500.$$

ii) Suppose $C = 60 + 0.8Y$ and $I = 70$. Find out equilibrium income. If investment increases by 10 then find out the value of the expenditure multiplier.

Equilibrium condition is given by $Y = C + I$

$$= 60 + 0.8Y + 70$$

$$Y(1 - 0.8) = 130$$

$$\text{or } Y = 650.$$

This is the value of initial equilibrium income.

Now, MPC = b = 0.8

Value of multiplier can be obtained as $\frac{\Delta Y}{\Delta I} = \frac{1}{1-b} = \frac{1}{1-0.8} = \frac{1}{0.2} = 5$

iii) If investment falls by 10 and MPC is 0.6, then find out the change in equilibrium output and change in consumption spending.

We know

$$\frac{\Delta Y}{\Delta I} = \frac{1}{1-b}$$

$$\text{or } \Delta Y = \frac{1}{1-b}\Delta I$$

It is given that b = 0.6 and $\Delta I = 10$

$$\therefore \Delta Y = \frac{10}{1-0.6} = 25.$$

So, if investment falls by 10, Y will fall by 25 following a multiplier effect.

Change in consumption expenditure is the difference between change in output and change in autonomous investment, such that $\Delta C = \Delta Y - \Delta I$.

$$\therefore \Delta C = 25 - 10 = 15$$

6.6 Equilibrium with induced investment expenditure

So far, we have assumed aggregate investment as exogenous, but now we can modify the system by assuming that investment has an induced component as well. In other words, investment can be an increasing function of Y, given by $I = I(Y); I' > 0$. I', the ratio of change in investment to the change in income, is termed as marginal propensity to invest (MPI). Equilibrium condition with income dependent investment expenditure can be rewritten as

$$Y = C(Y) + I(Y) \tag{6.9}$$

Alternatively,

$$Y - C(Y) = I(Y) \text{ or } S(Y) = I(Y) \tag{6.10}$$

For simplicity we may consider linear forms of saving and investment functions. In linear form, the saving function can be written as

$$S = -a + sY; 0 < s < 1. \tag{6.11}$$

Where s represents marginal propensity to save (MPS) which is nothing but the slope of the saving function.

Investment function in linear form is given by

$$I = I_0 + iY; 0 < i = MPI < 1 \tag{6.12}$$

Substituting (6.11) and (6.12) in equilibrium condition (6.10) we can write

$$-a + sY = I_0 + iY.$$

Solving, we get

$$Y_e = \frac{I_0 + a}{s - i} \tag{6.13}$$

The following diagram shows the determination of equilibrium income with *S* and *I* schedule, where investment is income dependent. Both *S* and *I* curves are rising, though the *S* curve is steeper than the *I* curve. Equilibrium is attained at point *E*.

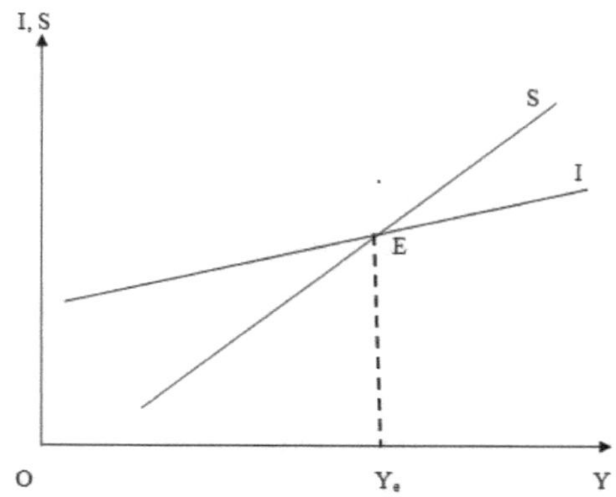

Figure 6.7 Equilibrium with *S* and *I* curve

If $(s-i)>0$, then the economy will achieve equilibrium at a positive Y. This is the sufficient condition for the existence of equilibrium. It can also be shown that $(s>i)$ is nothing but the stability condition of the model. For stability, excess demand should vary inversely with Y. Therefore, $\frac{d[I(Y)-S(Y)]}{dY}<0$, or $I'<S'$ or Marginal propensity to invest < Marginal propensity to save. Alternatively, for stability, the saving function should be steeper than the investment function corresponding to the equilibrium point. This condition is satisfied at point E in the previous figure.

6.6.1 *Impact of increase in autonomous investment expenditure — the super multiplier*

Equilibrium condition with income dependent investment expenditure is given by $Y=C(Y)+I(Y)$ which can be rewritten in linear form as

$$Y=a+bY+I_0+iY \tag{6.14}$$

$$\text{or } Y(1-b-i)=a+I_0$$

$$\text{or } Y_e=\frac{a+I_0}{(1-b-i)} \tag{6.15}$$

Equation (6.13) and (6.15) give the same result. Sufficient condition for the existence of equilibrium at a positive Y, here, is $(b+i)<1$. In words, the marginal propensity to spend should be less than unity, which is an alternative way of saying $(s>i)$.

Now suppose autonomous investment is raised by ΔI. It is evident that $\frac{\Delta Y}{\Delta I}=\frac{1}{(1-b-i)}$ which is termed the *super-multiplier*. As $(1-b-i)<(1-b)$, we have $\frac{1}{(1-b-i)}>\frac{1}{(1-b)}$. Thus, the *value of the multiplier is larger when investment is income dependent* as compared to a situation when it is exogenously given. The multiplier derives its value from induced expenditure In fact, in this situation, when Y increases as a result of an increase in autonomous investment, both induced consumption expenditure as well as induced investment expenditure increase. This additional investment gives a boost to the multiplier effect.

6.6.1.1 *Example*

Suppose $C=50+0.6Y$ and $I=30+0.2Y$. Determine the value of equilibrium income in this closed economy without government model. If autonomous investment rises from 30 to 40, find out the value of expenditure multiplier.

In equilibrium

$$\begin{aligned} Y &= C+I \\ &= 50+0.6Y+30+0.2Y \\ &= 80+0.8Y \end{aligned}$$

$$\text{or } 0.2Y=80$$

or $Y_e = 400$;
this is the value of equilibrium value of income.

Given $\Delta I = 10$, $b = 0.6$, and $I = 0.2$; we have the result

$$\frac{\Delta Y}{\Delta I} = \frac{1}{(1-b-i)} = \frac{1}{(1-0.6-0.2)} = 5$$

6.7 Limitations of the Keynesian multiplier

Following criticisms are raised against the Keynesian multiplier:

First: this multiplier is static in nature as it doesn't consider the element of time. It just compares two equilibrium incomes. The theory doesn't delve into the intricacies of income generation. To grasp the dynamics of income generation, one must turn to a dynamic analysis that incorporates the dimension of time.

Second: if MPC = 1 or MPC > 1, the analysis becomes invalid in static theory.

Third: when the government intervenes in the economy by imposing taxes, the consumption function becomes contingent on disposable income. This taxation serves as a leakage in the multiplier process, diminishing the value of the investment multiplier. Similarly, in an open economy, a portion of the generated income exits the country to meet import expenses, constituting another leakage in the multiplier process.

Last: the Keynesian investment multiplier assumes a universal "MPC", maintaining a constant value applicable to the entire economy. However, distinct sectors within an economy may exhibit varying MPCs. Consequently, the multiplier values can differ across sectors, leading to diverse outcomes for the overall economy.

6.8 Conclusion

This closed economy without government model depicts the determination of equilibrium income in a simplified manner. Output is demand determined in this model such that output expands only when demand increases. As there is no role of government, impacts of government's policy changes could not be captured here; instead the impact of autonomous expenditure change is described using the concept of a multiplier. Stability analysis of the model is also carried out to check the stability condition. To have a more practical, realistic, and generalised model we need to introduce the government sector, which we will do in Chapter 7. However, modification in the value of multiplier incorporating foreign transactions is done in Chapter 18 of this book.

Summary

- The present chapter addressed the simple Keynesian system by the help of autonomous investment expenditure and showed the way of determination of equilibrium national income of a capitalistic economy.
- The stability of the equilibrium of the aggregate economy was discussed and the multiplier analysis was done which showed that an increase in autonomous investment (or consumption) expenditure would lead to increase in income at a rate greater than the increase in the amount of expenditure.

- The model further was extended to incorporate induced investment expenditure and showed the magnified multiplier result.
- We came to know the effectiveness of the aggregate demand component in the economy to rescue of the economy from depression.

Keywords

Consumption expenditure
Investment expenditure
Marginal propensity to save
Marginal propensity to invest
Autonomous expenditure multiplier
Stability analysis
Super-multiplier
Marginal propensity to consume

Multiple choice questions and answers

1. Keynes was especially concerned with explaining the

    (a) Recession of 1920–1921.
    (b) Low level of output and employment during the Great Depression.
    (c) Strong economic growth of the 1920s.
    (d) High unemployment in Great Britain during 1920s.

2. In the simple Keynesian model of aggregate output determination, an equilibrium level of output below that necessary to maintain full employment can be explained by

    (a) Minimum wage laws.
    (b) A generous level of unemployment benefits.
    (c) Relatively low aggregate demand.
    (d) All of the above.

3. The simple Keynesian model illustrates the idea that the economy can come to rest at a level of aggregate output

    (a) Only at the full employment level.
    (b) Below the full employment level.
    (c) Only when the price level is fixed.
    (d) Only when wages are stable.

4. If the consumption function is $C = 20 + 0.5\,Y$, then an increase in income by 100 will result in an increase in consumer expenditure by

    (a) 25.
    (b) 70.
    (c) 50.
    (d) 80.
    (e) 100.

5. If consumption expenditure falls by 160 when disposable income falls by 200, the MPC is

    (a) 2.0.
    (b) 1.6.
    (c) 0.8.
    (d) 0.4.
    (e) Cannot be determined.

6. If unplanned investment is positive, firms will ______ production and output will____

(a) Cut; rise.
(b) Cut; fall.
(c) Increase; rise.
(d) Increase; fall.
(e) None of the above.

7. If aggregate demand exceeds actual output, using the simple Keynesian model, we would predict that

(a) The level of unemployment is likely to rise.
(b) The economy will experience an increase in inflation.
(c) The economy will experience a recession.
(d) The level of output will rise, due to declining inventories.

8. For a marginal propensity to consume of 0.75, the value of the multiplier is

(a) 3.00.
(b) 3.75.
(c) 0.25.
(d) 4.00.
(e) 5.00.

9. In the simple Keynesian framework, the price level

(a) Varies inversely with wages.
(b) Is fixed.
(c) Is indeterminate.
(d) Varies directly with unemployment.

Answers

1. (b); 2. (c); 3. (b); 4. (c); 5. (c); 6. (b); 7. (d); 8. (d); 9 (b).

Review questions

1. If the MPC of an economy is 0.8, by how much should government spending rise to increase the equilibrium output by 2,220?
2. Explain the role of unplanned inventory changes in bringing about equilibrium in SKM.
3. In SKM an increase in autonomous expenditure will cause equilibrium income to increase by a multiple of it. Explain the process by which this happens.
4. Suppose the consumption function is $C = 100 + 0.8Y_d$, while investment is given by $I = 50$.

a. What is the equilibrium level of income in this case?
b. What is the level of saving in equilibrium?
c. If, for some reason, output is at the level of 800, what will the level of involuntary inventory accumulation be?
d. If I rises to 100, what will the effect be the equilibrium income?

e. What is the value of the multiplier here?
f. Draw a diagram indicating the equilibria in both (a) and (d).

5. a. Obtain the equilibrium values, of Y and S for $C = 25 + 0.7Y$, $I = 5 + 0.2Y$ in an economy where there is no government.
   b. Show that the equilibrium S falls if autonomous C falls to 20. (Any attempt to save more causes an actual decline in S.)

6. Why is the Keynesian cross a stable equilibrium? Find out the condition of stability.
7. Suppose investment falls by 40 units. MPC is 0.8.

   a. Find out the change in equilibrium output.
   b. What will be the induced change in consumption spending?

8. Suppose the consumption function is nonlinear. If consumption increases as income increases but at a diminishing rate,

   a. How is the equilibrium condition affected?
   b. How is the investment multiplier affected?

9. In the short run, it makes no difference whether consumption increases (the consumption function shifts upward) or whether investment increases (the investment function shifts upward). In the long run, it makes a difference. Explain.

7 Introduction of the government sector into the simple Keynesian model (Model II)

7.1 Introduction of the government sector into the SKM

According to Keynes, massive unemployment in Great Britain and the United States during the 1930s was the result of a deficiency in aggregate demand. This calls for desirability of expansionary fiscal policy action which would increase output and employment. Such policies would not work in the classical system, where output and employment were not demand determined. The government's activities can influence the level of overall economic activity in a number of ways. The level of economic activity may be altered by strict government regulation, imposition of taxes and subsidy, changes in the level of government's spending, etc. For the time being we concentrate entirely on the impact of government spending and taxes on the economy. Government spending, which is the expenditure item of the government's budget, includes purchases of goods and services by the government and transfer payments made by it. Taxes, which are the income item of the government's budget, are the reverse of transfer payments. The difference between taxes and transfer is often called net taxes. If government purchases exceed net taxes, then it will have a deficit budget. To finance this excess expenditure the government has to borrow or print money. Thus, to make the model more realistic in this chapter we introduce the government's activity by incorporating government purchase and (net) taxes. However, prices are still assumed to be constant as before. With this modification we will examine the impacts of different fiscal policies of the government on the level of demand and hence output using the concept of a multiplier.

7.2 Equilibrium under the SKM with government intervention

Now we will extend the model considering an economy that does not participate in foreign trade but has three sectors – household, firm, and government. We also assume that there exist unutilised resources in the economy. Price level and wage rates are also assumed to be constant throughout the analysis. Introduction of government sector affects the level of equilibrium in two ways: i) by purchasing goods and services (G) which are components of planned expenditure and ii) by altering taxes and transfer payments and thereby affecting consumption spending by changing disposable income (Y_d). In addition to the purchase of goods and services, governments often make transfer payments, as discussed in national income chapters, which affect disposable income. To finance these expenditure, the government imposes taxes which reduce aggregate disposable income. But changes in government purchases, transfers, and taxes are often the result of political process. It is found to be adjusted for reasons associated with the economic condition of

DOI: 10.4324/9781003501138-10

the country. For the sake of analytical simplicity, we will temporarily assume government purchases, transfers, and taxes to be fixed at specific levels. So, $G = G_0$; $T = T_0$ (all taxes are lump sum in nature); and $TR = 0$ (assuming no transfer on the part of the government). Y_d is the net income available for spending by the household after paying taxes (*T*) and receiving transfer (*TR*) from the government, that is, $Y_d = Y - T + TR$. As we have assumed no transfer payments, that is $TR = 0$, the Keynesian consumption function can be rewritten as $Y = C(Y - T)$.

Hence, for given values of *G*, *I* and assuming that a constant amount is collected as income tax (also known as lump-sum tax), planned expenditure can be expressed as $E = C(Y - T_0) + I_0 + G_0$ (*G* and *T* are exogenously given). Aggregate supply is aggregate actual expenditure on goods and services and is represented by the 45-degree line. Thus, the equilibrium condition in SKM with government can now be written as

$$Y = C(Y - T_0) + I_0 + G_0 \tag{7.1}$$

Considering the consumption function in linear form we can write, $Y = a + b(Y - T_0) + I_0 + G_0$. Solving for the equilibrium value of income, we get

$$Y_E = \frac{a - bT_0 + I_0 + G_0}{1 - b} \tag{7.2}$$

If, instead of lump-sum tax, income tax (of the form $T = tY$) is considered, then the equilibrium condition can be rewritten as

$$Y = a + b(1 - t)Y + I_0 + G_0 \tag{7.3}$$

Here t = tax rate, and $0 < t < 1$. Solving (5.3) we get

$$Y_E = \frac{a + I_0 + G_0}{[1 - b(1 - t)]} \tag{7.4}$$

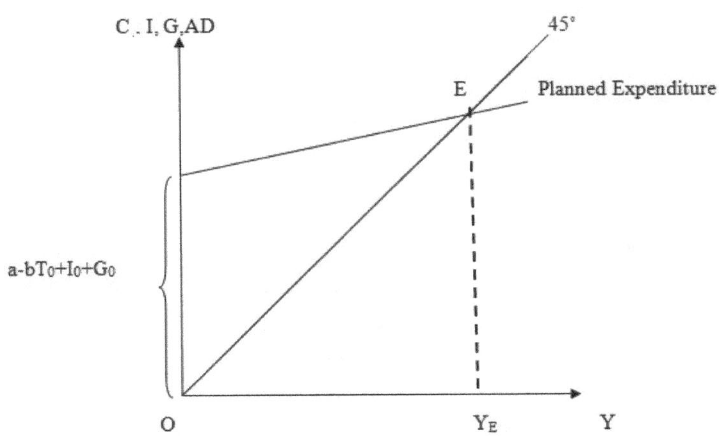

Figure 7.1 Equilibrium under SKM with government

The equilibrium condition with the government sector can also be represented in terms of saving investment equality as follows. In equilibrium, the value of output produced is equal to AD having three components: consumption demand, investment demand, and government demand for goods and services. As mentioned earlier, in a closed economy with government equilibrium, the condition can be expressed as

$$Y = C + I + G. \quad (7.5)$$

Again, national output which also measures national income, assumed to be paid to households in return for factor services, is partly consumed, partly saved, and partly paid in taxes. Hence

$$Y \equiv C + S + T. \quad (7.6)$$

But Equation (7.6) is a definitional identity though Equation (5.5) holds only in equilibrium. Thus, in equilibrium we can write $C + I + G = Y \equiv C + S + T$

Equivalently,

$$I + G = S + T. \quad (7.7)$$

Equality presented by Equation (7.7) can be interpreted in the following manner. As investment and government expenditure are inflows (injections) in the system and taxes and saving are outflows (leakages), the previous equation explains that the system is in equilibrium when flow of output will be such that the sum total of injections $(I + G)$ is just balanced by sum total of leakages $(S + T)$.

One point should be made clear in this connection. I, in equilibrium condition (7.5), represents planned or desired investment. Additionally national product (Y) is equal to the sum total of consumption (C), realised investment (I_R), and government spending (G), which is

$$Y \equiv C + I_R + G. \quad (7.8)$$

Combining (7.5) and (7.8) we have

$$I = I_R. \quad (7.9)$$

Hence only in equilibrium is planned investment equal to realised investment. Equation (7.9) gives another way of stating the equilibrium condition.

7.3 The paradox of thrift

In a closed economy, people in a bid to save more may sometimes cause a decline in income and consumption with no increase in saving at all or even have their savings lowered. This paradoxical phenomenon is called the *paradox of thrift* where thrift means desire to save more. SKM being a demand-determined model gives this paradoxical result where additional savings may be hoarded.

Suppose people become thriftier so that everyone in the economy saves more than before and spends less. As total spending falls, firms are unable to sell their output, and inventory holding increases as a result. Consequently, firms are bound to cut down their production. Actually, in SKM, though saving is a source of investment, saving and investment decisions are independent of each other. Diagrammatically, more saving at each level of income will be represented by an upward shift of the saving curve.

We can explain the effect of such an increase in desire to save graphically by considering the Figure 7.2. In the figure, national income is plotted on the horizontal axis and saving and investments are plotted on the vertical axis. As I_0 and G_0 are exogenously given, the I_0+G_0 curve will be a horizontal straight line, and on the other hand the S_0+T_0 curve will be rising as saving increases with income. The initial equilibrium point is given by E_0 where the S_0+T_0 curve intersects the I_0+G_0 curve with equilibrium national income Y_0. An increase in desire to save more will shift the S_0+T_0 curve upward to the left to S_1+T_0. New equilibrium income falls to Y1, though saving remains unchanged. An increase in desire to save raises saving (shifting saving curve upward), but fall in income reduces saving to restore the equilibrium condition $S_1+T_0=I_0+G_0$ with the higher saving function. There has been no change in saving despite an increase in thriftiness.

If investment becomes an increasing function of income, as we have shown earlier, then it can be observed that aggregate saving also declines along with income as a result of a rise in propensity to save. Suppose we consider investment function as $I=I(Y);I'>0$, then the $I(Y)+G_0$ curve, unlike the previous case, will be rising.

As shown in Figure 7.3, both $(S + T)$ and $(I + G)$ curves are rising. An increase in desire to save more will shift the $S_0(Y) + T_0$ curve upward to $S_1(Y) + T_0$. As a result, equilibrium aggregate income falls from Y_0 to Y_1 and aggregate saving is also reduced from E_0Y_0 to E_1Y_1. Hence, in Keynesian opinion, saving is desirable from an individual point of view, but it is undesirable from a social point of view. But for stability the $(S + T)$ curve has to be steeper than the $(I + G)$ curve. Which means $s>i$ or $b+i<1$. Thus, stability requires propensity to spend $(b+i)$ be less than unity.

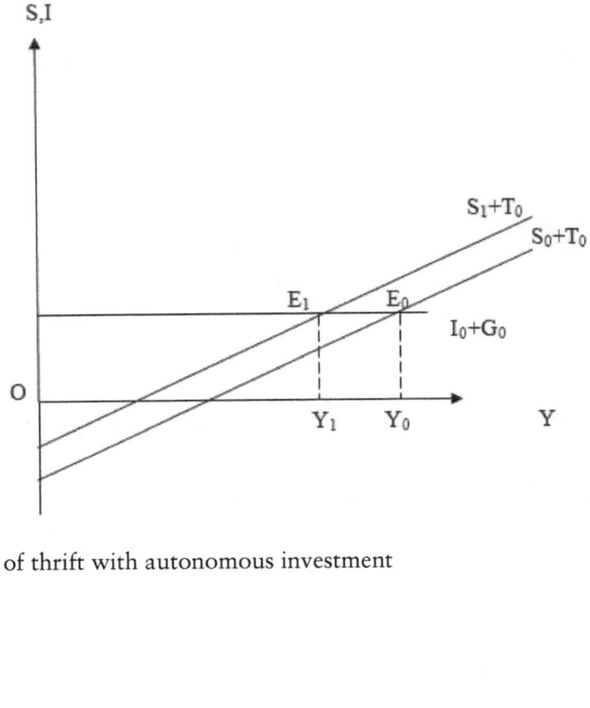

Figure 7.2 Paradox of thrift with autonomous investment

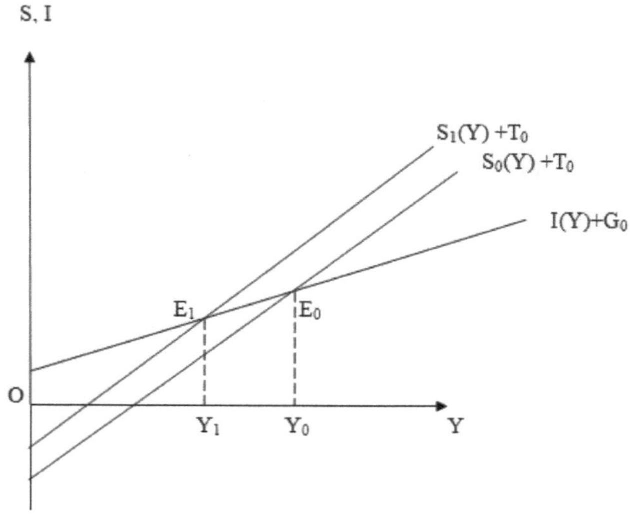

Figure 7.3 Paradox of thrift with income dependent investment

We can show this result mathematically as follows. Assuming linear saving and investment functions $S = -a + sY$ and $I = \overline{I} + iY$, the equilibrium condition can be written as

$$-a + sY + T_0 = \overline{I} + iY + G_0$$

$$\text{or, } sdY + Yds + dT_0 = d\overline{I} + idY + Ydi + dG_0$$

$$\text{or, } (i - s)\ dY = Yds \text{ (Putting } d\overline{I} = di = dG_0 = dT_0 = 0)$$

$$\frac{dY}{ds} = \frac{-Y}{(s-i)} < 0 \text{ (as, } s > i).$$

The previous inequality shows that income decreases with increase in propensity to save.
Differentiating the investment equation and using (i) we get

$$dI = idY + Ydi = idY = \frac{i(-Y)ds}{s-i}$$

$$dI = (\frac{-iY}{s-i})ds < 0.$$ Aggregate investment falls as MPS increases.

Again, differentiating the saving equation, one gets $dS = sdY + Yds$.

$$\text{or, } dS = (Y - \frac{sY}{s-i})ds$$

$$\frac{dS}{ds} = (\frac{-iY}{s-i}) < 0,$$ aggregate saving also falls with an increase in saving propensity.

The reason behind this paradoxical result should be found in the role of demand in the Keynesian model. In Keynesian model, it is the investment that determines savings, not the other way around. SKM considers a demand-deficient economy with the existence of unemployed resources. Hence, anything that changes demand and income in the short run is purely determined by demand factors. When saving rises (given income), it will lead to a fall in consumption. We know that one individual's consumption expenditure generates income of the other. So aggregate demand and hence income will dampen following a rise in saving propensity. Given the MPC, the multiplier process will work, multiplying the initial decrease in saving. Diagrammatically also it can be observed that, when saving propensity increases, at the previous equilibrium income level (Y_0), ($S + T$) exceeds ($I + G$). In other words, total supply of goods and services is greater than total demand for goods and services. So, some amount of goods and services will remain unsold, inducing producers to decrease its production. This process will continue until new equilibrium is established corresponding to a lower level of income. Actually, some people whose incomes are intact do save more, but some people also lose jobs and find their income reduced. So national saving will not rise. Hence, in a demand-deficient economy, saving is not a virtue. Though thriftiness is beneficial from the point of view of an individual, it might be harmful for the society as a whole. One point should be remembered in this respect. Though the paradox of thrift theory is applicable for developed countries, it is not applicable in underdeveloped countries where lack of capital stock is the basic economic problem. In developed countries unemployment exists because of insufficient effective demand. Capital goods remain idle because of lack of demand. But in developing countries, employment cannot increase because of shortage of capital. Thus the nature of unemployment in a developing economy is different from that of a developed economy. A higher saving rate thus helps the underdeveloped economies to prosper by formation of capital. So the same prescriptions cannot be applied to both types of economies.

7.4 Multiplier theory in the presence of a government sector

After discussing the concept of a multiplier in the context of a closed economy without government, now we reexamine the same concept in the presence of a government sector. As already mentioned, the government of a country engages in economic activities which gives rise to a separate head of expenditures. Though the total amount of government expenditure is assumed to be fixed at a specific level ($G = G_0$), the government also imposes taxes to meet its expenditure.

Let us rewrite the equilibrium condition of the national income determination of a closed economy in the presence of the government sector, assuming only lump-sum taxes and no transfer on the part of the government, as

$$Y = C(Y - T_0) + I_0 + G_0 \text{ (assuming, } T = T_0 \textit{ and } TR = TR_0). \tag{7.10}$$

Now, taking total differential of the previous equation, we have

$$dY = C'(dY - dT_0) + dI_0 + dG_0 \quad (C' \text{ represents MPC here}).$$

Starting from a situation of equilibrium suppose there is an increase in autonomous investment only [*i.e.* $dI_0 > 0$ but $dG_0 = dT_0 = 0$]

$$dY = C'dY + dI_0$$

$$\text{or, } \frac{dY}{dI_0} = \frac{1}{1 - C'} > 1. \tag{7.11}$$

This is the value of (autonomous) investment multiplier in SKM which shows that income changes by $[\frac{1}{1-MPC}]$ if investment changes by one unit, all other variables hold constant. If MPC = 0.6, the value of multiplier will be 2.5. Clearly the size of the multiplier depends on marginal propensity to consume. The higher the value of MPC, the greater will be the value of the multiplier.

The result that the value of the investment multiplier is greater than unity can also be illustrated graphically with the help of Figure 7.4. With investment I_0 and government expenditure G_0, initial equilibrium income is Y_0. As a result of increase in investment from I_0 to I_1, the AD schedule shifts up from AD_0 to AD_1. The new equilibrium income becomes Y_1 where income is equal to a higher value of AD. Clearly $E_0R = \Delta Y$.

From ΔE_0RE_1, we see that $E_0R = E_1R$ (as E_0 and E_1 both lie on the 45-degree line)

Again $E_1R = E_1N + NR = \Delta I + NR$ Also $E_0R = \Delta Y$.

Hence, we can write, $\Delta Y = \Delta I + NR$

$$\therefore \frac{\Delta Y}{\Delta I} = 1 + \frac{NR}{\Delta I},$$

as $\frac{NR}{\Delta I} > 0, \frac{\Delta Y}{\Delta I} > 1$. The economy thus multiplies the change in investment into an even larger change in income through the multiplier process.

Actually, income increases for two reasons: i) due to initial increase in autonomous investment (primary effect) and ii) due to an induced increase in consumption as a result of an increase in income (secondary effect).

If instead of lump-sum tax income tax is considered, then the value of multiplier will be modified as follows. The income dependent tax function can be written as

$$T = t(Y); 0 < t' < 1 \tag{7.12}$$

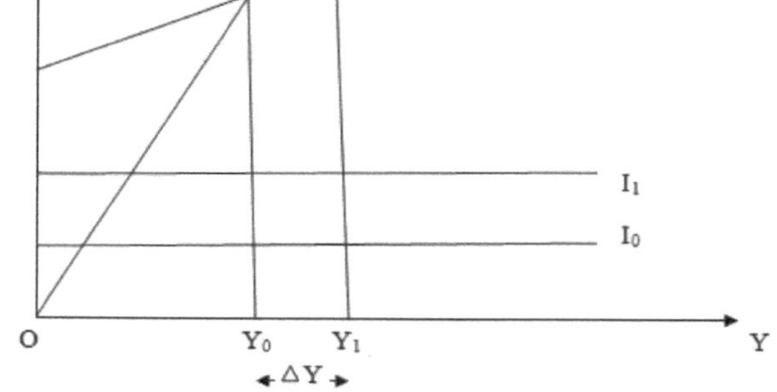

Figure 7.4 Effect of increase in autonomous expenditure on *Y*

Here t' represents the tax rate. Inserting Equation (7.12), the equilibrium condition (7.10) can be rewritten as:

$$Y = C[Y - t(Y)] + I_0 + G_0. \tag{7.13}$$

Taking the total differential of Equation (5.13), we have

$$dY = C'[dY - t'(Y)dY] + dI_0 + dG_0$$

$$\text{Or, } dY(1 - C' + C't') = dI_0 + dG_0$$

$$\text{Or, } \frac{dY}{dI_0} = \frac{1}{1 - C'(1 - t')} \text{ (assuming } dG_0 = 0\text{)}. \tag{7.14}$$

Since $[1 - C'(1 - t')] < 1$, $\frac{dY}{dI_0} > 1$

Comparing (7.11) and (7.14) it is observed that $\frac{1}{1 - C'} > \frac{1}{1 - C'(1 - t')}$, implying that inclusion of an income tax reduces the value of the multiplier, thereby reducing the fluctuation in income. Income tax reduces the induced increase of consumption as a result of income change. In fact, in the first situation (lump-sum tax case) there is only one leakage from circular flow, namely saving. But in the latter situation (income tax case) there are two leakages, saving as well as tax leakage. Proportional income tax will have a contractionary effect on Y through a reduction in propensity to consume. As the level of income rises due to rise in autonomous investment, tax yield (leakage from circular flow) also increases, dampening the expansionary effect. For this reason, it is often called an *automatic* or *built in stabiliser*. Graphically it can be shown that income tax reduces the slope of the consumption function and hence the AD function, dampening the increase in Y. This dampening effect will be stronger the higher the tax rate.

7.4.1 The government expenditure multiplier

Let us now discuss how changes in *G* affect the economy. Suppose there is an increase in government purchase leading to an increase in PE for a given level of income. In Figure 7.5, we see that an increase in government spending by ΔG shifts up the PE (or AD) schedule by the same amount from $\{C(Y - T_0) + I_0 + G_0\}$ to $\{C(Y - T_0) + I_0 + G_1\}$. The economy moves from point A to B. The figure shows that an increase in G leads to a greater increase in Y (equal to distance RS), that is $\Delta G < \Delta Y$. Hence the government expenditure multiplier, $\frac{dY}{dG}$, is greater than unity. The multiplier process for an increase in *G* is same as for *I*. An increase in Y, following an increase in G, also increases consumption. This leads to further increase in *Y* due to secondary effects via consumption spending.

To construct the value of government expenditure multiplier, let us resort to algebra. Assuming only lump-sum taxes and zero transfer, equilibrium condition of SKM in general form can be expressed as

$$Y = C(Y - T_0) + I_0 + G_0 \text{ (assuming all taxes are of lump sum in nature).}$$

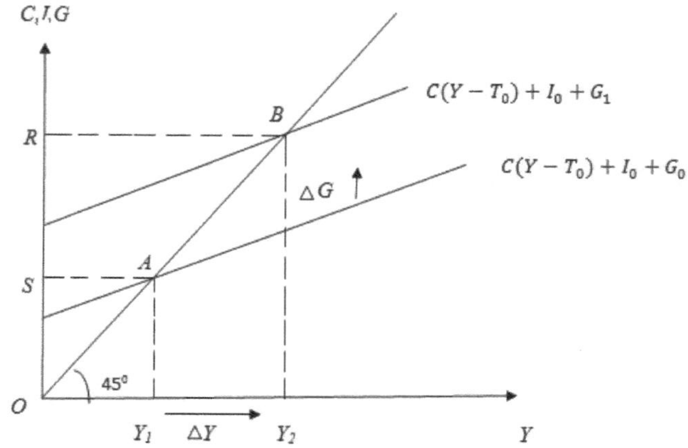

Figure 7.5 Effect of increase in G on Y

Taking the total differential of the previous equation,

$$dY = C'(dY - dT_0) + dI_0 + dG_0$$

If we consider the changes in government expenditure only, then $dG_0 > 0$ but $dT_0 = dI_0 = 0$.

$$dY = C'dY + dG_0$$

$$\frac{dY}{dG_0} = \frac{1}{1-C'} \geq 1 \tag{7.15}$$

It can easily be shown that if taxes are income dependent, instead of being lump sum, the value of government expenditure multiplier will be reduced to $\frac{dY}{dG_0} = \frac{1}{1-C'(1-t')}$. Here t' represents tax rate and C' is MPC. Inclusion of income tax reduces the value of the multiplier because it reduces the induced increase of consumption out of income change, on one hand and it flattens the aggregate demand curve, on the other. When tax becomes a function of income, an increase in G raises the level of disposable income by only $(1-t')$ times increase in income, as t' % of increase is immediately returned to the government as tax collection. Thus only $[(1-t')C']$, a fraction, instead of C', is spent on consumption which lowers the responding in each round. As a result of this reduced MPC, the multiplier takes on the lower value as described previously.

7.4.2 *Lump-sum tax multiplier*

A tax cut policy increases the disposable income which raises aggregate demand and generates multiplier effect. If the government cuts (lump-sum) taxes from T_0 to T_1 by an amount ΔT, disposable income increases by the same amount for any given level of disposable income leading to an increase in consumption expenditure. The PE or AD schedule shifts upward by MPC times ΔT. Unlike a change in G, ΔT in tax shifts the AD

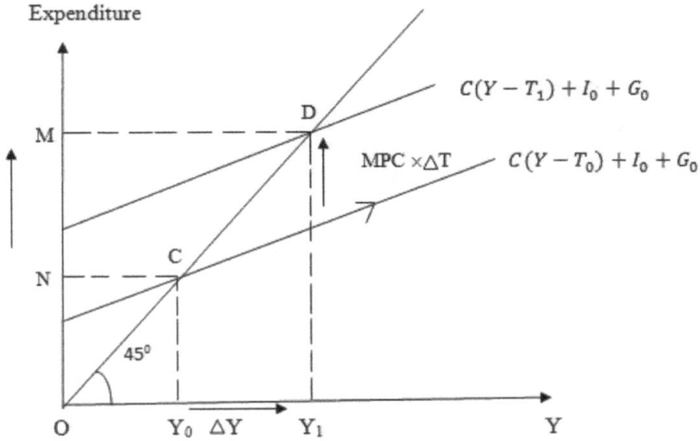

Figure 7.6 Effect of tax cut on Y

curve by only a fraction (MPC) of change in tax. A cut in taxes by ΔT raises disposable income by ΔT but raises consumption by only $(MPC\Delta T)$. As illustrated in Figure 7.6, the equilibrium point shifts from C to D and equilibrium income increases from Y_0 to Y_1 as a result of this tax cut.

Let us find out the value of the tax multiplier algebraically. Differentiating the equilibrium condition $Y = C(Y - T_0) + I_0 + G_0$ totally and substituting $dG_0 = dI_0 = 0$, we have

$$dY = C'(dY - dT_0)$$

$$\text{or, } \frac{dY}{dT_0} = \frac{-C'}{1 - C'} < 0. \tag{7.16}$$

This is the lump-sum tax multiplier. The negative sign implies that income rises if tax collection is reduced. If MPC = 0.6, for example, $\frac{dY}{dT} = -1.5$. A cut in tax by Rs. 1 raises equilibrium income by Rs. 1.5.

7.4.2.1 *Economic logic for greater value of a government expenditure multiplier*

One important distinction should be noted in this connection. Absolute value of a government expenditure multiplier is greater than that of a lump-sum tax multiplier. When the government increases its own expenditure, it raises AD directly (primary effect) and then via change in induced consumption (secondary effect). The resulting increase in income will be equal to $\frac{\Delta G}{(1 - MPC)}$. So both the primary and secondary effects are present there.

But tax change affects AD indirectly by changing disposable income and hence consumption. When the government reduces (lump-sum) taxes by the same amount $(\Delta G = \Delta T, \text{say})$, the disposable income of the individuals increases by the same amount of decrease in taxes. Given the value of MPC, the initial increase in consumption expenditure of the individuals will be $(MPC\Delta T)$. The multiplier effect will work on this initial increase in consumption expenditure. Hence, we will get only secondary effects; the primary effect is absent here. As the value of $(MPC\Delta T) < \Delta G$ (even if $\Delta G = \Delta T$), the absolute value of final increase in income resulting from reduction in tax $(\frac{MPC}{1-MPC}\Delta T)$ will be less than that from increase in government expenditure $(\frac{1}{1-MPC}\Delta G)$ by the same amount.

7.4.3 *Income tax multiplier*

Let us now consider the effect of change in tax rate (t) on equilibrium income, keeping I and G unchanged. Substituting tax and consumption functions of the following linear forms $T = tY$, $o < t < 1$ and $C = a + b(1-t)Y$; $a > 0$; $0 < b = MPC < 1$ respectively in the equilibrium condition, we have

$$Y = a + b(1-t)Y + I_0 + G_0 \tag{7.17}$$

Differentiating totally and putting $dG_0 = dI_0 = 0$, we can write:

$$dY = bdY - btdY - bYdt$$

$$\text{or, } (1-b+bt)dY = -bYdt$$

$$\text{or, } \frac{dY}{dt} = \frac{-bY}{1-b(1-t)}. \tag{7.18}$$

Equation (7.18) shows the value of the income tax multiplier in SKM. The negative sign implies that as tax rate increases, income falls. If the government raises the marginal tax rate, disposable income and hence consumption will fall, which in turn will reduce aggregate demand. Interestingly, the multiplier here depends on initial level of income and initial tax rate. The lower the initial tax rate, the higher will be the change in Y as a result of income tax rate change.

7.4.4 *Balance budget multiplier*

The government cannot control consumption and investment directly. It can influence consumption indirectly through tax changes as explained earlier. G and T are policy parameters of the government. An increase in G, ceteris paribus, raises AD. An increase in T, ceteris paribus, on the other hand, lowers consumption and hence AD by reducing disposable income. An interesting case occurs when G and T increase by the same amount, that is, $dG = dT$ (a balanced budget increase). It can be shown that an increase in G fully financed by increase in T raises equilibrium income by the same amount, which is $dG = dT = dY$. The multiplier effect on Y of an equal (balanced budget) increase in G and T is known as the balanced budget multiplier (BBM).

Balanced budget theorem states that in the context of a closed economy with government intervention, having considerable amount of unutilised or underutilised resources, a balanced (equal) increase in government expenditure and tax revenue will result in an exactly equivalent increase in national income (assuming no change in the volume of autonomous investment and slope of the consumption function). The multiplier in this case is equal to unity. W. A. Salant pointed out that in case of an increase in government purchase by ΔG, NI is raised by an amount ΔG directly and then indirectly via the series of increase in consumption spending giving the total charge in Y as,

$$\Delta Y_1 = \Delta G_0 + b\Delta G_0 + b^2\Delta G_0 + \ldots$$

But the tax increase by an amount ΔT does not enter directly into the NI on the very fast round. It affects NI through reduction in consumption expenditure and then via the series of further reductions in spending. We will get only the secondary effect; the primary effect is absent here. Hence, change in income in this situation becomes

$$\Delta Y_2 = -b\Delta T_0 - b^2\Delta T_0 - \ldots$$

Here, b = MPC and $\Delta T_0 = \Delta G_0$ due to balanced budget change. Adding the previous two series we get $\Delta T_0 = \Delta G_0 = \Delta Y$, where $\Delta Y_1 + \Delta Y_2 = \Delta Y$ = Net effect on Y. Thus, $(\frac{\Delta Y}{\Delta G_0})_{BBM} = 1$

To derive the result mathematically, we will start from the equilibrium condition $Y = C(Y - T_0) + I_0 + G_0$ (assuming all taxes are lump-sum tax, independent of the level of income and transfer earning is zero). Differentiating equilibrium condition totally, assuming $dI_0 = 0$, we get

$$dY = C'(dY - dT_0) + dG_0 \,.\; (C' = \text{MPC, here})$$

Putting $dG_0 = dT_0$ the previous equation can be rewritten as

$$dY(1 - C') = dG_0(1 - C')$$

$$\text{or, } \frac{dY}{dG_0} = \frac{(1 - C')}{(1 - C')} = 1 \tag{7.19}$$

The ratio of change in real income to the change in government expenditure, when government expenditure and tax revenue are changed by equal amount, is unity. In other words, equilibrium income goes up by the same amount as G and T.

An intuitive explanation of the balanced budget theorem given by P. A. Samuelson in his “The simple mathematics of income determination” is as follows. Subtracting T from both sides of the equilibrium condition $Y = C(Y - T_0) + I_0 + G_0$ gives $(Y - T_0) = C(Y - T_0) + I_0 + (G_0 - T_0)$.

$$\text{or, } Y_D = C(Y_D) + I_0 + (G_0 - T_0).$$

Here, assuming TR = 0, Y_D represents disposable income. The previous equation determines Y_D uniquely. Therefore, so long as $(G_0 - T_0)$ and I_0 remain constant, Y_D must also remain constant. An increase in G and T by the same amount with an unchanged I, therefore, leaves Y_D unchanged. Hence Y must increase by the same amount of increase in T. Thus, the balanced budget multiplier is exactly unity.

7.4.4.1 *Some special cases*

7.4.4.1.1 CASE I) BBM < 1

In a closed economy, BBM may be less than unity, if *tax depends on income*. Suppose we consider a tax function of the following form $T = T_0 + tY$, which is, tax function has an autonomous component and an induced component. So there is an additional leakage from the circular flow of income. If certain portion of every extra rupee earned (due to an increase in G) is taxed away, then consumption will not increase as much as it would otherwise. Considering the linear form of the consumption function, the equilibrium condition can be rewritten as

$$Y = a + b\left[Y - (T_0 + tY)\right] + I_0 + G_0 .$$

Differentiating totally, we have

$$dY = bdY - bdT_0 - btdY - bYdt + dI_0 + dG_0$$

$$\text{or, } dY = \frac{dG_0 - bdT_0}{1 - b(1-t)} \text{ (assuming no change in } t, I_0, \text{ and } G_0).$$

In the case of balanced budget change, which is $dG_0 = dT_0$, we have

$$\frac{dY}{dG_0} = \frac{1-b}{1-b(1-t)} < 1. \tag{7.20}$$

7.4.4.1.2 CASE II) BBM > 1

Suppose we consider a closed economy, *but investment is an increasing function of income* such that $I = I(Y), I' > 0$. Hence, the equilibrium condition can be rewritten as

$$Y = C(Y - T_0) + I(Y) + G_0$$

Differentiating totally, we get,

$$dY = C'(dY - dT_0) + I'dY + dG_0 .$$

Putting $dG_0 = dT_0$, as we are considering BBM,

$$\frac{dY}{dG_0}\Big|_{(dG=dT)} = \frac{(1-C')}{(1-C'-I')} > 1 \cdot \tag{7.21}$$

Here output sensitivity of investment is making the multiplier effect stronger.

7.4.4.1.3 CASE III) BBM ≠ 1

Let us now consider two different income groups having different values of MPC: b_1 and b_2.

Suppose only one group is taxed and the tax proceeds are used to finance government expenditure.

Total Income (Y) is distributed between the two income groups such that $Y = Y_1 + Y_2$. Let $\frac{Y_1}{Y} = \alpha$ and $\frac{Y_2}{Y} = 1-\alpha$, where "α" is an income distribution parameter. Suppose that group 1 is taxed. Assuming linear consumption function equilibrium condition can be written as follows

$$\begin{aligned} Y &= a_1 + b_1(Y_1 - T) + a_2 + b_2 Y_2 + I + G \\ &= A + b_1(\alpha Y - T) + b_2(1-\alpha)Y + I + G \end{aligned}$$

[where $A = \alpha_1 + \alpha_2$],

differentiating we get

$$dY = b_1(\alpha dY - dT) + b_2(1-\alpha)dY + dG[\text{assuming, } dA = dI = 0]$$

$$or,\ dY\{1 - b_1\alpha - b_2(1-\alpha)\} = dG - b_1 dT = dG(1-b_1)\ [\text{Since } dG = dT]$$

$$\frac{dY}{dG}\bigg|_{(dG = dT)} = \frac{1-b_1}{1-\alpha b_1 - (1-\alpha)b_2}. \tag{7.22}$$

The right-hand side of Equation (7.22) is not necessarily unity. It may be greater than or less than unity depending on the values of MPC.

7.5 Budget deficit and fiscal policy

A budget is an account of the government's receipts and expenditure. Stabilisation is an important objective of the government's budget where the government tries to neutralise fluctuation in output using fiscal instruments. A budget deficit (BD) is the excess of government expenditure over income, which can be expressed as $BD = G + TR - T$

An increase in government expenditure, though it raises income via the SKM multiplier process, will lead to an increase in income tax collection. It can be observed that the primary effect will outweigh the secondary effect, making the net effect of G change on BD positive. To check the impact of G increase on BD we assume for simplicity that there is proportional taxation (i.e., $T = tY$) and transfer payment is zero.

$$\Delta BD = \Delta G - t\Delta Y$$

$$= \Delta\frac{1}{2}G - t\{\frac{1}{1-b(1-t)}\}\Delta G$$ (substituting the value of government expenditure multiplier with income dependent tax function and linear form of consumption function)

$$\frac{\Delta BD}{\Delta G} = [1 - \frac{t}{1-b(1-t)}]$$

$$\frac{\Delta BD}{\Delta G} = \frac{(1-b)(1-t)}{1-b(1-t)} > 0. \tag{7.23}$$

Similarly, we can consider the effects of an increase in the tax rate on the budget surplus. An increase in tax rate (with unchanged G), on the other hand, raises tax revenue at an unchanged Y. Again, Y falls, following the multiplier effect. What will happen to budget surplus, BS, (the negative of BD) depends on the relative strength of these two effects. We know that income tax acts as automatic stabiliser reducing the value of the multiplier. The higher the tax rate, the higher will be the dampening effect. It can be shown that net effect is an improvement in BS.

$BS = T - G - TR$. Assuming, for simplicity, that there is proportional taxation (i.e., $T = tY$) and transfer payment is zero, we have $BS = tY - G$.

$$\frac{\Delta BS}{\Delta t} = t\frac{\Delta Y}{\Delta t} + Y$$

$$= [Y - \frac{bYt}{1-b(1-t)}] \text{ (substituting the value of } \frac{\Delta Y}{\Delta t})$$

$$\frac{\Delta BS}{\Delta t} = \left[\frac{(1-b)Y}{1-b(1-t)}\right] > 0. \qquad (7.24)$$

So an increase in tax rate raises BS, despite the fall in income caused by the initial increase in "t".

7.5.1 *Budget deficit multiplier is not unique*

We do not get any unique budget deficit (BD) multiplier because the impact on the budget deficit will depend on the nature of the BD, that is, whether the deficit is created by increasing G keeping T unchanged or by changing T keeping G constant.

Let us consider the following situation,

$$Y = C + I + G$$

$$Y = a + b(Y - \bar{T} + \bar{TR}) + \bar{I} + \bar{G}$$

$$\text{or, } dY = b(dY - d\bar{T}) + d\bar{G} \text{ (as, } d\bar{I} = d\bar{T} = 0)$$

$$\text{or, } dY = b\{dY + d(BD) - d\bar{G}\} + d\bar{G} \text{ (as, } - d\bar{T} = d(BD) - d\bar{G})$$

$$\text{or, } (1-b)dY = (1-b)d\bar{G} + bd(BD)$$

$$\text{or, } dY = d\bar{G} + \frac{b}{1-b}d(BD) \qquad (7.25)$$

Now, if T changes but G does not, then $d\bar{G} = 0$, $d\bar{T} \neq 0$; we get

$$\frac{dY}{d(BD)} = \frac{b}{1-b}$$

Suppose G changes but T is constant so that $dT = 0$ and $d(BD) = dG$. From Equation (7.25),

$$dY = d(BD) + \frac{b}{1-b}d(BD)$$

$$\text{or, } \frac{dY}{d(BD)} = \frac{1}{1-b}$$

Now if both G and T change, then the value of the BD multiplier can be obtained from Equation (7.25) and $\frac{b}{(1-b)} \leq \text{BD Multiplier} \leq \frac{1}{1-b}$. Hence, *we will not get any unique budget deficit multiplier.*

7.5.2 *The concept of full employment budget surplus*

Often it seems that BS is a simple measure of the overall effect of fiscal policy on the economy. When the budget is in deficit then we would say that the fiscal policy in expansion. However, BS suffers from a serious defect as a measure of the direction of the fiscal policy. It can change because of changes in autonomous private spending also. In case of an income-dependent tax structure, $BS = tY - \bar{G} - \overline{TR}$. An increase in BD or reduction in BS does not necessarily mean that the government has changed its policy. As we frequently want to measure the way in which fiscal policy is being used to affect the level of income, we require a more sound or powerful indicator. Such a measure is provided by *full-employment BS, denoted by BS**. The full employment BS measures BS at the full employment level of income. Hence it can be expressed as $BS = tY^{*} - \bar{G} - \overline{TR}$, where Y^* denotes full employment level of income. But one point should also be noted in this connection: there is no certainty as to the true full-employment level of output. On the other hand, the full-employment surplus is also not a perfect measure of the thrust of fiscal policy. There are several reasons for this. A change in government spending with a matching increase in taxes may leave BS* unchanged, even if in this situation income increases (implying expansionary fiscal policy). Expectations about future fiscal policy changes can also affect current income, leaving BS* unchanged.

7.6 Illustrative examples

1. Let $C = 200 + 0.75(Y - T)$, $I_P = 100$, $G = 100$, $T = 100$.

   a. Find the equilibrium level of income.
   b. If G increases to125, what will be the new equilibrium?
   c. What level of G is needed to achieve an income of 1,600?

   Ans.

   a. We know

$$
\begin{aligned}
Y &= C + I_P + G \\
&= 200 + 0.75(Y - 100) + 100 + 100 \\
\text{or, } Y - 0.75Y &= 200 - 75 + 100 + 100 \\
\text{or, } 0.25Y &= 400 - 75 = 325 \\
Y_e &= 1{,}300
\end{aligned}
$$

   b. Substituting $G = 125$, we have

$$
\begin{aligned}
Y &= 200 + 0.75(Y - 100) + 100 + 125 \\
\text{or, } 0.25Y &= 350 \\
\text{or, } Y_e &= 1{,}400.
\end{aligned}
$$

c. New income has to be equal to 1,600. Substituting in the equilibrium condition, we have

$$1{,}600 = 200 + 0.75(1{,}600 - 100) + 100 + G$$

$$1{,}600 = 200 + 0.75(1{,}500) + 100 + G$$

$$1{,}600 - 1{,}425 = G$$

$G = 175.$

$G = 175.$

is needed to achieve an income of 1,600.

2. Suppose marginal propensity to consume is 0.9 and tax rate is 0.3. Find out the multiplier. If investment decreases by Rs. 10 billion, by how much will GDP decline?

Ans:

Product market equilibrium condition is: $Y = C + I + G$
Taking linear form, we get,

$$Y = a + b(1 - t)Y + I + G$$

Then investment multiplier is: $\frac{dY}{dI} = \frac{1}{1 - b(1-t)} = \frac{1}{1 - 0.9(1 - 0.3)} = \frac{1}{1 - 0.63} =$ $\frac{1}{0.37} = 2.70$. The value of multiplier is 2.7

So, $dY = .7 \times dI$

When investment decreases by Rs. 10 billion, dI = 10 billion.

So, $dY = (2.7 \times 10)$ billion = 27 billion.

Thus GDP will decline by 27 billion.

3. Let $C = 35 + 0.80(Y - T)$, $I = 70$, $G = 65$, $T = 0.10Y$

a. Find the equilibrium level.
b. What are tax revenues at equilibrium output? Does the government have a balanced budget?
c. If I rises to 90, what will be the new equilibrium output?
d. What has happened to the government budget now?

Ans.

a. As $Y = C\ (Y - T) + I + G$, we have

$$Y = 35 + 0.80(Y - 0.10Y) + 70 + 65$$

or, $Y_e = 607.14$

b. $T = 0.10Y = 0.10 \cdot 607.14 = 60.71$.
So the government budget is in a deficit as $G = 65$ exceeds $T = 60.71$
$BD = 4.29$

c. If I rises to 90, then $Y = 35 + 0.80(Y - 0.10Y) + 90 + 65$

or, $Ye = 678.57$

d. Now tax revenue has increased to 67.86 which is greater than $G = 65$
So, there is a surplus, and $BS = 67.86 - 65 = 2.86 > 0$.

7.7 Conclusion

SKM overstates the role of demand-side factors in determining income. According to Keynes, any change in autonomous component of AD changes equilibrium income through the multiplier process. The multipliers developed in this model show changes in equilibrium income following changes in autonomous components of investment, government purchase, tax collection, etc. Operation of the multiplier is crucially dependent on the assumption of existence of unutilised resources. Output can increase in response to rise in demand without putting any pressure on price. But the situation might be different if the supply of some crucial input is exhausted. Increase in demand will lead to price rise then.

Multiplier theory gives only the end result; it does not show the time path of income. Marginal propensity to consume (MPC) is assumed to be fixed and specific throughout the analysis. The value of the multiplier will not be fixed if MPC varies for some reason. Again, the multiplier is obtained as the sum of an infinite geometric progression. Hence, if autonomous expenditure increases, the full multiplier effect will be obtained only after an infinite period of time. Hence the whole multiplier effect cannot be achieved in any finite period of time.

The model illustrates that equilibrium income is low because AD is low. It completely ignores the role of supply-side effect. According to supply-side economics, fiscal actions like tax cuts induce people to work hard which might lead to an increase in aggregate output. Such supply-side effects might be significantly strong.

The model also ignores the role of the money market and fails to explain the behaviour of prices and wages. Output can change here with no effect on price level. Yet this useful simple closed economy model can be extended in many directions to cover up many deficiencies and to capture macroeconomic reality.

Summary

- The present chapter covered the effect of inclusion of government sector into the SKM.
- It was observed that inclusion of government expenditure will push up the value of national income like that of the increase in private sector's investment.
- An increase in savings was proved to be making reduction of national income as well as savings. It was known as the paradox of thrift.
- The chapter highlighted the effect of different types of taxes upon national income. It found that there would be a reduction of national income due to imposition of different types of income taxes.
- Further, the combined effects of tax and government expenditure (or the budget) upon national income were observed, and it was found that there might not be an additional income effect.

Keywords

Paradox of thrift
Government spending
Tax multiplier
Balanced budget multiplier
Government expenditure multiplier
Fiscal policy
Budget surplus
Budget deficit

Multiple choice questions

1. Keynes believed that changes in autonomous spending was dominated by changes in

   (a) Consumer expenditure.
   (b) Autonomous consumer expenditure.
   (c) Investment spending.
   (d) Taxes.
   (e) None of the above.

2. A tax cut

   (a) Increases consumption expenditure by an amount greater than the tax cut.
   (b) Increases consumption expenditure by an amount equal to the tax cut.
   (c) Increases consumption expenditure by an amount that is less than the value of the tax cut.
   (d) Has no effect on consumption expenditure.
   (e) Reduces consumption expenditure by an amount that is less than the value of the tax cut.

3. In the simple Keynesian framework, declines in planned investment spending that produce high unemployment can be offset by raising

   (a) Taxes.
   (b) Government spending.
   (c) Consumer confidence.
   (d) Business confidence.

4. If the consumption function is $C = 20 + 0.5\ Y_d$ then an increase in disposable income by 100 will result in an increase in consumer expenditure by

   (a) 25.
   (b) 70.
   (c) 50.
   (d) 80.
   (e) 100.

5. By "paradox of thrift", Keynes meant that an increase in desire to save would lead to

   (a) Decrease in income.
   (b) Increase in income.
   (c) Decrease in income as well as savings.
   (d) Decrease in savings.
   (e) None of the above.

6. In the Keynesian model, an increase in government spending increases –

   (a) The money supply by an equal amount.
   (b) The money supply by a multiple amount.
   (c) Aggregate demand by a multiple amount.
   (d) Aggregate demand by an equal amount.

Answers

1. (c); 2 (c); 3. (b); 4. (c); 5. (c); 6. (c).

Review questions

1. Explain how an increase in government purchases results in an increase in income greater than the initial increase in government purchases.
2. Define tax multiplier. Show that the effect of tax increase on the equilibrium income is contractionary in nature.
3. Suppose that the government increases taxes and government purchases by equal amounts.

   What happens to the interest rate and investment in response to this balanced-budget change? Does your answer depend on the marginal propensity to consume?
4. Consider the impact of an increase in thriftiness in the Keynesian cross. Suppose the consumption function is $C = C_0 + c(Y - T)$, where C_0 is a parameter called autonomous consumption and c is the marginal propensity to consume.

   a. What happens to equilibrium income when the society becomes more thrifty, as represented by a decline in C_0?
   b. What happens to equilibrium saving?
   c. Why do you suppose this result is called the paradox of thrift?
   d. Does this paradox arise in the classical model? Why or why not?

5. Consider a closed-economy model given by the following equations:

   $$Y = C + I + G$$
   $$C = 160 + 0.8Y_d$$
   $$Y_d = (1 - t)Y - T_0$$

   Investment and government spending are exogenous and each is equal to 200. The tax system has two components: a lump-sum tax denoted by T_0 and an income tax of rate t.

   a. Assume T_0 is equal to 200 and t is .25. Find the level of income that satisfies spending balance. How much does the government collect in taxes at that level of income? What is the level of government spending?
   b. Suppose the lump-sum tax is reduced to 100. Find the new level of income that is consistent with spending balance. What is the lump-sum tax multiplier? What are the new levels of tax collections and government saving?
   c. If G rises to 250, what is the new equilibrium level of output? What will be the value of the government expenditure multiplier?

6. Consider two cases in the context of the simple Keynesian model for a closed economy. In one investment demand is autonomous while in the other it is an increasing function of aggregate income (*Y*). Suppose the government wants to raise *Y* by a given amount and thus it seeks to achieve by lowering its tax collection ($\overline{T}$). In which case will it have to lower $\overline{T}$ by a larger quantity and why? Explain.
7. $C = 100 + 0.5Y_d$, $I = 50 + 0.1Y$, $G = 100$, $T = 0.2Y$. Find out the equilibrium values of *Y*, *I*, *C*, and the government budget deficit. How will an increase in the tax rate from 0.2 to 0.3 affect aggregate domestic savings? Can you call this result a "paradox of thrift"?
8. Suppose the consumption function is $C = 100 + 0.75y$. Investment is $I = 50 + 0.2y$. If MPC decreases to 0.5, what should be the impact on equilibrium, income, and aggregate savings? Does it explain the paradox of thrift?
9. Explain why an increase in income tax rates will lower the expenditure multiplier. Explain why an increase in marginal propensity to consume will raise it.
10. Explain why a budgetary deficit may be misleading with regard to the measurement of the thrust of fiscal policy.

Additional readings

Keynes, J. M. (1936). *The General Theory of Employment, Interest, and Money*, Chapter 8–10. London: Palgrave Macmillan.

Rakshit, M. (1989). *Studies in the Macroeconomics of Developing Countries*. Delhi: OUP.

Salant, W. A. (1967, May). "Taxes, income determination, and the balanced budget theorem". *The Review of Economics and Statistics*, 39(2), 152–161.

Samuelson, P. A. (1966). "The simple mathematics of income determination". in *Income Employment, and Public Policy: Essay in Honour of Alvin Hansen*; reproduced in M. G. Muller (ed), *Readings in Macroeconomics*. Delhi: Surjeet Publications (First Indian Print published in 1978).

8 Product market equilibrium (Model III)

8.1 Introduction

The SKM of equilibrium income determination was restricted to a single market, namely the commodity market. Since the financial sector was excluded from the model, we did not observe the interplay between the real and the financial sides of the economy. SKM also makes a simplifying assumption that the level of planned investment is fixed. But this is not sufficient to make the model realistic and thereby to explain short run fluctuations. For this purpose, we need to extend the model by introducing interest rate as another variable (more specifically, making investment dependent on (r) and by incorporating the financial sector which will interact with the product market. Through such incorporation, we will be able to show how the government's fiscal policies and the central bank's monetary policies interact and influence the entire economy. This extended model can be captured in terms of IS-LM model, built by J. R. Hicks on the Keynesian foundation, which will also help us to analyse short run macroeconomic fluctuations in an economy. Price levels remain exogenous and constant in this model. Therefore, inflation and expected inflation are assumed to be zero.

Economist Hicks first introduced this model in 1937. IS-LM refers to two curves, the IS investment saving curve which represents equilibrium in the goods market and the LM liquidity of money curve which represents equilibrium in the money market. The model shows how the real and the monetary sectors are linked together and also help us to understand how repercussions in the real sector get transmitted to the monetary sector and vice versa. It gives a short run view of the economy as price level is considered to be exogenously given and aggregate supply curve is horizontal in the price-output space. Equilibrium output is thus determined by the position of aggregate demand curve. The expansionary policy of the government will lead to an increase in the aggregate demand for goods and services which will shift the aggregate demand curve rightwards, thereby increasing both employment and output and eliminating the excess demand. Despite several weaknesses, it is a very popular model of monetary economics, which helps us to understand the role of money in the determination of real variables like employment and output.

In this chapter we concentrate only on the product market or real sector in the context of a closed economy. Let us first establish the relationship between rate of interest and investment, then we insert that investment demand function into the product market equilibrium condition to derive the IS curve. The IS curve in the context of open economy is derived in Chapter 18 of the book.

DOI: 10.4324/9781003501138-11

8.2 Investment as a function of interest rate

Investment refers to addition to capital stock, such as purchase of durable goods like plants, machinery, equipment, etc. A firm undertakes an investment in an income-earning real asset (say, a machine) because it expects an income stream in the future. Most of the investment decisions are long term in nature as they are used for a number of years from the time of purchase. It is a flow concept measured over a period of time. According to Keynes, investment decisions depend on business expectations, hence they show greater fluctuations than other components of GDP, like consumption, government expenditure, etc. Investment is the only component of final demand through which people's expectations regarding the future affect the present. Investment may be autonomous or induced. Autonomous investment is that type of investment which is not influenced by changes in interest rate or income. Induced investment takes place either due to change in the level of income or due to change in interest rate.

Investment is partly financed through borrowing. The cost of borrowing can be measured by the interest rate that the firm has to pay to borrow or to forego (opportunity cost) in case of using their own funds. So, whether the funds are available or borrowed makes no difference. The higher the cost of borrowing, the less the incentive to borrow to finance investment. This explains why aggregate planned investment is a decreasing function of interest rate. This explanation will suffice for the present. We will discuss the reason for this inverse relationship between investment and rate of interest in detail in a separate chapter on investment function. Here, we assume that interest rates on all the different types of loans are the same and denote this common interest rate by "r". The level of investment can therefore be expressed as a decreasing function of the rate of interest such that

$$I = I(r),\ I' < 0 \tag{8.1}$$

For simplicity we may consider linear form of the investment demand function as

$$I = I_0 - gr,\ (I_0, g > 0) \tag{8.2}$$

For small changes this linear form is very useful as it reduces the complexity of calculations.

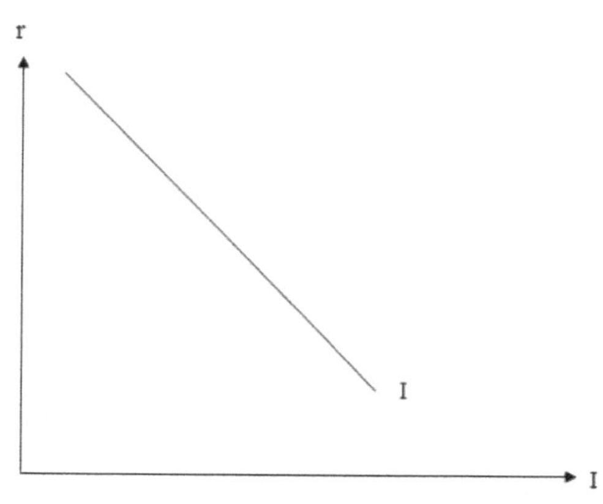

Figure 8.1 Linear investment curve

Here coefficient "g" measures the responsiveness of investment spending to the interest rate. I_0 denotes autonomous investment spending. Slope of the investment curve depends on "g". If investment is highly responsive to interest rate (g is large), then a relatively small decline in r generates a large increase in investment spending. Hence, the schedule is relatively flat. Conversely the schedule will be steeper if the responsiveness of investment to rate of interest is lower (g is small). I_0, on the other hand, is a shift parameter. An increase in I_0 shifts the curve rightward, meaning that at each level of r, firms invest more.

8.3 Establishing product market equilibrium through IS function

Now we incorporate this investment function to modify the aggregate demand function. Just like SKM, for simplicity, we assume that government expenditure is exogenously given, total tax revenue collected by the government is of lump-sum type, planned consumption is a function of disposable income, and the economy considered here is closed with no foreign transactions. Given these assumptions, the equilibrium condition of the product market can now be written as

$$Y = C(Y - T_0) + I(r) + G_0. \tag{8.3}$$

Where Y = GDP, T_0 = lump-sum tax revenue collected by the government, G = government expenditure, C = planned consumption expenditure, and I = planned investment expenditure. Corresponding to every prespecified value of r, we get a value of Y that equilibrates the goods market as a function of r, given the values of exogenous variables. Therefore, we shall get an infinite number of combinations of Y and r that keep the commodity market in equilibrium. Plotting all these combinations in the (Y, r) plane in a graph we get the *IS curve*. This curve is a graphical representation of the product market equilibrium condition which shows the level of income that will yield equality of planned investment and saving at different possible interest rates. From the previous equation it is clear that for a given level of income, an increase in r reduces investment spending and hence aggregate demand.

8.3.1 *Formal derivation of IS curve using the Keynesian cross*

IS curve is the locus of the combinations of rate of interest (r) and level of income (Y) at which the commodity market of the economy is in equilibrium. Alternatively, the IS curve shows, for any given rate of interest, the level of income for which the commodity market is in equilibrium.

To derive the IS curve through the Keynesian cross model, we consider the following three figures in Figure 8.2.

According to the Keynesian view, planned expenditure of households, firms, and the government is the key determinant of total income in the short run. In Figure 8.2a, interest rate is assumed to decrease from r_1 to r_2 which causes increase in investment expenditure from I_1 to I_2, since investment expenditure is an inverse function of interest rate. This increase in investment expenditure causes an increase in planned expenditure or aggregate demand which is shown in the diagram by the upward shift of the aggregate demand or PE curve from ($C + I_1 + G$) to ($C + I_2 + G$). Accordingly, equilibrium income increases from OY_1 to OY_2 (in Figure 8.2b). Likewise, if we consider successive reduction

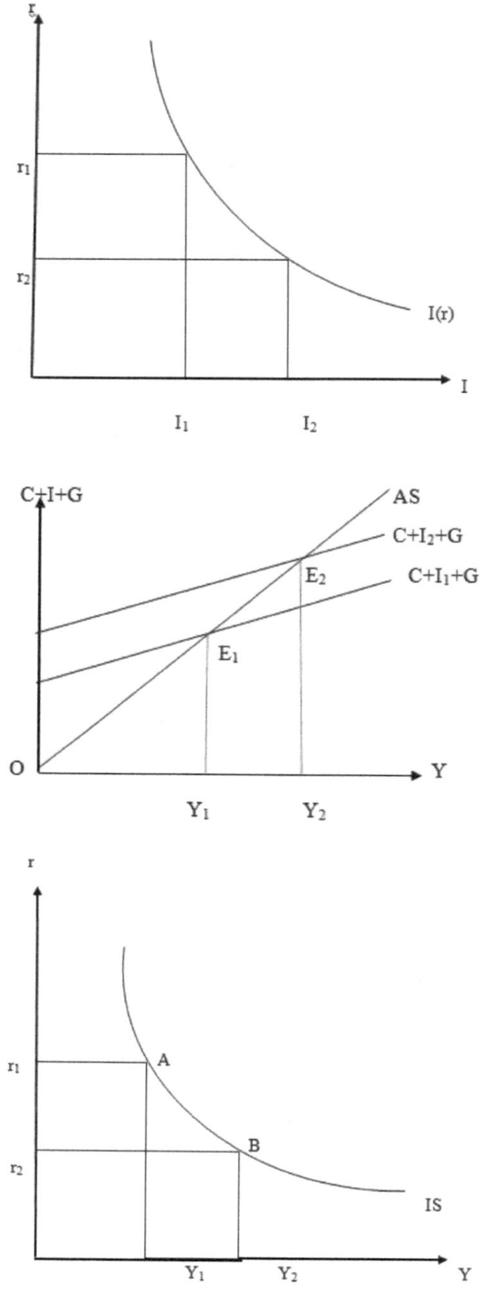

Figure 8.2 Derivation of IS curve

(a) The graph represents a downward-sloping investment demand curve showing a negative relationship between real interest and investment demand in the (Y, r) plane. As r falls from r_1 to r_2, investment demand increases from I_1 to I_2.

(b) As a result of increase in I, the $(C + I + G)$ curve shifts parallelly upward, leading to an increase in equilibrium income from Y_1 to Y_2.

(c) Joining equilibrium combinations like (Y_1, r_1), (Y_2, r_2) etc., the downward-sloping IS curve is obtained in the (Y, r) plane, all points of which represent equilibrium in the commodity market.

in interest rate we will get successive increase in equilibrium income, all of which will satisfy the product market equilibrium condition, which is $Y = C(Y - T) + I(r) + G$. Now locus through these equilibrium combinations in the (Y, r) plane provide us a smooth curve (in Figure 8.2c) which is downward sloping, popularly known as the IS curve. Each point on the IS curve represents product market equilibrium. As an increase in interest rate causes planned investment to fall, the IS curve slopes downward.

8.3.2 *Derivation of IS curve using a loanable funds approach*

In macroeconomics all financial markets can be grouped into a single *loanable fund* market. The loanable funds market is the aggregate of all the individual financial markets. In the previous chapter we derived $I = (S + BS) - NX$, where $(S + BS)$ represents the sum of private and government saving, which is national saving. The equation thus states that national saving and foreign borrowing are used to finance investment. In the loanable fund market there is only one interest rate, which is an average of interest rates of all the different types of financial assets. Interest rate, which is the equilibrating variable in this market, is nothing but the opportunity cost of loanable funds. We are now going to analyse how loanable funds markets determine real interest rate, saving, and investment.

The equality between the supply of and the demand for goods and services can be equivalently demonstrated by the equality of supply of and demand for the loanable funds. This equivalence shows another way to interpret the IS curve. Product market equilibrium condition gives $Y = C + I + G$

$$\text{or, } Y = C(Y - T_0) + I(r) + G_0 \text{ (assuming lump-sum tax only)}$$

$$\text{or, } Y - C(Y - T_0) - G_0 = I(r) \tag{8.4}$$

$$\text{or, } Y - T_0 - C(Y - T_0) + (T_0 - G_0) = I(r). \tag{8.5}$$

Here $\{Y - T - C(Y - T)\}$ represents private savings and $(T - G)$ is government saving. Hence, the left-hand side of Equation (8.5) can be interpreted as the *supply of loanable funds* (also national saving) which depends on income and fiscal policy parameters. The quantity of loanable funds supplied is the total funds available from private and government saving. The quantity of loanable funds demanded is the total quantity of funds demanded to finance investment during a given period. The right-hand side of Equation (8.5) shows the *demand for loanable funds* which depends on interest rate only.

Inflows into the financial market (private and public saving) must balance the outflows from the financial markets (investment). Interest rate is the equilibrating variable here. We can draw a saving curve or supply of loanable fund schedule for a given level of income, given the values of fiscal policy parameters T and G. Clearly, it will be a vertical line (independent of r) for a given level of income. We can also draw the investment curve which is negatively sloped in the (r, I) plane, implying the lower the interest rates, the greater the quantity of loanable funds demanded will be. Changes in the expected profit from investment will shift the demand-for-loanable-funds curve. Similarly, a change in disposable income, expected future income, and wealth will shift the supply-of-loanable-funds curve. These two curves intersect at a point E_1 in Figure 8.3, which produces equilibrium interest rate r_1. At this interest rate investment plans of borrowers and saving plans of lenders are consistent with each other. Clearly, adjustment in the interest rates ensures equilibrium in this market. Given r_1, one can get an equilibrium income Y_1 from the following figure, for which a supply-of-loanable-funds curve can be drawn.

Now, as income rises from Y_1 to Y_2, other things remaining the same, national saving or supply of loanable funds also rise and the supply of loanable funds schedule shifts rightward from $S(Y_1)$ to $S(Y_2)$. As a result of this shift, rate of interest falls because, given the demand for loanable funds, as supply of loanable funds rises, the rate of interest decreases from r_1 to r_2. Thus, we get (r_2, Y_2) combinations in Figure 8.4. Applying the same procedure, if we increase the level of income successively, we will get consecutive reduction in r. Now locus through all such equilibrium (r, Y) points plotted in (r, Y) space produces a smooth downward-sloping IS curve showing higher income (also higher saving) associated with a lower equilibrium rate of interest.

In this structure it also can be shown that a change in fiscal policy will shift the IS curve. An increase in G or decrease in T reduces national saving for any given income level, which is, $S = [Y - T - C(Y - T) + (T - G)]$ will fall. In case of an increase in G, the result is straightforward, as government saving will fall with private saving remaining unchanged. But in case of a tax cut, interpretation will be easier if we consider $S = [Y - C(Y - T) - G)]$ (as given in the left-hand side of Equation 6.4). A tax cut here raises disposable income which in turn raises consumption leading to a decrease in national saving, for a given level of G and Y. Again reduction in S raises r which equilibrates the market. Since r is now

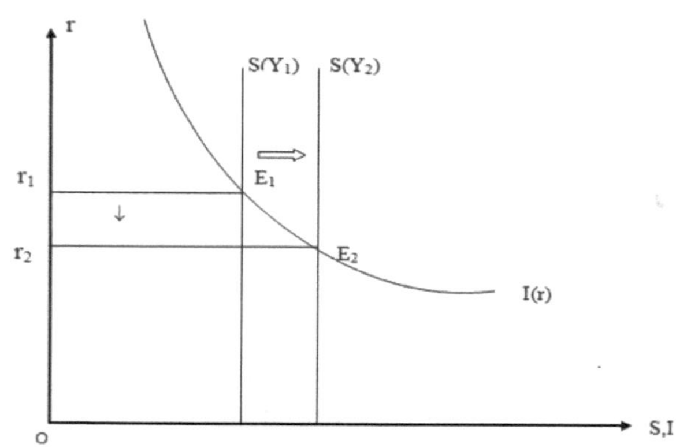

Figure 8.3 Shift of supply-of-loanable-funds curve

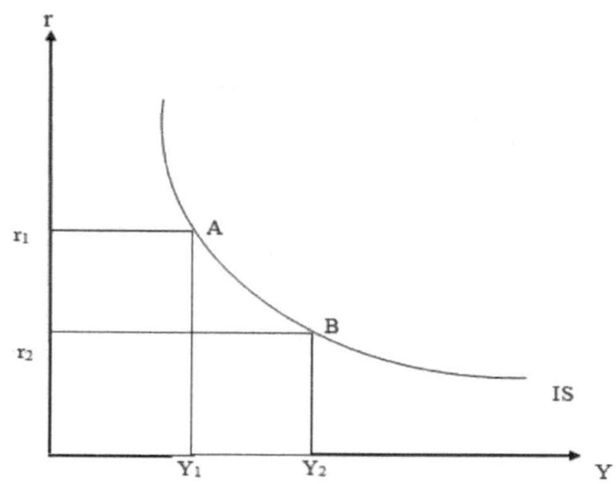

Figure 8.4 IS curve

higher for any given level of income, the IS curve shifts upward in response to expansionary fiscal policy.

8.3.3 Alternative derivation of IS: fourth quadrant case

IS curve can also be derived using four quadrant diagrams as shown in Figure 8.5. From a goods market equilibrium condition of a closed economy with government we get $C + I + G = Y = C + S + T$; alternatively, $I + G = S + T$. This equation represents the saving investment balance implicit in the basic GNP relation. Real income is measured on the right horizontal axis. As investment is an inverse function of rate of interest and G is exogenously given, the $[I(r) + G]$ curve can be represented by a downward sloping curve in the $[(I + G), r]$ plane as shown in the second quadrant of the figure. The $(S + T)$ curve will be an upward sloping line (with a negative intercept) in the $[Y, (S + T)]$ plane, assuming saving as a function of disposable income and tax is of lumpsum variety, as depicted in the following diagram.

A goods market equilibrium is established in quadrant three with the help of a 45-degree line at every point of which $(I + G) = (S + T)$. When $r = r_0$, goods or commodity market equilibrium is satisfied for $Y = Y_0$. Thus, $A(Y_0, r_0)$ represents a point on the IS curve. Likewise, for r_1 interest rate, Y_1 income ensures commodity market equilibrium. Thus, $B(Y_1, r_1)$ represents another point on the IS curve. Joining points like A, B, etc. we generate the IS curve in the first quadrant, representing an equilibrium condition in the commodity or goods market. The shape of IS can be linear or nonlinear, depending on the shapes of $(I + G)$ and $(S + T)$ curves. As we have drawn both $(I + G)$ and $(S + T)$ as linear curves here, the corresponding IS becomes linear.

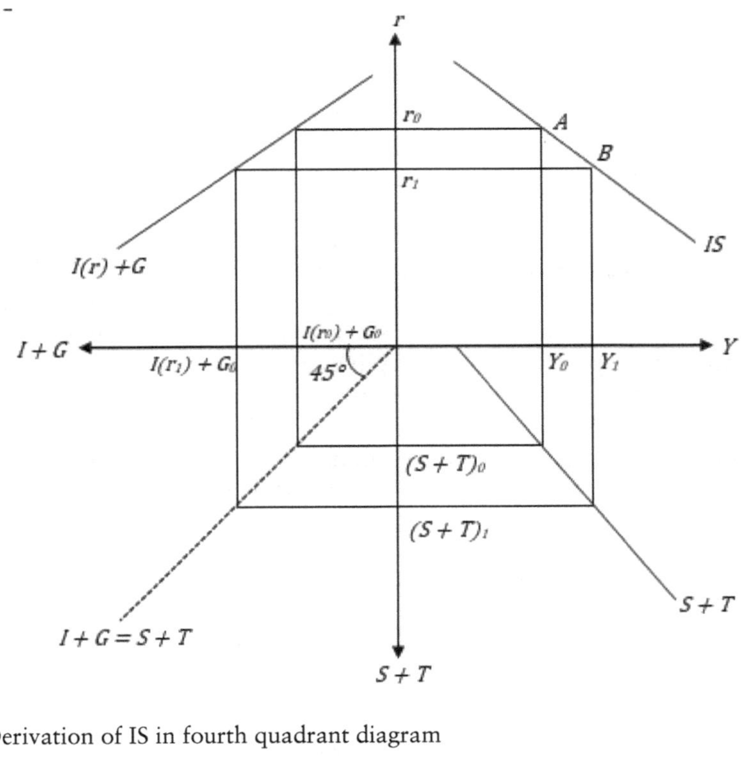

Figure 8.5 Derivation of IS in fourth quadrant diagram

8.4 Slope of the IS curve

8.4.1 *Interpretation of slope of IS in a closed economy without government*

Let us first find out the slope of the IS curve assuming that there is no government. We write an interest-dependent investment function of the following form $I = I(r)$; $I' < 0$ and assume consumption depends only on *Y*. Commodity market equilibrium condition without government can be written as

$$Y = C(Y) + I(r).$$

Differentiating we get

$$dY = C'dY + I'dr$$

$$\text{or } \frac{dr}{dy} = \frac{1 - C'}{I'} < 0. \tag{8.6}$$

Considering the linear consumption function $C = a + bYs$ and the linear investment function

$$I = I_0 - gr, (I_0, g > 0; \text{ and } \frac{dI}{dr} = -g), \text{ we get}$$

$$Y = (a + bY) + (I_0 - gr)$$

$$\text{or } dY = bdY - gdr$$

$$\text{or } dY = -\frac{g}{1-b}dr$$

$$\frac{dr}{dy} = -\frac{1-b}{g}$$

$$\frac{dr}{dy} = -\frac{MPS}{g} < 0. \tag{8.7}$$

So, the IS curve here is a negatively sloped straight line with slope [–*MPS* / *g*], where *MPS* is marginal propensity to save and "*g*" is interest sensitivity of investment. Clearly the steepness of the curve depends on how sensitive investment spending is to changes in the interest rate and also depends on the multiplier.

A reduction in interest rate leads to an increase in the investment (as investment is inversely related to r). An increase in "*I*", on the other hand, leads to an increase in equilibrium income (via the simple Keynesian multiplier process). Suppose we start with a change in interest rate by *dr*; then change in *I* will be $dI = -gdr$. So the change in equilibrium income is

$$dY = \text{simple Keynesian multiplier} \times dI$$

$$\text{or, } dY = \frac{1}{1-b} \times (-gdr)$$

Therefore, the change in income resulting from a change in the rate of interest depends on two things:

i) How much I changes following a change in r (measured by $-g$)
ii) How much Y changes following a change in I (represented by SKM multiplier)

If g is large then a given change in the interest rate produces a large change in AD resulting in a large shift in the $(C + I + G)$ curve in the previous diagram. This will produce a correspondingly large change in the equilibrium level of income, making the IS curve flatter. Similarly, if g is small, then IS will be relatively steep. Again, given the value of g, the magnitude of change in Y as a result of a change in r and hence I depends on the value of the SKM multiplier. The larger the value of the multiplier, the larger the change in Y will be following a change in r. Hence, the larger the multiplier, the flatter the IS curve will be.

8.4.2 *Interpretation of slope of IS in a closed economy with government*

In a closed economy with government, commodity market equilibrium condition becomes

$$Y = C(Y - T) + I(r) + G.$$

Assuming $G = G_0$ and $T = t(Y)$, (income dependent tax) we have the IS equation as

$$Y = C(Y - t(Y)) + I(r) + G_0. \tag{8.8}$$

Totally differentiating, we get

$$dy = C^{/}(dY - t^{/}dY) + I^{/}dr + dG_0$$
$$\text{or, } \{1 - C^{/}(1 - t^{/})\}dY = I^{/}dr, \text{ (assuming } dG_0 = 0)$$
$$\frac{dr}{dY} = \frac{1 - C^{/}\left(1 - t^{/}\right)}{I^{/}} < 0; \text{ (as } I^{/} < 0). \tag{8.9}$$

$\therefore$ IS curve is negatively sloped.

If we consider the linear forms of the C, I, and T function, then we get

$$Y = a + b\{Y - tY\} + I_0 - gr + G_0. \tag{8.10}$$

(where, $C = a + b(Y - T); 0 < b < 1.$

$I = I_0 - gr,\ g > 0;$

$T = tY,\ 0 < t = \text{tax rate} < 1;$).

Totally differentiating, we can write

$$\{1 - b(1 - t)\}dY + gdr = 0$$
$$\text{or, } \frac{dr}{dY} = \frac{-1 - b(1 - t)}{g} < 0. \tag{8.11}$$

This is the value of the slope of the IS curve with government in a closed economy, which is clearly negative. also

From Equation (8.11) it is evident that larger the value of "g" and the larger the value of "b", the flatter the IS curve will be. Higher "g" means Y is highly sensitive to r as well. A small change in r leads to a large change in Y; as a result the IS curve will be relatively flat. The converse of the result is also true. Similarly the larger the MPC (b) the larger the change in income will be resulting from a given change in interest rate leading to a flatter IS curve. Differently speaking, the larger the multiplier, the larger the change in income produced by a given change in interest rate. Hence, the higher the sensitivity of investment spending to the interest rate and the larger the MPC, the larger the multiplier, the flatter the IS curve.

8.5 Shifting of IS — the roles of demand side parameters

The IS curve will shift if the parameters of the IS equation change. Any change in autonomous expenditure of the economy will shift the IS curve. If G rises or T (tax) falls, then the IS curve will shift outward. On the other hand, if G falls or T rises, then IS will shift inward.

Let us check what happens to the IS curve if G changes. Suppose government expenditure increases by ΔG, then at constant rate of interest, which is a constant level of investment, the AD increases by ΔG in the first round; $\{b(1-t)\Delta G\}$ in the second round, and so on (where t is the tax rate, less than unity) following the multiplier logic. So, at any constant interest rate, income increases by $\frac{\Delta G}{1-b(1-t)}$, which means IS shifts to the right. Thus the change in income as a result of the change in autonomous spending is just the expenditure multiplier times the change in autonomous spending.

The numerator of the expression gives the amount of excess demand that is created at any r on the initial IS following an increase in G by ΔG. Equilibrium will be restored in the goods market, with r remaining unchanged, when Y rises to such an extent that the

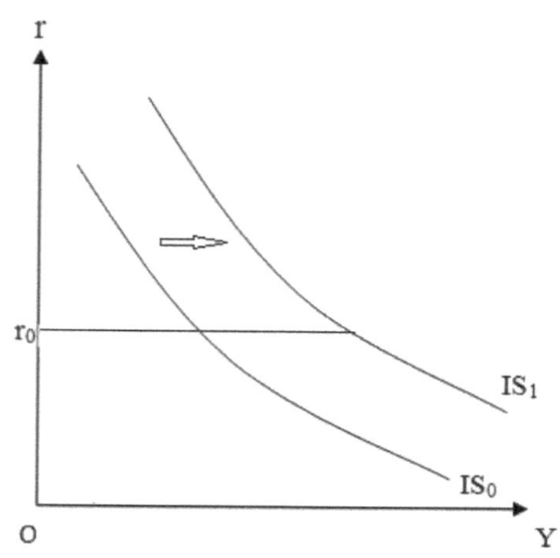

Figure 8.6 Shift of IS

excess demand falls in absolute value by ΔG. With unchanged r, excess demand falls by $[1-b(1-t)]$ when Y rises by one unit. Therefore, excess demand falls in absolute terms by ΔG when Y rises by $\frac{\Delta G}{1-b(1-t)}$. Hence, corresponding to a given rate of interest, IS shifts horizontally by an amount $\frac{\Delta G}{1-b(1-t)}$. The shift is parallel because the magnitude of the shift does not depend on Y and r. The shift depends on the marginal propensity to save since that determines how much income must rise in order to generate the additional savings needed to offset the increase in G. A reduction in government spending shifts the IS curve to the left.

The same logic is true in case of a reduction in lump-sum tax, where again IS will shift rightward parallel from IS_0 to IS_1. If lump-sum tax is reduced by ΔT, then, corresponding to a given rate of interest, IS shifts rightward horizontally by an amount $(\frac{b\Delta T}{1-b})$. Fiscal policy variables are not the only factors that can shift the IS schedule. Any autonomous change, like change in autonomous investment, may be due to a change in profitability of investment, which will also shift the IS curve. Here also the IS curve will shift horizontally by a distance equal to the multiplier times the change in autonomous spending.

8.6 Points off the IS curve

Every point on the IS curve implies equilibrium in the commodity market whereas a point off the IS curve represents disequilibrium in the commodity market. To ascertain the state of

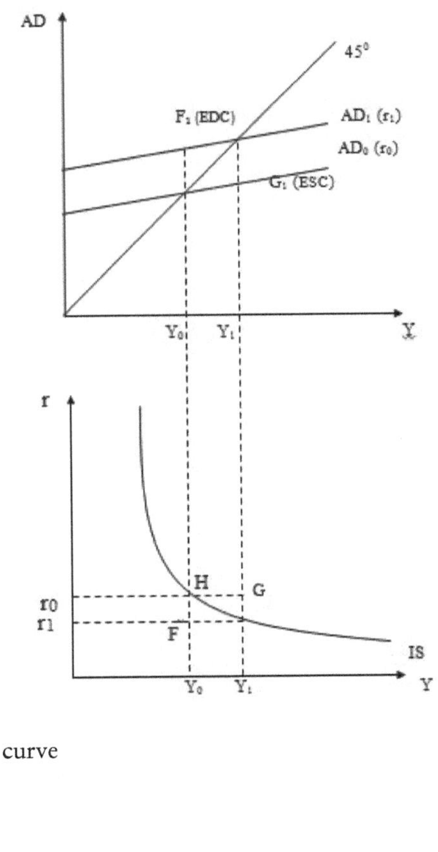

Figure 8.7 Point off the IS curve

the commodity market at any point off the IS curve, one has to compare the given point on the IS to another point which has either the same *Y* or the same *r*. Consider the following diagram to examine the position of a point off the IS curve. Let us take point *F* which lies below the IS curve (shown in the lower panel). At *F*, income is Y_0 and interest rate is r_1, so the commodity market is not in equilibrium. To check the position of the state of the commodity market at *F* we have to compare it with point *H*, having the same *Y* but higher *r*.

Corresponding to r_1 interest rate, aggregate demand is AD_1. Therefore, point *F* in the lower panel corresponds to point F_1 in the Keynesian cross diagram of upper panel. But at F_1, aggregate demand exceeds aggregate supply. In other words, F_1 represents a point where there is excess demand in the commodity market. Similarly, it can be deduced that any point to the right of the IS curve (like *G* in the lower panel) represents excess supply in the commodity market.

8.7 Nonconventional IS curves

Case I: in the *extreme situation*, if investment is completely insensitive to interest rate ($g = 0$), then the investment schedule and hence the *IS curve will be vertical.* An increase

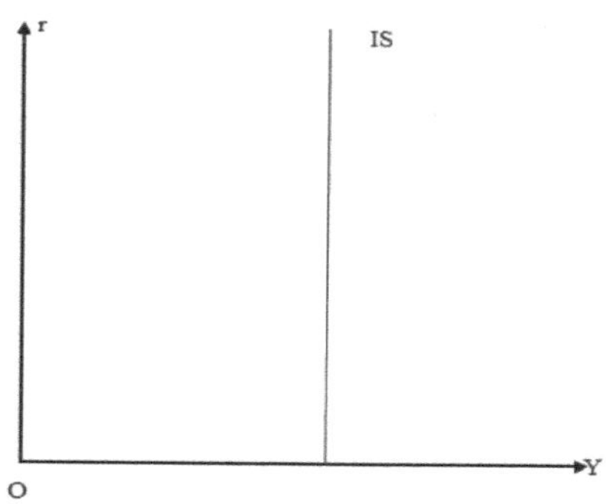

Figure 8.8 Vertical IS

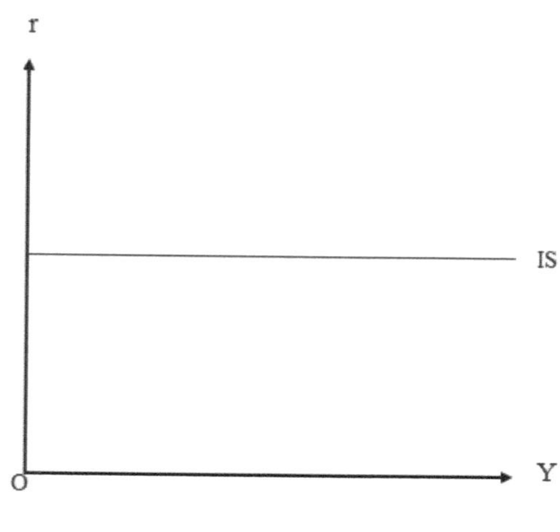

Figure 8.9 Horizontal IS

in r would not lead to a fall in investment at all. As a result, equilibrium in the product market requires the same level of income.

If investment spending is unrelated to rate of interest, then the IS equation becomes

$$Y = a + b\{Y - tY\} + I_0 + G_0$$

Clearly it is independent of r, hence the schedule is vertical.

Case II: if g is undefined, then the investment schedule is horizontal, implying that any amount of investment is feasible with a given rate of interest. Thus, any amount of Y is compatible with a given r. The slope of IS, $\frac{dr}{dY}$, becomes zero. The IS curve becomes horizontal in this situation as shown in the following diagram.

8.8 Conclusion

In this chapter we have extended the SKM of the previous chapter by making interest rate an endogenous variable. Spending or aggregate expenditure became dependent, as a result, on interest rate because of the sensitivity of investment to the interest rate. Two approaches were adopted in this respect: the Keynesian cross approach and the loanable fund approach. With investment dependent on interest rate, we found that an equilibrium level of income exists for each interest rate for which commodity market is in equilibrium. But, to determine the unique equilibrium level of income, the market rate of interest must be known. In order to tell the full story of the interest rate we need to consider the money market. For this we need to move to Chapter 9. Though we will restrict our analysis temporarily for a closed economy; it can easily be extended for an open economy also. This has been done later in Chapter 18 of this book.

Summary

- In this chapter, investment is made dependent on the real interest rate. A higher interest rate discourages some investment projects and lowers total investment.
- Product market equilibrium condition is given by $Y = C + I + G$.
- The IS curve, which represents product market equilibrium, is downward slopping in the interest rate aggregate income space as an increase in interest rate causes planned investment and hence Y to fall.
- The IS curve shifts to the right with an increase in government expenditure and its magnitude depends on the marginal propensity to save.
- An increase in taxes increases aggregate savings and the nominal interest rate declines, thereby shifting the IS curve downwards.
- The lower the responsiveness of investment spending to the interest rate, the steeper the IS curve.

Keywords

Investment function	Interest rate
Vertical IS curve	Horizontal IS curve
Loanable fund	Points off the IS

Multiple choice questions

1. Like the simplified Keynesian model, the full Keynesian ISLM model

   (a) Examines an equilibrium in which aggregate output produced equals aggregate demand.
   (b) Assumes a fixed price level.
   (c) Assumes that interest rates are fixed.
   (d) Does all of the above.
   (e) Does only (a) and (b) of the above.

2. When the interest rate rises,

   (a) Planned investment falls.
   (b) Planned investment rises.
   (c) Planned investment will be unaffected.
   (d) Equilibrium income increases.

3. The _____ traces out the points for which total quantity of goods produced equals total quantity of goods demanded.

   (a) LM curve.
   (b) IS curve.
   (c) Consumption function.
   (d) Investment schedule.

4. The _____ describes points for which the goods market is in equilibrium.

   (a) LM curve.
   (b) IS curve.
   (c) Consumption function.
   (d) Investment schedule.

5. When investment is negatively related to the rate of interest, equilibrium output in the goods market

   (a) Is unrelated to the rate of interest.
   (b) Is inversely related to the rate of interest.
   (c) Is positively related to the rate of interest.
   (d) Falls as the rate of interest decreases.

Answers

1. (e); 2. (a); 3. (b); 4. (b); 5. (b).

Descriptive questions

1. Derive the IS curve using supply and demand schedule for loanable funds.
2. Why is the IS curve negatively sloped?
3. When would the IS curve be relatively steep?
4. What are the determinants of the position of IS curve?

5. Suppose $C = 150 + 0.8(Y - T)$, $T = 100 + 0.1Y$, $G = 300$, and $I = 210 - 100r$. Derive the equation of the IS curve and find out its slope. Explain its meaning. How much will IS shift horizontally if G changes by 5 units?
6. Why is the IS curve a depiction of equilibrium in the product market? What factors cause the IS curve to shift and in what direction?

9 Money market equilibrium (Model IV)

9.1 Introduction

After discussing product market equilibrium in Chapter 8, we now concentrate on the money market. Money is the most liquid of all assets. Keynesian theory suggests that money affects income via the interest rate. Interest rate can be considered as the return for sacrificing liquidity. According to Keynes rate of interest is a monetary phenomenon which depends on demand for and supply of money. The average amount of money that the economic agents want to keep in hand is known as demand for money. The money market will be in equilibrium if demand for money equals supply of money. Diagrammatic representation of the money market equilibrium condition can be made with the help of the LM curve. For different rates of interest, the LM curve specifies the level of income which makes demand for money equal to the supply of money. The name LM follows a notion introduced by John Hicks, where he referred to the demand for money as desired liquidity (L). Setting desired liquidity equal to the supply of real money balances M (i.e. $L = M$) which results in a schedule where the money market is in equilibrium.

9.2 Money market equilibrium and the LM curve

Let us try to identify combinations of income and interest rate that equilibrate the money market, ignoring the commodity market temporarily. *The LM curve shows the combinations of interest rate and income for which the money market is in equilibrium.* To derive the LM curve, we first try to determine interest rate through the *liquidity preference theory*. The liquidity preference theory states that an individual holds money because of its liquidity. This explanation is called the theory of liquidity preference because it posits that the interest rate adjusts to balance the demand and supply for the economy's most liquid asset, which is *money*. According to Keynes, interest rate is a reward for parting with liquidity for a certain period. Just as the Keynesian cross is a building block of the IS curve, the theory of liquidity preference is a building block of the LM curve.

9.2.1 Liquidity preference theory

In this theoretical framework, we try to determine interest rate by considering interaction between supply of money (supply of real balance) and demand for money (or demand for real balance). First, we will explore the nature and the determinants of the supply of and demand for real balance.

If P stands for price level or the average price of goods and services and M stands for the supply of money, then M / P is the supply of real money balances. According to the theory

DOI: 10.4324/9781003501138-12

of liquidity preferences, supply of real balance is considered to be determined exogenously by the central monetary authority of the concerned country, which is by the central bank of the economy. The central bank has other names in other countries. Therefore, supply of real balance is independent of the rate of interest and the level of income (note that the price level is also exogenous in this short run model). If we plot supply of real money against interest rate then the relevant graph will look like the following (Figure 9.1).

If $\overline{M}$ is the nominal money supply determined by the central bank and $\overline{P}$ represents the constant price level, then

$$\overline{m} = \frac{\overline{M}}{\overline{P}}. \tag{9.1}$$

Where, $\overline{m}$ = supply of real money balance, which is exogenously given.

Demand for real money balance is the amount of money which people wish to hold at a particular point in time. Demand for money is considered to be influenced by income level and the rate of interest. According to the theory of liquidity preference, interest rate is another important determinant of how much money people choose to hold. Interest rate can be viewed as the *opportunity cost of holding money* – it is what we forgo by holding some of our assets as money, which does not bear interest, instead of an interest-bearing financial asset, like bonds. If interest rate rises, the opportunity cost of holding money rises. Then the demand for real balance will decrease because people will put more of their wealth into interest-bearing financial assets, say bonds. In other words, the higher the interest rate, the more costly it is to hold money and accordingly less cash will be held at each level of income. Hence demand for real balance, for a given income level, is likely to be a decreasing function of the rate of interest.

On the other hand, demand for real balance depends on the level of real income because individuals hold money to pay for their purchases which in turn depends on income. When income is high expenditure is also high, so people engage in more transactions that require use of money. Thus, greater income implies greater money demand. So, the demand for real balance is a positive function of income level and inverse function of rate of interest. We can write the money demand function as

$$L^d = L(r, Y);\ L_r < 0, L_Y > 0 \tag{9.2}$$

and in the (r, L) plane it looks like Figure 9.2.

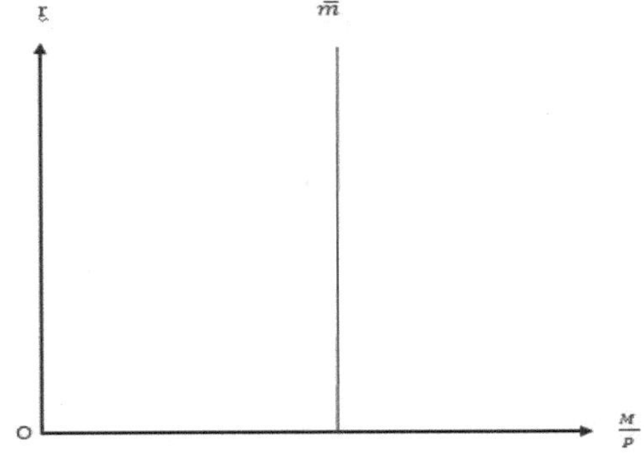

Figure 9.1 Money supply function

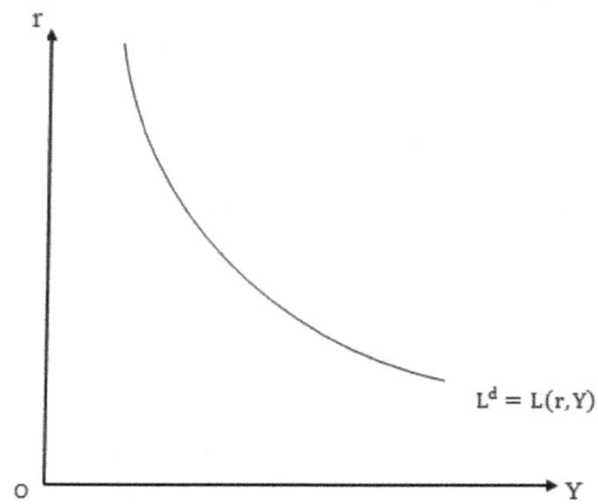

Figure 9.2 Money demand function

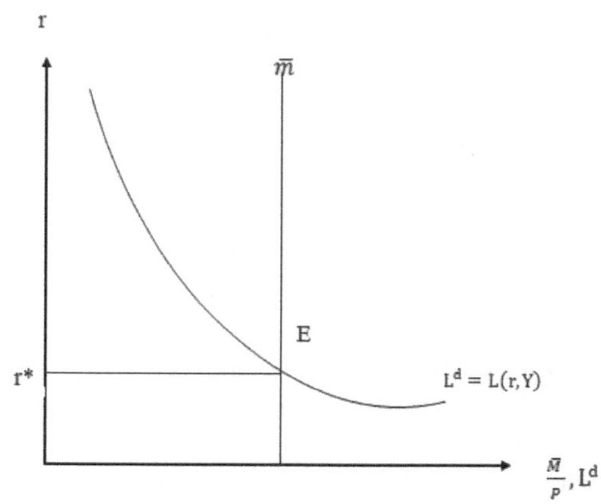

Figure 9.3 Equilibrium in the money market

In money market equilibrium, the supply of real balance is equal to demand for real balance. The money market equilibrium condition is therefore given by

$$\overline{m} = L(r, Y). \tag{9.3}$$

To determine the equilibrium interest rate graphically, we superimpose demand for real balance curve on the vertical supply of real balance curve.

Equilibrium rate of interest is determined at the point of intersection between demand for real balance and supply of real balance schedule. In the following diagram, *E* is the equilibrium point and r^* is the equilibrium rate of interest.

If the rate of interest now goes above the equilibrium level, the supply of money exceeds the demand for money. People have more money at their disposal than they desire to hold and will be eager to convert some of it into interest earning in banks or interest-earning assets. Banks and asset issuers will take advantage of this opportunity and offer low interest rates. Ultimately as a result of this excess supply pressure, the rate of interest will fall to its equilibrium rate

9.2.2 *Derivation of LM schedule from liquidity preference theory*

Now we are in a position to derive the LM curve. The LM curve is a locus of all combinations of Y and r for which the money market is in equilibrium. The derivation of the LM curve, in a closed economy, can be shown with the help of the following figure:

In Figure 9.4, we draw $L^d = L(r, Y)$ curve, which is the demand for real balance curve, which is negatively sloped. The supply of real balance curve $\bar{m} = \frac{\overline{M}}{\overline{P}}$, which is a vertical straight line, is also drawn there. Two curves intersect at intersect at E_1 and the

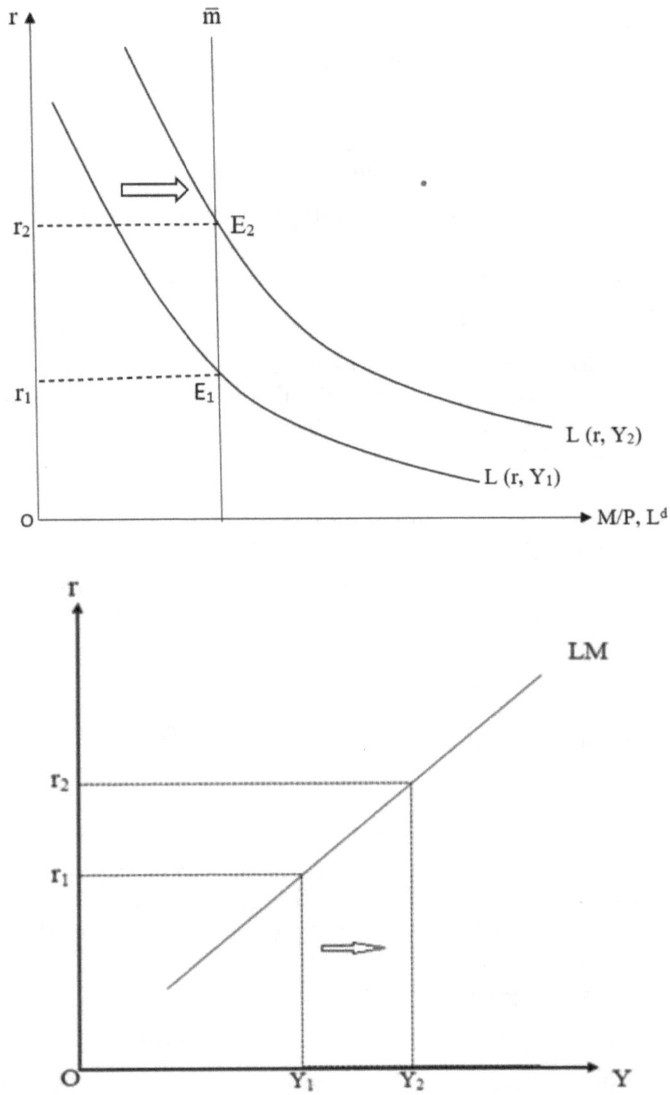

Figure 9.4 Derivation of LM curve

equilibrium rate of interest r_1 is determined in the money market. Let this demand for real balance correspond to the real income Y_1. Therefore, in the right-hand panel, we plot the (r_1, Y_1) equilibrium combination. Suppose, now, that income level increases exogenously from Y_1 to Y_2. This will shift the demand for real balance curve to the right from $L(r, Y_1)$ to $L(r, Y_2)$ with an unchanged supply of real money balance. As income increases, the transaction demands for money increase because people need more to spend on goods and services. The interest rate must now rise from r_1 to r_2 to equilibrate the money market. Therefore, according to the theory of liquidity preference, with a higher income (Y_2), a higher interest rate (r_2) equilibrates the money market. In right panel of the previous figure, (r_2, Y_2) is another combination of interest rate and income for which the money market is in equilibrium. Joining these equilibrium combinations, we get the LM curve, which is clearly rising. This is the LM schedule in the context of a closed economy where there is no foreign transaction, like exports and imports. The open economy counterpart of this analysis has been incorporated in a later chapter.

9.2.3 *Alternative derivation of LM: four-quadrant case*

In order to derive LM curve using a four-quadrant diagram we slightly modify the money market equilibrium condition as follows: $k(Y) + l(r) = m_0$. Here LHS represents the total demand for money consisting of transaction and speculative balances and RHS shows the exogenously given real money supply.

In second quadrant we draw the speculative demand, $l(r)$, curve and in the fourth quadrant the transaction demand the $k(Y)$ curve. When $r = r_0$, the speculative demand for money (l_0) is equal to AB. According to the figure the supply for real balances, (m_0) is OB. So, to keep the money market in equilibrium the transaction demand for real balances should be equal to OA, and for that income should be Y_0. So, (Y_0, r_0) is a point on the LM curve.

In third quadrant, the 45-degree line with respect to each axis is drawn and distance from the origin on each axis is equal to the total exogenously given real money supply (m_0). Transaction demand and speculative demand always add up to total money supply on each axis. Any point on the 45-degree line directly represents money market equilibrium condition.

For $r \geq r_{\max}$, $l(r) = 0$ and Y_{max} is constant, so for $r > r_{\max}$, LM is vertical. For $r = r_{\min}$, $l = \infty$ and any Y is possible, so LM is horizontal. Note, Y_{max} is the maximum amount of income that can be financed by the given supply of real balances.

Thus, the LM curve has three segments

i) The horizontal segment, corresponding to the horizontal segment of the $l(r)$ curve, known as the *extreme Keynesian zone* where the speculative demand for money is infinitely interest elastic. This kind of situation prevail in deep depression.
ii) The upward sloping segment, corresponding to the negatively sloped part of $l(r)$, known as the *intermediate* or *Keynesian zone*.
iii) The *vertical part*, corresponding to zero speculative demand (when $l(r)$ is vertical), known as the *classical zone*. The equation of LM becomes $Y = \frac{m_0}{k}$. Here, $\frac{m_0}{k}$ is the maximum amount of income that can be financed by given supply of real balance (m_0). "r" is at such a high level that everyone prefers to purchase bonds (speculative demand for money equals zero).

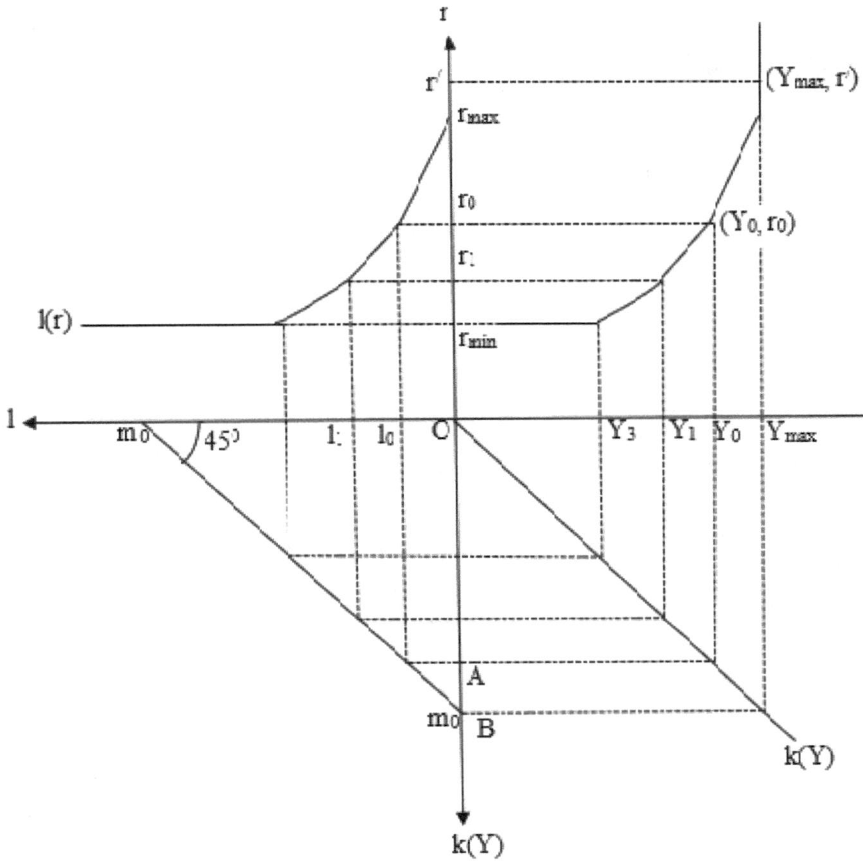

Figure 9.5 Derivation of LM: four-quadrant case

9.3 Slope of an LM curve

Money market equilibrium condition is given by $L(r,Y) = \overline{m}$. Taking the total differential of this equation treating all exogenous variables as given, we get

$$L_Y dY + L_r dr = 0 \tag{9.4}$$

LHS shows the change in demand for real balance and RHS shows the change in supply of real balance. From the previous equation we can write $dr = \frac{-L_Y}{L_r} dY$. This expression shows the amount of change in r needed to keep money market equilibrium when Y changes by dY. Therefore

$$\frac{dr}{dY} = \frac{-L_Y}{L_r} > 0 \text{ (as } L_r < 0, L_Y > 0). \tag{9.5}$$

Expressions L_Y *and* L_r denote income sensitivity and interest sensitivity of real balance respectively. Let us consider the linear forms of money demand and money supply functions

$$L^d = kY - lr \text{ (where k, } l > 0) \tag{9.6}$$

$$\overline{m} = \frac{\overline{M}}{\overline{P}} \tag{9.7}$$

In equilibrium,

$$\overline{m} = kY - lr \tag{9.8}$$

This is the equation of LM curve in linear form whose slope is $\frac{dr}{dY} = \frac{K}{l} > 0$.

As already mentioned, "l" is interest sensitivity of real balance and "k" is income sensitivity of real balance. As both are positive, *LM is rising*.

If Y rises, aggregate demand for real balance goes up with an unchanged r, supply of real balance remaining at the previous level. Hence at the given r there emerges an excess demand for real balance. To bring the system into equilibrium at this higher r, interest rate has to be increased which will reduce demand for real balance. Hence, as the level of income rises higher, interest rates are required to restore money market equilibrium. Thus there is a direct relation between Y and r. One can check that to the left of LM curve there is excess supply of money and to the right of LM there is excess demand for money.

Clearly the slope of LM depends on the values of l and k. Lower the value of income sensitivity of demand for money, k, and raise the value of interest sensitivity of demand for money, l, and the LM curve will be flatter. A small value of k means only a small change in r is necessary to offset the small increase in demand for money caused by a change in Y. So the LM curve is relatively flat. If the demand for money is interest inelastic, the LM curve will be fairly steep. In this case, a shift in money demand caused by an increase in Y leads to a large change in r. In the extreme situation if money demand is completely interest insensitive ($l = 0$), it depends only on income; LM will be *vertical* as shown in the following figure.

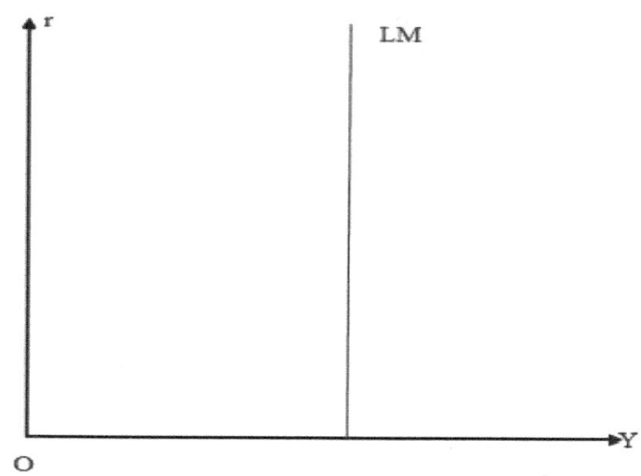

Figure 9.6 Vertical LM

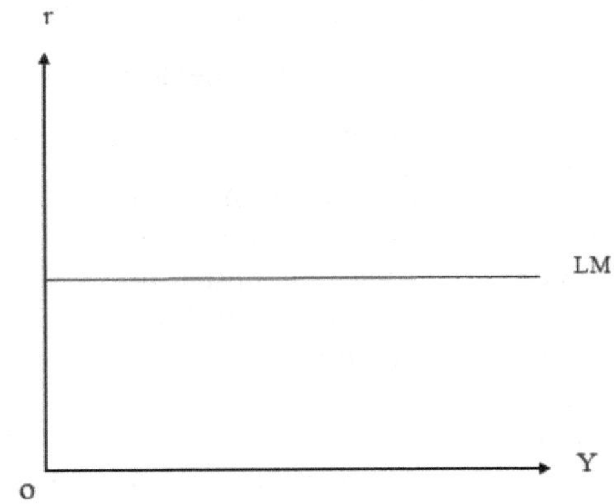

Figure 9.7 Horizontal LM

We may refer this case as the ***classical case*** because in the classical theory, as in this situation, money demand depends only on income and not on interest rate.

Another extreme situation occurs when demand for money is extremely sensitive to the interest rate and thus l is very large. Money demand will be almost infinitely elastic, then, at a very low interest rate. A small change in the interest rate must be accompanied by a large change in the level of income in order to maintain money market equilibrium. Infinitely elastic money demand will lead to *horizontal* LM curve. This is also termed the *Keynesian liquidity trap case*. Everybody holds their wealth in the form of money (as bond price is very high) here. Additional money supply will be absorbed in the individual's portfolio at the prevailing r.

9.4 Shift of the LM curve

LM curve can shift due to changes in two factors. One is exogenous change in the fixed supply of money and the other is shift in the money demand function. Money supply is a policy instrument, hence an increase in money stock means setting this policy instrument to a higher level. Demand for money or liquidity preference curve, on the other hand, changes if money demand changes for given level of income or interest rate. This may happen due to changes in the economic condition or uncertainty. Now we consider the impact of these two situations, which is changes in money supply and changes in the demand for money, on the LM curve one by one.

9.4.1 Effect of change in the supply of money

The LM curve is drawn for a given supply of real money balances, which is assumed to be fixed by monetary authority of the concerned country. If real money supply changes, then we get a shift of the LM curve. As price level is assumed constant throughout the analysis, any change in nominal money supply will lead to an increase in real money supply. In case of an increase in $\bar{m}$, without any change in the amount of income and hence demand for real balance, LM shifts rightward. On the other hand, if there is a fall in real money supply, we have the leftward shift in the LM curve, indicating that at each level of income, the interest rate is now higher.

Let us start from an initial equilibrium in the money market, E_0, as shown in Figure 9.8. Now consider an increase in money supply, given the demand for real balance. There will be an excess supply in the money market. As $m(=\frac{M}{P})$ increases due to an increase in nominal money supply (M), to maintain money market equilibrium, either Y will rise or r will fall so as to satisfy the money market equilibrium condition $\bar{m} = kY - lr$. Suppose, initially, the LM_0 curve was consistent with the initial money stock. Along this LM curve an interest rate r_0 would reflect an equilibrium point for income level Y_0. Thus (Y_0, r_0) is a point (point A) on the LM_0 curve. The corresponding money market equilibrium position is shown by point E_0 in the left panel. If we hold "r" constant at the particular value r_0, then Y must increase to maintain money market equilibrium, after the increase in nominal money supply. r_0 can be the equilibrium interest rate in the money market only if Y increases to Y_1.

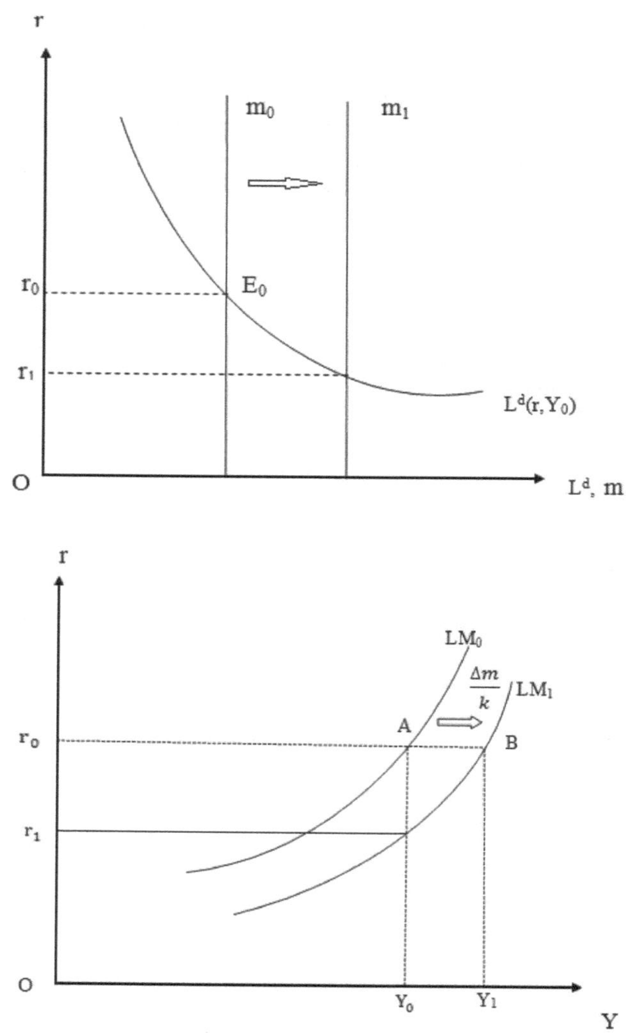

Figure 9.8 Shift of LM

This is shown by point *B* on the new LM curve LM_1. Clearly the new equilibrium point on the LM schedule LM_1 must lie to the right of point A. Hence for each *r*, Y must increase to maintain money market equilibrium, leading to a rightward shift of the LM curve. The magnitude of the horizontal shift depends on the size of the increase in the money supply and the value of the k ratio. In other words, $\frac{\Delta m}{k}$ measures the amount of the horizontal shift in the LM curve.

Following similar logic, it can be said that, with unchanged *Y*, *r* has to fall to r_1, to restore equilibrium, again leading to an outward shift of LM schedule. At each level of income, the equilibrium interest rate has to be lower to induce people to hold a larger quantity of money. A decrease in the price level does exactly the same thing to the LM curve as an increase in money supply (though price level is assumed constant in the IS LM framework). A fall in *P* raises the supply of real balance, shifting the vertical $\bar{m}$ line rightward. This increase in real money supply creates excess supply in the money market at the initial income and interest rate leading to a fall in equilibrium interest rate. Thus for any given level of income, a fall in *P* reduces the money market equilibrium interest rate, shifting the LM curve rightward.

9.4.2 *Effect of change in the demand for money*

One can also verify that a shift in the demand for real balance function (rightward), at an unchanged *r* and Y, shifts the LM schedule (upward to the left). Assume that there is an increase in money demand for a given level of income and the interest rate. A possible reason for shift might be loss of confidence in other financial assets. The left panel of Figure 9.9 shows an initial equilibrium in the money market corresponding to income level Y_0. Initially, money demand is designated as $L_0^d(r, Y_0)$. The equilibrium interest rate is r_0, as shown at point *P* on the initial LM curve LM_0 in Figure 9.9 (right panel). Now we assume that the money demand function shifts to $L_1^d(r, Y_0)$ implying that more money is demanded for the same level of income. At the unchanged level of income, Y_0,

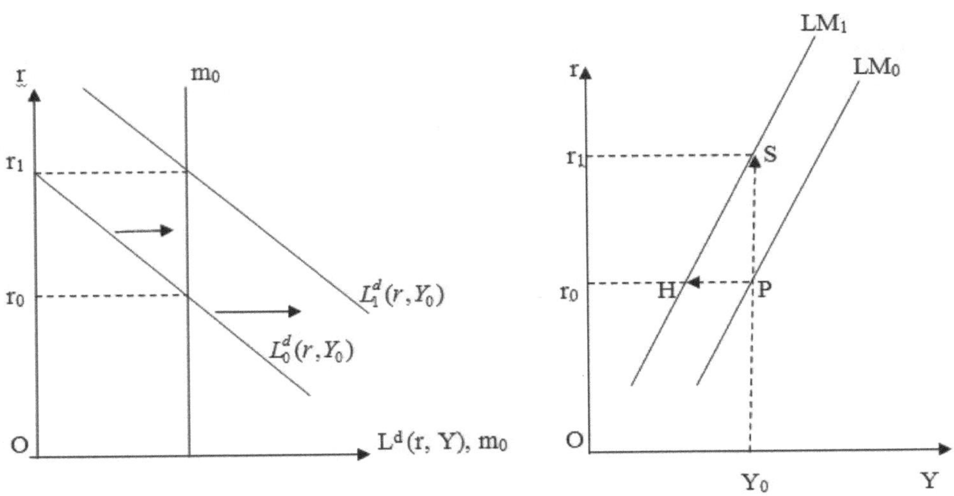

Figure 9.9 Shift of money demand and LM curve

equilibrium in the money market requires an interest rate of r_1. The point on the new LM curve, LM_1, in the left panel of the diagram, for a given level of income Y_0 will be above the old LM schedule. This point is shown as point *S* in the figure. Similarly, maintaining equilibrium in the money market at r_0 after the shift in the money demand curve would require a fall in income to a level below Y_0. This would shift the L^d schedule in figure in the left panel back down to the level of the original $L_0^d(r, Y_0)$ line.

Thus, the point on LM_1 at r_0 is to the left of LM_0. This point is shown as point *H* in the right panel of the diagram. A shift in the money demand function that increases the demand for money at a given level of both the interest rate and income shifts the LM schedule upward and to the left. A reverse shift in money demand lowering the amount of money demanded at given levels of income and the interest rate shifts the LM curve downward to the right.

9.5 Points off the LM curve

Every point on the LM curve implies equilibrium in the money market whereas a point off the LM curve represents disequilibrium in the money market. To ascertain the state of the money market at any point off the LM curve, one has to compare the given point on the LM curve to another point which has either the same *Y* or the same *r*.

Consider the diagram Figure 9.10 to examine the position of a point off the LM curve. Let us take any point to the left of LM curve, say *A′*. At *A′*, rate of interest is r_2, but level of income is Y_1, which is less than Y_2. Corresponding to r_2 interest rate, Y_2 income is needed to maintain money market equilibrium. Panel A shows that when $r = r_2$ and $Y = Y_1$ there exists excess supply of money. But point *A′* in panel B corresponds to point *A* in panel A. Likewise, if we take a point to the right of the LM curve, say *B′*, then from panel A it is evident that total demand for money will be greater than total supply of money. Therefore, to the right of the LM curve there exists excess demand in the money market. Only

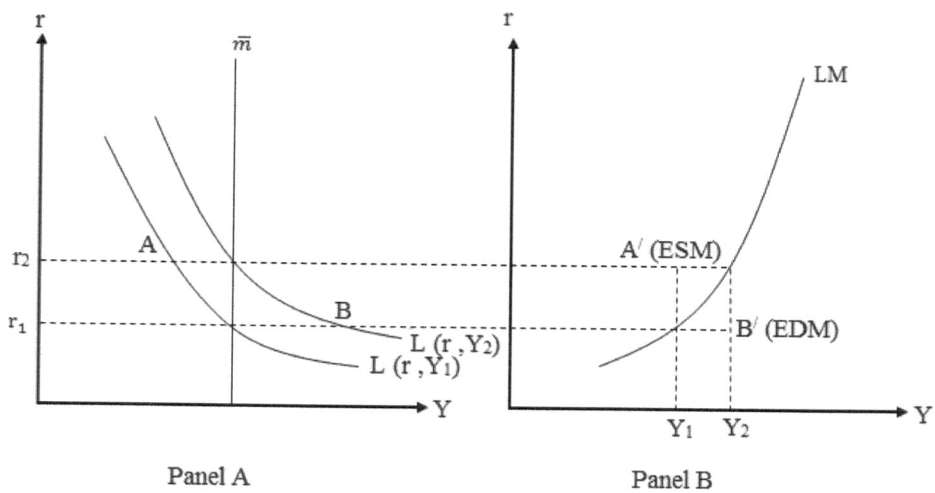

Figure 9.10 Point off the LM curve

along the LM curve is there no excess supply or excess demand in the money market, which means the money market is in equilibrium.

9.6 Interest sensitivity of money supply and the LM curve

If money supply becomes interest sensitive (i.e. endogenous), then we can write,

$$\frac{M}{\overline{P}} = m(r),\ m'(r) > 0 \tag{9.9}$$

The effect of interest sensitivity of money supply on LM curve can be explained in terms of Figure 9.11. Suppose initial income Y_1 is consistent with the demand for money curve which is $L^d(r, Y_1)$. With an initial money supply $\overline{m}$, initial equilibrium interest rate is given by r_1, as shown in the left panel of the previous diagram. Now, let income level increases exogenously from Y_1 to Y_2. L^d curve shifts rightward to $L^d(r, Y_2)$. Given the fixed money supply, $\overline{m}$, interest rate will rise to r_3 to maintain money market equilibrium. But if money supply becomes sensitive to interest rate (rising function of interest

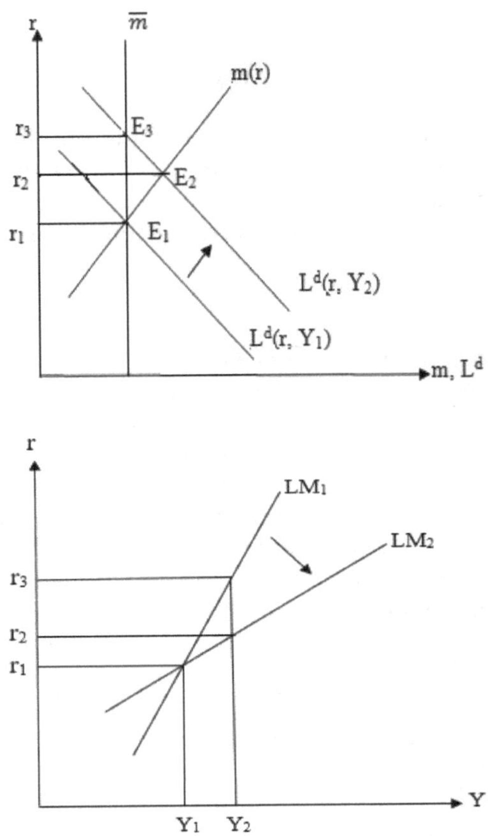

Figure 9.11 Effect of interest sensitivity of money supply on LM curve

rate such that $m'(r) > 0)$, then interest rate will rise only to r_2 instead of r_3. Thus, the interest elasticity of money supply reduces the increase in interest rate needed to maintain money market equilibrium with a given increase in Y (from Y_1 to Y_2). Thus, *LM curve will now be flatter or more interest elastic* than the original LM curve, as is evident from the left panel of the diagram.

The money market equilibrium gives us the following equation of the newly modelled LM function as

$$m(r) = L(y, r) \tag{9.10}$$

Taking total derivatives of the above equation we have

$$(\partial m / \partial r) . dr = (\partial L / \partial y) . dy + (\partial L / \partial r) . dr$$
$$Or, \ [(\partial m / \partial r) - (\partial L / \partial r)] . dr = (\partial L / \partial y) . dy$$
$$Or, \ (m_r - L_r) . dr = L_y . dy \tag{9.11}$$

The slope of the new LM is

$$dr / dy = L_y / (m_r - L_r) > 0 \tag{9.12}$$

Terms L_Y, L_r and m_r denote income sensitivity of real balance, interest sensitivity of real balance, and interest sensitivity of money supply, respectively. The LM is still positively sloped like the exogenous money supply model but with some differences in magnitudes. Comparing (9.12) and (9.5) it can be said that, as $M_r > 0$ term has been added to the denominator of the slope expression of (9.12), the slope of the modified LM will be flatter compared to the old LM function with the exogenous money supply system.

9.7 Conclusion

In this chapter we considered demand for and supply of money and derived the LM curve from the money market equilibrium condition. The LM curve, analogous to the IS curve in the commodity market, shows all equilibrium combinations of income and interest rate for which the money market is in equilibrium. We are now ready to discuss the joint equilibrium of the product and the money markets. To find out the unique equilibrium level of income, the equilibrium market interest rate must be known. For this we need to consider both the markets simultaneously and superimpose the LM curve onto the IS curve. This has been done in the next chapter. Again, we will restrict our analysis for a closed economy temporarily; it can easily be extended for an open economy also.

Summary

- This chapter introduces the money market where the interest rate is determined by demand for and supply of money using the liquidity preference theory
- The LM curve, all points on which represents money market equilibrium, is upward sloping in the nominal interest rate-aggregate income space as an increase in income raises the demand for real money balances which results in a rise in the interest rate.

- The LM curve is inelastic (elastic) when the demand for money is interest inelastic (elastic). When the demand for money is sensitive to changes in the interest rate an increase in the demand for money for transactions that accompanies an increase in income does not result in a large change in the interest rate. The resulting LM curve will be flat.
- The LM curve shifts to the right if there is an increase in the money supply, and if there is a fall in real money supply the LM curve will shift leftward. The magnitude of the horizontal shift depends on the size of the money supply change
- Interest sensibility of money supply will make the LM curve more elastic.

Keywords

Money market	Interest sensitivity of money supply
Liquidity preference	Opportunity cost
LM curve	Money demand
Liquidity trap	Real money balance

Multiple choice questions

1. The demand for money is

   (a) Positively related to output and the rate of interest.
   (b) Negatively related to output and the rate of interest.
   (c) Negatively related to output and positively related to the rate of interest.
   (d) Positively related to output and negatively related to the rate of interest.

2. The _____ describes the combinations of interest rates and aggregate output for which the quantity of money demanded equals the quantity of money supplied.

   (a) IS curve.
   (b) LM curve.
   (c) Consumption function.
   (d) Investment schedule.

3. As interest rates rise, the opportunity cost of holding money _____ and the demand for money _____.

   (a) Rises; rises.
   (b) Rises; falls.
   (c) Falls; rises.
   (d) Falls; falls.

4. The demand curve for money is downward sloping because

   (a) At lower interest rates, people want to hold more money and fewer bonds.
   (b) At higher interest rates, people want to hold more money and fewer bonds
   (c) At lower interest rates, bonds are more attractive.
   (d) At higher interest rates, holding money is desirable.

5. If the demand for money is perfectly interest-inelastic, the LM schedule will be

   (a) Rising.
   (b) Downward sloping.

(c) A horizontal line.
(d) A vertical line.

6. Liquidity trap is a situation when

(a) All potential investors expect the rate of interest to rise in future.
(b) All potential investors expect the rate of interest to fall in future.
(c) Natural rate of interest is above the critical rate of interest.
(d) Demand for money for speculative purpose is interest inelastic.

7. In the liquidity trap, the money demand curve

(a) is vertical.
(b) is horizontal.
(c) is positively sloped.
(d) is negatively sloped.

8. In the Keynesian system, liquidity preference refers to the –

(a) demand for consumer goods.
(b) demand for capital.
(c) supply of money.
(d) demand for money.

Answers

1. (d); 2. (b); 3. (b); 4. (b); 5. (d); 6. (a); 7. (b); 8. (d).

Descriptive questions

1. Define the LM curve and explain why it slopes upward.
2. What does a point to the left of the LM curve indicate?
3. Explain the shape of the LM curve when money demand is extremely sensitive to the interest rate.
4. What will be the shape of the LM curve if money demand does not depend on income?
5. What will be the impact on the slope of the LM curve if money supply becomes positively related to interest rate?

10 Interactions of fiscal and monetary policies in IS-LM models (Model V)

10.1 Introduction

Chapter 8 and 9 discussed equilibrium in the product and money markets respectively in the context of a closed economy. The present chapter considers joint equilibrium of both the markets. For simultaneous equilibrium, level of income and rate of interest should be such that both the product and money markets are in equilibrium. Price level is still assumed to be exogenous and constant, as in the previous chapters, implying inflation and expected inflation to be zero. This IS-LM model allows us to understand the immediate impact of monetary and fiscal policy in an economy where resources are not fully utilised. Hence there is no supply constraint in this model; rather lack of demand is the constraint on output. In the Keynesian cross model aggregate demand is governed by the autonomous expenditure without any role of money supply. In contrast, in the IS-LM model, developed by Hicks (1937), transforming the Keynesian model, the demand is influenced not only by all components of autonomous expenditure but also by money supply. To understand the workings of the model clearly, we will consider a disequilibrium state where the level of income and the rate of interest are different from their equilibrium values and then conduct the stability analysis of the model. Impact of fiscal and monetary policies are then discussed along with some of the determinants of the relative effectiveness of these policies. For simplicity we assume a closed economy without any foreign transaction. Extension of the model incorporating an open economy can be obtained in Chapter 20.

10.2 Short run macroeconomic equilibrium in the IS-LM model

We know the IS curve shows all combinations of (r, Y) for which a commodity market is in equilibrium and the LM curve shows all combinations of (r, Y) for which the money market is in equilibrium. The point of intersection of two curves represents simultaneous equilibrium in both product and money market. Two equations representing the complete IS-LM model (already derived in the previous two chapters) are:

$$Y = C(Y-T) + I(r) + G \quad \text{(IS curve)}$$

$$\frac{M}{P} = L(r, Y) \quad \text{(LM curve)}$$

Solving these two equations, equilibrium values of two variables r and Y can be determined.

In Figure 10.1 we find that simultaneous equilibrium in both the money and product market is attained at the point of intersection between IS and LM curves, which is

DOI: 10.4324/9781003501138-13

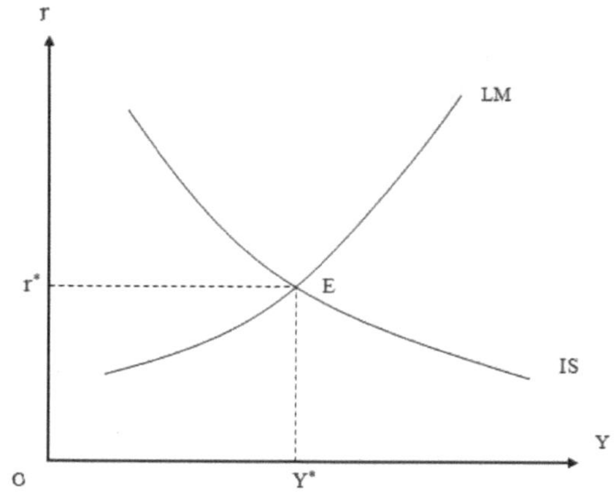

Figure 10.1 Equilibrium in IS-L model

at point E where equilibrium interest rate and income are $r^*$and Y^* respectively. This equilibrium is valid for given values of government expenditure (G), taxes (T), supply of money (M), demand for money (L^d), price level (P), and propensity to consume (MPC). So, any variation in any of these factors may cause variation in equilibrium. Government expenditure (G) and taxes (T) are fiscal policy parameters and supply of money (M) is a monetary policy parameter.

All points on LM, except E, represent commodity market disequilibrium and all points on IS, except E, would result in money market disequilibrium. At point E only is there no excess demand or supply in either the money or commodity market. Hence, there is no pressure for income or interest rate to change. Hence, E represents simultaneous equilibrium in both the money and product markets.

10.2.1 *Stability analysis*

Let us now investigate whether the equilibrium is stable or not. An equilibrium is said to be stable if economic forces tend to push the market towards it. Consider points like A, D, etc. which lie above the LM curve in the following figure. At these points the interest rate is too high for money market equilibrium to be achieved. This means that the supply of money exceeds the demand for money and so downward pressure is exerted on interest rate. This is true for all points above the LM curve. Similarly, upward pressure will be exerted on interest rates at all points below the LM curve (like points C, B, etc.) as there is excess demand for money.

Now we examine the same points with respect to the IS curve. At points such as A and B, which lie to the right of the IS curve, output exceeds aggregate demand. Investors find their stock of inventories piling up. As a result, firms will reduce their output. This is true for all points to the right of or above the IS curve. Similarly, for all points to the left of IS curve there is excess demand for goods and thus there is pressure on income to rise.

Consider point D in Figure 10.2, where there is excess supply in both the product and money markets. To be clear, money market interest rate will fall immediately before any adjustment in Y takes place. Thus economy will move to D_1 on the LM curve. At D_1, the

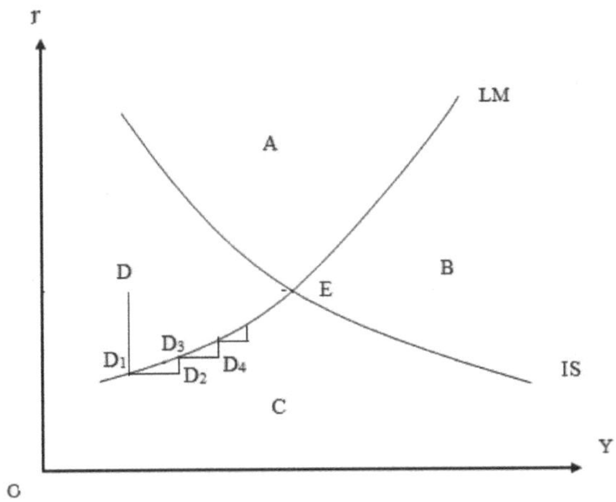

Figure 10.2 Stability analysis of IS-LM model

money market is in equilibrium though there is excess demand in the product market. Excess demand pressure will raise Y which will give rise to excess demand in the money market. This will drive up interest rate to D_3 on the LM curve. In this way market adjustments will take place along the LM curve until the equilibrium point E is reached.

10.3 Comparative static analysis — policy issues

Let us now analyse the effects of policy actions on the equilibrium levels of income and interest rate. The factors that change equilibrium levels of r and Y are those that shift IS and LM curves. We often use linear algebraic formulations, for simplicity, to find out the exact magnitude of different changes, including that of the value of multipliers. Henceforth, without loss of generality, linear IS-LM curves will be used for graphical presentation.

10.3.1 Fiscal policy and government expenditure multiplier

Let us consider how changes in fiscal policy alter economy's short run equilibrium. Changes in fiscal policy influence fiscal instruments like G and T, which can affect planned expenditure, leading to a shift in the IS curve. First, we examine the effects of one policy change, an increase in G. To analyse its impact, we consider the following IS-LM framework algebraically.

Product market equilibrium condition is given by:

$$Y = C(Y - T) + I(r) + G$$

Rewriting this equation in linear form (assuming $T = tY$, i.e., tax depends on income proportionally)

$$Y = a + b\{(1-t)Y\} + I_0 - gr + G_0. \tag{10.1}$$

Totally differentiating the previous equation

$$dY = b(1-t)dY - gdr + dG_0 \text{ (assuming, } dG_0 > 0\text{, } da = dI_0 = 0\text{)}. \tag{10.2}$$

Rewriting the money market condition $\overline{m} = L(r, Y)$ in linear form, we have

$$\overline{m} = kY - lr \; (k > 0, l > 0).$$

Totally differentiating this, we can write
(money supply remaining constant)

$$\Rightarrow dr = \frac{k}{l}dY. \tag{10.3}$$

Substituting the value of dr from Equation (8.3) in Equation (8.2) we get

$$\{1-b(1-t)\}dY = -g\frac{k}{l}dY + dG_0$$

$$\Rightarrow \left\{1-b(1-t)+g\frac{k}{l}\right\}dY = dG_0$$

$$\Rightarrow \frac{dY}{dG_0} = \frac{1}{\{1-b(1-t)+gk/l\}}. \tag{10.4}$$

Equation (10.4) gives the value of the government expenditure multiplier in the context of the IS-LM model.

Clearly,

$$\frac{1}{\{1-b(1-t)+gk/l} \le \frac{1}{[1-b(1-t)]}$$

The value of government expenditure multiplier under the IS-LM model is less than that under SKM. This is because $g\frac{k}{l} > 0$, since g, k, and l are positive, in the normal Keynesian zone of the LM curve.

The effect of expansionary fiscal policy can be explained diagrammatically as follows.

In the following diagram, initial equilibrium position is given by E_0, and initial equilibrium level of income and interest rate are Y_0 and r_0 respectively. Now consider an increase in G. This will shift the IS curve out to the right from IS_0 to IS_1. Given the LM curve, we get a new equilibrium at E_1 where equilibrium income becomes Y_1 and interest rate r_1. Clearly, after an increase in G by an amount ΔG, both equilibrium Y and r increase as a result.

As G rises, income will also rise by the familiar multiplier process, at the same rate of interest. With the rise in G, initially, aggregate demand rises both directly and then indirectly following income-induced increase in consumer expenditure. Increase in planned expenditure stimulates production, which causes total output (income) to rise. Now as Y rises in the goods market, demand for real balance in the money market will also push

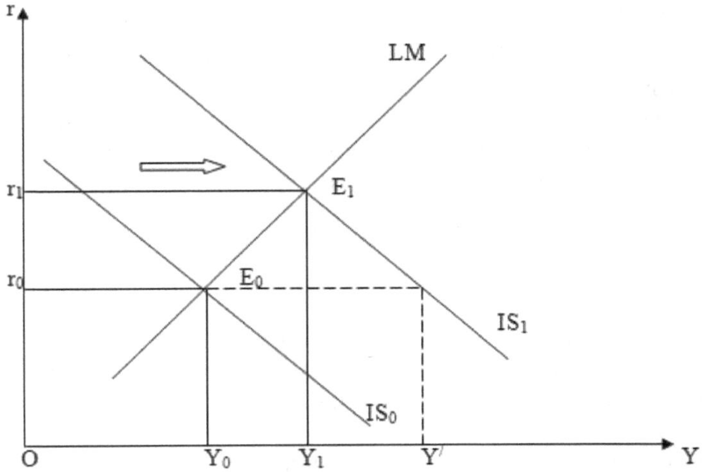

Figure 10.3 Expansionary fiscal policy through *G* change

up corresponding to every interest rate. Supply of money remaining constant, higher money demand will cause equilibrium interest rate to go up. At the new equilibrium, interest rate must rise sufficiently to keep money demand unchanged even though income is higher. This increase in *r* will reduce investment in the goods market which in turn will reduce income following the multiplier process. So, the favourable effect of an increase in *G* is partly offset by the adverse effect of fall in private investment. However, fall in income due to fall in investment will be smaller than the initial increase in income due to increase in government expenditure. In terms of the diagram, initial increase in income due to increase in *G* is $Y_0Y^/$ (i.e. $\Delta Y = \frac{1}{[1-b(1-t)]}\Delta G$ in case of income-dependent tax and $\Delta Y = \frac{1}{[1-b]}\Delta G$ in case of lump-sum tax) but fall in income due to fall in investment is $Y^/Y_1$. Rise in *r* has choked off a part of increase in *Y*. Therefore, the final increase in income due to increase in *G* is Y_0Y_1. In other words, the government expenditure is crowed out by the private investment. The tendency of the stimulative effects of fiscal policy to be offset by an induced decline in private expenditure is called *crowding out.* The effect of this crowding out (offsetting of expansionary fiscal action through a rise in the rate of interest) is the reduction in income by $Y^/Y_1$. In SKM this crowding out does not happen because there we consider only the goods market of the economy (also investment was assumed to be fixed there). The crowding out arises due to a rise in the rate of interest in the money market of the economy. Rise in *r* dampens the impact of fiscal action by reducing private investment. A combination of high *g* (interest sensitivity of investment) and high *k* (income sensitivity of money demand) strengthen the crowding out effect. In other words, low *g* and low *k* make fiscal policy more effective. Due to this crowding out phenomenon, increase in income in response to a fiscal expansion is smaller in the IS-LM model than in the SKM. So the multiplier effect in the IS-LM model is less than that in the SKM. Fiscal policy instruments may be used by the government either to stimulate the economy using expansionary fiscal policy or to control expansion in the economy using contractionary fiscal policy.

10.3.2 *Lump-sum tax multiplier in the IS-LM model*

In the IS-LM model, changes in taxes affects the economy almost in the same way as changes in government purchase do. But in this case, tax change affects expenditure via consumption. For instance, a *cutback in lump-sum tax* collection by an amount ΔT raises disposable income, which encourages consumers to spend more. It therefore increases aggregate expenditure. At any given interest rate, this change in tax policy raises the level of income by $\Delta T \times (-\frac{b}{1-b})$ (as shown by distance AC in Figure 10.4).

Therefore, the IS curve shifts to the right by this amount ($\Delta Y = -\frac{b}{1-b}\Delta T > 0$, as $\Delta T < 0$). But the equilibrium of the economy moves from point A to point B. The tax cut raises both income and interest rate. As the higher interest rate depresses investment, partially offsetting the stimulating effect, crowding out arises. Increase in income is again smaller in the IS-LM model than in the SKM.

We can measure the impact of change in lump-sum tax on the equilibrium level of income mathematically as follows:

$$\text{IS: } Y = C(Y-T) + I(r) + G.$$

Rewriting the previous equation in linear form (setting, $G = G_0$, and $T = T_0$) we have

$$Y = a + b(Y - T_0) + I_0 - gr + G_0 \tag{10.5}$$

$$\text{LM: } \overline{m} = L(r, Y).$$

Rewriting in linear form we get

$$\overline{m} = kY - lr. \tag{10.6}$$

Totally differentiating (10.5) and setting $dG_0 = dI_0 = da = 0$,

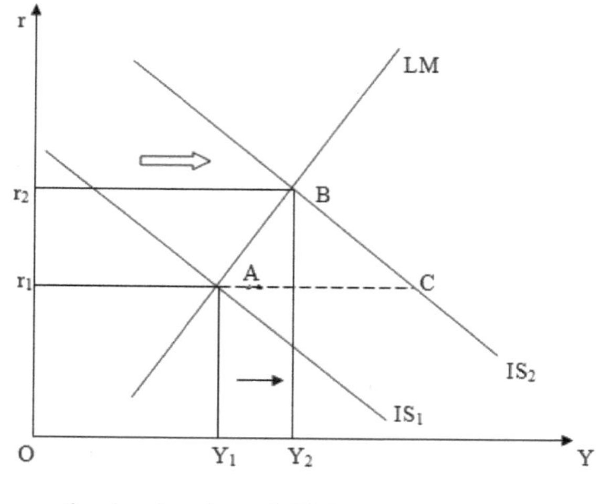

Figure 10.4 Expansionary fiscal policy through T change

we get

$$dY = bdY - bdT_0 - gdr. \tag{10.7}$$

Similarly, from the LM equation we get

$$dr = \frac{k}{l}dy.$$

Substituting the value of dr, Equation (8.7) can be rewritten as

$$(1-b)dY = -bdT_0 - g\frac{k}{l}dy$$

$$\Rightarrow \left(1 - b + g\frac{k}{l}\right)dY = -bdT_0$$

$$\Rightarrow \frac{dY}{dT_0} = -\frac{b}{(1 - b + g\frac{k}{l})}$$

(as we have considered lump-sum tax here $t = 0$ and $T = T_0$). (10.8)

This is the value of the lump-sum tax multiplier in the IS-LM model. Thus, again, the value of the fiscal policy multiplier in the IS-LM model is lower than that in the SKM. The tax multiplier is negative because taxes act as a leakage from the circular flow of income.

10.3.3 *Contractionary fiscal policy*

If there is overexpansion in the economy leading to a high level of inflation, then government expenditure may be reduced or tax can be increased as it will cause reduction in income and output along with a decrease in r. An increase in lump-sum tax collection, for example, lowers disposable income which causes consumption to decline. It therefore reduces aggregate expenditure and shifts the IS curve leftward. In Figure 8.5 this is shown

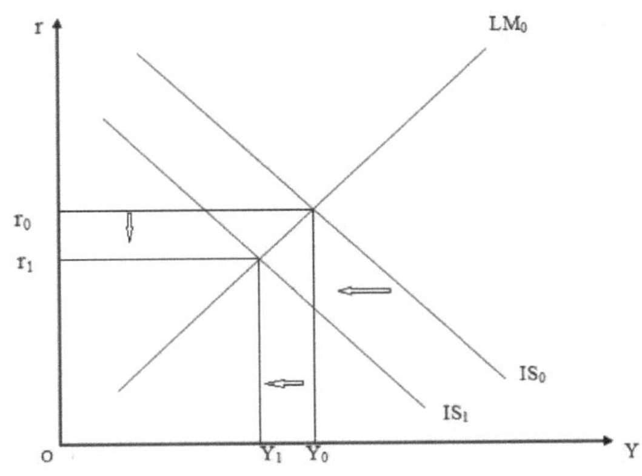

Figure 10.5 Contractionary fiscal policy

by a downward (leftward) shift of the IS curve from IS_0 to IS_1. As a result of this contractionary fiscal policy, Y falls from Y_0 to Y_1 and r falls from r_0 to r_1.

The horizontal distance by which the IS curve shifts with a change in tax is equal to $dY = -\frac{b}{(1-b)}dT$, though the actual change in Y is less than this shift. The reason is that, as a result of tax increase, when Y initially decreases, money demand and hence r also decrease. This causes investment to rise, partially offsetting the decline in consumption caused by the tax increase. This offsetting leads to *crowding out* effect. On the other hand if, instead of fiscal policy, autonomous investment expenditure is reduced, then corresponding to the original level of r, investment falls, causing the IS curve to shift leftward. We get the same result for a fall in equilibrium income and equilibrium interest rate.

10.3.4 *Effectiveness of fiscal policy depending upon the slopes of IS and LM curves*

In this subsection we analyse how effectiveness of fiscal policy is affected as a result of change in the slopes of IS and LM curves. We examine the impact of slope change of the IS curve and then that of the LM curve on the effectiveness of fiscal policy. To check whether the effectiveness of fiscal policy is more or less, the impact of the policy action on the output or income level for a given level of interest rate needs to be examined. The slope of IS curve may be different, as already discussed, due to difference in interest sensitivity of investment. Similarly, the slope of the LM curve will be different depending on the interest sensitivity of money demand.

Figure 10.6 shows the impact of expansionary fiscal policy, increase in government spending, say, on the income with two different types (with different slopes) of IS curves. Horizontal distance E_0A measures the magnitude of the fiscal policy multiplier without crowding out, which we get in SKM, as it represents change in income for the given interest rate. A steep curve, IS_0, represents less interest sensitivity of investment than that of IS_1. Now, as autonomous expenditure increases, income increases, and interest rate

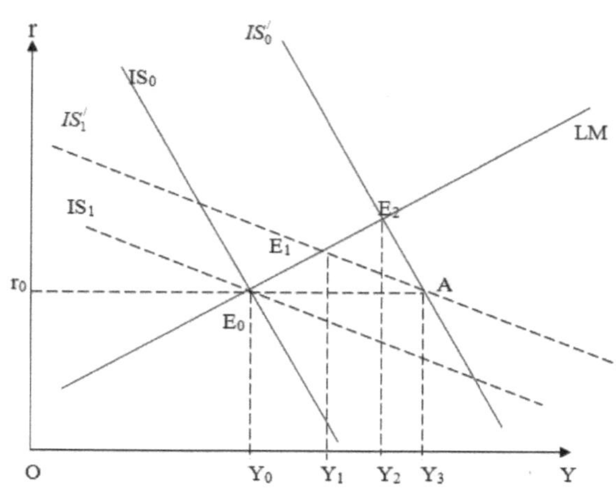

Figure 10.6 Slope of IS and effectiveness of fiscal policy

will rise to maintain money market equilibrium. If investment is not very sensitive to changes in the rate of interest, investment will fall by lesser amount. Crowding out will be smaller and income will increase more. This is what is happening with the IS_0 curve; income increases from Y_0 to Y_2, leading to a crowding out of Y_2Y_3. Clearly when interest sensitivity of investment is high (as in the case of IS_1), crowding out is larger (Y_1Y_3), and ultimate impact on income is less (Y_0Y_1). Hence *fiscal policy is more effective when the IS curve is steeper* (maybe due to low interest elasticity of investment), and its effectiveness reduces with its slope.

Let us now investigate what happens to the effectiveness of fiscal policy as the slope of the LM curve changes. With the help of the following diagram, we can show that the expansionary impact of fiscal policy will be higher if the LM curve is relatively flat. The LM curve may become flat due to higher interest sensitivity of money demand or because of interest sensitivity of money supply, as already discussed in the previous chapter.

Figure 10.7 depicts the magnitude of crowding out as well as the impact on income of an expansionary fiscal policy, when the demand for or supply of money is interest elastic (and the relevant LM curve is LM_2) vis-a-vis the case when the demand for or supply of money is interest inelastic (and the relevant LM curve is LM_1). The increase in autonomous expenditure, say, government expenditures, at the initial interest rate expands income from Y_0 to Y_3. This extra income will push up the rate of interest via the money market channel. Increase in rate of interest will swallow a part of income increase. However, crowding out, when money demand or supply is interest inelastic (and LM is steep), is Y_1Y_3, which is larger than the crowding out of Y_2Y_3 when money demand or supply is interest elastic (and LM is flat). Thus, if money demand or supply function is more sensitive to change in rate of interest, only a small increase in r is required to restore equilibrium in the money market. As a result, little crowding out of private investment takes place; income rises by relatively larger amount. Thus, *fiscal policy is more effective when LM curve is flatter.*

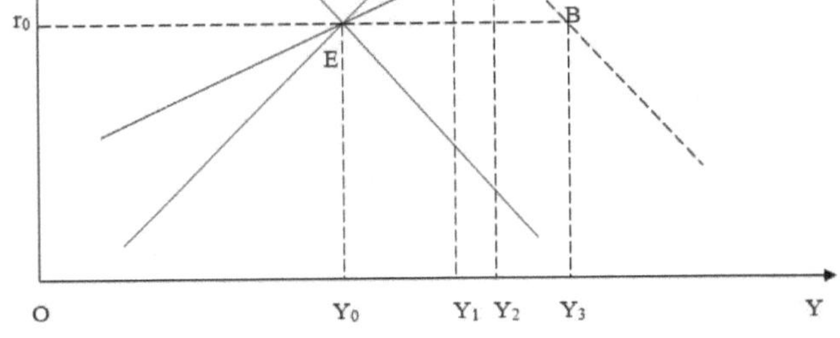

Figure 10.7 Slope of LM and effectiveness of fiscal policy

Considering only lump-sum tax and general forms of investment, saving, money demand and money supply functions, the government expenditure multiplier expression, *with interest-sensitive money supply*, now becomes

$$dY / dG|_{new} = 1 / \left[S_y + \frac{I_r L_y}{(L_r - m_r)} \right] > 0$$

Terms L_r, m_r, and I_r respectively denote interest sensitivity of real balance, money supply, and investment respectively. S_Y and L_Y represent income sensitivity of saving and real balance.

The corresponding expressions under the fixed money supply system were

$$dY / dG|_{old} = 1 / \left[S_y + \frac{I_r L_y}{L_r} \right] > 0 .$$

The logic behind more income increase is due to the positive effect of interest rate on money supply. That means the magnitude of crowding out effect under the new money supply condition is smaller than the older one. Extra income is generated by extra money supply induced by rate of interest increase.

10.3.5 *Extreme cases*

10.3.5.1 *Case 1*

In an extreme situation, if money demand function becomes perfectly interest inelastic ($l = 0$), the LM curve becomes vertical. This is also referred as the classical case. A shift of IS in this situation will only affect *r*, leaving income unchanged. This is shown in the following diagram. As a result of fiscal expansion, IS shifts right from IS_1 to IS_2 but it fails to change *Y*. It is completely crowded out by the rise in *r* as shown in Figure 10.8.

Intuitively, suppose *G* increases, putting an upward pressure on AD and hence on *Y* (at a given *r*). This attempt to increase *Y* raises money demand, which will increase *r* to

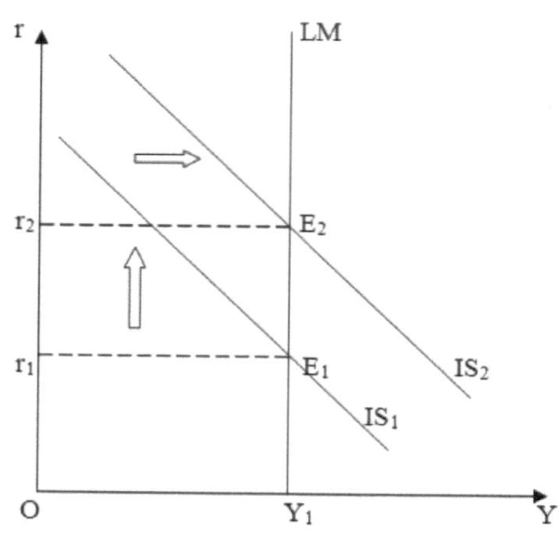

Figure 10.8 Vertical LM and fiscal policy

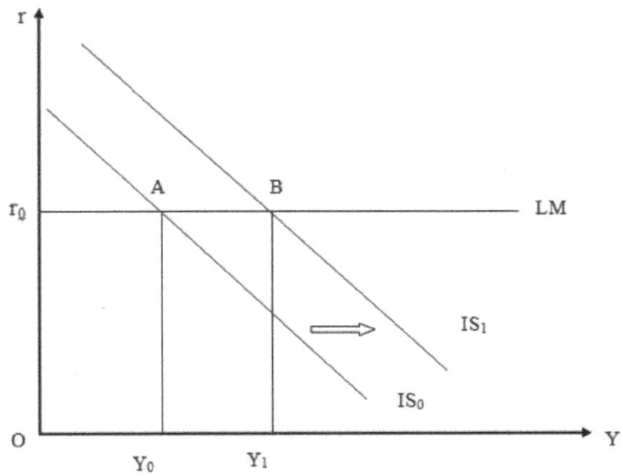

Figure 10.9 Horizontal LM and fiscal policy

regain money market equilibrium. Consequently, investment falls to bring Y back to the initial level. A situation of *full crowding out* occurs. So, *fiscal policy is completely ineffective* if LM becomes vertical.

10.3.5.2 *Case 2*

Another extreme situation occurs when the money demand function becomes perfectly interest elastic ($L_r = l \rightarrow \infty$, *liquidity trap case*). Here $\frac{dr}{dY} = 0$ and LM becomes horizontal as shown in the following diagram. If G increases, increasing Y through the multiplier process, money demand will not be affected at all. r will also remain unaffected without any consequent reduction in I and hence Y. Income rises by nearly the full amount of the horizontal shift in the IS curve. This is a case of zero crowding out, with two multipliers (SKM and IS-LM) having the same value. *Fiscal policy is fully effective* in raising Y in this extreme Keynesian situation or liquidity trap case.

Combining the previous two cases (case 1 and 2) it can also be said that, given other factors, the flatter the LM curve, the less the crowding out effect is, the greater the effectiveness of fiscal policy is.

10.3.5.3 *Case 3*

If interest elasticity of investment is zero or investment is completely interest insensitive (i.e. $I_r = g = 0$), then IS will be vertical. An expansionary fiscal policy will shift IS rightward as shown in Figure 10.10, without any crowding out effect. Expansionary fiscal policy causes interest rate to rise but it does not result in any decline in investment. Income increases by the full amount of the distance of the horizontal shift in the IS curve. Here also two multipliers (SKM and IS-LM) have the same value. Fiscal policy is fully effective here though monetary policy will be completely ineffective in affecting output.

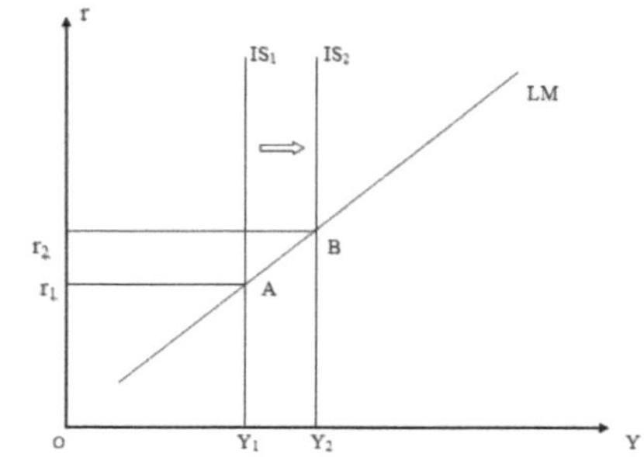

Figure 10.10 Vertical IS and fiscal policy

10.3.5.4 Comparison between Fiscal instruments in terms of effectiveness

In influencing economic activities, the impact of G change is more certain than that of T change because in case of T change the impact on Y is not direct; it is indirect in nature. Variation in disposable income (Y_d) and thereby variation in consumption by MPC times variations in Y_d affect aggregate demand and hence income. Besides, high value of MPS may also have negligible impact on Y in case of T change. But these problems are absent in case of impact of G change on Y.

10.4 Balance budget multiplier (BBM) under the IS-LM model

Balance budget change means an increase (decrease) in government expenditure matched by an equal increase (decrease) in taxes. The BBM theorem states that, under certain conditions, as a result of a balance (equal) increase in G and T, the increase in income will be equal to $dG(= dT)$.

Under SKM only the product market is considered, and investment is assumed to be autonomous. The product market equilibrium condition is given by $Y = C(Y - T) + I_0 + G$ and the value of BBM was unity. But in the IS-LM model both product and money markets are considered simultaneously and investment is assumed to be a function of rate of interest. Here the equation of the IS curve becomes $Y = C(Y - T) + I(r) + G$ (only lump-sum tax is assumed here) and that of LM is $\overline{m} = L(r, Y)$

Rewriting the equation of LM in linear form $\overline{m} = kY - lr$ and differentiating it we get $dr = \frac{k}{l}dy$.

Rewriting the IS equation in linear form $Y = a + b(Y - T) + I_0 - gr + G$ and differentiating it, we can write $(1-b)dY = -bdT - g\frac{k}{l}dy + dG$ (after substituting the value of dr). Assuming $dT = dG$ (balanced budget change)

$$(1-b)dY = (1-b)dG - g\frac{k}{l}dy$$

$$\Rightarrow \frac{dY}{dG} = \frac{1-b}{1-\mathrm{b}+g\frac{k}{l}} < 1 \text{ as } g\frac{k}{l} > 0. \quad (10.9)$$

Clearly, the *value of BBM under IS-LM is less than that in SKM.*

As already discussed, investment in SKM is assumed to be fixed (independent of r). So, increase in G results in an increase in Y via the multiplier process without affecting r and hence the full value of the multiplier is obtained. However, in IS-LM the effect of increase in income due to increase in G on the money market is considered. Increase in income in this situation leads to an increase in demand for money, and as a result "r" increases. As I is an inverse function of r, this leads to a fall in I. Hence Y will decline, at least partially. Thus, we cannot get the full effect of simultaneous increase in G and T. The net increase in income can be obtained by subtracting the fall in income due to increase in r from the initial increase in income due to increase in G and T. Final expansion of Y is less than the initial $dG(= dT)$. Therefore, the value of BBM will be less in the IS-LM model than that in SKM.

We know that the LM curve is horizontal if demand for money is extremely sensitive to the interest rate ($L_r = l \to \infty$, liquidity trap case) and IS curve is vertical if investment is completely insensitive to interest rate ($I_r = g = 0$). In these two situations, the expression $g\frac{k}{l} = 0$, crowding out will be zero. Hence, the value of BBM under IS-LM will be equal to unity, which is equal to the value of BBM under SKM as well.

10.5 Monetary policy under IS-LM

Through the monetary policy, the central bank of the country in consultation with the government changes the supply of money, shifting the LM curve and thereby affecting interest rate and income in the economy. The effect of increase in money supply on r and Y can be shown with the help of the following diagram.

The initial equilibrium point is represented by E_0 where IS_0 and LM_0 intersect each other. Corresponding to the LM curve, the LM_0 real money supply is m_0. Given the

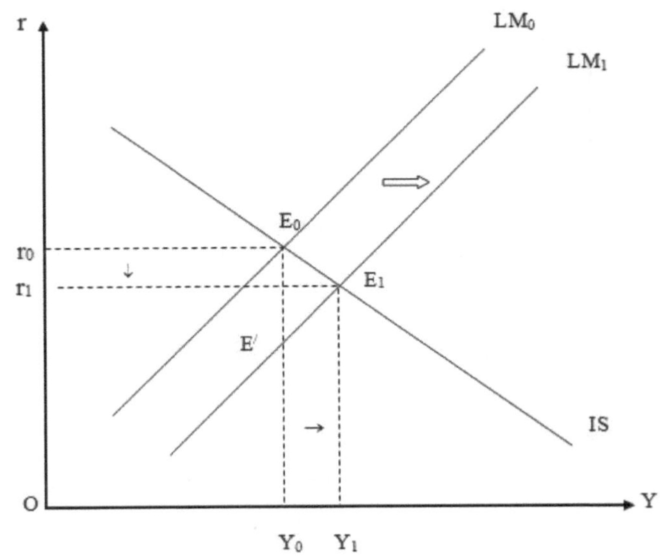

Figure 10.11 Monetary expansion

price level, as nominal money supply increases, other factors remaining unchanged, the real money supply will increase. As a result, the LM curve will shift rightward from its initial position LM_0 to LM_1. Thus, at the initial equilibrium point E_0 (corresponding to the same r, i.e. r_0), excess supply of money appears, to which public will adjust by reducing their money holding through buying other assets like bonds or start depositing extra money in banks. In this process asset prices increase and yields decline. Interest rate will then fall until people are willing to hold all the extra money created by the central bank. This brings the money market to a new equilibrium. We move immediately from E_0 to E', where the money market clears due to assumption that money and asset markets adjust instantaneously. Reduction in interest rate, again, has ramifications for the goods market. As interest rate declines, given the initial income, investment demand and hence aggregate demand increase, which will run down inventories. So, at E', there is excess demand in the goods market. In response to this, output expands and we start moving up along the new LM_1 curve. A new equilibrium is achieved when the fall in r and rise in Y jointly increase money demand by an amount equal to the increase in money supply. Ultimately, a new equilibrium will be attained point E_1 with a lower rate of interest and higher level of income than the initial equilibrium point E_0.

If the government finds that there is unnecessary overexpansion in the economy causing economic hazards like inflation, then the government may take recourse to contractionary or tight monetary policy by decreasing the supply of real balance. A decline in money stock has just the opposite effects. Accordingly, the LM curve shifts leftwards which leads to higher interest rates that cause reduction in output and income of the economy.

As shown in Figure 10.12, after a reduction in money supply, the equilibrium point shifts from E_0 to E_1, leading to a rise in interest rate from r_0 to r_1 and fall in income from Y_0 to Y_1.

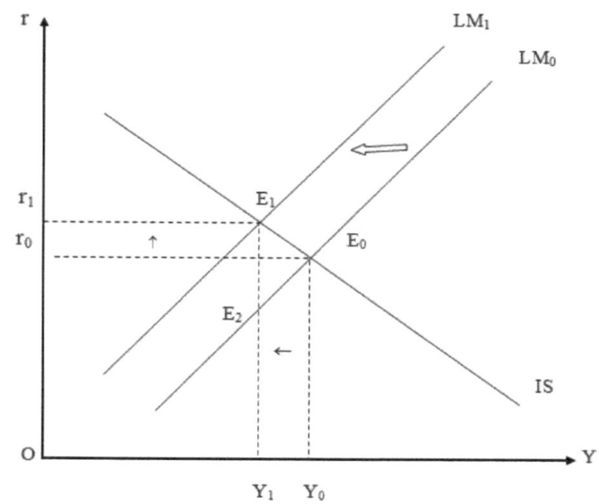

Figure 10.12 Monetary contraction

10.5.1 Mathematical derivation of the money multiplier in the IS-LM model

The money multiplier shows how much an increase in the real money supply increases the equilibrium level of income, keeping fiscal policy unchanged. Let us now derive the value of the money multiplier mathematically as follows.

Equation of IS curve is:

$$Y = C(Y - T_0) + I(r) + G_0.$$

Rewriting in linear form

$$Y = a + b(Y - T_0) + I_0 - gr + G_0. \tag{10.10}$$

The equation of LM is $\overline{m} = L(r, Y)$.

Rewriting in linear form we have

$$\overline{m} = kY - lr. \tag{10.11}$$

Taking the total differential of Equation (10.10)

$$dY = bdY - bdT_0 - gdr + dG_0 \text{ (assuming } dI_0 = 0). \tag{10.12}$$

Taking the total differential of the LM equation, Equation (10.11)

$$ldr = -d\overline{m} + kdY$$

$$\text{or } dr = \frac{-d\overline{m} + kdY}{l}. \tag{10.13}$$

Now substituting the value of dr in Equation (10.12) we have

$$(1 - b)dY = \frac{-g(-d\overline{m} + kdY)}{l} + dG_0 - bdT_0$$

$$\Rightarrow \frac{dY}{d\overline{m}} = \frac{g/l}{1 - b + g\frac{k}{l}} \text{ (putting } dT_0 = dG_0 = 0)$$

$$\Rightarrow \frac{dY}{d\overline{m}} = \frac{g}{l(1 - b + g\frac{k}{l})} \geq 0. \tag{10.14}$$

We know g, k, and l all are positive and $b < 1$, therefore monetary policy is effective in raising the level of output. Clearly when l is infinitely high (liquidity trap case) the value of the money multiplier becomes zero.

The process by which changes in monetary policy affect aggregate demand is called the *monetary transmission mechanism* (MTM). There are two steps in the MTM: the *first* is that an increase in money supply (keeping P unchanged) and hence real balance generates portfolio disequilibrium. At the prevailing interest rate and income people now hold more money than they want. This causes portfolio holders to attempt to reduce their money holdings by buying other financial assets and thereby raising asset prices and reducing yield. In other words, changes in money supply alter interest rate. The *second* stage of transmission process occurs when the disturbance spills over from the money market to the product market, as investment spending adjusts to the changing interest rate. The change in spending or aggregate demand in turn leads to income adjustment. As Y increases, L^d increases, thereby reducing the excess supply in the money market initially created. One point should be noted in this connection. If portfolio imbalance does not lead to significant changes in interest rates, or if spending does not respond to changes in interest rates, the link between money and output does not exist.

10.5.2 Effectiveness of monetary policy depending upon the slope of IS and LM curves

This subsection analyses how effectiveness of monetary policy is affected as a result of change in the slopes of IS and LM curves. The impact of slope change of IS and LM curves on the effectiveness of monetary policy is examined here. Effectiveness of monetary policy means the size of the effect on income of a given money supply change. We have already discussed in the context of fiscal policy that two important determinants of slope of IS and LM curves are interest sensitivity of investment and interest sensitivity of money demand respectively.

Following this discussion, with the help of Figure 10.13, proves that the lower the interest sensitivity of investment, the steeper the IS curve will be, the smaller the effectiveness of monetary policy will be. With expansion in money supply by monetary authority of the country, the LM curve shifts from LM_0 to LM_1 by an amount E_0N. In case of a flatter IS curve (IS_2), income increases by a larger amount, Y_0Y_2, as the magnitude of crowding out is lower here. But in the case of a steeper IS curve (IS_1), impact on Y is much less due to a larger crowding out effect. In this case, income increases only by the amount Y_0Y_1. In fact, as mentioned earlier, monetary expansion lowers interest rate, which in

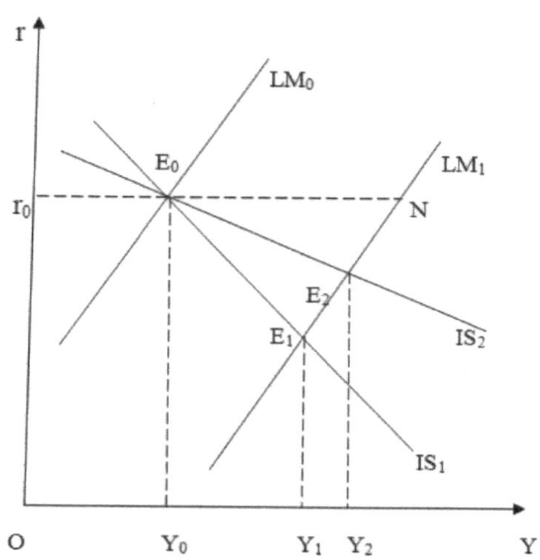

Figure 10.13 Monetary policy effectiveness and slope of IS curve

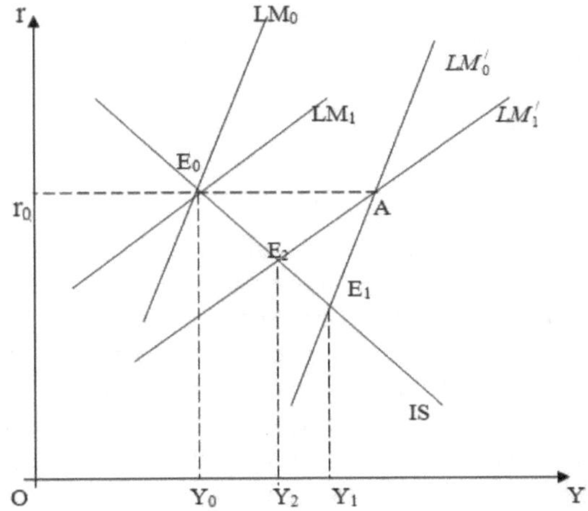

Figure 10.14 Monetary policy effectiveness and slope of LM curve

turn raises investment demand. If interest sensitivity of investment is lower (hence IS is steeper), then investment will increase by a relatively lesser amount.

Consequent expansion of *Y* will also be lower, reducing the effectiveness of monetary policy. Following a similar argument, monetary policy is more effective if the IS curve is relatively flat.

Figure 10.14 demonstrates the relationship between steepness of LM curve and effectiveness of monetary policy. As in the previous analysis, money supply expansion shifts LM curves rightward by an amount E_0A at constant rate of interest. In case of flatter LM (LM_1), interest sensitivity of money demand is higher than that of LM_0. Clearly, in case of flatter LM curves, expansion in income and fall in rate of interest are lower; monetary policy is less effective as a result.

In conclusion, it can be said that when interest elasticity of money demand is low (LM curve is relatively steeper), effectiveness of monetary policy is high and that of fiscal policy is less. Likewise, effectiveness of monetary policy increases and that of fiscal policy decreases as the IS curve becomes flatter (and interest elasticity of investment demand is larger).

10.5.3 Extreme situations

Thus, expansionary monetary policy implemented by increasing the supply of real balance shifts LM rightward, leading to a lower rate of interest from initial situation. This reduction in *r* causes increase in investment and hence income and output in the economy. The positive impact on *Y* will be small if interest elasticity of money demand is high or interest elasticity of investment is low. In this respect we can point out the following extreme situations.

10.5.3.1 Case 1

The higher the value of interest elasticity of investment, *g*, the larger the increase in investment will be following a drop in *r*. We know that high value of *g* implies a flatter IS curve. Thus, *the flatter the IS, the more effective the monetary policy will be*. In an extreme situation when *IS is vertical*, investment is not affected by monetary policy as investment demand does not depend on the interest rate ($I_r = g = 0$). Increase in money stock has no effect on equilibrium income.

Figure 10.15 shows that monetary expansion is powerless to affect output. It only reduces r, output remaining unchanged. The steeper the IS curve, the less effective the monetary policy.

10.5.3.2 Case 2

It can be shown that monetary policy is more effective when the LM schedule is steeper. If money demand is very interest sensitive (higher value of l), a small drop in r is required to remove money market disequilibrium that occurred as a result of monetary expansion. Consequently, the increase in investment and hence income will be small. If, on the other hand, money demand function becomes perfectly interest inelastic ($l = 0$), *the LM curve becomes vertical.*

A fall in interest rate itself, in this situation, does nothing to increase the demand for money and restore equilibrium in the money market. However, a fall in interest rate raises investment and income. This is the maximum possible increase in income for a given increase in money supply. None of the additional money is siphoned off as an increase in speculative demand with the fall in r. As shown in Figure 10.16, as a result

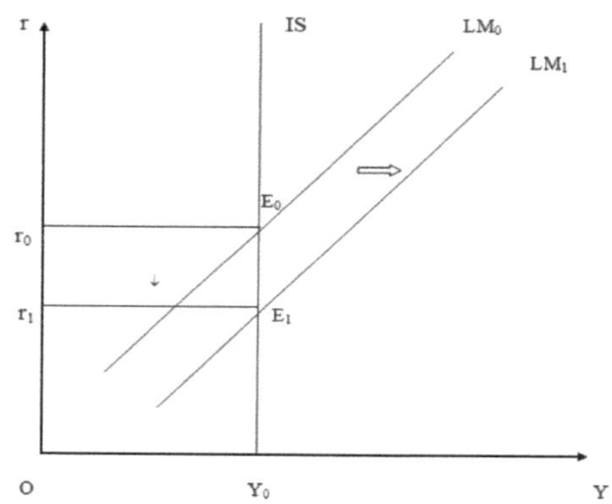

Figure 10.15 Vertical IS and ineffectiveness of monetary policy

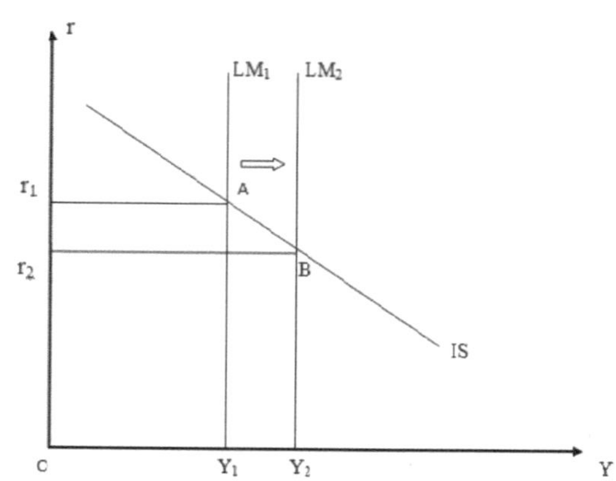

Figure 10.16 Vertical LM and monetary policy

of monetary expansion, output increases to its full extent from Y_1 to Y_2 though r falls from r_1 to r_2. Hence, in the case of vertical LM, monetary policy is fully effective, with no crowding out.

10.5.4 *Relative effectiveness of monetary and fiscal policy*

A smaller value of g (interest sensitivity of investment) implies a small effect of the money supply on Y as the IS curve is very steep in this situation. A shift in the LM curve does not cause much of a change in income. So, monetary policy is less effective in this situation. Again, when g is small there is little crowding out effect and fiscal policy is more effective in raising Y.

On the other hand, if l (interest sensitivity of money demand) is small, LM is almost vertical and fiscal policy has little effect on Y. Changes in money supply also have a large effect on Y as a result of little crowding out. Thus, a small value of l makes monetary policy more effective and fiscal policy less effective.

10.6 Monetary fiscal policy mix

Fiscal and monetary actions may interact with each other, the impact of which will depend on the interdependence. It was already discussed that, in the case of monetary expansion, rate of interest declines and investment rises. On the other hand, fiscal expansion reduces investment by raising interest rate. This is an important difference because investment is a major determinant of long-term growth of an economy. Sometimes the government may have more than one target (e.g. stabilisation and growth). In this situation the government has to use a combination of both the monetary and fiscal policies to achieve its goal.

10.6.1 *Case I*

In an economy, for example, application of expansionary fiscal policy causes a crowding out effect when money supply is kept constant. In this situation the government of the concerned country may desire to check the rising trend of interest rates and for that purpose, along with fiscal expansion, monetary expansion may be adopted. The policy of keeping interest rates constant is popularly known as monetary fiscal policy mix or accommodating monetary policy.

In terms of the diagram, we find that simultaneous adaptation of fiscal expansion (a tax cut, say) and monetary expansion causes rightward movement of both the IS and LM curve in such a way that interest rate remains unaltered at the initial level though the desired effect on Y is completely achieved. As shown in Figure 10.17, the two policy actions would increase output from Y_0 to Y_1 with the interest rate remaining at r_0. This policy cancels out the crowding out effect completely by appropriate monetary action.

Here the objective of the government is to keep interest rate unaltered. If the government undertakes fiscal policy, where the fiscal policy instrument is lump-sum tax, then $-\frac{b}{1-b}\Delta T = \Delta Y$, which shows the rise in Y as a result of cut in T with an unchanged r. Again, $k\Delta Y = \Delta m$ measures the accommodating change in money supply needed to raise Y by the same amount (ΔY), keeping r unchanged. So, to eliminate crowding out by fixing interest the rate target, we require $\Delta m = \frac{bk}{1-b}\Delta T$. This measures the

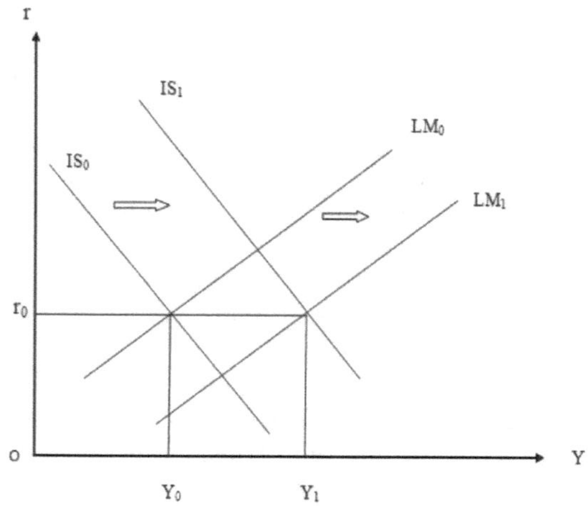

Figure 10.17 Policy mix for interest rate targeting

accommodating change in money supply needed to keep r unchanged and to neutralize the crowding out effect. Similarly, for "G" change the condition $\frac{k}{1-b}\Delta G = \Delta m$ needs to be satisfied to fix the interest rate target.

10.6.2 *Case II*

Sometimes the government of an economy may desire to raise an interest rate with a targeted income level in order to control overexpansion. Suppose an initially expansionary fiscal policy is adopted. This will shift IS rightward from IS_0 to IS_1, as a result of which both r and Y will increase (see Figure 10.18). Now to control overexpansion the government may undertake a contractionary monetary policy to keep Y unchanged.

10.6.3 *Case III*

Suppose the government raises taxes to reduce budget deficit but does not want income to fall. The IS curve shifts downward from IS_1 to IS_2 as a result of tax increase, as depicted in Figure 10.19. Both r and Y will fall as a result. The downward pressure on Y can be neutralized by increasing money supply in appropriate manner. The LM curve shifts rightward from LM_1 to LM_2 to offset the leftward shift of the IS curve. Here a tax increase does not lead to a recession, but it does cause a large fall in r, from r_1 to r_2 as shown in the following diagram. Ultimately the equilibrium point shifts from A to B with unchanged Y. Though Y remains unchanged as these two opposite effects balance, there is a change in the composition of Y.

Higher tax reduces consumption, but lower r stimulates I. Here recession is avoided by the mix of fiscal contraction accompanied by monetary expansion. Hence contraction in Y is avoided by making appropriate use of monetary and fiscal measures.

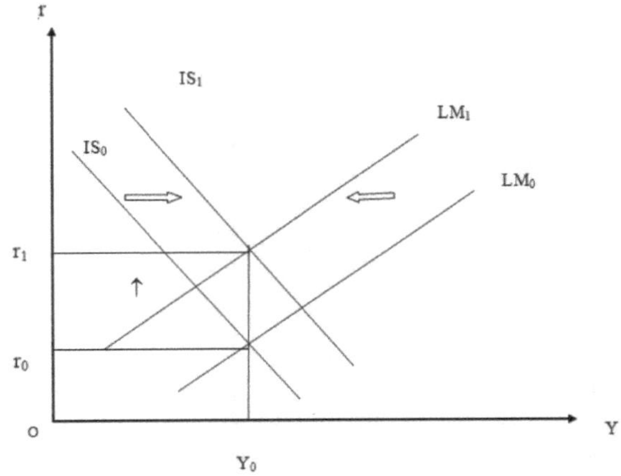

Figure 10.18 Policy mix for income targeting

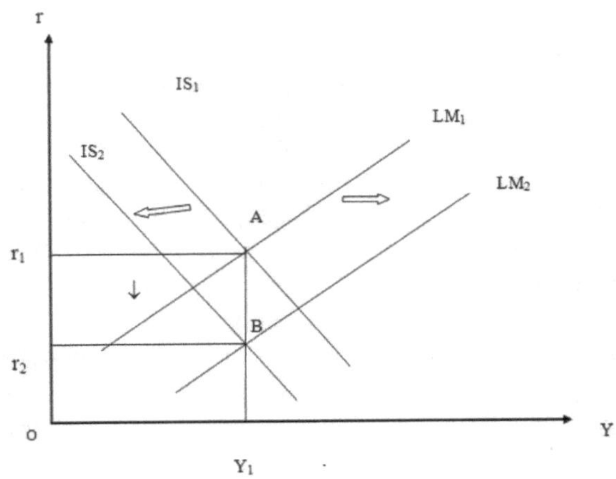

Figure 10.19 Keeping Y constant through monetary expansion and fiscal contraction

10.6.4 Case IV

Suppose Y_f is the full employment level of output and Y_1 is the aggregate demand-side output given by the combination of the goods and monetary sectors. The demand-side aggregate output is less than the full employment level of output. That means there is internal imbalance in the economy in the sense that the population size desires less output than the economy's capacity to produce. The situation of the economy has been presented in Figure 10.20.

To achieve the full employment target, the economy needs to expand its demand either from the goods sector or monetary sector or both. If expansionary fiscal policy is undertaken, only then can the economy reach full employment at point *F* but with an increase in rate of interest that can push up general price level, creating price instability. On

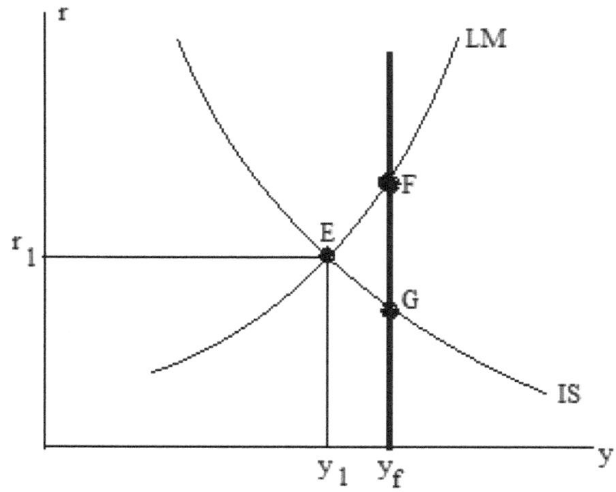

Figure 10.20 Policy composition for full employment targeting

the other hand, an expansionary monetary policy could be an ideal choice in such a sub-optimal situation. By increasing the money supply, it is possible to shift the LM curve to the right to G which can raise aggregate demand-side output to full-employment level and reduce the rate of interest which can enable price stability.

Finally, a combination of the two policies can be used to enable the economy to reach the point of full employment. The final equilibrium of the economy in this situation will be somewhere between *F* and *G* along the full-employment line. What is important here is that the choice of a policy may be made on the basis of the choice of the government to alter the composition of output, without changing its total. An expansionary monetary policy can be used to stimulate the interest-elastic component of aggregate demand, mainly the investment spending. In contrast, the effect of fiscal policy depends on exactly what goods the government buys or what changes it incorporates in the tax transfer programs.

10.7 Impact of investment subsidy in the IS-LM framework

We have already analysed the impact of increase in autonomous private investment expenditure in terms of shift in IS curve. But the government can sometimes boost investment expenditure, if required. It is possible for the government to raise investment spending by giving an investment subsidy, the impact of which is shown in the following figure.

The government can subsidize investment through an investment tax credit, whereby a firm's tax payments are reduced when the concerned firm increases its investment spending. Government investment subsidies actually reduce the firm's cost of investment, thereby encouraging total investment expenditure. An investment subsidy increases investment at each rate of interest, shifting the investment schedule rightward. At each interest rate, firms now plan to invest more, and aggregate demand increases as a result. In Figure (10.21), the IS schedule shifts from IS_0 to IS_1 by the amount of the SKM multiplier times the increase in autonomous investment brought about by the subsidy. The equilibrium point shifts from E_0 to E_1. At new equilibrium both Y and r are higher

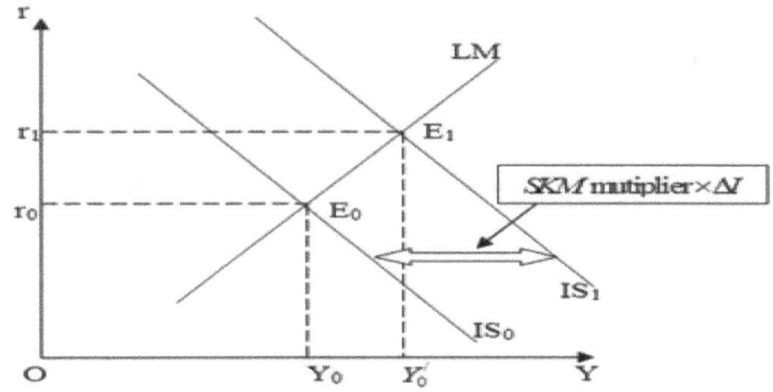

Figure 10.21 Investment subsidy and impact on Y

than the initial position. Interest rates have risen, but interestingly, investment has also increased at new higher r. The interest rate increase dampens but does not reverse the impact of the investment subsidy. This is an example in which both induced consumption and investment rise as a consequence of expansionary fiscal policy.

10.8 Possibility of crowding-in as a result of loan-financed increase in government expenditure

Let us now consider an interesting case where the government uses the loan to finance its expenditure, G. In order to explain this impact of government's internal borrowing to finance an increase in G, we rewrite the IS and LM equations as follows:

$$\text{IS: } Y = C(Y-T) + I(r,Y) + G;\ 0 < \frac{\partial C}{\partial Y_d} < 1, Y_d = Y - T;$$

$$I_r = \frac{\partial I}{\partial r} < 0 \text{ and } 0 < I_y = \frac{\partial I}{\partial Y} < 1$$

$$\text{LM: } \bar{m} = L(r,Y).$$

In the IS equation, investment is made sensitive to both rate of interest (r) and income (Y). One justification for why investment is positively related to Y might be like this. An increase in Y brings about a higher rate of utilisation of the existing capacity and therefore a higher profit rate. This will encourage producers to undertake more investment.

We explain it with the help of the following diagram.

IS and LM curves are plotted in the right panel of the diagram. Initial value of Y is obtained through the intersection between IS_0 and LM curves and is given by Y_0. In the left panel, investment is measured along the horizontal axis in the leftward direction. $I(r, Y_0)$ represents the initial investment function. An increase in government expenditure financed with an internal loan shifts IS rightward to IS_1, LM remaining unaffected. Equilibrium values of r and Y go up. Accordingly, equilibrium level of investment falls from I_0 to $I_0^/$. Again, as Y increases, investment schedule will shift to the left as investment is an increasing function of Y. The new investment schedule is given by $I(r, Y_1)$. Investment in the new equilibrium may be larger, as shown in the figure, despite the rise in interest

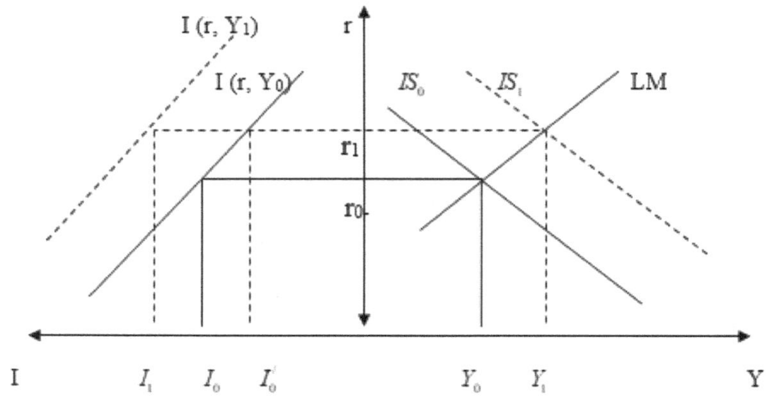

Figure 10.22 Loan financed increase in G and crowding in

rate from r_0 to r_1. Thus, a loan financed increase in G may exert a "*crowding-in*" effect on private investment along with the "crowding-out" effect. However, the former may be stronger than the latter so that we may have a situation where increase in G raises private investment.

10.9 Conclusion

The IS-LM model presents a theory of short-term fluctuation in output where real output is governed purely by effective demand. The Keynesian version of the model treats output and the interest rate as endogenous, assuming the price level as fixed until full employment is reached. The government adopts short run stabilisation policies to control recession and overexpansion. The fiscal policy is powerful but its strength is reduced by the crowding out feature. The monetary policy is effective but its effectiveness is impaired by the liquidity trap. Keynes criticized the classicists and undermined the role of monetary policy by emphasising the liquidity trap and interest insensitivity of investment. Within these constraints, stabilisation policies could be used to control any business cycle. Again, this model is based on the liquidity preference theory of interest rate, which focuses only on the money market. It derives the equilibrium value of interest rate from the money market equilibrium condition alone and relegates the loan market to the background. The neglect of the loan market is responsible for some of the major weakness of this model. It cannot show how final expenditures are financed. Again, it does not take into account the process of money creation. Hence, it cannot show how monetary authority can change money supply. Also, this model considers only the goods and product markets and ignores the role of the labour market. But without considering the labour market and production function, output cannot be determined. In this way it ignores the supply side of the model.

This model is entirely concerned with positions of static equilibrium. We have not got a dynamic specification which allows us to trace the time path of the endogenous variables. As any economy always faces random shocks, it is always out of comparative-static equilibrium. It is thus extremely important for policymakers to know the adjustment path followed by the economy. Knowledge of comparative-static equilibrium properties is not sufficient for the successful implementation of macroeconomic policies. Though the analysis is restricted for a closed economy, in this chapter, its useful extension in the context of open economy has been done in Chapter 22. In addition to that, in Chapter 26, the environmental sustainability function has been inserted in the traditional IS-LM model to determine the optimum income and rate of interest and accordingly the demand management policies like expansionary fiscal and monetary policy, and export promotion are also attempted and a set of mixed results is obtained on equilibrium income and rate of interest.

Applications

1. Suppose that the money demand function is $(M / P)^d = 1{,}000 - 100r$, where r is the interest rate in percent. The money supply is 1,000 and the price level P is 2 (fixed).

   a. What is the equilibrium interest rate?
   b. If the central bank wishes to raise the interest rate to 7%, what money supply should it set?

   Ans:

   a. Here $M^s = 1{,}000$, $P = 2$
   So, $(M^s / P) = 1{,}000/2 = 500$.
   The money market equilibrium condition is:

   $L^d = (M^s / P)$

   So, $1{,}000 - 100r = 500$
   i.e. $100r = 500$
   i.e. $r = 5$.

   So, equilibrium interest rate is 5%.

   b. When $r = 7$,

   $L^d = 1{,}000 - 100r = 1{,}000 - 100 \times 7 = 1{,}000 - 700 = 300.$

   The money market equilibrium condition is:

   $L^d = (M^s / P)$

   Putting $L^d = 300$, $P = 2$, we get

   $300 = (M^s / 2)$
   i.e. $M^s = 600$.

   So money supply should be Rs. 600.

2. In the context of the IS-LM model, how is the efficacy of fiscal policy affected when consumption depends on both rate of interest and income?

   Ans: here product market equilibrium condition is:

   $$Y = C\{(Y-T),\ r\} + I(r) + G;\ C'(Y-T) > 0, C'(r) < 0, I'(r) < 0.$$

   Taking linear form we can write

   $$Y = a + b(1-t)Y - hr + I_0 - gr + G.$$

Total differentiating both sides and assuming $dG > 0, da = dI_0 = 0$ we get

$dY = b(1-t)dY - hdr - gdr + dG$ (i).

Now the money market equilibrium condition is

$\bar{m} = L^d(r, Y)$.

Taking linear form we can write (ii)

$\bar{m} = kY - lr; k, l > 0$.

Total differentiating both sides, we get

$d\bar{m} = kdY - ldr$

So, $dr = (k / l)dY$; (as $d\bar{m} = 0$). (iii)
Substituting (iii) in (i), we get

$$\frac{dY}{dG} = \frac{1}{1-b(1-t)+(g+h)k/l} \leq \frac{1}{1-b(1-t)+gk/l}$$

Fiscal policy is less effective when C is interest sensitive than when C is independent of interest rate.

Summary

- The IS-LM model is appropriate for the short run where wages and prices do not change and there is underutilisation of capacity.
- The intersection of the IS and LM curves ensures general equilibrium of product and money markets.
- An expansionary monetary policy in the IS-LM model which is more effective the more interest inelastic is the demand for money as long as private expenditure on consumption and investment are not interest inelastic.
- An expansionary fiscal policy in the IS-LM model is more effective the more interest inelastic private investment and consumption expenditure are and the more interest elastic the demand for money is.
- Crowding out occurs when the stimulative effects of fiscal policy are offset by a reduction in consumption and investment due to the rise in the interest rate.
- Crowding out is larger the larger the interest sensitivity of investment and consumption expenditure is, the larger is the income sensitivity of money demand is, and the smaller the interest sensitivity of money demand is.

Keywords

Balanced budget multiplier
Tax multiplier
Crowding-out
Crowding-in
Fiscal policy
Stability analysis
Monetary policy
Liquidity trap

Multiple choice questions

1. When the IS and LM curves are combined in the same diagram, the intersection of the two curves determines the equilibrium level of _____ as well as the _____.

   (a) Aggregate output; price level.
   (b) Aggregate output; interest rate.
   (c) Money supply; price level.
   (d) Consumer expenditures; interest rate.

2. If the economy is on the IS curve but is to the left of the LM curve, aggregate output will _____ and the interest rate will _____.

   (a) Rise; rise.
   (b) Rise; fall.
   (c) Fall; rise.
   (d) Fall; fall.

3. If the economy is on the LM curve but is to the right of the IS curve, then the _____ market is in equilibrium, but aggregate _____ exceeds aggregate _____.

   (a) Goods; output; demand.
   (b) Goods; demand; output.
   (c) Money; output; demand.
   (d) Money; demand; output.

4. Crowding-out occurs when

   (a) A decrease in money supply raises the rate of interest which crowds out interest-sensitive private sector spending.
   (b) An increase in taxes for the private sector reduces private sector disposable income and spending.
   (c) A reduction in income taxes results in a higher interest rate, which crowds out interest-sensitive private sector spending.
   (d) A reduction in government spending induces less consumption spending.

5. A change in money supply has a greater effect upon output

   (a) The more interest-sensitive the private sector spending is.
   (b) The less interest-sensitive the private sector spending is.
   (c) The smaller the expenditure multiplier is.
   (d) The more interest-sensitive money holdings are to the rate of interest.

Answers

1. (b); 2. (b); 3. (c); 4. (c); 5. (a)

Descriptive questions

1. Explain why government expenditure multiplier in the IS-LM model is usually smaller than that in SKM. Explain under what circumstances their values are same.
2. What will be the impact on the slope of LM curve if money supply is interest sensitive?
3. Explain the impact of an investment subsidy with the help of an IS-LM diagram.

4. Suppose $T = \bar{T} + tY$

   a. How does this tax system change the way consumption responds to changes in GDP?
   b. How does this tax system alter the government purchase multiplier?
   c. How does this alter the slope of the IS curve?

5. Consider an economy where the consumption function is given by $C = 200 + 0.75(Y - \bar{T})$. The investment function is $I = 200 - 25r$. Government purchases and taxes are both 100.

   a. For this economy, graph the *IS* curve for r ranging from 0 to 8.
   b. The money demand function is given by $(M / P)^d = Y - 100r$. The money supply M is 1,000 and the price level (P) is 2. For this economy, graph the *LM* curve for r ranging from 0 to 8.
   c. Find the equilibrium interest rate r and the equilibrium level of income Y.
   d. Suppose that government purchases are raised from 100 to 150. What is the new equilibrium income and interest rate?

6. Suppose that the demand for real money balance depends on disposable income. That is, the money demand function is $M / P = L(r, Y - T)$. Using the IS-LM model, discuss whether this change in the money demand function alters the following:

   a. The analysis of changes in government purchases.
   b. The analysis of changes in taxes.

7. Use the *IS-LM* diagram to describe the short run and long run effects of the following changes on national income, the interest rate, the price level, consumption, investment, and real money balances.

   a. An increase in the money supply.
   b. An increase in government purchases.
   c. An increase in taxes.

8. Suppose that consumption function is $C = 220 + 0.63Y$, investment function is $I = 1{,}000 - 2{,}000R$, net export function $X = 525 - 0.1Y - 500R$ and money demand $M = (0.1583 - 1{,}000R)P$, where income Y, consumption C, investment I, net export X, and interest rate R are endogenous variables, government purchases G and money supply M are exogenous variables, and price level P is a predetermined variable.

   a. Find the numerical equations of the IS curve and LM curve.
   b. Solving for Y, find the level of income that satisfies the IS-LM model.

9. Do you think that the IS-LM framework violates neutrality of money?

Additional readings

Friedman, M. (1968). "The role of monetary policy". *American Review*, 58, 1–17.
Krugman, P. (2000). "Thinking about the liquidity trap". *Journal of Japanese and International Economics*, 14(4), 221–223.
Smith, W. L. (1970). *Macroeconomics*. London: Richard D. Irwin, Inc, pp. 267–279.

11 Aggregate demand and supply analysis

11.1 Introduction

So far, in the previous chapters, it is assumed that price level remains constant, in the short run. Chapter 10 dealt with two equations, that of IS and LM and two endogenous variables, rate of interest and real income or output. This fixed price model suffers from two significant flaws. First, it doesn't explain how the aggregate price level is determined and, second, it ignores the role of aggregate supply assuming that output is not limited by resources and technology. But both assumptions are highly untenable even in the short run. So, it is time to study how changes in the price level affect aggregate real output and expenditure in a closed economy. The level of aggregate expenditure associated with different price levels is called the aggregate demand function. With price level becoming an active player, the first section of this chapter derives the aggregate demand (AD) curve for the economy from the IS-LM model. Also, in a fixed price model, aggregate supply is assumed to be perfectly elastic, having no role in equilibrium output determination. But in reality, the AS curve shows the amount of outputs that firms plan to supply at different price levels. The next portion of this chapter analyses how behaviour of firms determines the shape of the AS curve. In other words, we will be able to understand how the AS curve can be derived from the micro foundation of macro analysis. This analysis assumes that wages and prices are sticky or adjust slowly in the short run due to the contractual nature of various agreements. Last, we combine the theories of aggregate supply and demand to form a more complete model of theory of income determination, called the AD-AS model. The IS-LM model is useful to examine the effect of different shocks that change interest rate and hence saving, investment, etc. But to discuss issues related to price change or inflation and unemployment, an AD-AS framework is more convenient.

11.2 Derivation of Keynesian aggregate demand from product and money markets

In this section, as already mentioned, we relax the assumption of constancy of price level in the short run to explain the determination of aggregate price level through the interplay between AD and AS. The AD curve for an economy shows the inverse relation between aggregate price level and national income or output at which product and money markets are simultaneously in equilibrium. We will consider the IS-LM model to derive the AD curve. The following diagram is used to examine the effect of rise in P on Y.

In the upper panel of Figure 11.1, IS and LM_0 curves in the (r, Y) plane intersect at E_0. Hence, Y_0 is the equilibrium level of real income. For given price level, the equilibrium

DOI: 10.4324/9781003501138-14

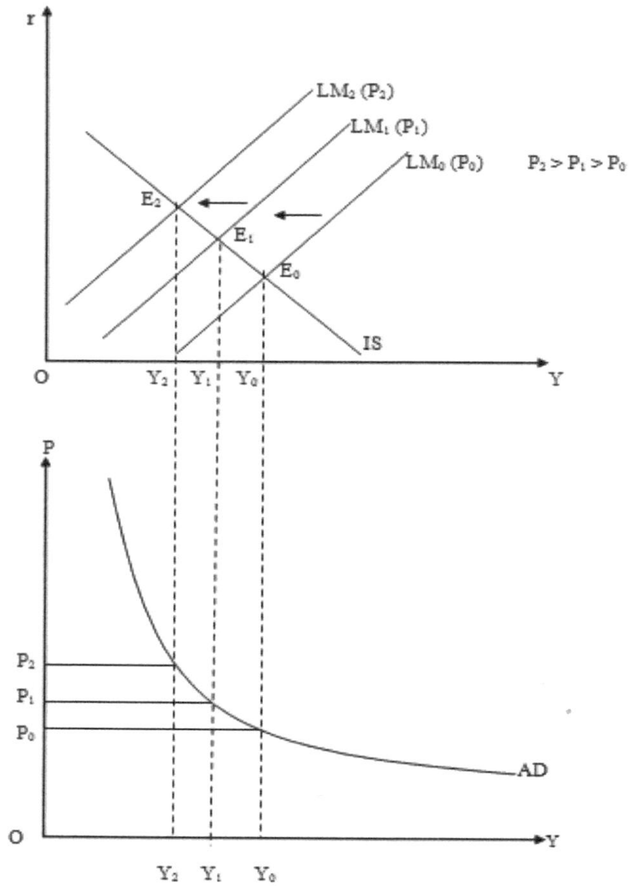

Figure 11.1 Derivation of AD curve

level of real income or output, Y_0, represents aggregate demand also. Furthermore, it is also known that a particular LM curve is drawn on the basis of a particular value of real money supply (M / P). Hence, if price level changes, keeping the nominal money supply unchanged, then the real money supply will also change.

Let LM_0 correspond to price level P_0. If nominal money supply is M_0, then real money supply will be (M_0 / P_0). Suppose, now, price level increases to P_1; real money supply will fall as a result and the LM curve will shift leftward to LM_1, IS remaining unchanged. The new equilibrium is established at E_1 at which real income is Y_1, which also represents aggregate demand at new higher price. Thus, as price level increases, aggregate demand decreases. Similarly, if price level increases from P_1 to P_2, the real value of money supply will decrease once again and the LM curve will shift leftward to LM_2; reaching a new equilibrium point at E_2. Real income or aggregate demand falls further. Clearly, we get an inverse relationship between price level and aggregate demand. By joining (P_0, Y_0), (P_1, Y_1), and (P_2, Y_2) combinations in price, in the aggregate output plane in the lower panel of Figure 11.1 we get the AD curve. It must be noted that the AD curve, derived in this way from the IS-LM model, is a locus of points showing alternative combinations of P and Y that are consistent with the general equilibrium of both product and money markets.

11.2.1 *Mathematical derivation of slope of the AD curve*

The equation of the IS curve is: $Y = C(Y - \overline{T}) + I(r) + \overline{G}$. (11.1)

Rewriting Equation (11.1) in linear form we get

$$Y = a + b(Y - \overline{T}) + I_0 - gr + \overline{G}. \quad (11.2)$$

The equation of LM is

$$\frac{M^S}{P} = L(Y, r) = \overline{m}. \quad (11.3)$$

Rewriting Equation (11.3) in linear form, we get

$$M^S = kPY - Plr. \quad (11.4)$$

Taking the total differential of Equation (11.2) we have

$$dY = b\,dY - b\,d\overline{T} + dI_0 - g\,dr + d\overline{G}$$

$$\text{or } dY = b\,dY - g\,dr \text{ (assuming } d\overline{T} = d\overline{G} = dI_0 = 0)$$

$$\text{or } dr = \frac{-(1-b)dY}{g}. \quad (11.5)$$

Differentiating (11.4) and assuming no change in money supply, we get

$$0 = kP\,dY + kY\,dP - lr\,dP - lP\,dr \text{ (as } dM^S = 0)$$

Substituting the value of dr we get

$$(kY - lr)dP + kPdY + \frac{lP(1-b)}{g}dY = 0$$

$$\Rightarrow \overline{m}dP = -[kP + \frac{lP(1-b)}{g}]dY$$

$$\Rightarrow \frac{dP}{dY} = -P[\frac{gk + l(1-b)}{g\overline{m}}]$$

$$\Rightarrow \frac{dP}{dY} = -P[\frac{g\frac{k}{l} + (1-\mathrm{b})}{\frac{g}{l}\overline{m}}] < 0. \quad (11.6)$$

So, in a normal situation $\frac{dP}{dY} < 0$, which is, the AD curve will be negatively sloped. For the sake of simplicity, we have used linear forms of IS and LM functions.

Figure 11.1 and the previous expression clearly depict an inverse association between price and quantity. A *negative slope* of AD curve can be explained as follows. An increase in price level leads to a fall in supply of real money balance. Demand for real money balance is still associated with initial income level. To eliminate this discrepancy between demand and supply of money balances, individuals will sell other financial assets, like bonds. This causes the rate of interest to rise at the given level of income, to maintain money market equilibrium. This rise in interest rate reduces investment as *r* and *I* are inversely related, leading to a fall in Y. This fall in income is associated with a higher level of price, resulting in a negative slope of AD.

11.3 Impact of expansionary policies on the AD Curve

Aggregate demand curve of an economy represents various levels of equilibrium AD (considering both product and money market) at different price levels. As shown earlier, AD is derived from the intersection of IS and LM curves. So any factor that causes intersection points of IS and LM curves to shift to the right, at a constant price, will raise AD. It can easily be shown that an expansionary fiscal and monetary policy of the government will lead to a rightward shift of the AD curve. It means that, corresponding to each price level, aggregate demand will increase due to expansionary fiscal and monetary policy. We use Figure 11.2 to examine the impact of expansionary fiscal policy on AD.

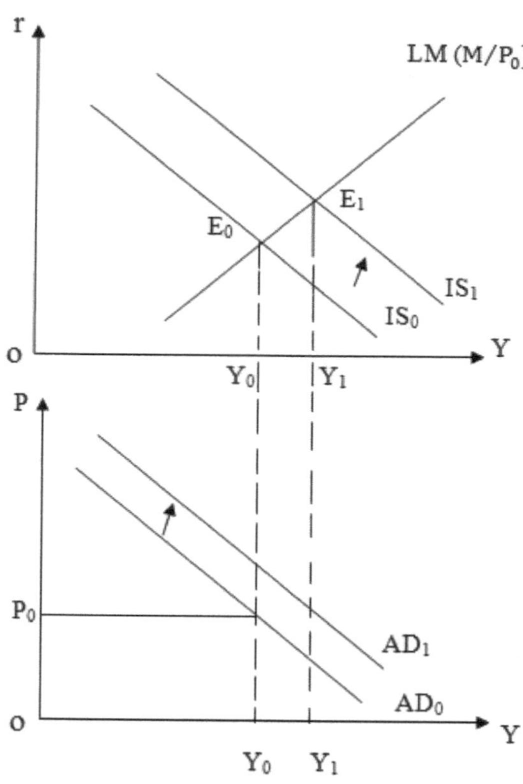

Figure 11.2 Fiscal policy and shift of AD

In upper panel of Figure 11.2, the initial equilibrium point is shown at E_0, where IS_0 intersects LM corresponding to which real money supply is given by (M / P_0). Hence when price level is P_0, equilibrium aggregate demand and hence income is Y_0. Now, suppose the government adopts expansionary fiscal policy, so the IS curve will shift from IS_0 to IS_1, LM remaining the same. A new equilibrium is established at E_1. So the corresponding aggregate expenditure and hence income is Y_1 which is greater than the previous level, Y_0. In this way, we can show that at each price level, AD for output will increase due to expansionary fiscal policy. In the lower part of the figure, AD_0 corresponds to the IS_0 curve. When the IS curve shifts to IS_1, the AD curve shifts to AD_1 showing that at each price level AD increases due to an expansionary fiscal policy of the government.

AD also depends on real money supply. In Chapter 9 it was observed that LM shifts rightward as money supply increases. We can now show that an *expansionary monetary policy* of the central bank will also lead to a rightward shift of the AD curve.

In left-hand panel of Figure 11.3, the initial equilibrium point is E_0 where LM_0 intersects IS. The LM_0 curve is drawn on the basis of real money supply (M_0 / P_0). Now suppose that the central bank increases nominal money supply from M_0 to M_1. Price level remaining constant at P_0, the real money supply will increase from (M_0 / P_0) to (M_1 / P_0), as a result of which LM will shift rightward from LM_0 to LM_1. At the new equilibrium point E_1, AD and hence real income is Y_1. Thus, it is seen that corresponding to each price level, like P_0, an expansion of money supply will result in an increase in AD. Thus, in the right-hand panel of Figure 11.3, the AD curve shifts from AD_0 to AD_1 due to an increase in money supply.

It may, thus, be concluded that expansionary policies such as increase in government spending, tax cuts, and increase in money supply shift the aggregate demand curve rightward. A reduction in real money demand, likewise, perhaps due to increased use of credit cards, will shift both LM and AD rightward. Consumer and investor confidence may also affect the AD curve. When confidence increases, the AD curve moves to the right; on the other hand, if confidence drops, AD shifts to the left.

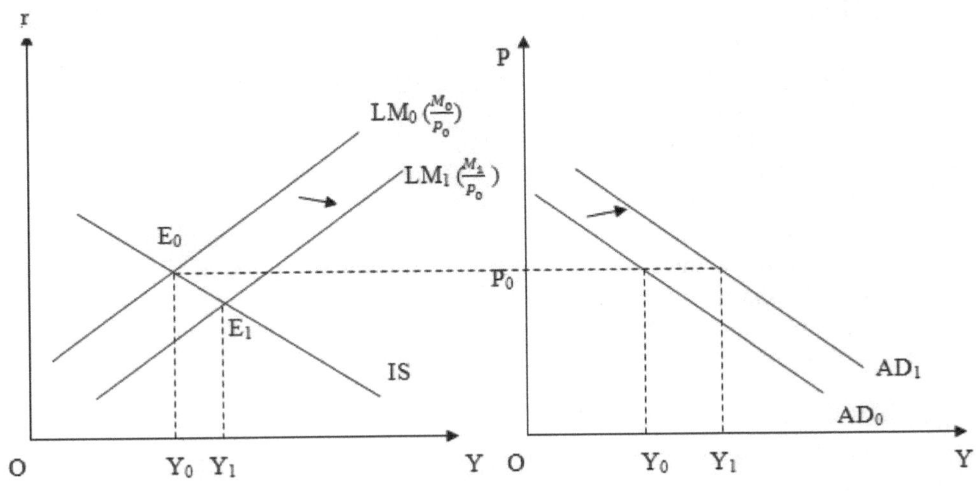

Figure 11.3 Monetary policy and shift of AD

11.4 Micro foundation of macroeconomics and SRAS curve

We have already observed that price level in the economy is determined by the interplay between AD and AS. The AS curve describes, for each given price level, the quantity of output that the firms are willing to supply. It represents the total output of goods and services that firms wish to produce, assuming that they can sell all they wish to sell, at the going price level. Thus, the nature of AS depends on the actions of firms as well as on the behaviour of factor markets. Factor markets might be complicated due to the varying beliefs about the flexibility of wages and prices and also about the nature of information with the workers and firms (perfect or imperfect) prevailing in the market. Thus, the supply side of the product market is not as straightforward as its demand side.

It is useful to distinguish between two types of AS curves. SRAS curve shows the quantity of output that firms would like to produce and sell at each price level on the assumption that price of all inputs remain constant. The long run AS (LRAS) curve, on the other hand, plots the desired quantity of output that firms would like to produce after the input prices have been fully adjusted to any exogenous shift of AD. So the AS curve behaves differently in the short run than in the long run.

In LR, the prices and wages are fully flexible and the AS curve becomes vertical. In this case, a shift in the AD curve affects the price level but output of the economy remains at the natural rate. On the other hand, in the SR, the prices are sticky and the AS curve is upward rising. In this case, the shift in AD curve affects the price level as well as causes fluctuations in output. Economists have developed various models which can be used to derive an upward sloping SRAS curve. Many economists who believe in the assumption of short run inflexibility of prices agreed to accept the SRAS relation as:

$$Y = \overline{Y} + \alpha\ (P - P^e)); \text{ where } \alpha > 0. \tag{11.7}$$

Here, Y is the actual output or real income, and $\overline{Y}$ is the natural rate of output or potential output or output corresponding to the full employment level. P is the actual price and P^e represents expected price level, which is given in the short run. α is a (positive) parameter which indicates how much output (GDP) responds to unexpected changes in the price level. The higher this sensitivity, the flatter the slope of AS ($1 / \alpha$) will be. The previous relation, usually called the *Friedman-Lucas AS curve*, in honour of these economists' contribution to the AS function, states that output deviates from its full employment level or natural rate when actual price level deviates from the expected price level. Deviation of Y from $\overline{Y}$ is directly related to the deviation of P from P^e. Graphical representation of SRAS curve for a given price expectation is shown in Figure 11.4. Any change in the price expectation (P^e) would shift the curve.

New Keynesian macroeconomists have tried to focus on the *micro foundation* behind various *imperfections* in the markets which lead to upward slope of the short run AS (SRAS) curve. The shape of the SRAS curve can be explained theoretically with the help of the following four models by looking into the frictions of macroeconomics that cause short run fluctuations in output.

- The sticky wage model
- The workers' misperception model
- The imperfect information model
- The sticky price model

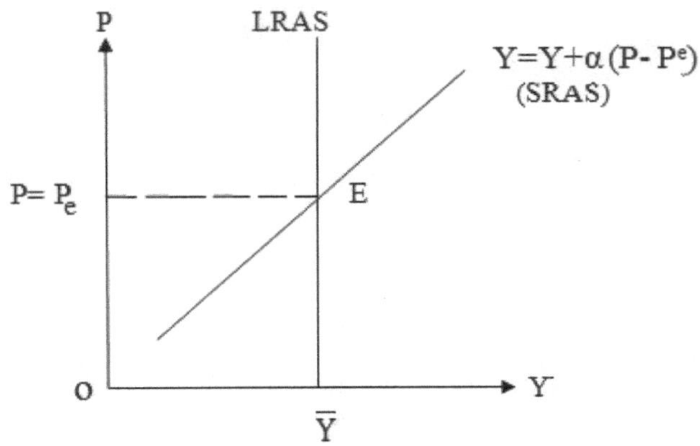

Figure 11.4 Short run AS curve

Analysing the behaviour of firms and households, all the models discuss some kind of market imperfection that causes the output of the economy to deviate from its full employment level. As a result, instead of being vertical, the SRAS curve is upward sloping. Though it is not possible to say which one is the most plausible, the main proposition of all the models is same – money is neutral in its effect only in the long run, not in the short run.

11.4.1 *The sticky wage model*

This model emphasizes the sluggish adjustment of nominal wages to explain why the SRAS curve is upward sloping. In many industries, nominal wages are set by long-term contracts between the labour unions and the management. Such contracts are made once in a while but they remain valid until the next settlement. So wages cannot adjust quickly when the economic condition changes. Even in industries not covered by formal contracts, implicit agreement between workers and firms may limit wage changes. Money wages may also become rigid because of the minimum wage law, efficiency wages, notions of fairness, social norms, etc.

Labour market imperfection in the sticky wage model implies that money wage is determined by the bargaining between workers and employers, not by forces of demand and supply in the labour market. Money wage prevailing in a period is determined at the beginning of that period. But, at the beginning of that period, neither the workers nor the employers know the price level that will prevail within the period. We assume a uniform expected price (P^e) for both employers and workers. Money wage is so contracted that the expected real wage is equal to the fair or targeted real wage mutually agreed to among the workers and the employers. In other words, nominal wage rate is set on the basis of the expected inflation rate, expected by workers and employers. That is,

$$W^m / P^e = \omega. \tag{11.8}$$

Here (W^m / P^e) is expected real wage and ω represents targeted or fair real wage. Hence,

$$W^m = P^e . \omega. \tag{11.9}$$

Labour supply is assumed to be perfectly elastic at the contracted money wage. Such a type of contractual market assumption suggests that the workers suffer from money illusion.

After the nominal wage has been set and before labour has been hired, firms learn the actual price level (P). Thus, real wage turns out to be:

$$W^m / P = \omega.\left(P^e / P\right). \qquad (11.10)$$

That is, Actual real wage = Targeted real wage × (Expected price level) / (Actual price level). This equation shows that real wage deviates from the targeted level if actual price level differs from the expected price. It should be pointed out here that the labour market is subject to nominal wage inflexibility but the product market is competitive with complete price flexibility. If the actual price level turns out to be higher than the expected one, that is, $P > P^e$, then the actual real wage is less than its targeted level. That is if $P > P^e$ or $(P^e / P) < 1$ then $\omega > W^m / P$.

Now we describe the firm's hiring decisions by the labour demand function:

$$L_d = L_d\left(W^m / P\right) \qquad (11.11)$$

Where $L_d^{/}$ (slope of L_d curve) is negative. This equation states that the lower the real wage, the more labour will be hired by the firm, so the labour demand curve is negatively sloped. Since labour supply is assumed to be perfectly elastic at the given wage, actual employment will be demand determined:

$$L = L_d \qquad (11.12)$$

It is important to note that the labour market doesn't clear in this model. The labour market normally clears by money wage adjustment and money wage is contractually fixed in this present model.

Output is a function of actual employment, that is

$$Y = F(L),\ F^{/} > 0; \text{ and } F^{//} < 0. \qquad (11.13)$$

This production function states that more output is produced by hiring more labour.

From Figure (11.5 a), it is clear if $P^e = P_1$, which means the value of actual price turns out to be P_1 which is also equal to expected price, then $W^m / P_1 = \omega$ (from equation iii). Corresponding equilibrium employment, which is demand determined, becomes $\bar{L}$; as $\bar{L} = L_d(\omega)$ (from equation iv). Equilibrium output for $\bar{L}$ employment can be obtained from production function $\bar{Y} = F(\bar{L})$ (as shown in Figure 11.5 b). Here, $\bar{Y}$ represents the natural rate of output.

Any *unexpected change in price level* (from P_1 to P_2 in Figure 11.5c) moves the real wage away from the targeted real wage. This change in real wage influences labour hired and output produced. If actual price turns out to be higher than the expected one, the real wage rate falls below the targeted level. So, the firms, who learn quickly about the new prices, will hire additional labour and produce more than the natural level of output. This would cause an upward pressure on nominal wage rate, though wage rate would go up slowly due to the long-term contracts. In contrast, if the actual price is less than the expected price, the real wage rate would be higher than the targeted level. Profit maximising firms will hire fewer workers then and produce an output below their natural level.

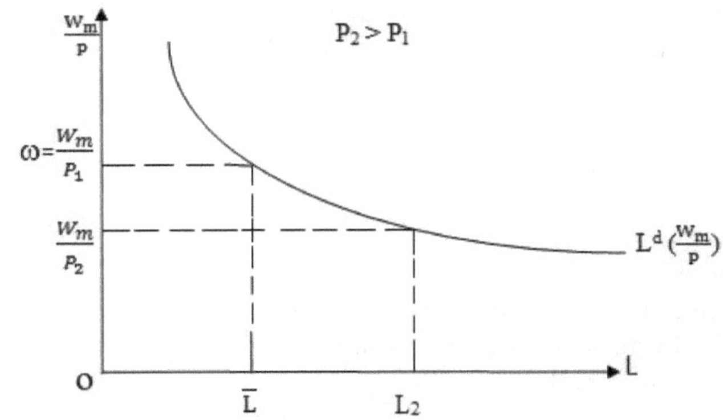

Figure 11.5a Labour market

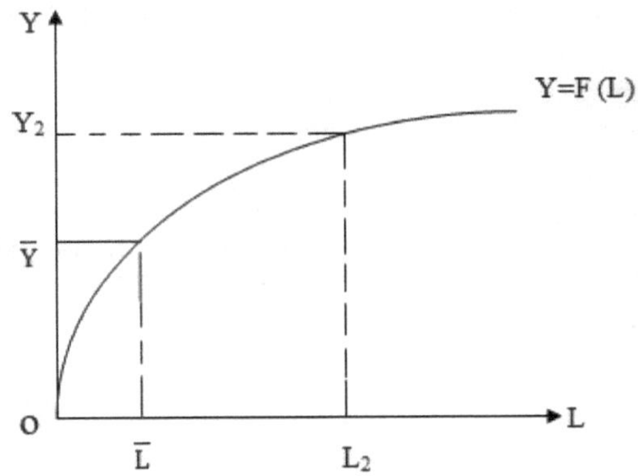

Figure 11.5b Production function

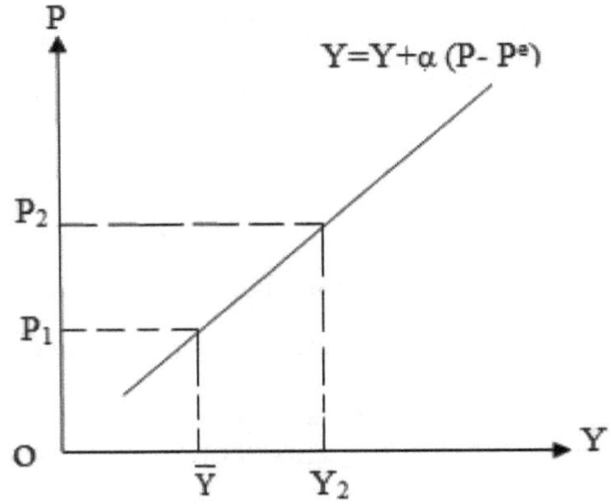

Figure 11.5c SRAS Curve

Hence, we can say that the higher the value of $(P - P^e)$, the higher $(\omega - W^m / P)$ will be, leading to higher $(Y - \overline{Y})$. Taking proportionality form, we can write:

$$(Y - \overline{Y}) \propto \left(P - P^e\right)$$

$$\text{or } (Y - \overline{Y}) = \alpha\ (P - P^e)$$

$$\text{or } Y = \overline{Y} + \alpha\left(P - P^e\right) \tag{11.14}$$

where α is proportionality constant. Equation 11.14 is the equation of SRAS curve which is shown in Figure 11.5c. It tells that as output deviates from natural level price level deviates from its targeted level.

Here, $dP / dY = 1 / \alpha > 0$ represents the slope of the SRAS curve.

11.4.2 *The workers' misperception model*

The worker's misperception model, presented by Friedman, unlike the sticky wage model, is based on the assumption that the wages can be adjusted freely and quickly to equilibrate the labour market. Workers suffer from some sort of *money illusion* in this model, in the sense that *they do not perceive price change*, rather temporarily equating a rise in nominal wage as a rise in real wage. So, they misperceive money wage change as real wage change. Thus, unexpected movements in the price level influence labour supply. Though the quantity of labour demanded by firms depends on actual real wage, the quantity of labour supplied by workers depends on the perceived real wage, which is nominal wage (W) deflated by the given expected price level (P^e). Labour demand and supply functions are as follows:

$$L_d = f\left(\frac{W}{P}\right), L_d^{\prime} < 0 \tag{11.15}$$

$$\text{and } L_S = g\left(\frac{W}{P^e}\right), L_S^{\prime} > 0 \tag{11.16}$$

The reason for this type of labour supply function is that, while deciding how much labour to supply, workers know their nominal wage but not the overall price level (P). Hence, they supply labour on the basis of expected real wage. Expected real wage can be expressed as the product of actual wage $(\frac{W}{P})$ and $(\frac{P}{P^e})$:

$$\frac{W}{P^e} = \frac{W}{P} \times \frac{P}{P^e}. \tag{11.17}$$

Equation (11.17) represents the relationship between actual and perceived real wage. $(\frac{P}{P^e})$ in this model reflects workers' misperception of the price-level. If $(\frac{P}{P^e}) > 1$, then $P > P^e$, which is, actual price exceeds the expected price. If $P < P^e$, the converse is true. Now substituting Equation (11.17) in Equation (11.16), we get:

$$L_S = g\left(\frac{W}{P} \times \frac{P}{P^e}\right). \tag{11.18}$$

Equation (11.18) represents constructed or converted labour supply function. It shows that the quantity of labour supplied depends on the real wage as well as on the worker's misperception of the price level. Asymmetric information plays an important role in this model in the sense that, though employers or firms can correctly perceive the price change, workers cannot.

Labour market clearance condition is given by $L_S = L_d$ (11.19)

Let us initially consider $P = P^e$. The initial equilibrium point in the labour market is given by E in Figure 11.6. Market clearing real wage and employment are given by $\overline{(\frac{W}{P})}$ and $\overline{L}$ respectively. Now we see what happens if the price level increases unexpectedly such that $(\frac{P}{P^e}) > 1$.

Immediately, as real wage falls, labour demand increases though labour supply remains unchanged as workers do not perceive this price change in the short run. Excess demand appears in the labour market by an amount AB, in Figure 11.6. This excess demand pressure will push money wage upward leading to an increase in expected real wage. The labour supply curve will now shift right and the market will reach a new equilibrium point E' with higher employment and output than the initial equilibrium. So, the actual output deviates from its natural rate when actual price level deviates from the expected price level. From Figure 11.6 also it follows that $(Y - \overline{Y})$ increases with $(P - P^e)$. Taking proportionality form, we have $(Y - \overline{Y}) \propto (P - P^e)$.

$$(Y - \overline{Y}) = \alpha(P - P^e)$$

$$\text{or } Y = \overline{Y} + \alpha(P - P^e) \tag{11.20}$$

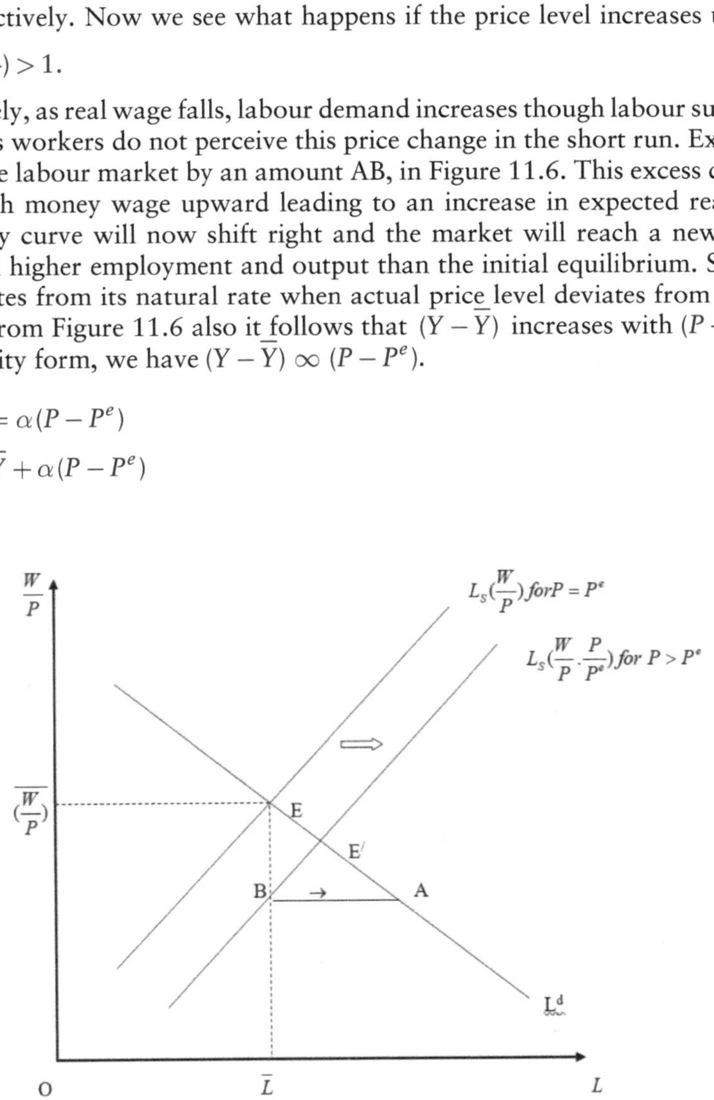

Figure 11.6 Impact of unexpected increase in price level

So, the equation of the short run aggregate supply (SRAS) curve is the same as in the previously explained sticky wage models.

Both the "sticky wage" and "workers' misperception" models are based on the assumption of *labour market imperfections*. However, the two forms of misperceptions are different and there is an important consequence of this difference. In the sticky wage model, the labour market does not clear, whereas in the workers misperception model money wage adjusts to clear the market.

11.4.3 The imperfect information model

The imperfect information model assumes that, instead of being sticky, all wages and prices are flexible and free to adjust in response to forces of demand and supply in the labour and commodity market to ensure equilibrium. This assumption is generally compatible with the long run. Yet we get an upward rising AS curve in short run because of the *temporary misperceptions about movements in absolute and relative prices*. This model assumes that *firms have difficulty in getting information about prices* in the economy other than the price of their own output.

This imperfect information model is based on the realistic assumption that each firm in the economy produces a single good but consumes many goods. As innumerable goods are produced in the economy, suppliers cannot observe the movement of all prices regularly. It has to be noted that suppliers of certain goods are consumers of other goods also. Hence, they keep a close watch on the prices of the products they produce but observe less closely the prices of all the goods they consume. So, there are temporary information barriers through which firms cannot see what is going on in other markets. They are relatively uninformed about developments in other markets and learn slowly what is happening there. Because of this imperfect information, they sometimes confuse changes in the overall level of prices with changes in relative prices. This confusion influences decisions about how much to supply and it leads to a positive relationship between the price level and output in the short run.

Suppose all prices in the economy rise by the same amount, but each firm will observe the increase in the price of its own product only. So, the firm has to make a guess about the prices of other products. If the firm doesn't adjust to its guess and thinks that its own relative price has increased, then the firm will produce more. If some other firms behave mistakenly in the similar manner, then they all produce more as a result of a general price rise.

To be more specific, let us consider an example. Consider a corn producer who earns income from selling corn and uses this income to buy goods and services. So, the amount of corn the farmer chooses to produce depends on the price of corn relative to the price of other goods and services in the economy. If the relative price of corn is high, the farmer will work harder and produce more. Unfortunately, because of imperfect information, the farmer doesn't know the relative price of corn when he makes his productive decision. As a corn producer, he monitors the corn market closely and always knows the nominal price of corn, but he doesn't know the prices of all other goods in the economy. Therefore, he must estimate the relative price of corn based on his expected prices. Now suppose all the prices in the economy, including that of corn, increase. In this case, if the firm guess this correctly, then his estimate of relative prices of corn will remain unchanged. So, he doesn't work any harder. The other possibility is that the farmer did not expect the price level to increase (or to increase by that much). So, when he observes the increase in the level of price of corn, he is not sure whether other prices have only risen or it's only the price of corn which has risen. In the latter case, the relative price of corn will be higher. Therefore, the rational influence is that some of each has happened. In other words, the farmer infers from the increase in the nominal price of corn that he must work harder to earn more.

So, when price level rises unexpectedly, all suppliers in the economy observes increase in price of those goods that they produce. So, they all predict rationally but mistakenly that the relative prices of the goods have risen. So they work harder and produce more. Thus, this model says that when actual prices exceed expected prices, suppliers raise their output. This explains the upward rising supply curve whose equation is:

$$Y = \overline{Y} + \alpha\left(P - P^e\right)$$

11.4.4 The sticky price model

The sticky price model is a *non-market clearing product market model*, based on the assumption that *firms do not instantaneously adjust the prices they charge in response to changes in demand.* Often prices are set by long-term contracts (formal or informal) between firms and customers. Frequent price changes create confusion and annoyance among regular buyers which might lead to loss of goodwill. Moreover, there is the *cost of changing prices*. New prices are to be printed, they are to be announced through newspapers, new catalogues or price list are to be distributed to retailers and customers all over the country (these are called *menu costs*). These are all costly affairs in terms of time lost and money spent. So, the sticky price model assumes that *firms have some monopolistic or oligopolistic control over the prices* of their products, hence deviate from perfect competition where a firm is a price taker.

A typical firm's desired price, ρ, depends on two macroeconomic variables – cost of production, reflected by overall price level (P) and state of demand, reflected by the level of aggregate national income (Y).

i) A high overall price (which is a weighted average of all individual prices) implies that the *firm's costs* are higher. Hence, the higher the P, the higher the price of the product charged by any firm will be.
ii) A higher level of *national income* widens the market for a firm's product. Since marginal cost increases with increase in the volume of production, the greater the demand, the higher the firm's desired price.

The firm's desired price can be expressed as:

$$\rho = P + b(Y - \overline{Y}) \tag{11.21}$$

This equation states that *desired price* ρ depends on the general price level and the divergence of actual output from its classical benchmark, which is its full employment (natural rate) level. The parameter b, which is positive, measures the degree of responsiveness of a firm's desired price to the level of aggregate output. So, the first term represents the cost influence and the second one the influence of demand.

11.4.4.1 *Diverse price behaviour*

Let us assume that there are two types of firms. Some have *flexible prices*, because they set prices according to Equation (11.21). Others have sticky prices, in the sense that they announce their prices in advance on the basis of their expectation about future economic condition, that is, on the basis of whether they expect the economy to speed up or slow down.

The price-fixing strategy of firms with sticky prices can be expressed by the following equation:

$$\rho = P^e + b(Y^e - \overline{Y^e}) \tag{11.22}$$

Here also the first term represents the expected cost influence and the second one represents the expected state of demand.

Suppose, for the sake of simplicity, that these firms expect output to be at its natural rate, then the last term, at $(Y^e - \overline{Y^e})$, disappears. Then these firms set the price

$$\rho = P^e \tag{11.23}$$

This means that firms with sticky prices set their prices on the basis of what they expect other firms to charge.

If we are to derive the AS curve, we have to find out the overall price level in the economy, which is the weighted average of prices set by the two groups of firms. If s is the proportion of firms with flexible prices, then the overall price level is

$$P = [sP + sb(Y - \overline{Y})] + (1 - s)P^e \tag{11.24}$$

Here $(1 - s)P^e$ is the price of the sticky-price firms weighted by their proportion in the economy and the first term in the previous equation is the price of the flexible price firms, weighted by their fraction.

$$P = P^e + [\frac{sb}{(1 - s)}](Y - \overline{Y}) \tag{11.25}$$

This equation gives the value of overall price level which depends on the expected price level and on the level of output. Rearranging this we have

$$(1 - s)(P - P^e) = sb(Y - \overline{Y})$$

$$\text{or } Y = \overline{Y} + \alpha\left(P - P^e\right), \text{ where } \alpha = \frac{(1 - s)}{sb}$$

In this way we can convert the aggregate pricing equation into the standard form of the aggregate supply equation, presented by Equations (11.7), (11.14) and (11.20) in three other models. Thus, the sticky price model also suggests that the deviation of output from the natural rate is directly related to the deviation of price from the expected price level.

If no firms have flexible price, which means $s = 0$, then slope of the AS curve will be $\frac{1}{\alpha} = \frac{sb}{(1 - s)} = 0$. SRAS will be horizontal in this situation.

After explaining the reason for the upward slope of the supply curve we now turn to two extreme cases where the AS curve will not necessarily be upward rising; instead, it may become horizontal or vertical.

11.5 Keynesian aggregate supply curve

According to Keynesian economists the AS curve will be *horizontal* as shown in Figure 11.7. In the short run, firms are reluctant to change prices and wages when demand shifts. Accordingly, they are willing to supply as much as is demanded at the existing price level. This might be due to the fact that there exist unemployed resources for which firms can get as many factors of production (labour) as they want at the current wage. The average cost of production, therefore, does not change as output level changes. Firms are accordingly willing to supply any amount at the existing price level in the short run. The Keynesian assumption holds good for low levels of output in the short run.

An increase in AD in this situation increases output and employment only without any change in price. There will be no dampening effect of expansionary policy.

11.6 Classical aggregate supply curve

The classical AS curve is *vertical*, as shown in Figure 11.8, implying that output is always at the full employment level. Vertical AS curve in the long run is based on the assumption that wages and prices are fully flexible and real wage adjusts instantly to ensure full employment all the time. If all the factors of production are already employed, overall production will not increase following an increase in overall demand.

In this situation, expansionary policy can not affect output, as we see in the next chapter, though price level depends on the interaction of supply and demand. If firms try to hire more labour to meet excess demand, it only bids up wages and cost of production, as all factors of productions are fully employed. So, they only charge higher prices, output remaining unchanged.

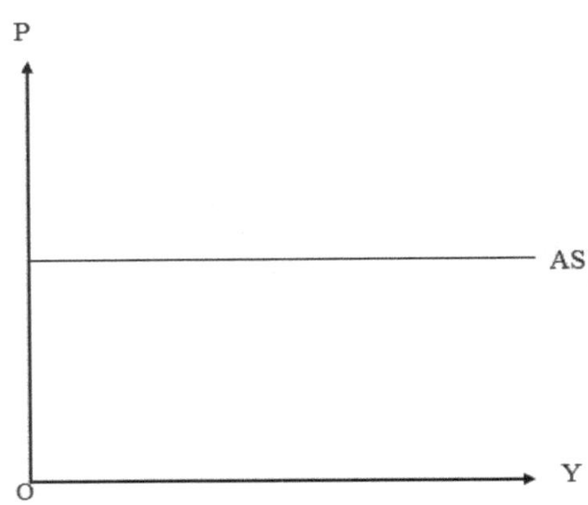

Figure 11.7 Horizontal SRAS curve

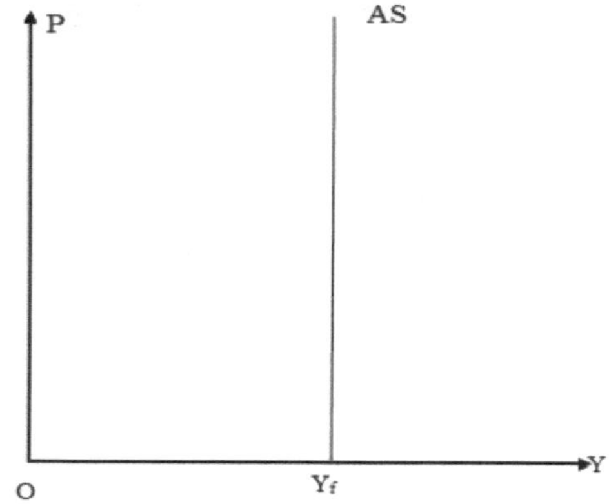

Figure 11.8 Vertical LRAS curve

Hence from the previous two extreme situations it is clear that in Keynesian zone, where wage and prices are fixed, AS is horizontal, and in the classical zone, where wage and prices are perfectly flexible, AS is vertical. In the intermediate zone AS will be rising.

11.7 Shift of the aggregate supply curve

One reason for shift of the supply curve is adverse or favourable supply shock. *Shocks* disrupt the economic wellbeing by pushing output and employment away from their natural rate. Normally there are three types of shocks that result in economic fluctuations. *Private demand shocks* are where modification of consumption and investment spending are influenced by expectations about the future course of the economy. Another type of shock is *policy shocks* which affect the demand side of the economy. These policy shocks include changes in the money supply, fiscal policy, etc. Third there are *supply shocks* that affect the production or supply side of the economy. They includes climatic change, natural disasters (earthquakes, flood, and drought), technical innovation, change in the supply of an essential input (say oil), change in productivity (introduction of new techniques, new management practices, change in quality of inputs), etc. Adverse supply shocks lead to reduction in output and employment, whereas favourable supply shocks raise them. A sudden fall in the supply of an important intermediate input, say petroleum, might be an example of adverse supply shock. This will make petroleum costlier, leading to a leftward shift of the AS curve. A sudden fall in labour productivity is another example of adverse supply shock. Fall in labour productivity will raise cost of production without any change in real wage. This will reduce employment and shift AS leftward. Figure (11.9 a) shows that as a result of such negative supply shock the AS curve shifts left from AS_1 to AS_2.

A reduction of tax on labour income which encourages work effort and improvement in labour productivity are sources of favourable supply shocks which might shift the AS curve rightward. Output will increase at each price as a result of such shift, as shown in Figure (11.9 b).

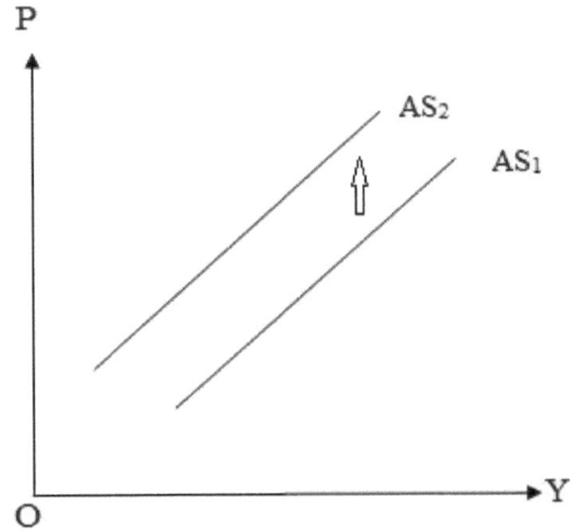

Figure 11.9a Leftward shift of AS

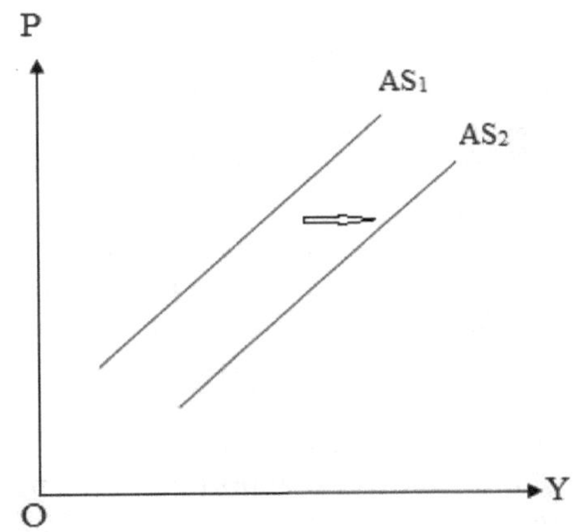

Figure 11.9b Rightward shift of AS

11.8 Determination of equilibrium price and output

AD curve shows the combinations of price and output for which both product and money markets are simultaneously in equilibrium. AS curve, on the other hand, shows the quantity of output that firms are willing to supply corresponding to each price. The intersection of AD and AS determines the equilibrium price and output for the economy. Figure (11.10) shows simultaneous determination of equilibrium price P_E and equilibrium quantity Y_E.

At point E, workers and firms in pursuit of their self-interest produce Y_E output at price P_E. Changes in any factor that shifts either AD or AS will result in different macroeconomic equilibrium.

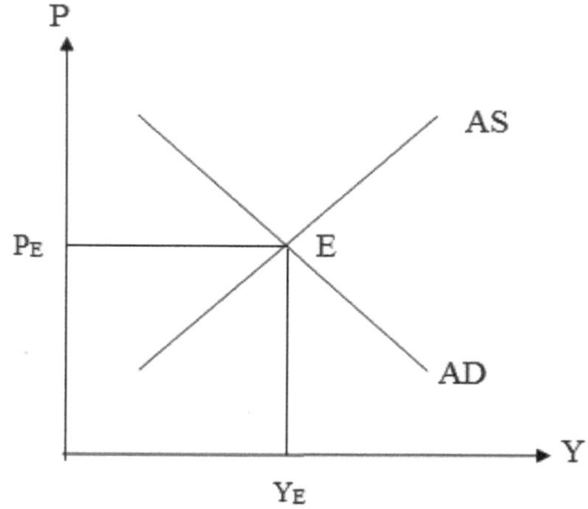

Figure 11.10 Intersection of AD and AS

11.9 Demand and supply shocks in AD-AS model

Sometimes economic shocks might disrupt macroeconomic equilibrium causing economic fluctuations. After discussing the macroeconomic equilibrium, we will now investigate the impacts of aggregate demand and supply shocks. An aggregate demand shock is some event other than a change in policy that shifts the AD curve. Introduction of a new type of credit card, for example, might reduce the need for cash holding. Demand for money schedule shifts inward, as a result, for each interest rate which has the same effect as an increase in money supply. This will shift the AD curve rightward, affecting real output immediately. There can be unexpected shifts in spending also leading to demand shock. For example, the amount of investment undertaken by businesses at any given interest rate might rise. These are examples of *favourable demand shock*. Similarly, adverse demand shock will shift the demand curve inward. The disturbance might be temporary or permanent. This distinction is important to the policymakers. A temporary disturbance might be ignored as its effect will disappear soon. But in reality, it is difficult to distinguish between temporary and permanent shocks.

Favourable demand shock, as shown in Figure 11.11, shifts the AD curve rightward from AD_0 to AD_1. Equilibrium of the economy will move from its initial position E_0 to a new position E_1 as a result. Price level rises from P_0 to P_1 and the level of output from Y_0 to Y_1, in the short run. Both output and price level rise as a result, causing an economic boom. The amount by which price level changes depends on the slope of the AS curve as well as the extent to which AD shifts. If AS is relatively flat, *P* moves very little; *Y* does most of the adjustment. Just the opposite situation will materialize if AS becomes relatively steeper.

However, monetary authority can eliminate the impact of demand shocks if it can control the money supply properly. It can dampen the boom by reducing money supply which would stabilize AD.

Now consider the opposite situation of *adverse demand shock*. Suppose increase in uncertainty about the future increased the need for cash, which in turn raised the demand for money. It would have same effect as a reduction in the supply of money, which would shift the AD curve to the left from AD_1 to AD_2, as shown in Figure 11.12. This will reduce both price level from P_1 to P_2 and output from Y_1 to Y_2.

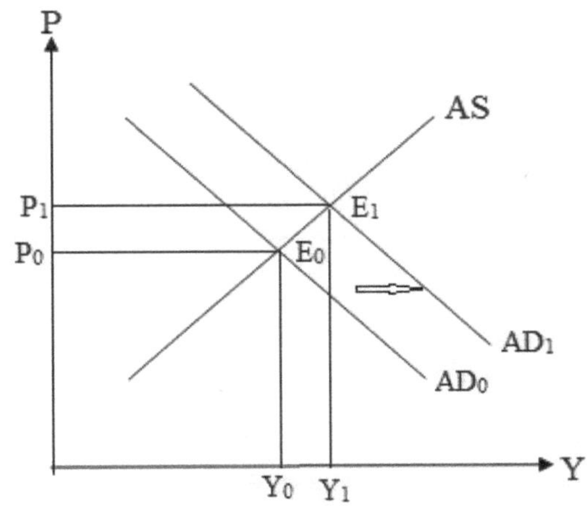

Figure 11.11 Impact of favourable demand shock

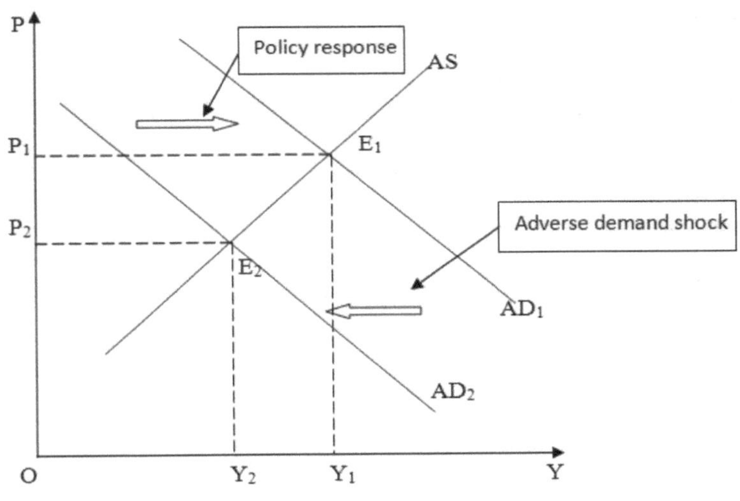

Figure 11.12 Adverse demand shock and policy response

Appropriate policy response in this situation would be to increase money supply to match the increase in money demand. This would exactly offset any leftward movement in the aggregate demand schedule. The economy will restore its initial position E_1 as a consequence. This type of demand management policy is known as *countercyclical stabilization policy*. It attempts to counter those disturbances to the economy that would otherwise cause cyclical fluctuation in output and price level.

An *adverse supply shock*, also described in previous chapter, shifts the AS curve leftward, reducing output and raising price level. Embargo in the export of crude oil by oil exporting countries, decline in labour productivity, a new environment protection law, a drought that destroys crops, etc., are examples of such shocks. The US economy faced two major oil price shocks in 1970s. The first shock struck the economy during 1971–1974, whereas the second one accelerated inflation in 1979–1980. During the first shock the oil price went up by about 80%. Since oil happens to be the major source of energy for the production of almost all goods and services, the oil price hike aggravated the adverse supply shock. The Vietnam War further aggravated the situation. Consequently, the world as a whole faced *stagflation* – simultaneous occurrence of both evils. The oil price hike raised the cost of production of the firms, so they were willing to supply output at a higher price. Figure 11.13 illustrates the effect of negative or adverse supply shock on the economy. The economy moves from E_1 to E_2 as the AS curve moves leftward to AS_2, reducing output and employment and accelerating inflation.

The extent to which price and output respond to this kind of supply shock depends on the slope of the AD curve as well as on the extent to which AS shifts. If AD is relatively flat, most of the adjustment will be done by Y; P moves little. It will be reversed if AD is very steep.

In response to adverse supply shocks, policymakers can increase AD to prevent a reduction in output. The monetary authority is said to have accommodated the supply shock if the increase in AD coincides with the shock to AS. The cost of this policy is a permanently higher level of prices. In no way can both price stability and full employment (if the economy is in full employment level initially) be attained. This is the limitation of stabilisation policies in dealing with the twin evils of unemployment and inflation simultaneously. Rather, a relatively better remedy for an adverse supply shock lies in reversing it through favourable supply shock of the same amount. This might be done through incentives given by a cut in the income tax rate of workers, a cut in the corporate profit tax rate of firms, etc.

A favourable supply shock (might be caused by technological improvements), on the other hand, shifts the AS curve rightward, leading to a fall in price and increase in output. In such a situation, if the government of the concerned country shifts AD

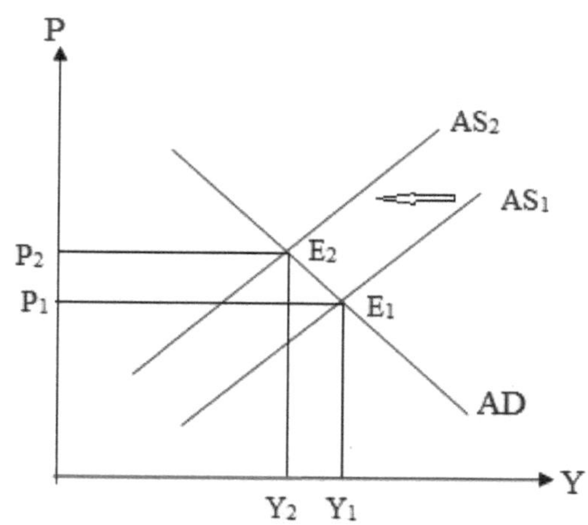

Figure 11.13 Impact of adverse supply shock

rightward by undertaking an appropriate accommodating policy measure to maintain parity with the permanent rightward shift of AS, then the economy might experience smooth growth in the absence of high unemployment with lower inflation. During 1981 to 1986 oil prices fell sharply as a new source of oil became available and the OPEC cartel weakened. This was a favourable supply shock. Another large shock in oil prices came in August 1990, following Iraq's invasion of Kuwait. The price of oil shot up as Kuwaiti oil production was halted and the United Nations placed an embargo on Iraqi oil exports. But the oil price declined rapidly after the victory of the United Nations in early 1991.

11.10 Special cases

In this section we consider two different types of AS curves – already discussed in a previous chapter – and examine the impact of demand shocks on the economy in these two situations.

11.10.1 The classical case

We have already discussed that in the classical case the AS curve is vertical at the full employment level of output. Wage price flexibility ensures this full employment all the time. Figure 11.14 shows the impact of favourable demand shock under this kind of supply assumption. As AD shifts rightward from AD_0 to AD_1, at the initial equilibrium price, spending in the economy (and demand for goods) would rise. But firms cannot obtain more labour to produce more output in response to higher demand. As firms try to hire more labour, wage rates and hence cost of production will increase. So, firms must charge a higher price for their product. Increase in demand therefore results in a higher price with unchanged output. The increase in price reduces the spending to a level consistent with full employment output (Y_f). The economy moves from E_0 to E_1. Hence classical economists were non-interventionists in the sense that they did not

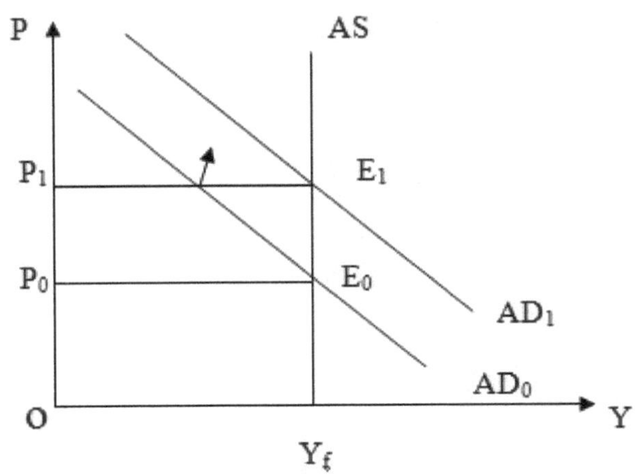

Figure 11.14 Classical AS curve and shift of AD

advocate for active monetary and fiscal policies to stabilise the economy due to its self-adjusting nature.

One point should be noted in this connection. If this expansion in AD is caused by sudden monetary expansion, then it is evident from the discussion that money cannot influence real output or employment. Hence *money is neutral* in this long run situation. The vertical long run supply curve thus satisfies the *classical dichotomy* since it implies that the level of output is independent of money supply. The classical situation holds true in the *long run* when the time frame is a decade or more and the economy approaches full capacity production.

11.10.2 *The Keynesian case*

In the Keynesian case, AS is horizontal such that firms can produce any amount of output at the given price and they hire just enough labour to produce the amount demanded. As aggregate demand rises, leading to a shift of the AD curve from AD_1 to AD_2 (as shown in the following diagram), output and employment will increase, price remaining unchanged. After a sudden rise in AD, firms are stuck with prices that are too low. With demand high and prices low, firms sell more of their product, which causes them to increase employment and production. There is no dampening effect on output through rise in *P*. The economy will move from E_1 to E_2 as shown in Figure 11.15.

The Keynesian situation becomes reasonably accurate for low values of *Y* in the short run. Keynesian economists were interventionists in the sense that they believed that appropriate use of demand management policies would reduce the undesirable fluctuations in output and employment thereby stabilize the economy effectively.

Hence, the analysis can be summarised as follows. Over very short periods of time, prices are sticky, the AS curve is horizontal, and changes in AD affect the output of the economy. Over a long period of time, prices are flexible, AS curve is vertical; changes in AD affect only the price level. Thus, changes in AD have different effects over different time periods.

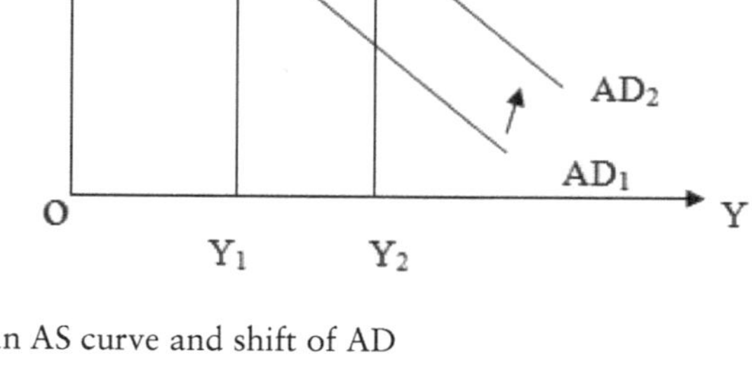

Figure 11.15 Keynesian AS curve and shift of AD

11.11 Conclusion

The aggregate demand-supply model derived in this chapter is a more generalised version of the IS-LM model in the sense that it incorporates the supply side of the economy while determining aggregate output and price level as not fixed. The model explains how AD and AS curves are used to determine equilibrium levels of price and output endogenously. The mechanism of derivation for AD and AS curves explores how different markets of the economy are interconnected. Four prominent models have been presented here to explain the upward slope of short run supply curve, though it is not possible to say which one is best. The model also depicts how any exogenous effect can shift AD and AS curves, leading to changes in the output and overall price level. Aggregate demand is not only influenced by money supply as in the classical model (presented in Chapter 3) but also by several exogenous factors, like autonomous government expenditure, autonomous taxes, autonomous investment, etc. Unlike the classical model, aggregate supply is also subject to supply shocks. Last, we use aggregate demand and supply tools to study the short run output fluctuations and the fluctuation of the price level in terms of the static model. The impact of government policies intended to smooth output fluctuations and to maintain stable prices and demand supply shocks on the average price level and output have also been explored.

Applications

1. Why is the neoclassical aggregate supply schedule vertical?

   Neoclassical analysis assumes that any price level change is incorporated immediately into the labour demand and supply schedule. Because of an immediate price adjustment, the number of workers employed is unaffected by the price level. The full employment condition in the labour market results in an aggregate supply schedule independent of the price level. Hence, the AS curve in neoclassical analysis is vertical.

2. Explain why unexpected deflation might have redistribution effects which could further dampen aggregate demand.

   Unexpected deflation (the concept of inflation and deflation has been discussed in Chapter 13) increases the real indebtedness of borrowers and the real wealth of lenders. Since borrowers or debtors are more likely to have a higher marginal propensity to consume than creditors or lenders, unexpected deflation is likely to reduce consumption. This will shift the AD curve leftward and reduce the output.

Summary

- The AD-AS model demonstrates the determination of the equilibrium levels of output and prices.
- The AD curve shows the relationship between the quantity of output and the general prices level for which products and money markets are in equilibrium. The AD curve is derived from the equilibrium condition in the goods (IS curve) and the money market (LM curve).
- It is a downward sloping curve.

- Change in any variable, other than the price level, that shifts the IS and LM curves, such as fiscal and monetary policy, consumption spending, or private investment, shifts the AD curve.
- The AS curve shows at each level of prices the quantity of real output that firms are willing to supply. It is upward rising when the expected price diverges from the actual price, maybe due to market imperfections or due to misperception regarding price change.
- While deriving the supply curve, it is assumed that wages are inflexible due to a long-term contract between firms and workers for a certain period. It is also taken into account that wage changes are not coordinated among firms.
- Favourable demand shock shifts the AD curve outward, leading to an increase in output, employment, and price level. The extent to which price and output will rise following AD change depends on the slope of AS curve.
- Unfavourable supply shock shifts the AS curve leftward, leading to a fall in employment and increase in price.

Keywords

Aggregate demand	Aggregate supply
Keynesian aggregate supply curve	Keynesian aggregate supply curve
Imperfect information	Price stickiness
Worker's misperception	Sticky wage

Multiple choice questions

1. An increase in price level

   (a) Reduces the real money supply and shifts the LM schedule rightward.
   (b) Reduces the real money supply and shifts the LM schedule leftward.
   (c) Increases the real money supply and shifts the LM schedule rightward.
   (d) Increases the real money supply and shifts the LM schedule leftward.

2. The slope of aggregate demand becomes flatter

   (a) The more sensitive investment spending is to the rate of interest.
   (b) The more sensitive the demand for money is to the rate of interest.
   (c) The smaller the value of expenditure multiplier.
   (d) The larger the nominal money supply.

3. The aggregate supply curve is

   (a) The total quantity of raw materials offered for sale at different prices.
   (b) The total quantity of final goods and services offered for sale at the current price level.
   (c) The total quantity of final goods and services offered for sale at different price levels.
   (d) The total quantity of intermediate and final goods and services offered for sale at different price levels.

4. When aggregate supply is positively sloped and there is an increase in per-unit cost of materials, aggregate supply shifts

   (a) Rightward, the price level falls and output increases.
   (b) Leftward, the price level falls and output level increases.
   (c) Rightward, the price level increases and output decreases.
   (d) Leftward, the price level increases and output decreases.

5. Which of the following statements about the labour markets is false?

   (a) The imperfect knowledge model contends that nominal wages adapt to changes in the price level.
   (b) In a rational expectations model, aggregate supply may be positively sloped in the short run because of forecasting errors.
   (c) In the "new classical" macroeconomics, aggregate supply is positively sloped in the long run.
   (d) Contemporary Keynesian macroeconomics attributes the positively sloped aggregate supply schedule to nominal wage contracts.

6. The long run aggregate supply curve is

   (a) A vertical line through the non-inflationary rate of output.
   (b) A vertical line through the current level of output.
   (c) A vertical line through the natural rate level of output.
   (d) A horizontal line through the current level of output.

7. When there is full employment and AS is vertical, a decrease in taxes

   (a) Increases the price level and real output.
   (b) Increases the price level but has no effect on real output.
   (c) Increases real output but has no effect on price level.
   (d) Has no effect on the price level or real output.

Answers

1. (b); 2. (a); 3. (c); 4. (d); 5. (c); 6. (c); 7. (b)

Descriptive questions

1. What factors are responsible for the negative slope of the AD curve?
2. If money demand is independent of the rate of interest, what effects will a rise in G have on the AD curve?
3. Why is the classical AS curve vertical? Explain the mechanism that ensures full employment in this situation.
4. What is the difference between an economy's short run and long run supply curve?
5. Derive the aggregate supply in the short run when nominal wages are set by long run contracts between the trade unions and the firms.
6. Construct a sticky price model of aggregate supply. What will be the nature of aggregate supply if i) no firms have flexible price or ii) the desired price does not depend on aggregate output?

7. What is the essence of the workers' misperception model?
8. How would you justify the asymmetric information assumption in the workers' misperception model?
9. Suppose initially there is full employment equilibrium. If new technology shifts the AS curve rightward i) explain how the economy adjusts to its increased capacity through a change in the price level and ii) what happens to the components of aggregate output?

12 Aggregate supply, inflation and Phillips curve

12.1 Introduction

The last chapter, emphasising the supply side of the economy, explained that aggregate supply of an economy will differ from potential output in the short run because of market imperfections. The impact of government policies and demand supply shocks on average price level and output were also explored there. After doing so, the concept and nature of the Phillips curve, both short run and long run, showing relation between inflation and unemployment, will be introduced in the present chapter. We will also explore how the expectation augmented Phillips curve can be derived from SRAS curve. Discussions are also carried out to show that a rising long run Phillips curve results from the inability of the individuals to adjust their expectations perfectly and instantaneously. Invoking the concept of rational expectation, this chapter tries to explain policy irrelevance result and the phenomenon called painless disinflation.

12.2 The Phillips curve

British economist A. W. Phillips, in 1958 introduced the concept of Phillips curve which originally was an inverse relationship between the rate of unemployment and the nominal wage rate. The Phillips curve postulates an empirical relationship regarding inflation-unemployment trade-offs and is not a complete theory of inflation as it involves the unemployment rate, which is itself an endogenous variable that needs to be explained. As unemployment declines, the bargaining power of workers increases and they are able to increase wages at a higher rate. Alternatively, when there is excess supply of labour in the economy, the wage rate will fall. The original Phillips curve is used to exhibit a linear inverse relationship between rate of change in nominal wage and rate of unemployment. As nominal wage rate is positively related to the rate of inflation, this concept was later modified and incorporated in modern macroeconomics to describe a link between the rate of unemployment and the rate of inflation. This short run relationship can be expressed as

$$\pi = F(u),\ F^{\prime} < 0. \tag{12.1}$$

Equation (12.1) postulates that a lower rate of unemployment can be achieved by permitting inflation rate to rise. Low unemployment is associated with tightness in labour markets and high levels of consumer income and demand. Thus, the conditions for rapid wage and price increases are present on both the demand side and cost side. Consequently, low unemployment is associated with a rapid rate of inflation. Thus, society can opt for price stability but at the cost of a high unemployment rate.

DOI: 10.4324/9781003501138-15

Let us now concentrate on the *dynamic version* where the wage price adjustment procedure will be analysed to derive the Phillips curve. In a Keynesian setup employment is determined where $W = P\,f_L$. Taking the log, $\log p = \log W - \log f_L$. Differentiating both sides with respect to t,

$$\frac{1}{p}\frac{dp}{dt} = \frac{1}{W}\frac{dW}{dt} - \frac{1}{f_L}\frac{df_L}{dt}. \tag{12.2}$$

This shows that the rate of price change is equal to the difference between the rate of wage change and the rate of change of labour productivity. As unemployment pressure causes money wages to fall, we can write

$$\frac{1}{W}\frac{dW}{dt} = \bar{\alpha} - \beta\frac{1}{U}\frac{dU}{dt}. \tag{12.3}$$

Where, $\beta > 0$, and for simplicity the linear relationship is assumed in Equation (12.3).

Substituting (12.3) in (12.2) we can write $\frac{1}{p}\frac{dp}{dt} = \bar{\alpha} - \beta\frac{1}{U}\frac{dU}{dt} - \frac{1}{f_L}\frac{df_L}{dt}$

$$\text{or } \pi = \bar{\alpha} - \beta u - \rho. \tag{12.4}$$

Equation (12.4) represents the linear version of Equation (12.1); clearly, $u = \frac{1}{U}\frac{dU}{dt}$ represents unemployment rate and $\pi = \frac{1}{p}\frac{dp}{dt}$ is the inflation rate, and they are inversely related ($\rho = \frac{1}{f_L}\frac{df_L}{dt}$ represents the growth in labour productivity). The curve (12.4) is downward sloping, as β is positive. Also, the *position of the Phillips curve depends on the growth of labour productivity*. An increase in marginal productivity of labour (f_L and hence ρ) lowers the rate of inflation for a given u. So, an increase in productivity, ρ, other factors remaining unchanged, *shifts the Phillips curve* towards the origin.

The graphically short run Phillips curve (SRPC) can be demonstrated as follows:

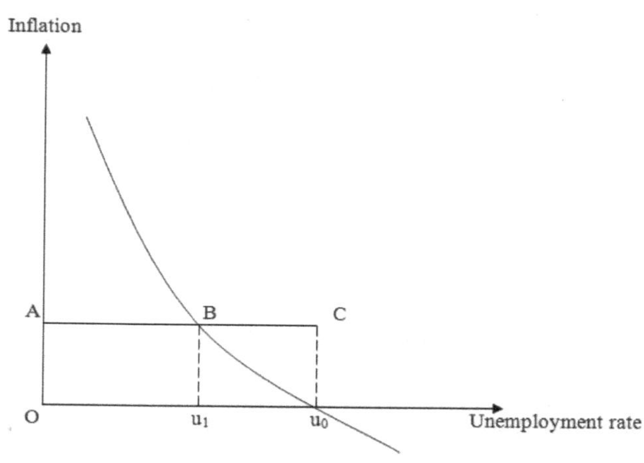

Figure 12.1 Short run Phillips curve

In the diagrammatic approach we have drawn nonlinear Phillips curves to give a generalised flavour of the analysis. However, consideration of a straight-line Phillips curve will in no way affect the main results. The point of intersection with the horizontal axis shows the rate of unemployment consistent with price stability, when real wages neither rise nor decline. Milton Friedman called this level of unemployment the non-accelerating inflation rate of unemployment (NAIRU). This is the lowest sustainable unemployment rate and represents a floor to the rate of unemployment in the long run. Any effort to reduce it by means of fiscal and monetary policies may succeed in the short run but may become frustrating in the long run. As mentioned in Chapter 1, *NAIRU* refers to a situation when all the unemployment is frictional, structural, and seasonal (but is no cyclical unemployment) and is *consistent with labour market clearance.* If true unemployment exceeds this NAIRU level, then that is due to the existence of cyclical unemployment, $(u - u_n)$, and the wage rate will be adversely affected in this situation. Cyclical unemployment increases when there is a slowdown in economic activity and an overall decline in labour demand during business cycle downturn.

Initially we start from a position that unemployment is at natural rate with zero inflation (point u_0 in the figure). This unemployment rate coincides with full employment output Y^*, mentioned earlier. If the government is dissatisfied with this unemployment rate and raises aggregate demand by expansionary policy measure, then this extra demand will cause inflation to rise from 0 to OA. If money wages do not adjust to this price rise (maybe due to existing labour contracts or maybe because the fact that price rise has not been properly anticipated by workers), real wage will be reduced. This will prompt firms to expand production and hire more labour. Unemployment falls to u_1, and the economy moves to a new short run equilibrium B with reduced unemployment rate and higher inflation. This movement is upward to the left along the Phillips curve. This also explains the *negative slope* of the short run Phillips curve (SRPC) graphically.

The Phillips trade-off between inflation and unemployment is likely to be a short run phenomenon, because it depends on the time lag between the rise in inflation and resulting money wage revision. In other words, a point like B is unsustainable. As soon as workers realise that inflation has actually risen to OA and they are working for a lower real wage, they increase their nominal wage demand. When contracts are renegotiable, money wages rise to catch up to the rise in prices. If workers succeed in pushing wage up to the full extent of the hike in prices, real wage and unemployment return to their initial natural rate only with higher inflation. The economy moves from B to C, and labour market is again cleared at the pre-existing real wage. Inflation is now built into the economy as wages and prices both have risen. If, however, the wage revision is partial, real wage stays below the original level and some reduction in unemployment can be maintained at the cost of higher inflation.

However, during the late 1960s it was observed that inflation and unemployment rates started moving in the same direction in countries like France, Malaysia, and the UK and in a mixed pattern in some other industrialised countries, signifying positive or no correlation between these two variables. Formation of a cartel by oil exporting countries, OPEC, in mid-1960 to eliminate competition among themselves, again leads to a significant increase in crude oil price, fuelling huge increase in the cost of production and a stagflationary situation. Friedman and Phelps famously predicted that as inflation rate increases, inflation expectations begin to play a major role in wage negotiation. As their predictions came true, both of them own a Nobel Prize. Since workers try to protect their real income, they are concerned with the wage adjusted for any expected change in the price level (expected real wage). Hence, workers' expectations about inflation are a major factor that determines wage changes. But when the wage contract is made, actual inflation for that period is not known, hence it is done on the basis of expected inflation, π^e. When expected inflation is higher, they bargain for higher wages and employers are also willing to grant a raise because the prices of the products they sell are expected to rise. This actually raises costs and prices. Incorporating this expectation factor, Equation (10.3) can be modified as

$$\frac{1}{W}\frac{dW}{dt} = \bar{\alpha} - \beta\frac{1}{U}\frac{dU}{dt} + \gamma\,\pi^e$$

Substituting this in (10.2), (10.4) can be rewritten as

$$\pi = \bar{\alpha} - \beta u + \gamma\,\pi^e - \rho\,. \tag{12.5}$$

Here $\beta > 0$ and $0 \le \gamma \le 1$. When $\gamma = 1$, workers are both rational (do not suffer from money illusion) and can fully adjust their money wages to compensate for expected price increase and $0 \le \gamma < 1$ if they only partially adjust their money wage. In general form the *expectations-augmented Phillip curve* can be written as

$$\pi = F(u) + \gamma\,\pi^e,\ F' < 0. \tag{12.6}$$

In the previous two equations, expected inflation (π^e) appears as a shift parameter. A rise in π^e will cause the curve to shift up by pushing up actual inflation even if unemployment stays the same. In response to changing expectations of firms and workers (π^e), the height of the SRPC moves up and down. Thus Equation (12.5) or (12.6) represents a family of Phillips curves, one for each value of π^e. If the inflation persists, people come to expect inflation in the future and the SRPC moves up.

Clearly expectation of inflation is the phenomenon that drives the movement of SRPCs. The most common way to formulate the expectation of inflation is as a function of past inflation rates. This is the idea of adaptive expectation. In the simplest form it is assumed that anticipated inflation for period "t", π_t^e, equals previous periods if actual inflation, π_{t-1}. Incorporating it in Equation (12.5), we can write

$$\pi_t = \bar{\alpha} - \beta u_t + \gamma\pi_{t-1} - \rho. \tag{12.7}$$

In the long run inflation will converge to the stationary state where $\pi_{t-1} = \pi_t = \pi$ and $u_t = u_n = u$. So Equation (12.7) can be rewritten as

$$(1-\gamma)\pi = \bar{\alpha} - \beta u - \rho \tag{12.8}$$

$$\text{or } \pi = \frac{\bar{\alpha} - \rho}{(1-\gamma)} - \frac{\beta}{(1-\gamma)}u. \tag{12.9}$$

This gives the equation of the *long run Phillips curve* (LRPC) which, having absolute slope $\frac{\beta}{(1-\gamma)}$, is clearly greater than the absolute slope of SRPC, β. Hence *LRPC is steeper than SRPC*, both having negative slope, as shown in Figure 12.2.

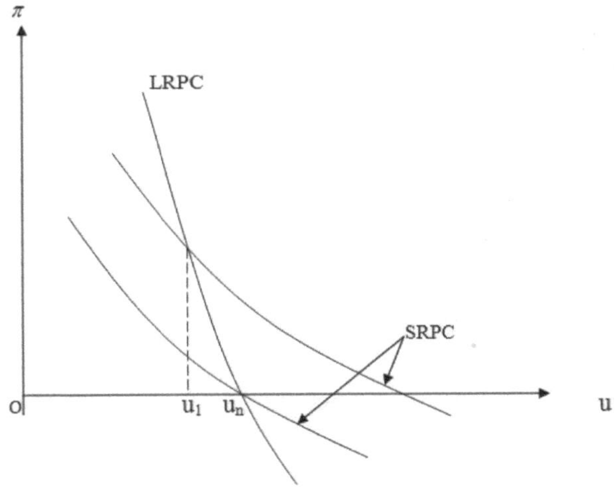

Figure 12.2 Downward sloping long run Phillips curve

If wages are perfectly and instantaneously negotiated in terms of expected wage to compensate for expected inflation, the economy will always tend towards the same natural rate of unemployment, with actual inflation equalling expected inflation. In this situation $\gamma = 1$, and *LRPC will be vertical* (evident from Equation 12.8), and the trade-off between inflation and unemployment will vanish. From (12.8) we see that if $\gamma = 1$, then $\bar{\alpha} - \beta u - \rho = 0$.

Solving this, we get $u = u_n = \dfrac{\bar{\alpha} - \rho}{\beta}$. (12.10)

This is the value of natural rate of unemployment.

With $\gamma = 1$, from Equation (12.7) we have $\pi_t = (\bar{\alpha} - \rho) - \beta u_t + \pi_{t-1}$

Substituting the value of $u_n \beta = (\bar{\alpha} - \rho)$ from natural rate expression mentioned earlier, we can write

$$\pi_t = \beta(u_n - u_t) + \pi_{t-1} \tag{12.11}$$

Considering general form we have

$$\pi_t = \pi_t^e - \beta(u_t - u_n). \tag{12.12}$$

If inflation is not fully anticipated $\pi_t \neq \pi_t^e$ a temporary trade-off between inflation and unemployment exists. But if inflation is perfectly anticipated, $\pi_t = \pi_t^e$, as in the long run, then the trade-off vanishes. *The long run Phillips curve will be vertical* at $u = u_n$.

Now we concentrate on the *long run adjustment procedure* and derivation of the long run Phillips curve with the help of the following diagram. Each SRPC is drawn for a given expected rate of inflation as given by Equation (12.5) or (12.6). To keep the mathematical formulation simple, as already mentioned, we have considered linear wage and price adjustment equations and derived a linear relationship between inflation rate and unemployment; in the case of graphical representation we will generalise by drawing nonlinear curves without affecting the results of the model. We start from a position of stable price level and constant money wages. For simplicity we further assume that meanwhile there is no growth in labour productivity ($\rho = 0$). The lowest curve, $SRPC_0$ passing through u_n (natural rate) is based on an expectation of stable prices ($\pi^e = 0$). If the government stimulates aggregate demand to reduce unemployment to u_1, then in the short run, employment increases. As the rise in price following the rise in aggregate demand is not immediately anticipated by the workers and their expected price remains the same and real wage falls as a consequence. The economy will move from N to M in the short run with π_1% inflation and u_1% unemployment ($u_1 < u_n$). It can be concluded thus: expansionary policies will move the unemployment rate temporarily below the natural rate.

However, as workers anticipate that prices have risen by π_1%, they put pressure for a rise of π_1% in nominal wage. Once they succeed, real wage (and hence unemployment) comes back to its original level and the economy moves to *T* on a higher Phillips curve, $SRPC_1$ (with $\pi^e = \pi_1$%), which will pass through the point (u_n, π_1). The policymakers who are not satisfied with this return of unemployment to its natural rate may still pursue a target unemployment rate below the natural rate, like u_1, by stimulating AD further through expansionary policies. Suppose this time inflation rises to, say, π_2%. Until workers come to anticipate further increase in inflation, unemployment falls below u_n. After a certain time, workers will anticipate the higher inflation rate and the SRPC will again shift upward ($SRPC_2$ with $\pi^e = \pi_2$%). The economy will come back to its natural rate with π_2% rate of inflation at point S. If policymakers again attempt to do this, then eventually, they will understand that anticipated inflation fails to generate any reduction in unemployment. Accelerating inflation through expansionary policy will ultimately stop. The long run Phillips curve showing the relationship between inflation and unemployment, when inflation is fully anticipated, is *vertical*. The negative relationship

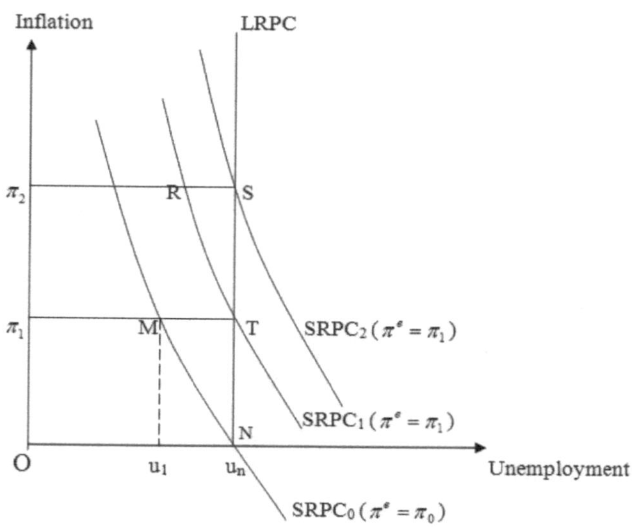

Figure 12.3 Vertical long run Phillips curve

between unemployment and inflation no longer exists. If policymakers attempt to reduce the unemployment rate to a level less than the natural rate, they may be successful for the time being. But as workers adjust their expectations in regard to the new higher rate of inflation, the short run relationship shifts, and the trade-off between inflation and unemployment evaporates. Keynesians ignored this price expectation and thus could not visualise LRPC.

Apparent contradiction of late 1960s and early1970s can be resolved with this concept of the expectation-augmented Phillips curve. In the absence of oil price shock or any other adverse supply shock, the relation between inflation and unemployment was negative. But when any adverse supply shock struck the economy leading to lower output and employment and higher unemployment, people revised their inflationary expectation upward as well. This leads to upward shift of SRPC, resulting in higher inflation as well as higher unemployment.

12.3 Duality between aggregate supply and Phillips curve

In the previous section we derived the equation of the expectation-augmented short run Phillips curve, where actual inflation depends inversely on unemployment rate and inflation expectation acted as a shift parameter. Normally there are two types of inflation: demand-pull and cost-push. In Chapter 5 we discussed in detail the causes and effects of these types of inflation on the economy. As the Phillips curve establishes the relationship between inflation and unemployment, it should incorporate different sources from which inflation can arise into its equation. *Demand-pull inflation* has already been taken care of by the term $(u - u_n)$, representing cyclical unemployment, deviation of unemployment from its natural rate. As unemployment falls below its natural rate, aggregate demand rises, pulling the price level upward. This explains demand-pull inflation. The coefficient β of the cyclical unemployment term, in Equation 12.12, measures the responsiveness of inflation to *cyclical unemployment*. The minus sign before β explains that high unemployment reduces inflation. But the equation of the Phillips curve given by Equation (12.12) has not considered another important source, which is cost-push inflation (discussed in detail in Chapter 5), which arises mainly due to adverse supply shock. We have, though, discussed the impact of supply shocks in terms of AD-AS analysis. One way to incorporate it is to add a supply shock term (ε) in the Phillips curve equation such that, whenever $\varepsilon > 0$ due to adverse supply shock, inflation will increase. A favourable supply shock $(\varepsilon < 0)$, on the other hand, will cause the rate of inflation to fall.

After making this small adjustment to inflation unemployment short run trade-off, Equation (12.12) can be modified as (ignoring subscript "t" to concentrate on the static version only)

$$\pi = \pi^e - \beta(u - u_n) + \varepsilon. \tag{12.13}$$

It is evident from expectations-augmented Phillips curve equation mentioned earlier that actual inflation depends on three factors:

i) Expected inflation (π^e).
ii) Cyclical unemployment, which leads to demand-pull inflation $(u - \mathrm{u}_n)$.
iii) Supply shock which is a source of cost-push inflation (ε).

Our motive to introduce the concept of the Phillips curve in this chapter is to establish the relationship between aggregate supply curve and the Phillips curve. According to the SRAS equation, output is related to unexpected movements in the price level whereas, according to the Phillips curve, equilibrium unemployment is related to unexpected movement in the inflation rate. If we consider movement upward along the AS curve, both price and output and hence employment levels increase. In other words, for movement along the AS curve in an upward direction, inflation rises and unemployment falls; which are similar to the upward movement along the negatively sloped short run Phillips curve. Thus, the Phillips curve and aggregate supply curve can be viewed as *two sides of the same coin.*

The equation of Phillips curve can be derived from the aggregate supply (AS) equation following three simple steps – *subtraction, substitution, and addition.*

The equation of the AS curve, previously presented by Equation (11.7), is:

$$Y = \overline{Y} + \alpha(P - P^e)$$

$$Y = \overline{Y} + \alpha P - \alpha P^e$$

$$\alpha P = \alpha P^e + Y - \overline{Y}$$

$$P = \frac{(\alpha P^e + Y - \overline{Y})}{\alpha}$$

$$P = P^e + b(Y - \overline{Y});\ \text{where } b = 1/\alpha. \qquad (12.14)$$

Now, *subtracting* previous period's price (P_{-1}) from both sides of (12.14) to arrive at the annual inflation rate, we have

$$P - P_{-1} = \left(P^e - P_{-1}\right) + b(Y - \overline{Y})$$

Or $\pi = \pi^e + b(Y - \overline{Y})$, where π is actual inflation and π^e is expected inflation in the current year. π^e is the difference between the expected price today minus the previous period's actual price. Note, $\pi^e$and π are defined in the static sense here.

From Okun's law, we know that there exists an inverse relationship between real GDP and unemployment. It says that the deviation of actual output (Y) from its natural rate $\overline{Y}$ is inversely related to the deviation of unemployment from its natural rate. Symbolically, in general terms, it can be written as:

$$Y - \overline{Y} = \psi\ (u_n - u),\ \psi' > 0$$

$$\text{whenever } Y > \overline{Y};\ u_n > u.$$

Substituting this, we get:

$$\pi = \pi_e + \varphi(u_n - u);\ \varphi' > 0. \qquad (12.15)$$

Now let us *add a supply shock* to represent exogenous events that affects inflation, denoted by ε. Hence, we get, $\pi = \pi^e + \varphi(u_n - u) + \varepsilon$

This is the equation of the *expectation-augmented Phillips curve.* More specifically, rewriting in linear form we get same expression as Equation (12.13): $\pi = \pi^e - \beta(u_n - u) + \varepsilon$ where β is the adjustment coefficient representing inflation elasticity of cyclical unemployment.

The previous equation shows that a fall in π is associated with increase in u or fall in aggregate income of the economy, as $d\pi / du = -\beta$. Also, when $u_n = u$, then $\pi = \pi^e$; at natural rate of unemployment actual inflation perfectly matches the expected rate.

Both SRAS and short run Phillips curves establish a link between real and nominal variables, leading to breakdown of the concept of classical dichotomy (explained in Chapter 3 of the book) in the short run.

12.4 Adaptive expectation and inflation inertia

To derive short run trade off we have so far assumed that expectations of inflation are based on past inflation rates. So, whenever inflation accelerates, expectations of inflation lag behind the actual rate. This type of expectation formation is termed as *adaptive expectation hypothesis* by Friedman. This hypothesis assumes that the expected rate of inflation is revised in the light of past errors in anticipating inflation.

$$\text{Formally, } \pi_t^e - \pi_{t-1}^e = \lambda(\pi_{t-1} - \pi_{t-1}^e) \tag{12.16}$$

$$\text{or } \pi_t^e = \pi_{t-1}^e + \lambda(\pi_{t-1} - \pi_{t-1}^e)$$

$$\text{or } \pi_t^e = \lambda\pi_{t-1} + (1-\lambda)\pi_{t-1}^e. \tag{12.17}$$

Equation (12.17) states that expected inflation formed at the beginning of the current period for the current period is simply a weighted average of the actual inflation of the last period and expected inflation of the last period.

λ is an adjustment parameter or coefficient of adaptation that lies between 0 and 1, representing the speed with which price expectation will be adjusted. A lower value of λ implies sluggish adjustment of expectations. If $\lambda = 0$, then $\pi_t^e = \pi_{t-1}^e$, which means expected rate of inflation never changes and is unaffected by the actual movement of prices. Some inflation rate is regarded as normal; any deviation from that is assumed to be temporary. If $\lambda = 1$, on the other hand, then $\pi_t^e = \pi_{t-1}$, which means people expect the previous period's actual inflation to prevail throughout current period. In this case the expected rate of inflation adapts completely to changes in the actual rate of inflation.

Alternatively, if people expect at the beginning of this period that this year's prices will rise at the same rate as they did last year, then this year's expected inflation will be the same as last year's actual inflation, which is $\pi_t^e = \pi_{t-1}$. Substituting this, Equation (12.13) can be rewritten as

$$\pi_t = \pi_{t-1} - \beta(u_t - u_n) + \varepsilon_t \tag{12.18}$$

This clearly states that current inflation depends on past inflation, cyclical unemployment, and supply shock.

The term π_{t-1} in Equation (12.18) represents ***inertial inflation***. That means if unemployment is at its natural rate, $(u_t = u_n)$ and if there are no supply shocks ($\varepsilon_t = 0$) then inflation keeps on going; it neither speeds up nor slows down. Inflation inertia arises because past inflation influences the expectation of future inflation and these expectations on the other hand influence the wages and prices that people set. In an AD-AS model, inflation inertia can take place due to persistent upward shift of AD and AS curves. We know that the position of the AS curve depends on expected price level. Thus, if prices have been rising quickly, people will expect the same trend to continue.

The SRAS curve will continue to rise upward as a result. Inertial inflation can persist for a long time, as long as people expect the inflation rate to remain unchanged. In such a situation inflation is built into the system. But economic history suggests that inflation does not remain undisturbed for long. Due to adverse or favourable supply shocks, the actual inflation rate moves above or below the inertial rate and inflationary expectations will also be changed.

12.5 Sacrifice Ratio and Disinflation

When inflation reaches an alarming level, it becomes a problem for the entire economy. To reduce this inflation, high unemployment is to be accepted as observed by the short-term Phillips curve relationship. Before deciding whether to use any demand management policy to reduce inflation or not, policymakers must know how much output would be lost during the transition to lower inflation. This cost should be compared with benefit of lower inflation. In discussion of the cost of disinflation, the concept of *sacrifice ratio* is used. It is measured as a percentage of the year's real GDP that must be forgone to reduce inflation by one percentage point. The sacrifice ratio can alternately be defined as cumulative percentage loss of output incurred during disinflation divided by reductions in the inflation rate. Suppose a policy reduces inflation from 12% to 6% over a 3-year period at the cost of levels of output that are 8% below potential in the first year, 6% below potential in the second year and 4% below potential in the third year. Therefore, total loss of GDP is 18% and sacrifice ratio is (18 / 6 =) 3.

It has been estimated by some economists that reductions in inflation by 1% cause a sacrifice of real GDP by 5%. For example, we assume that inflation is running at almost 11% year. To reach moderate inflation, say at 5% per year, would mean reducing inflation by 6% points. If each percentage point costs 5% of the economy's annual output, then reducing inflation by 6% points would require sacrificing 30% points of annual output.

Using Okun's law, we know a rise in one percentage point in the unemployment rate causes the economy to lose 2% of its output. So, 1% reduction in inflation rate leads to 2.5% increase in unemployment rate. In this way the sacrifice ratio concept can also be used to calculate cost of disinflation in terms of unemployment.

This estimated value may vary depending on the nature of the data set. Hence, we can use the sacrifice ratio to estimate by how much and for how long unemployment must rise to reduce inflation.

12.6 Rational Expectation Hypothesis and Disinflation

We have so far used the adaptive expectation hypothesis (AEH), where individuals make systematic errors in forecasting the rate of inflation. Rational expectation theorists argued that rational people do not make systematic errors continuously. According to them, rational agents must use all the relevant information in a logically consistent manner at the time of forming expectations. The rational expectation hypothesis was popularised by Robert Lucas. Under REH, people optimally use all the available information including that of current government policies to forecast the future. We have seen that monetary and fiscal policies influence inflation by influencing AD. Thus, inflation expectations should also depend on the monetary and fiscal policies in effect. REH, thus, tells that a change in the monetary and fiscal policies must be incorporated in the set of information used to form expectations rationally. So, if the government persists in attempting to maintain a below-natural rate through demand management policy, the policy change will be anticipated. There will be no effect of the policy on the economy. So, when expectations are formed rationally, government policy is ineffective in its attempt to affect economy. This is known as ***policy ineffectiveness proposition.***

Now we use the rational expectation hypothesis (REH) to see how the sacrifice ratio is affected as a result of this change. If people do form their expectations rationally, then inflation may have less inertia than it appeared at first sight. Advocates of REH believe that if policymakers are credibly committed to reducing inflation, rational people will understand the commitment and will quickly lower their expectations of inflation. So, under a credible policy, the cost of reducing inflation may be much lower than the estimates which sacrifice ratio suggests. In other words, sacrifice ratio will be very small here. In an extreme situation if the policymakers have a reputation of keeping their commitments, the inflation can come down even without a rise in unemployment or causing any recession at all. This is known as *painless disinflation.* So, the theory of REH says that traditional estimates of the sacrifice ratio for evaluating the impact of alternative policies become irrelevant. This painless disinflation has two requirements:

- The plan to reduce inflation must be announced before the agents or individuals who set wages and prices and form their expectations.
- The individuals must have faith in the announcement; otherwise, they will not revise their inflationary expectation downward.

If the previous two requirements are met, the announcement will immediately shift the short run Phillips curve downward, as shown in Figure 12.4, permitting a lower rate of inflation without higher unemployment. Surprise or unexpected policy change leading to unanticipated inflation can only reduce unemployment in this situation.

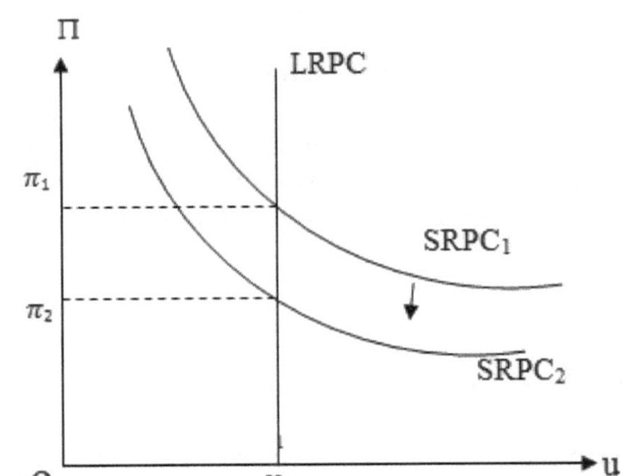

Figure 12.4 Painless disinflation

12.7 Natural-rate hypothesis and hysteresis

According to the *natural-rate hypothesis*, fluctuations in aggregate demand affect output and employment only in the short run. In the long run, the economy returns to the natural rate of employment, output, and unemployment. It was observed during 1973 to 1988 that the US unemployment rate stayed well above the natural rate. Also, in Europe unemployment rates averaged 4.2% in the 1970s and nearly 10% in the 1980s. These observations contradict the natural rate theory, that the unemployment rate over long periods cannot move too far from the natural rate. This induces some economists to challenge the natural rate hypothesis. According to critics of the natural rate hypothesis, prolonged periods of high unemployment might have raised the natural rate in both the United States and Europe in the 1980s, leading to a phenomenon known as *unemployment hysteresis*.

This happens when a long period of unemployment changes an individual's attitude towards work and reduces his desire to find employment. With high unemployment rate, unemployed people might lose skills, get accustomed to laziness, and feel too disheartened to even look for jobs. They might find out about unemployment benefits, how to obtain them, and how to spend the day doing odd jobs. The unemployed may become discouraged and apply less than full effort to finding a job. Also, during recessions, unemployment often goes up as the wage rate is maintained at a relatively higher rate by workers (a smaller group of insiders) who care more about wage rate rather than high employment. The recession may thus permanently push real wages further above the equilibrium level and raise the amount of structural unemployment. The problem may be reinforced by the actions of potential employers. For instance, employers may believe that the longer a person has been unemployed, the more likely it is that the person lacks the energy and qualifications to work. Long unemployment spells are thus a signal to the firms that the worker is undesirable, and, accordingly, firms refrain from hiring such workers. Hence, the longer the unemployment spells, the more unbreakable the vicious cycle lengthening unemployment spells. One important implication of this theory is that hysteresis raises the sacrifice ratio by greatly increasing the cost of recession, because output is lost even after the period of disinflation is over.

Thus, because the unemployment rate was high in previous years, it is high even today. Under the opposite situation, when the unemployment is low and the most people are working, workers improve their job skills through the job and put in their best efforts to find new jobs quickly if they lose their old ones. Accordingly, the unemployment rate becomes low if it was low in past. Many economists suggest that the natural rate of unemployment has fallen in the US and in Europe due to this hysteresis theory. The term hysteresis here refers to the long-lasting influence of history on the natural rate.

12.8 Conclusions

Analysis of the Phillips curve, showing the relationship between inflation and unemployment, has been introduced in the chapter, to establish a link between the AS curve and Phillips curve. But detailed analysis of inflation, including that of demand-pull and cost-push varieties, has already been carried out in Chapter 5. Aggregate supply curve can be converted to expectation-augmented Phillips curve following three steps of subtraction, substitution, and addition. Analysis also depicts that the shape of the long run Phillips curve will depend on the individual's ability to adjust price expectations with changing situations. Concepts of adaptive and rational expectations have been introduced in the last portion of the chapter. Movement from AEH to REH helped explain the phenomenon called painless disinflation. However, the models developed here are relatively simple as we have ignored the government budget constraint and also assumed simplified consumption and investment functions. Hence some predictions of the model may be inaccurate. Also, the model predicts only the direction of change of endogenous variables as a consequence of a change in exogenous variables. But as the parameters or coefficients of the model are not known, we cannot estimate the magnitude of change. Hence to get more accurate and specific results we need to concentrate on the complex econometric model.

Applications

1. Suppose that an economy has the Phillips curve $\pi = \pi_{-1} - 0.4\ (u - u_n)$ where $u_n = 0.5(u_{-1} + u_{-2})$.

   a. Suppose that the central bank follows a policy to reduce inflation permanently by 1%. What effect will that policy have on the unemployment rate overtime?
   b. What is the value of the sacrifice ratio?

   Ans:

   i. If policymakers permanently reduce π by 1%, rational people will understand the commitment and quickly revise their expectation of inflation downward which causes SRPC to shift downward. This will allow a lower rate of inflation without causing any unemployment. This is known as painless disinflation.
   ii. $\frac{d\pi}{du} = -0.4$ i.e. $\frac{du}{d\pi} = -2.5$. As π falls by 1%, u increases by 2.5%. According to Okun's law, 1% increase in u implies 2% fall in GDP, for example, a 2.5% increase in u implies a 5% fall in GDP. So, the sacrifice ratio = 5.

2. Inflation is running at 12%. The central bank wants to reduce it to 6%. Give two scenarios that will achieve the goal.

   Ans: suppose the rate of inflation in the economy is 12% and the government decides to fight high inflation, intending to get the economy down to the inflation rate of 6%. Governments often face this problem of how to deflate. This is known as inflation targeting. Two alternative strategies for disinflation are:

   a. Gradualism
   b. Cold turkey

   In the gradualist strategy, the growth rate of money is initially reduced only slightly and the economy never moves far away from the natural rate of unemployment. But the inflation rate comes down only slowly. The cold turkey strategy by contrast starts with a huge cut in growth rate of money supply and a deep recession takes place. The recession is much worse in this case than in the gradualist strategy but the reduction in inflation rate is much more rapid. The choice of the correct *strategy is a complex task.*

3. Why is a change in the nominal money supply neutral when aggregate supply is vertical and output is at its full employment level?

   Ans: in the case of a vertical AS curve, changes in nominal money supply cause proportional changes in the price level, real money supply remaining unchanged. Output and employment remain unaffected. So, nominal money supply change is neutral in the sense that it has no effect on the rate of interest or on the level and composition of the output.

4. Why might inflation be inertial?

   Ans: inflation is inertial because of the way people form expectations. It is plausible to assume that people's expectations of inflation depend on recently observed inflation. These expectations then influence the wages and prices that people set. For example, if prices have been rising quickly, people will expect them to continue to rise quickly. These expectations will be built into the contracts people set so that actual wages and prices will rise quickly. In addition, both the Phillips curve and the short run aggregate supply curve show that inflation and unemployment move in opposite directions.

5. Under rational expectation, the Phillips relation fails to hold. Why? What is the implication of this failure for the supply curve?

   Ans: the advocates of rational expectations argue that the short run Phillips curve does not accurately represent the options that policymakers have available. They believe that if policymakers are credibly committed to reducing inflation, rational people will understand the commitment and will quickly lower their expectations of inflation. Then, inflation can come down without a rise in unemployment and fall in output. This is known as "painless disinflation". According to the theory of rational expectations, traditional estimates of the sacrifice ratio are not useful for evaluating the impact of alternative policies. Under a credible policy, the costs of reducing inflation may be much lower than estimates that the sacrifice ratio suggest. Hence, under rational expectations the traditional relation of the Phillips curve fails to hold due to the constancy of unemployment at its natural rate.

   We know that the Phillips curve is considered an alternative expression for the aggregate supply (AS) curve. Under rational expectation, a reduction in inflation is powerless to affect the level of unemployment. It implies that the relevant Phillips curve will be vertical at the natural rate of unemployment (u_n). Thus the aggregate supply curve, which is an alternative expression of Phillips curve, will also be vertical, implying that any unexpected change in price level can't affect the level of output produced in the economy.

Summary

- Aggregate supply relationship between price and output can be transformed into a Phillips curve relationship between inflation and unemployment.
- The Phillips curve says that inflation depends on expected inflation, deviation of unemployment from its natural rate, and supply shocks. Adjustment of workers' expectation to inflation gives a vertical Phillips curve in the long run.

- If people have rational expectations, then a credible announcement of a policy change might lead to reduction in inflation without reducing output or without causing a recession. This is known as painless disinflation.

Keywords

Adverse supply shock	Favourable supply shock
Phillips curve	Rational expectation
Painless disinflation	Hysteresis
Natural rate hypothesis	Sacrifice ratio

Multiple choice questions

1. The trade-off between unemployment and inflation is the result of an aggregate supply curve that is

   (a) Horizontal.
   (b) Vertical.
   (c) Upward sloping.
   (d) Downward sloping.

2. The Phillips curve shows

   (a) An inverse relationship between real and nominal wages.
   (b) An inverse relationship between the rate of inflation and the rate of unemployment.
   (c) A positive relationship between the nominal wage and the rate of unemployment.
   (d) A positive relationship between the rate of inflation and nominal wage.

3. Lower unemployment and lower inflation rates can best be achieved with a

   (a) Rightward shift of the Phillips curve.
   (b) Rightward shift of the aggregate demand curve.
   (c) Rightward shift of the aggregate supply curve.
   (d) Leftward shift of the aggregate supply curve.

4. Which of the following will cause the Phillips curve to shift to the left?

   (a) Eliminating price controls.
   (b) Reregulating the country.
   (c) Increasing the marginal tax rate on excess profit.
   (d) Job-search assistance.

5. AW Phillip's wage-inflation unemployment trade-off is based on

   (a) Static expectations hypothesis.
   (b) Adaptive expectations hypothesis.
   (c) Extractive expectations hypothesis.
   (d) Rational expectations hypothesis.

Answers: 1

1. (c); 2. (b); 3. (c); 4. (d); 5. (b)

Descriptive questions

1. What is the Phillips curve? How do you derive the aggregate supply curve from the Phillips curve?
2. Use an AD-AS diagram to differentiate between

    a. Negative supply shock and demand contraction.
    b. Positive supply shock and demand expansion.

3. What is the relation between unemployment and the rate of change of money wage in the short run? Does the relation hold in the long run also?
4. Explain the impact of fiscal policy in the short and long run in the expectations-augmented Phillips curve model.
5. There is a trade-off between inflation and unemployment in the short run. There is no such trade-off in the long run. True or false – explain.
6. Explain how the ability of inflation expectations to shift the Phillips curve helps the economy to adjust automatically to aggregate demand and supply shocks.
7. Show that the Phillips curve is an alternative way to express the aggregate supply curve.
8. What is disinflation? What is sacrifice ratio? Why does the sacrifice ratio become relevant in the context of painless disinflation?
9. What is inertial inflation? Why does it occur?
10. What is the essence of rational expectation hypothesis?
11. What is hysteresis? How does it challenge the natural rate hypothesis?
13. Suppose an economy has the Phillips curve $\pi = \pi_{-1} - 0.5(u - 0.06)$

    a. What is the natural rate of unemployment?
    b. Graph the short run and long run relationship between inflation and unemployment.
    c. How much cyclical unemployment is necessary to reduce inflation by 5% points? Using Okun's law, capture the sacrifice ratio.

Additional readings

Friedman, M. (1975). *Unemployment Versus Inflation*. London: Institute of Economic Affairs.
Friedman, M. (1977). "Nobel lecture: Inflation and unemployment". *Journal of Political Economy*, 85(3).
Godfrey, L. (1971). "The Phillips curve: Incomes policy and trade union effects". in H. Johnson and A. Nobay (eds), *The Current Inflation*. London: Macmillan, pp. 99–124.
Phillip, C. (1965). *Determinants and Effects of Changes in the Stock of Money, 1875–1960*. New York: National Bureau of Economic Research.

13 Complete Keynesian model

13.1 Introduction

The classical school of thought miserably failed when its serious flaws were observed through their incapability to explain the causes of the Great Depression of the 1920s and its continuation up to the early 1940s and also their failure to prescribe any proper remedy to pull the world's capitalistic economies out of this crisis. John Maynard Keynes criticised against the classical orthodoxy by providing an antithesis to this orthodox concept of automatic full employment without any intervention of the governments of the countries in the economic activities. Keynes provided the answer through the writing of his famous book in 1936, *The General Theory of Employment, Interest and Money*. In spite of the continuous downward movements of money wage rate, which have been postulated by the classical perfect flexibility of wage rate and price level, there were significantly high degrees of unemployment in the advanced economies. That means a variable money wage could not manage to restore full employment and even if there was a supply of goods, there was deficiency of demand, which meant Say's law failed. The unemployment rate in the United States rose from 3.2% of the total labour force in the year 1929 to 25.2% in 1933 and the GNP fell by 30% between 1929 to 1933. The average unemployment rate in the United Kingdom for the same period was around 10% of the total workforce. There was no answer from the classicists.

According to Keynes, such a high unemployment rate in the US and Great Britain was the result of a deficiency of aggregate demand. Aggregate demand was too low because of low investment demand. So, he traced the policies of raising aggregate demand to combat unemployment. Keynesian favoured the application of fiscal policies, mainly government spending on public works projects to stimulate demand. In fact, he traced both fiscal and monetary policies to work together to reduce unemployment. That is why he criticised the classical school in respect to both the product as well as monetary sectors. The government should actively participate in economic activity by means of different developmental projects to boost effective demand of the sluggish economies. No automatic market mechanism like the classical economy would work. According to him, the classical assumptions are perfectly fit for the long run where we are all dead. The classical approach completely bypassed the short run problems of the economy that affected the business cycle and Keynes took a grip on the problem from the perspective of short run system. If the short run problems are solved by continuous government interventions (by both fiscal and monetary policies) then, according to Keynes, the economies can reach the long run solution like the classical model. According to Keynes, the diminishing demand for labour was due to diminishing aggregate demand. He traced the role

DOI: 10.4324/9781003501138-16

of government spending which would raise income as primary effect or direct effect and raise consumption demand and therefore income as an indirect effect, thus generating employment directly and indirectly.

The role of demand in the situation of excess supply during the phase of the depression has been primarily captured in the Keynesian system in the nomenclature of the simple Keynesian model (SKM) which has been addressed in Chapter 3 of this present book. Successively we have modified the demand components and formed the aggregate demand in the chapters covering the IS-LM analysis. The role of supply was taken as immaterial since there was abundance in the supply of goods during the phase of depression. Hence, the commodity prices in general form were taken as fixed and the aggregate supply function was a horizontal line. But to determine the general price level of goods and services, particularly of labour, it is necessary to address the aggregate supply system in the Keynesian model. Hence, we need to discuss the labour market and production system in the Keynesian model and we will group the aggregate supply with the aggregate demand and form the complete Keynesian model. The following sections will highlight all the issues in some detailed versions.

13.2 Employment and output in Keynesian model

Keynes argued that the prevailing unemployment situation during the period of depression was due to the deficiency of aggregate demand and he termed this particular type of unemployment as involuntary in nature, not voluntary, as the workers were willing to work at the existing market wage rate but did not get the job. He further argued that, in the short run, certain institutional factors bar the money wage from moving freely, at least in the downward direction. This is called sticky wage or rigidity of money wage which keeps the difference between the desire to supply the labour force and the desire of the producers to hire and use the labour force. Keynes believed that the money wage would not adjust sufficiently in the short run to keep this economy at full employment. So the labour contract would be for money wage which is assumed to be rigid in the downward direction due to the following reasons.

i) Relative wage hypothesis: workers contract for their money wage, not real wage, and they try to maintain their relative wage position with respect to the other. Any reduction of wages of a concerned work group will not be possible on the uncertainty that other sectors of money wage will be cut. The contract for money wage in the Keynesian model allows us to know that the workers in the Keynesian model are assumed to suffer from money illusion. *Money illusion* is the situation where the workers contract for the nominal value of the wage rate, not in terms of how much that wage rate is effective for leading lives. Any increase in money income makes the worker better off whatever be the price level of the basket of goods they consume.
ii) Short term contract: this is for the contract which is set for a given time period. The workers and the producers follow a fixed wage rate in a short period's contract. Even if there is fluctuations in the aggregate demand, there will be no changes in the wage rate as it is fixed in a short period of time.
iii) Maintaining goodwill of the employers: to maintain goodwill or to meet the future uncertainty regarding availability of the labour force, in the time of property, the employers generally do not reduce money wage; rather they fix it as a given level.

iv) Trade unions movements: according to Keynes, a trade union has significant power to bargain for the wage rate at a preferable rate. Due to the fear of workers' strikes and other uncertainties from the attendance of workers in the production point, the employers maintain a fixed wage rate.
v) Government's law: there are certain legal restrictions like minimum wage laws in countries that bind the employers to pay a fixed wage rate whatever be the productivity of the workers. Suppose in India the minimum wage rate has been fixed for the workers working in the MGNREG projects where the government of India and all the state governments are spending thousands of crores rupees in building a rural infrastructure base of the country.

13.3 Aggregate supply system

We are now in a position to develop the aggregate supply system under the Keynesian model under the condition of variable price level of the goods. The aggregate supply system is comprised of a labour market equilibrium and aggregate production function. Again, the labour market equilibrium will be discussed with the help of the equality between aggregate demand for labour and supply of labour.

13.3.1 Aggregate demand for labour and production function

The Keynesian concept of aggregate demand for labour is similar to that of the classical model. The demand for labour by the employers is determined on the basis of marginal productivity theory and the wage rate is determined at the point where the money wage rate is equal to the value of marginal productivity (= price × marginal productivity of labour). The optimising behaviour of the firms/employers is identical in both the Keynesian and classical model. The demand for labour function is thus

$$w = P.\, dY / dN \tag{13.1}$$

where Y is nominal income, N is unit of employment, P is price level, and "w" is money wage rate. dY / dN is marginal productivity of labour, which is positive and declining, which is $d^2Y / dN^2 < 0$. This alternatively means that the aggregate production function is positively sloped and concave with respect to the employment axis. The production function is thus

$$Y = f(N, K_0) \tag{13.2}$$

where K_0 is the fixed quantity of stock of capital which bars the quantity of production to change infinitely in the short run system of production.

13.3.2 Aggregate supply of labour

The Keynesian labour supply has fundamental differences from the classical labour supply function. Under the classical model, the working of flexible money wage and commodity price levels produced an upward sloping supply of labour without any restriction. The labour owners who wanted to do the job at the existing market wage rate would definitely get the job and therefore there was no involuntary unemployment in the classical model. But the outbreak of the great depression rejected the free market full employment concept and Keynes put forward the concept of money wage rigidity which created the situation of involuntary unemployment in the sense that at the fixed money wage rate, all the workers did not get the jobs. The only grounds was the deficiency of aggregate demand. Hence, the labour supply function in the short run at the rigid or sticky wage rate (w_0) is horizontal and it eventually converges to the classical upward sloping shape representing labour supply as a positive function of wage rate. The equation of labour supply function under Keynes is

$$w = w_0 + w(N) \tag{13.3}$$

The previous function follows that w (N) is zero for $N < N_f$, and w' (N) > 0 for $N > N_f$, where N_f stands for full employment level. At the minimum money wage rate w_0, N_f workers are willing to work. When the actual employment is less than or equal to the full employment level, the money wage rate is constant. Note that the term "actual employment" in the Keynesian model means the employment is determined by the demand side or by the producers; there is no role like that in the supply side of the classical model to determine quantity of employment. But if the volume of employment is greater than the full employment level, the wage rate will increase as employment increases, which resembles the classical labour supply function. Hence, the Keynesian labour supply function is first horizontal, corresponding to w_0 and then takes upward movement. Figure 13.1 containing three panels presents the aggregate supply side of the Keynesian model.

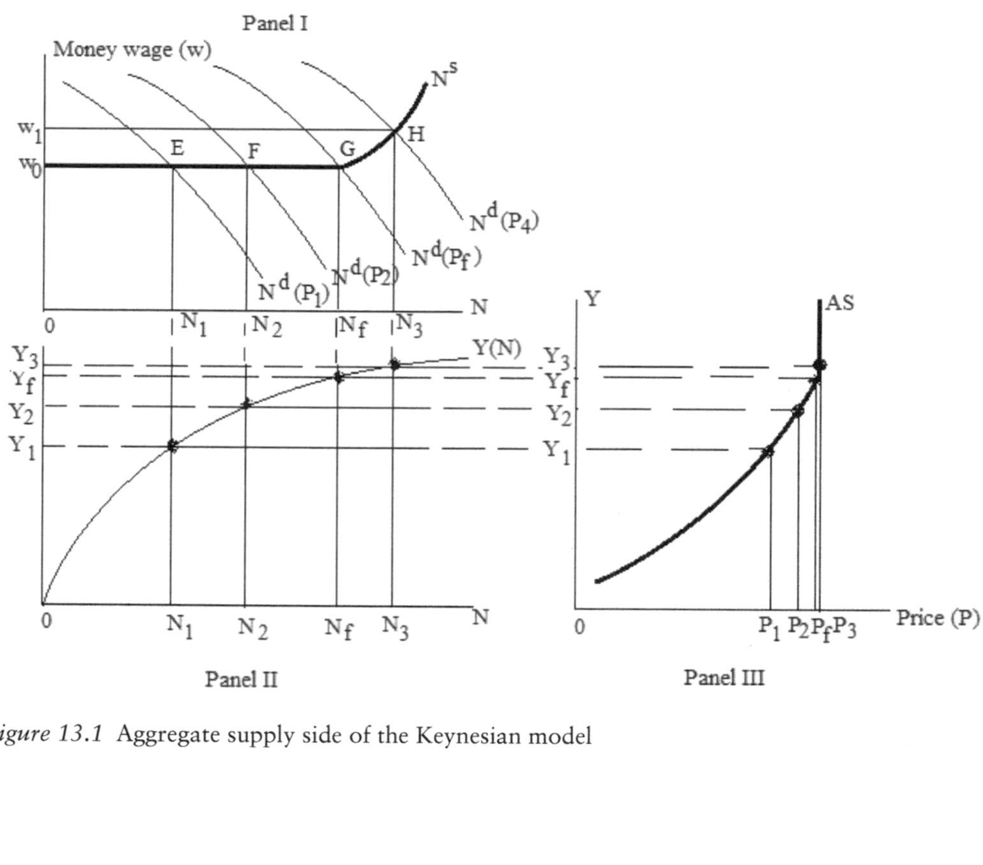

Figure 13.1 Aggregate supply side of the Keynesian model

Panel I presents the labour market equilibrium with the usual labour demand function and a two-part labour supply function; first horizontal at the rigid money wage rate and second the upward sloping part which is above the rigid wage. Panel II presents the aggregate production function of the economy with the usual properties as stated earlier and Panel III presents the aggregate supply function which again has two parts: upward sloping and vertical. N_f is the full employment level and Y_f is the aggregate output at full employment. In Panel I, we have drawn four labour demand functions at four price levels, $P_1 < P_2 < P_f < P_4$. At price P_1, the labour market equilibrium occurs at point E on the horizontal labour supply function where N_1 units of labour force are absorbed. The gap, $(N_f - N_1)$, is called involuntary unemployment. The total quantity of output produced by the N_1 units of employment is Y_1 is observed in Panel II. In Panel III, we get a combination (Y_1, P_1) on the aggregate supply function. Keynes prescribed that the extent of involuntary unemployment can be reduced only by the expansionary fiscal or monetary policies. There is no guarantee that full employment will be automatically achieved in the labour market. As expansionary policies are undertaken, new demand will be created and price level will increase which will push up the labour demand. For example, with increase in demand, the new price is P_2 which shifts out the labour demand function to N^d_2 which as a result leads to increase in employment level to N_2. That means prescription for expansionary demand policies creates reduction of the magnitude of involuntary unemployment. The quantity of output and income also increases, leading to more supply at high price. According to Keynes, if such policies are continuously executed, then the full employment level can be achieved and the economy can be pulled out of the depression. Once the full employment level is reached, additional policy prescription will not be able to generate more output and income; only the price level will increase at the full extent of demand increase. Therefore, the Keynesian aggregate supply function is positively sloped under the sticky wage model and it becomes vertical like the classical model once the full employment level is reached. An upward rising aggregate supply function, thus, means that both the roles of demand and supply factors are present in deciding output and employment in the Keynesian model which is just opposite to the claim of the classical school. Two important policy conclusions are obtained from the Keynesian model.

- Fiscal and monetary policy effects are not neutral.
- Active intervention of the government is supported.

13.4 Aggregate demand system

The aggregate demand system in the Keynesian model has been discussed in detail in the IS-LM chapters but with some exceptions related to the shapes of the IS and LM functions. The IS and LM functions have been taken as linear in the previous chapters, but from this chapter onwards we consider them to be nonlinear; that means they have the usual slopes like before but are shaped like curves. The interactions of the commodity and money markets give us the aggregate demand schedule which is negatively sloped. In short, the goods market equilibrium (or the IS function) is given by

$$S(Y)+T=I(r)+G. \tag{13.4}$$

And the money market equilibrium (or the LM function) is given by

$$M = L(Y) + L(r)$$
$$\text{or } M = k \,.\, PY + L(r). \tag{13.5}$$

The combination of Equations (13.4) and (13.5) is called the *commodity-money* (CM) sector. By varying price level, the aggregate demand function can be derived under the Keynesian system. Figure 13.2 presents it briefly.

As price increases, real balance falls with money supply (M) fixed, and the LM curve shifts leftward, producing low income at the unchanged position of the goods market. Again as price falls, real balance rises, which creates a rightward shift of the LM curve which generates more income. So we can derive the aggregate demand curve from the change in position of the LM function with a given IS function. The locus of E', F', and G' gives the aggregate demand function which is negatively sloped. Unlike the demand function under the classical model, the Keynesian demand function contains the components of goods as well as the money market.

13.5 Complete Keynesian model

We discuss the complete Keynesian model under two different conditions – flexible price and sticky wage rate and both flexible price and wage rate. Keynes postulated that, in both the conditions, the involuntary unemployment problem is a demand deficiency phenomenon and can be solved by active interventions of the government.

13.5.1 *A flexible price and sticky wage model*

Let us present the complete Keynesian model *under the condition of sticky (rigid)wage and flexible commodity prices*. By the term "complete Keynesian model" we mean the determination of relevant macroeconomic variables, output, employment, price level, and rate of interest in the system of combining the aggregate demand and aggregate supply factors. We will show how the supply as well as demand factors play a role in

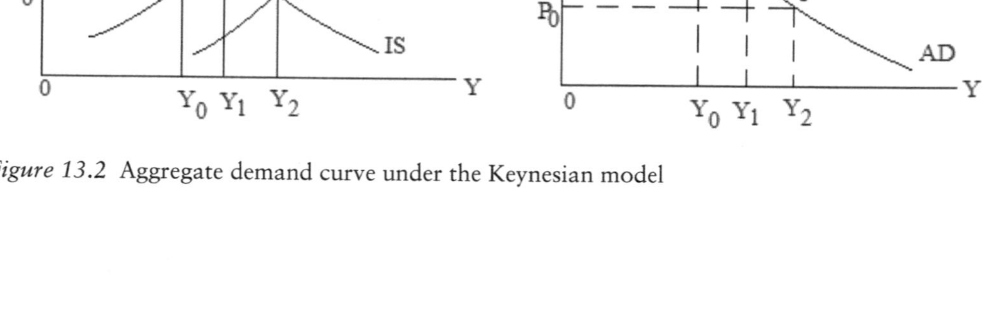

Figure 13.2 Aggregate demand curve under the Keynesian model

deciding the economic variables and prove the classical model invalid in discussing the short run phenomenon of the business cycle during the depression. The complete Keynesian model is presented through a set of equations covering the commodity market, money market, and labour market and aggregate production function.

The commodity market has the following three equations:

The saving function as

$$S = S(Y), \tag{13.6}$$

the investment function as

$$I = I(r), \tag{13.7}$$

the equilibrium condition in the commodity market as

$$S(Y) = I(r), \tag{13.8}$$

the equations under the money market as:

money demand function

$$M^d = k \,.\, PY + L(r), \tag{13.9}$$

And money supply function

$$M^s = M_0, \tag{13.10}$$

equilibrium condition in the money market as

$$M^d = M_0$$
$$\text{or } M_0 = k \,.\, PY + L(r). \tag{13.11}$$

The labour market has following set of equations:

Labour demand function as

$$w = P \,.\, dY / dN, \tag{13.12}$$

labour supply function as

$$w = w_0 + w(N), \tag{13.13}$$

labour market equilibrium condition

$$P \,.\, dY / dN = w_0 + w(N), \tag{13.14}$$

aggregate production function

$$Y = f(N, K_0). \tag{13.15}$$

There are, thus, ten equations (13.6 to 13.15) in the complete Keynesian model. We trim it to four to determine the central variables, *Y*, *N*, *r*, and *P*. We have thus four equations, Equation (13.8), (13.11), (13.14), and (13.15) which can be used to determine four variables, *Y*, *N*, *r*, and *P*. Hence, the complete Keynesian model has deterministic solutions (the readers can solve for the four variables by the help of these four equation by applying the Cramer's Rule). But there is underemployment equilibrium in the Keynesian system. Figure 13.3 and Figure 13.4 depict the complete Keynesian model.

Figure 13.3 has three panels. Panel I presents the labour market equilibrium, Panel II the aggregate production function, and Panel III the commodity and money market equilibriums. Panel I and II together constitute the supply side of the economy and Panel III constitutes the aggregate demand side of the economy. Suppose initially *H* is the commodity and money market equilibrium which generates demand-side output Y_1 and at the initial supply condition P_1 is the price level (refer to Figure 13.4). *E'* is the initial equilibrium of the economy which is corresponding to points *H*, *E*, and *G* in Figure 13.3. The level of employment is N_1 where labour demand and labour supply meet at price P_1. There is underemployment equilibrium and $N_f - N_1$ is the magnitude of involuntary unemployment. The sticky money wage rate has caused the appearance of involuntary unemployment. Keynes opines that the involuntary problem can be solved by active fiscal

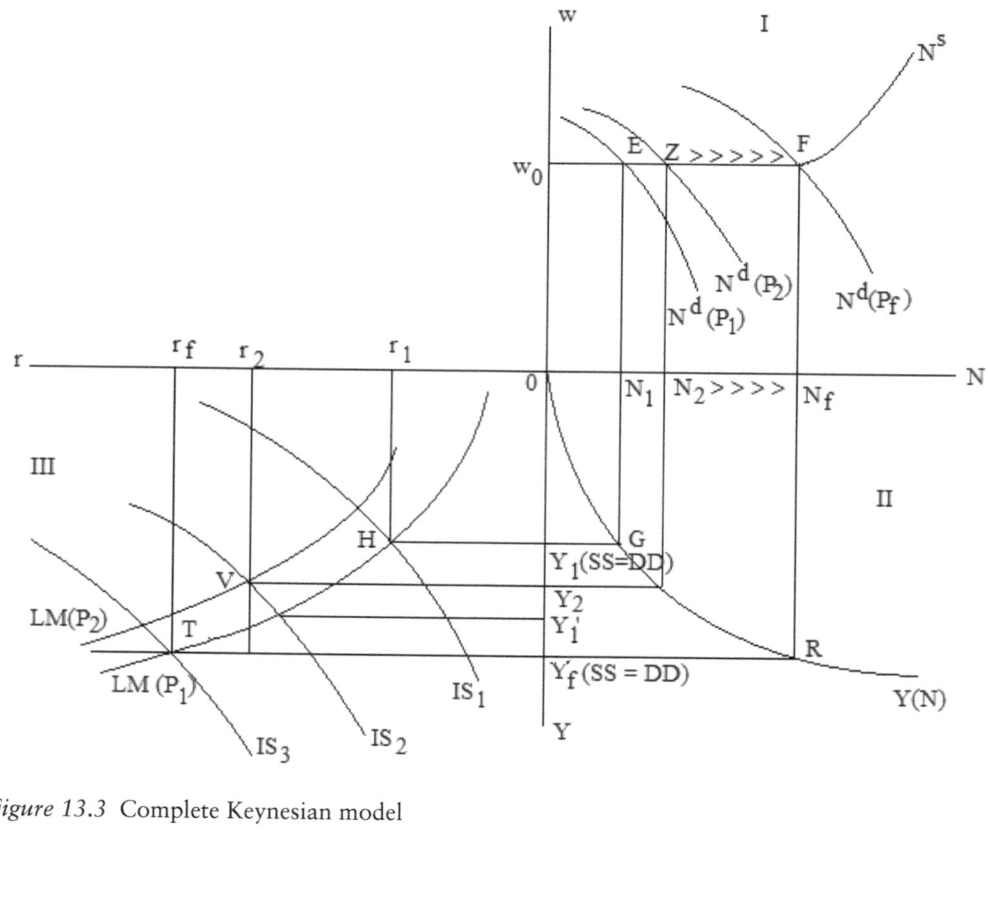

Figure 13.3 Complete Keynesian model

and monetary policies; no supply-side policies can solve the problem as it is undesirable during the phase of depression.

13.5.2 *Fiscal and monetary policy effects under sticky wage model*

Suppose the government spends more than before – the IS function shifts to IS_2. New equilibrium demand-side income rises to Y_1'. There is excess demand for goods (since $Y_1 < Y_1'$) that leads to increase in price level. Increase in price level has two effects: one, the labour demand function (N^d) function shifts rightward and two, the LM function shifts leftward. As the N^d function shifts rightward, the new labour market equilibrium happens at point Z where the level of employment rises to N_2 and supply of the output rises to Y_2. So, there is reduction of magnitude of excess demand from Y_1' to Y_2. Again, rightward shifting of LM leads to rise in interest rate to r_2 making a new demand-side equilibrium at *V* where fall in investment demand causes reduction of income to move to Y_2. The magnitude of involuntary unemployment falls from $(N_f - N_1)$ to $(N_f - N_2)$. This is why Keynes proposed continuous fiscal impetus to reduce the magnitude of depression of the business cycle. The continuous shifting of the aggregate demand functions towards AD_3 in Figure 13.4 have the capability to generate real effects in Keynes' model which is unlike the classical approach. That means a change in the demand parameters lead to real effects upon *N*, *Y*, *r*, etc. and there is no dichotomy like in the classical system. So all the sectors in the Keynesian system are interlinked from either the demand side to the supply side or the supply side to the demand side. Once the vertical part of the aggregate supply function is reached at point F′, additional demand will fully push up the price level to absorb the additional demand. At this point, the Keynesian and classical results are identical which corresponds to the long run solution.

13.5.3 *A flexible price and flexible wage model*

In assumption of flexible price and flexible wage in establishing the output and employment determination it seems that the Keynesian model is the opposite side of the same

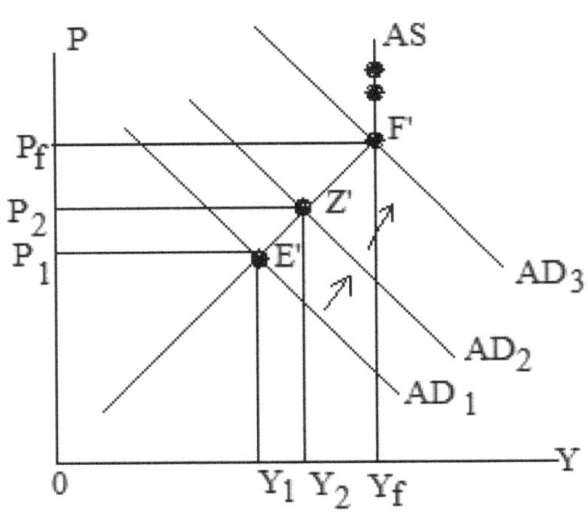

Figure 13.4 Aggregate economy's equilibrium

coin in the sense that the classical and Keynesian results will be identical. But this is not right to assume in advance. There is a notable difference in the anticipation about the future price level in both the models. While the classical model assumes that there is no difference between actual price and expected price and actual real wage and expected real wage, the Keynesian model assumes that there is a difference between actual real wage and expected real wage as the labourers expect the price and wage rates in some lagged period's adjustments. This is the novelty of the Keynesian model since there is asymmetry of information which forces the labourers to imperfectly anticipate the price as well as wage rates. But the classical model assumed perfect information of all the economic agents.

We examine here the difference in the Keynesian and classical views of labour supply functions in the flexible wage-price model.

In the classical supply assumption, both "w" and P are perfectly known to all the agents of the economy. That is, the cost of collection of information, known as transaction cost, is zero. Hence, in the classical flexible wage-price model, the attainment of full employment is a general phenomenon. The labour supply function under the classical model is

$$N^s = f(w / P) \tag{13.16}$$

Here, the slope of the function is $f' > 0$.

In the Keynesian view, since the labour bargain is in terms of the money wage, we can assume that workers know the wage rate but not the price. There is a positive transaction cost (bounded rationality) of collecting information of prices. Thus, Keynes postulated that the workers expect an average price level for the contracted period where the expectation is made on the basis of past experience regarding prices. So, the expression for expected price is

$$P^e = \alpha_1 P_{-1} + \alpha_2 P_{-2} + \alpha_3 P_{-3} + \ldots\ldots\ldots\ldots \tag{13.17}$$

where $\Sigma\alpha_i = 1$ and "α" stands for weight given upon different past periods.

Therefore, the labour supply is a function of expected real wage (w / P^e). The mathematical form of the labour supply function is

$$N^s = g(w / P^e) \tag{13.18}$$

The slope of the supply function is still positive, $g' > 0$. Keynes assumed that P^e slowly adjusts to change in current price, P, in the short run. That is, P^e is kept constant in the short run. The purpose of analysis is to show that even if money wage is perfectly flexible, with the Keynesian version of labour supply curves, the aggregate supply curves for the goods would not be vertical. Output and employment would not be completely supply determined; aggregate demand would also play a role. In reality the Keynesian belief is that the money wage is sticky in the downward direction, and much of the unemployment we observe is the result of the catastrophe of the money wage to create equilibrium in the labour market. Imperfect information about prices is, therefore, a pivotal factor in the Keynesian model to explain fluctuation of output and employment in the business cycle.

13.5.4 Derivation of aggregate supply function under flexible wage-price model

We can now derive the aggregate supply function in the Keynesian model under the flexible wage-price condition. We use the labour demand function as given in Equation (13.12) and the labour supply function as given in Equation (13.18) to derive the aggregate supply from the labour market equilibrium and production function of the whole economy. We keep the figure for the aggregate production function implicit and intuitively derive the aggregate supply function from the labour market equilibrium. The labour demand function is based on the marginal productivity principle like before but the labour supply function is not two-stepped like in the situation of the sticky wage model. It is upward sloping and is positively dependent upon the flexible money wage rate, but the barrier is imperfect information on the expected price level. Therefore, $N^s(P^e)$ is upward sloping. Figure 13.5 describes the derivation. It has two panels; Panel I depicts the labour market equilibrium and Panel II depicts the aggregate supply function.

From the labour market's initial equilibrium point *E*, we have N_1 *as* the initial employment when price is P_1. The corresponding output is Y_1 which is also the aggregate supply of output as shown in Panel II. But here is a question: does such employment correspond to full employment level? It is not clear; we have to check it.

Let us introduce an increase in price from P_1 to P_2. The labour demand curve shifts rightward as the firms are now capable of hiring more labour power. Since expected price, P^e, cannot properly adjust to actual change of price, $N^s(P^e)$ does not make changes to the new labour market equilibrium which produces $N_2 > N_1$ level of employment. Full employment would arise or N_1 would be the full employment, if a rise in price would be capable of shifting $N^s(P^e)$ leftward in such a way that the rise in employment demand would be completely washed out, keeping N_1 intact. Since such a possibility did not appear, we can conclude that there is unemployment (involuntary) even under flexible money wage and prices. Another indication of the existence of unemployment is the slope of the supply function which is rising, indicating the importance of aggregate demand in deciding output and employment. If it would have been vertically sloped, then the existence of unemployment in the Keynesian flexible wage-price model would be nil.

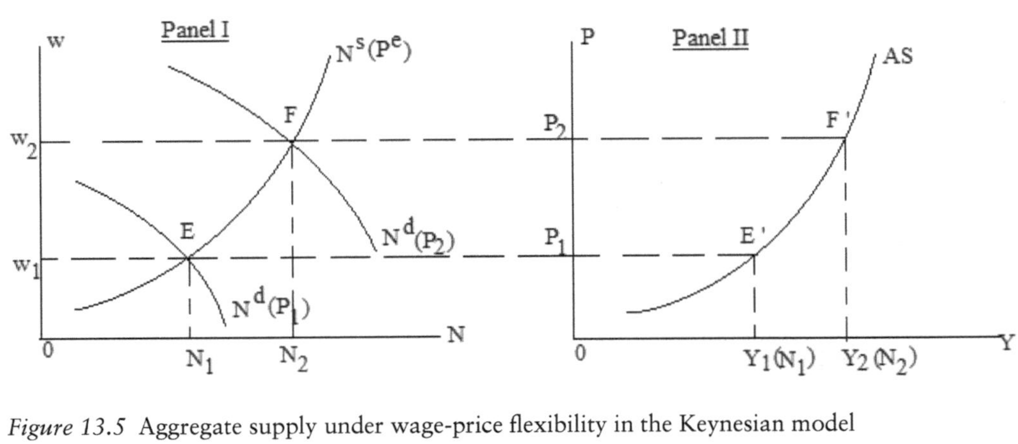

Figure 13.5 Aggregate supply under wage-price flexibility in the Keynesian model

13.6 The classical system under rigidity in money wage

Let us have a look at the repercussions to the classical conclusions if the assumption of rigid money wage is introduced into it. We have seen in the previous analysis and chapter on classical economics that the assumption of a perfectly flexible money wage resulted in a supply-determined full employment level of output. If we incorporate the sticky wage condition, then the classical model can also show the existence of the unemployment situation.

When money wage rate is kept fixed at w_0 then the labour demand and labour supply functions are functions of price levels and there is $N^S{}_1$ as units of supply of labour and $N^D{}_1$ as demand for labour with $N^S{}_1 > N^D{}_1$ (refer to Panel I of Figure 13.6). Therefore, at a rigid wage rate there is unemployment of the magnitude $N^S{}_1 - N^D{}_1$. But the labour market is cleared at a relatively low money wage rate w_0' with N_1 units of employment. Again, at w_0 and price P_1, with higher real wage $(w_0 / P_1) > (w_0' / P_1)$, the firms hire $N^D{}_1$ amount of labour, but with higher real wage the workers desire to sell $N^S{}_1$ amount of labour. This shows that there is demand-determined labour employment and output, nullifying the conclusion of the classical orthodoxy.

Let us see the effect of increase in price levels from P_1 to P_2. In this case we will find that the output and employment determination will not solely be supply determined. Let us see how. As price rises to P_2, the real wage rate falls, which will push up the demand for labour which will create an upward shift of the function to $N^D{}_2$ (refer to Panel II of Figure 13.6). Again, as real wage rate falls, the suppliers of labour will reduce their supply. N^S will thus shift leftward to $N^S{}_2$. Now the new employment rises to N_1 from $N^D{}_1$ where $N^S{}_2 = N^D{}_2$ which again corresponds to our previous equilibrium employment N_1 where the real wage rates are equal $[(w_0 / P_1) = (w_0' / P_1)]$. So we see that as price rises, employment rises and output rises, which means the aggregate supply function under the classical system with money wage rigidity is no longer vertical, it is rather upward rising up to P_2 (refer to Panel III of Figure 13.6). After P_2 (from where $N^S = N^D$), the supply function again is vertical.

Why price changes? With money stock being fixed at M_1, with income Y_1, the price is fixed at P_1. Now as price rises to P_2, employment rises to N_1 and supply of output rises to Y_2. But from the demand side, such equilibrium will be attained until money supply increases to another level, say to M_2. So there is the role of aggregate demand in determining output and employment in the classical model under the rigid money wage situation.

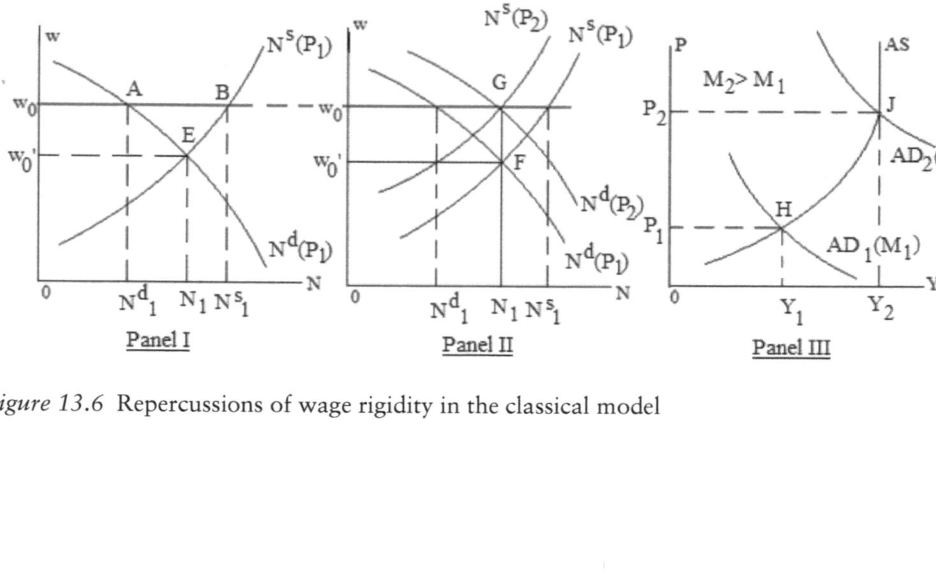

Figure 13.6 Repercussions of wage rigidity in the classical model

As previously mentioned, at P_2, employment does not change (since money wage changes proportionately with price, w / P = fixed) and so income is fixed. Hence, any additional money supply will raise the proportional amount of commodity price which leads to the restoration of neutrality of money result. Therefore, with money wage rigid, the classical model provides a Keynesian solution. Therefore, we can say that *money wage rigidity is the necessary condition* of producing underemployment equilibrium in both the Keynes and classical models. But it is not the only condition of producing underemployment equilibrium in the Keynesian model. We discuss these conditions in the following sections.

13.7 Different sources of underemployment equilibrium in the Keynesian model

Not only the contractual differences in the labour market, but the prevalence of underemployment situation in Keynesian model had several sources arising out of the demand side of the economy.

Source 1: money wage rigidity with price variable

We have already shown this case in the previous analysis of the chapter in the head of the complete Keynesian model; refer to Equations (13.6) to (13.15) and Figure 13.3. (N_1 – N_f) was the magnitude of involuntary unemployment, and Y_1*was* supply of output at underemployment equilibrium with price P_1. That means underemployment equilibrium was caused by money wage rigidity.

Source 2: Money wage and price are variable

Here the underemployment equilibrium is explained under following three sub sources

i) The labour supply function is such that the labour contract is made in terms of expected real wage in the short run. That means, in spite of variable price, the workers expect the future price for their wage contract in respect to the expected price, not with respect to the actual price. Under this expectation model, the underemployment equilibrium is possible under the Keynesian framework that we have discussed in the previous section (refer to equation 13.17 and 13.18 and Figure 13.5).
ii) Even with a classical labour supply function (where actual real wage is the determinant for labour supply), the unemployment equilibrium in the Keynesian model is reached when $L_r \rightarrow -\infty$. This is the situation of a *liquidity trap* where individuals hold money in cash form to use it for lucrative assets. Note that speculative or liquidity preference theory is neither necessary nor sufficient for underemployment equilibrium. But the money demand function in the liquidity trap region may result in underemployment equilibrium in the Keynesian model

In this situation, as wage is cut above equilibrium (Figure 13.7), there is excess supply. That means, at the initial demand given by the intersection of LM in its liquidity trap region and the IS curve at point *E*, there is excess supply since $Y_f > Y_1$ (refer to Panel I). The excess supply situation leads to a fall in price level which will again lead to an increase in real wage since change in money wage rate is greater than change in price level (or $dw > dP$). If MPC <1, there is lesser magnitude of increase in aggregate demand which means there is a gap between aggregate supply of goods and aggregate demand for goods (Panel III). According to Keynes, such an inconsistency between supply and demand can

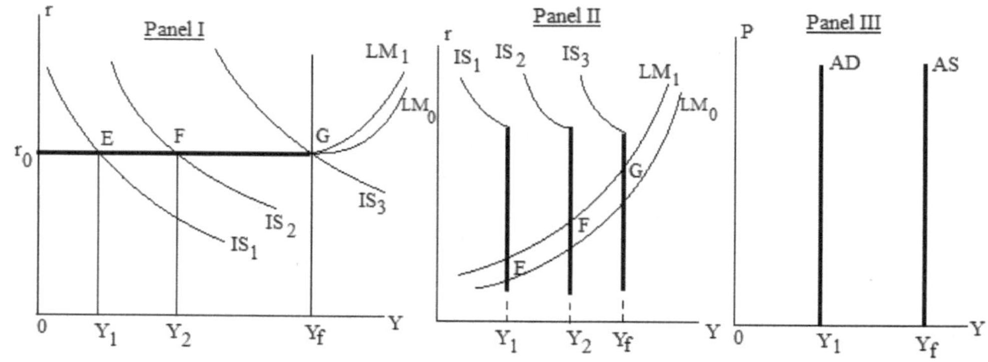

Figure 13.7 Underemployment situation under liquidity trap region and interest insensitive investment function

be managed by taking the money market into consideration, because with normal shapes of IS and LM, as price falls, LM shifts rightward to LM_0 giving a higher demand-side output which ultimately matches with the supply of goods. But if the economy operates under a liquidity trap, such a decrease in price will not induce the rate of interest to fall and thereby will raising investment as well as income in the aggregate demand side. Hence, under the condition of $L_r \rightarrow -\infty$, there can be underemployment equilibrium in the Keynesian model. It is sometimes called the *Keynesian crisis*.

iii) With variable money wage and price, there is another case that is $I_r \rightarrow 0$ or interest in sensitivity of investment demand or vertical IS function, where we may find the underemployment equilibrium. As with the case in ii), here also a cut in money wage rate leads to increase in supply and accordingly fall in price level of the goods (Panel II of Figure 13.7). Reduction of price level will shift the LM function rightward which will again lead to a fall in interest rate. There will be no change in investment demand because investment is insensitive to rate of interest which keeps aggregate demand at the initial level, generating further a gap between aggregate demand and aggregate supply like in Panel III. Hence, we get another *Keynesian crisis* situation where the involuntary unemployment (of magnitude $N_f - N_1$) problem persists.

Therefore, we conclude that wage rigidity is not the only cause of producing underemployment equilibrium in the Keynesian model; there can be the same result under the condition of $L_r \rightarrow -\infty$ and $I_r \rightarrow 0$ with wage-price flexibility.

13.7.1 *How to solve the underemployment problems under source 1 and source 2 (1, 2, 3)*

The crisis can be managed by following *stabilisation policies* – intervention policy and non-intervention or market-based policy.

Intervention policy: in the case of all sources of underemployment equilibrium, Keynes provided the intervention of the government to induce aggregate demand continuously. In the case of wage rigidity, there is no problem of equilibrium since the negatively sloped aggregate demand curve meets with the aggregate supply function. But there is underemployment equilibrium. As government spending is raised continuously (Figure 13.8), the economy can reach the full employment level (point *F* or *F'* in two parts of the diagram) which is why Keynes called it general theory.

In the case of a liquidity trap situation, as government expenditure is increased continuously, the IS function will shift continuously towards full employment and the aggregate demand function shifts rightward towards full employment supply (Panel I and Panel III of Figure 13.7). Again, for the case of an interest-insensitive IS function, increase in public spending will lead to a rightward shift of the vertical IS function along the usual LM function, which creates a reduction of unemployment problem, and ultimately the economy can reach the full employment level (Panel II and Panel III of Figure 13.7) and the AD function meets the AS function by shifting rightward.

Market-based policy – the real balance effect: according to neoclassical economists like Pigou and Patinkin, even without the government's intervention through the fiscal front or the inability of the monetary policy in case of $L_r \rightarrow -\infty$ and $I_r \rightarrow 0$, there may be a rightward shifting of the IS function through the real balance effect. The *real balance effect* (also known as the *Pigou effect*) shows that falling commodity price levels during the phase of unemployment will lead the consumers to be wealthier in terms of real values which is measured by (M / P). It is also known as wealth effect. In this approach, the consumption expenditure of the households is a positive function of real balance besides income, and as real balance increases, increase in consumption expenditure $([dC / d(M / P)] > 0)$ will lead to a rightward shift of the IS function and ultimately the problem of unemployment can be solved and the system can be stabilised. No government intervention will be required as it may be more disturbing, according to the classicists' claim. We can refer to Panel I of Figure 13.7 where we can think of the shifting of the IS function not by increase in government spending but through increase in the real values of the assets/wealth. The readers can verify that the slope of the IS function remains unchanged after the incorporation of the real balance term into the consumption function; only the intercept of the consumption function gets changed. We can now conclude from the previous analysis that wage rigidity, is both the necessary and sufficient condition for explaining underemployment equilibrium; other sources of unemployment are temporary as they can be solved by a market-based neoclassical approach.

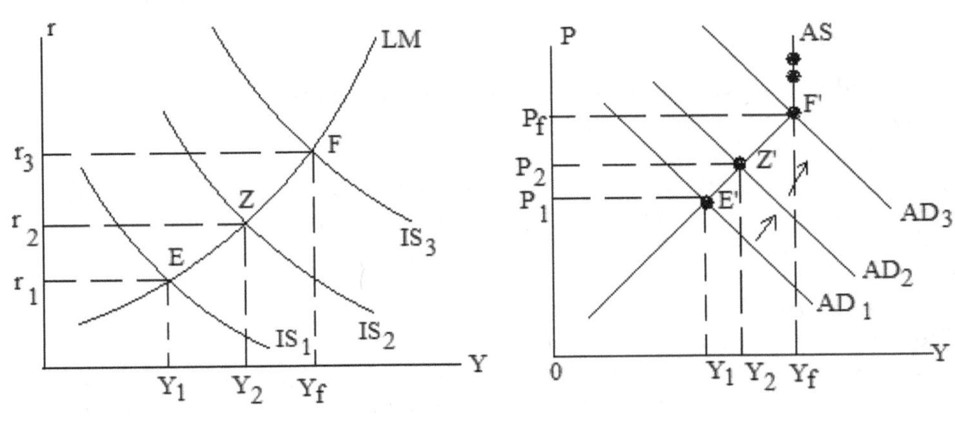

Figure 13.8 Effect of government intervention

13.7.2 Criticisms of the Keynesian model

There are some general criticisms made by the opponent groups comprising the monetarists and the new classical economists against the Keynesian model.

First, the Keynesian model is "too aggregative" in the sense that it does not take into account the micro basis of the economic behaviour of the agents.

Second, this model is too static. It means that the model does not consider the short run dynamics of income change and that it is unsuitable in the analysis of long-term economic growth.

Third, the Keynesian demand management policies were successful in preventing unemployment like that experienced in the 1930s, but, unfortunately, after the end of World War II they tended to give rise to the phenomenon known as stop-go.

Fourth, the Keynesian model fails to take into account the problem of inflation. Indeed, the basic model assumes that prices and wages are fixed and the only time they are allowed to rise is after the attainment of full employment. Experience in the 1970s has shown us that high rates of inflation can co-exist with high rates of unemployment (which is also known as stagflation) and no explanation is provided in the Keynesian theory.

Finally, the monetarists claimed that without government interference the economy will tend towards a natural rate of unemployment.

13.8 Conclusion

The present chapter discussed the Keynesian model in complete form in the way of incorporating both the aggregate and supply side of the capitalistic economies. The novelty it established was that rigidity in the money wage and imperfect information produced the underemployment equilibrium, and to rescue the economy from the short run depression it prescribed strong intervention of the government sector into economic activities. The classical long run model with perfect market conditions also fails if the sticky wage condition is imposed on it.

Summary

The complete Keynesian model that we discussed in the present chapter has the following points to note.

- It emerged as the sharp contrast school of thought against the classical orthodoxy. It pointed out the existence of rigidity in money wage was the sole explanation of involuntary unemployment.
- Even if both wage rate and commodity prices are allowed to be flexible, the informational asymmetry causes the labour supplier to negotiate a contract of labour on the basis of expected real wage, not in terms of actual real wage like the classicists. Because the expected prices adjust slowly to the actual prices, the involuntary unemployment is again a natural occurrence in the Keynesian model.
- The complete Keynesian model shows how the main determinants in a macroeconomic framework are determined by the combinations of aggregate demand and supply factors, unlike the completely supply-determined system of the complete classical model.

- Active government intervention by increasing public spending in a continuous form can remove the fluctuations in the business cycle, as proposed by Keynes.
- Besides a sticky money wage rate, the position of a liquidity trap and interest insensitivity of investment can also produce underemployment equilibrium in the Keynesian model. But the real cause of unemployment is the money wage rigidity in the Keynesian model.
- Even if we introduce the wage rigidity condition in the classical model, there can be the same underemployment equilibrium.
- The real balance effect is an alternative to the intervention policy as proposed by the neoclassical economists, which can work when the monetary policy fails to remove the unemployment problem.

Keywords

Aggregate demand
Money wage rigidity
Underemployment equilibrium
Fiscal policy
Real balance effect
Aggregate supply
Labour contract
Involuntary unemployment
Monetary policy

Multiple choice questions and answers

1. If both the commodity prices and money wage rate are kept fixed, then the aggregate supply function under the Keynesian system will be

   (a) Usually upward sloping.
   (b) Vertical.
   (c) Horizontal.
   (d) None of the above.

2. If wage and price are perfectly flexible with perfect information, then the aggregate supply function will be

   (a) Usually upward sloping.
   (b) Vertical.
   (c) Horizontal.
   (d) None of the above.

3. If there is money wage rigidity in the labour market and commodity prices are variable, then the aggregate supply function of goods will be

   (a) Usually upward sloping.
   (b) Vertical.
   (c) Horizontal.
   (d) None of the above.

4. According to complete Keynesian model, the problem of involuntary unemployment can be solved unambiguously by

   (a) Expansionary monetary policy.
   (b) Contractionary tax policy.
   (c) Expansionary public spending.
   (d) Both (b) and (c).

5. Real balance effect leads to

   (a) The aggregate consumption expenditure being dependent on the real value of wealth.
   (b) The IS function shifting to the right.
   (c) Both (a) and (b).
   (d) None of the above.

Answers

1. (c); 2. (b); 3. (a); 4. (d); 5. (c)

Review questions

1. What is a "sticky price" model? Mention some grounds for justifying sticky wage as per Keynes.
2. Write down the equation of the labour supply function under rigid money wage. Draw the labour market equilibrium in the Keynesian model and prove that there is underemployment equilibrium.
3. Show how the main determinants in a macroeconomic framework are determined by the combinations of aggregate demand and supply factors in a complete Keynesian model.
4. Explain how fiscal and monetary policy combinations make possible the removal of involuntary unemployment in the Keynesian model. Are both the policies always capable of removing the fluctuations in the business cycle? Discuss.
5. Justify the statement with the proper arguments – "Money wage rigidity is necessary as well as a sufficient condition of producing an underemployment equilibrium" in the Keynesian model.
6. What are the variables involved in the complete Keynesian model? Explain the effects of expansionary fiscal policy in a complete Keynesian model.
7. Draw the IS and LM functions when investment is completely interest insensitive and money demand is infinitely elastic. Show that monetary policy does not work to remove the involuntary unemployment problem under these two conditions in the Keynesian model.
8. What is real balance effect? Explain how it can work as a substitute for unnecessary government intervention in the economic activities to control for fluctuation in a business cycle.

Additional readings

Keynes, J. M. (1936). *The General Theory of Employment, Interest, and Money*. London: Palgrave Macmillan.
Patinkin, D. (1948). "Price flexibility and full employment". *The American Economic Review*, 38(4), 543–564.
Pigou, A. C. (1943). "The classical stationary state". *Economic Journal*, 53(212), 343–351.

Part IV

Micro foundations of macroeconomics – the consumption and investment behaviours

14 Consumption function

14.1 Introduction

In the analysis of aggregate income determination in a simple or general equilibrium model, we have considered in the previous chapters that consumption expenditure and investment expenditure in particular were aggregative in nature. We did not consider how they were determined in an economy. Economists have shown that these two heads of expenditure in a macroeconomic system have their route in microeconomics where they are determined by consumers' (or households') and investors' (or firms') optimisation of utility and profit respectively over different time periods. In the present chapter, we will discuss different models, rather hypotheses, of consumption expenditure, and the investment behaviour will be discussed in the next chapter.

Consumption function describes a relationship between consumption and disposable income, the personal income net of taxes. The concept was introduced into macroeconomics by J. M. Keynes in 1936 upon writing his general theory. To study the process by which equilibrium income of an economy is determined, Keynes primarily stressed the aggregate volume of consumption expenditure derived from the total households in the economy. Keynes believed that households make consumption and savings decisions on the basis of fundamental psychology, which is better termed *fundamental psychological law*, without taking into account why such behaviour works. Keynes postulated that aggregate real consumption expenditure depends in a stable way upon the aggregate absolute incomes of the households in the economy, hence its name is *absolute consumption hypothesis*. Empirically it has been proven that the short run property of the Keynesian consumption function does hold good, but if the growth of income is allowed to continue then the theory cannot explain the time series nature of the consumption function. That means, whatever is true and consistent for the cross section of households in the short run, it is not true for the long run version of time series of both consumption and income. Simon Kuznets (1946) has shown empirically by the existing data of the industrially developed countries of the world, particularly of the USA, that in the long run there should be a proportional relation between absolute consumption and income, and hence, as income rises continuously, there should be the equality or balance between the average and marginal propensity of consumption.

In the post-Keynes and Kuznets developments of consumption behaviour, many hypotheses are developed by eminent economists to justify the factors responsible for the short run variability and long run constancy properties of a consumption function. For example, Irving Fisher explained how one person allocates his total budget upon consumption in a current period and in future periods (i.e. savings today or abstaining from

DOI: 10.4324/9781003501138-18

current consumption) so that his utility is maximised. In another side, James Duesenberry developed the *relative income hypothesis* in the year 1949 where the individual households behave in the way that keeps up with the other members of the society. Later, Milton Friedman was awarded the Nobel Prize in Economics for his invention of consumption theory in the year 1957 on the basis of permanent income that was capable of explaining both the short run and long run empirical reality. After that, Ando and Modigliani developed the consumption behaviour on the basis of the total income generated in the total life cycle of a household and also justified the empirical facts of consumption. Both Friedman and Ando and Modigliani used the intertemporal budget studies of Fisher to develop their models. We will discuss all these models in the following section starting with the Keynesian consumption function.

14.2 Keynes on absolute consumption hypothesis

Keynes' writing of the general theory came in the advent of the classical crisis in the name of the Great Depression of the 1930s where there was massive unemployment and excess supply in the general economic system which was a strong departure from the automatic full employment conclusion. Keynes thought that the prevalence of unemployment and general excess supply was resultant from the deficiency in aggregate demand generated from the private capitalistic system. He emphasised increasing the volume of aggregate demand by means of consumption and private investment expenditure in a simple economic system under the condition that the supply side is completely elastic, meaning the aggregate supply function of goods was horizontal. Hence, any increase in aggregate demand through increase in consumption and/or investment would definitely lead to increase in aggregate income and employment of the economy and if the process was continued by means of all sorts of expenditure (e.g. consumption, investment by both private and public sectors) then eventually the economy would get out of the crisis in the short run phase and reach the long run solution of full employment level of output.

Keynes' consumption function is known as the *absolute income hypothesis*. Consumption demand depends on income and propensity to consume (it is the response of consumption to an extra unit change in income). Propensity to consume again depends on various factors such as price level, interest rate, stock of wealth, and several subjective factors. Since Keynes was concerned with the short run consumption function, he assumed price level, interest rate, stock of wealth, etc. to be constant in his theory of consumption. The two main variables concerned in the Keynesian consumption function are the aggregate households' consumption expenditure and aggregate absolute income of the economy net of tax and transfer payments. The Keynesian consumption function considers consumption as a function of income. It is expressed as

$$C = C(Y) \tag{14.1}$$

where C is aggregate consumption and Y is aggregate absolute income. The important properties of Keynesian consumption function are as follows:

- Aggregate consumption expenditure in real terms is a stable and increasing function of aggregate real national income. That is, $dC / dY > 0$, where dC / dY is the marginal propensity of consumption (MPC) (which is also the slope of the consumption function) and is positive. Additionally, as income rises by one unit, consumption expenditure rises by less than one unit or $0 < MPC < 1$. This is a very crucial condition in the Keynesian demand-side model and it holds for *fundamental psychological law*. The Keynesian fundamental psychological law is an intuitive concept which means an individual always consumes less than his income during the working or earning phase since he has to pay past borrowing (i.e. consumption before entering into the earning phase) and a part is kept to meet future expenses (i.e. consumption after the end of the earning phase up to the end of life). That means, during the working phase, $C < Y$ or $Y - C > 0$ since total income is spent upon consumption and savings expenditure. That is $S > 0$. That means individuals have to make positive savings during the working phase to manage past and future expenses. The amount of consumption in the pre-earning phase (that is with income zero) is known as *autonomous consumption* (this is always positive since people cannot live without consumption) which is done by borrowing or negative savings ($S < 0$) (Figure 14.1).

Assuming average life expectancy of 70 years, the positive savings phase falls in the earning phase of 25–60 years and negative savings or borrowing phases are 0–25 and 60–70 years of total life.

- As income continues to increase, the ratio of consumption to income or the average propensity to consume (APC) will go down or the savings ratio will go on increasing and there will be a gap between average and marginal propensity of consumption in the way that APC > MPC. This is the short run feature of the Keynesian consumption function which happens when there is a drift in consumption function and it starts above the origin through the consumption axis. The property also means that there will be short run variability in consumption that creates deviation from average in the marginal values of consumption.

Let us explain these two properties by the help of a simple mathematical form of the short run consumption function along with its diagrammatic presentation. Suppose the consumption function in the short run is linear in the following form:

$$C = a + bY. \tag{14.2}$$

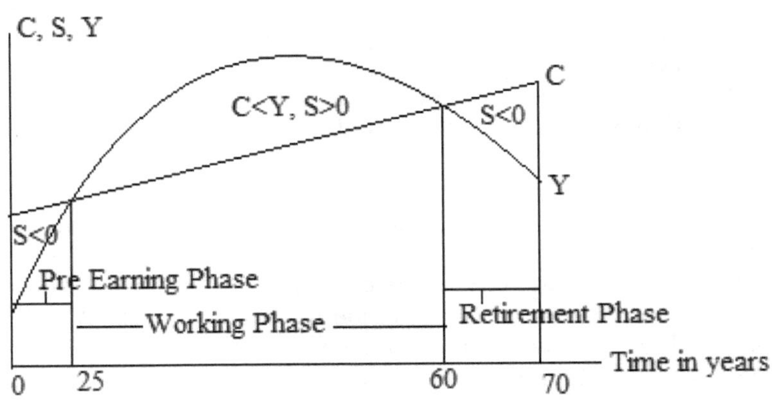

Figure 14.1 Income-consumption composition in total life

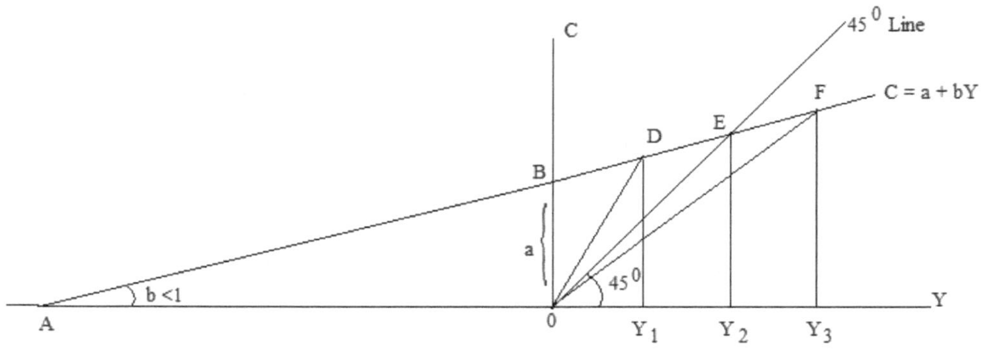

Figure 14.2 Linear nonproportional consumption function in the short run

where "*a*" stands for drift (or intercept) parameter which is known as autonomous consumption and is always positive (this makes the function nonproportional) and "*b*" represents MPC (as well as the slope of the consumption function) which lies between zero and unity. The term "*bY*" is the induced consumption expenditure. Figure 14.2 presents a linear nonproportional consumption function in the short run. The function starts from the vertical axis and the drift or intercept of the function ($= a > 0$). It is an upward sloping straight line with slope given by b = MPC, which is less than one. A line through the origin has been drawn with an angle of 45 degrees to compare the slope of it with the consumption function. We know the slope of the 45-degree line is tan 45° = 1 and hence the consumption function will cut the 45-degree line from above.

The consumption function starts actually from point *A* (with negative Y axis) and its slope at any point of income is equal to b which is again equal to $dC / dY = DY_1 / AY_1 = EY_2 / AY_2 = FY_3 / AY_3 =$ and so on and so forth for all higher values of income. This feature of consumption function satisfies the first property that consumption increases less equi-proportionately than income increase. The second property, that is as income rises, APC (= C / Y) falls and APC > MPC, is also satisfied by this consumption function. From the diagram, APC at any point can be measured by the slope of the ray connecting the origin and the point on the consumption function. For example, the slope of the ray, OD, at income Y_1 is DY_1 / OY_1. As income rises to Y_2, the APC becomes EY_2 / OY_2. Comparing the APC at Y_1 with that of Y_2 gives us the result that $DY_1 / OY_1 > EY_2 / OY_2$. That means, as income increases, APC falls and vice versa. Again comparing the values of APC and MPC at all levels of income, it is observed from the diagram that $DY_1 / OY_1 > DY_1 / AY_1$ or APC > MPC and it holds for all levels of income. Mathematically, we can show this. We have the consumption function as $C = a + bY$. So, MPC = $dC / dY = b$ and APC = $C / Y = a / Y + b = a / Y +$ MPC. Since, $A > 0$, and Y is always positive, APC > MPC. Therefore, the short run properties of the Keynesian consumption function are satisfied by this diagram.

The short run variability property of the consumption function of Keynes gives the indication that as income increases, consumption-income ratio or the APC falls, so there should be increased ratio of savings. If this is so, for very high levels of incomes tending towards infinity, the consumption ratio should tend towards zero and the savings ratio should infinitely go up. But the empirical data show that in the developed countries like the USA, the savings ratio is not infinitely large. Hence, the Keynesian short run property does not hold in all situations. This may be called the *consumption puzzle*.

14.2.1 Consumption function puzzle

Empirical studies based on long-term times series data of the US economy for the period 1869–1938 made by the noted economist Simon Kuznets (1946) estimated a consumption function dating back to the Civil War which contradicts Keynes' consumption function which was found to be correct on the basis of cross sectional studies of household budget data and short-term time series data. This contradiction between Kuznets' empirical findings and Keynes' consumption function has been called the consumption function puzzle. Kuznets' observation pointed out two important aspects of consumption behaviour. First, for such a long time series data on consumption and income, the APC or the consumption-income ratio did not show any downward trend for the so-called developed countries like USA (Figure 14.3 on C / Y and S / Y) and so the MPC will be equal to APC. Second, during the boom period, the periods when APC was below the long run average and during the slump period, APC lies above the long run average value of consumption. This tendency Kuznets termed the happenings during the cyclical fluctuations. Hence, besides the already developed Keynesian short run nature of consumption function supported by Kuznets, he additionally developed the long run property of the consumption function which is known as the constancy property where APC = MPC for all values of income. The consumption function in this case is proportional with no drift and it starts from the origin but lies below the 45-degree line because MPC < 1.

Suppose the proportional consumption function is $C = bY$, $0 < b < 1$. Here, APC = MPC = b for all values of income. Figure 14.3 presents two types of consumption functions.

It is observed from the figure that the short run consumption functions with drifts, a, a', ($a' > a$) are flatter and originated from the vertical axis producing the feature of APC > MPC and $dAPC / dY < 0$ and the long run consumption function showing the feature of APC = MPC at all levels of incomes since the ratios of all the heights and bases of the respective triangles are always equal to unity.

Efforts have been made by several economists to resolve this puzzle and new theories of the consumption function have been put forward to resolve the conflict between the Keynesian intuitive consumption function of the short run and Kuznets' empirical findings in the long run. These new theories have been put forward by James Duesenberry's

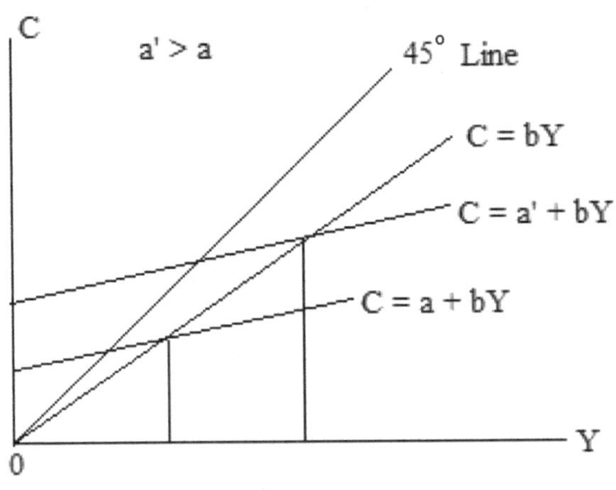

Figure 14.3 Short run and long run consumption functions

Relative Income Hypothesis in 1949, Milton Friedman's *Permanent Income Hypothesis* in 1957, and Ando and Modigliani's *Life Cycle Hypothesis* in 1963. The last two hypotheses followed Irving Fisher's concept of intertemporal choice of consumption of a rational consumer under the objective of utility maximisation subject to a present value constraint. The first model differs from the other two in the way that it compares the behaviour of a consumer with respect to their peer group and past consumption behaviour at its peak. In the following sections we discuss the models one by one.

14.3 Duesenberry's relative income hypothesis

In his relative income hypothesis, James Duesenberry developed the consumption behaviour of households that satisfies the short run as well as the long run features. His analysis is based on two relative income hypotheses. First, consumers are not concerned with their absolute level of consumption, rather with their consumption relative to the rest of the population in the society or group, called the peer group. The consumers' target under the Duesenberry approach is to maximise utility which is a function of ratios of consumption to average of the consumption of the rest of the population. Suppose C_0, $C_1 \dots C_T$ is the series of consumption at period 0, 1, 2 . . . T and P_0, $P_1 \dots P_T$ is the series of weighted averages of the consumption of the rest of the population; then the utility function, unlike the intertemporal utility function, is as follows:

$$U = U\left(C_0 / P_0,\ C_1 / P_1,\ \dots\dots,\ C_T / P_T\right). \tag{14.3}$$

It shows that the utility of an ith household increases only if the individual's consumption rises relative to that of the average of the rest of the population.

Second, present consumption is not only motivated by the present levels of absolute or relative incomes but also by the levels of consumption in the previous period which is a peak. It is much more difficult for a family drastically to cut down its consumption from a previous peak level. This is known as *consumption ratchet* in the Duesenberry model.

There is a tendency on the part of the people to imitate or emulate the consumption standards maintained by their peer group. Specifically, people with relatively low incomes attempt to "keep up with the Joneses" – they consume more and save less. This imitative nature of consumption has been described by Duesenberry as the *demonstration effect.*

The outcome of these two hypotheses of relative income is that the individual household's APC depends on its relative position in income distribution. Households with relatively high incomes in the group experience lower APCs and households with relatively low incomes experience high APCs. That means, as income rises, APC or the consumption to income ratio falls and vice versa. This satisfies the short run property of the consumption function. If, on the other hand, income distribution is relatively constant, as in keeping each household's relative position unchanged while incomes of all households rise equi-proportionately, Duesenberry then argues that APC will not change along income and it will be equal to MPC. Thus, in the aggregate we get a proportional relationship between aggregate income and aggregate consumption.

Let us discuss the short run fluctuation and long run constancy property of the consumption function by the Duesenberry approach in a mathematical and graphical way. In the short run, households treat their consumption and savings behaviour on the basis of the ratio of present income to the income of the peak period of the past. That means, when present income, Y, exceeds the previous peak, Y^*, then consumption as a ratio of income will fall and correspondingly the ratio of savings to income will rise. That is, the savings ratio is expressed as

$$APS = S / Y = a + b.\, Y / Y^* \tag{14.4}$$

The function shows that $d(S / Y) / d(Y / Y^*) = b > 0$ which means, as present income rises relative to the previous peak income, APS will increase, and if relative income compared to the peak income falls, APS also falls.

The reverse happened for the consumption function which is derived by the residual income after savings. That means

$$APC = C / Y = 1 - APS = (1 - a) - b.Y / Y^*. \tag{14.5}$$

The relation shows that $d(C / Y) / d(Y / Y^*) = -b < 0$ (since $b > 0$) which means that as present income rises relative to the previous peak income then APC will decrease and vice versa. A part of the short run property is, hence, explained. Now derive MPC from the previous relation by converting C / Y into the consumption function. The consumption function is thus

$$C = (1 - a).\, Y - b.Y^2 / Y^*. \tag{14.6}$$

Now MPC = $dC / dY = (1 - a) - 2b.\, Y / Y^*$. Comparing APC and MPC we get that

$$MPC = (1 - a) - b.Y / Y^* - b.Y / Y^* = APC - b.\, Y / Y^*. \tag{14.7}$$

Since $b > 0$, $Y / Y^* > 0$, so APC > MPC. This proves the short run property of the consumption function depicting the cyclical fluctuations.

On the other hand, in the long run, as income grows along a trend, previous peak income will always be the notion of last year's income and hence the ratio of Y / Y^* will remain constant for all levels of income. That means the drift part of the consumption and savings function will vanish. Hence, the consumption ratio functions will be the following as

$$C / Y = APC = -b.\, Y / Y^*. \tag{14.8}$$

And

$$dC / dY = MPC = -b.\, Y / Y^*. \tag{14.9}$$

Hence, APC = MPC. This proves the long run constancy property of the consumption function. Figure 14.4 presents the short run and long run behaviour of the consumption function under relative income hypothesis.

The figure shows the consumption ratchet which is the outcome of the short run and long run behaviours of the consumption function. As income grows along the trend, the ray through the origin representing long run consumption function, there is constancy of the values of APC and MPC. But, when there is fluctuation of Y relative to Y^*, the functions flatten to the long run function, APC outweighs MPC, and the consumption to income ratio falls over the values of income when there is $Y > Y^*$. Hence, the relative

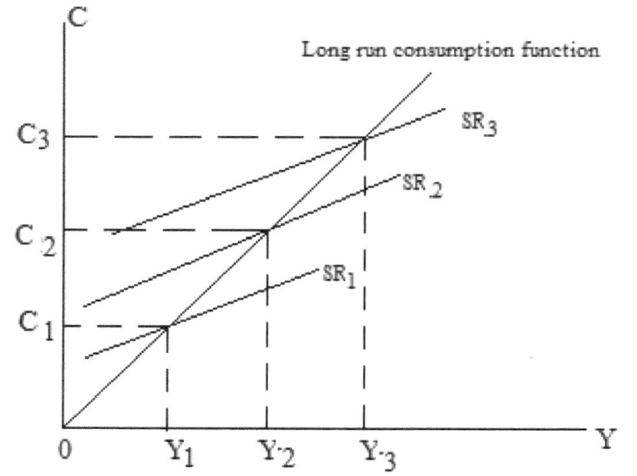

Figure 14.4 The consumption ratchet

income hypothesis of Duesenberry is capable of explaining, rather reconciling, the short run fluctuations and long run constancy property of the consumption function.

14.3.1 Criticisms against Dusenbery

Although Duesenberry's theory made a fantastic reconciliation of the apparent contradictions between the short run and long run time series studies, it suffers from a number of deficiencies. Some of them are addressed here.

i) The relative income hypothesis assumes the direct relation between consumption and income in all situations of the economy. But the empirics do not justify this. Recessions and booms in the business cycle do not always lead to decline and increase in consumption.
ii) This hypothesis assumes a proportional increase in income and consumption at all levels of employment position of the economy. But increases in income along the full employment level do not always lead to proportional increases in the consumption.
iii) The theory assumes that the distribution of income remains unchanged with the progress of the economy. If favourable redistribution occurs with increases in income, the APC of the households belonging to the relatively poor and relatively rich classes will tend to be reduced leading to no changes in the drifts. Hence, the short run property cannot be sustained.
iv) Thinking of the previous peak period's income while making consumption of the current period does not work always and hence previous peak income would have less effect on current consumption. According to Michael Evans, the consumer behaviour is slowly reversible over time, instead of being truly irreversible.
v) The hypothesis did not consider the income and consumption pattern of a family or an individual on the basis of total income earned in the total life period. Friedman, Ando, and Modigliani incorporated this phenomenon in establishing their income-consumption hypotheses on the basis of Irving Fisher's model of optimum consumption of a household on the basis of present values of income and consumption in one's life span.

14.4 Irving Fisher on optimum consumption

Irving Fisher (1930) developed a model of optimum consumption with respect to the utility function subject to intertemporal budget function in a two-period framework or the present value of income in a total life span. Let us think of the formulation in the case of an individual consumer. His utility function is like the following-

$$U = U(C_0, C_1, C_2, \ldots\ldots, C_T) \tag{14.10}$$

where the total time period in life is zero to T. Besides, the consumer calculates his present value of income and consumption in the total period which are respectively

$$C_0 = \overset{t=0}{\underset{T}{\Sigma}} C_0 \,/\, (1+r)^t \text{ and } Y_0 = \overset{t=0}{\underset{T}{\Sigma}} Y_0 \,/\, (1+r)^t \tag{14.11}$$

where "r" is the rate of discount of the future period's consumption and income and C_0 and Y_0 are the respective present values of consumption and income. The objective of the consumer is to maximise total utility subject to the constraint that the present value of his income does not fall short of the present value of total consumption. Hence, the lifetime consumption problem of the consumer is as follows:

$$\max U = U(C_0, C_1, C_2, \ldots\ldots, C_T)$$

subject to

$$\overset{t=0}{\underset{T}{\Sigma}} C_0 \,/\, (1+r)^t = \overset{t=0}{\underset{T}{\Sigma}} Y_0 \,/\, (1+r)^t$$

The constraint function shows that the consumer does not oversave or undersave in his total life period. To present the consumer's problem in a two-dimensional diagram like what we usually do in microeconomics, the problem is reduced to two periods, 0 and 1. The problem is then reduced to

$$\max U = U(C_0, C_1)$$
$$\text{subject to } C_0 + C_1 \,/\, (1 + r) = Y_0 + Y_1 \,/\, (1 + r)$$

The utility function is represented by the usual indifference curves with negative slope and strict convex curvatures. The intertemporal budget function is given by the negatively sloped straight line (Figure 14.5) with the intercept along the Y_0 axis as $Y_0 + Y_1 / (1 + r)$ and along the Y_1 axis as $Y_1 + Y_0{}^*(1 + r)$ and the slope the function as $dY_1 / dY_0 = -[Y_0 + Y_1 / (1 + r)] / [Y_1 + Y_0{}^*(1 + r)] = -(1 + r) < 0$.

The consumer attains equilibrium at E where the indifference curve (depicted by U_3) is tangent to the intertemporal budget function. At this point the slope of the indifference curve, $-MUC_0 / MUC_1$, is equal to the slope of the budget line, $-(1 + r)$. That means, in absolute terms, the ratio of marginal utilities is equal to the rate of time preference, or,

$$MUC_0 \,/\, MUC_1 = (1+r). \tag{14.12}$$

This means, at the optimum decision, the consumer will not change his consumption plan across the two periods. If the consumer would otherwise stay at the intersection point

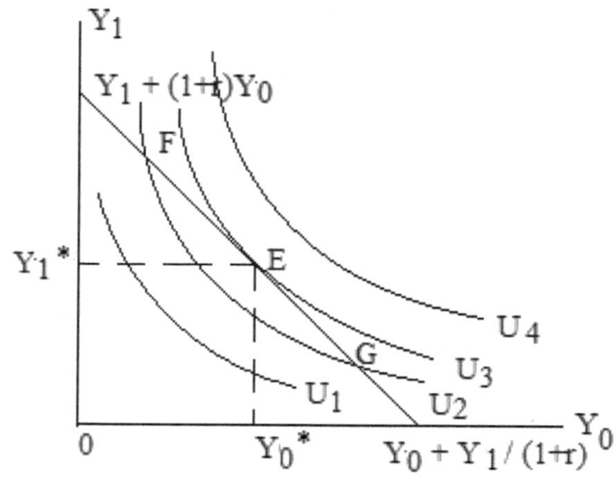

Figure 14.5 Optimum consumption in an intertemporal budget constraint

like F then it would be better for him to change his consumption plan in favour of the current period and against the future period. That means consumption is preferred to savings (that is, of the future period's consumption). On the other hand, at point G, the consumer's optimum decision will be to prefer savings to consumption during the current period. Hence, the optimum consumption combination is Y_0^* and Y_1^* which exhausts his lifetime income.

The important implication of Fisher's model of optimum consumption in a lifespan gives us the general formulation of the consumption function which says that the consumption expenditure at any time "t" is a positive function of the present value of the income stream. That is

$$C_t = f(PV_t) \tag{14.13}$$

where $PV_t = \sum_{t=0}^{T} Y_0 / (1+r)^t$ and $f' > 0$.

Friedman, Ando, and Modigliani used this formulation of consumption function in explaining the short run and long run natures of the consumption function through their hypotheses.

14.5 Friedman's permanent income hypothesis

Milton Friedman, a Nobel laureate in economics, developed the *permanent income hypothesis* (PIH) in 1957 to solve the consumption puzzle of the difference between the short run and long run behaviour of the consumers. He used Fisher's intertemporal choice theory that says that optimum consumption expenditure depends directly on the present value of income. Moreover, he argues that consumption expenditure should not depend on current income alone, but the permanent income hypothesis emphasises that people experience random and temporary changes in their income from year to year. This part of random income follows a probability distribution but the permanent income is a stable income which is known to the household. Hence, total consumption is dependent on permanent income in the long run whereas it depends also on the random income which is known as transitory income. The transitory income in Friedman's approach is the factor which explains the short run behaviour of the consumption function. Therefore,

$$Y = Y_P + Y_T \tag{14.14}$$

where Y is total income, Y_P is permanent income or average income, and Y_T is transitory income which is a deviation from the average income as it is unexpected. According to Friedman, consumption should primarily depend on permanent income, because consumers use saving and borrowing to smooth out consumption in response to transitory changes in income. For example, if an individual receives a permanent rise of INR 20,000, his consumption would rise by about as much. But if he would win the same money in betting or gambling, he would not consume it all in one year. Instead, he would spread the extra money over the rest of his life. Thus, consumers spend their permanent income, but they save most of their transitory income.

Friedman's formulation of the consumption function hence is $C = kY_P$, where k is a constant proportion indicating the marginal propensity of consumption out of permanent income where Y_P is a function of present value of the income.

Similarly, he distinguishes between permanent consumption (C_P) and transitory consumption (C_T). Transitory consumption may be regarded as the unanticipated spending like unexpected illness, pickpocketing, etc. Thus, measured consumption is the sum of permanent and transitory components of consumption. That is,

$$C = C_P + C_T. \tag{14.15}$$

Let us prove, rather reconcile, the consumption puzzle by means of Friedman's approach. First consider the long run property. For this purpose, we recall that permanent consumption is a proportional function of the permanent income, which is $C = kY_P$. It follows from the relation that APC and MPC out of the permanent income are constant, which is equal to k. That means, in the long run APC = MPC. Hence, the permanent income hypothesis proves the long run constancy property of average and marginal values of consumption that were observed from the US data.

Let us consider the case of short run variability in consumption around the average values of permanent income. Friedman assumes that there is no correlation between Y_P and Y_T, between Y_T and C_T, or between C_P and C_T. That means the covariances are zero. We write down them as

$$\text{Cov}\,(Y_P, Y_T) = 1 / n[\Sigma(Y_P . Y_T) - \bar{Y}_P . \bar{Y}_T = 0$$
$$\text{Cov}\,(Y_T, C_T) = 1 / n[\Sigma(Y_T . C_T) - \bar{Y}_T . \bar{C}_T = 0$$
$$\text{Cov}\,(C_P, C_T) = 1 / n[\Sigma(C_P . C_T) - \bar{C}_P . \bar{C}_T = 0$$

where the bars carry the mark for the average for all concerned variables. The previous relations show that the transitory part of income or consumption does not have long run effects; rather it has short run effects.

Since Y_T is uncorrected with Y_P, the fact follows that a high (or low) permanent income is not correlated with a high (or low) transitory income. For the entire group of households from all income groups, transitory incomes (both positive and negative) would cancel each over out so that average transitory income would be equal to zero. This is also true for transitory components of consumption. Thus, for all the families taken together, the average transitory income and average transitory consumption are zero, that is, $\overline{Y_T} = \overline{C_T} = 0$. Hence, it follows that income and consumption are of permanent nature in overall sense. That is $Y = Y_P$ and $C = C_P$.

Now consider that some families in the society have above-average measured incomes because of their unexpected incomes. This means their transitory incomes are positive and $Y_P < Y$ (or $C < C_p$). On the other hand, if some families have below-average income because of some loss in gambling, say, then the reverse incidence arises. That is, negative transitory incomes lead to $Y_P > Y$ (or $C > C_p$). These two situations help in resolving the cross section conflict.

When $C < Cp$ then we can write $C - C_p = C_T$.

Or $C = C_P + C_T$
or $C = kY_P$ + a positive number
or APC = $C / Y_P = k$ + a positive number.

This means APC > k

Since, MPC is equal to k, so APC > MPC and as income rises, APC falls.

Figure 14.6 presents all the short run and long run features of Friedman's consumption function. The line $C_p = kY_P$ shows the proportional relationship between permanent consumption and permanent income which is flatter than the 45-degree line. This line cuts the short run consumption line (i.e. $C = kY_P + B$, where $B > 0$) at point E which corresponds to the average measured income of the population at which there is no transitory income. We get the corresponding average or permanent consumption, C_P, on average income. Hence, we get APC = MPC along the proportional consumption line, a ray through the origin.

Let us explain the cross sectional results of the consumption and income relation which takes into account the transitory parts of income and consumption. If a sample

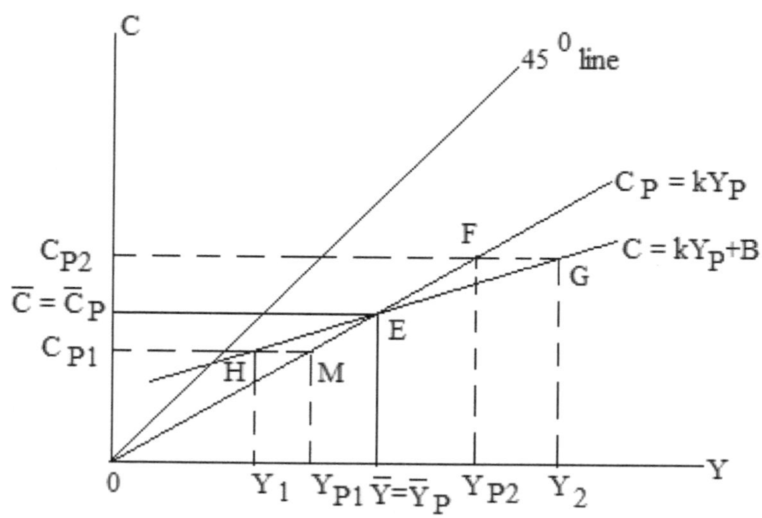

Figure 14.6 Consumption function under permanent income hypothesis

group of population has an average income above the population average, its transitory income is positive. The horizontal difference between the short run and long run consumption functions (points *F* and *G*) describes the transitory income. On the other hand, when the sample population has less than the average income of the population, then transitory income is negative and the difference between the short run and long run consumption function is given by the points *H* and *M*. This consumption function gives an MPC that has a value less than the long run proportional consumption function, $C_p = kY_p$. Thus, in the short run, Friedman's hypothesis yields a consumption function similar to the Keynesian one, that is, MPC < APC. And over time, as the economy grows, transitory components reduce to zero for the society as a whole. So the measured consumption and measured income values are permanent consumption and permanent income and along the $C_p = kY_p$ APC is fairly constant, and APC = MPC. Therefore, the consumption puzzle has been resolved by Friedman on the basis of his permanent income hypothesis.

14.5.1 *Criticism of permanent income hypothesis*

Criticism of the PIH has centred on two main assumptions.

i) Economists like Friend and Kravis have objected to Friedman's assumption of constant APC. They maintain that households with a low level of permanent income are under much heavier pressure to consume than households with a much higher level of permanent income. Therefore, from a theoretical standpoint, APC of a low-income household should exceed that of a high-income household.
ii) Various economists have also objected to Friedman's assumptions of MPC from transitory income being equal to zero. Empirically much evidence suggests that MPC from transitory income is positive, as in $cov\ (c^t, y^t) > 0$.
iii) From an empirical point of view this hypothesis is hard to test because of the difficulty of measuring permanent income and permanent consumption.

Despite all these limitations, PIH has some important implications.

14.6 Ando—Modigliani's life cycle hypothesis

Albert Ando and Franco Modigliani in their seminal work on "The Life Cycle Hypothesis of Savings" in 1963 reconciled the short run and long run properties of the consumption function in line with the Fisher's intertemporal utility maximisation. According to the life cycle hypothesis (LCH) of Ando–Modigliani, consumption is a function of lifetime expected income of the consumer which consists of the resources available to him, the rate of return on capital, the spending plan, and the age at which the plan is made. The present value of his resources includes income from assets or wealth or property and from current and expected labour income. Thus the total resources of the consumer in total life consist of his income and wealth. The objective of the consumer is to maintain a slightly increasing level of consumption throughout his life subject to the condition that the present value of his total income does not fall below the present value of his total consumption. This principle can work when the consumer dissaves during the pre-earning and post retirement phase and saves during the earning phase to repay the debt in the pre earning phase and keep aside a fund for future security after retirement (Figure 13.1). Therefore, intuitively the life cycle hypothesis says that, in a cross section of consumers, the high-income group in the society will contain a higher-than-average proportion of consumers who are at high levels of income since they are in the earning phase of their lives and hence they have a relatively low consumption-to-income ratio. That is C / Y (= APC) will be falling with income. On the other hand, the low-income groups who are in the post-retirement phases of their lives have relatively high APC. Therefore, the Ando–Modigliani hypothesis says that in the cross section model, as income rises, APC falls and vice-versa and APC > MPC. But if we consider the trend of income of the consumers, then the model shows that there is a constancy property of consumption, which is APC = MPC.

Let us discuss the model in detail. Reconsidering Fisher's version, consumption of any consumer, i, at any time period, t, depends positively and proportionately on his present value of income and consumption, PV^i. That means

$$C^i_t = k^i \,.\, PV^i_t \tag{14.16}$$

where $0 < k^i < 1$. k^i stands for the proportion of present value of income spent on the consumption of the ith consumer. If the population distribution is equitable in age and income (which has been observed in US economy) and all the consumers maintain a stable taste pattern in present as well as future periods, then the aggregate consumption of the entire population is the simple horizontal summation across all the ith consumers. Therefore, in aggregate, the consumption function is as follows:

$$C_t = k \,.\, PV_t \,. \tag{14.17}$$

Ando and Modigliani attempted to measure the present value by means of present values of observed incomes which are obtained from the labour supply and present values of the volumes of assets/wealth possessed by the consumers. Hence, for the consumers with life span of 0 to T, the present value of income is

$$PV_0 = \Sigma Y_t^L / (1+r)^t + \Sigma Y_t^A / (1+r)^t \tag{14.18}$$

The life cycle hypothesis assumes that the asset market is perfect and hence the present value of asset income is the value of the asset itself, which is say A0. It is thus the actual quantity of asset income. That is

$$PV_0 = \Sigma Y_t^L / (1+r)^t + A_0. \tag{14.19}$$

Further, the hypothesis splits the entire labour income into observed current income and the expected labour income for the period 1, 2 . . . . . ., T. That means,

$$PV_0 = Y^L{}_0 + \Sigma Y_t^L / (1+r)^t + A_0 \tag{14.20}$$

where $Y^L{}_0$ is the observed current period's labour income. Again, the hypothesis assumes that the average expected income from labour service in the current period, $Y^e{}_0$ is the expected value for the time span 1, 2 . . . ., T which is expressed as

$$Y^e{}_0 = [1/(T-1)].\, \Sigma Y_t^L / (1+r)^t \tag{14.21}$$

or

$$\Sigma Y_t^L / (1+r)^t = (T-1).\ Y^e{}_0. \tag{14.22}$$

Hence, the present value expression is derived from the previous relations as

$$PV_0 = Y^L{}_0 + (T-1).\ Y^e{}_0 + A_0. \tag{14.23}$$

One term is still immeasurable in the previous expression, which is the expected income. Ando and Modigliani assumed that expected labour income is some positive function of current income, which is

$$Y^e{}_0 = \alpha.\ Y^L{}_0. \tag{14.24}$$

where $\alpha > 0$. Hence, the final expression for the present value function (from 14.23 and 14.24) is

$$PV_0 = Y^L{}_0 + (T-1).\ \alpha Y^L{}_0 + A_0 \tag{14.25}$$

or

$$PV_0 = Y^L{}_0\left[1+(T-1)\ \alpha\right] + A_0. \tag{14.26}$$

As now all components of the present value function are observable and statistically testable, the consumption function at current period can now be derived as the following:

$$C_0 = k\left\{\left[Y^L{}_0\left[1+(T-1)\alpha\right] + A_0\right\}. \tag{14.27}$$

This is rearranged as

$$C_0 = k\left[1+(T-1)\alpha\right]Y^L{}_0 + kA_0. \tag{14.28}$$

The previous consumption function (14.28), according to Ando and Modigliani, best fits the US data in the post-world war periods. The variable part of consumption comes out of the labour income and the fixed part of consumption or the drift part arises out of the asset incomes. In the short run, the asset income part, kA_0, works as the intercept of the consumption function and remains fairly constant and the MPC out of the labour income is $k[1 + (T - 1)\ \alpha]$ which is less than unity, since k, $\alpha < 1$ and APC falls as income rises and APC > MPC. Hence, the short run consumption function passes through the vertical (i.e. consumption) axis with the positive drift of kA_0. On the other hand, in the long run, with more and more savings leading to more and more asset generation, the magnitudes of drifts increase over time and there is one optimum consumption-income relation along a particular short run, and the locus of all such optimum points gives us the long run consumption function, which is a ray through the origin but flatter than the 45-degree line. Along this ray through the origin, there is a proportional relation between consumption and labour income and APC and MPC are fairly constant and APC = MPC. The line OP in Figure 14.7 is the long run consumption function and SRC_1, SRC_2 and SRC_3 represent the short run consumption functions with respective drifts, kA_1, kA_2, and kA_3.

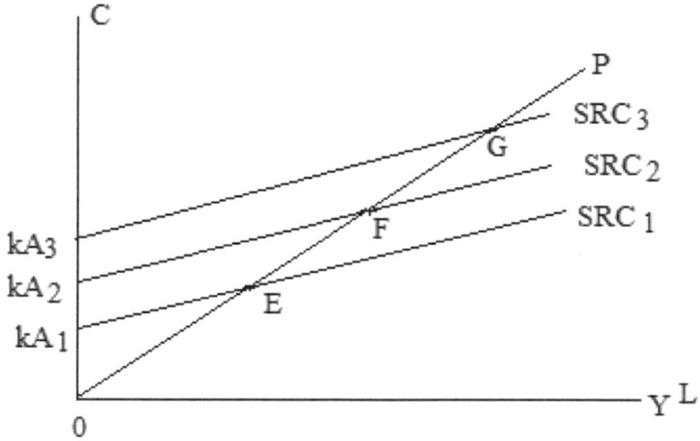

Figure 14.7 Consumption functions under life cycle hypothesis

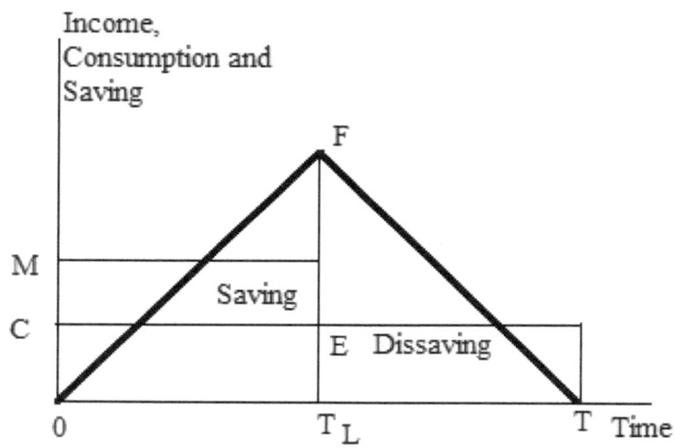

Figure 14.8 Prediction sketch of life cycle hypothesis

Empirically the Ando–Modigliani consumption function based on the US data for the post world war period is $C_t = 0.7\ Y^L_t + 0.06\ A_t$, where the MPC is 70% out of the labour income and 6% out of the asset income.

The life cycle model makes many other predictions as well. It implies that saving varies over a person's life in a predictable way. If the consumer smooths "*C*" over his lifespan, he will save and accumulate wealth during his working years and then dissave and run down his wealth during retirement time, T_L out of his total life of $0T$.

Figure 14.8 describes this phenomenon. The consumer saves in the entire working period of T_L out of his income, say *OM*. In each period, he consumes *OC* amount and saves the rest. For each period up to the age of his demise, *T*, he has the wealth/asset accumulation function which looks like *OFT*. After T_L time, his income falls short of consumption and thus he dissaves. He keeps nothing for his heirs.

14.6.1 *Comparisons between LCH and PIH*

The LCH differs from PIH in a number of ways.

i) The LCH pays more attention to the motives of saving than PIH does and provides convincing reasons to include wealth in the consumption functions. LCH is also concerned explicitly with the role of asset accumulation and the effect of age on household consumption. PIH, on the other hand, pays more attention to the way in which persons form expectations about their future incomes.
ii) PIH is less satisfactory than the LCH in the sense that assets are only implicitly taken into account as a determinant of permanent income, and it relies on less-observable aspects of income – permanent and transitory – than the LCH which separates out observable components – labour income and income from assets. Therefore, LCH might be more useful to econometric model buildings and forecasting.

In spite of these differences, the focus and methodology of two models are closely related. Both are based explicitly on intertemporal utility maximising behaviour by household. Persons with high transitory income in PIH would be the persons staying in the middle years of the LCH and persons with negative transitory income could be the ones at the beginning or end of the life cycle. Thus the LCH could be one explanation of the distribution of Friedman's transitory income.

14.7 Robert Hall and the random-walk hypothesis

The permanent income hypothesis is based on Fisher's model of intertemporal choice. It builds on the idea that forward-looking consumers base their consumption decisions not only on their current income but also on the income they expect to receive in the future. Thus, the permanent income hypothesis highlights that consumption depends on people's expectation. Research on consumption by Robert Hall in 1978 on "Stochastic Implications of the Life Cycle-Permanent Income Hypothesis: Theory and Evidence" has combined this view of the consumer with the assumption of rational expectations. Hall's approach to the consumption function originates from the Lucas critique. The *Lucas critique*, named after Robert Lucas, argues that it is naive to try to predict the effects of a change in economic policy entirely on the basis of relationships observed in historical data, especially highly aggregated historical data. More formally, it states that the decision rules of the Keynesian consumption function cannot be considered as structural in the sense of being invariant with respect to changes in government policy variables. The critique further suggests that, if we want to predict the effect of a policy experiment, we should model that the deep parameters relating to preferences, technology, etc. are assumed to govern individual behaviour. If these models can account for observed empirical regularities, we can then predict what individuals will do, taking into account the policy changes and then aggregate the individual consumption decisions to calculate the macroeconomic effects of the policy change.

Robert Hall was the first to derive the implications of rational expectations for consumption. He showed that if the permanent income hypothesis was correct and if consumers had rational expectations, then changes in consumption over time should be unpredictable. According to Hall, the combination of the permanent income hypothesis and rational expectations implies that consumption follows a *random walk*.

According to the permanent income hypothesis, consumers face fluctuating income and try their best to smooth their consumption over time. At any moment, consumers choose consumption based on their current expectations of their lifetime incomes. Over time, they change their consumption because they receive news that causes them to revise their expectations. For example, a person getting an unexpected promotion increases consumption, whereas a person getting an unexpected demotion decreases consumption. In other words, changes in consumption reflect "surprises" in income. If consumers are optimally using all available information, then they should be surprised only by events that were entirely unpredictable. Therefore, changes in their consumption should be unpredictable as well. The consumption function that Hall presented looks like the following equation:

$$C_2 = C_1 + U_1 \tag{14.29}$$

where C_2 is the consumption expenditure in period 2 that is generated from the past period's consumption, C_1 plus a random disturbance term U_1 which may be treated as innovation term. The consumption model by Hall is a time series process where the present period's consumption is derived from all the past values of consumption the consumer can manage to consider in rationalising his consumption decision. Generalising this model, we can write the consumption function as

$$C_t = C_{t-1} + \varepsilon_t \tag{14.30}$$

where ε_t is the random shock that can explain the consumption expenditure which we proxy as an innovation term in the earlier equation. The consumption function, as per time series concept, is a non-stationary series.

The rational expectation approach to consumption has important policy implications also. If consumers obey the PIH and have rational expectations, then only unexpected policy changes influence consumption. Policy changes will be effective when they change the public's expectations. Hence, if consumers have rational expectations, policymakers influence the economy not only through their actions but also through the public's expectation of their actions.

14.8 Arthur Smithies on the reconciliation of the puzzle

Arthur Smithies, a Keynesian economist, put forward the roles of factors other than income in nomenclature like that of the hypotheses of Duesenberry, Friedman, and Ando–Modigliani, on the determination of consumption expenditure to justify the Keynesian short run nonproportional consumption and income relation and to convert the relation into proportional or long run relation by means of the roles of the shifted factors. These other factors, according to him, are population increase in the urban areas due to rural-urban migration, population distribution in favour of old and young ages below the earning age, etc. Duesenberry, Friedman, and Ando–Modigliani in their theories did not consider these consumption-influencing factors like Smithies. According to Smithies, under the condition of other nonchangeable factors under ceteris paribus restrictions to determine consumption expenditure other than income, the consumption function passes through the vertical axis with a positive intercept fixed by the parametric values of the other factors (Figure 14.9). Along this consumption function (A_1CS_1), as income rises, the

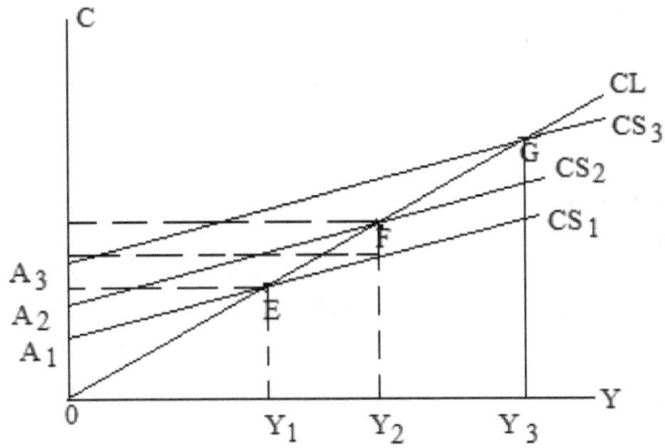

Figure 14.9 Smithies consumption function

C / Y ratio falls and $C / Y > dC / dY$ or APC > MPC. Hence, the consumption function under ceteris paribus restriction is nonproportional.

Smithies also opined that if the other factors imputed within the ceteris paribus restriction are allowed to change continuously, then the short run consumption function will shift upwards (from A_1CS_1 to A_2CS_2, A_3CS_3, etc.) continuously with the increase in these factors and for each such increase there will be one optimum combination of consumption and income (like *E*, *F*, and *G*) and they each will be corresponding to the points on the long run consumption function. Hence, we get the proportional consumption function passing through the origin along which, as income increases, the C / Y ratio will be constant and APC will be equal to MPC. In the figure, OCL is such a consumption function.

14.9 Factors affecting consumption expenditure

In the previous section we saw that the Keynesian absolute income hypothesis postulated that aggregate real consumption expenditure depended on aggregate real (absolute) national income, other things remaining constant. The factors that belong to those other things play the role of shifting of the consumption function. The factors other than the level of income affecting consumption expenditure of households can be divided into three groups: (*A*) subjective, (*B*) objective and (*C*) structural.

14.9.1 Subjective factors

Subjective factors are psychological ones that cannot be quantitatively measured. They are attributes and can be qualitatively measured or ordered. Examples of some of the subjective factors are basic values, states of mind, attitudes, etc. According to Keynes, there are several motives for saving, such as precaution, foresight, enterprise, pride and greediness, enjoyment, short-sightedness, generosity, etc. determining the shifting of the consumption function. In the short run, according to Keynes, these subjective factors are likely to be nonchangeable in the way that one's positive expectation regarding the future price or income growth, say, is neutralised by others' reverse expectation on these variables.

14.9.2. Objective factors

Objective factors are economic variables that can be measured quantitatively. There are some crucial objective factors which influence the consumption expenditure in the economy.

Volume of wealth: the consumption function looks like $C = C(Y, W_0)$ where W_0 is the volume of wealth. As volume of wealth increases through rise in savings expenditure, the consumers feel better and consume more (i.e. $dC / dW > 0$). This means that if a person already has a great volume of wealth or money, his propensity to consume will be high. This is also true for the whole economy. This is known as *real balance effect* of Pigou and Patinkin. It helps the economy overcome the persistent unemployment problem.

Rate of interest: another important objective factor after income is the rate of interest, r. The consumption function then is $C = C(Y, r)$. A rise in the interest rate with given income creates reduction of aggregate consumption expenditure and vice-versa. That is, $dC / dr < 0$. This happens due to reduction of bond prices – thereby discouraging the consumption propensities of the bondholders – and due another to more savings discouraging consumption and consumers preferring future consumption to the current period's consumption. The reverse effect appears when there is reduction of rate of interest.

Expectations regarding the future: if the consumers expect the commodity prices to increase in future periods they will definitely go for more consumption in the current period. If there are uncertainties in the future periods to foresee the price changes, aggregate consumption expenditure may increase, decrease, or remain constant.

Advertising: advertising for the producers' products in real or artificial forms also affects the consumption decisions of the consumers as it discloses some information about the products to the consumers. Other things remaining the same, the greater the volume of advertising expenditure the greater the consumption expenditure will be.

14.9.3 Structural factors

Structural factors include aspects particularly relevant for the problem of aggregation. The first important structural factor is income distribution. We know that the marginal propensity to consume of low-income people is substantially higher than the marginal propensity to consume of high-income people. Hence, when there is redistribution of income from rich income groups to poor income groups, this will increase consumption expenditure in an economy even if the level of income remains unchanged.

Increase in population of a country leads to increase in consumption expenditure as a whole. There are certain demographic factors like family size, spatial aspect of the population, etc. that cause shifting of the consumption expenditure function. For example, other things remaining the same, the spending of big families must be greater than that of smaller families. Rural families spend less than urban families. Families with young children are likely to spend more than those without small children.

Fiscal and monetary policies and international trade policies also affect the consumption expenditure of a country. Expansionary fiscal and monetary policies in line with Keynes' model generate more income for the country which ultimately leads to increase in consumption. A favourable open trade policy leading to export promotion may also lead to more consumption since export income makes the economy wealthy and the consumption in aggregate increases. If the government raises more money through taxation, it will reduce the disposable income and hence the consumption expenditure will fall. Similarly, if the government reduces taxes or makes more transfer payments, the disposable income will increase and hence the consumption expenditure will also increase. Even if the national income remains unchanged, disposable income may change because of the fiscal operation of the government and, thereby, may change consumption expenditure as well.

It is of note that most of the previous types of factors remain unchanged in the short run, hence the short run aggregate consumption expenditure may be regarded as a function of income. When any of these factors that are assumed to remain constant change, the consumption function will shift as well and a continuous upward shift lead to the long run nature of the consumption function.

14.10 Conclusion

In the present chapter we have made discussions about the households' consumption behaviour on the basis of microeconomic foundations. We started with the Keynesian absolute income hypothesis and defined short run and long run properties and there are some other models that tested the properties empirically. What was made clear is that in the short run there will be fluctuations in consumption due to APC > MPC and in the long run there will be consistency of consumption with income due to the condition of APC = MPC.

Summary

- Aggregate consumption expenditure is a positive function of income with marginal propensity to consume lying between zero and unity.
- As income increases, average propensity to consume falls and average propensity to consume is greater than marginal propensity to consume – it is the short run property
- In the long run, average propensity to consume is equal to marginal propensity to consume. These two features form the consumption puzzle.
- James Dusenbery explained the puzzle by means of relative income hypothesis, Milton Friedman explained it by permanent income hypothesis, and Ando and Modigliani explained it by the life cycle hypothesis. All have come to a similar conclusion to that of Keynes and Kuznets
- There are subjective factors, objective factors, and fundamental factors in explaining aggregate consumption expenditure

Keywords

Consumption function
Marginal propensity to consume
Absolute income hypothesis
Relative income hypothesis
Permanent income hypothesis
Life cycle hypothesis
Intertemporal consumption
Random walk hypothesis

Multiple choice questions and answers

1. Under the Keynesian Absolute Income Hypothesis, consumption expenditure is a stable function of

   (a) Absolute income.
   (b) Nominal rate of interest.

(c) Both (a) and (b).
(d) None of the above.

2. Under the short run system, the consumption function bears the property that

(a) APC > MPC.
(b) APC falls with income and APC > MPC.
(c) APC = MPC.
(d) All of the above.

3. The long run property of consumption function says that

(a) APC = MPC.
(b) Consumption function will be a ray through the origin and lies below the 45-degree line.
(c) APC remains constant with income.
(c) All of the above.

4. According to the permanent income hypothesis, the correlation between permanent income and transitory income will be

(a) Positive.
(b) Negative.
(c) Zero.
(d) None of the above.

5. The ratchet effect is found in

(a) Life cycle hypothesis.
(b) Permanent income hypothesis.
(c) Absolute income hypothesis.
(d) Relative income hypothesis.

Answers

1. (a); 2. (b); 3. (d); 4. (c); 5. (d)

Review questions

1. Suppose a consumption function is $C = a + by$; give the economic interpretation of the terms "a" and "b". Discuss the objective factors affecting consumption expenditure. Mention also the subjective factors determining consumption expenditure.
2. Define a consumption function. What are the basic properties of the Keynesian consumption function? Draw the diagram of the consumption function given by $C = 200 + 0.75\ Y$. How its position will change if it is replaced by $C = 400 + 0.85.\ Y$?
3. What is the consumption puzzle? Explain how the puzzle has been explained by the relative income hypothesis.
4. Differentiate "permanent income" from "transitory income". Explain how Professor Friedman proved the validities of the short run and long run phenomenon of consumption behaviour with the help of these two concepts of income.
5. What is meant by "life cycle" of an individual? Explain the life cycle hypothesis to reconcile the short run and long run behaviour of consumption expenditure.

6. What is a random walk? Explain how Professor Hall used this concept in explaining households' consumption behaviour.
7. Suppose the consumption function is given by $C = a + by$. Derive the savings function from it and prove that APC + APS = 1 and MPC + MPS = 1. Can consumption and savings functions be parallel? Discuss.
8. What is intertemporal consumption? Explain how optimum consumption decision is taken by a household in a two-period framework.

Additional readings

Ando, A. & Modigliani, F. (1963). "Life cycle hypothesis of saving: Aggregate implications and tests". *The American Economic Review*, 53(1).

Fisher, I. (1930). *The Theory of Interest, as Determined by Impatience to Spend Income and Opportunity to Invest It*. London: Macmillan.

Friedman, M. (1957). "The permanent income hypothesis". NBER Working Paper. http://www.nber.org/books/frie57-1.

Hall, R. (1978). "Stochastic implications of the life cycle-permanent income hypothesis: Theory and evidence". *Journal of Political Economy*, 86(6).

Kuznets, S. (1946). *National Income and its Composition*, vol. II. New York: NBER.

15 Theories of investment demand

15.1 Introduction

Investment demand is an important component of aggregate output of an economy after consumption in the Keynesian as well as classical models; in fact, it carries more weight in the first model compared to the second. We have already seen the role of investment in Keynesian and classical economics in determination of output and employment in an economy. The Keynesian model emphasised its active role in determining output and employment through the multiplier process whether it was made by privately owned capitalistic firms or the government of the economy. On the other hand, in the classical model, investment plays the role of determining rate of interest conjugative with savings and the determination of rate of interest by savings and investment is independent from the other sectors of the economy. This is known as one form of dichotomy in the classical model. In the following sections we will discuss different concepts of investment and different theories of investment to establish its role.

It is hard to find any general type of investment function prevailing in the world economies even if there is a bilateral causal relation between investment and profit or income of the firms or of the economies. We already know from the multiplier analysis that higher investment leads to higher profits and also equilibrium income of the economy. But higher profits/income again lead to higher investment through some unspecified investment functions. Since investment adds to the existing productive capacity of the economy, the expected increase in the potential capacity of output leads further to a feedback effect upon the volume of investment. In the following discussion, we will concentrate on the channels of output to investment primarily and then another determinant, that is rate of interest, upon the investment demand. There are some intermediate theories in between the two previous theories which will also be covered under the discussion on important theories of investment. Before visiting them in detail, we will address some concepts of investment.

15.2 Concepts of investment

Investment refers to real investment or capital formation which adds to capital equipment plus change in stock of unsold product which is known as inventory. It includes new plants and equipment; construction of public works like roads, buildings, dams, schools, colleges, bridges, canals, etc.; net foreign investment, inventories; and stocks and shares of new companies. Capital, on the other hand, according to Bohm Bawerks,

DOI: 10.4324/9781003501138-19

is a "produced means of production", those means which are produced by labour. In this sense, capital is sometimes termed frozen labour. It refers to real assets like factories, plants, equipment, and inventories of finished and semi-finished goods. It is any previously produced input that can be used in the production process to produce other goods. The amount of capital available in an economy is the stock of capital. Thus, capital is a stock concept.

Suppose stock of capital in time t is K_t and the stock in the last period $t - 1$ is K_{t-1}, then the amount of investment in period t is given by the following relation:

$$I_t = K_t - K_{t-1}. \tag{15.1}$$

Net addition to capital stock arises when $K_t > K_{t-1}$, which means I_t is positive when capital in the current period outweighs the amount of depreciation of the old capital. On the other hand, net subtraction or loss to capital stock arises when $K_t < K_{t-1}$, which means I_t is negative when capital in the current period falls short of the amount of depreciation of the old capital. This situation is called disinvestment or negative investment which erodes the stock of capital of the business institution that narrows down the size of business and output of the firm as well as that of the entire economy. For example, Reliance Telecommunications has total capital of Rs. 1,000 crore in the year 2015 and the management decides to purchase Rs. 1,500 crore of capital in the year 2016. Then total investment in the year 2016 is 1,500 – 1,000 = 500 crore. That means Reliance Telecommunication has added to its stock of capital by Rs. 500 crore in 2016.

15.2.1 Gross investment vs. net investment

Gross investment is the total volume of capital formation which is derived from the addition of capital stock plus inventory accumulation of unsold finished products and the products which remain in the process. Inventory accumulation may be positive or negative depending on the volume of excess demand or excess supply of the entire economy. If there is excess demand for the good under consideration then inventory accumulation will be negative since the stock in the warehouse will be cleared to meet the extra demand. On the other hand, if there is excess supply or recession in demand then surplus products will be added to the stock in the warehouse. Hence,

$$Gross\ investment\ (I) = Addition\ to\ capital\ goods + inventory\ accumulation. \tag{15.2}$$

On the other hand, *net investment* (or net capital formation) is the net addition to capital stock plus inventory accumulation. The term "net addition" arises since capital goods depreciate over time or over their usage. Depreciation (D) is defined as the physical wear and tear of machinery, equipment, etc. Hence,

$$Net\ investment\ (NI) = Gross\ investment\ (I) - D. \tag{15.3}$$

If gross investment is just enough to replace the amount of depreciation, then there is actually no investment in net value. Net investment is positive when gross investment is greater than D and it is negative if D is greater than gross investment.

15.2.2 *Autonomous investment vs. induced investment*

Investment, whether in gross or net form, again has two types depending upon the nature of its determinants. *Autonomous investment* is the amount of investment which is fixed at a given level, say at I_0, under the condition that all the determinants of it are unresponsive. For example, Reliance Telecom India decided to invest \$1,000 billion into developing the 5G internet network without looking at how much of their profits/returns/output (*Y*) were obtained from the existing 4G networks or whether the central bank of India reduced the repo rate (*r*) or not; the company only has the feeling that the original founder of Reliance Industry, Mr. Dhirubhai Ambani, had such a desire in his living ages. The investment function will then look like the first one in Figure 15.1 which is a horizontal line through the (Y, r) axis where I_0 = \$1,000 billion.

On the other hand, when investment demand is dependent on any of the variables like the income of the company or GDP of the country (*Y*) and rate of interest (*r*, which may be induced by repo rates) then it is called induced investment. The shapes of the investment functions under two different variable structures will not be horizontal, rather upward sloping with respect to *Y* and negatively sloped with respect to *r*. The second and third part of Figure 15.1 show them.

15.2.3 *Income and interest sensitivity of investment*

Sometimes it is of interest to the investors or the business firms to know the magnitude of response of the changes in either income or rate of interest upon the quantity of investment to judge their business as well as capacity profiles. The sensitivity of investment with respect to income and rate of interest are usually measured by the slope of the investment functions in the respective variables. Hence, the income sensitivity of investment is measured by the term dI / dY and the interest sensitivity of investment is measured by the term dI / dr. The sign of the first term is positive and the sign of the second term is negative, but why? The detailed answer will be provided in a later part of the discussion. For the time being, it can be intuitively explained that income is a positive factor to investment and rate of interest is a negative factor or cost to investment (refer to Figure 15.1). The income sensitivity from the figure follows that $dI / dY = EG / FG > 0$ and the interest sensitivity is $dI / dr = JL / HJ < 0$. Suppose initial investment is INR 100, income is INR500, and rate of interest is 10%. If income increases to INR 600 (an increase by 100 units) and interest rate increases to 12% then investment in the first case increases to, say, INR 130

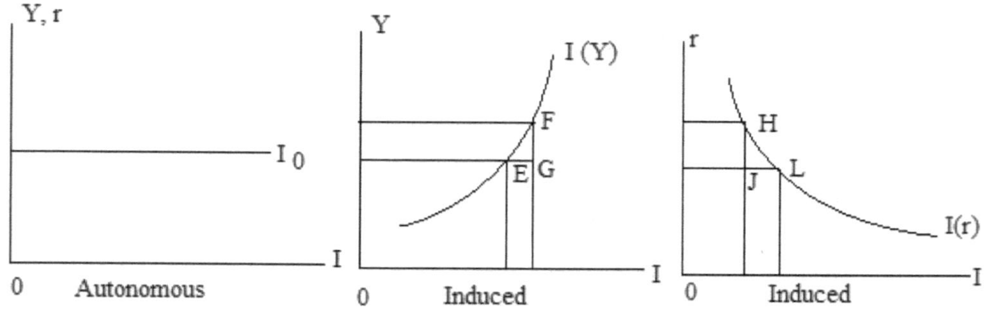

Figure 15.1 Different investment functions

and falls to INR 80 in the second case. Hence, $dI / dY = (130 - 100) / (600 - 500) = 30 / 100 = 30\%$ and $dI / dr = (80 - 100) / (12 - 10) = -20 / 2 = -10\%$.

15.3 Important theories of investment demand

In macroeconomics, we have a list of important theories on aggregate investment decisions made by all the firms in the economy in carrying out their production and income-generating activities contributing to national output. There are four such important theories of investment demand made by a capitalistic economy depending upon different economic indicators. They are *the accelerator theory of investment, the internal funds theory of investment, the neoclassical theory of investment*, and *the Keynesian theory of investment*. We discuss here the previous theories in a nutshell.

15.3.1 The accelerator theory of investment

The *accelerator theory* of investment, in its simplest form, is based upon the notion that a particular amount of capital stock is necessary to produce a given output. The factor, output or national income (Y), as we mentioned earlier, now plays the role of determining the amount of capital and investment expenditure of an economy. The *accelerator principle* is one of the principles of determining investment of an economy through changes in capital stock backed by the volume of output or income of an economy. The accelerator theory is an economic hypothesis that investments made by firms or companies augment when either the volume of aggregate demand or income/output increases and vice versa. Further it suggests that when there is an excess aggregate demand in the economy, firms or companies have two options to meet them. One is by increasing prices to decrease demand or increase investment up to the level of increased demand. The accelerator theory is based upon the second one that the firms or companies naturally choose to increase production or income, thereby increasing profits. This growth, in turn, attracts further investors which works to accelerate growth of the firms as well as the entire economy. The theory further assumes that there is no excess capacity enjoyed or preserved by the firms or the economy.

This simplest form of the accelerator theory was invented by J. M. Clark in 1917. According to this theory, investment is inherently unstable since any temporary change in output could lead to a significant change in investment spending. According to this, when income or consumption increases, investment will increase by a multiple amount which will allow a greater amount of the commodities to be produced. This will require more capital in an induced or endogenous system to produce them if the already given stock of capital is fully used.

The *accelerator* is the numerical value of the relation between the increases in investment resulting from an increase in income. That means $v = I_t / dY_t = dK_t / dY_t$, where "stands for the accelerator. Again, "v" can be termed as the incremental capital–output ratio, which shows how many capitals are required to produce one extra unit of output. It alternatively represents the inverse of marginal productivity (or efficiency) of capital. A low value of "v" means the capital is highly efficient or productive and a high value of it means the capital is less efficient and a zero value means the capital remains the same in efficiency. This argument on the accelerator has been widely applied in the neoclassical and Harrod-Domar theories of growth. The net induced investment will be positive if national income increases and induced investment may fall to zero if the national income or output remains constant and negative if national income decreases. That means $dI_t >$ 0, = 0 and < 0, depending upon whether $dY_t > 0$, = 0 and < 0.

Let us come to the acceleration principle in detail. If an economy desires to produce a given amount of output, it requires a certain amount of capital. If Y_t output is required to be produced at time t and v is the capital–output ratio, the required amount of capital to produce Y_t output will be given by the following equation:

$$K_t = vY_t \tag{15.4}$$

where K_t stands for the stock of capital at time t. It is assumed in the acceleration principle that the capital–output ratio v is constant. Therefore, under the assumption of constant capital–output ratio, changes in output are made possible by changes in the stock of capital in a proportional way. For example, $v = 2$ means, to produce one unit more of output, additional capital requirement is 2 units. If we address the same relation for the one period lag, $t - 1$, then required stock of capital at $t - 1$ period will be $K_{t-1} = vY_{t-1}$.

Hence, the required increase in the stock of capital in period t is given by the following relation:

$$K_t - K_{t-1} = vY_t - vY_{t-1} = v(Y_t - Y_{t-1})$$
$$\text{Or } dK_t = v \,.\, dY_t. \tag{15.5}$$

Since increase in the stock of capital in a year ($K_t - K_{t-1}$) represents investment in that year, so we can rewrite the previous equation as

$$I_t = v \,.\, dK_t \tag{15.6}$$

which says that the amount of investment (or change in capital stock) at time t will be v times more than the increase in income. Hence, it is "v", which is capital–output ratio which represents the magnitude of the accelerator. Hence, we get that the amount of investment in an economy in a given time is a function of change in income from the previous year or $I = f(Y)$, $I_y > 0$.

Let us take the case of India to explain in simple arithmetic the workings of the acceleration principle. Total capital has been made proxy by the amount of gross domestic product (GDP of India) under the assumption that one unit of GDP can be produced by two units of capital. In other words, the value of the accelerator is taken as fixed at 2. We use the data of the World Bank on the GDP and take, for instance, that 1/8th of the required capital stock in the previous period is necessary to replace the existing capital which we call "depreciation". The data series on GDP is in current price in US billion dollar units (1 billion = 100 crore). Table 15.1 gives the acceleration process in case of India for the period 2001–2013.

We observe from the table that the required capital stock (column 4) has been derived as the transformation from GDP by the multiple of 2 (since $K_t = v \,.\, Y_t$), the value of the accelerator and gross investment by the summation of net investment and depreciation (since $NI = I - D$). Figure 15.2 shows the charts of all the series from 2001 (t) to 2013 ($t + 12$).

It is observed from the figure that all the series are upward sloping but have a common dip around 2008–2009 for the global financial crisis that originated from the US. The trends of I and NI are again downward due to the ramifications of the crisis. Hence,

Table 15.1 Acceleration process

Period	*Time*	*GDP(Y)*	*Required capital (K)*	*Depreciation*	*Net investment (NI)*	*Gross investment (I)*
2001	*t*	492.3	985	123.075	0	123.075
2002	*t* + 1	522.8	1,046	123.075	61	184.075
2003	*t* + 2	617.5	1,235	130.7	189	320.1
2004	.	721.5	1,443	154.375	208	362.375
2005	.	834.2	1,668	180.375	225	405.775
2006	.	949.1	1,898	208.55	230	438.35
2007	.	1,238.7	2,477	237.275	579	816.475
2008	.	1,224	2,448	309.675	−29	280.275
2009	.	1,361	2,722	306	274	580
2010	.	1,684.3	3,369	340.25	647	986.85
2011	.	1,847.9	3,696	421.075	327	748.275
2012	.	1,858.7	3,717	461.975	22	483.575
2013	*t* + 12	1,876.7	3,753	464.675	36	500.675

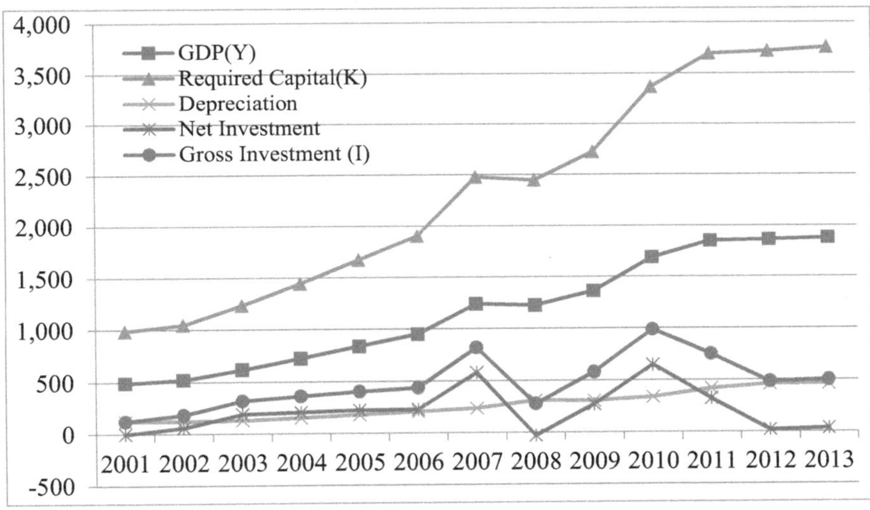

Figure 15.2 Trends of GDP, capital stock, and investment

we can say that the acceleration principle worked for the period 2001–2007 and gets disturbed thereafter due to the fluctuations in the business cycle.

15.3.1.1 *Limitations of the accelerator theory*

Although the acceleration principle is of great importance in establishing the way by which investment demand is made by a firm or a country, it has suffered from a series of limitations pointed out by eminent economists. Some of the crucial limitations are pointed out here:

i) Prof. Kaldor pointed out that assumption of a constant value of the accelerator throughout the trade cycle is very simplistic in the sense that an increase in output or income by an amount must always give rise to a multiple increase in investment.

ii) The assumption of zero excess capacity existing in consumer goods industries further allows the firms to go for no more purchase of capital (hence investment) if there is any temporary increase in demand. This is a very restrictive assumption in modern industries enjoying some degrees of imperfections. If there were excess capacity and extra shift working was possible, the supply of goods could be increased with the existing equipment without further investment and the accelerator principle would not come into play. For example, in a festival season, the garment producers do not usually invest extra money on purchasing additional sewing machines; rather they try to use the existing machines over their optimum capacity as the increased demand is purely temporary and the additional cost of new machines may not be covered by additional sales.

iii) The principle assumes further that there is surplus productive capacity in the capital goods sector to meet additional demands for the capital goods from the firms to produce extra quantities of consumer goods. This is again a highly restrictive assumption as the capital goods industries are mostly comprised of a few firms with sufficient degree of market controlling powers so that they can charge more prices on their produced capital goods rather than going for more production. Hence, there is no more supply of capital goods in spite of more demand, there is no extra investment, and hence the acceleration principle fails to work at least in the short run.

However, in spite of the aforementioned limitations of the acceleration principle, economists like Samuelson, Hicks, and others have shown how the accelerator combined with a multiplier provides an adequate and acceptable theory of trade cycles happening in the capitalist economies.

15.3.2 *The internal funds theory of investment*

The internal funds theory of investment, by name, is the funding for new desired capital stock or investment which is financed by the internal sources. The internal source of this fund is profits in expected or realised levels. Several explanations have been offered for justifying the source of internal funding. For example, Jan Tinbergen opines that realised profits perfectly reflect expected profits. Hence, investment may be decided by expected profits as well as realised profits in a positive way in the sense that as realised profit increases, investment demand increases and vice versa. If π is the realised profit, then $I = f(\pi)$ where $dI / d\pi > 0$.

Alternatively, it has been argued that managers have a decided preference for financing investment internally. Some of the reasons for internal funding are that they are less risky and under control of the firms, and there is no need for collateral like what is required in outside financing. The shareholder's part of the profit may also be used without any constraint, etc.

There is a list of internal funding for investment which includes retained earnings, depreciation expense, which is provisioned to recover the plants and equipment from depreciating, and different types of borrowing like sales of bonds, etc.

15.3.2.1 *Comparison between acceleration principle and internal fund theory*

Let us have a look at the comparison between the accelerator theory and the internal fund theory in terms of the determinants and policy perspectives. According to the accelerator theory, investment is determined by output or income whereas investment in the internal fund theory is determined by the levels of profit earned by the firm or the total economy as a whole. Since the two theories differ with respect to the determinants of investment, they are also different in policy prescriptions and their effectiveness.

If the policymakers have the target to increase investment, the internal funds theory says that the policies designed to increase profits directly are the most effective ones. These policies include the device to reduce firms' tax burden. For instance, reductions in the corporate income tax rate; allowing firms to depreciate plants and equipment more rapidly, thereby reducing their taxable income; allowing investment tax credits; and a law allowing the use of more funds under undistributed profits for further investments, among others, are the most suitable policies to attract investment under the internal funds theory.

Contrastingly, the policies designed under the accelerator theory are to influence investment directly, but under the internal funds theory they will be ineffective. For example, a reduction in the corporate tax rate will have little or no effect on investment because, under the accelerator theory, investment depends on output, not the availability of internal funds. On the other hand, the demand influencing policies like increases in government purchases or reductions in personal income tax rates will be successful in motivating investment through their impact on aggregate output.

There is a reconciliation between the two, despite the differences. The proponents of the internal funds theory admit that the importance of the relationship between investment and output works especially in the long run, and the internal funds approach is an important determinant of investment, particularly during recessions or a slump in the economic system.

15.3.3 The neoclassical theory of investment

The neoclassical theory of investment behaviour is based on the optimal capital accumulation which is determined by relative prices of factors of production. According to the theory, the desired capital stock is determined by output/income and the price of capital services relative to the price of output. Again, the price of capital services depends on the price of capital goods, the interest rate, and the tax treatment of income from business sources.

Let us see how the investment in the neoclassical theory is generated by the optimum capital stock. We first discuss how optimum capital stock is generated. Firms use capital along with labour to produce and sell goods and services. The firms decide not only upon the prices of how much of labour and capital are to be used for production but also the contributions they make to the production and revenue of the firms. According to this theory, investment (or addition to the stock of capital) in an economy is determined by marginal product of capital (MP_K) and user cost of capital which is also known as real rental cost of capital. Marginal product of capital measures the addition to the production by using an additional unit of capital ($= dy / dK$), labour and technology remaining constant. Real rental cost (or r / p), on the other hand, is the rental cost (r) as a part of price of the goods and services (p). Due to the operation of the law of diminishing returns, marginal product of capital declines as more units of capital are used for production, the other factors being held constant.

The optimum capital stock is determined by the profit maximising principle of the firms. Suppose the production function to be $Y = f(L, K)$, with $f_L, f_K > 0$ and $f_{LL}, f_{kk} < 0$.

The cost function for the two factors is $C = w \,.\, L + r \,.\, K$ where w is the wage rate and r is the nominal rent on per unit capital. The relevant profit function is

$$\pi = p\,.\,Y(L,\,K) - w\,.\,L - r\,.\,K. \tag{15.7}$$

The optimum capital stock will be determined when

$$d\pi\,/\,dK = 0 \Rightarrow p\,.\,MP_K(K) = r$$
$$\text{or } MP_K(K) = r\,/\,p \tag{15.8}$$

or optimum capital stock will be determined from the condition where the value of marginal productivity of capital (VMP_K) is equal to the nominal rent or marginal productivity of capital (MP_K) is equal to the real rent ($= r\,/\,p$). Therefore, as long as the value of marginal product of capital exceeds the rental or user cost capital, it will be profitable for the firm to add to its stock of capital. Unless we know the nature of the production function, we cannot determine the optimum stock of capital. For operational easiness, let us consider a Cobb-Douglas production function of the following type

$$Y = AL^{\alpha}K^{1-\alpha} \tag{15.9}$$

where the notations are of usual meanings with A being the parameter measuring the level of technology and α and $(1 - \alpha)$ being the parameters that measure labour and capital's share of output as well as their respective output elasticity. Marginal product of capital can be obtained by differentiating the production function with respect to capital. Thus, we have

$$MP_K = dY\,/\,dK = (1-\alpha)\,.\,A\,.\,L^{\alpha}K^{-\alpha}$$
$$or,\ MP_K = (1-\alpha)\,.\left[A\,.\,L^{\alpha}K^{1-\alpha}\right]/\,K$$
$$\text{or } MP_K = (1-\alpha)\,.\,Y\,/\,K. \tag{15.10}$$

From the profit maximising condition, we have $MP_K\,(K) = r\,/\,p$, so

$$(1-\alpha)\,.\,Y\,/\,K = r\,/\,p$$
$$\text{or } K^{*} = (1-\alpha)\,.\,(p\,/\,r)\,.\,Y \tag{15.11}$$

where K^* indicates the optimum stock of capital. The previous equation shows that the desired stock of capital (K^*) depends on the size of output (Y_1) directly and real cost of capital ($r\,/\,p$) inversely. That means the greater the expected output (Y_t) is, greater the desired capital stock will be, and the higher the rental cost of capital (r) is, the lower the desired capital stock will be and vice versa in both the determinants.

We have presented the determination of optimum capital stock in Figure 15.3. We have measured the amount of capital along the horizontal axis and marginal productivity of capital and rental cost along the vertical axis.

Initially at the rental price of capital r_1, the firms' desired capital stock is at K_1 at the corresponding parametric output Y_1. As the rental price falls, the desired capital stock

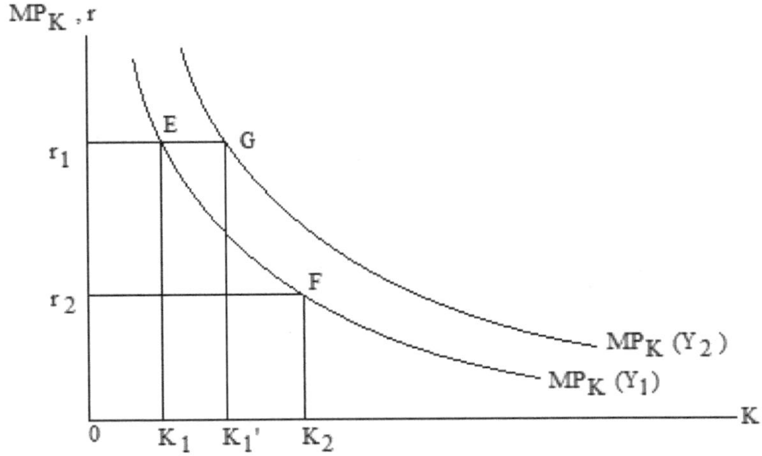

Figure 15.3 Determination of capital stock under the neoclassical model

rises to K_2 because of the profit maximising condition. If the expected income increases over Y_1 to Y_2 (say) then the MP_K function will shift rightward at the constant rental price leading to further increase in desired capital stock like K_1' at the initial rental price r_1. Once the desired capital stock is determined by the previous process, the optimum investment will be decided by the additional stock of desired capital.

15.3.3.1 *Fiscal and monetary policy implications of the neoclassical theory of investment*

Whether fiscal and monetary policies are at all effective in the decisions to invest depends upon whether the increase in demand parameters like governments' increased expenditure leads to increase in rate of interest or not. If it does, then there will be a drop in private investment which is popularly known as the crowding out effect. The neoclassical theory of investment postulates that if expansionary fiscal policy is combined with a tax reduction/credit policies like subsidies then the rental cost of capital will fall which will further boost capital stock or investment. The crowding out effect can then be nullified. However, if there is corporate tax or profit tax, then there will be increase in rental cost of capital which will further discourage investment. The reverse will happen if there is reduction in corporate tax.

On the other hand if there is expansionary monetary policy, the real rate of interest will go down which will pull down the rental cost and hence the additional capital stock or investment will be in the economy. Thus expansionary monetary policy stimulates private investment.

15.3.4 *The Keynesian theory of investment*

In the general theory, J. M. Keynes stressed upon the central role of investment in determining aggregate output and employment in a depression sick economy. According to him, the decisions of investment are made by comparing the marginal efficiency of capital (MEC) or the yield with the real rate of interest (r). Profit expectations of the firms play the central role in the determination of investment decisions and these decisions are affected by the investment in the present period since this is one of the important determinants of the profits in the present period. This is a strong departure from the earlier theories of investment.

Before going on to explain the investment theory of Keynes, we need to explain first the concepts of present discounted value of returns in future periods and cost of capital and marginal efficiency of capital since they are the foundation of the theory.

Present discounted value (*PDV*): the PDV of any investment project is the value of the stream of future returns or incomes discounted by the rate of interest. Just think of a reality. If you hold Rs. 100 today and you want it to roll in the market to get additional earning which is known as rate of interest or rate of discount (r). Suppose "r" is 10% per annum. That means Rs. 100 today is worth $100 + 100 \times r = 100(1 + r) = 100 + 100 \times 10 / 100 = 100 + 10 =$ Rs. 110 next year. Alternatively we can say that Rs. 110 in the second period is Rs. 100 in the current or present period. That means the present value of Rs. 110 is $110 / (1 + r) = 110 / (1 + 0.10) =$ Rs. 100. This is the simple formula for deriving the present value of the future value of the asset/return in a two-period model. The present value is alternatively termed present discounted value in the sense that Rs. 110 in period 2 has been discounted by "r". The rate of interest "r" may be called the rate of discount. As the value of "r" increases, the PDV falls and vice versa. If the asset/investment has "n" numbers of periods with a stream of returns $R_1, R_2, \ldots\ldots, R_n$ then the PDV of all the "n" periods will be as follows:

$$PDV = R_1 / (1+r) + R_2 / (1+r)^2 + R_3 / (1+r)^3 + \ldots\ldots + R_n / (1+r)^n \quad (15.12)$$

$$\text{Or } PDV = \Sigma R_i / (1+r)^i. \quad (15.13)$$

Cost of capital (*C*): is the market price or supply price of the capital good/s purchased for investment purpose. For example, Tata Company planned to invest or purchase all materials including land, machinery, technical and managerial personnel, etc. which was valued at Rs. 1,000 crore. This is the cost of capital. Upon this amount of investment, the company expected a series of return (sales volume or profit) for a number of periods.

Net present discounted value (*NPDV*): The investor's decision to undertake any project depends upon the weightage of PDV and C or the net present discounted value. That means:

$$NPDV = PDV - C$$

$$\text{or } NPDV = R_1 / (1+r) + R_2 / (1+r)^2 + R_3 / (1+r)^3 + \ldots\ldots + R_n / (1+r)^n - C \quad (15.14)$$

Investors have to make the decision whether the project can be undertaken or not depending on whether NPDV is positive or not. If $PDV > C$ or $NPDV > 0$, then the stream of returns discounted to the present period is greater than the cost of capital and hence it will be worth it to undertake the investment decision on the said project. If $NPDV < 0$ then the project should not be undertaken. Finally, if $PDV = C$ or $NPDV = 0$ then the investor is indifferent between undertaking the project or investing the said fund upon alternative assets.

The marginal efficiency of capital (MEC): It is the rate of discount which equates the present value of a series of expected returns from the income-generating asset like a machine over its entire economic life to the cost of the machine. It is further the rate of return at which a project is expected to break even (sums of all discounted $R = C$). MEC can also be termed internal rate of return which means the rate of discount at which NPDV = 0. We can derive the rate of such discount or the MEC by the following algebra. To do this we assume now that the expected returns during all the prospective years are equal, that is $R_1, R_2, \ldots\ldots, R_n = R$ (say) and rate of discount is δ which is different than rate of interest, r. The formula for MEC is thus

$$C = R/(1+\delta) + R/(1+\delta)^2 + R/(1+\delta)^3 + \ldots\ldots\ldots + R/(1+\delta)^n + R/(1+\delta)^{n+1}$$

$$\text{or } C = R(1+\delta)^{-1} + R(1+\delta)^{-2} + R(1+\delta)^{-3} + \ldots\ldots\ldots + R(1+\delta)^{-n} + R(1+\delta)^{-(n+1)}. \quad (15.15)$$

Multiplying both sides by $(1 + \delta)^{-1}$ we get

$$C(1+\delta)^{-1} = R(1+\delta)^{-2} + R(1+\delta)^{-3} + R(1+\delta)^{-4} + \ldots + R(1+\delta)^{-n} + R(1+\delta)^{-(n+1)}. \quad (15.16)$$

Subtracting the last one from the equation just preceding it we get

$$C - C(1+\delta)^{-1} = R(1+\delta)^{-1} + 0 + 0 + \ldots + 0 + R(1+\delta)^{-(n+1)}$$

$$\text{or } C - C(1+\delta)^{-1} = R(1+\delta)^{-1} + R(1+\delta)^{-(n+1)}.$$

Let us assume that as n tends to infinity, $R(1+\delta)^{-(n+1)} \to 0$. Hence, we have

$$C\left[1-(1+\delta)^{-1}\right] = R(1+\delta)^{-1}$$

$$\text{or } C\left[(1+\delta-1)/(1+\delta)\right] = R(1+\delta)^{-1}$$

$$\text{or } C\,.\,\delta = R$$

$$\text{or } \delta = R/C. \quad (15.17)$$

This value of δ is called optimum rate of discount (or MEC) which is derived from the condition of NPDV = 0. If this discount rate is greater than the rate of interest, r, then the project will be undertaken and the intention of the firm in investing the funds in alternative business earning rates of interest will be forgone. If the firm has different projects in mind and needs to select the best one out of them, it has to calculate the series of MECs for each of the projects and the project in which the NPDV is highest or in which MEC is greater than r; only that will be accepted. If the reverse happens, which is MEC is less than r, the project should not be accepted.

There is an inverse relation between MEC and units of investment. Because of a diminishing rate of return on capital, as the number of units of capital is added or more is

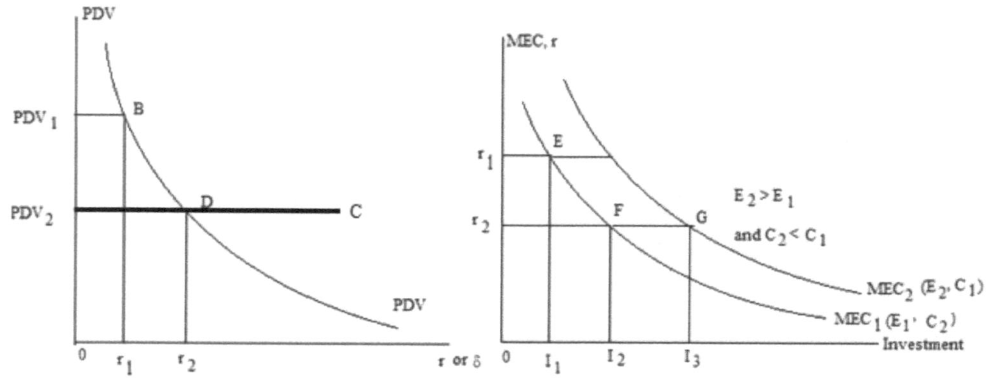

Figure 15.4 PDV-*r* and MEC-investment relation

invested, then the efficiency of the last unit of capital will go down. Hence, MEC is a decreasing function of investment. Figure 15.4 shows the PDV and MEC schedule.

The first part (left side) of the diagram shows the PDV and rate of discount (δ) / rate of interest (r) relation which shows the inverse relation between PDV and δ or r. The thick horizontal line represents the fixed cost of capital or supply price of capital. D is the equilibrium where NPDV = 0. Hence, r_2 is the value of MEC which makes NPDV = 0 or PDV = C. The second part of the diagram (right side) shows the MEC schedule which is declining with respect to level of investment given the expected return (E) and cost of capital (C), both of which are assumed to be constant under the MEC criterion. With initial expected return (E_1) and cost of capital (C_2), an interest rate of r_1 allows investment of I_1 amount of capital through the MEC schedule. As the rate of interest falls to r_2, with the same expected return and cost of capital, more investment is made at I_2.

We now came to know the factors determining the MEC schedule. They are: expected returns/incomes/profits/revenues (all R's) and cost of capital (all C's). The MEC schedule shifts rightward if at the same rate of interest the volume of expected returns increases. This follows from our derived relation, $\delta = R / C$. In the diagram, it has been denoted by $E_2 > E_1$. On the other hand, as the cost of capital becomes lower, or the capital goods like machines are cheaper, then the MEC will shift rightward at the existing rate of interest. In the diagram, it has been denoted by $C_1 > C_2$.

Example: Decision to purchase assets/capital goods

Suppose Sachin Tendulkar wants to purchase 25% of the share of the Mumbai Indians Cricket Team from Mukesh Ambani at Rs. 20 crore and he expects equal returns for the next 3 years at Rs. 8 crore. If the market rate of interest is 10%, is Sachin's decision to invest right?

We have $C = 20$ crore, $R = 8$ crore, $r = 10\% = 10/100 = 1/10$

Now, we have to see whether NPDV > 0 or MEC is greater than r.

$$\text{NPDV} = 8 / (1 + 1 / 10) + 8 / (1 + 1 / 10)^2 + 8 / (1 + 1 / 10)^3 - 20$$
$$= 7.27 + 8 + 8.8 - 20 = \text{Rs. } 24.07 - 20 = \text{Rs. } 4.07 \text{ crore}$$

Hence, Sachin should purchase the share of the cricket franchise.

By our derived relation we can say that $\delta = R / C = 8 / 20 \times 100 = 40$. We see that "40" is well above the rate of interest of 10%. Hence, the decision will be to invest.

What happens if we remove the assumption of fixed supply price of capital at all levels of demand for capital asset (or investment)" The answer cannot be obtained from the Keynesian MEC theory of investment. What is true for an individual firm in deciding on investment through the MEC principle may not be true for all the firms or the economy's investment as a whole? That means, if all the firms see that they are getting positive investment as per the MEC rule with a constant supply firm, all of them will go for purchasing more and more capital goods leading to increase in aggregate demand for the capital goods (or machines) which will push up the supply price of the capital goods and will further pull down the value of MEC (since $\delta = R / C$) since expected returns from the streams are constant. In such a situation, the firms have to pull off their additional demand for capital and they have to make the optimum decision so that they can make the capital stock reach towards the optimum point. Hence, a new concept of investment theory emerges to deal with the issue. This is known as marginal efficiency of investment (MEI) used by K. E. Boulding and G. Ackley.

15.3.4.1 Marginal efficiency of investment (MEI)

Under the MEC principle the supply price of capital (which is determined by the replacement level of investment) was taken as fixed and the situation was the decision making by a single firm. It is hard to find any single firm influencing supply price of capital unless it is a very big firm having, say, about 80% of industrial concentration, an extreme imperfect market condition. Rather, the case in the industry usually consists of several firms having moderate size of industrial concentration. Therefore, in the case of the whole economy, the supply price of capital can be moved upward if the firms need new capital, having used the full capacities of the old capital. If the firms do not use their existing capital at below the full capacity, then supply price of capital may not increase. But if the capital goods producing the industry run with decreasing returns, then the supply price will be variable and will follow a rising shape. This means more capital demand, which is the investment, increases with supply price of capital. There are, therefore, different supply prices with different capital stocks or investments. Given the prospective yields, the computation of MEI is based upon increasing supply price of capital. MEI is that rate of discount that will make the present value of the expected net returns from the capital asset just equal to its supply price in the presence of variable supply price even in the short run assuming the constant cost assumption does not work like in the case of MEC. The MEI principle allows us to determine the rate of discount at which the actual capital stock moves or inches towards the optimum capital stock. The MEI schedule is also negatively sloped like the MEC. The MEC schedule refers to the stock of capital whereas the MEI schedule refers to the flow of investment. In brief, the MEC is a concept that describes the expected rate of return on investment, given the supply price of capital. The MEI is the expected rate of return on investment for additional units of investments made over a period, given the induced changes in demand for capital.

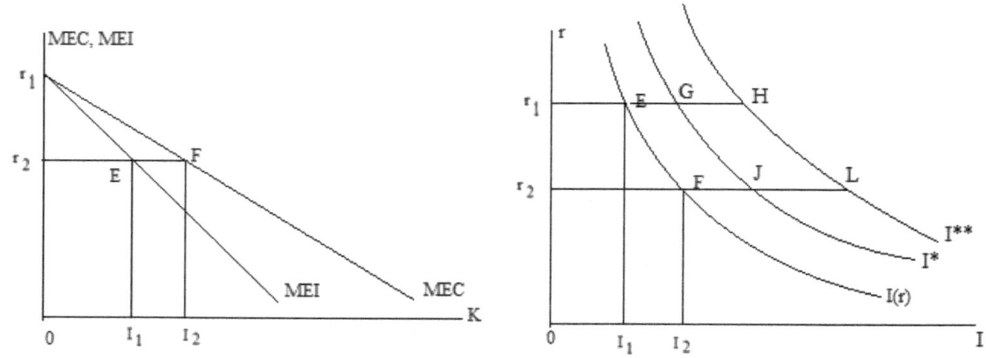

Figure 15.5 MEC, MEI, and investment schedules

The MEI will be different from the different levels of investment. As the rate of investment increases, cost of capital also increases and the MEI decreases. The MEC schedule thus refers to stock of capital and the MEI schedule refers to flow of investment. Figure 15.5 shows the distinction between the two.

Let us first assume that the market rate of interest is r_1 in the first part of the diagram. This rate of interest makes it worthwhile for the firm to replace worn out capital. Further, it is such a rate where there is no difference between MEC and MEI. Now assume that the rate of interest drops from r_1 to r_2 ($r_2 < r_1$). This will induce each of the firms to expand its capital stock. As a result of that, total demand for capital/investment will increase to I_2 on the MEC schedule. Implication of this over demand for investment will push up the supply price of capital which, in turn, will lead to a fall in the MEC of all firms for all of the projects since $\delta = R / C$. This will further lead to low actual investment of I_1 instead of I_2, as is shown by point E on the MEI schedule. Hence, the difference between the MEC and MEI lies in the difference between desired investment (I_2) on the MEI schedule and actual investment (I_1) at the rate of interest r_2. The process will be similar if the rate of interest falls further. The gap between MEC and MEI will be wider as rate of interest falls. Thus, it is clear that the MEC schedule adequately represents the economy's investment-demand schedule. Like MEC, the MEI schedule is also negatively sloped but relatively steeper than the MEC schedule. Hence, we get a negatively sloped investment function with respect to rate of interest, which is $I = I(r)$ and $dI / dr < 0$. The second part of the diagram (right side) shows the investment function.

15.3.4.2 Shifting of the MEI curve

Out of the relation between I and r in a MEI schedule there are some parameters upon the relation which cause the MEI schedule to shift from its original position. Some such exogenous factors are business expectations and animal spirits, technology and innovations, user cost of capital, availability of credit, fiscal policy, etc. Out of them, business expectations and animal spirits, technology and innovations, availability of credit, and expansionary fiscal policy work in favour of shifting the investment schedule upward (from I to I^* to I^{**}, etc.), making additional investments of the amount FJ or JL and EG or GH with the original rate of interests r_2 and r_1 respectively (right-hand side of

Figure 16.5). On the other hand, increase in user cost of capital leads to decrease in investment as shown by the leftward shifting from I^{**} to I^* or to I.

15.3.5 *Tobin's q theory of investment*

James Tobin, a Nobel Prize winner, developed the idea of investment decisions made by the firms on the basis of the value of their market shares as a ratio of the values of the assets they have to use for production of the goods carrying market values in the stock/share markets. Hence, it is a ratio named q which can be written as:

$$q = V / C = V / p \,.\, K \tag{15.18}$$

where V is the value the stock marketplaces on the firm's asset, C is the cost of producing those assets, p is the price of capital goods/assets per unit, and K is the total quantity of asset. The idea behind this postulate is that the firm needs money or funds for investment in capital goods which are used for production of the goods by the firms. The money or fund can be raised either by borrowing from financial institutions or from the public by selling their shares, equity, etc. When the firm sells the share, the buyer buys the share to earn a capital gain from the increase in the market value of the shares. The "q" thus simply means that the companies should be justified by the amount they can replace the cost.

What is the decision rule to invest? The decision to invest depends on the values of "q", whether it is greater, less than, or equal to one. If $q > 1$, then $V > C$. That means the return from shares or values of the stocks exceeds the cost of acquiring them. That means the firm should make investment decisions in a positive way. Now, if $q < 1$, then $V < C$ which means the return from the shares are less than the cost of the assets to produce the goods holding the shares. It is not justifiable to invest under this condition. Again, if $q = 1$, $V = C$. That means the firm should be indifferent to make investment decisions. Therefore, only the case of $q > 1$ leads the firm/s to make investment decision.

How can we relate investment demand with the rate of interest with the help of Tobin's q theory? There is still an inverse relation between investment and rate of interest. We have to recall the PDV formula. Like any physical capital, any particular share or stock of a company has a stream of future returns whose discounted value is called the present value of the share. Also we know that as rate of interest (or rate of discount) increases, the PDV decreases which leads to fall in V and vice versa. Hence, we have a chain of relation: $V = V(\text{PDV})$ with $V' > 0$, $\text{PDV} = f(r)$ with $f' < 0$ and investment $I = I(V)$ with $I' > 0$ and $I = I(r)$ with $I_r = dI / dr < 0$. The investment function will look like the second part of Figure 16.5.

Example of Tobin's q theory

Suppose Company A has a capital asset of 100 units each with cost Rs. 1 crore. The company has outstanding shares of 100,000,000 units each with a value of Rs. 50. Check whether the investment decision will be fruitful for the company.

We have C = 100 × 10,000,000 = 1,000,000,000 and V = 50 × 100,000,000 = 5,000,000,000. Hence, q = 5,000,000,000 / 1,000,000,000 = 5 > 1. Hence the investment decision by the company will be fruitful.

The clear-cut decision to invest based upon the previous conditions (i.e., whether $q > 1$, < 1, or $= 1$) depends upon whether the stock market is efficient or not. If efficient, then the share prices will perfectly reflect V and then stock price and quantity of investment will be positively associated or the correlation coefficient between V (stock price) and investment will be positive. But this is a theoretical possibility. In practice, that positive correlation may not happen for all the firms in all the countries since stock value influences many assets and it is thus very difficult to segregate the effects. This is a research question which is to be handled by appropriate methods.

15.4 Supplementary topics on investment

In the recent developments in the literature on investment opportunities, the residential investment and inventory investments have demanded special attention to the building of economic theories. We address the issues in a conceptual way in the following section.

15.4.1 Residential investment

Residential investment includes the purchase of new housing both by people who plan to live in it themselves and by landlords who plan to rent it to others. Let us assume, for simplicity, that all housing is owner-occupied.

First, we consider the market for existing stock of houses. The relative price of housing (P_H / P) is determined by the supply and demand for the existing stock of houses. At any point of time, the supply of houses is fixed, given by a vertical line. The demand curve for houses slopes downward. High prices cause people to live in smaller houses, to share residences or sometimes even to become homeless. The price of housing adjusts to equilibrium supply and demand (Figure 15.6).

Construction firms buy materials and hire labour to build houses and then sell the houses at the market price. Their costs depend on the overall price level (P) and their revenue depends on the price of housing (P_H). The higher the relative prices of housing (P_H / P), the greater the incentive to build houses and the more houses are built. The flow of new houses, which is residential investment, depends on the equilibrium price set in the market for existing houses.

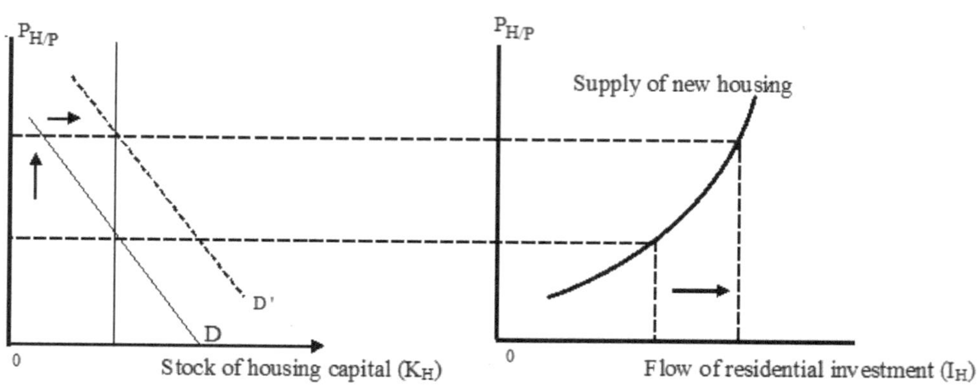

Figure 15.6 Residential investment

When the demand for housing shifts, the equilibrium price of housing changes and this change in turn affects residential investment. An important determinant of housing demand is the real interest rate (r). Many people take out loans to buy their homes, which implies that r is the cost of the loan. Even if the people do not borrow but use their own funds, r is the opportunity cost of holding their wealth in housing rather than putting it in banks. A reduction in r, therefore, raises housing demand which implies $\frac{P_H}{P}$ rises which implies residential investment also rises.

15.4.2 *Inventory investment*

Inventory investment is the stock of goods that business firms put aside in storage. Though it is a negligible component of aggregate spending, it is very volatile in nature. During recessions, firms stop replenishing their inventory as goods are sold and inventory investment becomes negative.

Inventories are held for the following reasons:

i) *Production smoothing*: firms often experience temporary booms and busts in sales. Rather than adjusting production to match the fluctuation in sales, the firms may find it cheaper to produce goods at a steady rate. When sales are low, the unsold goods are put into inventory. When sales are high, the firm takes goods out of inventory.
ii) *Inventories as a factor of production*: inventories may allow a firm to operate more efficiently. Retail firms, for example, can sell items more effectively if they have goods on hand to show to customers. Manufacturing firms keep inventories of spare parts to reduce the time that plants are shut down when a machine breaks. The larger the stock of inventories a firm holds, the more output it can produce.
iii) *Stock-out avoidance*: firms often have to make production decisions before knowing the level of consumer demand. If demand exceeds production and there are no inventories, the goods will be out of stock for a period and the firm will lose sales and profit. To avoid running out of goods, firms hold inventories.
iv) *Work in process:* many goods require a number of steps in production and therefore take time to produce. When a product is only partly completed, its components are counted as a part of inventories.

15.5 Conclusion

The discussion we have made so far in the present chapter provided us with concepts of investment and different theories of investment. We covered major theories of investment which are notably the accelerator theory, internal funds theory, neoclassical theory, Keynesian theory, and Tobin's q theory of investment. In the accelerator principle, capital stock or investment demand depends on output produced and more output leads to more investment. The internal fund theory proposes that investment depends on internal resources like profit in either nominal or actual form. More profit means more investment. The neoclassical theory of investment is based upon the marginal productivity theory and that optimum investment is determined at a point where marginal productivity of capital is equal to real rent on capital. The Keynesian theory of investment is a new idea on investment demand which states that decisions of investment are made by comparing the marginal efficiency of capital (MEC) or the yield with the real rate of interest (r). In modern globalised economies, a new theory of investment known as the q theory of James Tobin has been developed which states that investment decisions made by the firms depend on the value of their market shares as a ratio to the values of the assets they have to use for production of the goods carrying market values in the stock/share markets.

Summary

The present chapter on investment demand has summary results as noted below:

- Investment is defined as the addition to capital stock where capital is defined as the produced means of production.
- Autonomous investment is the amount of capital accumulation which does not depend on any economic indicators but induced investment depends on income or rate of interest like economic variables.
- Gross investment is the investment inclusive of depreciation but net investment is exclusive of depreciation.
- Acceleration principle states that investment demand depends on output produced and more output leads to more investment.
- The internal fund theory proposes that investment depends on internal resources like profit in either nominal or actual form. More profit means more investment.
- The neoclassical theory of investment states that optimum investment is determined at a point where marginal productivity of capital is equal to real rent on capital.
- The Keynesian theory of investment proposes that decisions of investment are taken by comparing the marginal efficiency of capital (MEC) or the yield with the real rate of interest (r).
- The q theory of James Tobin states that investment decisions taken by the firms depend on the value of their market shares as a ratio to the values of the assets they have to use for production of the goods carrying market values in the stock markets.

Keywords

Investment
Accelerator principle
Internal funds
Marginal productivity of capital
MEC
MEI
Present discounted value
q theory

Multiple choice questions and answers

1. Net investment can be zero when

   (a) Gross investment outweighs depreciation.
   (b) Gross investment is equal to depreciation.
   (c) Gross investment is outweighed by depreciation.
   (d) All of the above.

2. Suppose a firm has the stock of capital in two periods such that $K_{t+1} < K_t$, then the firm has

   (a) Positive investment.
   (b) Zero investment.
   (c) Disinvestment.
   (d) None of the above.

3. The acceleration principle says that as income increases, capital accumulation happens. What about investment? It

   (a) Rises.
   (b) Falls.
   (c) Remains unchanged.
   (d) None of the above.

4. A firm takes a positive decision on investment if

   (a) NPDV > 0.
   (b) PDV > Cost of capital.
   (c) PDV – Cost of capital > 0.
   (d) All the above are true.

5. In Tobin's q theory of investment, the term "q" refers to the

   (a) Ratio of stock market value of the assets of the firm to cost of producing the assets.
   (b) Ratio of cost of producing the assets to stock market value of the assets of the firm.
   (c) Ratio of PDV to cost of capital.
   (d) Ratio of quantity of investment to profit.

Answers

1. (b); 2. (c); 3. (a); 4. (d); 5(a)

Review questions

1. Define the concepts: gross investment, net investment, induced investment, depreciation, interest elasticity of investment.
2. Explain the accelerator principle of investment in detail. Point out major limitations of the theory.
3. Give a brief note on the internal funds theory of investment. What are the limitations?
4. Define present discounted value and net present discounted value of returns. Construct a hypothetical firm's investment decision with values of the concerned variables of your own choice. Calculate net present value from the hypothetical problem.
5. What are MEC and MEI? Explain the Keynesian theory of investment and point out major limitations of the model.
6. Suppose Reliance Jio wants to purchase 30% of share of the Vodaphone at Rs. 200 crore and it expects equal returns for the next 3 years at Rs. 50 crore. If the market rate of interest is 8%, is the decision of Reliance Jio to invest right? Explain it from the PDV postulate.

7. What is marginal productivity of capital? Explain the neoclassical theory of investment decision on the basis of marginal productivity theory.
8. Discuss Tobin's q theory of investment. What is the optimum condition of investment under this approach? Taking a time series data of a listed company in the SEBI, calculate the values of "q" over time.

Additional readings

Tobin, J. & Brainard, W. C. (1977). "Asset markets and the cost of capital". in *Economic Progress, Private Values and Public Policy*, Essays in Honor of William Fellner. Amsterdam: North-Holland Publishing Company, pp. 235–262.

16 Demand for money

16.1 Introduction

Everybody needs money in daily life. This is a common phenomenon. Do you know how your predecessors would lead their lives some centuries back? They had no money, but there was the barter system which would maintain the economic and social relations in those days. A *barter system* is a mode of exchanging goods and services among the people, families, groups, classes, etc. where goods were exchanged for goods and services were exchanged for services; no role of money was there. In fact, the concept of money was not there. The concept is like, say, you exchanged apple in your Tiffin hours with orange of your friends, and your friend also did the reverse so that both of you are better off after making a commodity-to-commodity exchange. The history of bartering dates all the way back to 6000 BC. Introduced by Mesopotamia tribes, bartering was adopted by Phoenicians. Phoenicians bartered goods to those located in various other cities across oceans. Babylonians also developed an improved bartering system. Goods were exchanged for food, tea, weapons, and spices. In the middle ages, Europeans travelled around the world to barter crafts and furs in exchange for silks and perfumes. Colonial Americans exchanged musket balls, deer skins, and wheat. Due to lack of money, bartering became popular in the 1930s during the Great Depression. It was used to obtain food and various other services. It was done through groups or between people who acted similar to banks. A barter system is more than creating a social bond but fails on economic grounds. With increase in population and volumes of exchanges of goods and services, the traditionally operated barter system was inappropriate and insufficient. Asymmetric information regarding the qualities of the goods and services exchanged has made the system obsolete. Money, then, was introduced as a strong alternative to the barter system. Nobody is vulnerable to the exchange of bad/fraud items when they are made in terms of money.

Now the question is why one needs money or why one demands money. Economists differed on the roles of money. The classical economists believed that money played the role of medium of exchange; here money plays an active role. The role of money, according to the classical approach, is based on the current period's use in the sense that it is used as and when required; there is no need to hold it for future use. The modern economists, like Keynes, defended that money had stored value, that is, it had a passive role. People keep or hold money to get more benefit in a future period compared to the current period. Taking into account the debates between the classical approach and the Keynesian approach on the roles of money, one thing that can be addressed here is that money has some alternative uses or it has some opportunity costs. In line with the classicists, use

DOI: 10.4324/9781003501138-20

of money in active purpose or as medium of exchange means people lose the opportunity to use it in the future, and in line with Keynes, storing money for future use means people lose the liquidity power of money for current use. These are two polar extremes of use of money. There is the approach like that of Tobin, a Keynesian economist, who believed that people should use money for active and passive balances in an optimum manner. The theory is popularly known as portfolio balance approach. Besides, money works as a unit of measurement in the sense that we can value any good and service in terms of money. All the approaches on the role of money believe in this particular role of money, there is no difference of opinion on these grounds.

What is the opportunity cost of money? Think of a real situation. Suppose the price of a toy remains same for the month of January and February. Your parent gave you Rs. 500 for either purchasing the toy (assume cost of one toy is Rs. 100) in January or to keep it for February. You, being a rational lad, may purchase the toy in either of the months. If you see that the toy is beneficial to you right now, you will use Rs. 500 to purchase five toys in January. Your money gets exhausted. On the other hand, you can lend out the money as loan to your friend who commits to give you extra Rs. 100 in February. That means, if you hold the money or store it with your friend for a month; you will be able to purchase six toys instead of five since you will have Rs. 600 in February. That additional hundred rupees or one additional toy is the opportunity cost of Rs. 500 in January. We alternatively term the opportunity cost or Rs. 100 as rate of interest on the money held for future use. But there are uncertainties on whether your friend will pay you the additional money at all or whether the toy will be available in February, etc. Hence, if you go by the previous two extreme cases, you may be a loser. That is why another alternative is that you can purchase some toys in January and keep (i.e. loan or invest) the balance part for future purchase in an optimum way to avoid the uncertainty.

Let us use the technical terms for usages of money. The active use or money as medium of exchange is the demand for cash or liquidity and the passive use of money is the holding of money in a financial asset which is called a bond. Hence, we have cash/money and bond. A bond is a financial asset which earns fixed returns in maturity and the fixed earning is accrued by interest earning. As the rate of interest rises, the price of the bond (Fixed returns / r, where r is the rate of interest) falls and demand for bonds rises. If people demand more bond due to rise in interest rates, they will demand (or need) less money for active balance which is now called *transaction motive*. Investing some money on a bond is called the processing for using the stored money on lucrative financial assets in the future. That motive of earning additional income from the lucrative assets is called *speculation* or *speculative demand for money*. The reverse logic will work when rate of interest falls. On the other hand, if people are now richer, they have more money; they will go for more transaction of goods and services. Hence, we see that demand for money is twofold – transaction and cash vis-a-vis bond. The economists since the Great Depression have developed theories on demand for money on different lines which provided different answers as noted earlier to a common question: *if a bond earns interest and money does not, then why should people hold money*? The answers to this common question bring out the different theories of demand for money that we will discuss in the following sections.

As per the variables concerned in determining demand for money, we can write down the demand for money function in the following form containing two broad roles of money:

$$M^d = M / P = L(y) + L(r) \tag{16.1}$$

where M^d or M / P is the real balance which is the money balance the individuals want to hold in the form of cash or bank deposits narrowly defined as M_1 (non-interest-bearing holdings) or for money in the broader sense of M_2 or M_3, y is the real income and r is the real rate of interest. $L(y)$ stands for the money as active balance which is a positive function of y (it is the transaction demand) and $L(r)$ stands for money playing a passive or idle role which is a negative function of r (it is the speculative demand). Thus the demand for money or the demand for real balance is some combinations of active or idle balances. In extreme cases, M / P may be just equal to $L(y)$ or M / P may be just equal to $L(r)$. We discuss in detail the important theories of demand for money that explain the combinations of the roles of money as cash or bond or both.

The macroeconomic literature to date has offered five theories of demand for money. They are:

- Quantity theory of money by the classical economists like Fisher, Marshall, and Pigou
- Liquidity preference theory by Keynes
- Regressive expectation theory attributed to Keynes and developed by Tobin
- Portfolio balance approach of Tobin
- Inventory theoretic approach to transaction demand of Baumol–Tobin
- Modern version of quantity theory of money by Friedman

Let us discuss all of the aforementioned six theories of demand for money.

16.2 Classical theory

The classical economists believed that people need or demand for money for making day-to-day transactions of goods, services, purchase of raw materials, etc. We have already given some explanations on this topic earlier; we are recalling here some relevant parts of the theory of classical demand for money. Money is treated here as an asset promptly helping in making different types of economic transactions, hence, money demand is called demand for active balance. The term "balance" means people need to hold cash/money for transaction since there is usually a time gap between receipts of income and payments of income.

Suppose P is the overall price of transacted items in the economy and T is the number or units of transactions, then total requirement of cash (or demand for money) is

$$M^d = P.T. \tag{16.2}$$

Again, the source of money, according to all schools of economists, is

$$M^s = M.V \tag{16.3}$$

where M is the total quantity of money kept in circulation by the central bank of the country and V is the number of times said money rolls within the economy from hand to hand. It is called velocity of money; an increase of V indirectly implies more supply or circulation of money with a given quantity of money, M. Hence, the balancing condition leads us to the following relation (or identity)

$$M^d = M^s$$
$$Or,\ MV = PT. \tag{16.4}$$

Writing M as demand for money, M^d, we have

$$M^d = PT / V. \tag{16.5}$$

The previous relation gives out to the classical demand for money. What we observe from the equation is that demand for money is directly proportional to price level, P, which means as price increases, people need more money to smooth out transaction since T and V are constants. Again, M^d is proportional to T since, ceteris paribus, as unit of transactions rises, people need more cash money. But M^d is inversely proportional to velocity of money, V, since if money rolls speedily then people may need less money for transactions.

We can derive the demand for money function in the (T, P) plane by rewriting the previous equation as follows:

$$M . V = P . T$$
$$\text{or } M_0 = P . T \tag{16.6}$$

where M_0 is the fixed quantity of money stipulated by the central bank of the country. Therefore, we get the relation that as P increases, T falls and vice versa. Hence, the demand for transaction function is negatively sloped (Figure 16.1).

Again, replacing T with real income, Y, as classical economist assumed, we have

$$M^d = P . y \tag{16.7}$$

The transaction demand or total demand for money in the classical model, is an upward sloping function with respect to income. As income or output in the

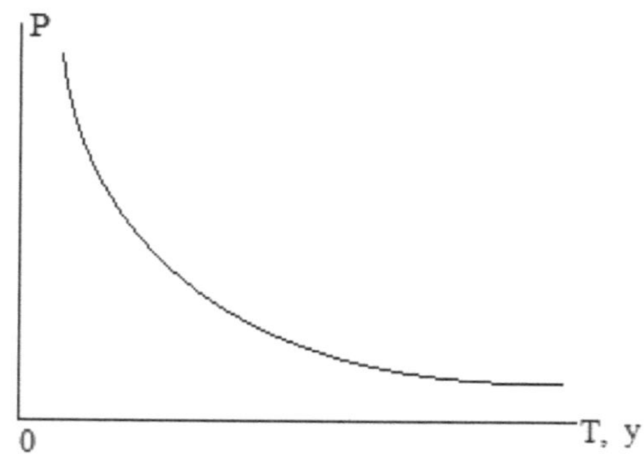

Figure 16.1 Demand for money

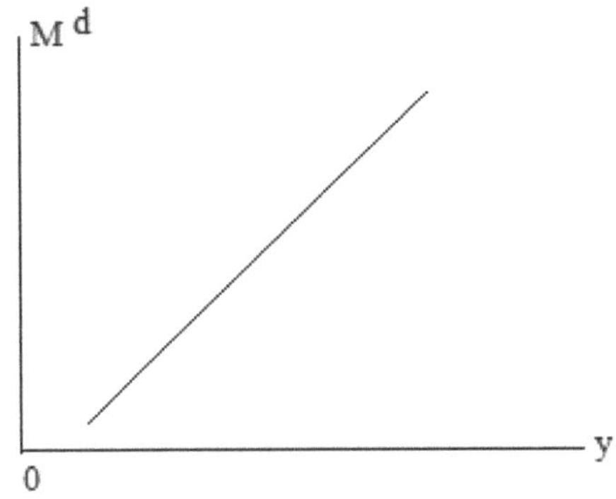

Figure 16.2 Transaction demand for money

economy increases, people need more money/cash for transactions and vice versa (Figure 16.2).

16.3 Keynesian theory of liquidity preference

Prof. Keynes, till the phase of the Great Depression, also believed in the classical approach of demand for money as to meet the active transaction requirements, but he shifted his stand during the post-depression phase when he wrote his general theory. To him, people demand liquid money to satisfy three purposes – transaction purposes, precautionary purposes, and speculative purposes. Money plays an active role or plays as a medium of exchange when it is used for transaction and precautionary purposes and it behaves idly or as a store value when it is used for speculative purposes. The optimum allocation of money for active and idle balances provides the liquidity preference theory. Postulation for speculative demand for money is a unique departure from the classical idea.

16.3.1 Transaction demand

Like the classical approach, people hold cash money for neutralising the gap between receiving payments and execution. This process of holding liquid cash is equally applicable to business enterprises where they need money all the time in order to make payments for booking and purchasing of raw materials, meeting transport requirements, current expenses like wage and salaries, etc. How much the consumers and businesses will hold cash depends on the level of income they potentially earn. Therefore, transaction demand for money function is $L^T = L^T(y)$ where "y" is the income level and $dL^T / dy > 0$. This means the transaction demand function is rising. A rich person should hold a larger amount as cash compared to a poor person (Figure 16.2).

16.3.2 Precautionary demand

People sometimes hold money for meeting certain transactions that are not perceived before the time of transaction. There are certain transactions which are uncertain to be predicted beforehand. To guard against this type of unforeseen contingencies, people hold cash prior to meeting execution. There is always a risk of an accident or the risk of bad weather and earthquakes that can hamper the consumption and production decisions of consumers and firms respectively. These expenses cannot be accommodated for by the transaction motive because the transaction motive works when there is certainty of receiving flow of money and execution for several purposes. As income level is high, demand for holding cash under precautionary motives will also be higher. Therefore, like the transaction motive, the precautionary demand function also directly depends on *y*. The demand function becomes

$$L^P = L^P(y) \tag{16.8}$$

where $dL^P / dy > 0$.

The summation of transaction and precautionary demand for money for any income level gives rise to the demand for active balances. Hence, active demand for cash balance

$$L = L^T(y) + L^P(y) = L\ (y) \tag{16.9}$$

where $L_y = dL / dy > 0$.

16.3.3 *Speculative demand*

This particular part of demand for money is an invention of Keynes. It arose due to the fact that money in cash form earns nothing but if it is invested, it earns return or rate of interest. According to him people sometimes hold some idle cash under the motive of applying it for lucrative earnings from assets that may appear in the future. According to him, cash held for speculation purpose is used to make gains by dealing in bonds which fluctuate in price. There is an inverse relationship between bond price and rate of interest. As rate of interest falls, price of bond rises. Demand for bond falls, and demand for cash rises. This implies the speculative demand function is negatively sloped.

The demand for speculation is, thus,

$$L = L\ (r) \tag{16.10}$$

where $Lr = dL / dr < 0$.

There is a range of interest rate (and so bond price P_b). When rate of interest is maximum (r_{max}), bond price is minimum (P_{bmin}) and demand for bond is maximum (closely equal to total money held) and demand for cash for speculation is close to zero. Over this range of interest, the speculative demand function coincides with the vertical axis (where slope of the function L_r tends to zero). This is known as the classical zone of the speculative function. At r_{min}, bond price is very high which leads to very low (close to zero) demand for bond and so the demand for speculative balance is infinity ($L_r \rightarrow \infty$). This is the pure Keynesian zone. In such a zone, all demand for money is speculative and hence liquidity is trapped in this zone. This is hence called the *liquidity trap*. The speculative demand function is horizontal (infinitely elastic). With $r_{min} < r < r_{max}$, the speculative demand function is negatively sloped (Figure 16.3).

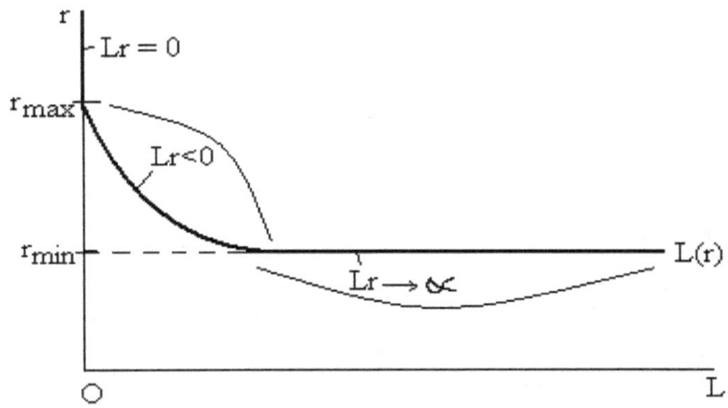

Figure 16.3 Speculative demand for money

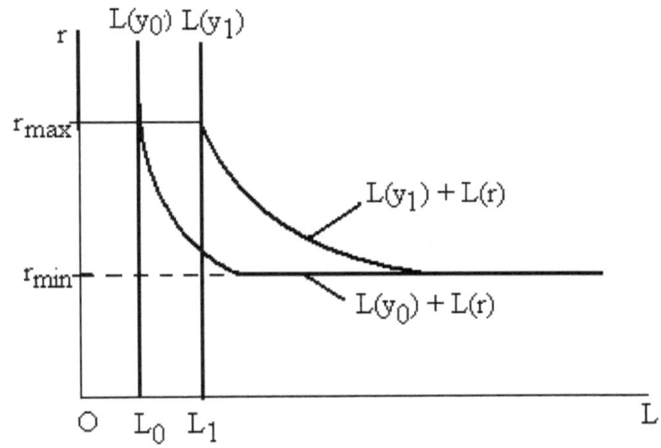

Figure 16.4 Aggregate demand for money

16.3.4 Derivation of aggregate demand for money schedule

Aggregate demand for money is now the summation of transaction demand (including the precautionary demand and speculative demand i.e., $M^d = L(y) + L(r)$ where M^d is the aggregate demand for money. Aggregate demand for money consists of two unknowns, y and r, so how can we add them up? Keynes opined that y is determined by the commodity market; no role of monetary factors work behind its determination. Since the commodity market is not considered for determining r, it is so taken that y is fixed. As y is fixed, transaction demand for money is also fixed. So total demand for money M^d depends only on rate of interest.

Suppose y_0 is the fixed level of income and $L(y)$ is the corresponding transaction demand for money. The transaction demand for money is vertical. The summation of $L(y_0)$ and $L(r)$ gives us the M^d schedule $[L(y) + L(r)]$ which is downward sloping like the speculative demand function, but the vertical part is away from the vertical axis by the amount of the fixed transaction demand $[L(y_0) = OL_0]$ (Figure 16.4). If level of income rises from y_0 to y_1, transaction demand for money rises to $L(y_1)$ at a given rate of interest. The new transaction demand for money function moves rightward horizontally to OL_1. The sum $L(y_1) + L(r)$ further moves to the right because of income rise. The new demand schedule is negatively sloped like before. $L(y_1) + L(r) = M^d$ schedule is also known as the liquidity preference schedule.

16.4 Regressive expectation theory

The *regressive expectation theory* is attributed to Keynes but described by James Tobin in his work on liquidity preference. According to this theory, people need money either to make transactions or to store. On the other hand, money is needed for transaction or investment since investment gives returns in terms of rate of interest and money in cash form does not provide any interest income. Again, people hold money for investment purposes if bond price is expected to fall in the future or interest rates are to rise in the future, and people hold cash when bond price is expected to rise or interest rate to fall in the future. That means the expectation works in a regressive direction.

A bond gives the holder two types of expected returns: one is the interest payment which is called yield (say r) and a potential capital gain (say g). Hence, total expected return (R) is $r + g$. As we have already mentioned, there is an inverse relation between price of bond (P_b) and rate of interest (r). Again, price of bond is the yield as a ratio to rate of interest. Suppose Rs. 100 is the price of the bond and it gives a fixed return of Rs. 10 annually, then 100 / 10, that is 10%, is the rate of interest. As the price of the bond increases to 200, then to get Rs. 10 as fixed yield, (10 / 200) *100, that is, 5% should be the rate of interest. Hence, we can write

$$P_b = Y / r. \tag{16.11}$$

Again, capital gain is defined as the rate of change of expected price of the bond with respect to the current value of price of the bond. In other words,

$$g = \left(P_b^{\,e} - P_b\right) / P_b. \tag{16.12}$$

Since expected price of the bond depends on the expected rate of interest and the current price of the bond depends on current rate of interest, the previous expression for g can be written as

$$g = \left[\left(Y / r^e - Y / r\right)\right] / \left(Y / r\right) \tag{16.13}$$

$$\text{or } g = \left(r / r^e\right) - 1. \tag{16.14}$$

This is the expression of capital gain. If $r > r^e$ then g will be positive, and if the reverse, then it will be negative. There will be no capital gain or loss if $r = r^e$. But how will the money/bond holder gain if the expected rate of interest falls short of the current rate of interest? The answer is here. As expected rate of interest rate falls, expected bond price increases and it is more than the current price of the bond, which is corresponding to the current rate of interest. On the other hand, if r^e is greater than r, then expected bond price will be less than current bond price and hence there will be capital loss.

Now, referring back to the total, the expected rate of return on holding of bonds is given as

$$R = r + g. \tag{16.15}$$

Substituting the expression for "g" we get

$$R = r + \left(r / r^e\right) - 1. \tag{16.16}$$

This is the crucial expression for defining the demand for money by an individual household or by the individuals of the aggregate economy.

Let us introduce how the regressive expectation hypothesis works for individuals or the economy as a whole. The previous expression says that people will hold total money in bonds if $R > 0$ and alternatively in full cash if $R < 0$. They will be indifferent if $R = 0$. People think of the income-earning position of their money with respect to the long run rate of interest which is called normal rate or average rate of interest which does not usually change. Now see what happens to the individual behaviour and then to the aggregate behaviour.

16.4.1 *Individual demand for money*

The individual perceives the expected return on bond to rise in the future if the current rate of interest is less than the long run average rate and to fall if the current rate is more than the long run rate. There is a rate of interest where there is neither increase nor decrease compared to the normal average rate. This particular rate is called *critical rate of interest*, r^c. Corresponding to the "r^c", R is equal to zero. That means

$$r + \left(r / r^e\right) - 1 = 0$$

$$\text{or, } r.r^e + r - r^e = 0$$

$$\text{or, } r\left(r^e + 1\right) = r^e$$

$$\text{or } r = r^e / \left(r^e + 1\right) = r^c = \textit{critical } r. \tag{16.17}$$

The critical rate of interest is less than the expected r at all positive values of interest rates. An individual's decision to hold a bond will depend on the relation between r and r^c. When current (or actual) rate of interest will be greater than the critical rate of interest (i.e. $r > r^c$) then it is expected that the individual will hold all of his money in bonds and when $r < r^c$ then he will put all of his money in cash form for transaction purposes. We can now derive the individual demand for money or real balance function with the help of the aforementioned relations between actual r and critical r. Figure 16.5 shows this phenomenon.

The figure shows three distinct parts of the individual demand for money function depending on the position of the critical rate vis-a-vis the actual rate. When $r > r^c$ then the individual puts all of his wealth on bond and so the demand for money or real balance will be zero and the function will coincide with the vertical axis. Again when $r < r^c$ all the money will be held as cash; no demand for bond will be there. The individual will be indifferent when $r = r^c$. The individual demand for money is a *step function*.

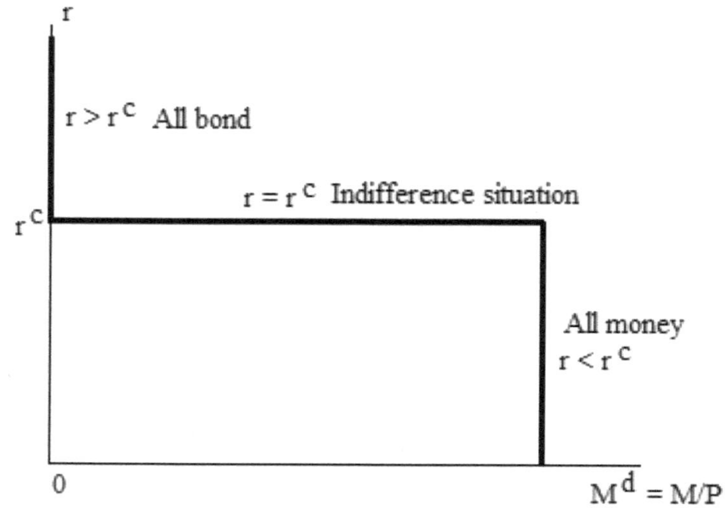

Figure 16.5 Individual demand for money

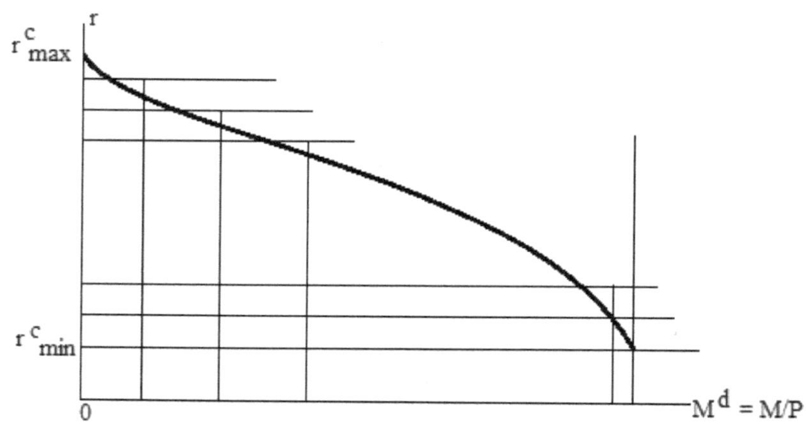

Figure 16.6 Aggregate demand for money

16.4.2 Aggregate demand for money

An economy's total requirement of money depends on the summation of all individuals' requirement for money. Like individuals' investment of money, we can think of investment of money in its entirety but with a bit difference in analysis. Figure 16.6 presents the aggregate demand for money in a regressive expectation model.

All individuals in an aggregated system may not have equal preference for liquidity. That means, at the extreme value of critical rate of interest, there may be one or more individuals and at the same time there may be one or more at the lower strata of the critical rate of interest. There may be some in the middle range of the critical interest rate. Suppose r^c_{max} is the maximum value of the critical rate for one individual or many homogeneous individuals. At that maximum value, there will be a preference for bond and all the money will be held for bonds and no money for cash. We get one point on the aggregate demand for money function. Now suppose the maximum value of the critical rate is below the earlier maximum value of the critical rate. Here we again get that some individuals in this zone will hold their money in bonds, nothing as cash. Doing the same analysis for all the remaining low rates of the critical values up to r^c_{min}, there will be similar types of bond and money combination. Joining all such points like A, B, C, D, etc. we get aggregate demand for money function, which is not a step function like the individual demand function but rather a smooth negatively sloped downward sloping function with respect to rate of interest.

16.5 Portfolio balance approach

In the regressive expectation theory, the individuals behaved as holding all of their money in bonds or in the form of cash or safe bank deposits, not any combination of both of bond and cash money. The underlying assumption was certainty regarding the future expectations. James Tobin, in his theory on *portfolio balance approach*, argues that the future is uncertain and it will be costlier for an individual to keep all of his assets in either bonds or money. Rather, in a real-world situation, individuals hold some combinations of the two in the uncertain world. Individuals always try to avert risk and want to get more benefit. But to get more benefit, individuals have to take risk. If there is zero risk, there will be no bonds but all money in cash form, providing zero returns. How much of his total wealth will be distributed on bond and cash depends on the preference in risk and return framework and the budget constraint of the individual. Here return or gain is captured by the average return or mean return (or expected return), and risk is captured by dispersion or standard deviation.

16.5.1 Indifference curves under different risk conditions

Just as the indifference curve is derived under the case of certainty under the fulfilment of certain axioms regarding an individual consumer's behaviour, we can also derive the indifference curve under uncertainty subject to the fulfilment of the axioms set under the von Neumann-Morgenstern expected utility functions. To derive IC under uncertainty we need to define the variables through which the equal preference relation or indifference relation will be drawn. For any risky asset there is on the one hand a positive side (like the character of a good) which is his expected gain ($E(x) = \mu$) from the risky asset and a negative side (like the character of a bad) which is the degree of variability or the probability which is captured by the measures of standard deviation ($SD = \sigma$). We have the idea from the ordinal approach of the consumer's theory that for a good the marginal utility is positive and for a bad it is negative, so we put positive marginal utility for μ and negative marginal utility for σ. The IC under uncertainty is, therefore, defined as the combinations of expected return (μ) and variability or SD of return (σ) that keeps the utility or satisfaction level of the consumer at a fixed level. The equation of the IC may be written as

$$U(\mu, \sigma) = U_0 . \tag{16.18}$$

where U_0 is the fixed level of utility. The marginal utility of expected return is $dU / d\mu > 0$ and marginal utility of SD (i.e. risk) is $dU / d\sigma < 0$. If we measure expected return along the horizontal axis and SD along the vertical axis then slope of the IC is

$$MRS = -d\sigma / d\mu = -\ [dU / d\mu] / [dU / d\sigma] = -\ MU\mu / MU\sigma > 0. \tag{16.19}$$

This means the ICs are upward sloping in a good and a bad framework. But the curvatures of the ICs depend on the nature of the consumer regarding taking risks. If the consumer is a risk averter, he will always want risk protection. In that case he will try to get high returns with fewer and fewer relative risks to be as well off as before.

That means the IC will look like convex shapes with respect to the risk or SD axis or concave with respect to the return or mean axis (Figure 16.7). The more the ICs are away from the SD axis or closer to the mean axis, the more the level of utility will go on increasing. If, on the other hand, the individual loves more risk relative to his return (the case of a risk lover), his IC will be convex to the return axis and concave to the SD axis (Figure 16.8). Again, if he loves risk and return, in a weak sense he is a risk neutral and in that case the IC is an upward sloping straight line (Figure 16.9). The utility levels are denoted by U_0, U_1, U_2, and U_3 and ranked by $U_0 < U_1 < U_2 < U_3$.

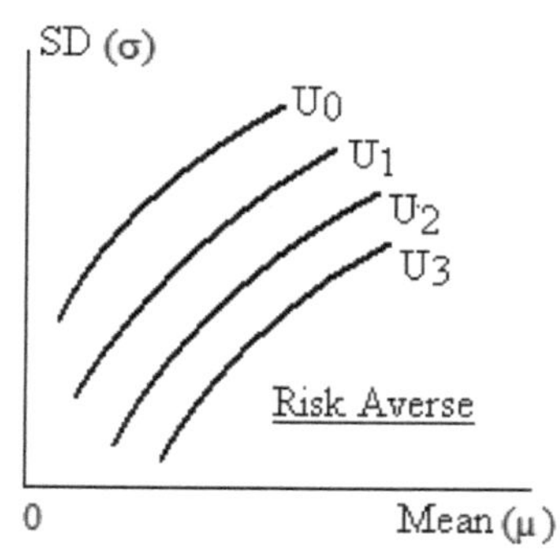

Figure 16.7 Risk averter

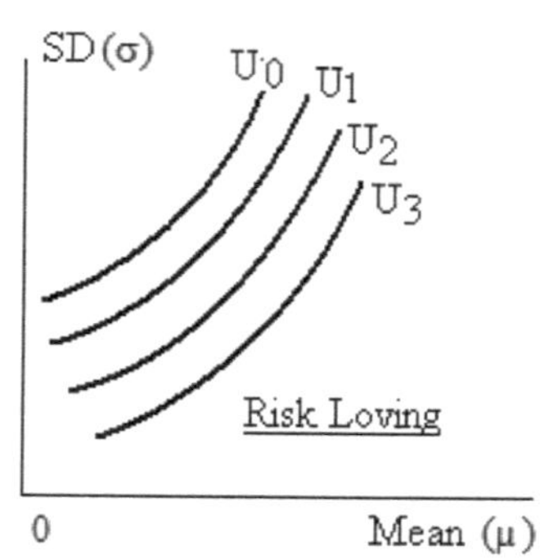

Figure 16.8 Risk lover

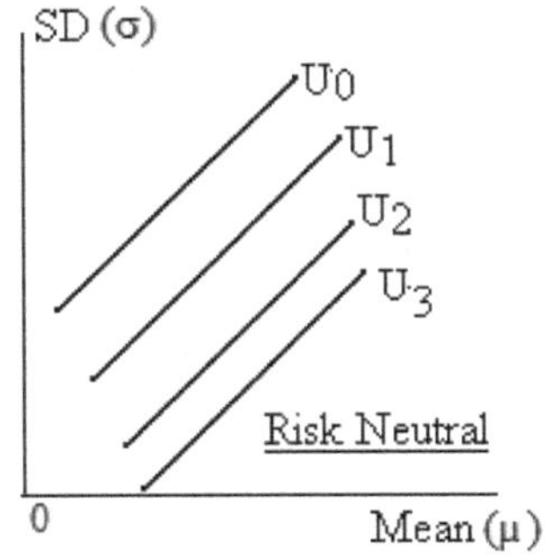

Figure 16.9 Risk-neutral person

16.5.2 *Budget function*

Let us consider the risk-free asset *S* (*S* for "sure") and the risky asset *R*. The expected return from the risk-free asset is equal to the actual return and we denote it *RS*. The risky asset has the expected return *RR* and the actual risky return is *RA*. Since the stock asset has a chance factor and is risky, then we can expect its return to be higher than the return from the safe asset i.e. $RR > RS$. If not, the risk-averse investors will not go for purchasing any stock asset but only certain assets. Now we have to see how the individual does allocate his entire fund on these two types of assets. Let θ be the share of total surplus fund invested upon the risky asset and the remainder $(1 - \theta)$ invested upon the safe asset. The individual will face the expected or mean return from the entire diversified package (*RD*) which is

$$RD = \theta.\ RR + (1-\theta)\ RS. \tag{16.20}$$

Let us measure the riskiness of the asset by the SDD (SDD is the standard deviation for diversified asset) where

$$SDD^2 = E[xi - x]^2 = E[squared\ deviation\ of\ actual\ return\ from\ the\ mean\ return)$$

$$Or, SDD^2 = E[\theta.\ RA\ +\ (1-\theta)RS - RD]^2 \tag{16.21}$$

We have to convert the expected value of diversified return in respect of actual return. Hence,

$$RD = E[\theta.\ RR + (1-\theta)\ RS] = E[\theta.\ RA\ +\ (1-\theta)\ RS] = \theta.\ E(RA)\ +\ E[(1-\theta)\ RS]$$

$$Or,\ RD = \theta.\ RR + (1-\theta)\ RS \tag{16.22}$$

Now substituting the value of *RD* into the expression of SDD^2 we get

$$SDD^2\ =\ E[\theta.\ RA + (1-\theta)RS - \theta.\ RR - (1-\theta)\ RS]^2$$

$$Or,\ SDD^2\ =\ E[\theta\ (RA - RR)]^2$$

$$Or,\ SDD^2\ =\ \theta^2.\ SDR^2$$

$$Or,\ SDD^2\ =\ \theta^2.\sigma^2$$

$$Or,\ SDD\ =\ \theta.\sigma. \tag{16.23}$$

This means the total standard deviation of the diversified asset is θ times the standard deviation of the risky asset. The optimum choice of the individual demanding the asset will be on the basis of the trade-off between expected return from the diversified asset $RD(\mu)$ and the risk faced in purchasing stocks $SSD(\sigma)$. The individual's optimum choice will be made at a point where the upward sloping budget function will be tangent to the upward sloping indifference curve in the μ and σ plane.

We can now derive the budget function from the original equation of expected return from the risk-free and risky assets. That is

$$RD = \theta.\ RR + (1-\theta)\ RS$$

$$Or,\ \mu = \theta.\ RR + (1-\theta)\ RS. \tag{16.24}$$

Also we have the relation $SDD = \theta.\ \sigma$. Substituting this relation into the expected return equation we have the budget equation as

$$\mu = RS + (RR - RS).\ SSD / \sigma. \tag{16.25}$$

Rearranging the budget equation, we get

$$\sigma.\ RD + (RS - RR).SSD = \sigma.\ RS. \tag{16.26}$$

The price of RD is the σ and price of SSD is $(RS - RR)$. The intercept along the horizontal or RD axis is obtained when $SSD = 0$. This means $RD = RS$ and also $\theta = 0$. This means for a risk-free asset expected return is the total return when all funds are invested upon treasury bills. This means the budget function will originate from the RD axis at a value RS.

Now slope of the budget function is obtained as

$$dSSD / dRD = d\sigma / d\mu = -\ \sigma / (RS - RR) = \sigma / (RR - RS) > 0. \tag{16.27}$$

That means the budget line is an upward sloping straight line. This means as amount of risk rises the expected return should increase, otherwise the investor will not go for risky assets (Figure 16.10). The slope of the budget line may also represent the price of risk. OB is the budget line which starts from the origin where there is zero risk and zero return.

16.5.3 Optimal portfolio allocation

A risk-averse investor will move to that point along the line OB which enables him to reach the highest attainable indifference curve. At that point he ends up choosing that portfolio which he intends to choose and, thus, maximises his utility. The individual's total wealth function is

$$W_0 = Bond + Money = B + M \tag{16.28}$$

where W_0 is the total amount of wealth that he can use on different combinations of bond (B) and money (M). In Figure 16.10, the individual's optimum portfolio choice has been presented.

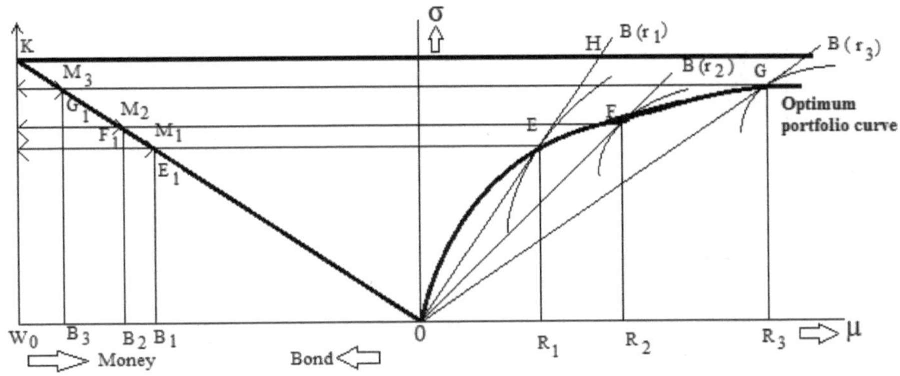

Figure 16.10 Optimal portfolio allocation

Initially at rate of interest rate r_1, $B(r_1)$ is the budget function of the individual and E is the equilibrium of the concerned individual where the budget line is tangent to the indifference curve (right panel of the diagram). In the left panel of the diagram, the optimum combination of bond and money has been shown. At r_1 interest rate, B_1 is the amount of bond holding and the remaining part, i.e. $W_0 - B_1$ equals M_1 unit of the wealth held as cash money. The arrows show the directions of bond or money holdings. If the indifference curve would not make tangency with the budget line at E, rather intersect the origin, then there would be zero holding of bond and all wealth would be held as money. On the other hand, if it would pass through point H then total wealth would be used for bonds and no residual would be left for cash money and the corresponding point would be at K. Point K and origin "0" are the situations under the regressive expectation approach. Under the portfolio balance approach the distribution of total wealth will lie between these two extremes.

Let us allow rate of interest to increase from r_1 to r_2. The budget line will shift rightward towards the average return (μ) axis. New equilibrium of the individual will be at F which makes more bond holding of B_2 since bond price has fallen. And accordingly the demand for money has fallen to M_2. If rate of interest further increases to r_3 then new equilibrium occurs at G and bond demand becomes B_3 and money demand M_3. In short, as the interest rate rises, a given increase in risk, which corresponds to a given increase in the amount of bonds in the portfolio, will result in a greater increase in expected return on the portfolio. The locus of E, F, and G is called the optimum portfolio curve of the individual and the locus of E_1, F_1, and G_1 gives the optimum combinations of money and bond.

We can now derive the demand for money function under the portfolio balance approach. The combination of r and M from the figure gives the demand for money function which has been depicted in Figure 16.11. The demand for money function is negatively sloped which justifies the shapes offered by the earlier approaches. Tobin's approach provides sound explanations to the negatively sloped speculative demand function.

We can make some useful simplifications in the portfolio balance approach where the demand for money function is $M^d = M / P = f(y, r)$. First, the demand function uses real income "y" as a proxy for wealth (W). Second, the only return variable it includes is the

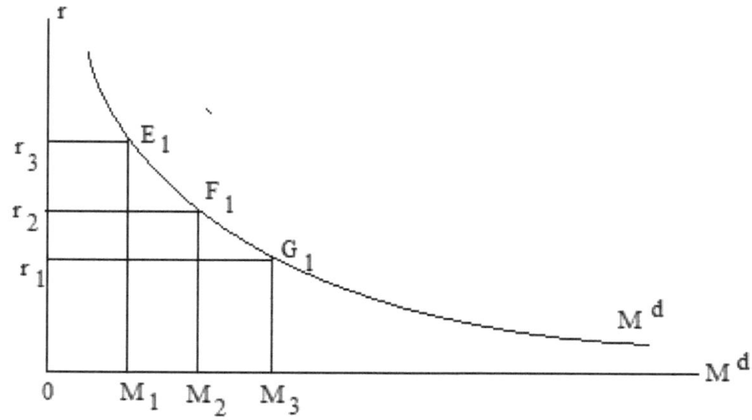

Figure 16.11 Demand for money function under portfolio balance approach

nominal interest rate, which is the sum of the real return on bonds and expected inflation. Therefore, Tobin's theory suggests that the demand function for money should also include the expected returns on other assets as well.

16.6 Inventory theoretic approach to transaction demand

W. J. Baumol and J. Tobin in their joint postulation challenged the classical and Keynesian versions of transaction demand for money as it was made related to the income or output of the economy. People hold some money as cash for transaction purposes since there is a gap between payment and execution of income. They treat the money balance held for transaction purposes similar to how a producer treats and uses its inventory of goods. As businesses maintain inventories of goods and materials to facilitate transactions or exchange in the context of changes in demand for them, Baumol and Tobin emphasise that individuals also hold an inventory of money because this facilitates transactions of goods and services. In other words, according to them, transaction demand is like inventory accumulation that can be used at any time as per requirements. As there is a cost to be incurred on holding inventories of goods, there is need for keeping optimal inventory of goods to reduce cost. Similarly, individuals have to keep optimum inventory of money for transaction purposes. Individuals also incur cost when they hold inventories of money for transaction purposes. The cost here is the foregone interest earning that could have been earned by shifting a part of the transaction balance on savings bank deposits or fixed deposits or on bonds. Hence, no additional or surplus money should be held for transaction purposes, rather a part of the transaction balance can be deposited in a savings bank account which earns a nonzero interest rate and can be withdrawn at any time. In this sense Baumol and Tobin stressed that transaction demand for money was not independent of the rate of interest, rather it was inversely related to rate of interest. As rate of interest rises, people should hold less money for transaction and hence less demand for transaction purpose and vice-versa. That is why individuals should compare the costs and benefits of funds in the form of money with the interest-bearing saving deposits or fixed deposits. According to them, the cost which people incur when they hold funds

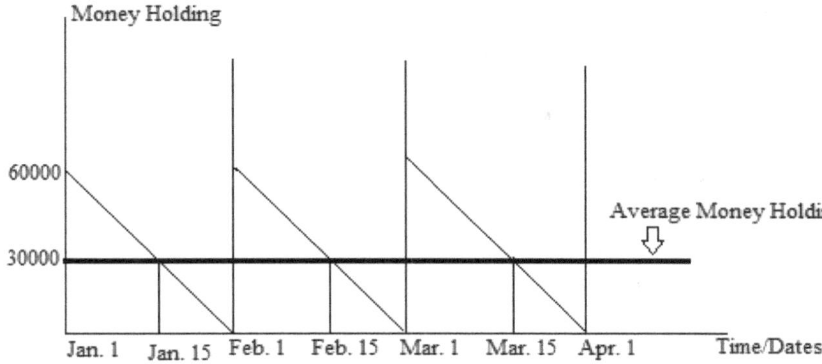

Figure 16.12 Money holding by the individual

in money is the opportunity cost of these funds which is again the foregone interest income by not putting them in secured saving deposits.

Let us see how the transaction demand for money can be linked to the inventory approach by means of segregating the total units of income held as transaction balances to optimise the combination of cash and deposit (or investment on bonds) so that the individual ultimately gains more than the cost of holding money. We have started assuming that the individual withdraws Rs. 60,000 per month on the first day of the month and he holds 50:50% of the total income for the first 15 days and last 15 days so that he can carry out all of his transactions. Also he gradually spends the total sum daily throughout the month with Rs. 2,000 per day so that at the end of the month he is left with no money balance. Hence, his average money holding in the month will be Rs. 60,000 divided by 2 which is Rs. 30,000. That means he will have more than Rs. 3,0000 before fifteenth of the month and less than Rs. 30,000 after the fifteenth day of the month. Average holding of money equal to Rs. 30,000 has been shown by the thick line in Figure 16.12. Here we get two cash management phases; one is the first half and the other is the second half.

Now, the natural question arises whether it is the optimal strategy of managing money. Put simply, the answer is no since the individual is losing interest earning by holding all the money in liquid cash form which he could have earned if he had deposited some funds in interest-bearing saving deposits instead of withdrawing all his salary in cash on the first day. He can manage his money balances so as to earn some interest income as well. That is why the concept of income-bearing inventory management comes into play.

Instead of withdrawing his entire salary on the first day of the month, suppose he withdraws only Rs. 30,000 (which is half of his total salary) in cash and deposits the remaining amount of Rs. 30,000 in a saving account which gives him interest of 4%, say. But his per-day expenditure for transaction purposes remains constant at Rs. 2,000. Figure 16.13 illustrates this situation of segregation.

It is observed from the diagram that the individual's money holdings of Rs. 30,000 will be reduced to zero at the end of the fifteenth day of each of the months. Now, he can withdraw Rs. 30,000 on the morning of sixteenth of each month and then spend it gradually at the rate of Rs. 2,000 per day for the next 15 days of a month. Average money holdings will be Rs. 30,000 / 2 which is equal to Rs. 15,000. The individual gets a better position now than before since his remaining balance of the last 15 days can earn

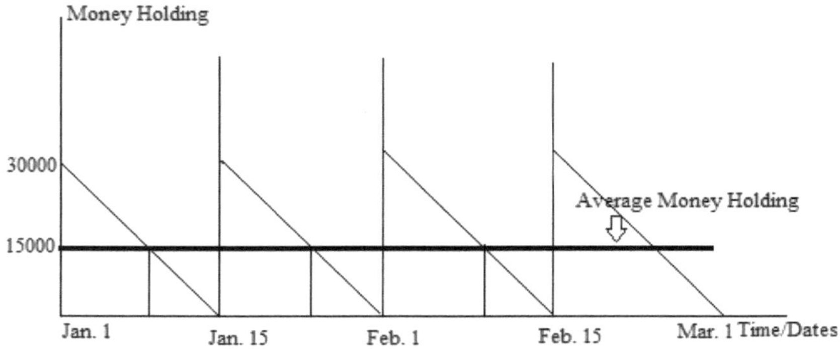

Figure 16.13 Segregation of periods

interest income which is 30,000 × 0.04 = 1,200. Therefore, he gets Rs. 1,200 additional money for the remaining half of the month. This is, therefore, a better method of managing funds.

Similarly, the individual can break the first 15 days into, say, three more slots each with five days' interval and the average holding then will be 15,000 / 3 = 5,000 and he can earn interest income from the rest of the 10,000 amount (5,000 + 5,000). The process can be continued for infinite periods. But there are some costs of these additional earnings which are called *transaction costs*. They are like additional brokerage fees for purchasing and selling bonds, spending a lot of time in the queues in the banks, transportation costs to do all these activities, etc. Hence, the individual will have to optimise the cash and investment schemes so that his net earnings (income less cost) are maximised or total cost is minimised.

Suppose the monthly salary amount is Y, the average amount of the cash the individual withdraws each time from the bank is C, the number of times he goes to the bank is T (= Y / C), and each brokerage fee is b. Total brokerage fee is b. T and total interest income foregone or lost is r. C / 2 (where C / 2 is average money holding in a two-phase distribution). Thus total cost (TC) of holding money for a transaction is given by the following equation:

$$TC = b \,.\, T + r \,.\, C/2$$

$$Or,\ TC = b \,.\, Y/C + r \,.\, C/2. \tag{16.29}$$

The individual's objective will be to minimise TC by fragmenting the total salary. This will happen when dTC / dC = 0.

$$Or,\ -b.Y/C^2 + r/2 = 0$$

$$Or,\ C = (2bY/r)^{1/2} = C^*. \tag{16.30}$$

C^* is the optimum amount of cash the individual will withdraw from the bank. The expression for C^* shows that the average amount of cash withdrawal which minimises cost is the square root of the two-time brokerage fee multiplied by the size of individual's income (Y) and divided by the rate of interest.

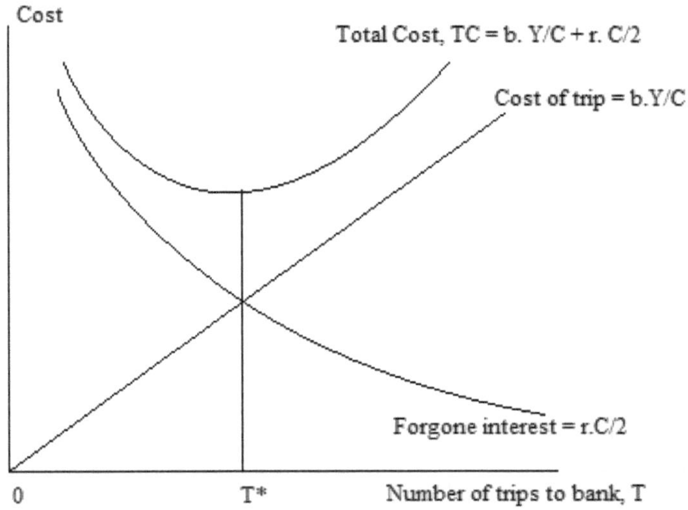

Figure 16.14 Cost function for transaction

Figure 16.14 presents the total cost function of making transactions under the inventory approach. The cost-of-trip function is upward sloping with the number of trips and the forgone interest income inversely related to the number of trips. The total cost (TC) curve is U-shaped because it incorporates the transaction costs and the interest forgone. The optimal number of visits is T^*that minimises the total cost of transaction· because at $N^*$the TC is minimum.

What follows from the expression is that, as brokerage fee rises, average amount of cash withdrawal from the bank will rise since bond investment will not be so worthwhile. Again, as monthly salary increases, the amount of withdrawal will increase for transaction purposes which is a normal phenomenon of transaction demand for money in classical and Keynesian lines. Finally, what is more important is that, as rate of interest rises, the amount withdrawn for transaction purposes falls and vice-versa. This particular phenomenon explains that the transaction demand for money for an individual is inversely related to rate of interest.

What about the aggregate demand for money function? To get its functional form, let us say there is another person who is a producer and the first person is a consumer. The producer holds different fractions of money for business transactions and holds a part of it in bonds that earn interest income. Hence, the roles of two individuals regarding demand for money are similar. Hence, we can take sum of the previous expression of C (= C^*) twice to get the aggregate demand for money or multiply it by 2. Hence, the aggregate demand for money function is –

$$C = 2(2bY / r)^{1/2} = C^*. \tag{16.31}$$

This means the aggregate demand for money for transaction follows the square root formula. Hence, the transaction demand for money under Baumol-Tobin's approach is as follows:

$$L^T = L(r,\ Y_0). \tag{16.32}$$

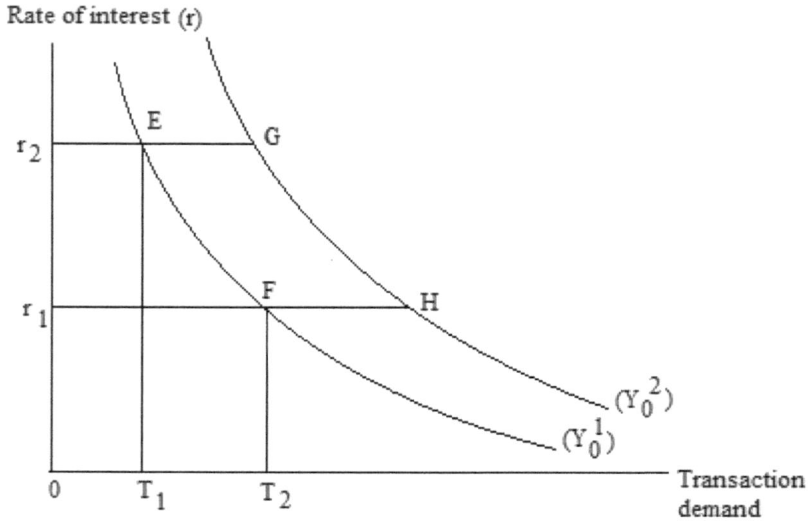

Figure 16.15 Transaction demand function under Baumol's approach

where Y_0 is a fixed level of income. Figure 16.15 presents the negatively sloped transaction demand for money.

At interest rate r_1, the transaction demand for money is T_2, given the salary income of Y_0^1. As rate of interest increases from r_1 to r_2, at the same level of income, transaction demand falls from T_2 to T_1. Again we see that at the given interest rates, as income level increases from Y_0^1 to Y_0^2, the transaction demand increases which has been shown by the upward shifting of the inventory form of the transaction demand function.

16.6.1 *LM function under interest-sensitive transaction demand*

We can now re-establish the money market equilibrium under the inventory theoretic approach to the demand for money. The money market equilibrium condition is now

$$M = T(y) + T(r) + L(r) \tag{16.33}$$

where $T(y)$ is the transaction demand for money with $T_y > 0$ as usual, $L(r)$ is speculative demand for money with $L_r < 0$ as usual, and the new term $T(r)$ represents the interest-sensitive transaction demand for money with $T_r < 0$. The equation of the LM function is now obtained by taking the total differentiation to both sides of the equation which is

$$dM = T_y.\, dy + T_r.dr + L_r.\, dr\,. \tag{16.34}$$

The slope of the new LM function is

$$\partial r / \partial y = -\, T_y / (T_r + L_r) > 0\,. \tag{16.35}$$

The LM function is still positively sloped but it is flatter than the slope of the curve under the perfectly interest-insensitive transaction demand function. The additional term, T_r, has been added to the denominator of the slope expression and that has caused the slope to be lower.

We can give some clues here to the effectiveness of fiscal and monetary policies under this new LM function. The flatter shape of the LM functions is a reminder that the monetary policy will not be effective to influence output of the economy; rather, the fiscal policy has such power to produce real effects. The readers can verify this by means of mathematical and diagrammatical analyses.

16.7 Consumer and producer goods approaches to money

In a strong departure from the traditional approaches of demand for money meant for transaction or speculation, Milton Friedman considered the role of money from the viewpoint of microeconomic foundations. According to him, money is like a consumer or producer's good. A consumer holds money to get utility or satisfaction and a producer needs money to purchase raw material and other factors the combined effect of which makes output or the producer's goods. It may be noted that the service rendered by money is that of a general purchasing power so that it can be conveniently used for buying goods and services. Friedman considers the demand for money merely as an application of a general theory of demand for capital assets.

According to Friedman, the consumer's demand for money should be a demand for real balance just like the consumer's demand for a real consumer's good; no money value of the goods arises or the situation of money illusion does not arise at all. The consumer's demand for real balance thus should depend on their real income and the returns from different alternative investments like on bonds and consumer's durables. On the other hand, the producer's demand for real balance also depends on the real output and real price of capital or relative returns on the alternative roots of capital investments. Suppose y is the real income (or output) and r_1, r_2, ..., r_n is the series of returns from "n" number of assets which are alternatives to money, then the demand for money or real balance is as follows-

$$M^d = M / P = f(y, r_1, r_2, \ldots\ldots\ldots, r_n). \qquad (16.36)$$

If values of real incomes are non-changing or less fluctuating, then we can side out the value of y from the functional values and so the demand for money only depends on different returns from different assets. Friedman considers three rates of interest, namely r_m, r_b and r_e, which determine the demand for money. r_m is the own rate of interest on money. Here it is important to note that money kept in the form of currency and demand deposits does not earn any interest income. But money held as saving deposits and fixed deposits earns certain rates of interest and this is captured by r_m in the money demand function. Given the other rates of interest or return, the higher the own rate of interest, the greater the demand for money. An individual's demand for money is derived by comparing the own return with the other rates of returns or the opportunity costs. The opportunity cost of holding money is the interest or return given up by not holding these other forms of assets. As rates of return on bonds (r_b) and equities (r_e) rise, the opportunity cost of holding money will increase, which will reduce the demand for money holdings. Thus, the demand for money is negatively related to the rate of interest (or return) on bonds, equities, and other such non-money assets. Friedman's money demand function is negatively sloped.

The model is an advanced approach in the sense that here we can incorporate the effects of inflation and velocity of money like factors in deciding the position of the money demand function. We have no such scope to incorporate all these issues in the present book. Interested readers are suggested to explore Friedman, M. (1959), "The Demand for Money: Some Theoretical and Empirical Results," Journal of Political Economy 67, no. 4, page 327–351.

16.8 Conclusion

We discussed in detail in the previous sections of the present chapter the issue of why people have demand for money and what the determinants of the demand for money are. Money has basically two roles – an active or transaction role and an idle or speculative role. The classical model defended their position through their invention of quantity theory of money that money is exclusively required for transaction purposes. Keynes, on the other hand, claimed that not only is money used for transaction, rather it has a store or idle value in the sense that it can be stored or held to use in the future for investing in assets like bonds which will provide lucrative returns. According to Keynes, the idle demand or speculative demand for money is inversely related to rate of interest and transaction demand positively depends on income. The regressive expectation theory is similar to that of Keynes and that developed by Tobin which shows that people expect the future bond price to move in a regressive way with respect to the current price of bonds or rate of interest. The individual demand for money is a step function here. But this theory does not include people's behaviour in that they can hold a combination of money and bonds to get optimum benefit from their money. It is Tobin's "portfolio balance approach". William Baumol criticised both the classical and Keynesian views on transaction demand for money being dependent only on the level of income and postulated that people can think of transactions like inventory and therefore transaction demand for money is inversely related to rate of interest. It is known as the inventory theoretic approach to transaction demand for money. Friedman postulated that money is like consumers' and producers' goods and from the perspectives of microeconomics he postulated that the consumer's demand for money should be a demand for real balance just like in the consumer's demand for real consumer goods no money value of the goods arises.

Summary

In the previous discussion we elaborately explained different theories of demand for money by individuals and aggregate economy. The summary outputs are:

- The classical theory of demand for money is based on the quantity theory of money of Fisher's equation of exchange and cash balance approach of the Cambridge school. According to the theory, money is used for only transaction purposes or as medium of exchange.
- Keynes, in his theory of liquidity preference, established that money has both active and idle roles. His novel idea is that people hold money in extreme situations to invest in bonds and the demand for money in this context, the speculative demand for money, is inversely related to the rate of interest.

- James Tobin, penetrating into the Keynesian liquidity preference theory, established that people hold money on the basis of regressive expectation and the individual demand for money is a step function but the aggregate demand for money is a negatively sloped smooth function with respect to the interest rate.
- Tobin's own invention of portfolio balance approach postulated that people hold or demand for money to invest in some combination of bonds and shares.
- William Baumol strongly criticised the classical and Keynesian theories on determinants of transaction demand for money and claimed that transaction demand for money is like a demand for inventory and, like producers' assets, it is inversely dependent on rate of interest. The LM function is relatively flatter under this form of money demand.
- Milton Friedman explained the demand for money on the microeconomic foundation and that consumer's demand for money should be a demand for real balance just like in the consumer's demand for real consumer goods no money value of the goods arises or the situation of money illusion does not arise at all.

Keywords

Money
Classical demand for money
Keynesian demand for money
Regressive expectations
Portfolio balance
Inventory theoretic approach
Consumer goods and producer goods

Multiple choice questions and answers

1. Which of the following is not true for the classical demand for money –
   (a) Money is required only to meet transaction purposes.
   (b) Volume of money supply should be identical to volume of transaction demand.
   (c) Money demand depends on rate of interest.
   (d) Quantity of money supply and commodity prices are proportionally related.
2. The speculative demand for money is generally related with the rate of interest in
   (a) A positive way.
   (b) An inverse way.
   (c) An independent way.
   (d) All of the above.
3. The individual demand for money function under the "regressive expectation model" is
   (a) An upward sloping function.
   (b) A smooth, negatively sloped function.
   (c) A horizontal line.
   (d) A step function.
4. The LM function under the inventory theoretic approach to transaction demand for money is positively sloped but
   (a) Relatively flatter than the usual LM function.
   (b) Relatively steeper than the usual LM function.

(c) With no change of magnitude of slope compared to the usual one.
(d) Maybe any of the above.

5. Under the portfolio balance approach, an individual holds money to invest

   (a) Only in bonds.
   (b) Only in shares.
   (c) Both bonds and shares.
   (d) None of the above.

Answers

1. (c); 2. (b); 3. (d); 4. (a); 5. (c)

Review questions

1. What is a barter system? Give a note on the evolution of methods of transaction from history to date.
2. What is meant by "money as medium of exchange and money as a medium of store"? Explain the quantity theory of money to establish the classical theory of demand for money.
3. What is speculative demand for money? Explain the Keynesian demand for money and explain the effect of increase in money supply on rate of interest.
4. Why is expectation regressive? Establish the demand for money with the help of the regressive expectation approach. Distinguish between the shapes of individual and aggregate demand for money functions.
5. What is the basis of keeping a portfolio of asset? Discuss the portfolio balance approach and determine the optimum combination of assets by an individual. Who is called a risk lover? Derive the utility function of a risk-loving individual.
6. Why is transaction demand called the demand for inventory? Explain the optimum transaction demand for money under the inventory theoretic approach of Baumol.
7. Derive the LM function when the transaction demand for money is interest elastic. Explain the effect of monetary policy under the reformulated LM function.
8. What are "consumer durables"? Give a brief note on Friedman's approach to the demand for money.

Additional readings

Baumol, W. J. (1952). "The transactions demand for cash: An inventory theoretic approach". *Quarterly Journal of Economics*, 66(4), 545–556.
Tobin, J. (1958). "Liquidity preference as behaviour towards risk". *Review of Economic Studies*, 25(2).

17 Theory of money supply

17.1 Introduction

In the previous chapters while dealing with money market equilibrium to determine income, rate of interest, and other related variables we assumed the money supply to be exogenously determined and the monetary authority had the exclusive role of deciding it. In the present chapter we relax this restriction and focus on the process by which money supply is determined in an endogenous manner. We will discuss here the roles of monetary institutions like the central bank and commercial banks of a country and the public who use money in different forms. We will also highlight the determinants of money supply, the money multiplier, and the credit creation of the commercial banks. Using specific countries' data, the present chapter will analyse different money supply components and instruments for controlling the inflationary situation of a country.

17.2 Definitions and types of money

Recalling our earlier discussions on money supply given in the chapters on money and inflation, "money" can be defined as a generally recognised medium of exchange for goods and services. Fundamentally anything can be considered as money, as long as it performs the three major functions of money which are medium of exchange, store of value and unit of account. There are different types of money throughout history. But in the practical world there are four most relevant types of money. They are commodity money, fiat money, fiduciary money, and commercial bank money. To help the readers to maintain flow of readings, we briefly discuss them again.

Commodity money relies on intrinsically valuable commodities that act as a medium of exchange. It is the money where face value and intrinsic (or material values) values are identical. Fiat money, on the other hand, gets its value from a government order. It is sometimes called legal tender money in the sense that the paper note or metal coin will carry the values which have been mentioned on them under some legal bindings. Its intrinsic values are much lower than their face values. For example, one Rs. 500 note takes the intrinsic value (or the printing cost) of Rs. 35 (say). The face value or the legal tendered value of this note is Rs. 500 but its intrinsic value is just Rs. 35. Usually the governor of the central bank of a country gives the common people such legal rights.

Fiduciary money depends for its value on the confidence that it will be generally accepted as a medium of exchange. Unlike fiat money, it is not declared legal tender by the government, which means people are not required to accept it as a means of payment. Instead, the issuer of fiduciary money promises to exchange it back for a commodity or fiat money

DOI: 10.4324/9781003501138-21

if requested by the bearer. Finally, commercial bank money can be defined as the claims against financial institutions that can be used to purchase goods or services. It is created through the fractional reserve banking. Fractional reserve banking is a process where commercial banks give out loans worth more than the value of the actual currency they hold.

We further classify money into *ordinary* and *high-powered*, both of which bear the aforementioned four types of money. We can now make distinctions between ordinary money and high-powered money.

17.2.1 Ordinary money vs. high-powered money

Narrowly we can define ordinary money as the sum of currency and demand deposits of commercial and central banks held by the public. It is sometimes called as narrow money. Suppose M denotes ordinary money, C is the total currency with the public and banks and DD is the total demand deposits in banks, then we have the relation for ordinary money as

$$M = C + DD. \tag{17.1}$$

On the other hand, high-powered money (H) refers to the money produced by the central bank and the government of the country and held by the public and banks. Sometimes the high-powered money is called *reserve money*. The H-money is defined as the sum of currency held by the public (C), cash reserves of banks (R), and other deposits of the central bank (OD). The historical data, for example the Reserve Bank of India, India's Central Bank, says that the other deposit part (OD) holds very low share compared to the total H-money and therefore we can avoid this head to deal with a simplistic formulation of high-powered money.

Therefore, the H-money is defined by the following relation as

$$H = C + R. \tag{17.2}$$

Let us compare previous two Equations (17.1 and 17.2) for the ordinary and high-powered money. We see that the difference between the two arises due to DD and R since "C" is the common term for both the forms of money. The difference between the two arises since demand deposits are produced by the banks which are counted as money like C. Again, to produce DD, banks have to maintain R, which is a part of H, which is the part and parcel of only the monetary authority and not by banks themselves. In a fractional reserve banking system, DD are a certain multiple of R and hence it lends to H the quality of high-poweredness over the ordinary money, M. It is the power of serving as the base for the multiple creation of DD. That is why H-money is also called *base money* or *monetary base* of a country.

17.2.2 Monetary aggregates in India

In our previous chapters on money and inflation, we have covered the discussion on different types of money supply from the point of view of general perspectives. In the present section we present the monetary aggregates used by the central bank of India. The monetary authority in India is the Reserve Bank of India which is the central bank of the country. Money supply is a stock concept whose values are measured in a particular point of time. RBI calculates four concepts of money supply in India which are known as monetary aggregates of the country. They are:

M_1 Money = Currency with the public (C) + Demand deposits of the public (D) = money supply in the *narrow sense*
M_2 Money = M_1 + Post office savings deposits
M_3 Money = M_1 + Time deposits of the public with the banks = *Broad money supply*
M_4 Money = M_3 + Total post office deposits

Besides the narrow and broad money concepts, M_2 and M_4 money are the money stock measures introduced by the RBI which contain all the deposits of post offices in the country. Although these two types of money constitute one form of liquidity to the public, RBI does not put much importance upon these two money supply concepts since it does not get regular information from the post office networks of the country. That is why these two concepts are irrelevant to the RBI but M_1 and M_3 moneys are relevant.

17.2.3 Data on monetary aggregates in India

The Reserve Bank of India, the country's central bank, maintains different monetary aggregates to date. We are here presenting the M_1 and M_3 money trends from the year 2000 to 2017 measured in billion rupees and rate of interest. The data are corresponding to March of every year. Table 17.1 presents the data series. We have computed the percentage changes of all of the three indicators over the years.

Figure 17.1 presents the line graph of M_1 and M_3 money components. Starting from Rs. 3,417.96 billion in 2000, the M_1 money ended up with Rs. 26,954.3 billion in 2017.

Table 17.1 Monetary aggregates in India (M_1 and M_3) (in billion INR) and rate of interest

Year	M_1	M_3	*Interest rate (r)*	*% Change of* M_1	*% Change of* M_3	*% Change of r*	*Term deposit*
2000	3,417.96	11,241.74	7	–	–	–	7,823.78
2001	3794.49	13,132.2	8	11.0162202	16.81643589	14.28571	9,337.71
2002	4,228.43	14,983.55	6.5	11.43605597	14.09779016	–18.75	10,755.12
2003	4,735.81	17,179.6	5.5	11.99925268	14.65640653	–15.38461	12,443.79
2004	5,787.16	20,056.76	5	22.2000038	16.74753778	–9.09090	14,269.6
2005	6,474.95	22,514.49	6	11.88475867	12.25387351	20	16,039.54
2006	8,263.75	27,295.45	6.25	27.62646816	21.23503575	4.16666	19,031.7
2007	9,659.89	33,159.93	7	16.89475117	21.48519259	12	23,500.04
2008	11,524.32`	40,175.73	7	19.30073738	21.15746324	0	28,651.41
2009	12,515.22	47,839.88	6	8.598338123	19.07656687	–14.28571	35,324.66
2010	14,907.04	56,019.95	4.25	19.11129009	17.09885142	–29.16666	41,112.91
2011	16,406.3	65,035	6.5	10.0573957	16.09257059	52.94117	48,628.7
2012	17,373.94	73,577.472	8.5	5.897978216	13.1351915	30.76923	56,203.531
2013	18,975.26	82,623.323	7.75	9.216792506	12.29432155	–8.823529	63,648.062
2014	20,597.62	94,554	7.75	8.549869672	14.43984198	0	73,956.38
2015	22,924.04	105,455.53	8	11.29460588	11.52942726	3.22580	82,531.494
2016	26,025.38	116,176.15	7.5	13.52876718	10.1660063	–6.25	90,150.770
2017	26,954.3	12,4308.25	6.75	3.569285059	6.999799694	–10	97,353.948
Correlation	**0.3719**	**0.4067**					**0.4150**

Source: Reserve Bank of India and the authors' calculations.

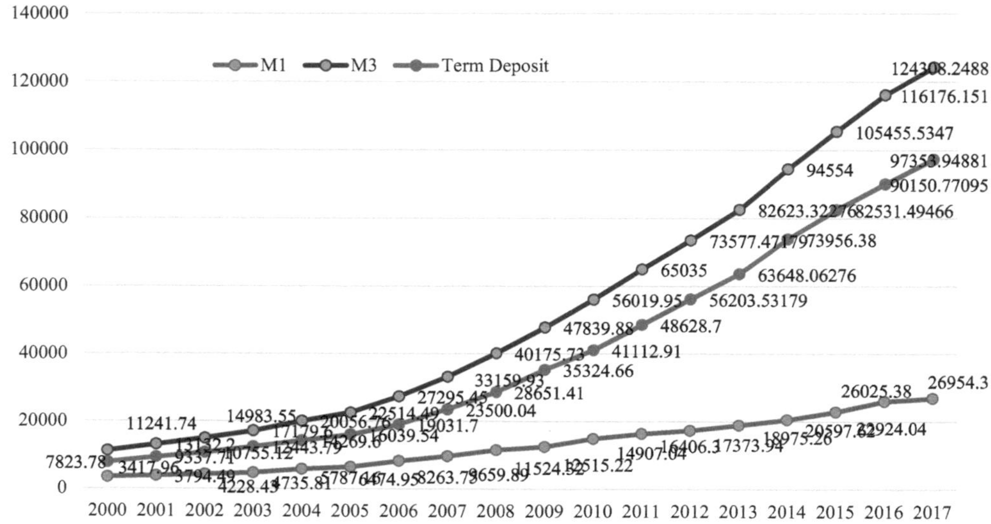

Figure 17.1 M_1 and M_3 money supply and the term deposit

On the other hand, the M_3 money or the broad money started from Rs. 11,241.74 billion in the year 2000 and reached Rs. 124,308 billion in 2017. Over time the gap between these two concepts of money supply widened. That means, the importance of time deposits of the public with the banks has risen over time and the values are increasing over time. The trend of the time deposit increases over time. Starting from Rs. 7,823 billion in 2000, the magnitudes of time deposit end up with Rs. 97,354 in 2017.

We have computed the relation between these two concepts of money supply with the rate of interest. We have justified them by the correlation coefficients between M_1 and "r" and M_3 and "r". The last row of the table shows the results. There are positive associations between the two monetary aggregates with the rate of interest but the latter is with high magnitudes of values. Hence, we get that $dM / dr = M_r > 0$.

17.3 Mechanism of deposit creation by banking system

In the previous sections we have pointed out that the commercial banking system of a country supplies money which is held by the common people in the form of currency and demand deposits. But we did not discuss how such a process works. Here we highlight this issue. Banks create deposits in two ways – the direct way which is known as primary deposit and indirect deposit which is known as derivative deposit. A primary deposit is the amount of money deposited by any individual in a bank and the derivative deposit is the money which is created by the bank when it gives a loan to any person. The important difference between these two types of deposits is that in the case of primary deposit total money supply remains the same whereas in the case of a derivative deposit the money supply in the economy increases. Every loan or credit creates deposit. Banks create deposit out of the excess reserves which they have. Excess reserve is the balance of funds held by the banks after deducting the minimum cash ratio (which is the reserve ratio required for dealing with regular transactions) from the total deposit made by the public with the banking system.

Let us explain the mechanism of deposit or money creation. Before explaining the mechanism, we need to assume some necessary conditions about the banking system. There are several banks with a standard reserve ratio fixed statutorily. Also, individuals do not hold any amount of money as cash, which means all money should be deposited into the banking system either by households or firms or both in any way. Suppose there are two banks, I and II; for the sake of simplicity each maintains the reserve ratio (that is reserve-deposit ratio) of "*rd*". Each bank provides a loan on the basis of excess reserves it holds statutorily to meet the regular demands of the depositors. The balance sheets of the two banks will together show the way of money supply creation. Suppose Bank I has excess reserve of ΔR equal to Rs. 1,000 and reserve-deposit ratio, *rd*, is equal to 20%. Bank I will create a loan of Rs. 1,000 (which is the derivative deposit). If the borrowers put this money in Bank II then Bank II will have Rs. 800 (= 1,000 – 20% of 1,000) as excess reserve which it can give as loans to the public. Similarly, the borrowers, say, deposit this Rs. 800 in Bank I again. Bank I will then have Rs. 640 (= 800 – 20% of 800) as excess reserve that it can give as loans to the public. Individuals will then withdraw the loan amount and deposit them in, say, Bank II which will have excess reserve of Rs. 512 (= 640 – 20% of 640) which again will be given as loans. The process continues for an indefinite period and the total money or deposit or credit created by the banks (ΔM) from the initial excess reserve of Rs. 1,000 is given as follows –

$$\Delta M = 1{,}000 + 800 + 640 + 512 + \dots\dots\dots\dots \tag{17.3}$$

The previous relation is an infinite GP series. It can be expanded into the following expression as:

$$\Delta M = 1{,}000 + 800 + 640 + 512 + \dots\dots\dots\dots \tag{17.4}$$

$$Or,\ \Delta M = 1{,}000 + 1{,}000 * [1 - 20/100] + 1000 * \left[1 - (20/100)^2\right] + 1{,}000 * \left[1 - (20/100)^3\right] + \dots\dots$$

$$Or,\ \Delta M = 1{,}000[1 + [1 - (20/100) + \left[1 - (20/100)^2\right] + 1{,}000 * \left[1 - (20/100)^3 + \dots\dots\dots\dots\right]$$

$$Or,\ \Delta M = \Delta R\ \left[1 + (1 - rd) + (1 - rd)^2 + (1 - rd)^3 + \dots\dots\dots\dots\right] \tag{17.5}$$

$$Or,\ \Delta M = \Delta R\ [1/\left(1 - (1 - rd)\right] \tag{17.6}$$

$$Or,\ \Delta M = \Delta R *\ [1/\ rd] \tag{17.7}$$

$$Or,\ \Delta M = (1/rd) * \Delta R \tag{17.8}$$

The previous expression is a reserve multiplier or deposit creation multiplier or credit creation multiplier. It shows that the amount of created money, ΔM, will be a multiple (=1 / *rd*) of the excess reserve, ΔR. This shows that as excess reserve is more in a bank then its created money will be more with a given reserve ratio. That is the money multiplier is

$$\Delta M / \Delta R = 1/rd > 1 \tag{17.9}$$

since $0 < rd < 1$.

On the other hand, if "*rd*" increases, that is, the commercial banks are required statutorily to hold more money as reserve, then created money will be less since the amount of loan (or deposit) created will be less than the situations with relatively lower values of "*rd*".

Now suppose people do not deposit all their borrowed money in the banking system, rather they hold "*b*" percent of the borrowed money. Then the capacity of the banks to create deposit will be less. Then the money creation series will be as follows:

$$\Delta M = \Delta R \left[1 + (1 - rd)(1 - b) + (1 - rd)^2 (1 - b)^2 + (1 - rd)^3 (1 - b)^3 + \ldots\ldots\ldots\ldots\right]$$

$$Or,\ \Delta M = \Delta R\ [1 / (1 - (1 - rd)(1 - b)] \quad (17.10)$$

$$Or,\ \Delta M = \Delta R\ [1 / (rd + b\ (1 - rd)]. \quad (17.11)$$

That is, the money multiplier is

$$\Delta M / \Delta R = 1 / (rd + b\ (1 - rd) > 1. \quad (17.12)$$

The magnitude of the multiplier is lesser than the earlier multiplier. As excess reserve increases, the created money will be lesser. If we assume "*b*" equals zero, then the money multiplier turns down to the earlier one. Hence, there are three factors responsible for money or deposit creation. They are excess reserve with $\delta M / \delta R > 0$, reserve to deposit ratio with $\delta M / \delta rd < 0$, and cash held with $\delta M / \delta b < 0$.

17.4 Determinants of money supply

In the literature on money supply by a central bank of a country there are mainly two approaches to money supply determinations:

- Balance sheet approach
- Money multiplier approach

17.4.1 *Balance sheet approach of money supply by the central bank*

Conventionally, money was created by either minting coins or printing currency. Nowadays, most money is stored electronically as account information. Before 1900, sovereign governments of the countries oversaw minting coins or printing currency – sometimes with disastrous results though. Nowadays, the supply of money is managed by the central banks as an autonomous body, not to satisfy the whims of politicians but to achieve specific well-established objectives, such as low inflation, maximum growth, or high employment. Money is usually created or destroyed electronically which is recorded in the central bank's balance sheet. Therefore, to understand the supply of money, one must understand how it is recorded in the central bank's balance sheet.

A central bank's balance sheet, like most balance sheets of the companies, is divided into assets and liabilities as the bankers' bank and assets and liabilities as the government's bank, as shown in Table 17.2. Broad money in a country is the sum of net foreign assets (NFA = Foreign assets – Foreign liabilities) and net domestic assets (NDA = Domestic assets – Domestic liabilities).

Table 17.2 Balance sheet of the central banks

	Assets	*Liabilities*
Bankers' bank	Loans	Bank accounts
Government's bank	Securities and foreign exchange reserves	Currency and government's accounts

Central bank assets include securities, which are mainly in the form of treasuries; foreign exchange reserves, which are mainly held in the form of foreign bonds issued by foreign governments; and loans to commercial banks. Out of them, the most important asset is securities, which the central banks use to directly control the supply of money in the countries.

On the other hand, the central bank liabilities include: currency, which is held by the public; the federal government's bank account, which the central bank uses just as anyone would use their own checking account, depositing its revenues – mostly in the form of tax revenues – into its account and paying its bills, mostly in electronic format; and commercial bank accounts, otherwise known as reserves, where commercial banks keep their deposits with the central bank. Vault cash, which is cash held in the banks' vaults, is also part of the commercial banks' reserves, because the cash is used to service its customers. Reserves can be further classified as either required reserves or excess reserves. Required reserves are reserves banks must hold as a legal minimum to ensure their financial soundness while excess reserve is the amount exceeding the required reserves, which banks keep to conduct their daily business or because they failed to lend it.

Because changes in the supply of money are revealed in the central bank's balance sheet, the balance sheet is the most important item that the central bank discloses. The Federal Reserve and most other central banks publish their balance sheets weekly to maintain transparency. When a central bank fails to publish its balance sheet, it often indicates trouble, usually in the form of increasing the supply of money at the request of the politicians of the ruling parties. Only a central bank can control its balance sheet at will, since only a central bank can create or destroy money. Because of the relationship between the supply of money and the bank's balance sheet, the creation of money is sometimes called expanding the central bank's balance sheet, because both its assets and liabilities increase; likewise, the destruction of money causes the contraction of the central bank's balance sheet.

17.4.2 Money multiplier approach

According to Friedman, money supply is a function of three exogenous variables. They are high-powered money (H) or the monetary base which is directly controlled by the central bank of the country, reserve to deposit ratio (rd), and currency to deposit ratio (c). From the definitions of H-money, we know that monetary base $H = B = C + R$. Again, $rd = R / D$ which is determined by the business policies of banks and the laws regulating banks. Finally, $c = C / D$ which is the amount of currency held by people (C) as a fraction of their holdings of demand deposits (D). Again the ordinary money as stated earlier is $M = C + D$.

Now

$$M / B = M / H = (C + D) / (C + R). \tag{17.13}$$

By some manipulations, the previous relation is converted into

$$M / B = [C / D + 1] / [C / D + R / D]$$

$$Or,\ M / B = (c + 1) / (c + rd) \tag{17.14}$$

$$Or,\ M = [(c + 1) / (c + rd)] * B = [(c + 1) / (c + rd)] * H. \tag{17.15}$$

Therefore, money supply depends on three exogenous variables: B or H, rd and c. Money supply is directly proportional to the monetary base (B) or high-powered money ($\delta M / \delta B > 0$). Again, money supply is inversely related to rd. As "rd" is lower then the loans given by the bank will be greater and thus the money supply will be greater ($\delta M / \delta rd < 0$). Finally, money supply is inversely related with "c" which means the lower the value of "c", the greater the credit creation and thus money supply since more "c" means less currency will be held by the public and more currency will be held by the banks ($\delta M / \delta c < 0$). Therefore, banks will be able to create more money.

17.4.2.1 Money supply and interest rate cohesion

Like the demand for money was dependent upon interest rates, supply of money can be made linked to rate of interest. And once it is done, the money market equilibrium condition will be changed and the LM function will be reoriented. The linking of money supply with the interest rates can be made by different concepts of reserves maintained by the central bank and commercial banks of the country. Till now we have the knowledge that money supply consists of currency in the hands of the public outside the banking system (non-banking system) and demand deposits with the commercial banks. Also we have the idea about excess reserves or borrowed reserves, which are used for deposit/money creation. On the other hand, the central bank provides un-borrowed reserves (UBR) by buying government securities in the open market operation. Again, the central bank provides borrowed reserves (BR) by lending to the commercial banks in terms of discounting. This rate of discount is known as repo rate in India; it is a type of bank rate charged by the central banks upon the commercial banks. Total reserve money is, therefore, $TR = UBR + BR$.

Again from the perspectives of the commercial banks, these reserves are allocated to three heads of usage. Commercial banks allocate their reserves to required reserves (RR) (it has been earlier noted as "rd" times demand deposit) depending on the demand for loan or to excess reserves (ER). Excess reserve is the residual of total bank reserves after deducting the required reserves. Besides, a part of reserves provided by the central bank will be held by the public in the form of currency (CP). Hence, total reserve will be on one hand the $UBR + BR$ and $RR + ER + CP$ on the other. Therefore, the common identity for the reserve money is

$$UBR + BR = TR = RR + ER + CP. \tag{17.16}$$

We can write the previous identity as

$$UBR = RR + (ER - BR) + CP. \qquad (17.17)$$

$$Or,\ UBR = RR + FR + CP. \qquad (17.18)$$

where FR is known as free reserves which is the excess reserve net of borrowed reserve. It is an important component of money supply which is responsive to rate of interest. It is an endogenous component of money supply since it depends on the loan opportunities and rate of interest. During the high loan demand relative to supply of UBR, the free reserve is expected to be negative and the banks will contract excess reserve. The opposite will happen if the demand for loan is slack. The association between the money supply and un-borrowed reserves depends on people's preference between currency and demand deposits (DDP) and banks' holding of excess reserves. Therefore, money supply is the sum of CP and DDP. That is

$$M = CP + DDP \qquad (17.19)$$

Suppose people hold β% of money in currency and $(1 - \beta)$% in demand deposits. Therefore, we have

$$CP = \beta \,.\, M \qquad (17.20)$$

and

$$DDP = (1 - \beta) \,.\, M. \qquad (17.21)$$

Now we present the expression for required reserve, *RR*, as earlier stated, in the following relation:

$$RR = rd \,.\, DDP. \qquad (17.22)$$

Substituting Equation (18.21) we have

$$RR = rd \,.\, (1 - \beta) \,.\, M \qquad (17.23)$$

where "*rd*" is the reserve to deposit ratio. Let us substitute (17.20) and (17.23) into the expression for un-borrowed reserves (Equation 17.18) and obtain the following relation to get the value of money supply, *M*:

$$UBR = rd \,.\, (1 - \beta) \,.\, M + FR + \beta \,.\, M$$

$$Or,\ M\ [\beta + rd \,.\, (1 - \beta)] = UBR - FR$$

$$Or,\ M = [UBR - FR] / [\beta + rd \,.\, (1 - \beta)]$$

$$Or,\ M = [UBR - FR] / [rd + \beta(1 - rd)] \qquad (17.24)$$

We see that money supply depends positively on un-borrowed reserves (that is $\delta M / \delta UBR > 0$) and negatively on free reserves ($\delta M / \delta FR < 0$), reserve ratio ($\delta M / \delta rd < 0$), and people's preference for currency ($\delta M / \delta\beta < 0$). As un-borrowed reserve is increased by the central bank of the country, money supply in the economy rises. Again, as reserve ratio increases statutorily then less money will be supplied as banks then hold more funds for cash transactions. Further, if the public prefers more currency over demand deposits then they will hold more money and the money supply from the system will fall. Finally, as amount of free reserves increases, then money supply will go down. Therefore, we get four determinants of money supply in an economy – un-borrowed reserves, free reserves, reserve ratio, and preference of the public towards currency. Out of the four, UBR and *rd* are institutionally fixed and β depends on the behaviour of the public which is again fixed at least in the short run. Hence, only the FR term is variable since it is dependent on the loan opportunities and rate of interest.

Let us relate free reserves to interest rate. We define two types of charges, rate of interest (r) charged by the commercial banks on the loan they create for the common people and business houses and discount rate (d) by which the central banks lend (or commercial banks borrow) reserves to the commercial banks. In Indian context, we can term "d" bank rate charged by the Reserve Bank of India. When $r > d$ or $(r - d) > 0$, commercial banks will clear excess reserves and increase their stock of reserve by borrowing more from the central bank. As a result of that, free reserve (FR) will fall since it is the difference between ER and BR. Hence, FR is inversely related to the interest rate differential $(r - d)$. That means the free reserve function is:

$$FR = f(r-d) = FR(r-d) \tag{17.25}$$

where $f' = \delta FR / \delta(r - d) < 0$.

By substituting (17.25) into (17.24) we get the money supply function as:

$$M = [UBR - FR(r-d)] / [rd + \beta\ (1 - rd)]. \tag{17.26}$$

As UBR, *rd*, and β are exogenous, money supply also depends on the difference $(r - d)$ via FR. As $(r - d) > 0$, the free reserve falls and money supply increases and as $(r - d) < 0$ then FR increases and money supply falls. Hence, we get the money supply function as positively related to the rate of interest prevailing in the market. The money supply function is thus

$$M = M\ (r-d) = M(r) \tag{17.27}$$

where $\delta M / \delta r > 0$. The money supply function is positively sloped which is a sharp contrast to the classical and Keynesian models of determining equilibrium output and interest rates. We will now remodel the LM function. Figure 17.2 presents the new money supply function vis-à-vis the earlier one.

The money supply function is vertical when it is interest insensitive and upward sloping when it is interest sensitive. The demand for money function is negatively sloped with respect to interest rate under the condition of a given level of income. E is the initial state of the monetary system with M_1 money supply and demand and r_1 rate of interest. Suppose there is an impetus from the product market by means of high level of income ($y_2 > y_1$). The demand for money function will shift rightward to $M^d(y_2)$. F is the money market equilibrium under the interest-insensitive money supply function and G is the

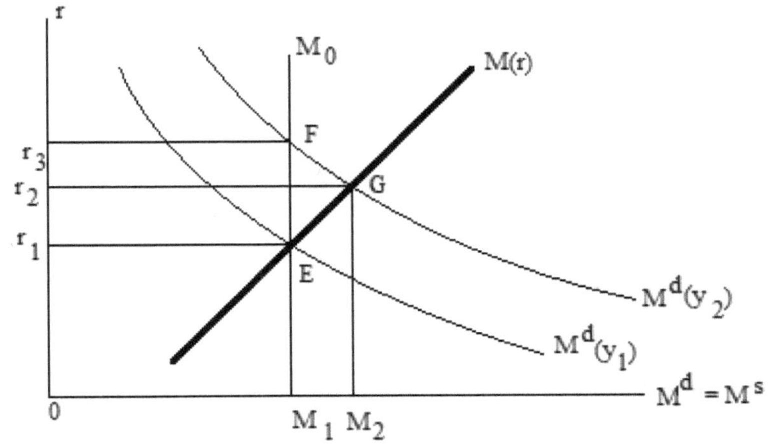

Figure 17.2 Different money supply functions

equilibrium under the interest-sensitive money supply function. Due to this rigidity of money supply, increase in income and excess demand for money lead to relatively high increase in rate of interest to r_3 but the increase in rate of interest rate for the case of variable money supply is relatively low (r_2). The reason for this is that excess demand for money induced by increase in income allows rate of interest to increase which also pushes up the money supply to M_2. The small magnitude of increase in rate of interest rate creates favourable investment conditions that allow more income to be generated in the goods market equilibrium.

17.5 Remodelling the LM function

In the complete classical and complete Keynesian models, we had determined the equilibrium income and interest rates on the basis of institutionally fixed money supply; not allowing it to vary with rate of interest. All the fiscal and monetary policies were attempted under this fixed volume of money supply. We will now remodel the LM function to re-establish the money market equilibrium and then go for policy implications.

Like before, the money market is in equilibrium when demand for money is equal to supply of money. The demand for money is written as

$$M^d = L(y, r) \tag{17.28}$$

where $L_y = \delta L / \delta y > 0$ and $L_r = \delta L / \delta r < 0$

where "y" and "r" represent real income and interest rate respectively.

The money supply function in real terms is:

$$M^s = M(r) \tag{17.29}$$

where $M_r = \delta M / \delta r > 0$

The money market equilibrium with $M^d = M^s$ gives us the following equation of the newly modelled LM function as

$$M(r) = L(y, r). \tag{17.30}$$

Taking total derivatives of the previous equation we have

$$\begin{aligned} &(\partial M / \partial r) \,.\, dr = (\partial L / \partial y) \,.\, dy + (\partial L / \partial r) \,.\, dr \\ &Or,\ \left[(\partial M / \partial r) - (\partial L / \partial r)\right] .\, dr = (\partial L / \partial y) \,.\, dy \\ &Or,\ (M_r - L_r) \,.\, dr = L_y \,.\, dy. \end{aligned} \tag{17.31}$$

The slope of the new LM is

$$dr / dy = L_y / (M_r - L_r) > 0. \tag{17.32}$$

The LM is still positively sloped like the exogenous money supply model but with some differences in magnitudes. Since $M_r > 0$ term has been added to the denominator of the slope expression, the slope of the modified LM will be flatter compared to the old LM function with an exogenous money supply system. Figure 17.3 presents the two types of LM function; one is interest insensitive with an exogenous money supply and the other is interest sensitive with an endogenous money supply system.

At the initial interest rate r_1, both the old and new LM functions intersect at E which generates y_1 level of output. As rate of interest increases to r_2, income increases to y_2 along the old LM since high level of interest rate reduces speculative demand for money and with fixed money supply (interest insensitive money supply) the money market equilibrium will be restored with high income that influences transaction demand for money. But such an increase in rate of interest will further push up income level to y_3 since along with the previous level of income, y_2, money supply will further increase (since $M_r > 0$).

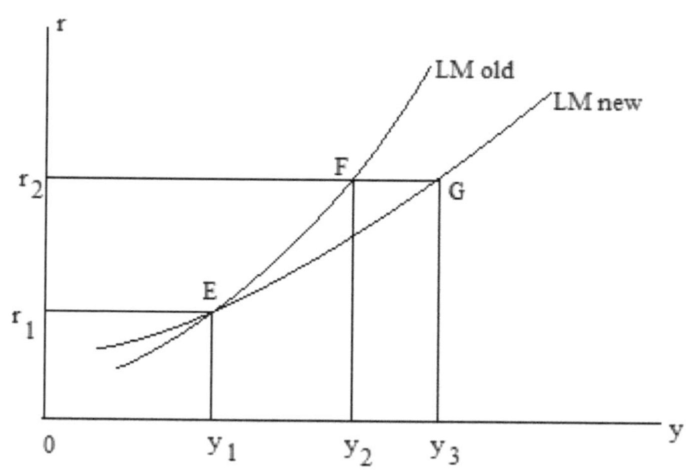

Figure 17.3 Different LM functions

Hence, interest sensitivity of money pushes up the income level if interest rate increases and vice-versa.

17.6 Revisiting aggregate demand-side equilibrium

We are now in a position to re-establish the aggregate demand-side equilibrium to determine income and rate of interest under the interest-sensitive money supply function in line with the design of the Hicks-Hansen model. Further recall that aggregate demand in an economy is comprised of the product and money markets with the supply side of the economy remaining unchanged. The product market equilibrium is given by the IS function and the money market equilibrium is given by the LM function. Also remember here that the LM curve under an interest-dependent money supply function is relatively flatter than the LM curve under the institutionally fixed money supply function.

The equation of the IS function is

$$S_0 + S(y) = I_0 + I(r) \tag{17.33}$$

where S_0 and I_0 represent respectively autonomous savings (which are negative of autonomous consumption) and autonomous investment. Again, S_y (= MPS) is greater than zero and less than unity and $I_r < 0$. IS function is negatively sloped ($dr / dy = S_y / I_r < 0$).

The equation of the LM function under the interest-sensitive money supply function is

$$M_0 + M(r) = L(y) + L(r) \tag{17.34}$$

where $L_y > 0$, $L_r < 0$ and $M_r > 0$ as usual. We have added the autonomous money supply (M_0) depending on the parametric values of un-borrowed reserves (UBR), reserve-deposit ratio (*rd*), and public preference for currency (β). The slope of LM is $dr / dy = L_y / (M_r - L_r) > 0$ which is flatter than the earlier one since its value is $dr / dy = -(L_y / L_r) > 0$. Figure 18.4 depicts the demand-side equilibrium under two LM functions.

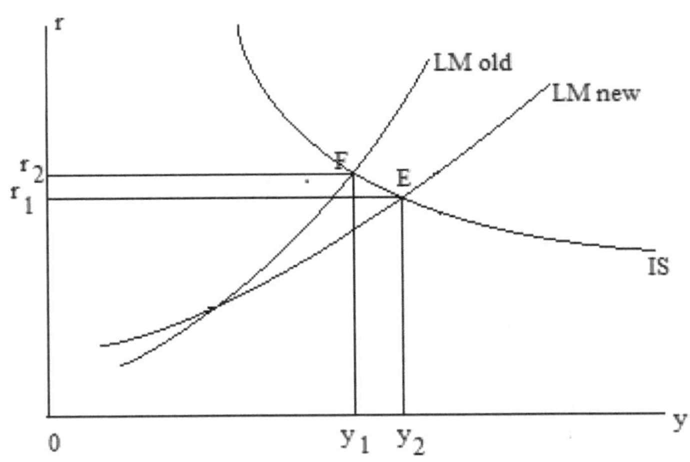

Figure 17.4 Demand-side equilibrium under two LM functions

E is the equilibrium (Figure 17.4) in the commodity and money market when money supply is interest-sensitive producing income, y_2, at rate of interest, r_1. On the other hand, F is the equilibrium under the interest-insensitive money supply function producing relatively less income, y_1, and relatively high rate of interest, r_1.

We can quantify equilibrium values of income and rate of interest by solving equations (17.33) and (17.34) (applying the Cramer's Rule). The values are as follows:

$$y = \left[(L_r - M_r) . (I_0 - S_0) + Ir . M_0\right] / \left[S_y . (L_r - M_r) + I_r . L_y\right] \tag{17.35}$$

and

$$r = \left[Sy . M_0 - Ly(I_0 - S_0)\right] / \left[S_y . (L_r - M_r) + I_r . L_y\right]. \tag{17.36}$$

Let us recall that the corresponding values of income and interest rate under the fixed money supply model (i.e. old model) were as follows:

$$y = \left[L_r . (I_0 - S_0) + Ir . M_0\right] / \left[S_y . L_r + I_r . L_y\right] \tag{17.37}$$

and

$$r = \left[Sy . M_0 - Ly(I_0 - S_0)\right] / \left[S_y . L_r + I_r . L_y\right]. \tag{17.38}$$

Comparing the values of "y" and "r" in both the new and old models we see that the new model gives more income and less interest rate and the old model gives relatively low income and relative high interest rate since the denominator of the new model is less than the denominator of the old model. Figure 17.4 shows these differences (i.e. point F vis-à-vis E).

17.7 Policy implications

Let us re-establish the fiscal and monetary effects in the new set up. We are now open to variable money supply function with respect to interest rate and a part with fixed money supply depending on the central banks policies regarding unborrowed reserves, reserve-deposit ratio, etc. The goods sector is as usual. We have seen that the introduction of interest sensitivity of money supply makes the LM function relatively flatter than that under the entirely fixed money supply conditions. In the static system of the goods sector and monetary sector interactions we have shown that increase in investment by private or public initiatives led to increase in income and rate of interest, but the magnitude of income increase was relatively lesser than that under no money market repercussions. Introduction of the money market made an increase in the rate of interest which crowded out a part of private investment, and the investment multiplier (or the fiscal policy multiplier) was truncated. On the other hand, an attempt for more money supply with no change in fiscal policy instruments had resulted into more income and less rate of interest. Now we come to the impact analyses of same policy tools in the interest sensitive money supply function.

17.7.1 *Fiscal policy effects*

Now recall Equation (17.35) and (17.36) for the initial equilibrium values of "y" and "r". To analyse the effect of increase in investment, assuming that the government of the country reduces corporate income tax rates or provides infrastructural facilities to the businesses that we usually observe in the system of special economic zones, we take the differentiation of "y" and "r" with respect to I_0. The results are as follows:

$$dy / dI_0 \,|_{new} = (L_r - M_r) / \left[S_y \,.\, (L_r - M_r) \;+\; I_r \,.\, L_y\right] > 0 \tag{17.39}$$

and

$$dr / dI_0 \,|_{new} = -\, Ly / \left[S_y \,.\, (L_r - M_r) + I_r \,.\, L_y\right] > 0. \tag{17.40}$$

The corresponding expressions under the fixed money supply system are

$$dy / dI_0 \,|_{old} = L_r / \left[S_y \,.\, L_r + I_r \,.\, L_y\right] > 0 \tag{17.41}$$

and

$$dr / dI_0 \,|_{old} = -Ly / \left[S_y \,.\, L_r + I_r \,.\, L_y\right] > 0. \tag{17.42}$$

We see that the income effect under the new money supply case is greater than that under the old money supply case. Besides, we see that rate of interest also increases after investment increase. The logic behind more income increase is due to the positive effect of interest rate on money supply. That means the magnitude of the crowding out effect under the new money supply condition is smaller than the older one. Extra income is generated by extra money supply induced by rate of interest increase. Figure 17.5 presents the differences in multiplier effects under the old and new situations.

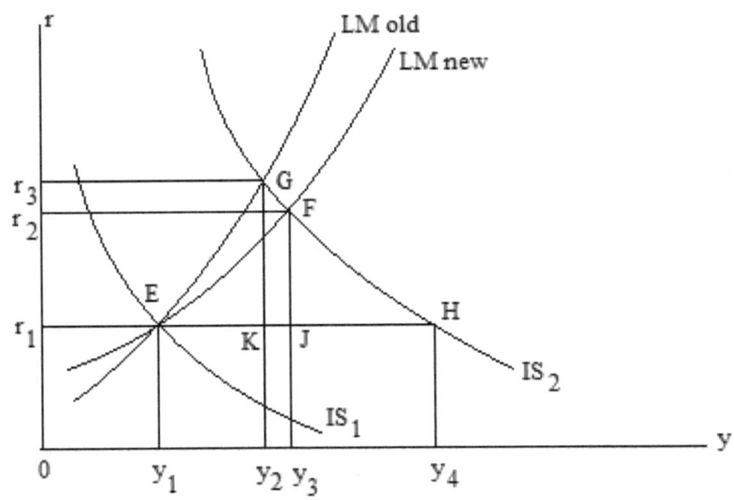

Figure 17.5 Effect of increase in investment expenditure

Initial demand-side equilibrium exists at point E where both the old and new LM functions and the initial goods market equilibrium meet. Equilibrium income is y_1 and rate of interest is r_1. Let us allow the expansion in the goods sector by means of increase in private (or public) investment expenditure. If the rate of interest is disallowed to change (i.e. the money market's role is absent) from r_1 then the full multiplier effect will be obtained by producing expansionary effects up to y_4. This extra income will push up the rate of interest via the money market channel and as a result of that investment demand will slide down from the magnitude of increase ($IS_2 - IS_1$). Increase in rate of interest will swallow a part of income increase. Hence, income increase will fall from y_1y_4 to y_1y_2 in the case of interest-insensitive money supply function (i.e. the old case) and y_1y_3 for the case of the interest-sensitive money supply function (i.e. the new case). "y_2y_4" and "y_3y_4" are the respective quantities of crowding out effects under old and new cases with the former being greater than the new one. Why? As the rate of interest increases due to money market repercussion, money supply under the new case will further increase since $M_r > 0$. Extra money supply will further make expansion in income through additional banking loans to the investors and public enterprises.

17.7.2 Monetary policy effects

An expansionary monetary policy under the usual conditions produces increase in income and fall in rate of interest. By usual the conditions we mean here the circumstances of neither liquidity trap nor the vertical LM functions. The logic behind the expansionary effect on income is that the fall in interest rate due to increase in money supply makes investment cheaper and the goods sector expands by means of increasing income. This is called the *money multiplier*. The expression for the multiplier can be derived from Equation (17.35) and (17.36) for the interest-sensitive money supply function and Equations (17.37) and (18.38) for the fixed money supply function. The expressions for the new case are as follows:

$$dy / dM_0 \,|_{new} = Ir / \left[S_y \,.\, (L_r - M_r) + I_r \,.\, L_y\right] > 0 \qquad (17.43)$$

and

$$dr / dM_0 \,|_{new} = Sy / \left[S_y \,.\, (L_r - M_r) + I_r \,.\, L_y\right] < 0. \qquad (17.44)$$

Again the expressions for the old case are:

$$dy / dM_0 \,|_{old} = Ir / \left[S_y \,.\, L_r + I_r \,.\, L_y\right] > 0 \qquad (17.45)$$

and

$$dr / dM_0 \,|_{old} = Sy / \left[S_y \,.\, L_r + I_r \,.L_y\right] < 0. \qquad (17.46)$$

The previous expressions show the desired signs of the monetary policy effects upon "y" and "r". Comparing the magnitudes of the income effects, we see that the magnitude of income increase is greater in the new case compared to the old case. Again, the interest rate will fall to a larger extent in the new case than the old case which justifies the

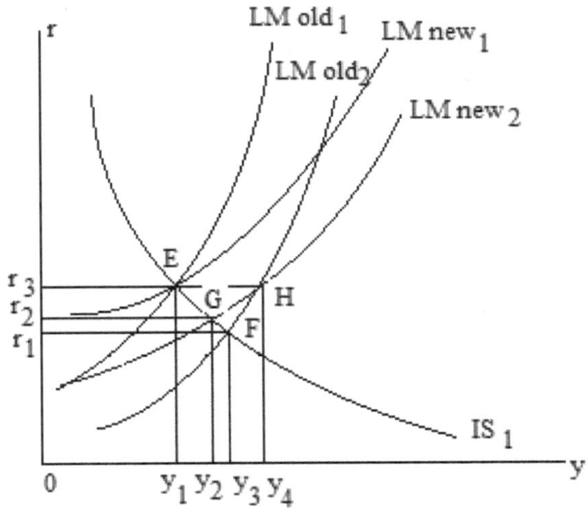

Figure 17.6 Monetary policy effects

magnificent income increase in the new case. Note that as "*r*" falls, money supply will also fall which will pull down the magnitude of income increase. Hence, we have two situations depending on the sensitivity of interest rates in the goods market and money market. If interest sensitivity of investment in the goods sector is less compared to the interest sensitivity of the money supply function, then an increase in money supply will produce relatively lower magnitudes of income increase in the new case compared to the old case. On the other hand, if the reverse holds, that is, the interest sensitivity in the goods sector is more than that of the money supply function, then magnitude of income increase will be less in the old case than that of the new case. Figure 17.6 presents the first possibilities.

In the first case (refer to Figure 17.6) the initial equilibrium, *E*, gets shifted to *G* and *F* respectively for the new and old cases. Also, the interest sensitivity of investment in the goods sector is less than the interest sensitivity of the money supply function which leads to more income increase ($y_3 > y_2$) and a smaller rate of interest ($r_1 < r_2$) in the case of the old LM function. The readers can verify the second possibility in the same way.

Suppose that, in the extreme case, the money supply function is infinitely interest elastic (i.e. $M_r \rightarrow \infty$), then the LM function will be nearly horizontal like what happens in the Keynesian liquidity trap region, and then an expansionary monetary policy will not be able to increase income. A fractional drop in the interest rate will reduce the money supply to the bottom level which will neutralise the income effect of money supply. Hence, expansionary monetary policy will not be effective in this circumstance but the expansionary fiscal policy will be fully effective. Again, if the investment function is infinitely elastic to rate of interest (i.e. $I_r \rightarrow \infty$), then the IS function will be horizontal and it can be seen, rather imagined, from Figure 17.6 that an expansionary monetary policy will be fully effective but the fiscal policy will not. However, which policy the government and monetary authority undertake depends on their ultimate target. What may be the ultimate target of the policymakers? One important policy target is to maintain full employment and price stability. That means we have to incorporate the supply side of the economy with the aggregate demand components. In the following sub section we highlight these issues.

17.7.3 Monetary and fiscal policy composition and full employment level of output

Suppose y_f is the full employment level of output and y_1 is the aggregate demand-side output given by the combination of goods and the monetary sector. The demand-side aggregate output is less than the full employment level of output. That means there is internal imbalance in the economy in the sense that the population size desires less output than the economy's capacity to produce. This situation of the economy has been presented in Figure 17.7.

To achieve the full employment target, the economy needs to expand its demand either from the goods sector or monetary sector or both. If expansionary fiscal policy is undertaken, only then can the economy reach full employment at point *F*, but an increase in rate of interest can push up the general price level, creating price instability. On the other hand, an expansionary monetary policy could be an ideal choice in such a sub-optimal situation. By increasing the money supply it is possible to shift the LM curve to the right to *G* which can raise the aggregate demand-side output to full employment level and reduce the rate of interest which can enable to price stability.

Finally, a combination of the two policies can be used to an enable the economy to reach the point of full employment. The final equilibrium of the economy in this situation will be somewhere between *F* and *G* along the full employment line. What is important here is that the choice of a policy may be made on the basis of the desire of the government to alter the composition of output without changing its total. An expansionary monetary policy can be used to stimulate the interest-elastic component of aggregate demand, mainly the investment spending. In contrast, the effect of fiscal policy depends on exactly what goods the government buys or what changes it incorporates in the tax transfer programmes.

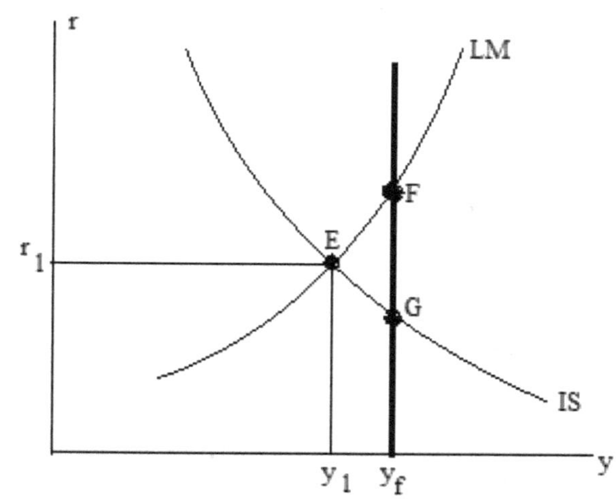

Figure 17.7 Policy composition and full employment

17.8 Instruments of monetary policy in India

Being the apex monetary authority, the central banks of different countries of the world perform the monetary functions to ensure growth and price stability. India's Reserve Bank of India (RBI) is not an exception in the list. Here we deal with major instruments the RBI uses in controlling money supply of the country. One thing we should be clear about is the fact that the ultimate objective of controlling credit or money supply is to keep inflation rate constant around a tolerable or benchmark level. There are two types of instruments the RBI uses to apply for controlling money supply – quantitative instruments and qualitative instruments. The quantitative control is an indirect method and the qualitative control is a direct and selective method.

17.8.1 Quantitative instruments

RBI applies different heads of quantitative restrictions on controlling the money supply of the country. Major heads are outlined in the following sections.

17.8.1.1 Bank rate policy

The commercial banks may face cash or fund crunch if the demand for credit or loan is high or the minimum cash reserve falls short of the statutory level. To manage the situation, the commercial banks have to take additional funds from the central bank by means of discounting their securities. The rate of discount in this case is called *bank rate*. Hence, bank rate is the interest rate charged by the central banks upon the additional fund demanded by them. The logic of bank rate working as one of the credit control instruments is that as bank rate increases, the cost of a loan from the central banks will increase, and the commercial banks will be forced increase the rate of interest which they charge upon their loan customers. Hence, the commercial banks will take a lesser amount of loan from the central bank and as a result, the capacity of the commercial banks to give loans to the general public (households, firms, etc.) will decrease. As amount of loan in the hands of the general public falls, the demand for goods and services will also fall which will pull down the general price level and reduce the inflationary pressure. On the other hand, as bank rate falls during the slump phase of the business cycle, the commercial banks will be eager to take additional funds at the cheaper rate from the central bank and their capacity to provide loans to the general public will increase which will further lead to increase in aggregate demand for goods and services. The general price level will then increase which will have beneficial effects for the producers.

17.8.1.2 Open market operations

Sometimes, the central bank of the country deliberately and directly buys and sells bills and securities in the money market to control money supply. This process is called *open market operations*. During the period of inflation or boom in the economy, the amount of money supply should be reduced, and during the slump phase the amount of money supply should be increased to incentivise the goods and service sectors of the economy. In the USA, the Federal Reserve, the central bank of the country, calls the first situation *quantitative restrictions* (QR) and the second situation *quantitative easing* (QE). During the global financial crisis of 2007–2009, the Federal Reserve applied the QE policy to provide additional funds to the banking system to fight against the crisis and the time now has come to them to apply the QR as the economy has recovered significantly from the crisis.

RBI, during inflationary period, may sell government securities to the commercial banks and others. Once the commercial banks purchase the securities, they have to pay for them out of their loanable funds. As a result of that, the credit opportunity of the commercial banks falls and hence the aggregate demand falls which ultimately pulls down the general price level. The reverse, that is, buying of securities by the RBI, works when there is a deflationary situation in the economy. The general price level boosts after the commercial banks get additional funds from selling securities to the RBI.

Which one is better? Strategically open market operations are more effective than the bank rate policy to control money supply and inflationary pressure since it is done exclusively by the central bank and no association or consultation with the commercial banks is required. But the process of discounting in case of bank rate policy needs the cooperation of the commercial banks to execute. It can also be said that the open market operations are used to make the bank rate policy effective. How? Suppose in the slump phase of the business cycle, the RBI will lower the bank rate to increase money supply. At the same time, the RBI will buy securities from the market and make available additional funds for the commercial banks to increase their loanable capacity so that money supply ultimately increases.

17.8.1.3 Variable reserve ratio

The central bank frames the guidelines for which proportion of the commercial banks' total deposit fund will be held as cash account or loanable account. The ratio is variable depending on the market conditions as well as the preference of the account holders in cash or savings. Variable reserve ratio is twofold – cash reserve ratio (CRR) and statutory liquidity ratio (SLR).

17.8.1.4 CRR

The commercial bank cannot use all of its deposits in lending to different sectors of the economy since the depositors may require cash for withdrawal for meeting transaction needs. Therefore, a part of the deposit is kept with the RBI in the form of reserves or balances. This proportion of cash is called CRR. It is thus clear that higher CRR with lower RBI will be the supply of money in the system and vice versa. RBI has been empowered to vary CRR between 15%and 3%. But as per the suggestion by the Narsimham Committee Report on the banking sector reforms in 1990–1991, the CRR was reduced from 15% in 1990 to 5% in 2002. After repeated sliding of the rates, it reached 4% at the end of 2016 (refer to Figure 18.8).

17.8.1.5 SLR

Besides CRR, all the financial institutions will have to maintain a certain quantity of liquid assets with themselves at any point of time in their total time and demand liabilities. Further, these assets have to be kept in noncash form such as approved government (central and state governments) securities like bonds etc. This particular ratio of the liquid assets to time and demand assets is called SLR. It is forced investment of the commercial banks upon government securities. Governments use this fund in their developmental projects.

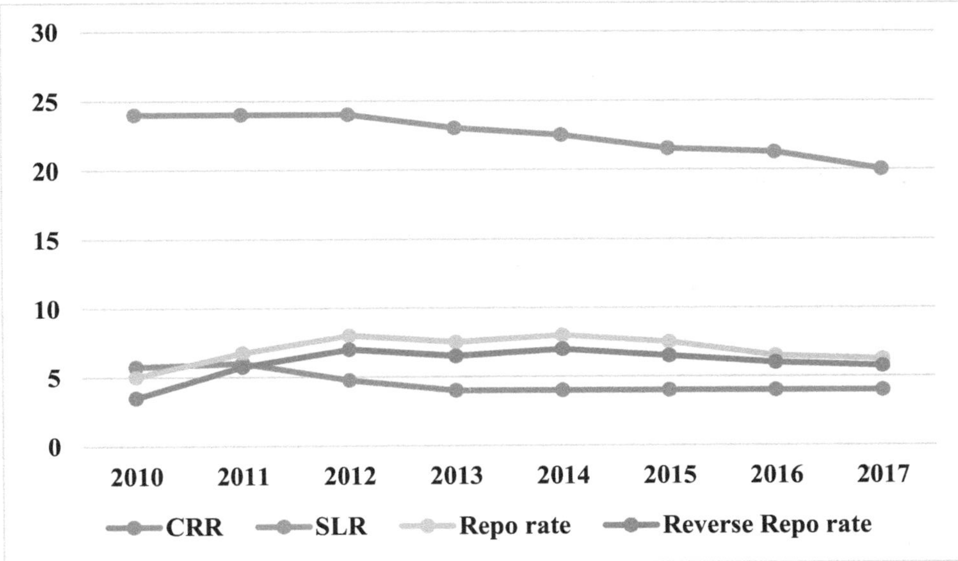

Figure 17.8 CRR, SLR, repo rate, and reverse repo rate

Source: RBI.

As the rate of SLR falls, more funds are available for private investors through loan and aggregate demand raises which further leads to increase in rate of inflation. The opposite logic works in case of increase in SLR. There was the recommendation by the Narsimham Committee to reduce SLR from 38.5% to 25% during the early 90s to improve the balance sheet of the commercial banks. Since investment in government securities provides the commercial banks returns with certainty, although with a relatively lower rate compared to the rate earned from the private investors, banks some time prefer to go for approved securities. The current SLR is around 20% (refer to Figure 17.8).

17.8.1.6 Repo rate and reverse repo rate

The RBI has introduced two new instruments for the last couple of years to control the monetary system. They are repo rate and reverse repo rate. *Repo rate* is the rate at which the RBI lends to commercial banks generally against government securities. Reduction in repo rate helps the commercial banks to get money at a cheaper rate and thus the rate of interest charged on their lending falls, and as a result, the aggregate demand as well as price level increase, creating a favourable business environment. On the other hand, increase in repo rate discourages the commercial banks from getting money as the rate increases and becomes expensive. On the other hand, *reverse repo rate* is the rate at which RBI borrows money from the commercial banks. The increase in the Repo rate will increase the cost of borrowing and lending of the banks which will discourage the public from borrowing money and will encourage them to deposit. As the rates become high, the availability of credit and demand decrease, resulting in decrease in inflation. This increase in repo rate and reverse repo rate is a symbol of tightening of the monetary policy. The easing of repo and reverse repo rates makes expansion in the money supply. Figure 17.8 highlights the trends of repo rate and reverse repo rates for the period March 2010 to March 2017. Up to the year 2012, both the rates increased and then fluctuated during 2013–2014 and thereafter decreased gradually.

17.8.2 Qualitative instruments

The aforementioned quantitative instruments for controlling money supply arbitrarily affect all sections of the economy depending upon bank credit. The reason is that, for example, as repo rate increases, all the borrowers will be hurt by increasing cost of borrowing, whether their activities have impacted price level increase or not. Therefore, it is reasonable to impose restrictions upon those particular sectors whose poor activities led to inflationary pressure. The qualitative control or selective credit control is treated as superior to the quantitative control as it pinpoints the target to control rate of inflation. There is a list of selective credit control instruments widely used by the central banks of different countries.

17.8.2.1 Moral suasion

This implies urging and request from the central banks to the commercial banks to follow the general credit control policy. During recession, the central bank may persuade the commercial banks to accept inferior quality of securities to expand the magnitudes of loans and advances. On the other hand, during the period of boom, the reverse is persuaded by the central banks to the commercial banks so that the credit magnitudes may be tightened.

17.8.2.2 Margin requirements

This is one of monetary control by which speculation in the stock market is checked. Generally, stockbrokers take loans from the banks in terms of collaterals of stocks to the banks. But a commercial bank cannot lend up to the full amount of securities and the remaining part of non-lending is called *margin*. If margin increases, the public will face more financial burden and as a result the money supply as well as inflation can be checked. The reverse will work for the lower margin.

17.8.2.3 Credit ceiling

In this operation, the RBI issues prior information or direction that loans to the commercial banks will be given up to a specified limit. Hence, the commercial banks will be constricted in advancing loans to the public. They will allocate loans to limited sectors. A few examples of the ceiling are agriculture sector advances, priority sector lending, etc.

There are other methods like regulation of consumers' credit, credit rationing, etc. that are popularly used by the central bank of the country.

17.9 Recent past explosion of monetary policy in India — the demonetisation

The Indian Prime Minister Mr. Narendra Modi made a remarkable and bold announcement on the evening of November 8, 2016 before the 125 crore people of the country as well as of the world communities that, from that day, the running 500 and 1000 denominations of notes would never again be legal tender as these two denominations born most of the black and counterfeit currencies in the country. In this sense, the pro BJP people are saying it is another surgical strike against the Pakistanis since it is widely believed by them that this country is the prime source of production of Indian counterfeit currencies of these two denominations. But, what happened after that decision? The people of India witnessed that the RBI and most of the growth forecasters all around the world concluded that India would face a drop of growth in its GDP by at least one percent point by March 2017. That means about rupees one and half lacs crores of GDP will be go out of the Indian economy which will cause disaster mostly in the unorganised sectors' employment and output.

Before going on to discuss on the impacts of the sudden policy announcements on different aspects of the Indian economy, we need to highlight how a monetary system of our country works. As an easy solution to the problems faced in the barter system of exchanges some years ago, the concept of exchange through monetary standard, was introduced and to date the system has been well accepted by all sorts of exchange makers in the world. But there was a natural question of how much money would be required to make smooth exchange of goods and services in an economy. The classical economists had proposed that quantity of money required for exchange would be the exact value of goods and services in an economy in a given time period where quantity of money is the product of quantity of money in circulation and the velocity of money in circulation. Hence, 500 and 1,000 denominations of money withdrawn from the public and kept within the banking system means there is increase in money supply in the monetary system that will lead to a fall in rate of interest, price levels, and overall GDP of the country. Besides, there is some unaccounted-for income in the hands of people in the form of black money and some fake currencies in circulation, both of which hamper the government's revenue collection as well as inflation levels. According to the RBI data and statement by the prime minister as of October 2016, there were about 17 lacs crore of money in all denominations in circulation to exchange 135 lacs crore of GDP out of which 86% was of 500 and 1,000 notes, and 6% of this 86% was black – that is, about 14.6 lacs crore of banned 500 and 1,000 notes and Rs. 88 thousand crores were black money (Table 17.3).

In addition to that, the prime minister announced that total fake and black currency would be around 3–4 lacs crore out of total 14.6 lacs crore. They thought this amount of black money would not be returned to the formal banking system because the black money holders would try to avoid conviction and punishments.

Hence, we need to identify some pros and cons of the demonetisation policy that intuitively follow from the macroeconomic theory.

Table 17.3 Data on money supply, GDP, velocity of money, and black money

Money SS (Rs. crore)	*GDP 2015–2016*	*Velocity of all*	*Velocity of 500*	*86% on* M1 *is*	*6% of 86% is black*
as on Oct. 2016	*in Rs crore*	*cash money(*M1*)*	*and 1,000 notes*	*of 500 (45%) and 1,000(41%) notes*	*in Rs crore*
1701380	13576086	7.979455501	9.278435361	1463186.8	87791.208

Pros

i) It will help the government to fight Black money, corruption, terrorism, and counterfeit currency with one single decision. Arms smuggling, espionage, and terrorist-related activities will be choked due to lack of funding.
ii) Heavy deflation that benefits the consumers in short term. Commodity price and gold price will fall.
iii) Rate of interest will go down as there is excess supply of money. Investment demand will rise which will raise inflation but not overnight. Deflation and inflation will balance each other out in the future.
iv) This decision will help institutionalise the real estate sector, bringing more transparency in the Indian real estate industry. This step would give the Indian real estate sector more credibility, making it more attractive to the foreign as well as domestic investors.
v) Housing prices could witness downward pressure, helping revive demand in the sluggish housing segment (this will give much needed blood life to the sector).
vi) The traditional benami transactions have already received a big blow as the new legislation has a provision for 7-year imprisonment and fine, replacing the 3-year jail term, or fine, or both.
vii) A cashless way to fight against black money and corruption and fake currency.
viii) More financial inclusion.
ix) Reduction in terrorist funding, arms smuggling, etc.

Cons

i) Deflation will hurt the producers.
ii) Inconvenience to the common people who will start running to the nearby bank to exchange the 500 and 1,000 currency notes. If we add the death of 100 persons standing in an ATM queue, the cost will be huge. That is loss of workdays + cost of death = total social cost since it is unrecoverable.
iii) Cost of replacing the 500 and 1,000 Rs. notes will be about 12,000 crore in terms of 100-rupee note production. Hence, it is a costly idea to scrap 500 and 1,000 notes.
iv) Very difficult for more than half the population who are not well versed in card transactions.
v) Employment will fall as an immediate effect. This move deeply impacts the working sections of society: drivers, maids, cooks, electricians, plumbers. Anybody who provides services in the informal sector and depends on monthly or bi-monthly cash payments.
vi) The small businesses will be affected, at least in the shorter run.
vii) The Jan Dhan scheme, UPI/digital payment stack, and payment banks are still in the nascent stage. It will be a long time before rural India moves to completely cashless transactions. In the short-term, people in rural India who have a significant amount of Rs. 500 and Rs. 1,000 notes but no official form of identification will have a tough time in exchanging their notes.
viii) Recession in agriculture and industrial activity, particularly of small and medium enterprises, will appear, which will further boost inflation in the next season.
ix) The big fish will be left out, whose black money is in the form of foreign currency and gold and is stashed away in tax havens.

x) Duplicity in the Jan Dhan A/Cs where the black money is deposited. If detected, the case will be settled in after a long duration because of poor governance. Hence, what is the utility of this move?

What the reality is today about 100 days from the declaration is that most of the currencies held by the public, as reported in some of the leading newspapers and channels in India, have been deposited into the banking system. The Income Tax Department has raided the sum of around Rs. 5,000 crores of money which they thought would have the possibility of being black nature. And interestingly, the central bank and even the finance ministry have not clearly unveiled the truth to date which made the common people more sceptical about the feasibility of such a policy announcement. Besides, if we make the cost-benefit analysis of such policy announcements, we can find in the immediate term that the magnitudes of cost (the cons items), including the costs of popular policies and imputed costs of deaths due to standing in a long queue before the ATMs and bank offices, will definitely supersede any benefits received to date by the common people. Although theoretically it is possible to get positive benefits from the recovery of black money in the long run, the existing judiciary system can take it up to the next generation at the cost of the current generation. That means the old get worse treatment than the young. Different institutions like the World Bank, IMF, and even the RBI have reduced the growth forecast of up to 1.5%. It is the long run effects which will answer to the effectiveness of the demonetisation policy.

17.10 Conclusion

We now conclude the entire chapter on money supply determination with the following points. Ordinary money or narrow money is defined as the sum of currency and demand deposits of commercial and central banks held by the public. On the other hand, high-powered money or reserve money is the money produced by the central bank and the government of the country and held by the public and banks. Different monetary aggregates of India have maintained increasing trends which showed the importance of currency money in countries like India. The deposit or credit creation multiplier by commercial function shows that the amount of deposit or credit to be generated is inversely related to the reserve-deposit ratio. The money multiplier is thus the reverse of reserve-deposit ratio. It is also shown that money supply is a positive function of rate of interest which is in contrast to the classical and Keynesian models of determining equilibrium output and interest rates. The LM function under the endogenous money supply condition becomes flatter compared to that of the exogenous money supply condition which makes the income effects under the fiscal and monetary policies greater than that under the exogenous money supply case. The recently announced demonetisation policy undertaken by the Indian government to date has produced large numbers of cons compared to the pros.

Summary

In discussing the money supply in an endogenous system the readers should note the following salient points:

- There are two concepts of money – ordinary and high-powered. Ordinary money is the sum of currency and demand deposits of commercial and central banks held by the public, and high-powered money is the money produced by the central bank and the government of the country and held by the public and banks.

- There are four monetary aggregates in India – M_1 Money = Currency with the public (C) + Demand deposits of the public (D) = Money supply in the *narrow sense;* M_2 Money = M_1 + Post office savings deposits; M_3 Money = M_1 + Time deposits of the public with the banks = *Broad money supply*; M_4 Money = M_3 + Total post office deposits.
- The deposit creation multiplier or money multiplier in general is defined as the inverse of the reserve-deposit ratio. As the banks hold more money as reserve, the value of the money multiplier will be smaller in the sense that the economy will get less money for productive purposes.
- Under the balance sheet approach, total money supply is measured by the sum of NFA and NDA.
- Money supply is positively dependent on rate of interest. The corresponding money market equilibrium generates a relatively flatter LM function. Fiscal and monetary policies are highly effective under the endogenous money supply system.
- There are quantitative and qualitative monetary policy control instruments applied by the central bank of India like bank rate policy, open market policy, repo rate, and reverse repo rate policy, moral suasion, etc.
- The recently announced demonetisation policy undertaken by the Indian government to date has produced large numbers of cons compared to the pros. It reduced growth rate by around 2% and employment in the informal sector by a severe rate.

Multiple choice questions and answers

1. High-powered money is defined as the

   (a) Money produced by the central bank and the government of the country and held by the public and banks.
   (b) Currency and demand deposits of commercial and central banks held by the public.
   (c) Demand deposits of commercial and central banks held by the public.
   (d) Currency of commercial and central banks held by the public.

2. M_4 Money in India is defined as

   (a) M_3 + Total post office deposits.
   (b) M_1 + Time deposits of the public with the banks + Total post office deposits.
   (c) Currency with the public + Demand deposits of the public + Time deposits of the public with the banks + Total post office deposits.
   (d) All of the above.

3. Commercial banks create deposit through a particular process. The derived deposit creation multiplier gives the

   (a) Direct relation between the extra money created and the reserve-deposit ratio.
   (b) Inverse relation between the extra money created and the reserve-deposit ratio.
   (c) Neither direct nor inverse relation with the reserve-deposit ratio.
   (d) Any one of the above.

4. If money supply is endogenous, then as interest rate increases, money supply will

   (a) Fall.
   (b) Be unchanged.
   (c) Rise.
   (d) None of the above.

5. When money supply is related to rate of interest then the LM function will be

   (a) Relatively flatter.
   (b) Relatively steeper.
   (c) Vertical.
   (d) Horizontal.

6. Demonetisation is a part of monetary policy of a country which means

   (a) Increase in supply of money to the public.
   (b) Decrease in supply of money to the public.
   (c) Control of inflation.
   (d) All of the above.

7. If NFA and/or NDA decrease then total money supply in the economy will

   (a) Increase.
   (b) Decrease.
   (c) Remain the same.
   (c) None of the above.

Answers

1. (a); 2. (d); 3. (b); 4. (c); 5. (a); 6. (b); 7. (b)

Review questions

1. Define M_1, M_2, M_3, and M_4 money. What happens to the money supply of an economy if M_1 money increases? Explain.
2. Distinguish ordinary money from high-powered money. Explain how commercial banks create deposit with the help of excess reserves and reserve-deposit ratio. What happens if people hold a part of the money in their hand without depositing it in the bank? Explain.
3. What is a money multiplier? Determine the factors upon which the value of the money multiplier depends.
4. What are the major determinants of money supply? Explain how money supply is interest dependent from the determinants of money supply.
5. Write down the money market equilibrium condition when money supply is interest sensitive. Derive the slope of LM function after incorporation of endogenous money supply function and compare it with that under the exogenous money supply functions considered in the classical and Keynesian models.
6. Derive the income and interest effects of fiscal and monetary policies when money supply is interest elastic. Compare these effects with the effects under exogenous money supply condition.

7. What is the credit control policy of a central bank of a country? What are the major instruments to control money supply of a country? Discuss critically the workings of different credit control policies adopted by the Reserve Bank of India.
8. What is demonetisation? Explain the possible advantages and disadvantages of the recently announced demonetisation policy of the Indian government from a theoretical background.
9. Define NDA and NFA. Explain how money supply is determined under the central bank's balance sheet.
10. Discuss the balance sheet approach and multiplier approach of money supply determination in an economy. How do they differ? Explain.

18 Schools of thought in macroeconomics

18.1 Introduction

Development of the subject of "economics" has been based on different schools of thought which have again been the outcomes of the shifting of paradigms. A paradigm is a conceptual framework for organising thought. There are competing paradigms for understanding the subject. In particular, paradigms influence thought in the way we attend to how we think about the economy. It started from the ancient period and ended up with the presently running system of the mixture of new classical and new Keynesian approaches. Ancient economic thought refers to ideas from before and during the Middle Ages. The earliest discussions of economics date back to ancient times, such as in Kautilya's *Arthashastra* or Xenophon's *Oeconomicus*. In those days, economics was not a separate discipline but part of philosophy. Religious beliefs and a concern for morality and ethics played a significant role in the views of early theorists.

The mercantilist approach originated from the rise of the nation-state in Europe during the sixteenth and seventeenth centuries. It believed in the myth that a country's progress was dependent upon the stock of precious metals like gold and silver, and favourable international trade (or merchandise exports over imports) could be the source of such stock of metals. This approach is called *bullionism*. Also, it believed that the state should take the necessary action to direct the development of the capitalist system. The monetary factor, thus, played a vital role in the development of an economy as per the approach of the mercantilists.

Till the age of mercantilism, there was no formal theory on economics. The first theoretical model on macroeconomics was developed by the *physiocrats* in France. The concept of circular flow of output among different sectors was established in the *Tableau economique* of Francois Quesnay in the middle of the eighteenth century. The physiocrats believed that the growth of an economy depended upon the growth of the agricultural sector. According to them, agriculture is the only sector to generate surplus which can further be used for economic development. They criticised the mercantilists on the grounds that the trade sector was unproductive and could not produce surplus.

A new group of economists emerged in the late 80s, after the mercantilists and physiocrats, who advocated that entire wealth of a nation could be managed and controlled by the operation of a free market mechanism; no state control or patronisation was required. This particular school of thought is popularly known as "classical" and the proponents are Adam Smith, David Ricardo, J. S. Mill, R. Malthus, etc. The free-market doctrine failed during the great depression of the 1920–1930s and the Keynesian Revolution emerged as a possible solution to the classical failure. The Keynesian approach

DOI: 10.4324/9781003501138-22

was of a short run system and there were the conditions of sticky prices and slump in aggregate demand that were identified as the cause of depression and thus he opined for the active intervention of the government sector into economic activities. It was established that an economy could be in equilibrium even under an unemployment situation. There was thus no immediate effect of demand increase by means of either expansionary fiscal or monetary policies upon the rate of inflation. There was remarkable success of the Keynesian postulates in combating depression and it continues up to the 1970s. It is popularly known in the macroeconomic literature as the "era of stabilisation optimism".

The serious flaw of the Keynesian system was observed in the 1970s when the US economy suffered from long-term stagflation (that is the combination of unemployment and inflation) which, according to the Keynes, should not appear. The new school pioneered by Milton Friedman emerged, named "monetarists", who strongly criticised the Keynesian orthodoxy and opined that economic agents' expectations on inflation should be given importance. They argued that most fluctuations in real output were caused by fluctuations in the money supply, rather than by fluctuations in consumption or investment spending. Besides, they maintained that a stable and consistent money supply policy could control price instability; no need of government intervention was desirable. The monetarists, thus, maintained the classical essence in partial form. Monetarist ideas attracted significant support during the 1970s and early 1980s, when the economy experienced high rates of unemployment and inflation, but the support declined during late 1980s and 1990s when the unemployment and inflation rate were relatively low.

The classical followers motivated by the monetarists and challenging the Keynesian orthodoxy formed a new school of thought called "new classical" which heavily depended upon the roles of rational behaviours of the economic agents in deciding their personal objectives. A popular theory, *rational expectation*, was developed by three well-known economists, Robert Lucas, Thomas Sargent, and Robert Barro. Policy ineffectiveness as a result was established by the theory because of rational behaviour of the economic agents and thus it justified the central proposition of the classical economists. The economic fluctuations during the 1980s pinpointed the failure of the rational expectation hypothesis. The proponents of real business cycle (RBC) theory like Edward Prescott and Finn Kydland agreed to the rational expectation hypothesis of the new classicists but did not agree as to why there were fluctuations in real GDP. According to them, it was the temporary shocks to productivity that explained fluctuations in real GDP. Real business cycle theory firmly rejects Keynesian and monetarists' postulates regarding the role of money.

The new classical school and their followers, the RBC theoreticians, tried to establish that Keynesian doctrine was dead and there was nothing to justify their positions regarding the economic fluctuations. James Tobin, an old follower of Keynes, reacted sharply to the claim of the new classicists and RBC theoreticians and established that the Keynesian economics was not dead, rather, it had a lot to offer. A new Keynesian school emerged through Robin Bade and Michael Parkin, Gregory Mankiw, and others, known as New Keynesian economics. They paid respect to the rational expectation hypothesis but developed the new theory on the basis of microeconomic foundations.

The new Keynesian school assumed a variety of market failures like the presence of market imperfections or monopolistic structure in price and wage setting to explain why prices and wages can become sticky. At the same time, the prevalence of different types of market failures creates dead weight loss or social cost that cannot be corrected by means of rational expectations. That means their claim of involuntary unemployment persists and thus the New Keynesians argued that macroeconomic stabilisation by the government using fiscal policy or by the central bank of the country using monetary policy would lead to a more efficient macroeconomic outcome than the classicists' laissez faire policy would. The economic events of the late twentieth century to date show the applicability of the combinations of the new classical and new Keynesian schools. The global financial crisis of 2007–2009 has been the failure of the market principle and the quantitative easing policy of the Federal Reserves in the United States has attempted to solve it which is a notion of state intervention.

Although there is a long history of development of the economics subject, the major developments of macroeconomics were started during the aftermath of the Great Depression of the 1930s. In the following sections we will present the salient features of different schools in macroeconomics starting from the classical orthodoxy to the new Keynesian system.

18.2 Agreements and disagreements among different schools of thoughts

18.2.1 Classical model

The classical model is based on some long run assumptions. The commodity prices and factor prices (mainly of wage rate) and rate of interest are assumed to be perfectly flexible in both upward and downward directions. The perfectly competitive structure in both the goods and factor markets always clear the market; no excess supply remains. Say's law operates which argues that supply creates its own demand always. The ultimate result of these assumptions is that the all-time full employment equilibrium and the aggregate supply curve is vertical along the full employment level. Any increase in demand induced only by the monetary sector leads to zero effect on output and employment and only the flexible price level gets adjusted upward by the full amount of increase in money supply. This effect is popularly known as *neutrality of money*, a type of policy ineffectiveness in the classical model. The phenomenon justifies that the classical model is completely a supply-side model and it discards the necessity of government intervention as it produces no real effects. Figure 18.1 explains the complete classical phenomenon.

The aggregate supply function is vertical along the full employment level of output, y_f. The aggregate demand function is negatively sloped and its position is fixed by the quantity of money. When the quantity of money is M_1 then E is the market clearing equilibrium

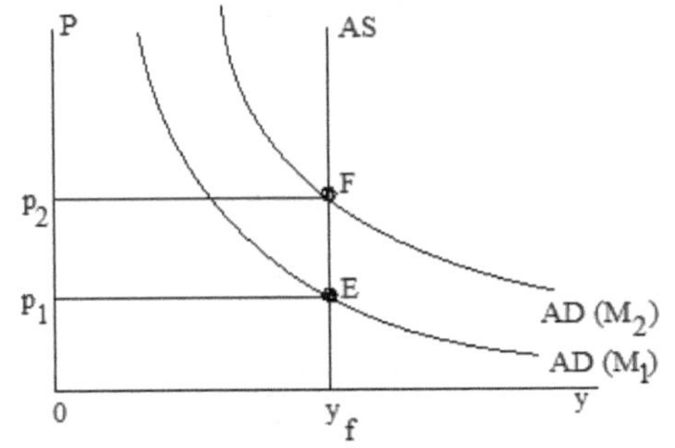

Figure 18.1 Classical model

point where p_1 is the general price level. An increase in the quantity of money from M_1 to M_2 shifts the aggregate demand function in an upward direction. The new equilibrium is *F* where it is observed that price level increases equi-proportionately to the increase in money supply. The quantity of real output remains the same due to increase in money supply; only the flexible price adjusts to this increased demand. This is known as neutrality of money. Full employment level is always restored; anyone left unemployed is termed by the classical school as voluntary, not involuntary, which is demand led.

18.2.2 *Keynesian model*

In his general theory, Keynes criticised the classical orthodoxy and explained the depressionary situation from the short run perspective. The market does not always clear and there is stickiness in wage rate and price level because of institutional bottlenecks and people's failure to perceive (or expect) perfectly the future wages and price levels. In a situation of excess supply, there is no role of the supply side in deciding output and employment, rather, the magnitude of effective demand determines output and employment. The supply function under this general excess supply condition is a horizontal line as depicted in Figure 18.2. The aggregate supply function under sticky price conditions is upward sloping which nullifies the neutrality effect under the classical model. It does not mean that Keynes completely rejected the full employment result at all stages of the economy. If proper public policies by active intervention of the government are continuously undertaken, then the institutional bottlenecks may be removed and ultimately full employment equilibrium can be reached. Hence, in the long run, after all corrections made in the short run, all the demand deficiency or involuntary unemployment problem of the economy can be reduced to zero and thus the aggregate supply curve will be vertical like the classical model. Therefore, we have presented the aggregate supply function first positively sloped and then vertical. The aggregate demand under the Keynesian system is determined by real as well as monetary factors. The negatively sloped effective demand function intersects the upward sloping as well as horizontal supply functions at point E and generates equilibrium output y_1 and price p_1. The notable outcome is that the equilibrium output under the sticky price model is well short of the full employment level. It justifies the underemployment equilibrium under the Keynesian system. An increase in the parametric values of either government

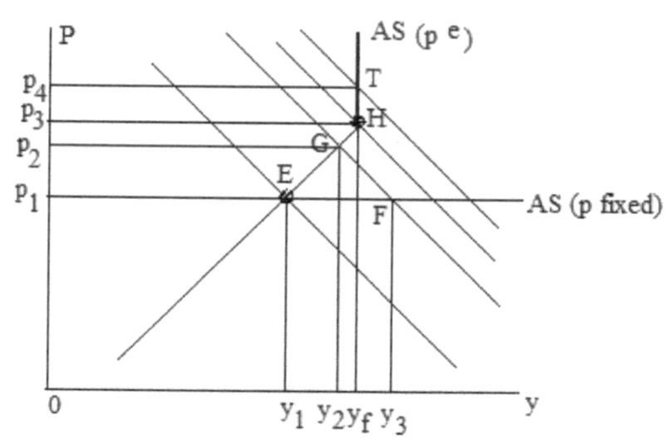

Figure 18.2 Keynesian model

spending or money supply will lead to a real effect as well as price effect. The equilibrium output level increases to the full extent of y_3 under the horizontal supply function and to y_2 under the positively sloped supply function. It is a departure from or disagreement with the classical result that under the Keynesian system additional demand leads to both output and price effect, not only the price effect as under the classical model. Hence, money or aggregate demand effects are not neutral under the Keynesian system. What we see is that the unemployment problem is getting solved with the expansionary fiscal or monetary policies. Once the economy reaches the full employment equilibrium at *H*, any additional fiscal or monetary impetus will not produce real effects; rather there will be full price effect and the neutrality effect will appear even in the Keynesian system. This is a clear consensus or agreement between the classical and Keynesian approaches that happen in the long run conditions. But they differ when short run conditions are taken into consideration in modelling their propositions (the details can be obtained from Chapters 3, 4, and 12).

18.2.3 Monetarists' model

The monetarists' counter revolution against the Keynesian system in the aftermath situation of World War II was on the grounds that the latter posited the role of money as not too strong because of the infinitely elastic money demand (or the liquidity trap) and the former argued that the role of money under the latter was unstable. The monetarists, through its pioneer, Milton Friedman, counterargued that the fluctuations in the business cycle was due to unstable and inconsistent money supply, and if it is made consistent then in the short run money supply can lead to changes in real income and price level unlike the classical conclusion. But in the long run, real variables like output and employment are determined by real factors, not by money supply. The monetarists thus extended the classical model and attacked the Keynesian model on the grounds of instability of monetary policy. Unlike most economists, Friedman is well known outside academic circles, a characteristic he shares with Keynes. Together with Keynes, Friedman has probably influenced macroeconomic theory and policymaking more than any other economist in the twentieth century. In recognition of his academic work, Friedman was awarded the Nobel Memorial Prize in Economics in 1976 for his successes in the fields of consumption analysis, monetary history, and theory and for his demonstration of the complexity of the stabilisation policy.

The core argument of Keynes' general theory is that capitalism market economies are intrinsically unstable and can remain in a state of less than full employment for lengthy periods of time. Keynes believed that changes in aggregate demand were the main cause of this instability. The mainstream Keynesian orthodoxy of the mid to late 1940s and 1950s focused on real disruptions (namely, changes in investment and autonomous consumption) as the primary driver of changes in money or nominal income, which mostly took the shape of shifts in real income. According to early Keynesians, a state of insufficient aggregate demand was reflected in the Great Depression, which was caused by a steep decline in investment and the terrible unemployment that followed. This contrasted with the previous quantity theory of money (QTM) approach, which saw changes in the money stock as the primary, if not the only, element explaining variations in money income. Milton Friedman, more than any other economist, was responsible for resurrecting the fortunes of the quantity theory of money during the 1950s and 1960s.

The monetarists' school centres around their discussions on the development of the theories in three consecutive models. The quantity theory of money (QTM) is the first (basics of it are given in Chapter 4) in the mid 1950s to mid 1960s, the expectation augmented Philips curve is the second (refer to Chapter 13) in the mid 1960s, and the monetary approach to balance of payments theory and exchange rate determination (details are in Chapters 17, 18, and 19) in the early 1970s. Here in this chapter, we focus mainly on the QTM version of the monetarist school of thought.

To justify their position, the monetarists remodelled the quantity theory of money which is attributed to the Cambridge version, not to the Fisher's version. The basic equation of the Cambridge version of quantity theory of money is

$$M^d = k \,.\, PY \tag{18.1}$$

where M^d stands for demand for money, P is price level, Y is nominal income, and k is the proportion of income held as money or income velocity of circulation which was kept fixed. Monetarists redefined the term k as it is not fixed and rather depended upon several factors consisting of nominal as well as real natures. The monetarists agreed to Keynesian assertion that money had asset value and thus people speculated between two options of money being used as cash or store value (as bond). According to them, "k" depends on returns on bonds (r_b), returns on equities or shares (r_e), and returns from stock of durable assets like domestic appliances, car, land, etc. (r_d). As the returns increase, people hold less money for transaction purposes and hence k falls. Therefore, the signs of dk / dr in all three heads will be negative. The money demand function as postulated by the monetarists is, thus, given as

$$M^d = k(r_b, r_e, r_d) \,.\, PY \tag{18.2}$$

The equilibrium condition in the money market under the monetarists approach is

$$M^s = M_1 = M^d = k(r_b, r_e, r_d) \,.\, PY$$
$$Or,\ M_1 = k(r_b, r_e, r_d) \,.\, PY \tag{18.3}$$

The relation (18.3) shows that money supply has positive effects upon nominal income (PY) and the proportion of holding money (k) through decrease in returns from different assets like bonds, equities, etc. This is a crucial difference between the classical quantity theory of money and Friedman's monetarists' version of quantity theory of money. The aggregate demand curve derived from the monetarists' approach is thus negatively sloped like the classical approach but the aggregate supply curve is not vertical, rather it is positively sloped like that of Keynes (Figure 18.3). But there are disagreements between Keynes and Friedman on the grounds that under the former, the money supply was unstable and the sensitivity of the demand for money with respect to rate of interest was infinite (i.e. liquidity trap) and monetary policy was nearly ineffective, and under the latter the money supply is more stable and the interest sensitivity of money with respect to rate of interest is inelastic which produces a relatively steeper LM function and the monetary policy is proved to be effective.

If any monetary expansion is done by the central bank (that is, increase from M_1), the aggregate demand curve will shift upward and it will lead to increase in income and employment on one hand and increase in goods prices on the other. This is the policy

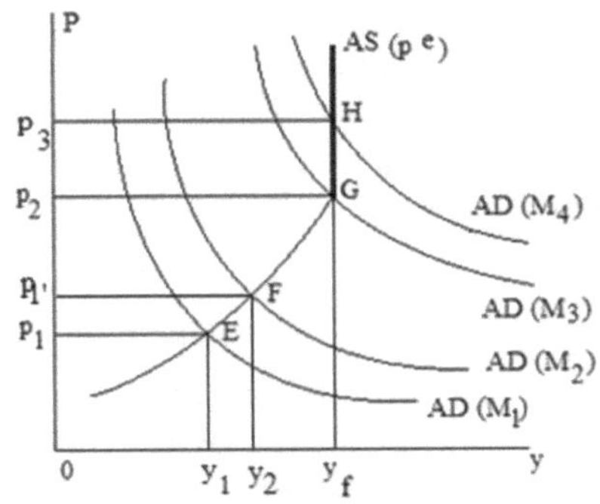

Figure 18.3 Monetarists' approach

Box I Link between monetary and real sectors in the monetarists' version

Utility-maximising individuals will reallocate wealth between different assets whenever marginal rates of return are not equal. This portfolio adjustment process is important to the monetarist description of the transmission mechanism by which changes in the money stock affect the real economy. This can be demonstrated by evaluating the impact of an increase in the money supply caused by monetary authorities' open market operations. An initial equilibrium is assumed, in which wealth is distributed among financial and real assets in such a way that marginal rates of return are equal. Following that, the public's money holdings will rise as a result of the monetary authorities' open market purchases of bonds. Given that the marginal return on any asset decreases as holdings increase, the marginal rate of return on money will be reduced as a result. Excess money balances will be bid up in price when they are exchanged for financial and real assets (such as consumer durables), until portfolio equilibrium is restored, when all assets are gladly kept and marginal rates of return are equal. Monetarists believe that, in contrast to orthodox Keynesian analysis, money is a substitute for a wide range of real and financial assets, and no one asset or collection of assets can be regarded a close equivalent for money. Monetarists credit a far bigger and more direct effect on aggregate spending to monetary impulses because they emphasise a much broader spectrum of assets and associated expenditures.

outcome of the monetarist model. But in the long run, if continuous money supply is increased, the economy can reach the full employment and no real effect will be obtained; only the price level will increase at the full extent.

Having a good theoretical base of the school of thought, the monetarists' approach was subject to lack of consensus with respect to its empirical validity. Although Friedman in his early empirical work on the demand for money claimed to have found that the interest rate was insignificant, practically all studies commenced thereafter have revealed that the interest rate becomes an important variable in the function. Indeed, in the later works Friedman acknowledged this. James Tobin, in his long debate with Friedman, has convinced most of the researchers in the field that the demand for money has an economically and statistically significant interest rate-responsiveness which means the LM curve is not perfectly inelastic or vertical like the classical orthodox thought. This argument of Tobin has been in support of discretionary fiscal policy having a role to play in stabilisation policy with the monetary policy. Further, though the certainty in a stable demand for money function was well supported by empirical evidence up to the early 1970s, since then several studies, both in the United States and other economies, have found evidence of seeming instability of the demand for money.

18.2.4 New classical model — rational expectation hypothesis

The new classical thought originated from the background of high magnitude of stagflation (a combination of high inflation and unemployment) in the 1970s. Their central philosophy was that of the classical economists and was in strong contrast to the Keynesian interventionist philosophy. They have similar thinking to the classical economists from before the Keynesian revolution, but they forwarded one additional argument known as *rational expectation.* It was developed by three well known economists, Robert Lucas, Thomas Sargent, and Robert Barro.

18.2.4.1 Intuitive explanations of the model

Under the *rational expectation* model, households (or workers) and firms form expectations of the future values of economic variables like inflation rate by making use of all available information they possessed in the past, and it is also taken into consideration that economic agents do not make repeated mistakes in their expectation formation. That is why the term rational expectation bears credit. If the economic agents, excepting the government sector, have rational expectations, then the aggregate supply curve will be positive functions of expected government expenditure (G^e), expected tax rates (T^e), expected private investment spending (I^e), expected money supply (M^e), etc. Hence, the aggregate supply function is

$$Y^s = Y\left(P \textit{ which is conditions upon } I^e,\ G^e,\ T^e,\ M^e,\ \ldots.\right). \tag{18.4}$$

On the other hand, the aggregate demand function will be negatively sloped under the parametric values of fiscal and monetary components. The aggregate demand function is like

$$Y^d = Y(P \textit{ which is conditioned upon } I, G, T, M, \ldots.) \tag{18.5}$$

Figure 18.4 presents the aggregate economy's equilibrium. One notable conclusion of the new classical school is the policy ineffectiveness result. *The policy ineffectiveness result was established by the theory because of rational behaviour of the economic agents and thus it justified the central proposition of the classical economists.* The initial equilibrium is at E where all anticipated demand is equal to all anticipated supply. The equilibrium output is yf and price is p_1. An increase in money supply or investment expenditure makes outward shift to AD' and makes new equilibrium at F where output increases to y_1 and at the same time price increases to p_1'. Since the individuals, specifically the labour class, are rational and anticipate the price increase, they will re-contract their agreement in such a way as to claim higher money wages. As a result of that wage hike, the producers' class will reduce demand for labour and as a result the aggregate supply function will shift leftward until the price level is further pushed up. AS' is such an aggregate supply function and new equilibrium is restored at G with output remaining unchanged at

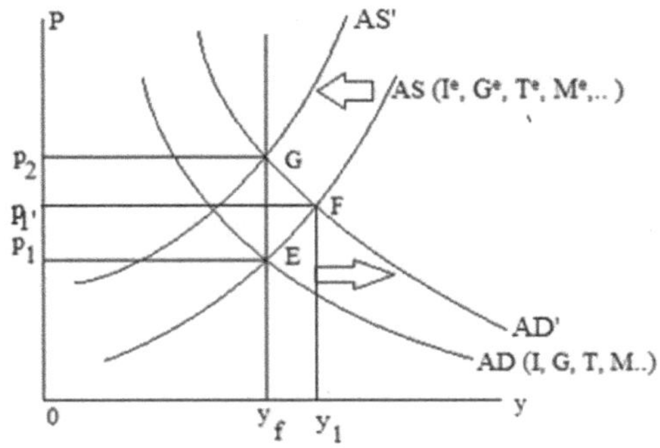

Figure 18.4 New classical model

y_f with the corresponding unchanged level of employment. The policy ineffective result is obtained even in the short run. But, if the policy changes are unanticipated (or like a shock) or are out of the reach of the information set of the economic agents, then there may not be policy ineffectiveness results in the new classical system. In that case, *F* would be the equilibrium, or there may be equilibrium in between *F* and *G* where the economy will get policy effective results. This is the point where new classical economists are in agreement with the Keynesian conclusion but still they do not believe in active intervention by the government into economic activities.

18.2.4.2 Mathematical expression of the rational expectation hypothesis

In the rational expectation hypothesis, it is argued that people use all the available information (INF) associated with the determination of the expected value of any economic variable, say price (*P*) at any point of time *t*, which is dependent upon the past value of *P*, which is *Pt* – 1 and the vector of other variables (*X*). Thus, the person who is formulating expectations about the value of *Y* in time "*t*" at the end of time point *t* – 1, his expression of *Y* can be written as

$$Y_t = a_0 + a_1 Y_{t-1} + a_2 X_{t-1} \dots\dots\dots\dots\dots\dots \quad (18.6)$$

According to the Lucas proposition, there is no impact of predictable macroeconomic policy such as anticipated money supply or anticipated public expenditure upon output and employment, while the unanticipated policies can produce relevant impacts upon output and employment. The first one is called the "policy irrelevant result" and the second one is called "policy relevant result". According to Robert Lucas and Thomas Sargent, once the unknowns are rationally expected, then any policy shock will not produce any economic effects as prices are correctly anticipated out of the positive policy shocks the failure of which leads to policy effective results.

The imperfect information model of Lucas has the following three structural/behavioural equations:

The aggregate supply (AS) equation is written as

$$Y_t = Y_f + (P_t - P_t^e);\ \beta > 0 \dots\dots\dots\dots\dots\dots\dots\dots \quad (18.7)$$

The AS equation shows that the output in period "t" is the sum of the full employment output (Y_f) and the deviations around the full employment level.

The aggregate demand (AD) equation is written as

$$m_t \cdot v_0 = p_t \cdot y_t$$

Taking the logarithm in both sides leads us to the following expression:

$$M_t + V_0 = P_t + Y_t$$

where M_t, V_0, P_t, and Y_t are the logarithmic values of m_t, v_0, p_t, and y_t. The velocity of money is taken to be fixed at V_0.

Suppose the monetary feedback mechanism works through the following mathematical relation-

$$M_t = \alpha Y_{t-1} + U_t$$

Where the stochastic disturbance term U_t follows normal distribution with zero mean and constant variance (σ^2). Money supply in the current period is determined by the past period's income and unknown factors. Here α is the anticipated part of the money supply while U_t is the unanticipated part of the money supply (e.g. any unforeseen circumstances like oil shock, war, drought, flood, etc.). We want to prove that the policy is ineffective, which is, anticipated changes in policy have no effect on real variables and only unanticipated changes can affect real variables, the output and employment.

From the previous logarithmic transformed equation we have

$$P_t = M_t + V_0 - Y_t$$
$$\text{or } P_t = \alpha Y_{t-1} + U_t + V_0 - Y_t \ldots\ldots\ldots\ldots\ldots \quad (18.8)$$

As the expectation is rational, we can write expected price $P_t^e = E(P_t \mid INF_{t-1})$. The expected prices are prices conditioned upon all the information available up to the point the expectations are made. Therefore,

$$P^e_t = \alpha Y_{t-1} + U_t + V_0 - Y_t$$
$$\text{or } P^e_t = E[(\alpha Y_{t-1} + U_t) + V_0 - Y_t \mid INF_{t-1}]$$
$$\text{or, } P^e_t = E[\alpha Y_{t-1} \mid INF_{t-1}] + E[U_t \mid INF_{t-1}] + E[V_0 \mid INF_{t-1}] - E[Y_t \mid INF_{t-1}]$$

Under the presence of rational expectation, the previous relation can be written as

$$P^e_t = \alpha Y_{t-1} + 0 + V_0 - Y_f$$
$$\text{or } P^e_t = \alpha Y_{t-1} + V_0 - Y_f \ldots\ldots\ldots\ldots\ldots\ldots\ldots \quad (18.9)$$

To get into equation (18.10) we make subtraction of (18.9) from (18.8) which gives-

$$P_t - P^e_t = Y_t - Y_f + U_t \ldots\ldots\ldots\ldots\ldots\ldots \quad (18.10)$$

Now substituting (18.10) into (18.7) we get

$$Y_t = Y_f + (Y_f - Y_t + U_t)$$
$$\text{or } (1 + \beta)\, Y_t = (1 + \beta)\, Y_f + \beta U_t$$
$$\text{or } Y_t = Y_f + \beta U_t \,/\, (1+ \beta) \ldots\ldots\ldots\ldots\ldots\ldots \quad (18.11)$$

It is observed from the previous equation that the monetary policy parameter (α) does not appear in the determination of output (as well as employment).

Here $dY_t \,/\, dM_t = 0$ when U_t is anticipated and $dY_t \,/\, dM_t \# 0$ when U_t is unanticipated. This proves that the anticipated part of the monetary policy leads to no change in the output level in the current period. This proves the policy ineffectiveness results. However, only the unanticipated part of the monetary policy (that is, the U_t) has an impact upon output and employment in the model. This proves the policy effectiveness results.

This strong policy ineffectiveness proposition has major implications for the controversy over the role and conduct of the macroeconomic stabilisation policies. If the money supply is determined by the authorities according to some "known" rule, then the authorities will be unable to influence output and employment even in the short run by pursuing a systematic monetary policy as it can be anticipated by agents. If, in practice, the money supply grew at a rate of some unknown unlike the "known rule" concept, the non-systematic (unanticipated) component of monetary expansion would cause output and employment to rise temporarily above their long run equilibrium (natural) levels, owing to errors in inflation expectations. Alternatively, the authorities might allow the money supply to be determined by a feedback rule (say, for example, in response to the changes in unemployment and output). Again, changes in the rate of monetary growth which arise from a known feedback rule will be anticipated by agents, making the feedback policy rule ineffective. Only departures from a known monetary rule (such as unforeseen changes in policy) which are unanticipated will influence output.

18.2.4.3 Nexus between monetary autonomy and inflation

From the market clearing assumption of the monetarists school of thought it is obtained that money supply influences price level (or the rate of inflation) in a proportional manner. If there is price instability then the monetary authority can stabilise it by means of appropriate monetary policy. The relation between money supply and the price level is given by the well-known quantity theory which is represented again by the following equation:

$$MV = PY$$

where the notations are of the usual meanings. Having the market clearing conditions, the output (Y) and velocity of money (V) are taken to be fixed and thus it is derived that

$$P = a \,.\, M$$

where $a = V \,/\, Y =$ constant.

Hence, $dP \,/\, dM = a =$ constant; a 1% increase in money supply leads to proportional increase in the rate of inflation and vice-versa. But the question is: are the monetary authorities or the central banks of the countries that independent in deciding inflation rates or price stability? The basics of the quantity theory as postulated by the classical economists and then reformulated by the monetarists are based upon the full autonomy of the central banks; no political or economic controls are dictated upon their policy-framing principles. In further detail, a monetary authority should be aware of the price stabilisation in the economy and that should be done on the basis of the movements of the leading fundamentals. But the reality is that no governments of the countries today allow their monetary authorities to work autonomously, rather they control their monetary authorities to some degree. Thus, there may be an inverse relation between monetary control and price stability in theory; as monetary control increases, rate of inflation increases. It is thus an empirical question too. Alesina and Summers (1993) and Alesina and Gatti (1995) have gone through the empirical validation of the same across the OECD countries. Later international monetary fund (IMF), in their working paper, has done the similar lines of works across the developing and emerging countries too. In order to construct a measure of central bank independence or the monetary authority's autonomy (MA), they have identified the ability of the central bank to select its policy objectives without the influence of the ruling government, the selection procedure of the governors of the central banks of the countries, the ability to use monetary instruments without restrictions, and the requirement of the central bank to finance fiscal deficits as key indicators. In theory the following relation holds

$$P = f(M(\text{Magnitude of Autonomy}))$$
$$dM / dMA < 0 \text{ and so } (\delta P / \delta M) * (\delta M / \delta MA) < 0.$$

As the magnitude of autonomy increases, the central banks make price stability in a greater way and a politically controlled monetary authority leads to price instability and high inflation rates. The aforementioned research empirically shows that in the 16 OECD countries, between 1955 and 1988, the political intervention increased upon the normal monetary performance and the inflation rate also increased. Countries like New Zealand, Spain, and Italy had very low scores of autonomy (i.e. high degree of political intervention) while Germany, Switzerland, and the USA had very high scores of autonomy (i.e. low degree of political intervention). As a result of that, the former set of countries faced very high rates of inflation while the latter set of the countries faced very low rates of inflation. IMF has shown that, between 1991 and 2003, countries like Brazil and India showed a relatively low score in autonomy and faced high magnitudes of inflation. Hence, there is a negative correlation between independence of the central banks and magnitude of inflation in a statistical sense. The facts makes ambiguities about the effectiveness of the policy results irrelevant as it depends upon the market clearing conditions.

18.2.5 Real business cycle model

The never-ending debate between the new classical school and the Keynesian school forced the two groups of thinkers to refine their model building and policy conclusions. The new classical group developed the real business cycle model and the Keynesians developed the new Keynesian approach from their own standpoints. The policies undertaken by the monetarists and the new classical schools were founded upon the belief that aggregate demand shocks were the main source of aggregate instability in the business cycle. In place of lobbying in favour of the persistent use of expansionary aggregate demand policies to achieve some target rate of full employment, both Friedman and Lucas advocated the use of supply-side policies. During the 1960s and 1970s, both Friedman and Lucas, in their explanation of business cycles, emphasised monetary shocks as the primary impulse mechanism driving the cycle. The real business cycle theorists have gone much further in their analysis of the supply side.

The *real business cycle* (RBC) model has been developed in line with the classical school's basic assumption, which is the effectiveness of the uninterrupted market clearing principle. The RBC model, developed by Edward Prescott and Finn Kydland, accepted the rational expectation hypothesis of the new classicists but did not agree to the causes of fluctuations in real GDP. Undeniably, the research of Kydland and Prescott represented a serious challenge to all previous mainstream accounts of the business cycle that focused on aggregate demand shocks, in particular those that emphasised monetary shocks. The result has been the development of a real business cycle theory which replaces the impulse mechanism of the earlier models (that is, unanticipated monetary shocks) with supply-side shocks in the form of random changes in technology. The real business cycle theory, as developed by its modern proponents, is built on the assumption that there are large random fluctuations in the rate of technological progress. These supply-side shocks to the production function generate fluctuations in aggregate output and employment as rational individuals respond to the altered structure of relative prices by changing their labour supply and consumption decisions. The transition from monetary to real theories of the business cycle was further stimulated by two other important developments. First, the supply shocks associated with the two OPEC oil price increases during the 1970s made macroeconomists more aware of the importance of supply-side factors in explaining macroeconomic instability. These procedures, together with the apparent failure of the demand-oriented Keynesian model to account sufficiently for rising unemployment accompanied by accelerating inflation, forced all macroeconomists to devote increasing research effort to the construction of macroeconomic theories where the supply side has coherent micro foundations. Second, the seminal work of Charles Nelson and Charles Plosser in 1982 titled "Trends and random walks in macroeconomic time series: Some evidence and implications" suggested that real shocks may be far more important than monetary shocks in explaining the path of aggregate output over time. They argue that the evidence is consistent with the proposition that output follows a path, which could best be described as a random walk. According to them, it was the temporary shocks to productivity that explained fluctuations in real GDP. The RBC model focuses on real factors like decline in the availability of oil or other raw materials, environmental degradation, natural resource depletion, or technological progress that make productivity shocks rather than changes in the quantity of money. RBC theory categorically rejects Keynesian economics and the real effectiveness of monetary policy as promoted by monetarists and the Keynesian economics.

In the following part we discuss the impacts of technology shock and demand shock upon income, employment, and other associated factors in an economy.

18.2.5.1 The nature of impacts of shocks – temporary or permanent

Any shock in the trend of the real GDP may be temporary or permanent. In the case of temporary shock, the effects are observed for the short period and the deviations due to the shock around the trend line die out to zero in a short interval; the movement off the trend due to the shock is brought back to the original trend, the long run path of the GDP. But for the permanent shock, the effects are observed for a long time, and the deviation from the trend due to the shock at any point of time "t" does not go back to the original long run trend, rather the series follows a drift from the path at time "t". The movement of this particular type of the series is called a random walk process. Nelson and Plosser, in their research into US data, have shown that its GDP trend follows a random walk. They view that reversible cyclical fluctuations can account for most of the short-term movements of real GDP can be represented by Equation (18.12) as

$$Y_t = A_t + bY_{t-1} + U_t \dots\dots\dots\dots\dots\dots \qquad (18.12)$$

where A and b ($0 < b < 1$) are constants and U represents random shocks which have a zero mean and constant variance. In the equation, A_t represents the underlying average growth rate of GDP which describes the deterministic trend. Assume there is some shock to U_t that causes output to rise above trend at time "t" which lasts for one period only. Since Y_t depends on Y_{t-1}, the shock will be transmitted forward in time, generating a serial correlation. But since $0 < b < 1$, the impact of the shock on output will eventually die out and output will return to its trend rate of growth (A_t). In this case, the output is said to be "temporary" or "trend-reverting" or "trend-stationary". The temporary impact of a shock on the path of income in the trend-stationary case is illustrated on the left side of Figure 18.5, where we assume an expansionary monetary shock (say) occurs at time t_1. Notice that Y eventually reverts to its trend path and therefore this case is synchronous with the natural rate hypothesis, which states that deviations from the natural level of output caused by unanticipated monetary shocks will be temporary. As the positive monetary shock ($dU > 0$) is given to the economy at time t_1, the GDP jumps up but comes back to the trend at time t_2 with the value of the GDP to Y_2. The shock dies out at time point t_2.

In contrast to the previous scenario, Nelson and Plosser argue that most of the changes in GDP that we observe are permanent, in that there is no tendency for output to revert

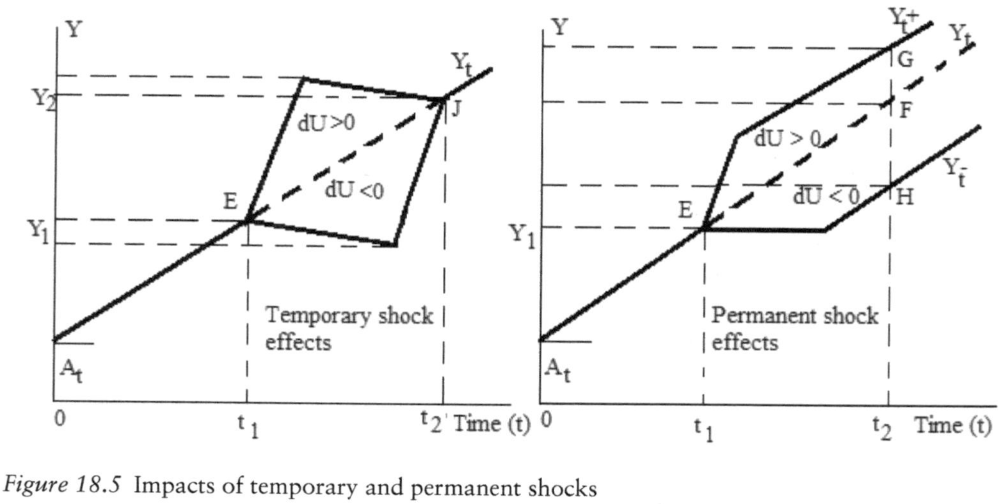

Figure 18.5 Impacts of temporary and permanent shocks

to its former trend following a shock. The trend equation for the series of DP will then look like

$$Y_t = A_t + Y_{t-1} + U_t \ldots\ldots\ldots\ldots\ldots\ldots \quad (18.13)$$
$$\text{or } Y_t - Y_{t-1} = A_t + U_t \ldots\ldots\ldots\ldots\ldots\ldots \quad (18.14)$$
$$\text{or } dY = \text{Drift} + \text{Shock}.$$

This is a random walk model which is always nonstationary in its nature. Since output in the next period is determined by output in period t_1, the rise in output persists in every future period. In the case of a random walk with drift, output is said to have a "unit root", that is, the coefficient on the lagged output term in equation (*) is set equal to unity, $b = 1$. This is a time series property which is largely discussed in the subject of time series econometrics. The readers are encouraged to capture the intuitive part of the random walk model for the time being. The right-hand side of Figure 19.5 explains the scenario. When there is positive unanticipated shock by $dU > 0$, then the rising trend of GDP continues after it initially jumps up at time t_1, and on the other hand, when there is negative unanticipated shock by $dU < 0$ then the declining trend of GDP continues after it initially jumps down at time t_1.

18.2.5.2 Effects of technology and demand shocks

In the following section we discuss the effects of technology shock and demand shock upon the real output in the economy around the trend of output. The shocks may be good or bad; we are analysing the effects of good shocks only in our discussion. The readers may try for the effects of the bad shocks on their own.

18.2.5.2.1 THE EFFECT OF TECHNOLOGY SHOCK

The new classical model failed to take into account that information barriers are too short to analyse and to explain the length and persistence of actual business cycle. In contrast the RBC model assumes that the supply shocks are persistent and prevail for years, die away smoothly, and then another shock appears. The economy, according to the RBC approach, reacts to these persistent supply shocks like that of the new classical framework. The firms accordingly decide how much labour to hire, and the households decide how much of consumption is to be made to obtain satisfactory levels of utility at the market determined wage rate, commodity prices, etc. In the following section we present the labour market adjustments to any of the technological shocks which affect productivity of labour either in upward or downward directions. Figure 18.5 with the left panel and right panel explains the effect of supply-side shocks upon the total output production and employment respectively. We have measured unit of employment along the vertical axis and unit of production along the horizontal axis in the left panel and real wage rate (money wage divided by price level = w / p) along the horizontal axis in the right panel. The initial production function is marked as Y (Good), indicating good technology and similarly for labour demand as N^d (Good). The labour supply function is upward sloping which is insensitive to technology shocks. The initial labour market equilibrium is at H where N_1 units of labour produce y_1 units of output corresponding to point E on the production function.

A favourable supply shock like technological progress will shift out the aggregate production function towards the right which represents the better technology (Y (Better)) compared to the initial production function with good technology. This technological development makes the labourers more productive and as a result the marginal productivity curve (or the labour demand curve) will shift rightward to N^d (Better). The new labour market equilibrium occurs at point T where real wage rate increases from $(w / p)_1$ to $(w / p)_2$ which further induces the labour suppliers to supply more labour. This upward shifting of the labour demand function makes higher output y_2 at point G on the new production function. Note that, if the labour supply function would be horizontal in the previous diagram, then technological development would not produce any employment effect. Therefore, the RBC model's capability to explain why employment increases (during favourable supply shocks) or decreases (during unfavourable supply shocks) during recession requires the labour supply function to be horizontal.

18.2.5.2.2 THE EFFECT OF DEMAND SHOCK

The households' labour supply function is derived under the utility maximisation hypothesis where utility function depends on real income and hours of leisure. The source of labour income is primarily the real wage rate ($w = W / P$) – as real wage increases, labour supply (N^s) increases and vice-versa. Besides, real rate of interest (r), which is derived from the commodity and money market interactions, acts as the parameter to the labour supply function in the sense that as real rate of interest increases, with the given real wage rate, the labour supply function shifts to the right, representing higher labour supply as households' asset incomes increase due to increases in the real rate of interest. On the other hand, the demand for labour (N^d) function is negatively sloped with the real wage rate. Changes in the rate of interest due to the demand shocks do not cause the business houses to change their labour demand due to the lag of adjustments of the latter with respect to the former.

The aggregate demand shock may be thought of as increase in the direct purchases of goods, capital, and services by the government of the country. Though there are other sources of demand shocks like tax rate reductions, transfer programs, etc. the case of the government's purchase is taken as the shock of having quick and direct impacts upon the business cycle to correct its downward fluctuations. As government purchases increase, with unchanged aggregate supply components (Y^s), the aggregate demand function of the economy (Y^d) will shift to the right, leading to increase in real income (Y) and real rate of interest. As a result, the labour supply will shift to the right leading to more employment and more output in the production sector following the production function, $Y = A \,.\, f(K, L)$. The downward fluctuations in the real business cycle can thus be corrected through the positive shock in the aggregate demand sector.

Figure 18.6 describes the possible impacts of an increase in government purchases in the economy. It has four panels; Panel I, Panel II, Panel III, and Panel IV respectively represent the labour market equilibrium, the production sector, the aggregate demand-side equilibrium (commodity and money sectors), and the aggregate demand-supply equilibrium as represented through the 45-degree line.

Let us start with the initial equilibrium position at point E in all the four panels of the figure. An increase in government purchases shifts the real aggregate demand curve from Y^d_1 to Y^d_2 in Panel III where the real output increases from Y_1 to Y_2, the real rate of interest rises from r_1 to r_2, and the real wage falls from w_2 to w_1 in response to an increase in

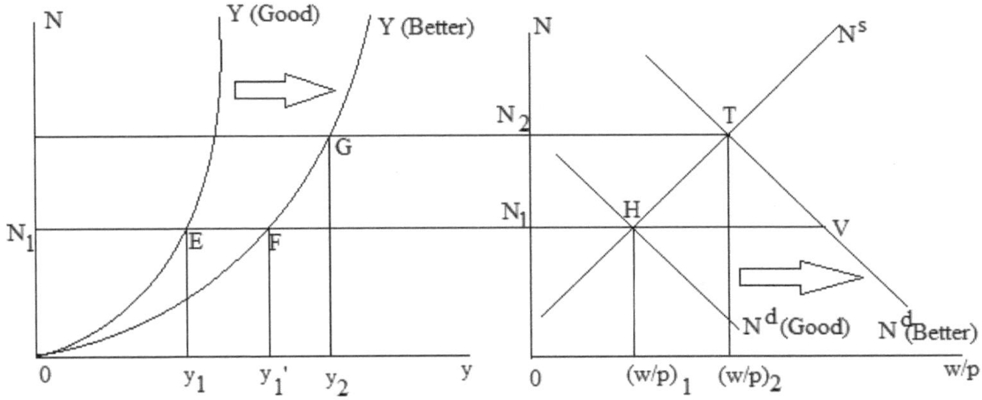

Figure 18.6 Effect of supply (technology) shock under RBC model

labour supply, with the labour supply curve shifting from N^s (r_1) to N^s (r_2) in Panel I. The new equilibrium considering all of these effects is given by point *F* in all four panels of the figure. Unlike the old classical model, with aggregate supply as perfectly inelastic and producing no real effects, the same is positively sloped in the real business cycle model representing the possibilities of accommodating economic changes, such as an increase in government purchases, as having positive effects on real output. In the RBC model, an increase in government purchases leads to an increase in real output because the induced rise in the real rate of interest encourages an increase in labour supply from N^s (r_1) to N^s (r_2) in Panel I, thereby increasing employment and real output. Thus, a positive demand shock through increases in the government's direct purchases have real effects unlike what we have seen in the old as well as new classical models.

18.2.5.3 Alternative effects of fiscal and monetary policies under the RBC model

As we know from the essence of the RBC model that the cyclical fluctuations in the business cycle have been due to the fluctuations in supply-side factors like technological progress, good/bad weather conditions, natural resource depletion, etc., the positive technology and positive demand shocks have the capacity to influence output and employment in favourable directions, leading to corrections in the business cycles.

Although direct public spending does have impacts, alternative fiscal policies like changes in income tax rates and government transfer programmes, can have problematic and inconclusive effects upon the labour supply function which can change its position to create real effects upon output and employment with ambiguous results. The labour supply function in the right panels of Figure 19.5 and Figure 19.6 will shift downward due to a transfer programme and upward due to a tax programme. But these policies may not be accepted by the households or the society as a whole since they create distortions which ultimately lead to social cost. Hence, there is the necessity for alternative support policies.

On the other hand, an increase in money supply cannot make corrections to the fluctuations in the business cycle as it proportionately makes an increase in the price level like the classical result. It is neutrality of money again. No effects on output and employment are created by the monetary policy. But there is again a distortion in a different form in the way that excess money supply unnecessarily creates an increase in the inflation level. The real income of the labour supplier and the firms gets reduced, leading to social cost.

What are the alternative policies mixes? If income tax rate is increased, labour supply will fall and people will enjoy more leisure and as a result there will be deposition of involuntary unemployment. An alternative monetary policy through increase in printing of new currency (which is called deficit financing) can help in balancing the fall in labour supply. This particular mechanism is popularly known as *seigniorage*. But, the fate of this policy mix depends upon the magnitude of new currency printing and income tax rates. If the former is greater than that of the latter, then there may be another form of social cost and the fluctuations in the business cycle will still be unsolved. Therefore, there should be an optimum policy mix to solve the fluctuations in the business cycle.

18.2.6 New Keynesian economics

The fall of the old Keynesianism or the Keynesian orthodoxy as claimed by the theoreticians, mainly the followers of the classical orthodoxy, has led to a debate on whether Keynesianism is dead. Despite positive developments within Keynesian economics in the labour market as well as institutional interventions, by the mid 1970s, Lucas and Sargent were of the view that the Keynesian model could not be patched up because the problems were much more fundamental were are related to the inadequate micro foundations which assumed non-market clearing conditions as well as incorporating the hypothesis of adaptive expectations rather than rational expectations hypothesis. Robert Lucas, in one of his articles titled "The Death of Keynesian Economics: Issues and Ideas", claimed that "people even take offence if referred to as Keynesians". By this time the USA's most distinguished "old" Keynesian economist James Tobin had already posed the question "How dead is Keynes"? When Paul Samuelson was asked whether Keynes was dead, he replied, "Yes, Keynes is dead; and so are Einstein and Newton". Later Tobin provided an unequivocal answer in his essay, "The Future of Keynesian Economics". According to him, one reason Keynesian economics has a future is that rival theories of economic fluctuations do not

> endanger the prediction that neither of the two species of business cycle theory offered by new classical macroeconomics will be regarded as serious and credible explanations of economic fluctuations a few years from now. Whatever cycle theory emerges in a new synthesis will have important Keynesian elements. . . . Yes, Keynesian economics has a future because it is essential to the explanation and understanding of a host of observations and experiences past and present, that alternative macroeconomic approaches do not illuminate.

The persistence of high unemployment in Europe during the 1980s and 1990s also called into question the plausibility of equilibrium explanations of the business cycle while also providing increasing "credibility to Keynesian theory and policy". Further, the global financial crisis in 2007–2009 has shown that agents do not fully understand the complexity of the world in which they live. On the contrary, their cognitive capabilities seem to be quite limited due to limited information or bounded rational behaviour. Numerous data and evidence indicate the importance of heterogeneous expectations in the general equilibrium models.

New Keynesian economics developed primarily as a response to the theoretical crisis facing Keynesian economics that emerged during the 1970s. In their brief survey of new Keynesian economics Gregory Mankiw and Paul Romer define new Keynesian economics with reference to the answer to a pair of questions: i) does the theory violate the classical dichotomy? That is, is money not neutral? ii) Does the theory assume that real market imperfections in the economy are crucial for understanding economic fluctuations? Only new Keynesians, out of all schools of thoughts in macroeconomics, answer both questions in the affirmative way where sticky prices explain non-neutralities and market imperfections explain the behaviour of sticky price. A key difference between the new classical model and new Keynesian model arises out of the price-setting behaviour. In contrast to the price taking behaviour of the new classical models, new Keynesian models assume price to make monopolistic, rather than perfectly competitive, firms. Both orthodox and new Keynesian approaches assume that prices adjust slowly following a disturbance. But, unlike the Keynesian cross or IS-LM approaches, which assumed fixed nominal wages and commodity prices, the new Keynesian approach aims to provide a microeconomic foundation for the slow adjustment of both wages and prices. In line with the choice-theoretical framework of new classical analysis, the new Keynesian approach assumes that workers and firms are respectively the rational utility and profit maximisers.

To respond to the classical and new classical attack about the interventionist policy and sticky wage model, a new group of Keynesian followers led by Gregory Mankiw created the new Keynesian club and re-established the initial claims of the old Keynesian economics. According to the old model, the product market was competitive unlike the labour market and money wage was rigid in a downward direction at least in the short run. Any fall in aggregate demand would push the optimising firms to cut down demand for labour and, as a result, money wage had to fall producing involuntary unemployment. The new Keynesian economists restored the claim with the help of some additional arguments. According to them the cause of wage rigidity was not only institutional but also due to the presence of imperfections in the product as well as labour markets. The optimising imperfect firms used to charge a commodity price far above the competitive (marginal cost pricing) price and used to pay less money as well as real wages to the workers. There is market failure situation in both the product and labour markets that keeps the wage rate fully unadjusted with economic changes. Hence, the concept of involuntary unemployment is safeguarded by the new Keynesians, and the necessity of government intervention which can (and should) accelerate the market's return to equilibrium is well felt again.

According to Tobin, the primary difference between the new classical and new Keynesian schools of thoughts is that the new Keynesians believe that deadweight losses and market failures are possible on a macroeconomic scale and can cause serious damage to the economy. Because of those phenomena, new Keynesian economists believe that government-prompted demand management policies can help the economy restore to equilibrium at a faster rate than is naturally possible.

The new Keynesian argument for the persistent involuntary unemployment problem has been explained by microeconomic foundations that justify money wage as well as real wage rigidity. These micro foundations include the sticky price or menu cost model, efficiency wage models, and the insider-outsider model.

In the *sticky price* or *menu cost* model, costs of changing prices prevent price adjustments during the period of demand-side recessions. Imperfect firms will not reduce the price and keep constant at the previous level which, as a result, leads to fall in output and employment. Therefore, the sticky price model advocates for the combination of fiscal and monetary policies to combat recession in demand. In the *efficiency wage* models, the firms set real wage rate above the market clearing level to attract good quality labourers who will maintain the efficiency standard. Thus, efficiency of workers depends positively on the real wage rate. Such a rigid real wage rate will allow the firms to employ relatively fewer units of labour and make a part of the job seekers unemployed. This is another notion of persistence of involuntary unemployment. Finally, the new Keynesians argued that present unemployment situation is dependent strongly on the past unemployment levels. This is alternatively termed by the economists as the *unemployment trap* or unemployment hysteresis. Hysteresis is a situation where, if any shock led to an unemployment situation then it will have no tendency to return to its initial full employment (or better employment) state. The insider-outsider model is a popular model of explaining the grounds for hysteresis. The labour union members are insiders and the job seekers are the outsiders. The insiders only are engaged in bargaining real wage. Once recession appears, the insiders lose jobs and they become outsiders, and the number of insiders falls and the number of outsiders rises. As a result, the firm can offer higher real wages to the few insiders and the ultimate result is the prevalence of the unemployment situation. Therefore, the new Keynesians maintained their claim from the earlier version that sticky prices led to the generation of involuntary unemployment through developing microeconomic foundations. Further, they defended their interventionist position to fight against fluctuations in business cycle.

18.2.6.1 Menu cost approach of new Keynesians

During the second half of the twentieth century, Keynesians were busy countering the neoclassicists and monetarists who were intruding onto their sacred ground: macroeconomics and the Phillips curve. New Keynesian Economics would keep on exploring market failure one breakdown at a time. They introduced the menu cost approach to explain fluctuations in the business cycle.

Menu costs are the costs that result from price changes. An easy way to understand menu costs is by means of a typical example: restaurants. When a restaurant manager wants to change prices, the cost of changing the menus (in order to show the new prices) must be taken into consideration. Therefore, the manager will need to assess whether the increase in prices will cover for the cost of printing new menus. As *Gregory Mankiw* demonstrates in his article “Small Menu Costs and Large Business Cycles: A Macroeconomic Model of Monopoly”, in 1985, these menu costs may lead to a non-socially *optimal situation*. Indeed, *Mankiw’s menu costs model* shows how higher menu costs may lead to a situation where prices remain unchanged, thus provoking so called price stickiness. Contrary to what economists from the *New Classical Macroeconomics* think, which is that *business cycles* are originated by shifts in supply (which originate mainly from technological shocks), *new Keynesian economists* believe that business cycles originate from price stickiness. This price stickiness might be explained by menu costs, since the slow adjustment of the economy may explain business cycles. Price stickiness, the suboptimal adjustment of prices in response to demand shocks, can result in business cycles.

There is a great debate over the following question: are these menu costs large enough to cause business cycles? Mankiw proved in 1985 in his article “Small Menu Costs and Large Business Cycles: A Macroeconomic Model of Monopoly” that sticky

Box II Probable reasons for price and wage stickiness

For price stickiness

i) Coordination failure – each firm waiting for others to change price first
ii) Cost-based pricing with lags
iii) Preference for varying product attributes other than price
iv) Implicit contracts – fairness to customers necessitates
v) Explicit nominal contracts Costly price adjustment – menu costs
vi) Constant marginal cost and constant mark-ups

For wage stickiness

i) Relative wage hypothesis.
ii) Short-term contracts.
iii) Trade union movements.
iv) Avoiding goodwill loss due to wage cut by the firms.
v) Institutional factors like minimum wage law.
vi) Low wage leads to low labour productivity.

prices can be both privately efficient and socially inefficient. In fact, as Mankiw points out, even small menu costs can cause large welfare losses. Later, economists like Daniel Levy demonstrated, using empirical evidence, that these menu costs are indeed large enough to cause business cycles. The authors use store-level data from five multi-store supermarket chains to directly measure menu costs. They find that the menu costs per store at those chains average more than 35% of net profit margins, which may be forming a barrier to price changes. When applying these findings to theoretical models of menu costs, he concludes that these menu costs are large enough to be capable of having macroeconomic significance. Furthermore, they believe that these menu costs may cause considerable nominal rigidity in other industries or markets, thus amplifying the effects on business cycles. These menu costs, they say, vary largely due to local and regional legislation, which may require, for instance, a separate price tag on each item, thus increasing menu costs.

Menu cost has microeconomic foundations to be explained. The new Keynesians countered the new classical as well as real business cycle theoreticians that Keynes is not dead. To that they forwarded the explanations to the business cycles by means of microeconomic foundations. Mankiw uses a static model of a monopoly firm's pricing decision, which starts by setting its price in advance and changes it ex post, incurring a small menu cost. The monopolist faces a constant cost function:

$$C = f(\text{value of output produced}) = f(p \,.\, q) = k \,.\, q \,.\, N \quad \text{......} (18.15)$$

Where C is total nominal cost of production, q is quantity produced, N is level of nominal demand which can be regarded as the overall price level, k is constant, and thus, $q \,.\, N$ is the nominal value of output which is the quantity times overall price.

The inverse demand function faced by the monopolist for the aggregate economy is

$$P = f(q) \, . \, N \ldots\ldots\ldots\ldots\ldots\ldots\ldots\ldots \quad (18.16)$$

Where P is the nominal price of the good produced by the monopolist.

N is a nominal scale variable, which denotes the exogenous level of aggregate demand. It can be regarded, for instance, as the overall price level. C and P increase proportionally to the level of nominal demand N.

Now, let us consider the cost per demand quantity $c = C / N = kqN / N$ and $p = P / N = f(q)N / N = f(q)$, which will turn the firm's problem independent of aggregate demand:

$$p = f(q) \ldots\ldots\ldots\ldots\ldots\ldots \quad (18.17)$$

In Figure 18.7, in the first panel, we see that the consumers' surplus (or social welfare, SW) is the triangular area AkE and in the second panel the producer surplus (profits earned by the firm), is equal to the rectangle between k and p_m. which is $PmFGk$. In the third panel, total surplus, which represents welfare, is the sum of consumer and producer surplus which is $AFGk$ and the magnitude of the dead weight loss (DWL) or the social cost is given by the area FEG.

The firm needs to set its price one period ahead based on expectations about future aggregate demand, being this price p_m . (N^e / N). If expectations are correct ex post, the

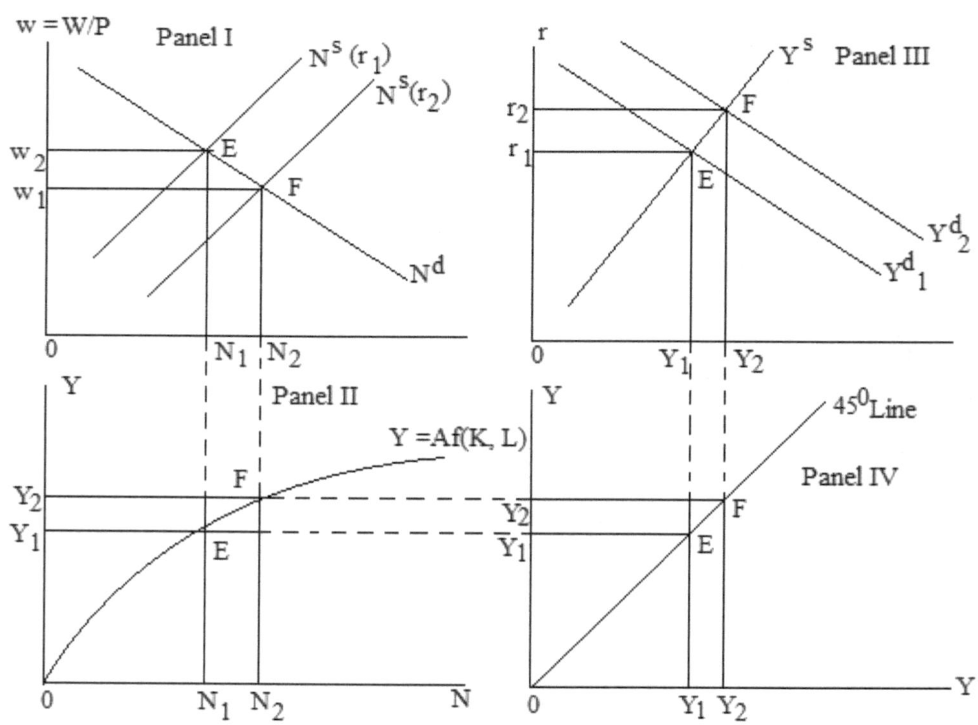

Figure 18.7 Effects of aggregate demand shock

observed price p_0 is p_m. If not, the observed price is $p_0 = p_m(N^e / N)$ where N^e / N is the demand differential due to expectation error and this expectation error leads to fluctuations in the business cycle. An expansion in aggregate demand may either increase welfare or reduce it but never more than the menu cost. On the other hand, a contraction in aggregate demand will reduce welfare, possibly in an amount much larger than the menu cost.

18.2.6.2 Credit rationing and the new Keynesian model

Like the imperfections in the goods and labour markets, the new Keynesians have also examined the consequences of credit market imperfections. Due to the imperfections in the credit or loan market, the risk-averse lenders are influenced to respond to recessions by shifting their portfolio towards safer activities. This behaviour can magnify an economic shock by raising the real costs of intermediation or the banking sector interventions. The resulting credit squeeze can convert a recession into a depression as many equity-constrained borrowers find credit expensive or difficult to obtain, and bankruptcy results. This is due to the fact that high interest rates can increase the probability of default; risk-averse financial institutions frequently resort to credit rationing. Whereas the traditional approach to analysing the monetary transmission mechanism focuses on the interest rate and exchange rate channels, the new paradigm emphasises the various factors that influence the ability of financial institutions to evaluate the credit worthiness of potential borrowers in the scenario of imperfect information. Indeed, in the new paradigm, banks are viewed as risk-averse firms that are constantly engaged in a process of reviewing and monitoring the customers. The situation has close links to the implications of the Great Depression that was caused among others, due to the breakdown of the economy's credit facilities, rather than a decline in the money supply.

Figure 18.8 explains the impact of credit rationing in an imperfect imperfection model. Initially, having no credit market imperfections and no or zero rationing condition, AS_1 and AD_1 were the aggregate supply and demand functions with equilibrium price P^* and output Y_1. An aggregate demand shock due to credit risk induces the aggregate supply curve to shift to the left to AS_0. The price level remains at P^*, even though output falls from Y_1 to Y_0. A shift of the aggregate supply curve to the left as the result of an increase in perceived risk will also shift the demand curve of labour to the left to AD_0. As a result, involuntary unemployment increases without any significant change in the real wage which magnifies the pervasiveness of the recessionary situation.

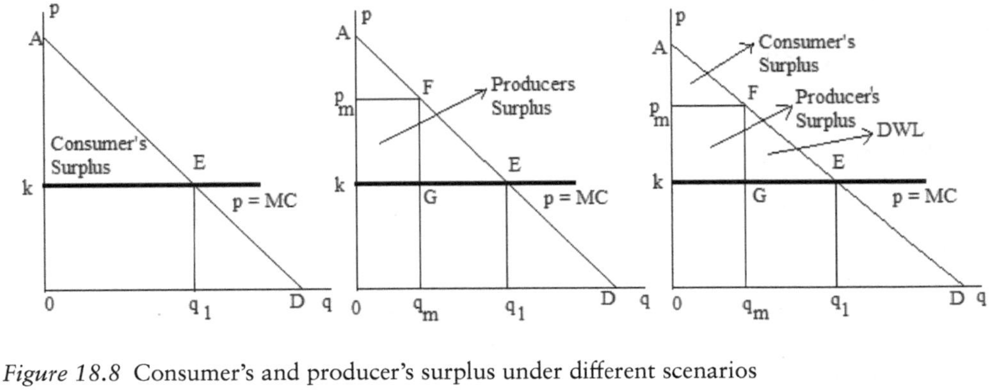

Figure 18.8 Consumer's and producer's surplus under different scenarios

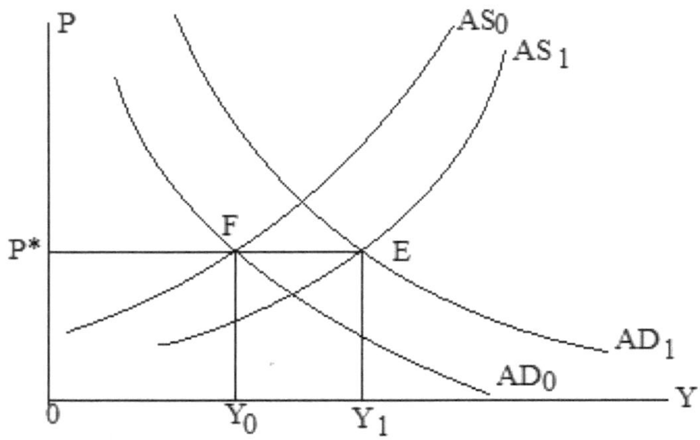

Figure 18.9 Credit shock leads to recession and depression

18.3 Conclusion

In the previous discussions we tried to capture different schools of thought in macroeconomics from the ancient period to the new Keynesian period. We detailed our discussion for the phase from classical to new Keynesian. The classical orthodoxy opined for an automatic full employment system with flexible price conditions. The market always clears there and it was purely a supply side model. The partial followers of the classical model are the monetarists, new classicists, and the real business cycle theoreticians who mainly maintained the long run classical full employment conclusions but they differed in their short run explanations. The new Keynesian economists modified the older Keynesian version and defended the involuntary unemployment problem on the basis of microeconomic foundations where the market fails to work. Further they heavily depended upon active interventions of the government to correct the fluctuation in business cycle.

Summary

The present chapter discussed the essential elements of different schools of thought starting from the classical model. Broadly there are two schools staying fundamentally different – the classical orthodoxy vis-à-vis the Keynesian thought. The subsequent developments of the subject on the basis of fluctuations in business cycle led to different ways of identifying the problems and providing policy suggestions. The essences of the models are as follows:

- Market clearing solution with flexible price, wage, and rate of interest led to automatic full employment output – a purely long run supply-side model of the classical school. Money has no role other than determining price level. It is called neutrality of money.
- Keynes criticised the classical orthodoxy on the grounds of their inability to explain the great depression. He opined for money wage rigidity as the cause of unemployment and prescribed active intervention of the government sector to correct the recessionary phase of the business cycle. Money has a positive role in determining output and employment –money is not neutral. The economy is demand as well as supply

determined. It is a short run model but it matches with the classical model in long run solutions.

- The monetarists criticised the Keynesian school as the latter considered money supply as unstable and argued that most fluctuations in real output were caused by fluctuations in the money supply, rather than by fluctuations in consumption or investment spending. Besides, they concluded that a stable and consistent money supply policy could control price instability; no government intervention was required.
- The new classical school developed the rational expectation model and concluded that people's expectations regarding the future in a rational manner make public policy ineffective.
- Another classical school as well as a partial Keynesian school named the real business cycle theory argued that fluctuations in the business cycle were due to fluctuations in real factors like productivity shocks, environmental degradation, etc. Hence, fiscal or monetary policy does not work in the usual sense, but a mixture of the two policies (known as seigniorage) may be attempted to generate real effect.
- Finally, the new Keynesian approach refined their involuntary unemployment concept and postulated that there is real wage rigidity due to sticky pricing, efficiency wage, etc. which are the causes of involuntary unemployment, and the government is required to correct the fluctuations.

Keywords

Mercantilism
Classical school
Supply side economics
Full employment
Keynesian model
Involuntary unemployment
Demand-side economics
Monetarists
New classical school
Real business cycle model
New Keynesian school

Multiple choice questions and answers

1. According to the mercantilist approach, economic progress depends on
   (a) Stock of capital.
   (b) Earnings of precious metals through trade.
   (c) Growth of the agriculture sector.
   (d) Growth of industrial activity.
2. The classical school of thought depends on Say's law which says that
   (a) Supply creates its own demand.
   (b) Demand creates its own sources of supply.
   (c) The sum of excess demand will be zero.
   (d) None of the above.
3. The concept of involuntary unemployment, according to Keynes, is due to
   (a) Perfectly flexible wage rate.
   (b) Perfectly flexible price level.
   (c) Money wage rigidity.
   (d) All of the above.

4. Under the new classical thought of rational expectation, a monetary policy will be

   (a) Effective always.
   (b) Partially effective.
   (c) Partially ineffective.
   (d) Fully ineffective.

5. The real business cycle model concludes that the fluctuation in output and employment is due to

   (a) Fluctuation in real factors like productivity shocks.
   (b) Fiscal policy misapplication.
   (c) Monetary policy misapplication.
   (d) None of the above.

Answers

1. (b); 2. (a); 3. (c); 4. (d); 5. (a)

Review questions

1. What is bullionism? Point out salient features of the mercantilists approach in establishing a school of thought in economics.
2. Mention basic assumptions of the classical model. Explain how the policy neutrality is explained in the model using the assumptions.
3. Explain wage rigidity in Keynesian line of thought. Explain briefly how different policies are effective under this model. Can increase in money supply lead to increase in price level to the full extent like the classical model? Explain.
4. What are the salient features of the monetarists' model? Can the monetary policy be effective under this model? Discuss. Explain autonomy of monetary authority and try to relate it to the price stabilisation outcomes.
5. What is rational expectation? Explain how the policy ineffectiveness result is justified by the new classical school of thought. What will happen to output and employment if there are unanticipated changes in money supply? Explain.
6. Define productivity shock. Explain how the productivity shocks justify the real business cycle model. Discuss appropriate policy combinations to remove the real shocks from the business cycle.
7. Explain how new Keynesians refined the old Keynesian position of wage rigidity. Can there be still involuntary unemployment and necessity of government intervention in the new Keynesian system? Justify your position.
8. Mention grounds behind the prevalence of sticky money wage in the Keynesian model. Discuss how underemployment equilibrium under Keynes is explained by the sticky money wage condition. Mention some other grounds of underemployment equilibrium under Keynes even if there is wage-price flexibility. Explain the real balance effect in this context.
9. Differentiate between adaptive expectation and rational expectation. Discuss how the rational expectation hypothesis works behind the policy irrelevant results.
10. Define menu cost. How are the imperfect market conditions explain under employment equilibrium in the New Keynesian set up?

Additional readings

Alesina, A. & Gatti, R. (1995). "Independent central banks: Low inflation at no cost?" *American Economic Review*, 85(2), 196–200.
Alesina, A. & Summers, L. H. (1993). "Central bank independence and 712 modern macroeconomics macroeconomic performance: Some comparative evidence". *Journal of Money, Credit, and Banking*, 25(2), 151–162.

Part V

Open economy macroeconomics

19 Open economy macroeconomics – concepts and applications

19.1 Introduction

In the progress of discussion on different macroeconomic issues in the preceding chapters so far, we were confined to the determination of aggregate output, employment, interest rates, and price level within a single economy which we termed domestic economy. Whatever was produced by the existing or available resources in the economy was consumed or used by the aggregated forms of different sectors/institutions within the economy. If there was overproduction or underproduction the domestic economy had to destroy them or some part of the population remained underserved or there was an unsatisfied demand. This domestic closed economic position is called autarky where no cross-border flow (both inflow and outflow) of goods and services were allowed. This is another way to say that the domestic economy did not have international linkages or trading relations with the foreign countries. The present chapter will address the conceptual issues related to the open economic relevance to the determinations of prime macro variables in both the domestic (or home) country and the rest of the world called together as foreign countries.

Now we need to analyse why there should be trading or exchanges of goods and services between a home country and a foreign country. From the general equilibrium model of exchange we know that a home country, say India, makes exchange of one good with another good of the foreign country, say the USA, when there arise three possibilities: the first is due to the differences in endowments, the second is due to differences in preferences, and the third is due to the differences in both endowments and preferences. By the term "endowment difference" we mean the differences in the stock of the goods held by both India and the USA. For example, there are two goods, jewellery and software. India has relatively more stock of jewellery than the USA and the USA has relatively more stock of software than India. Hence, India needs more software from the USA and the USA needs more jewellery from India. Therefore, there will be a flow of jewellery from India to the USA which is called *export* from India and flow of software from the USA to India which is called *import* to India. We can reversely say that there is *import* of jewellery and *export* of software by the USA. Again by the term "preference difference" we mean the differences in the desire to consume the goods by both India and the USA. Suppose the USA gets more satisfaction from consumption of jewellery than that of software and India gets more satisfaction from consumption of software than that of jewellery. Under the equal endowments of both the goods, the USA will thus need more jewellery from India and India will thus need more software from the USA. Again there are exports and imports of both the goods in opposite directions. Finally, there may be differences in

DOI: 10.4324/9781003501138-24

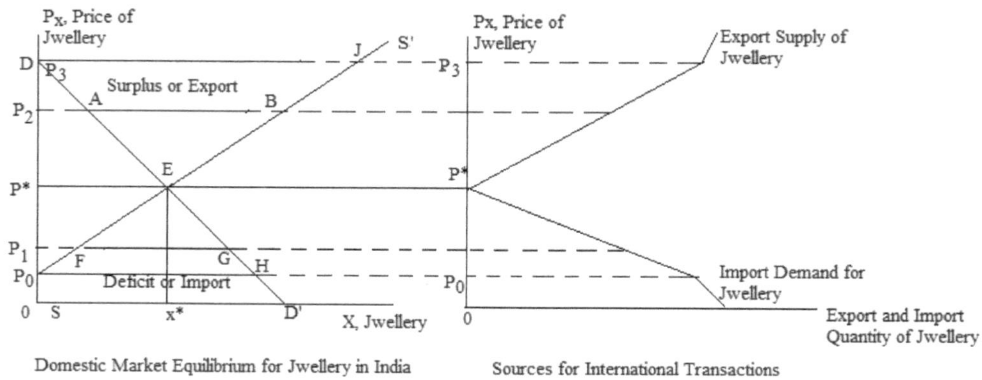

Figure 19.1 Scopes for export and import

both endowments and preference that may again lead to exports and imports in opposite directions. That means the home country is linked up with the foreign country by means of opening up of the intercountry boundaries.

Let us see how the magnitudes of export supply (or supply of exportables) and import demand (or demand for importables) are generated by the conditions of home markets' equilibrium for both the goods. Figure 19.1 illustrates this. The left side of the figure presents the market equilibrium and disequilibrium situation of the home country for the jewellery product. We see that the home market for jewellery is cleared at point E corresponding to the price P^*; neither the consumers nor the producers of the home country are dissatisfied with the price P^* and the optimum quantity bought and sold by the domestic consumers and producers is x^*. No question of cross border flow of jewellery is required by the home or the foreign country. So, the quantity of export and import is zero at P^*.

Now suppose there are deviations from the equilibrium point E towards any price greater or lesser than P^*. At any price greater than P^*, say at P_2, we find that the home (Indian) consumers demand P_2A amount but the home suppliers supply P_2B ($P_2B > P_2A$) of jewellery. That means, at that price, there is a surplus of jewellery of the amount AB which should be destroyed (or preserved in the stock room) if the autarky situation is considered. But the amount AB may be opened to the foreign (or US customers) consumers since their home endowment of jewellery is relatively low and hence its price is high. Hence, any excess quantity of jewellery in the Indian market over the price P^* can be termed as the schedule of export supply to the US consumers. It will start from P^* and is an upward sloping function, meaning that as domestic price of the good increases, the quantity of export will increase and vice versa (right part of the figure). Again, at any price smaller than P^*, say at P_1, we find that the home (Indian) consumers demand P_1G amount but the home suppliers supply P_1F ($P_1G > P_1F$) of jewellery. That means, at that price, there is a deficit of jewellery of the amount GF which should be unmet (or will be cleared from the stock room) if the autarky situation is considered. But the amount GF may be opened to be taken from any other foreign (except US) producers who have relatively more endowments of jewellery. Hence, we have a negatively sloped import demand schedule starting from price P^*. As the domestic price becomes lower and lower the demand for import will be higher and higher and vice versa (right part of the figure). If the price falls below $P0$ then no domestic suppliers will produce jewellery and the entire amount of demand (the falling part of the demand function *H* will coincide with the import demand function. It is thus relatively steeper than the import demand function above H where the domestic competing producers were producing a part of the home market demand for jewellery. On the other hand, any price above P_3 will allow the domestic suppliers to fully export jewellery to the foreign country and hence the upper part of the supply function from *J* will coincide with the export supply function. The same analysis can be done for the software product in the USA as their home market and India as the foreign market. Hence, the international linkages of the home country are started through the export and import channels. There may be exports or imports of goods or services and financial capitals.

Now a natural question arises: *how much will an importing country pay for the imported goods?* To have answers to this question we need to understand how the pricing of goods in the international market is adjusted with the currency values of the home country (i.e. importing country, say) vis-à-vis that of the foreign country (i.e. exporting country).

Referring to our example, India imports software from the USA. India will have to pay for US software at the price set by the US firms of the software industry. Suppose the price of software per unit in the US market is \$100 (\$ is the currency symbol of the US dollar). India will have to pay \$100 for each unit of imported software to the US companies. But India has its own currency, Rupee. How to get \$ from an Indian citizen? Now the concept that arises is the exchange rate. *Exchange rate* is the rate at which one currency is exchanged for the other. For example, the average exchange rate of one unit of \$ is Rs. 66 in the year 2016. That means, if any Indian has Rs. 66, he is entitled to get one \$ by exchange. On the other hand, the exchange rate of Rs. 1 in terms of \$ is 1/66 = \$0.015 = 1.5 cent. Comparison of the two currencies makes it clear that US dollar is a much stronger currency than the Indian Rupee. Now the Indians will have to pay \$100 = 66 * 100 = Rs. 6,600 for one unit of the software. Hence, pricing of the internationally traded goods and services is done by the adjustments of exchange rates of the currencies of the trading countries.

Box I Elasticity of demand for and supply of import

How much of import demand is influenced by the price of import item, and in reverse, the supply of import items that depends on the elasticity of import demand and import supply functions? Elastic import demand function is when increase in the imported good's price makes significant fall in the import demand and vice-versa. The import demand function is relatively flatter. On the other hand, if an increase in price of the imported good creates an insignificant fall in the demand for the imported good and vice-versa, then the import demand function is inelastic and the import demand function is relatively steeper. When do these conditions prevail? If the domestic country has different import opportunities from different countries of the same product as well as with many import competing industries, then the import demand function is relatively elastic. This phenomenon is usually observed in trading among industrially developed countries – *horizontal trade linkage*. On the other hand, if the importing country is less developed or developing with low degrees of (or limited) import substitutability, then increase in import price may not reduce the import demand at a greater extent and hence the import bill will rise. In the extreme case, if the domestic country is fully import-dependent like crude oil demand by India, then the import demand function will be perfectly inelastic or vertical. This is called *vertical trade linkage*. The left side of the following figure presents these different import demand functions.

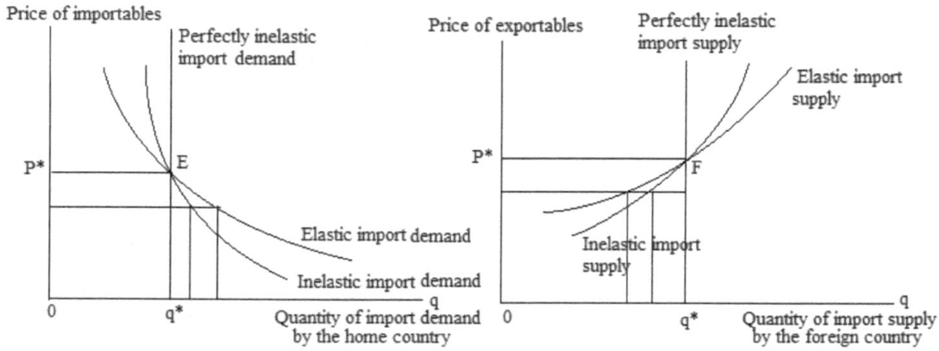

On the other hand, from the point of view of the suppliers of the import items (which is actually the supply of export items by the foreign country to the home country), we can see the similar types of elasticities but in line with supply functions, not with demand functions. If the exporting country, the USA in our example, has a variety of options to export the software products to different countries besides India, then the USA's supply elasticity of importables to India will be elastic. And if the USA has a limited option to sell the software products to other countries and they have to heavily depend on India, then the supply function will be relatively inelastic. Again in the extreme case, if the USA has a huge stock of software and it has no other market besides India, then it has to supply the product to India at any price. This is the situation of perfectly inelastic supply of importable items. The situations have been presented on the right side of the previous diagram.

Now there are questions on how the exchange rate is set and where from the foreign currencies available. Setting up the exchange rates between two or more currencies is done in two ways – one is by the monetary authority or the central banks of the countries and the other is by the equilibrium in the foreign exchange markets. The first one is called the *fixed exchange (or pegged) rate system* and the second one is the *floating (or variable) exchange rate system*. A fixed exchange rate denotes a nominal exchange rate that is set firmly by the monetary authority led by the central bank of a country with respect to a foreign currency or a set of foreign currencies. By contrast, a floating exchange rate is determined in foreign exchange markets depending on the interactions of demands for and supplies of foreign exchanges.

The central bank of a country procures or preserves different foreign currencies with greater acceptability like the US dollar, the euro of the European Union, pound sterling of Great Britain, etc. by its own management system. The central bank continuously takes part in the foreign exchange market for buying (that is selling of its own currency) and selling (that is buying of its own currency) of foreign currency, say \$. Once there is excess demand for \$ (or excess supply of Rupee), the price of \$ will go up which will destabilise the forex (i.e. foreign exchange) market, the central bank will start selling $ from its reserve, and as a result the price of $ per Rupee will go down or the Rupee will become more valuable. On the other hand, if there is excess supply of $ (or excess demand for Rupee), the central bank will start buying $ from the market and as a result the price of $ per Rupee will go up or the Rupee will become less valuable.

One thing now is clear: *a country needs foreign currency when it goes for import demand and earns foreign currency when it makes export supply to the foreign country.* Further, it is to note from our earlier discussion that when there is deficit in the domestic country for availability of the good there arises the possibility of importing the product from the foreign country and when there is surplus of the good in the domestic country then it goes for export supply. Hence, deficit in the domestic country for the good means there is demand for foreign exchange, and when there is surplus of the good in the domestic country there is supply of foreign exchange. Hence, the terms deficit/import demand and surplus/export supply are synonymous with the concepts of demand for and supply of foreign exchange respectively.

19.2 Exchange rate system

The *exchange rate system* is the system of setting the value of one country's currency with respect to the currencies of the other countries with whom the international flows of goods and services are made. We have also pointed out that there are fixed exchange rate and floating exchange rate systems where the former is managed by the central bank of the country and the latter is done by the interactions of demand and supply of exchange rate. Before discussing them in detail, we should know about the history of the exchange rate system. For centuries, the currencies of the world were backed by gold. In the 1930s, the US monetary authority set the value of the dollar at a single and fixed level in the way that one ounce of gold was worth $35. After World War II, other countries valued their own currencies on the US dollar (USD). Since USD was valued in gold, the value of any other currency against the dollar was also based on its value in gold. That means a currency worth thrice as much gold as a USD was, therefore, also worth three USD. But the USD suffered from inflation (that means its value decreased), while other currencies became more valuable and more stable. The pound sterling of the UK emerged as the leading and valuable currency over the USD. Eventually, the US Government officially reduced the value of $ to half so that one ounce of gold was then worth $70. Finally, in 1971, the USA took away the gold standard altogether. This meant that the dollar no longer represented an actual amount of a precious substance; market forces alone determined its value. From the end of the World War II and to date the global economy has faced two types of exchange systems – the fixed exchange rate system from 1944 to 1973 and the floating or flexible exchange rate system from 1973 to date. Besides, there is a third concept sometimes used by the countries or trading partners which is known as the hybrid exchange rate systems that is some mixtures of fixed and flexible exchange rate systems.

19.2.1 *Fixed exchange rate system — intervention by the central bank* — sterilisation

A fixed exchange rate is a country's exchange rate regime under which the government or central bank ties the official exchange rate to another country's currency or to the price of gold. The purpose of a fixed exchange rate system is to maintain a country's currency value within a very narrow band containing the ranges of deviations from the settled fixed exchange rates across the countries' currencies. Hence, the central banks of the countries have the role, which is called *intervention*, to manage the exchange rate around a pegged rate for any sort of deficit or surplus in the foreign currencies arising out of the international flow of goods and services. Fixed exchange rates provide greater certainty for exporters and importers, which also help the government to maintain low inflation, which in the long run will tend to keep interest rates down and stimulate increased trade and investment. Major industrialised nations have shifted to the flexible exchange rate systems since the early 1970s, while developing economies like India continue to have fixed exchange rate systems. Today, most fixed exchange rates are pegged to the US dollar because the dollar is used for most transactions in international trade. Besides, the dollar is used as the world's reserve currency. Countries also fix their currencies to that of their most frequent trading partners. Presently, according to Investment Frontier, (visitwww.investmentfrontier.com) 36 countries have pegged their home currency with different leading currencies like the US dollar and the Euro and some of the regional currencies. Most of them fall into the African region. The sample countries in the list are Cameroon, Gabon, Ivory Coast, Namibia, Niger, etc. and surprisingly most of them pegged their home currencies with the Euro. There are the countries like Hong Kong, Jordon, Cuba, and Venezuela who have fixed exchange rates with the US Dollar. We have presented here the fixed exchange rate scenario of the selected countries for the period 1950–1973 where the home currencies have been pegged around a band with respect to the US Dollar. Table 19.1 and Figure 19.2 present the data for the pre-floating rate regime for the UK, Italy, Japan, Korea, China, India, and Indonesia vis-à-vis USD. The column

Table 19.1 Pre-floating rate regime

Year	*USA*	*UK*	*Italy*	*China*	*India*	*Japan*	*Korea*	*Indonesia*
1950	1	0.357143	0.322584		4.7619	361.1	2.5	
1951	1	0.357143	0.322786		4.7619	361.1	6	
1952	1	0.357143	0.322786		4.7619	361.1	6	
1953	1	0.357143	0.322786		4.7619	360	18	
1954	1	0.357143	0.322786		4.7619	360	18	
1955	1	0.357143	0.322786		4.7619	360	50	
1956	1	0.357143	0.322786		4.7619	360	50	
1957	1	0.357143	0.322786	2.461809	4.7619	360	50	
1958	1	0.357143	0.322651	2.461809	4.7619	360	50	
1959	1	0.357143	0.320764	2.461809	4.7619	360	50	
1960	1	0.357143	0.322263	2.461809	4.7619	360	63.125	
1961	1	0.357143	0.322786	2.461809	4.7619	360	124.7917	
1962	1	0.357143	0.322786	2.461809	4.7619	360	130	
1963	1	0.357143	0.322786	2.461809	4.7619	360	130	
1964	1	0.357143	0.322786	2.461809	4.7619	360	213.8467	
1965	1	0.357143	0.322786	2.461809	4.7619	360	266.4008	
1966	1	0.357143	0.322786	2.461809	6.359125	360	271.3375	
1967	1	0.362103	0.322786	2.461809	7.5	360	270.5167	149.58333
1968	1	0.416667	0.322786	2.461809	7.5	360	276.645	296.29167
1969	1	0.416667	0.322786	2.461809	7.5	360	288.1608	326
1970	1	0.416667	0.322786	2.461809	7.5	360	310.5558	362.83333
1971	1	0.41092	0.320389	2.461809	7.491935	350.6777	347.1475	391.875
1972	1	0.40039	0.301207	2.245067	7.594468	303.1725	392.8942	415
1973	1	0.408171	0.3011	1.989416	7.742039	271.71	398.3217	415

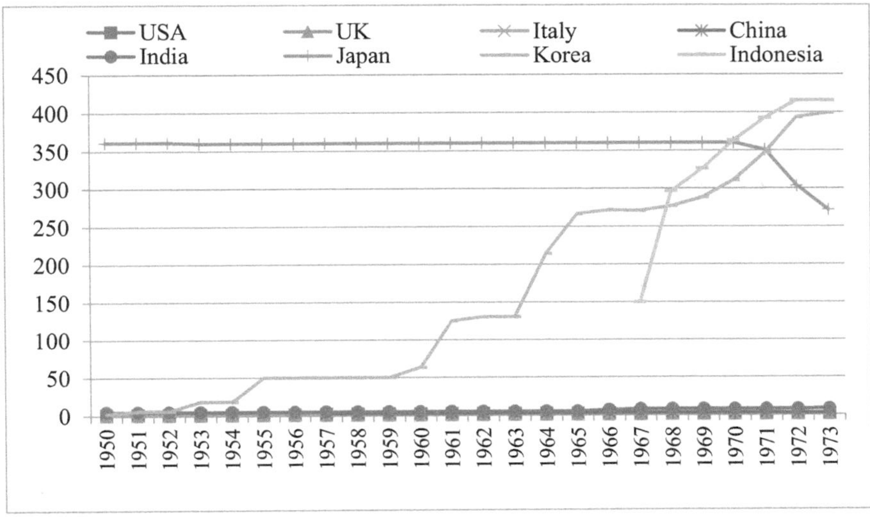

Figure 19.2 Pre-floating rate regime

for the USA in the table gives the value of 1 for all the years, which means the USD measures the other currencies, not the vice versa. The data for China and Indonesia are not available from the year 1950. All countries except Korea and Indonesia highly adjusted the exchange rate over time. Even India with other giants like the UK, Italy, Japan, and China, maintained a stable rate of its home currency with respect to USD at least up to 1965; thereafter, indication of fluctuation started.

Figure 19.2 diagrammatically presents the trends of the exchange rates of the countries during the regime of Bretton Wood Agreement which show that the series for Korea from the beginning and Indonesia from 1967 are rising by leaps and bounds. That means, the value of their home currencies, *Won* and *Rupiah* respectively, degraded with USD over time. That further means, their products became cheaper in the international market. Japan's *Yen* started improving since 1971 after maintaining a stable rate over time from the beginning.

19.2.1.1 Mechanisms of a fixed exchange system

Now we need to discuss how the fixed exchange rate system works and what mechanisms the central banks apply to peg it around a band. At first one thing the readers should know is that export of goods means inflow or earning of foreign currency, say USD, and import of goods means loss or outflow of foreign currency. Once USD comes through the business houses, they will sell it in the domestic market to convert it into home currency, say Rupee, to make payments for factors of the home country. The central bank (say the Reserve Bank of India, RBI) will then purchase USD at the fixed or pegged rate and sell the Rupee. That means inflow of USD means increase in supply of Rupee or supply of domestic money. In the reverse, as import demand rises, the businesses will demand more USD, so the central bank then will supply USD in exchange for Rupee from its reserve and thus the supply of Rupee will fall. Hence, there is a relation between demand (supply) for foreign currency and supply (demand) of home currency or simply supply (demand) of money. Also, it is clear why the central banks of the countries do reserve foreign currencies.

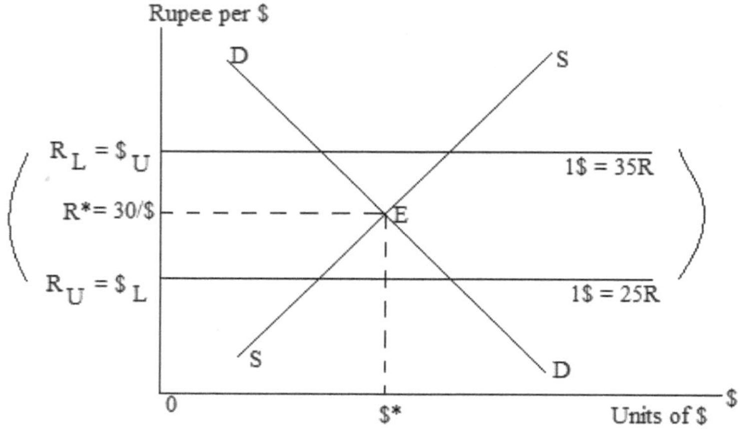

Figure 19.3 Fixed exchange rate system in a demand-supply model

Figure 19.3 presents the basic structure of a fixed exchange rate system in a classical demand-supply model of foreign currency, $, in respect to Rupees. *DD* is the demand for $ which is negatively sloped (since as Rupee for $ falls, that is, fewer Rupees are forgone for one unit of $, demand for more dollar rises, and vice versa) and *SS* is the supply of $ by the central bank which is positively sloped (since as Rupee for $ rises, that is more Rupees are forgone for one unit of $, supply of the dollar rises, and vice versa). Suppose, the RBI institutionally fixes Rs. 30 for one unit of $ depending on the existing demand for the dollar by the importers and the supply of the dollar by the reserve of $ itself. In the fixed exchange rate system, the preannounced rate may not coincide with the market equilibrium exchange rate. The central banks maintain reserves of foreign currencies which they can sell in order to intervene in the foreign exchange market to make up the excess demand or take up the excess supply. *E* is the equilibrium where R^* (= 30) units of rupee per dollar will balance $\$^*$ units of demand for and supply of the dollar. Importers and exporters make conversion of the home currency at the rate of R^*. If the RBI wants to increase the value of the Rupee to 25 per dollar, then it is called *revaluation* of the Rupee or *devaluation* of the dollar. Suppose Rs. 25 is the upper limit (R_U) of conversion of Rupees into dollars and it is also the lower limit ($\$_L$) of the dollar. On the other hand, if the RBI wants to decrease the value of Rupee to 35 per dollar, then it is called *devaluation* of the rupee or *revaluation* of the dollar. Suppose Rs. 35 is the lower limit (R_L) of conversion of the Rupee into the dollar and it is also the upper limit ($\$_U$) of the dollar. Hence, R^* lies within a band of exchange rate inside which the Rupee can be converted; no deviation over and under will be made by the central bank unless it is desired in any crisis. Therefore, we say that the exchange rate is fixed around a band indicated by the ( ) mark in the figure.

19.2.1.2 *Parametric effects*

Suppose the RBI wants to maintain the Rupee–dollar conversion rates within the band of Rs. 25 and Rs. 35. Also suppose that, within this framework, the parameters related to demand for dollar (or import) and parameters related to supply of dollar (or export)

get changed. One of the parameters for extra demand for the dollar is increase in income of the home country, India, and one of the parameters for extra supply of the dollar is increase in income of the foreign country, USA. A central bank maintains a fixed exchange rate by either buying or selling its own currency in the open market. If the exchange rate drifts too far above the fixed benchmark rate, then the central bank sells its own currency and buys foreign currency. This causes the price of the currency to decrease in value (devaluation). On the other hand, if it buys the currency it is pegged to, then the price of that currency will increase, causing the relative value of the currencies to be closer to the intended relative value (revaluation). If the exchange rate drifts too far below the desired rate, the government buys its own currency in the market by selling its reserves. This places greater demand on the market and causes the local currency to become stronger, hopefully back to its intended value. The reserves they sell may be the currency it is pegged to, in which case the value of that currency will fall.

We explain these two parametric effects upon the fixed exchange rate of rupee per dollar. Figure 19.4 presents the two situations.

First consider the effect of excess demand for the dollar. If the demand for the dollar rises from *DD* to *D'D'*, then G is the point where demand for and supply of the dollar meet, and at that point, the Rupee reaches its lower limit of 35, although the effect of excess demand falls within the band of 25–35. Therefore, excess demand for the dollar does not motivate the RBI to intervene into the exchange rate determination. But, if the magnitude of excess demand is very large, say by *D"D"* amount (the thick line), then the real magnitude of excess demand or the excess demand that influences the central bank to intervene is *GH*. The RBI will then sell *GH* units of extra dollars in exchange for Rupee to maintain the limit within the band. When the RBI sells out dollars in this manner, its official reserves of dollar will decline and domestic money supply will shrink (since sale of dollar means purchase of rupee). To prevent this dwindling money supply in the domestic market, the RBI may purchase government bonds (means supply of money) and thus meet the shortfall in money supply. This particular type of intervention is called *sterilisation* (a form of monetary action in which a central bank seeks to limit the effect

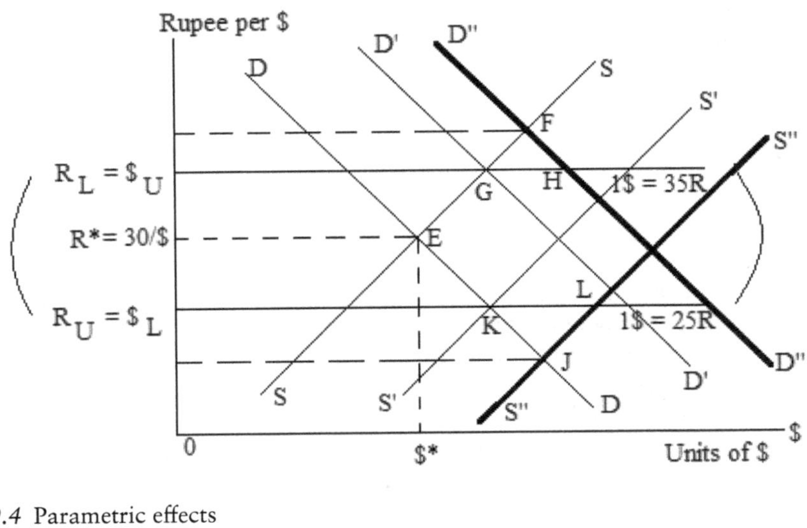

Figure 19.4 Parametric effects

of inflows and outflows of capital on the money supply by means of open market operations and is designed to offset the effect of foreign exchange intervention) in the foreign exchange market. But there may be *unsterilised* intervention which means the RBI will not go for open market operations and thus keep the short fall of money supply intact.

What happens if the rupee goes down in its value in terms of dollar at a greater magnitude? If such a thing happens then the central bank has to devalue its home currency in order to reduce the excess demand for dollars, which is, narrow the gap between the equilibrium and fixed rates (we will come to this in greater detail later).

Now consider the effect of excess supply of dollars. If the magnitude of excess demand is $S''S''$ then there is no need for the central bank to intervene. But excess supply by means of $S''S''$(= KL in the diagram) leads the central bank to purchase more dollars. That means, the price of the dollar will fall and the price of the Rupee will go up and the band ultimately will be maintained by the intervention. Again, any uncontrolled excess supply of the dollar may allow the central bank of the country to revalue its home currency (we will discuss the effect of revaluation later).

19.2.1.3 Relation among domestic credit, money supply, and international reserves

As per the Keynesian and monetarists' versions, the demand for money is positively dependent upon real income (Y) and negatively upon real rate of interest (r). The function looks like the following-

$$M^d = f(Y, r) \tag{19.1}$$

Here M^d is the demand for real balances. On the other hand, the money supply (M^s) function looks like

$$M^s = D + R \tag{19.2}$$

The supply of money is equal to the sum of domestic credit (that is, money created domestically = D) and money associated with changes in international reserves or the forex reserves (R). Any increase in domestic credit will be matched by an equal reduction in foreign exchange reserves, with no effect on the money supply. The money market will be in equilibrium when M^d must be equal to M^s so that:

$$M^d = D + R$$
$$\text{or } R = M^d - D \tag{19.3}$$

The forex reserves vary positively with demand for money and negatively with domestic credit.

From the previous monetary relations it is obvious that, in the case of a small country maintaining a fixed exchange rate with the rest of the world, the country's money supply becomes an endogenous variable, not an exogenous variable. Other things remaining the same, a balance of payments deficit leads to a reduction in a country's foreign exchange reserves and the domestic money supply and vice versa. In other words, where the monetary authorities follow a fixed exchange regime, changes in the money supply can arise not only from domestic sources (that is, domestic credit) but also from a balance of payments intervention policy to maintain a fixed exchange rate. From the money supply equation ($M^s = D + R$) it is revealed that domestic monetary policy only determines the division of the country's money supply between domestic credit and foreign exchange reserves, not the money supply itself. Other things remaining the same, any increase in domestic credit will be matched by an equal reduction in foreign exchange reserves, with no effect on the money supply which will have no influence on the domestic rate of inflation, interest rates, or the rate of growth of output. Monetary policy, in a small open economy, is thus completely impotent to influence any variable, other than foreign exchange reserves, in the long run. Domestic monetary expansion will have no influence on the domestic rate of inflation, interest rates, or the rate of growth of output; however, it can influence the rate of world monetary expansion and world inflation.

19.2.2 Flexible exchange rate system

The Bretton Woods Agreement was halted in the early 70s because the US economy suffered deficits in international transactions starting from the late 50s after maintaining surplus in the post-war phases. Periodic adjustments of $ vis-à-vis other leading currencies like pound sterling proved insufficient to pull the economy out from such deficits. The then President of USA, Richard Nixon, took the United States off the gold standard in 1973 and ushered in the era of flexible or floating exchange rates where the central bank will have no command in fixing the exchange rates; rather the market economic system will decide the rate of exchange in a demand-supply interaction mechanism. Any excess demand or supply of foreign exchange will automatically be adjusted like what we see in the price determination of a particular good in microeconomics.

Box II Collapse of Bretton Woods Accord

Soon after the Bretton Woods Accord, the US economy was making surplus in international trades with the negotiated countries. But by the late 50s and early 60s, the US dollar's fixed value against gold was seen as overvalued. A sizable increase in domestic spending on President Lyndon Johnson's Great Society programs and a rise in military spending caused by the Vietnam War gradually worsened the overvaluation of the dollar. In August 1971, US President Richard Nixon announced the temporary suspension of the dollar's convertibility into gold. While the dollar had struggled throughout most of the 1960s within the parity established at Bretton Woods, this crisis marked the breakdown of the system. An attempt to revive the fixed exchange rates failed, and by March 1973 the major currencies began to float against each other. Since the collapse of the Bretton Woods system, IMF members have been free to choose any form of exchange arrangement they wish and allow the currency to float freely.

In Figure 19.5 we have presented the mechanisms of a flexible exchange rate system in any country, say for India. Suppose, initially, the demand and supply functions for foreign exchange, US Dollar, are DD and SS respectively. The exchange market equilibrium occurs at point E where R^* is the equilibrium unit of Rupee required for one unit of $. Suppose this is Rs. 30/$ (i.e. 30 Rupees per dollar). There is no disagreement between the demand for

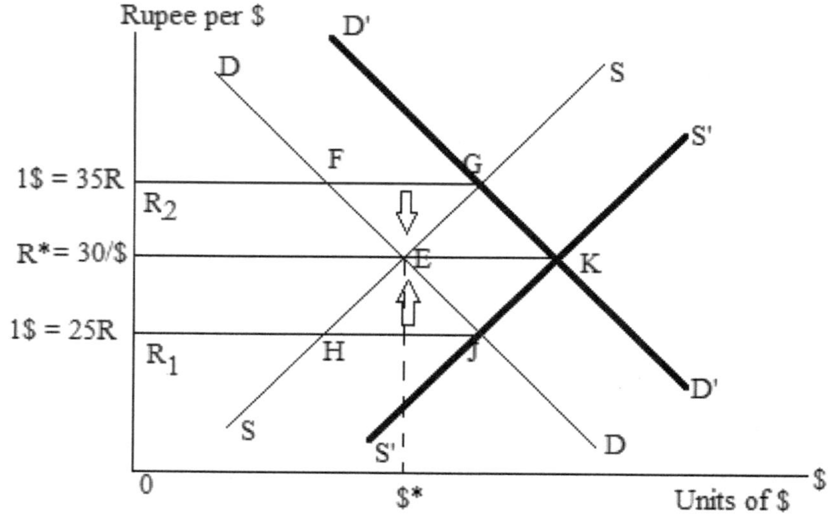

Figure 19.5 Mechanism of flexible exchange rate

dollar – that is the importers of goods and services in the home country from abroad – and the suppliers of dollar, that is, the exporters of goods and services to the foreign country. *E* is a stable equilibrium point in the sense that any deviation from it is brought back and the movements are shown by the arrows. Below *E*, there is excess demand (= *HJ* amount) for the dollar which makes the exchange rate rise from Rs. 25 to Rs. 30. This increase of exchange rate is called *appreciation* of the dollar or *depreciation* of the rupee. On the other hand, above *E*, there is excess supply (= *FG* amount) of the dollar which leads to fall in exchange rate from Rs. 35 to Rs. 30. That means, the Rupee appreciates and the dollar depreciates. Note that in the flexible exchange rate system we use depreciation (appreciation) of currency, not devaluation (revaluation) which is used in a fixed system.

We can also analyse the parametric changes in the same diagram. Suppose there is excess demand for the dollar with no change in supply of the dollar. The new demand curve shifts rightward to *D'D'*. *G* is the new equilibrium point where we see that the equilibrium exchange rate increased to R_2. On the other hand, if a greater supply of dollar occurs, then *J* will be the new equilibrium where the market adjustment will pull down the exchange rate to R_1. Finally, suppose that there are equal magnitudes of increase in demand for and supply of the dollar by both the importers and exporters (it is the situation when volume of trade of the concerned country increases). The new equilibrium will be at *K* where there is neither appreciation nor depreciation of foreign exchange, only the quantity of dollar-transacted increases to $R * K$. The readers can also verify that there will be different exchange rates if the magnitudes of shifting of demand and supply function for the foreign exchange are different.

19.2.2.1 *Clean floating vs. dirty floating*

A flexible exchange system does not necessarily imply the exchange market will operate in a freehand mechanism. Sometimes there are controls or management by the central bank of a country of the free movements of free exchange rates to avoid any sort of anticipated BOP imbalance. That means we have two subcategories under the flexible exchange rate – one is clean floating and the other is dirty or managed floating. When the exchange market fully adjusts, there are changes in excess demand for or supply of foreign exchange by means of currency depreciation and appreciation. No intervention, however, is required by the home country's central bank. That means the market exchange rate wipes out any excess demand for and excess supply of the foreign currency. Based on this logic, a clean floating system makes the BOP always in balance, i.e. neither in a deficit nor in a surplus. On the other hand, in a dirty or managed floating system, the free market mechanisms for exchange rate adjustments are barred by the central bank of the country; it allows partial flexibility in the exchange rate market. Most of the developed countries followed the dirty floating exchange system after the collapse of the Bretton Woods accord in the early 70s. Unstable behaviour of the economic fundamentals forced them to manage their flexible exchange systems.

19.2.2.2 Trends of exchange rates in the floating exchange system of selected countries

Here we present the trends of exchange rates of the selected countries, as mentioned in the fixed exchange system, for the period of 1974 onwards that captures the flexible exchange systems for most of the countries in the world. All the currencies of the selected countries have been expressed in terms of USD. Figures 20.6, 20.7, and 20.8 present the series for the UK, Italy, Japan, Korea, China, India, and Indonesia. We observe that the UK's pound sterling and Italy's lira have similar types of movements over time with respect to $. Both the trends are rising which means, in an overall sense, they have depreciated with $ over time, although there are some fluctuations at short term phases. For example (refer to Figure 20.6), there are depreciation phases during 1974–1977, 1980–1985 (steep depression), 1992–2001, and 2008–2016. Again there are the phases of appreciation of the Pound and Lira during 1977–1980, 1985–1992, and 2001–2008.

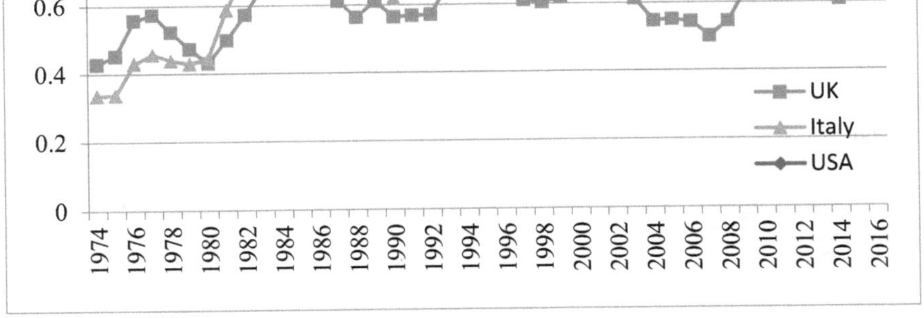

Figure 19.6 Trends of flexible exchange rates of countries

The series for India (refer to Figure 19.7) shows sustained depreciation of Rupee over time with minor improvements during 2002–07 while China has depreciation phase up to 1994 and maintained stability of Yuan during 1994–2005 and then improved against dollar. China's trade surplus during the phase has been accountable for this appreciation and that became one of the concerns of the US Government against China.

The series for Japan's yen (refer to Figure 19.8) has been appreciating over time against $ while for Korea, the won has been depreciating over time. But there is a huge

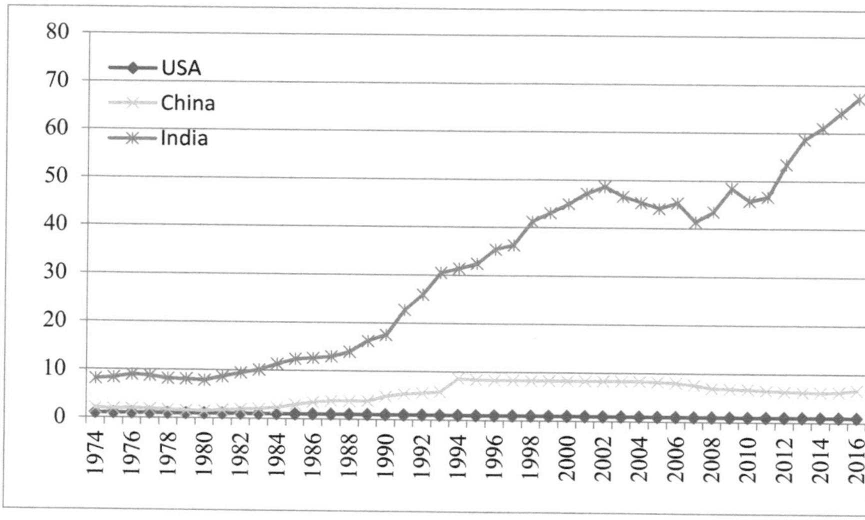

Figure 19.7 Trends of flexible exchange rates of countries

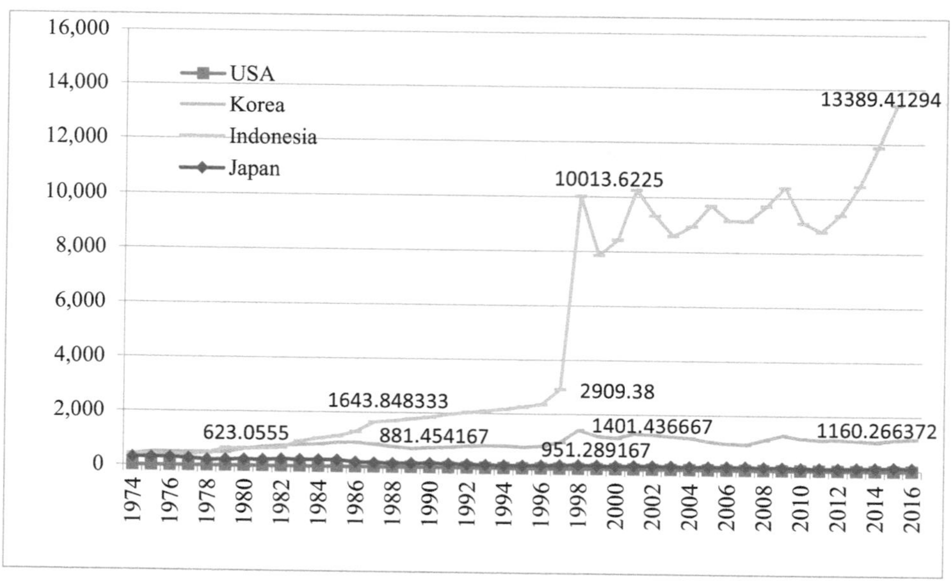

Figure 19.8 Trends of flexible exchange rates of countries

depreciation of Indonesia's Rupiah over time and there as a jump of depreciation on the magnitudes of 2,909 to 10,013 during 1997–1998. That particular jump has been related to the East Asia Financial Crisis (see Box III) that originated from the huge devaluation of Thailand's baht by 15–20% against the dollar in the early phase of 1997.

Box III East Asian financial crisis

The Asian financial crisis or the East Asian Crisis or the Asian Contagion was a period of financial crisis that gripped much of East Asia beginning in July 1997 which started in Thailand with the financial collapse of the Thai baht after the Thai government was forced to float the baht due to lack of foreign currency to support its currency peg to the US dollar. At the time, Thailand had acquired a burden of foreign debt that made the country effectively bankrupt even before the collapse of its currency. As a result of the devaluation of Thailand's baht, a large portion of East Asian currencies fell by as much as 38%. International stocks also declined as much as 60%. As the crisis spread, most of Southeast Asia and Japan saw slumping currencies, devalued stock markets and other asset prices, and a precipitous rise in private debt. The worst-hit countries of this crisis were Indonesia, South Korea, and Thailand. Relatively less-affected countries were Hong Kong, Malaysia, and the Philippines. Besides, there was a list of countries in the other Asian Zone along with some countries from the industrialised zone (USA, Europe, and Russia particularly) that were also hurt by the recession created by the crisis. The International Monetary Fund and the World Bank had to intervene and managed the turbulent situation.

19.2.3 Hybrid exchange systems

Both the fixed and flexible exchange rates are two polar extremes in the cross-country currency exchange system in the sense that in the former, the central bank has the exclusive power (institutional rigidities) to peg the home currency, and in the latter, the free market has to solve the exchange rate determination problem without considering the other fundamentals for the trading countries and it welcomes volatility in the exchange markets. Therefore, sometimes the countries choose a mixture of these two extremes in fixing their home currencies with the leading currencies. That particular form of exchange system is known a *hybrid exchange system*. Hybrid exchange systems have developed in order to combine the characteristics features of fixed and flexible exchange rate systems. They allow fluctuation of the exchange rates without completely exposing the currency to the flexibility of a free float. More specifically, under this system, the home currencies value is set at par with the weighted average of the basket of leading currencies. For example, India's five major trading partners during 2014–2015 are China, the USA, the UAE, Saudi Arabia, and Switzerland and their total trade volumes in millions of USD have been presented in Table 19.2. Here the basket of leading currencies is yuan, dollar, dirham, riyal and Swiss franc. We have calculated the concentration ratio (or weight of the currencies) by dividing the total volume of trade with the country (TRi, $i = 1, 2, \ldots, 5$) with the total volume of trade of India with all the countries (TR = summation for all the trading countries with India) besides the best five we have

Table 19.2 India's major trading partners and volume of trade during 2014–2015 (million USD)

Rank	*Country*	*Currency*	*Exchange rate (ei)*	*Export*	*Import*	*Total trade (Export + import)*	*Concentration ratio (TRi / TR)*
1	China	Yuan	10.3	9,010.35	61,706.83	70,717.18	0.093257
2	United States	Dollar	66	40,335.82	21,781.39	62,117.21	0.081916
3	United Arab Emirates (UAE)	Dirham	18	30,290.01	19,445.68	49,735.69	0.065588
4	Saudi Arabia	Riyal	17.5	6,394.23	20,321.33	26,715.56	0.035231
5	Switzerland	Swiss Franc	67	977.17	19,299.49	20,276.66	0.02674
6	**India's total trade volume in all countries**	Rupee	1	**262,290.13**	**381,006.63**	**758,301.08**	

Source: www.commerce.nic.in.

considered in our example. Therefore, the index of leading currencies in the basket is given in a formula as

$$I = e_1 * TR_1 / TR + e_2 * TR_2 / TR + e_3 * TR_3 / TR + e_4 * TR_4 / TR + e_5 * TR_5 / TR = \Sigma e_i * Tr_i / TR \quad (19.4)$$

where "e_i" stands for the exchange rate for the ith country.

We now calculate the basket of currency index in line with the previous formula for India which is as follows:

$$I = 10.3 * 0.093 + 66 * 0.081 + 18 * 0.066 + 17.5 * 0.0352 + 67 * 0.0264 = 9.95$$

Hence, the value of composite currency as per the leading trade partners is 9.95 which is very close to the currency of China. The use of this index will shortly be pointed out.

19.2.4 *Nominal, effective, and real exchange rates*

Economists usually make a distinction among three different concepts of exchange rates. They are *nominal, effective, and real exchange rates*. By nominal exchange rate we mean the nominal value of the home currency with respect to any foreign currency. It does not take into account the inflation figure prevailing in both the countries. For example, the nominal exchange rate for Rupee vis-à-vis USD is, say, 66. That means Rs. 66 will have to be exchanged to get one USD. We can say similar things about the nominal exchange rate of Rupee vis-à-vis the pound sterling, euro, yen, dirham, etc.

Effective exchange rate, on the other hand, is one type of inflation-free exchange rate like the nominal rate but it is calculated as the index of the basket of leading currencies with which the home country makes a major part of trading. We have already discussed the method of construction of hybrid exchange rate. Now we use it for calculation of effective exchange rate. Different countries' trade shares (TR_i / TR) are taken into account as weightage to nominal exchange rates, e_is. Therefore, the calculated "I" can be used as the notion for effective exchange rates.

Likewise we make a distinction between the nominal income and real income through the inflation rate or the value of the price index; the real exchange rate can also be the real or inflation-adjusted value of the nominal exchange rate. Therefore, real exchange rate tells how much the goods and services in the domestic country can be exchanged for the goods and services in the foreign country but nominal exchange rate means exchange of currencies. What is the expression for real exchange rate?

Suppose I is the real exchange rate which is defined as the ratio of the price level abroad (P_f) to the domestic price level (P), where the foreign price level is converted into domestic currency units via the current nominal exchange rate (e). The formula for R is thus

$$R = e.\left(P_f / P\right) = value\ of\ foreign\ currency\ in\ home\ currency * price\ of\ foreign\ good / home\ price\ \text{Or},\ R = Price\ abroad / Home\ price \tag{19.5}$$

where "e" is the nominal exchange rate of the home currency for one unit of the foreign currency. Price abroad (= $e.P_f$) may be alternatively called value of a foreign product. "R" thus can be treated as the measure of competitiveness of the home country's products. A decrease in R means appreciation of the real exchange rate (or home currency becoming appreciated which is not a good sign for the home country) and an increase means depreciation (which is a good sign for the home country). R can decrease if either "e" decreases or the foreign good is relatively cheaper than the home good (or $P_f < P$) and R can increase if the reverse conditions hold. Taking this differently, when $R > e$ then $e.(P_f / P) > e$. That means, $(P_f / P) > 1$ or $P_f > P$, which is home goods are cheaper than the foreign goods. That means import demand will decrease and export supply will increase which is beneficial to the home economy. On the other hand, when $R < e$ then $e.(P_f / P) < e$. That means $(P_f / P) < 1$ or the home good is costlier than the foreign good. That means import demand will increase and export supply will decrease which is detrimental to the home economy.

Box IV Example of real and nominal exchange rates

Suppose nominal exchange rate of Rupee per $ is 65. The price of a foreign good is $5 and of the home good is Rs. 20. The real exchange rate is $R = 65 * 5 / 20 = 325 / 20 = 16.25$. This implies 16.25 units of the Indian goods will be required to purchase one unit of American goods. So, what is Rs. 65 in nominal terms gets reduced to 16.25 in quantitative or real terms. Suppose foreign price increases to $10 with home price remaining the same, then $R = 65 * 10 / 20 = 650 / 20 = 32.5$. That means the real exchange rate increases which favours the Indian economy and disfavours the American economy.

In practice, changes of the real exchange rate rather than its absolute level are important. In contrast to the nominal exchange rate, the real exchange rate is always "floating", since even in the regime of a fixed nominal exchange rate "e", the real exchange rate R can move via price-level changes. If we repeat that the home country fixes its exchange rate in terms of the basket of leading currencies in real terms, then we can term it *real effective exchange rates*.

Relation: if any country has a single trading partner (or there is bilateral trade) then nominal exchange rate = effective exchange rate and real exchange rate = real effective exchange rate. Again, if the inflation levels are equal in both the countries (i.e. $P_f = P$) then nominal exchange rate = effective exchange rate = real exchange rate = real effective exchange rate.

19.2.5 Spot and forward exchange markets

Transactions in foreign exchange market are usually done in two forms – spot market and forward market. A *spot market transaction* (also known as FX spot) constitutes selling and buying foreign currencies where the sellers of the foreign currency (if goods market is dealt then we say seller of good) have to deliver the currency on the spot which is usually within two days of a selling agreement. Similarly, a buyer of the foreign exchange will receive the currency at the spot within two days after the buying agreement is done. No additional time is allowed in a spot transaction. But in a *forward market* the sellers of the foreign exchange agree to sell the stipulated units of the currency that are to be delivered on some future dates at the predetermined price during the contract. The usual span in the forward exchange is three months.

19.2.5.1 Link between spot and forward exchange markets – arbitrage, hedging, and speculation

Although the two terms of exchange markets have temporal differences, they are also closely linked. The ways by which they are linked are through interest arbitrage, hedging (or covering), and speculation. Arbitrage, hedging, and speculation are three distinct acts in market transactions in any items of trade – goods, securities, and currencies.

Arbitrage in the currency market refers to buying foreign exchange in one market at a low price and simultaneously selling it in another market at a higher price, profiting from a temporary difference in prices. This is considered riskless profit for the investor/trader. Interest arbitrage is the earning of extra interest incomes by buying the foreign exchange in a low interest country and selling it in a high interest country. If there is extra earning then it is called a premium and to forgo it is called discounting. Take an example. Suppose the spot exchange rate of Rupee for dollar is 50, which means Indian currency of 50 units is required to get one unit of US currency which holds equally in both the countries, but the forward rate of exchange may differ; it may be higher or lower than the spot rate. If the forward rate is higher than the spot rate of 50, say 55, then there is the opportunity of extra earning of Rs. 5 per dollar. That extra earning is called a *premium*. On the other hand, if the forward rate is lower than the spot rate, say, 45, then the loss is called *discount*. Symbolically, we can write the difference between the spot rate (R_s) and forward rate (R_f) as

$$Premium = R_f - R_s \text{ when } R_f > R_s \text{ and } Discount = R_f - R_s \text{ when } R_f < R_s$$

Now introduce the concept of interest arbitrage. Suppose that the short-term interest rate in the home market (India) is I_h which is equal to 8% and that in the foreign/away market (USA) is I_a which is equal to 6%. Then any currency trader holding currency with the same spot rate can get more earnings (premium) if he invests the currency in the Indian market by taking away the currency fund from the US market. The forward market rate in the US will go up and ultimately there will be equalisation of interest rates in both the countries. In reverse, if interest in the Indian market is 6% and in the US market is 8% then there will be discounting if the trader invests in the Indian market with the reverse logic for the interest equalisation. Therefore, a premium and a discount in interest arbitrage are given by the following relation

$$Premium = I_h - I_a \text{ when } I_h > I_a \text{ and } Discount = I_h - I_a \text{ when } I_h < I_a$$

where the premiums and discounts are related to the forward rate for the foreign currency, dollar.

Now we come to hedging or covering in the forex market. It arises when there is difference between the time of contract and time of delivery of any good or asset. An exporter can sign the contract to deliver the good, say after three months, taking into account that the currency exchange rate remains the same for the future three months. But there may be the chance that the exchange rate will change and the exporter in turn may lose. Hence to avert the risk of currency fluctuation, the exporter may cover the risk by hedging. He will sell the exportable goods in a fixed sum at the going forward rate for the dollar. That means he will not receive money at the time of contract, but after three months he delivers the good and gets payment. No change of exchange rate within these three months is a factor to the exporter.

Now come to speculation factor in relation to spot and forward rates of exchange. Speculation in the foreign exchange market is the operation of buying and selling the foreign currency under the conditions of uncertainty with the motive to earn a huge sum. Usually the speculators buy the currency when it is weak in value and sell when it is strong in value. Also, if the spot rate of the currency is expected to increase in the future, then the speculator buys forward and sell on the spot the currency bought by him. On the contrary, if the speculator anticipates a fall in the exchange rate, then he sells forward at the current rate and buys the spot when the currency is needed for the delivery.

From the previous discussion we say that there is a close link between the spot and forward rates via interest arbitrage. If the speculators expect the spot rate to increase they will go for buying forward leading to increase in demand for forward so that its price/return also increases. On the contrary, if the speculators expect the spot rate to fall, there will also be a fall in the forward rate. Hence, speculation in the forex market leads the spot and forward rates to move together.

19.3 Measures of openness

Openness is the free flow of goods, services, and financial assets across countries in a frictionless manner. A fully open country like Luxemburg has zero friction but a country with a subtle amount of international trade is North Korea. Today, a complete economic autarky or closeness is rare. A possible example of a current attempt at autarky is North Korea, based on the government ideology of self-sufficiency, which is concerned with maintaining its domestic localised economy in the face of its isolation. However, even North Korea has extensive trade with the Russian Federation, the People's Republic of China, Syria, and many countries in Europe and Africa. In between the two extremes there is a vast list of countries differing in degrees of openness. To measure *openness* the economists use some indices. The most common index is the ratio of total trade volume

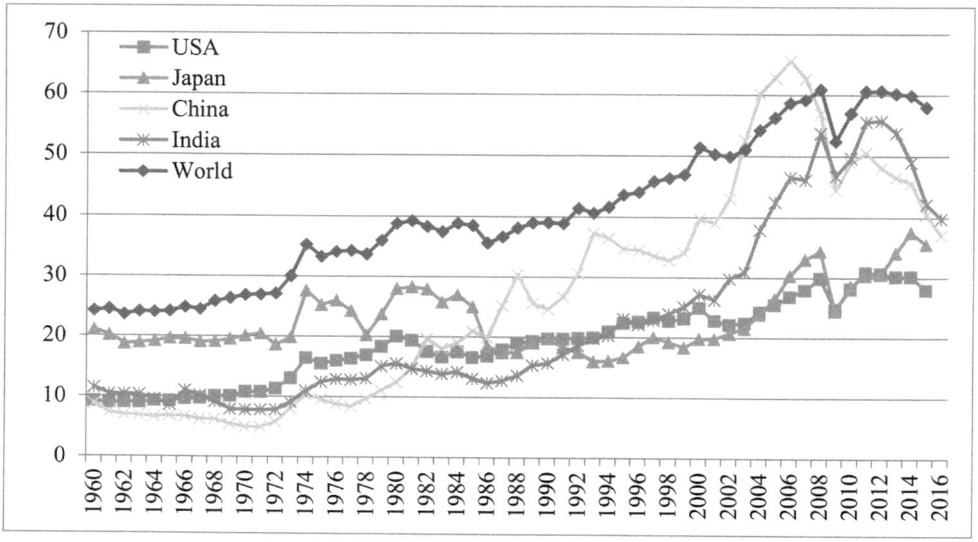

Figure 19.9 Trends of openness of selected countries

to the GDP of the country. Therefore, the economic openness (EO) by this concept is defined as

$$EO = Trade\ volume\,/\,GDP = (Export + Import)\,/\,GDP\,. \tag{19.6}$$

An increase in the trade volume relative to GDP means the degree of openness increases and a decrease in the trade volume relative to GDP means the degree of openness decreases. After the phase of globalisation, most countries' trade openness has increased over time. Figure 19.9 presents the trends of openness by means of the previous definition for the USA, Japan, China, and India and the world as a whole for the period 1960–2016.

We observe from the figure that the magnitudes of openness of all the countries along with the world level are growing over time, although Japan has sluggishness in its openness from 1960–1973 and 1986–2000. China jumped to a high degree of openness during 1978 for its liberalisation programme launched by Deng Xiaoping and the same for India during its liberalisation programme initiated in 1990–1991 by the Narasimha Rao Government. Starting for around 10% during 1960, China ended up with over 65% during 2006 and India with around 54% and after that every country experienced recession on a global level due to the outbreak of the global financial crisis. The recessionary effects still continued up to 2016 for all in the list.

Another measure of economic openness is the value of import duties (VID) as a ratio to the value of imports (VI), which is

$$EO = VID\,/\,VI\,. \tag{19.7}$$

Here the decision rule is reverse to that of the earlier. A reduction in the value of VID means more openness and increase in the value means less openness.

The recently developed index of openness was done by M. E. Waugh and B. Ravikumar in their working paper series of NBER in 2016. They opined that economic openness of a country should be proportional to trade potential (or potential gains from trade) of the country where trade potential measures how much each country can gain by moving from a current world with trade costs under autarky to a frictionless world. According to them, the trade potential (TP) of a country is proportional to the following term:

$$\left(A_i / Y_i\right)^{1/(1+\varepsilon)} \tag{19.8}$$

where A_i is country *i*'s observed home trade share, *Yi* is country *i*'s observed real GDP, and ε is the trade elasticity. Suppose *k* is the proportion, so we can write the openness as

$$TP = k.\ \left(A_i / Y_i\right)^{1/(1+\varepsilon)}. \tag{19.9}$$

As A_i increases relative to GDP and the trade elasticity becomes lower, the country's openness will increase and as a result the welfare cost under autarky can be reduced by means of open trade in a frictionless manner. That is why the poor countries have greater potential gains from trade.

19.4 Measures of international competitiveness

By the term *international competitiveness* we mean the capacity of a good to stay in the international competition and in an extreme case it swallows the market share of all the competing countries producing and selling in the international market. In a simple sense it gives the information on relative cheapness of the good compared to the other countries. We can measure the degree of international competitiveness of a country (say India as the home country) compared to another country (say USA as the foreign country) for a particular good "*i*" by the real exchange rate. We have already defined the real exchange rate as $R = e.(P_{fi} / P_i)$ where P_f is the foreign country's price of the traded good, *P* is the home country's price of the product, and *e* is the nominal exchange rate. Further, *R* can be expressed as the ratio of price abroad and home price. An increase in *R* means the foreign price is relatively higher than the home price which further means that India's good is more competitive in the international market than the US's good. On the other hand, if *R* falls then India's product is less competitive or India loses competitiveness to USA in the international market. But if *R* is constant or $P_f = P$ then there is no difference in the competitiveness of India's good and the US good; both the markets can be treated as a single market. Suppose there is a basket of goods traded between India and the USA with a different series of prices. Then the overall competitiveness of the home country can be determined in the same formula but the difference is that the prices in the home and away markets are the weighted averages of all the concerned prices or the inflation rates prevailing in both the countries.

What are the factors behind international competitiveness? In the formula for international competitiveness, *R*, we see that there are three direct factors adhered to this competitiveness measure. They are *e* (exchange rate), P_f (foreign price of the same good), and *P* (home price of the same good). There are positive relations between *R* and the exchange rate and foreign price of the good and the inverse relation between *R* and the home price of the good. As "*e*" increases, the home currency depreciates (that is, home customers will have to pay more for the foreign/imported good but the foreign customers will have to pay less for the home good) which means export from the home country will be cheaper and import from the foreign country will be dearer. That means the home country will gain competitiveness in the international market for his own products. The reverse situation or less competitiveness will arise when "e" goes down. Again, as the foreign good becomes costlier (i.e. P_f increases with e and P constant) then R will continue to increase which means the home country will gain competitiveness for their products and vice-versa. Finally, as a home good is cheaper (i.e. P falls with P_f and e remaining the same) then also the competitiveness of the home country will increase. The indirect factors for increasing international competitiveness are the factors which influence the values of "e", P_f, and P. They are, for example, political advantage of the home country at the international level for "e", fall in productivity in the foreign country leading to increase in P_f, and increase in productivity in the home country which lead to cost effectiveness of the home country's products, increase in income tax rate on the labourers of the foreign country, and exemptions in the home country. Recently a new dimension has taken shape in determining the competitiveness of the home country which is the "ease of doing businesses in the home country". If the government or the administrative system of the home country makes quick clearance of the business projects submitted by the private companies then the cost of production will be lower and as a result, the competitiveness of the home country will increase. You can add a list of indirect factors to influence R. According to the World Bank, the three top countries in ease of doing business are Singapore, Hong Kong, and New Zealand.

19.5 Conclusion

The present chapter discussed different concepts on international macroeconomics which are needed for explaining the linking of the internal economy with the external economy. There was the concept like exchange rate which was defined by the unit of domestic currency required to get one unit of foreign currency. If there is a fixed unit of home currency for each unit of foreign currency, then we have the system of fixed or pegged exchange rate. If the market decides it in a variable rate system, then it is called flexible or floating exchange rate. Sometimes a combination of these two is used which is known as hybrid exchange system. The chapter also explained the measures of openness and competitiveness of a country or a product in the international market.

Summary

The summary of the present chapter covers the following points:

- Import demand in the home country is generated when the home country's total supply is less than that of the demand.
- Export supply is generated when the home country's total supply is greater than that of the demand.
- Foreign goods are purchased in terms of the exchange rate of the home currency vis-à-vis the foreign currency.
- When home country's currency is exchanged at a fixed rate for one unit of the foreign currency then it is called fixed or pegged exchange rate. Again, if the market power decides the exchange rate, then it is called flexible or floating exchange rate. A combination of these two exchanges rates is called the hybrid exchange rate system.

- The economy's openness is mostly measured by a common index which is the ratio of total trade volume to the GDP of the country.
- International competitiveness is measured by the real exchange rate or the price of the foreign product abroad as a ratio to the home price of the product.

Keywords

Export supply
Import demand
Exchange rate
Fixed exchange rate
Flexible exchange rate
Nominal exchange rate
Real exchange rate
Openness
Competitiveness

Multiple choice questions and answers

1. Demand for import for any good arises when the domestic economy has

    (a) Surplus in the production of the import competing industry.
    (b) Deficit in the production of the import competing industry.
    (c) Balance in the production of the import competing industry.
    (d) None of the above.

2. Devaluation of home currency means

    (a) The home currency becomes stronger.
    (b) The foreign currency becomes stronger.
    (c) Neither home currency nor the foreign currency will be stronger.
    (d) All of the above.

3. If home currency gets devalued then the home country's BOP position will

    (a) Improve.
    (b) Get worse.
    (c) Remain unchanged.
    (d) None of the above.

4. In a flexible exchange rate, if home currency appreciates then the citizens of the home country will have to

    (a) Pay less for their imports.
    (b) Pay the fixed amount like before.
    (c) Pay more for their imports.
    (d) All of the above.

5. Openness of an economy in the international market is mostly measured by a common index. This is the

    (a) Ratio of GDP to total trade volume of the country.
    (b) Ratio of GDP to total volume of export of the country.
    (c) Ratio of GDP to total volume of import of the country.
    (d) Ratio of total trade volume to GDP of the country.

Answers

1. (b); 2. (b); 3. (a); 4. (c); 5. (d)

Review questions

1. What is international linkage? Explain how the import demand is generated from the domestic economy's capacity of production and capacity of consumption in diagrams.
2. Give brief notes on the following terms:
   a. Fixed exchange rate
   b. Flexible exchange rate
   c. Clean and dirty floating
   d. Nominal and real exchange rates
3. Define "sterilisation". Explain how the intervention of the central bank of a country works in the fixed exchange system.
4. Define spot and forward exchange markets. Explain in this connection the concepts of arbitrage, hedging, and speculation in the exchange market.
5. What is "openness of economy"? Discuss a popular measure of openness.
6. How can you measure international competitiveness? Explain the relation between international competitiveness and the difference between home and away price of a product.
7. What is hybrid exchange rate? Explain how it is measured.
8. Explain how the market for foreign currency operates under a floating exchange rate system. Discuss in this context the effect of excess demand for import for goods on the exchange rate of the home currency. What will happen if the reverse situation arises?

20 Accounting of international linkages – the balance of payments

20.1 Introduction

To see whether the flow of goods, services, and financial assets across the countries (which is broadly covered under the nomenclature "international linkages") is beneficial to the trading countries, that is both the home and foreign countries, we need first to account for the items of international linkages. The system by which we can account for all the cross-border movements of goods, services, and assets is known as balance of payments. *Balance of payments* (BOP) of a country is the systematic record of all economic transactions between the residents of the country and the rest of the world in a particular period, commonly over a year. These transactions are made by households, firms, and government bodies of a country. The accounting system is like a double entry (credit side and debit side) bookkeeping system in which every transaction or event changes at least two different nominal ledger accounts. The credit side in the open economy transactions includes all the items which earn foreign currency as incoming items and the debit side includes all the items in which foreign currency is to be paid for the items and thus are treated as outgoing items. Hence, one of the most important policy issues for the open economies is how to keep the BOP in equilibrium. It has been a pertinent question today since almost all the countries in the world have entered into the phase of globalisation. India has liberalised/globalised its economy during the period of 1991–1992 almost after a decade of Chinese liberalisation.

A country will face a favourable situation in its BOP if all the credit items supersede all the debit items in value terms. In reverse, there will be unfavourable BOP to the country if all debit items supersede all credit terms in value terms. If, by any chance, all the credit and debit items are identical, then we term it balance in the BOP. The first two cases stand for disequilibrium in BOP but the last case stands for equilibrium in BOP (it is the ultimate target of the policymakers).

20.2 Components of BOP

Broadly there are two components of BOP of a country in relation to its foreign counterpart depending on the flow and stock concepts. They are current account and capital account, where the first one is the flow concept that includes all transactions other than capital assets at a current period and the second one is the stock concept which includes all transactions of capital assets. Both of these two components have their own credit (incoming) sides and debit (outgoing) sides. But there is a puzzle in dealing with the credit and debit sides of current and capital accounts. The credit items in a current account

DOI: 10.4324/9781003501138-25

earn foreign currency through exports of goods and services (a movement from the home country) but the credit side in the capital account earns foreign currency through imports of capital (a movement to the home country from abroad). The readers thus will have to be careful in understanding the BOP system.

A. Current Account: captures exports (credit items) and imports (debit items) of all goods and services in international transactions along with unreturned transfers to and from abroad. When we have trade in goods without any service and transfers accounts then we call it *trade account* which includes all merchandise exports and imports of goods. These are the *visible items* in the current account. Similarly we have a service account which includes all returns from sale or export of factors, shipping service, banking and insurance service, etc. to the foreign country and its import counterparts from the foreign country to the home country. Finally we have transfer accounts which include receiving gifts and remittances from the relatives residing in foreign countries and its counterparts are the gifts, remittances from the home country to the foreign country. The service and transfer accounts constitute the *invisible items* in the current account. Therefore,

$$Current\ Account\ (CA) = Trade\ Account\ (TA) + Service\ Account\ (SA) + Transfer\ Account\ (TA)$$

$$Or,\ CA = Visible\ Account\ (=TA) + Invisible\ Account\ (SA+TA) \tag{20.1}$$

Similarly,

$$Current\ Account\ Balance\ (CAB) = TAB + SAB + TAB \tag{20.2}$$

$$Or\ CAB = (Export\ of\ goods - Import\ of\ goods) + (Export\ of\ service\ items - Import\ of\ service\ items) + (Export\ of\ transfer\ items - Import\ of\ transfer\ items)$$

$$Or\ CAB = Net\ exports\ of\ goods\ (NX) + Net\ export\ of\ service + Net\ inflow\ of\ transfers$$

$$Or,\ CAB = NX + Net\ transfers\ from\ abroad \tag{20.3}$$

where TAB is balance of trade account (BOT) which is NX, SAB is balance in service account, and TAB is balance in transfer account. We have taken all invisible transactions as transfer accounts.

Current Account Surplus and Deficit: surplus in the current account will arise if there will be surplus in any of the three items (trade, service, and transfer) or surplus in one item and deficits in other items but the sum of all surplus and deficits is positive. There may be any other combinations to justify surplus in CA. Surplus in the trade account is the situation when NX > 0, which is merchandise export value is greater than merchandise import value. Again surplus in transfer accounts means the home country gets more transfers and service income from abroad than what they pay the foreigners.

On the other hand, deficit in CA means the reverse. That means the sum of all the sectors' debit items will be more than the credit items.

Now here is a question. Does a country have anything to do if it experiences prolonged deficits and surplus in the current account? Yes, it has something to do. If the country faces long-term deficits, its importers will continue to demand foreign exchange to pay for import items and there will be depletion of forex reserves with the central bank of the country. That is not a good sign so far as economic sovereignty of the home country is concerned. At the same time, if there is prolonged surplus in the current account, then there will be extra forex reserve which may not be useful to the home country. Therefore, the home country needs to think about the deficit or surplus in the current account. The source which can adjust the deficits or surplus in the current account is the Capital Account Transaction which is another component of BOP.

B. Capital Account: like the trade and transfer accounts, home countries can get foreign currency as loan from abroad, sale of corporate bonds to the foreigners, banks' loan to the foreigners; all account for the inflow of foreign currency. In reverse, the foreign country can take a loan from the home country, sell their corporate bonds, and foreign banks can extend loans to the home residents that all account for outflow of foreign currency. All the aforementioned heads of transactions are recorded as capital account which deals with assets, not the goods.

Capital Account Surplus and Deficit: capital account surplus will emerge when receipts from sale of assets, government borrowings from foreign entities, etc. supersede the payment on purchase of assets, government lending to foreign entities, etc. Analogously, there will be a deficit in the capital account if receipts are less than payments.

Now BOP is the sum of A and B. That means

$$BOP = Current\ Account + Capital\ Account$$

$$Or,\ Balance\ in\ BOP = Balance\ in\ current\ account + Balance\ in\ capital\ account$$

$$Or,\ Balance\ in\ BOP = NX + Net\ transfer + Capital\ Account\ balance \tag{20.4}$$

BOP surplus and deficit: Surplus in BOP arises when there may be i) surplus in both the current and capital accounts, ii) surplus in the current account and deficit in the capital account, but the former outweighs the latter, and iii) deficit in current account and surplus in capital account, and the latter dominates the former. Again, the BOP will be in deficit, which is a major concern to most of the countries today, if there will be either deficits in both accounts or a deficit in either of them so that the net result is negative.

What happens if the BOP is in surplus or deficit? BOP surplus means BOP > 0 and all heads of both the current and capital accounts have income of foreign currency in an overall sense. So where will the surplus foreign currency go? At the same time, if BOP is in deficit, then BOP < 0 and there will be a net loss of the foreign currency reserve. So from where it will be adjusted? The answer can be given by the introduction of two concepts of capital flows: one is autonomous the other is accommodating. *Autonomous capital flows* are ordinary capital flows which take place regardless of the other items in the BOP. Transactions are said to be autonomous if their value is determined independently of the BOP. On the other hand, *accommodating capital flows* are the capital flows which take place specifically to equalise the balance of payments in the double entry bookkeeping system so that the BOP is balanced in the overall sense. Accommodating capital flows again are determined by the net consequences of the autonomous items. An autonomous transaction is one undertaken for its own sake in response to the given configuration of prices, exchange rates, interest rates, etc., usually in order to realise a profit or reduced costs. It does not take into account the situation elsewhere in the BOP. An accommodating transaction, on the other hand, is undertaken with the motive of settling

Table 20.1 A hypothetical example on BOP accounting

Sl. No.	*Credits*	*Amount ($)*	*Sl. No.*	*Debits*	*Amount ($)*
1	Exports of goods to foreign	1,000	1	Imports of goods by home	1,200
A1-Trade account	BOT = 1,000 – 1,200 = –200 => trade deficit by $200				
2	Exports of services	300	2	Imports of services	100
A2-Service account	SAB = 300–100 = + 200 => surplus in service account by $200				
3	Unreturned receipts and remittances from abroad	200	3	Unreturned receipts and remittances to abroad	400
A3-Transfer account	TAB = 200 – 400 = –200 => transfer account deficit of $200				
A = A1+A2+A3 = **Current Account**	–200 + 200 – 200	–200 => **current account deficit of $200**			
4-**Capital Account**- Autonomous capital flows	Capital receipts	1,000	4	Capital payments	1,500
B	CAB = 1,000–1,500 = –500 => capital account deficit by $500				
A + B = BOP	(1,000 + 300 + 200 + 1,000) – (1,200 + 100 + 400 + 1,500)	–700 => **BOP deficit by $700 => BOP imbalance**			
5	Accommodating capital receipts	700		Accommodating capital payments	0
BOP in bookkeeping sense	(1,000 + 300 + 200 + 1,000 + 700) – (1,200 + 100 + 400 + 1,500 + 0)	0 =>**BOP is balanced in accounting sense**			

the imbalance arising out of other transactions. Hence, through the concept of accommodating capital flows, we can say that *the balance of payments is always in balance in an accounting sense.*

Table 20.1 presents a hypothetical BOP accounting. There is BOT deficit of $200 (row 3), surplus in service account of $200 (row 5) and deficit of $200 in the transfer account (row 7). The current account (row 8) is therefore in deficit of $200. On the other hand, the capital account has deficit (CAB) of $500 which makes the BOP deficit (A + B) of the amount $700. The accommodating capital flow should be of $700 to keep the BOP in balance in a bookkeeping sense.

20.3 India's current account scenario

We present here the current account scenario of India for the period 1981–2017 in Figure 20.1 borrowed from the RBI database. India recorded a current account deficit of USD 34,300 million in the first three months of 2017, higher than the USD 300 million gap a year earlier due to higher imports. On the other hand, the services surplus widened to USD 176,000 million from USD 161,000 million due to higher earnings from travel, transport, construction, and other business services. The primary income deficit fell to USD 5,600 million from USD 6,600 million. Private transfer receipts, mainly representing remittances by Indians employed overseas, were at USD 15,700 million, barely unchanged from the preceding year.

Current account in India averaged –1791.84 million USD from 1949 until 2017, reaching an all-time high of 7,360 million USD in the first quarter of 2004 and a record low of –31,857. million 18 USD in the fourth quarter of 2012.

20.4 BOP imbalance and exchange rate adjustments

Now it is time to discuss the role of exchange rate adjustments in correcting BOP imbalance. We know that imbalance in BOP means either there is a deficit or surplus in the overall accounts of international linkages. At first, we discuss the role of fixed exchange adjustments.

Suppose there is a deficit in the BOP. That means the country of concern suffers from a foreign exchange crisis to meet its payments as it earns less foreign currency compared to its payments. There is excess demand for foreign currency, say $. The central bank will have to release $ from its reserves through intervention to maintain its currency exchange rate at a pegged rate. And if such deficit continues for long, there may be exhaustion of total forex reserves in the home country, say India. Hence, the central bank of the country will have to make a strong decision to boost the export volume so

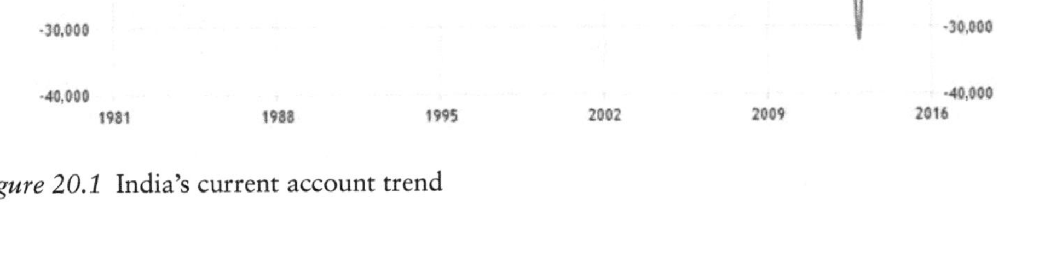

Figure 20.1 India's current account trend

that the deficits through more imports can be curtailed down. Most popular policy under the fixed exchange rate regime to boost export is *devaluation* of the home currency, the Rupee, vis-à-vis the foreign currency, the dollar. As we have already pointed out, devaluation makes the export goods cheaper and import goods dearer. Hence, devaluation will create inflow of foreign currency by more export and less import and will help in reducing the magnitude of the BOP deficit. On the other hand, suppose there is a surplus in BOP. That means there is excess supply of $. To peg the home currency at the fixed exchange rate, the central bank will have to purchase more dollars which means greater supply of Rupees which will boost commodity prices. Hence, the appropriate policy to reduce the magnitude of surplus into balance, in which the central bank will *revalue* the home currency, means now fewer rupees will be required to get one $. That means export will be dearer and import will be cheaper and ultimately the BOP surplus can be adjusted to zero. Besides the devaluation and revaluation mechanism in the current account, the country can also adjust through the capital account by means of loan from the foreign country, allowing foreign direct investment (FDI) and foreign portfolio investment (FPI) to the home country from foreigners during the deficit phase and giving loan to foreign individuals or FDI and FPI to foreign countries during the surplus phase.

Let us consider the flexible exchange system of adjustments. If the BOP faces deficit, more demand for $ can be mitigated by automatic *depreciation* of home currency through the free exchange market mechanisms. As home currency depreciates, export will be cheaper and import will be costlier. Therefore, the deficit problem of the BOP can be sorted out. On the other hand, if there is surplus in BOP, then home currency will *appreciate* which means its value will increase vis-à-vis $. Hence, exports will be fewer and imports will be more. So surplus in BOP can be handled through appreciation of currency. The adjustment process have been shown in Figure 19.3 (of Chapter 19) where deficit (or excess demand for $) takes the Rupee to Rs. 35 per dollar (point *G*) and surplus (or excess supply of $) takes the Rupee down to Rs. 25 per dollar (point *J*).

20.5 Convertibility of home currency

We know so far that international trade provides a scope of using home currencies for import of foreign goods, services, giving transfers and capital assets abroad, and earnings of foreign currencies through these channels. The first three items belong to the current account and the last one belongs to the capital account. Whatever be the requirements of foreign exchange receipts and payments, the question is how to get the foreign currencies by exchange of home currency or how to get the home currency from foreign currencies. The simple answer is by converting the home currency into the foreign currency and the reverse. But there is a question of whether all (i.e. 100%) the home/foreign currency in both current and capital accounts can be converted into the foreign currency. If this happens then it is called the situation of full currency convertibility or there is full convertibility of the home and foreign currencies in the transactions of both current and capital accounts. During the early phases of liberalisation of the economies, most of the countries had imposed restrictions upon convertibility of the home and foreign currencies. Over time, the home/foreign currencies required for goods imported through the trade account were allowed to convert and then a part of the current account was allowed to convert. After that, full current account convertibility was allowed but the requirements for the capital asset transactions were not allowed. India has now allowed full convertibility of Rupees since February 1992, but there are certain limitations/restrictions on capital account convertibility because macroeconomic parameters have to be stable before it is implemented. The low current account deficit should be sustained and the fiscal deficit needs to be contained. India's external sector was vulnerable till recently, with the current account deficit above the comfort level of 2.5% of the gross domestic product. It was 4.2% of GDP in 2011–2012 and rose to 4.7% in 2012–2013. After severe control, including restrictions on import of precious metals, the deficit fell to 1.7% in 2013–2014. In 2014–2015, it continued to stay low, with the third quarter showing a deficit of 1.6%. The fiscal situation remains fragile. The turning point was in 2007, the year of the global financial crisis. The fiscal deficit of the central government has been 4.6–6.5% in the past 6 years, before falling to 4.1% in 2013–2014. The government is committed to keeping the fiscal deficit low and the target of 3.9% has been retained for the year 2015–16. The deficit target was progressively reduced to 3.5 and 3% in 2016–17 and 2017–18, respectively. Experts believe paramount care should be taken along the path of convertibility. The government of India has set up the Tarapore II Committee to recommend suggestions for initiation of the full capital account convertibility. The committee recommended going for full convertibility in a phased manner: the first phase by 2006–2007, the second phase by 2007–2009, and the third phase by 2009–2011. India is still struggling for application of full capital account convertibility of the currencies.

The volatility and panic in other sectors of the East Asian economies widened the currency crisis in the zone during 1997–1998 and has warned the rest of the world about dealing with full capital account transactions in an unrestricted manner. The experience from the East Asian currency crisis could not hit India because of its restrictions on transactions in capital accounts. The developed countries have their historical evidence of full convertibility in all accounts of international transactions.

Box I Advantages and disadvantages of full convertibility in India

Advantages

- Indian consumers will have **better access to a variety of goods and services produced in different countries that can maximise their wellbeing.**
- Local businesses can benefit from easy access to foreign loans at comparatively lower costs (low interest rates). Companies will be able to directly raise equity capital from overseas markets.
- Indian businesses will be able to issue foreign currency-denominated debt to local Indian investors. Indian businesses will be able to hold foreign currency deposits in local Indian banks for capital requirements. Indian banks will be able to borrow/lend to foreign banks in foreign currencies.
- Regulators like to keep control of their territories. Free and open entry to an enormous number of global market participants would increase the risk of losing regulatory control due to large market size and huge flow of capital.
- Full capital account convertibility opens up the country's markets to global players, including investors, businesses, and trade partners through easy access to capital for different businesses and sectors, positively impacting a nation's economy.

With increased participation from global players, new businesses, strategic partnerships, and new employment opportunities across various industries, as well as nurturing entrepreneurship for new businesses, will arise.

Disadvantages

- The domestic commodity producing sectors may be worst hit by full convertibility of the rupee because import demand may increase and contraction arises in the import competing industries.
- In the midst of a lack of suitable regulatory control and rates subject to open markets with a large number of global market participants, high levels of volatility in forex rates may occur, challenging the country's economy.
- Businesses can easily raise foreign debt, but they are prone to the risk of high repayments if exchange rates become unfavourable.
- Increasing unregulated Rupees make Indian exports less competitive in the international markets. Once the regulations on exchange rates go away, India may face the risk of losing its competitiveness in the international market.
- Full capital account convertibility has worked well in well-regulated nations that have a robust infrastructure in place. India's basic challenges – high dependence on exports, explosive population growth, corruption, socio-economic complexities, and challenges of bureaucracy – may lead to economic setbacks after the full rupee convertibility.

20.6 Perfect and imperfect capital mobility

In the capital account of the BOP we saw that after international openness countries used to exchange capital assets among them. Now the question is – why are there movements of capital assets from one country to another? Is it only because countries need funds for investment? If so, what is the price of such capital? The answers are as follows:

Countries need additional capital from foreign sources to finance for their current account deficit. The channels of such capital flow, as we have already mentioned, are FDI, FPI, etc. Once funds flow to the home country from any foreign country, the foreigners expect returns on such capital investments. We take this return as *rate of interest* for simplicity. If there is the opportunity that the home interest rate is more than the foreign rate of interest, there will be interest arbitrage from the foreign country to the home country and vice versa. If the capital market is perfect, there will be no restrictions on the flow of capital funds from a low interest to a high interest country. If this process continues, the need of the home country for foreign capital will be fulfilled and rate of interest in the home country will start declining. On the other hand, there will be a relative shortage of capital in the foreign country which will push up the interest rate there. Hence, a scenario of *equalisation of rate of interest* will appear. This is the crucial feature of *perfect capital mobility*.

On the other hand, if there is any control or restriction in the free movement of capital from one country to another, then there arises the situation of *imperfect capital mobility*. In spite of shortage of capital in the home country and a related high rate of interest, the foreign countries are not allowed to enter into the home market and hence the scope of interest rate equalisation does not arise here. There is a perpetual difference in rate of interest remaining in the global markets.

Box II The eurozone crisis

The launching of the common currency, the euro, in the European Union in 1999 had as its motive stable economic growth in the zone that could challenge the dominance of the widely accepted US currency, the dollar. Unfortunately the vision was proved to be wrong. The investors heavily invested upon Spain and Ireland and lent out huge sums to Greece, Italy, and Portugal to support their budget challenges. But the outbreak of the global financial crisis during 2007–2009 originated from the fall of Lehman Brothers in USA and spread to the other countries that are highly interlinked with the USA. The worst hit were the countries of the eurozone, mainly Greece, Italy, Ireland, Portugal, and Spain (GIIPS countries) who faced the recession and sovereign debt crisis and the crisis was unmanageable for them because of the single common currency, the euro. For example, Greece experienced debt-to-GDP ratio of 105%, 113%, 129%, 134%, and 162% for the years 2008, 2009, 2010, 2011, and 2012. There was a loss of confidence of the investors and the consumers in the economies and hence there was little chance of recovery through large-scale investments. The business confidence index for Greece, for example, was 104, 68, 76, 69, and 68, and the consumer confidence index stood at –29, –55, –45, –66, and –83 for the years 2008, 2009, 2010, 2011, and 2012. The GIIPS countries faced huge deficits in their current account and there were limited scopes of balancing by the capital account transactions. Due to common currency, the countries could not follow the devaluation or increased money printing policies to handle the crisis and as a result the loss of competitiveness could not be recovered. Had there been a limited degree of openness and particularly of the capital account and separate currencies, then the countries could have been capable of saving their domestic economies.

20.7 Circular flow in a simple four-sector economy

We recall the flow of national output/income in a three-sector closed economy – households, firms, and government. A closed economy accounts for the flow of goods and services which are produced and used within the economic territory of the country; no components of international transactions (IT) are included. If we add the international transactions of goods, services, and financial assets, then the system turns into an open economy. In a simple system we take the open sector where only the current account transactions (i.e. trade, services, and transfer accounts) are dealt with. Figure 20.2 presents the circular flow of income in an open economy.

Since we have already given the flow concepts for three sectors in a closed economic set up, there no need to repeat them here, rather, we concentrate on the flow concepts under the international linkage sector. Firms export goods to the foreign market (IT) and in turn get export receipts and make the payments for imports of goods from abroad. On the other hand, the households sell factor services, the labour, and get remittances

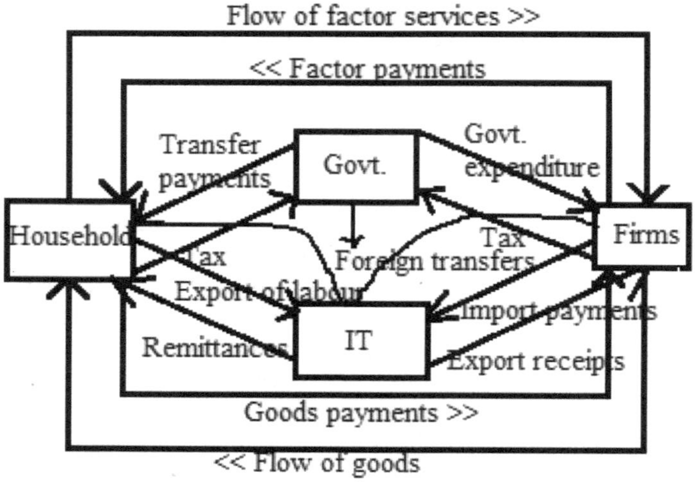

Figure 20.2 Circular flow of income in an open economy

from abroad. Households, firms, and the government net transfer to the foreign citizens (R_f) which balances the trade account, which is net exports ($NX = X - M$). The capital account transaction does not enter into the GNP accounting since it is not directly related to the current production, rather it involves only the transfers of capital assets. Therefore, the real GNP identity in an open economic system is:

$$GNP \equiv Y \equiv C + I + G + (X - M) \equiv C + S + T + R_f. \tag{20.5}$$

Export is an injection item and import and net foreign transfer are the leakage items in the open economy circular flow. Increase in X will expand the volume of GNP and increase in M or R_f will contract the volume of GNP. The left-side term, $C + I + G + (X - M)$, indicates aggregate demand or expenditure by the home and foreign sectors and the right-side term, $C + S + T + R_f$, indicates the aggregate supply or payments by the home and foreign sectors. Simplifying the previous identity we get

$$I + G + (X - M) = S + T + R_f \tag{20.6}$$

$$Or,\ I + G + X = S + T + (M + R_f) \tag{20.7}$$

or (Private + Public investment) $|_{\text{domestic}}$ + Foreign investment = Private + component of public savings) $|_{\text{domestic}}$ + components of foreign savings
or total incoming = total outgoing

20.8 Determinants of export and import

Export of products by the home country depends on the price of the home products (P) and exchange rate (e). We exclude the foreign income (GNP_f) from deciding export because it does not affect the circular flow and accounting of the home country's national income. Hence, the export function is

$$X = f\ (P,\ e) \tag{20.8}$$

where both dX / dP and dX / de are negative since as domestic price increases, foreigners will reduce export demand and as "e" increases, the home country's currency appreciates, export items become costlier, and hence export falls.

On the other hand, the import demand function by the home country depends on the home citizens' income, price of the competing products in the home market, and exchange rate. Hence, the import function is:

$$M = f(Y,\ P,\ e) = f(Y,\ P,\ e) / e \tag{20.9}$$

where dM / dY, dM / dP and dM / de all are positive. Since, as home country becomes richer, its citizens now have more money, import demand will rise; as price of the competing goods in the domestic market increases, import is then relatively cheaper and hence import will rise, and as exchange rate appreciates, import products are relatively cheaper and so import increases.

20.9 A simple Keynesian open economy model

Let us recall our simple Keynesian model (SKM) in a two-sector closed economy with autonomous government expenditure (G_0) supported by a lump-sum tax T_0 (for the sake of simplicity), and autonomous investment expenditure (I_0). The equilibrium output is balanced in the following equation:

$$Y = C + I + G$$

$$Or,\ Y = a + b.\ (Y - T_0) + I_0 + G_0 \tag{20.10}$$

where "a" (> 0) is the autonomous consumption expenditure and "b" is MPC ($0 < b < 1$). The equilibrium output is

$$Y = (a + I_0 + G_0 - b.T_0) / (1 - b). \tag{20.11}$$

We also get the autonomous expenditure multiplier as $dY / da = dY / dI_0 = dY / dG_0 = 1 / (1 - b) > 1$. That means the increase in autonomous expenditures from any head (C, I, or G) will lead to increase in national income at a multiplier rate and with such continuous expenditure-enhancing policies, the magnitudes of depression may be recovered. This is the essence of the Keynesian revolution.

Let us add the trade account component as the simplified model for an open economy Keynesian model. The income equilibrium relation is, thus, converted into

$$Y = C + I + G + X - M \tag{20.12}$$

$$Or,\ \ Y = a + b.(Y - T_0) + I_0 + G_0 + X_0 - M_0 - m.Y \tag{20.13}$$

$$Or,\ Y = a + (b - m).Y + I_0 + G_0 - b.\ T_0 + X_0 - M_0 \tag{20.14}$$

$$Or,\ Y = (a + I_0 + G_0 - b.T_0 + X_0 - M_0) / (1 - b + m) \tag{20.15}$$

where X_0 and M_0 are respectively the autonomous exports by countries abroad and imports by the home country which are positive and $0 < m < 1$ ($m = dM / dY$ = propensity to import = *MPI*), meaning increase in income induces more import and the increase in import should not exceed increase in income.

20.9.1 Effects of autonomous expenditure, export, and imports on domestic income

We can derive effects of autonomous expenditure on income (which is the open economy expenditure multiplier), export on income (which is the export multiplier = dY / dX_0) and import on income (which is the import multiplier = dY / dM_0) from Equation (20.16) by simple differentiation. They are as follows-

$$dY / da = dY / dI_0 = dY / dG_0 = 1 / (1 - b + m) \ < 1 / (1 - b). \tag{20.16}$$

We can also write the multiplier as $dY / da = dY / dI_0 = dY / dG_0 = 1 / (1 - MPC + MPI) = 1 / (MPS + MPI)$. The value of the open economy expenditure multiplier is positive and greater than unity because of the stability condition of national income equilibrium which is $(b + m) < 1$. But the magnitude of the open economy multiplier is less than that of the closed economy since mathematically the term $m > 0$ has been added to the denominator of the multiplier (17) which means, as autonomous expenditure in the home economy increases, national income will increase in the multiplier rate (since $1 / (1 - b) > 1$) and a part of this incremental income will be paid for with increased import demand which will further bring down the volume of *Y* since the home country's income outflows to the foreign country. Therefore, the value of the SK multiplier is reduced after the international linkages are considered. Figure 20.3 explains it.

The initial equilibrium in national income in the closed economy occurs at *F* and it shifts down to *E* when the open economy component (*NX*) is added to it. That means the equilibrium income goes down after import components are added. The aggregate demand function passing through *E* is flatter than that passing through *F* because import function swallows a part of income. Now we have exercised the autonomous expenditure multiplier in both closed and open economic situations through increase in I_0 by dI_0. The aggregate demand schedule shifts to *H* for a closed economy to *G* for open economic structure. The increase in income for a closed structure is by Y_2Y_4 and for open structure by Y_1Y_3. Both the changes are positive and greater than unity (the multiplier effect) but the magnitudes of increase in income are more in a closed structure than that of the open structure because of the import leakage item.

Now see what happens to the national income when autonomous export (X_0) increases by dX_0. Since export is an injection item to the open system circular flow, as its volume increases, equilibrium national income of the home country will increase at a multiplier rate like the autonomous expenditure multiplier. The export multiplier is thus:

$$dY / dX_0 = 1 / (1 - b + m). \tag{20.17}$$

The export multiplier is alternatively called the *foreign trade multiplier* as it boosts up the national income of the home country. It can be easily verified in the diagram in a way

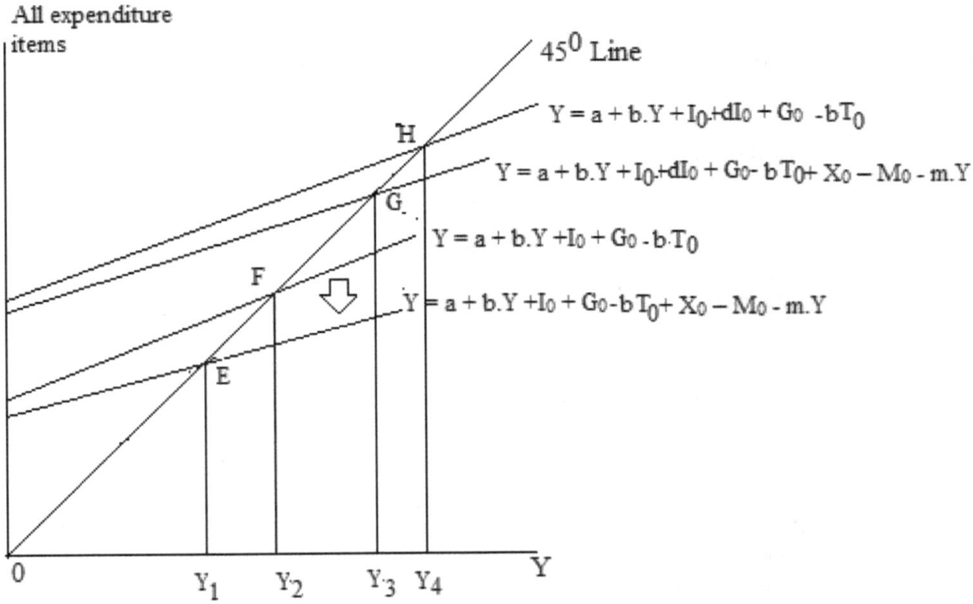

Figure 20.3 Open economy Keynesian expenditure multiplier

that replaces the increase in expenditure, dI_0, with dX_0 – then the diagram will be intact but the explanation will be like what we have given earlier.

Now attempt the effect of import increase upon the national income. It gives us the import multiplier which shows the effect of increase in autonomous import upon the income of the domestic economy and it is expressed as

$$dY / dM_0 = -1/(1-b+m) < 0. \tag{20.18}$$

The import multiplier is negative in sign which means as import increases there is outflow from the income stream like savings and taxation which pulls down the level of income. On the contrary, if import goes down, national income increases. That is why import is a debit item in the BOP. Diagrammatically the import multiplier can be shown by downward shifting of the aggregate demand function which will make the national income equilibrium at a lower level of income (the readers can try it on their own).

Box III

Example: suppose the consumption function is $C = 100 + 0.6Y$, autonomous investment expenditure is 200, government purchase of goods and services is 500, fixed export is 50, and import function is $M = 60 + 0.10Y$. Find out the autonomous expenditure multiplier under closed and open economic systems. Also find out the export and import multipliers.

Let us solve it. We have at equilibrium,

$$Y = C + I + G + X - M$$

Putting all the functional as well as non-functional values into the previous relation we get

$$Y = 100 + 0.6Y + 200 + 500 + 50 - 60 - 0.10Y$$
$$\text{or } Y = 790 + (0.6 - 0.10)Y$$
$$\text{or } Y(1 - 0.5) = 790$$

or $Y = 790 / 0.5 = 1{,}580$ = equilibrium income in an open economy. But the equilibrium income under a closed economy is $800 / 0.4 = 2{,}000 > 1{,}580$.

Now expenditure multiplier is $dY / da = dY / dI_0 = dY / dG_0 = 1 / (1 - b + m) = 1/(1 - 0.6 + 0.10) = 2 > 1$. This is also the foreign trade (export) multiplier. The result shows that one unit increase in investment or export will result in two units of national income. But the closed economy multiplier is $1 / (1 - b) = 1 / 0.4 = 2.5 > 2$. That means the closed economy expenditure multiplier is greater than that under the open economy multiplier since the import sector swallows a part of increased income. And the import multiplier is $dY / dM_0 = -1 / (1 - b + m) = -2 < 0$. It means one unit increase in import will reduce national income by two units.

20.9.2 The BOP equation

As we have already mentioned, BOP is the club of current account and capital account. Again, current account balance (CAB) is NX less net foreign transfer (R_f) (assuming the net transfer into import items). That means

$$CAB = NX - R_f = X - M - R_f\,. \tag{20.19}$$

We have the export function (from 9) as $X = f(P, e)$ and import function (from 10) as $M = f(Y, P, e) / e$. If "x" is the unit of home export at price P and "m" is the import quantity by the home country at price P_f, then CAB is transformed into the following relation:

$$X - M - R_f = P.f(P,\ e) - (P_f\,/\,e).\,f(Y,\ P,\ e)$$

$$Or,\ X - M = P.f(P,\ e) - (P_f\,/\,e).\,f(Y,\ P,\ e) \tag{20.20}$$

where the foreign transfer term has been included into the import function. The import function has been divided by the exchange rate since the home importers will have to convert their home currency into the foreign currency, otherwise they will have to depend upon the domestic goods in spite of their high-income levels.

Again capital account is $F = F(r)$ where $F' = dF / dr < 0$.

This shows that capital inflow to any country depends on the relative difference of the interest rate at home and abroad. For example, flow of capital from the US to India will be there if India's capital market provides more interest rate to the investors than that of the US capital market and vice-versa.

Hence, the BOP equation looks like

$$BOP = \text{Current account} - \text{Capital account}$$

$$Or,\ BOP = P.f(P,\ e) - (P_f / e).\ f(Y,\ P,\ e) - F(r). \qquad (20.21)$$

If BOP is in balance, BOP is equal to zero. That means current account balance (the first two terms) will be equal to capital account balance (the third term). With *P*, *Pf*, and *e* fixed, we get the BOP equation as the function in the (*Y*, *r*) plane. Any combination of (*Y*, *r*) can make BOP zero. Other combinations may create a BOP surplus or deficit. As *Y* increases, import will increase, which will reduce net export and hence current account deficit. To absorb the deficit, there should be surplus in the capital account that can be ensured by increase in rate of interest in the home market that will invite inflow of foreign capital. Therefore, as *Y* increases, *r* also increases and vice versa. Hence, the BOP (BP for short) line will be upward sloping. Mathematically we can derive the slope of the BP line from (20.22) by putting BOP = 0. That means,

$$P.f(P,\ e) - (P_f / e).\ f(Y,\ P,\ e) = F(r). \qquad (20.22)$$

Taking the derivative of "*r*" from the above equation with respect to *Y* we get

$$0 - (P_f / e).\ dM / dY = F'.\ dr / dY \ \left(since\ M = f(Y,\ P,\ e)\right)$$

$$Or,\ dr / dY\,|_{BOP=0} = -\ (P_f / e)\cdot dM / dY /\ F' > 0. \qquad (20.23)$$

since $dM / dY > 0$, and $F' < 0$. Figure 20.4 presents the BP line with balancing position (i.e. BP = 0).

The upward sloping line BP = 0 separates two zones – one is the BOP surplus zone which is left to the BP = 0 line and another is the BOP deficit zone which lies to the right of the BP = 0 line. Why? Let us take the case of the surplus zone. At any rate of interest, say r_2, the point *J* represents the BOP balance, but any point left to it, say *B*, represents low income ($Y_1 < Y_2$) which means the quantity of import of goods will fall and current account surplus will occur, not that at the fixed rate of interest r_2 there will be capital account surplus or deficit. Hence, BOP will be at a surplus in the leftward zone of the BP = 0 line due to the surplus in current account only. By the reverse logic, at any rate of interest, say r_1, the optimum level of income is Y_0 that keeps the BP in balance. For any income level more than Y_0 corresponding to r_1, say at point *A*, there is $Y_3 > Y_0$ and more income leads to more demands for import from the foreign country which ultimately results in current account deficit with unchanged position of the capital account. Therefore, there is a BOP deficit in the rightward zone of the BP = 0 line. The readers can verify the alternative arguments in explaining the two zones as surplus or deficit by taking income level as fixed and making variations in interest rates to make adjustments through the capital account, not the current account. *Note that the upward sloping BP = 0 line indicates the scenario of imperfect capital mobility*, which is $r \neq r_f$. We have differences in the interest rates of the home and foreign countries in a variety of ways.

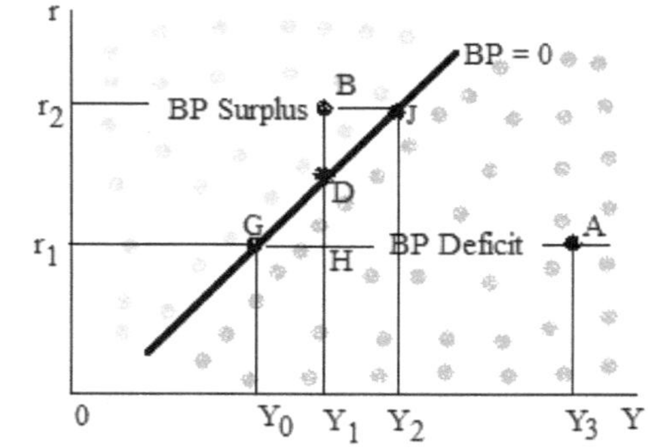

Figure 20.4 BP under imperfect capital mobility

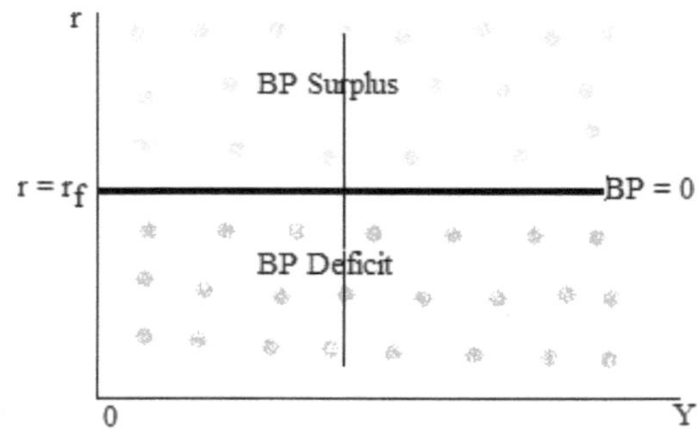

Figure 20.5 BP under perfect capital mobility

If we take the situation of *perfect capital mobility* then there will be automatic equalisation of interest rates in the home and away countries, which is $r = r_f$. The BP = 0 line will then be a horizontal straight line passing through the point at which $r = r_f$ (Figure 20.5). The home and foreign capitals are perfectly substitutable. Any increase in rate of interest of any country will immediately increase the flow of capital to the country from the other country with relatively low interest rates. The capital account will be in always balance since $F' = \infty$. From the slope of the BP line (Equation 20.23) we see that $dr / dY = 0$ (since $F' = \infty$). Therefore, the BP = 0 line is a horizontal line. Above the BP = line, there is a higher value of domestic interest than the foreign and there will be inflow of capital. Hence, there will be a surplus in the BOP and, contrastingly, below is the zone of deficit in BOP.

20.9.3 *Internal and external balance*

Prior to the discussions on the topic on international linkages, we were concentrating upon the equilibrium or balance in the closed economy or internal economy. The internal economy's balance refers to the situation of full employment of all the factors at the existing factor prices. Any economy falling short of full employment faces an unemployment problem, and on the other hand, if any economy reaches the position of more than full employment, it will face an inflationary situation. In both the underemployment and inflationary situations, the economy faces internal imbalance. In Figures 20.6 and 20.7, the internal balance is shown by the vertical line corresponding to the full employment output Y_f.

The external balance or the BOP = 0 lines have been shown as a horizontal line (Figure 20.6) because of perfect capital mobility and as an upward sloping line (Figure 20.7) because of imperfect capital mobility among the trading countries. In both the cases of perfect and imperfect capital mobility, *E* is the only point where both internal and external balances of the home country are ensured. There is neither unemployment nor inflation and neither BOP deficit nor surplus at *E*. Deviations from *E* (not along the internal and external balance lines) produce imbalances in either of the sectors. In Zone I of both the diagrams, there are unemployment and BOP surplus (i.e. unfavourable internal economy but favourable external economy); in Zone II, there is unemployment but a BOP deficit; in Zone III, there is inflation and BOP deficit; and in Zone IV, there is inflation in the internal economy but surplus in the external economy. All the economies

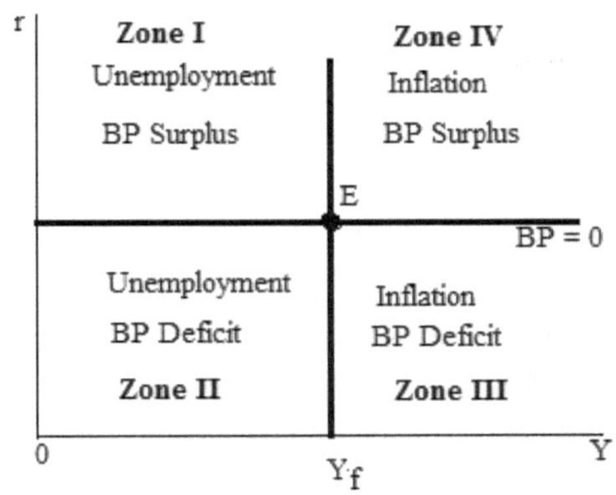

Figure 20.6 Internal balance with perfect mobility

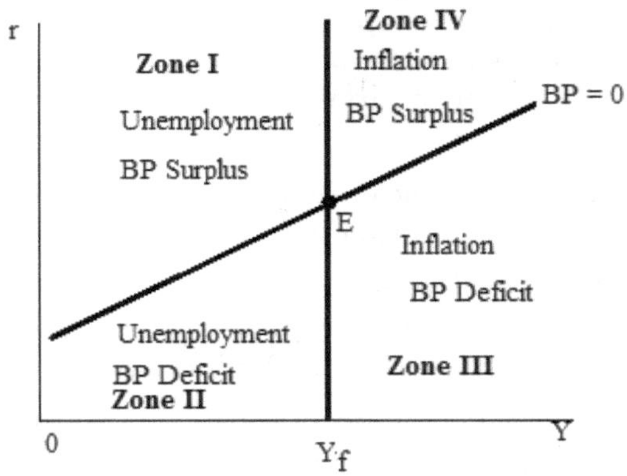

Figure 20.7 Internal balance with imperfect mobility

strive to reach *E* or to solve the internal and external imbalances by means of different policy prescriptions. The next chapter will cover the policy issues.

20.10 Some applications

1. Suppose that a country has a capital account surplus of Rs. 20 million and a current account deficit of Rs. 14 million.

   a. Calculate the balance of payment and state its situation.
   b. If the central bank intervenes, does it buy or sell the home currency?
   c. If the bank does not intervene, what will be the impact on the home exchange rate?

   Ans:

   a. Balance of payment surplus = Current account surplus + Capital account surplus
   Here, Current account surplus =RS (−14) million
   and Capital account surplus = RS 20 million
   So, Balance of payment (BOP) surplus = RS(−14 million + 20 million)
   i.e. Balance of payment surplus = RS 6 million.
   Thus, BOP is RS 6 million and it is in surplus.
   b. If the central bank intervenes, to maintain the BOP, it absorbs the surplus, which means it buys the home currency.
   c. If the bank does not intervene, then this BOP surplus increases supply of foreign exchange. So the supply curve of foreign exchange has a rightward shift which reduces *e*. So there is an appreciation.

2. Suppose that the rupee is appreciating steadily against the dollar. How would this affect your US friend who wants to visit India, (ii) an exporter of garments to the USA?

   Ans:

   a. When the rupee is appreciating steadily against the dollar, my US friend, who wants to visit India, has spend more in terms of dollars in this country. So it has an adverse effect on his expenditure during his visit to India.

b. When the rupee is appreciating steadily against the dollar, the price of exported garments in terms of the dollar rises, which reduces its demand. So the income of an exporter of garments to the USA falls. Thus it also has an adverse effect on India's exporter.

3. A decline in the price of oil in 1985–1986 led to a sharp depreciation of the currency of Mexico, a major oil exporter. Explain this fact using a suitable diagram.

Ans: a decline in the price of oil in 1985–1986 in Mexico causes increase in demand of oil in the USA, a country to which Mexico exports oil. As a result, the export of oil from Mexico to the USA rises. This increase in export of Mexico leads to an increase in the supply of the dollar in Mexico from the USA. So, the supply curve of foreign exchange of Mexico has a rightward shift and $e\ (=\frac{Peso}{\$})$ will appreciate (Figure 20.8). So, $\frac{\$}{peso}$ depreciates. This leads to depreciation of the currency of Mexico.

4. Suppose that money demand depends on disposable income, so that the equation for the money market becomes

$M\ /\ P = L\ (r,\ Y - T)$

Analyse the impact of a tax cut in a small open economy on the exchange rate and income under the floating exchange rates system.

Ans: a tax cut in a small open economy causes a rightward shift of the IS curve as the equation of the IS curve is

$$Y = C(Y - T) + I\ (r) + G + NX(Y,\ Y^*,\ e)$$

where Y^* = foreigners' income.
Since $M\ /\ P = L\ (r,\ Y - T)$, a tax cut also causes a leftward shift of the LM curve (Figure 20.9).

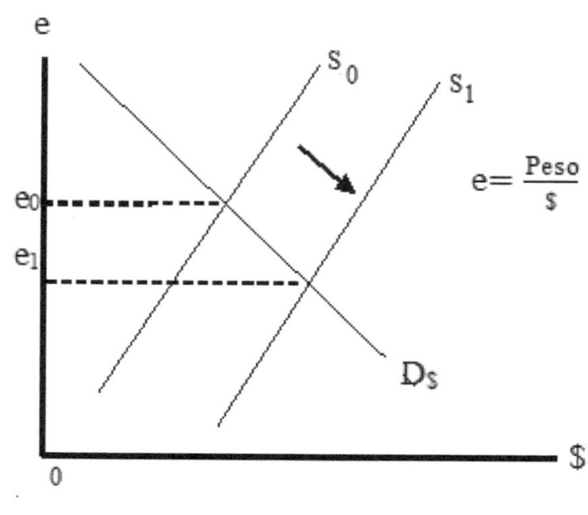

Figure 20.8 Oil price shock and its effects upon the exchange rate

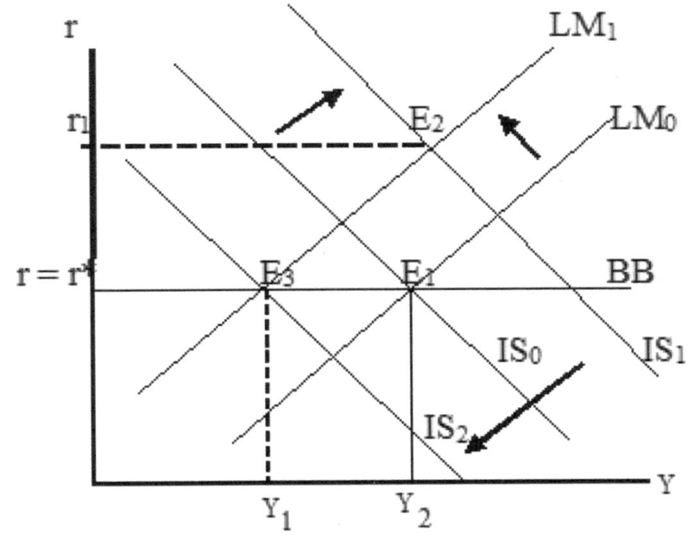

Figure 20.9 Impact of tax cut in an open economy

Thus both the IS and LM curve shift to E_2 from E_1. Now, r $(= r_1) > r^*$. It induces huge capital inflow in the country.

Under a flexible exchange rate, this capital inflow leads to an increase in the supply of foreign exchange, thus a rightward shift of the foreign exchange supply curve. It causes a fall in the equilibrium exchange rate, so there is appreciation of the exchange rate. Now, a fall in exchange rate encourages imports and discourages exports which causes a fall in net export (NX). This fall in NX causes a leftward shift of the IS curve until $r = r^*$ is restored. In this equilibrium, output falls. So here, expansionary fiscal policy under a flexible exchange rate reduces both income and exchange rate.

20.11 Conclusion

The present chapter threw light upon the accounting of international transactions in the name of balance of payments (BOP). The BOP has two broad heads – current account and capital accounts. If in an overall sense the sum of current account and capital account is in deficit, then we say BOP is in deficit and in the case of positive sum we say BOP is in surplus. Both deficit and surplus in BOP are the imbalance situations and they are to be corrected through proper policy. The popular policy is devaluation in case of deficit and revaluation in case of surplus. The circular flow of income was reoriented through the incorporation of the internal transactions and we showed that the autonomous government expenditure multiplier gets relatively low value due to increasing import demand function, and the export multiplier was positive. The internal and external balance conditions were discussed at a primary level. Whether a home currency can be fully converted into foreign currency has also been discussed in light of the Indian economy.

Summary

In the previous discussion on the accounting and related issues of open economic transaction we now have the summary results as follows:

- BOP has two broad items – current account and capital account. Current account has trade accounts and transfer accounts and capital account has all sorts of import and export of financial services.
- Current account deficit plus capital account deficit give rise to BOP deficit unambiguously. Again current account surplus plus capital account surplus give rise to BOP surplus unambiguously. These two features constitute BOP imbalance.
- Autonomous capital flow and accommodating capital flows are used to make the BOP always in balance.
- Introduction of open economic transaction into the Keynesian model gives the computation of national income in an open economy.
- Increase in government expenditure in the open economy model gives more income but with a lesser rate compared to the closed economic system because the import demand swallows a part of the increase in income.
- In the Indian economy, all the current account's transaction amounts can be fully convertible; capital account transactions are yet to be fully convertible.
- The BOP = 0 line is horizontal for perfect capital markets and BOP = 0 is rising for the imperfect capital markets. The area above the BOP = 0 line in both the cases indicates BOP surplus and the area below indicates BOP deficit.
- Internal balance is maintained along the full employment line. To the left of it represents the recession phase or deflationary phase and to the right of it represents the boom phase or inflationary phase.

Keywords

Current account	Rupee convertibility
Capital account	Internal balance
BOP	External balance
Export multiplier	Import multiplier

Multiple choice questions and answers

1. If there is deficit in the balance of trade, it refers to the situation where

   (a) Merchandise export is more than merchandise import.
   (b) Merchandise import is more than merchandise export.
   (c) Current account receipt is more than current account payment.
   (d) Current account payment is more than current account receipt.

2. A balance in BOP means

   (a) Current account is in balance.
   (b) Capital account is in balance.
   (c) Current account deficit and equal magnitude of capital account surplus.
   (d) All of the above.

3. Devaluation policy is applied for correcting the situation of

   (a) BOP deficit.
   (b) BOP surplus.
   (c) Capital account deficit.
   (d) None of the above.

4. If a system of an economy is such that the consumption function is $C = C_0 + C_y . Y$, investment is $I = I_0$, export is $X = X_0$, and import function is $M = M_0 + M_y . Y$, then the expression for the export multiplier will be

   (a) $dY / dX_0 = 1 / (1 - C_y - M_y)$.
   (b) $dY / dX_0 = 1 / (1 + C_y - M_y)$.
   (c) $dY / dX_0 = 1 / (1 - C_y + M_y)$.
   (d) None of the above.

5. Internal and external balance of an economy refers to a situation where there is

   (a) Unemployment and BOP deficit.
   (b) Boom and BOP deficit.
   (c) Full employment and BOP is zero.
   (d) Inflation and BOP surplus.

Answers

1. (b); 2. (d); 3. (a); 4. (c); 5. (c)

Review questions

1. Explain the terms: current account, capital account, and trade account. Taking a hypothetical example, show that BOP is always in balance.
2. What is meant by autonomous capital flows and accommodating capital flows? Use these terms to show that there is neither deficit nor surplus in balance of payments.
3. What are devaluation and depreciation of home currency? Explain in detail the effects of these two policies in restoring BOP equilibrium. Mention the conditions when these two policies will fail to correct BOP imbalance.
4. Construct a circular flow of income table in an open economy system. Identify the injection and leakage items in such a circular flow of income.
5. What is net export? Derive its slope with respect to income. Reorient the simple Keynesian model to incorporate net export function into it. Derive the equilibrium income in a simple Keynesian open economic system.
6. State the investment expenditure multiplier in a closed economy. Derive the equilibrium income under the functional relations: consumption function is $C = 200 + 0.6Y$, investment is $I = 100$, export is $X = 50$, and the import function is $M = 30 + 0.10.Y$.
7. Compare the investment expenditure multiplier under a closed economy and open economy. Explain why the results differ.
8. Derive the expression for export multiplier and import multiplier. Suppose the consumption function is $C = 200 + 0.65Y$, investment is $I = 100 + 0.20Y$, export is $X = 50$, and the import function is $M = 30 + 0.10.Y$. Derive the values of export and import multipliers. What will happen to equilibrium national income if autonomous export increases by 50 units and import increases by 10 units?

9. What is the "convertibility of the Rupee"? Give a note on the current status of convertibility of the Indian currency with respect to the major foreign currencies.
10. What are internal and external balances? Sketch the diagrams for presenting an economy's positions of internal as well as external balances under the conditions of both perfect and imperfect capital market conditions.
11. What are the important aspects of economic openness? What have been India's steps in trade liberalisation? How has its external sector policy changed since the early 1990s?
12. Define i) current account, ii) capital account, and iii) balance of payments. Capital account surplus means that domestic capital accumulation is being funded by loans from foreigners. Explain.
13. Current account deficit equals current account surplus. Explain.
14. Should a current account deficit always be cause for alarm? What are the forms of financing current account deficit?
15. Define nominal exchange rate, effective exchange rate, and real effective exchange rate. Currency appreciation has adverse effects on trade balance by stimulating imports and reducing exports. Explain.
16. Distinguish between the flexible exchange system and the fixed exchange system. Discuss the domestic adjustments called for to support an overvalued currency under a fixed exchange system.
17. Suppose that the RBI embarks on a tight money policy. What is the likely impact on India's exports under i) fixed exchange rate and ii) flexible exchange rate?
18. What is the relation between trade balance and the level of economic activity when the exchange rate is fixed? How does this relationship create a potential conflict between internal and external balance?
19. Unlike a closed economy, an open economy can raise its investment even if the domestic investment remains unchanged.
20. Do you agree that under perfect capital mobility and fixed exchange, monetary policy loses its effectiveness completely?
21. Do you think that fiscal action is more effective under a fixed exchange rate, given fall capital mobility? Give reasons for your answer.
22. Explore the foreign exchange market reform in India.
23. Why are countries reluctant to explore the use of nominal devaluation to improve balance of payments?

21 Interactions among commodity market, money market, and external market

21.1 Introduction

An economy should have balance in both the internal and external sectors. Internal sectors are the commodity producing sector and the monetary sector and their combination has the prime objective to ensure full employment. The external sector, on the other hand, is the transactions accounted for the heads of all sorts of exports and imports in the current and capital accounts that we have discussed in detail in the preceding chapter. Incorporation of the external transactions into the internal economy's output and employment determinations affects the product market, not the monetary sector. In the following sections we will first reorient the product market equilibrium in the presence of open economy transaction and introduce the balance of payment equilibrium condition into the internal economy's equilibrium to re-estimate the national output and rate of interest. This particular mode of analysis has been developed by Mundell and Fleming and is popularly known as the Mundell-Fleming model. Detailed policy analysis has also been done on all fronts to establish their effectiveness under different capital market conditions.

21.2 Product market equilibrium under open economy

The product market or goods sector of the closed economy is in equilibrium, as we know, when different combinations of Y and r make the supply of income equal to the demand for income. The diagrammatic representation of the product market equilibrium is given by the IS function with the equation as follows:

$$Y = C_0 + C(Y) + I_0 + I(r) + G_0 \tag{21.1}$$

where C_0, I_0, and G_0 represent the autonomous consumption, investment, and government expenditure respectively. The government is assumed not to impose any direct tax upon the citizens. Also $0 < C_y = dC / dY = \text{MPC} < 1$and $I_r = dI / dr < 0$ conditions hold. The derived equation of the IS function in a (Y, r) plane is:

$$dr / dY = (1 - C_y) / I_r < 0\,. \tag{21.2}$$

Let us introduce the international transactions into the product market equilibrium. Only the current account transaction will enter into the product market equilibrium condition since the goods market transactions deal with the current account, not the capital

DOI: 10.4324/9781003501138-26

account. Export will enter the system like any other expenditure item and import will enter as saving like a leakage item. The reformulated IS function is:

$$Y = C_0 + C(Y) + I_0 + I(r) + G_0 + X(P,\ e) - m(Y,\ P,\ e). \tag{21.3}$$

Taking the total derivatives on both sides and then differentiating r partially with Y gives us the slope of the open economy IS function which is as follows:

$$\delta r / \delta Y = \left[(1 - C_y) + \delta m / \delta Y\right] / I_r < 0. \tag{21.4}$$

The slope of the IS function is still negative since the numerator is positive (since $0 < C_y < 1$ and $\delta m / \delta Y > 0$) and the denominator is negative. But due to the addition of the term $\delta m / \delta Y > 0$ into the numerator of the slope expression, the IS function in the open economy will be steeper than the IS function under the closed economy (Figure 21.1). The closed economy IS function is IS_1 and for the open economy it is IS_0 which is steeper than the former.

We can also analyse the effect of the parameters upon the position of the IS functions. Parameters, as we know, cause shifting of the function. The shifting of the IS function now depends on autonomous export and import besides the parameters attached to the closed system like autonomous consumption, investment, and government expenditure. As export increases (due maybe to the increase in foreign income, fall in domestic price of the export items, etc.) the IS function shifts to the right and vice versa (i.e. $\delta Y / \delta X > 0$). On the other hand, as import rises (which may be due to increase in home income, currency appreciation or revaluation, etc.) the IS functions shifts to the left and vice versa (i.e. $\delta Y / \delta m < 0$).

We know that the increase in autonomous expenditure (or export) produces an income multiplier effect and its result leads to rightward shifting of the IS function. The new IS function after increase in autonomous expenditure (or consumption, private investment, public investment, or export) is IS_1' which shifted from IS_1 under the closed economy resulting in the multiplier value of $1 / (1 - C_y)$. The autonomous expenditure

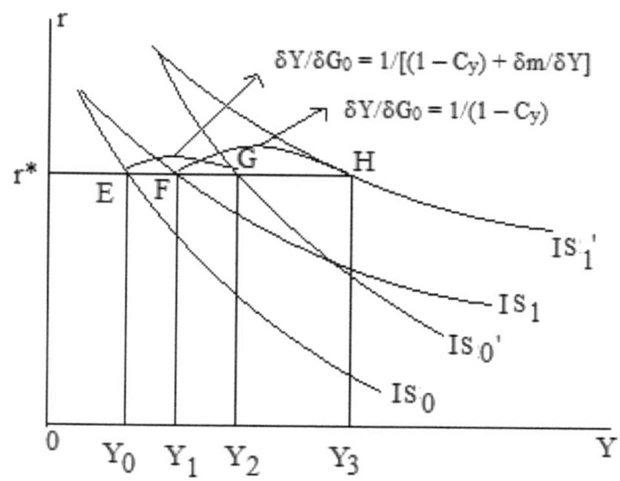

Figure 21.1 IS function under open economy

(or consumption, private investment, public investment, or export) multiplier under the open economy system generated through the changes in the product market equilibrium condition without any money market repercussions is thus:

$$\delta Y / \delta G_0 = 1 / \left[\left(1 - C_y\right) + \delta m / \delta Y \right] > 0) . \quad (21.5)$$

It means an increase in investment by private or public parties creates expansion of income still under the open economy set up but the magnitude of this open economy product market multiplier gets reduced more by the import propensity term added in the denominator than that of the closed economy (i.e. $dY / dG_0 = 1 / (1 - b)$). As Y rises through G_0, the home citizens get comparatively richer which influences them to go for more import demand that ultimately shrinks the domestic economy's expansion. The new IS function after the increase in autonomous expenditure (or export) shifts from IS_0 to IS_0'. The increase in output under the closed economy is Y_1Y_3 (= FH) which is less than Y_0Y_2 (= EG) under the open economy.

21.3 Money market equilibrium under the open economy

In a closed economic structure we know that the LM curve represents the relationship between Y and r that maintains the money market equilibrium where demand for money (= liquidity) is equal to supply of money or $M / P = L(Y, r)$ considering M as the amount of money offered; Y as real income and r as real interest rate; L as the demand for money, which is a function of r (determining the speculative part of money) and Y (determining the transaction or active balance part); and P as the price level. In an open economy, the interest rate is also determined by the equilibrium of supply and demand for money. Besides, the role of exchange rate must be taken into account since it affects money demand (investors may decide to buy or sell bonds in a country depending on the exchange rate). The equilibrium of the money market implies that, given the amount of money, the interest rate is an increasing function of the output level. When output increases, the demand for money rises, but, as we have said, the money supply is given. Therefore, the interest rate should rise until the opposite effects acting on the demand for money are cancelled; people will demand more money because of higher income and less due to rising interest rates. The slope of the LM curve is positive (or $\delta r / \delta Y = - L_y / L_r >$ 0 since $L_y = dL / dY > 0$ and $L_r = dL / dr < 0$).

21.4 Revisiting internal and external balance

Let us recall the concepts of internal and external balances. We pointed out in the previous chapter (Chapter 20) that the internal balance is maintained at a point where full employment of the factors is ensured. That means the potential demand for goods and money should be matched with the potential supply of goods. The potential demand is given by the intersection between the product and money market equilibriums (IS and LM) and the potential supply is given by the full employment level of output Y_f. E is the point where internal balance is restored (Figure 21.2 and Figure 21.3). Any deviation from that internal balance will cause either unemployment or inflationary situations. On the other hand, the external balance will be maintained where the BOP will be in balance. That is along the BP = 0 line. Any deviation from that will create either deficit or surplus (referred to in earlier discussions).

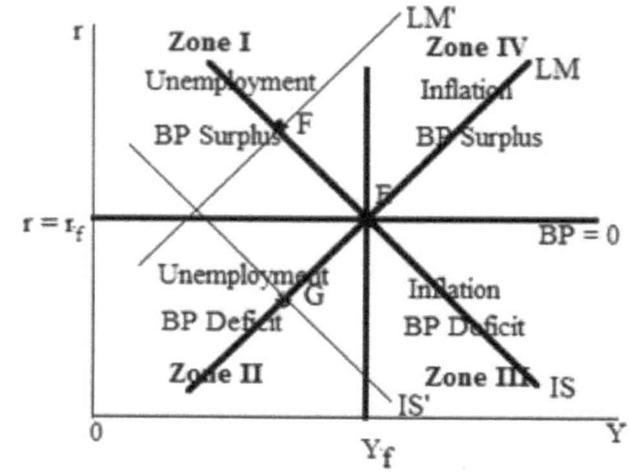

Figure 21.2 Internal balance under perfect mobility

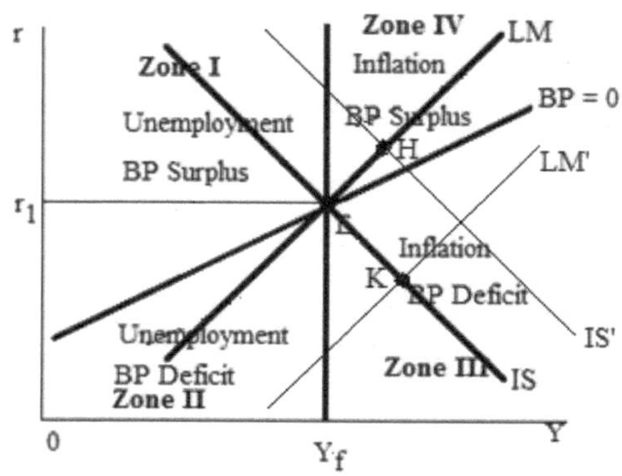

Figure 21.3 Internal balance under imperfect mobility

The figures present both the internal and external balances of an economy for perfect and imperfect capital markets leading to the horizontal and positively sloped BOP functions. One misconception may arise on the relative slope differences between the LM and BP = 0 line under an imperfect capital market. Both of them are positively sloped but their slopes are compared on the basis of empirical data. During the 1960s and early 1970s, both of them nearly maintained equal slopes in USA and Canada but the BP line got flatter than the LM after the onset of the floating exchange regime when different markets were integrated. We thus consider the BP = 0 line as relatively flatter than the LM curve in our following discussion. Also, we can say that a flatter BP = 0 line represents high magnitudes of capital mobility (nearer to the perfect mobility) and a relatively low degree of capital mobility (away from the perfect mobility) produces a steeper BP = 0 line.

It is not always guaranteed that an economy with internal balance will also maintain the external balance. Similarly, an economy may maintain external balance even with unemployment or inflationary situations at the domestic level. But the bull's eye of the economy is to maintain both the internal and external balances at the same time. We want to highlight all these issues now.

We observe from both the figures that E is the point that maintains both internal and external balances in both the capital market structures. But there are some departures also. In the left side of the diagram, let us imagine the *LM'* function which intersects with the IS at point *F* where there is balance in the internal system (since IS intersects LM and we take the output Y_f as the full employment output at all the points where both of them intersect) but imbalance in the external sectors in the sense that there is BOP in surplus. In a fixed exchange system, the surplus BOP can be handled by the central bank by purchasing more foreign currency and as a result supplying more money into the economy that will shift the LM out right and ultimately back to the point *E* where both the balances are maintained. If the system would be floating exchange, then BOP surplus would appreciate the home currency which would pull down export and pull up import which again makes adjustment towards *E*. Similarly, at point *G*, the IS function has been shifted down to *IS'*. There is internal balance but the BOP is in deficit meaning deficit in foreign currency to meet the debit items. In the same way as before, under the fixed exchange system, the central bank will do the opposite, which means it will sell foreign exchange by means of purchasing home currency that will lead to reduction in money supply which will result into more "*r*" and less *Y*. Both of them will lead to capital account surplus that solves the BOP problem and reduces import demand that brings back the *IS'* into IS and maintains internal balance as well. On the other hand, under the flexible exchange regime, a deficit in BOP will depreciate the home currency which will push up export and pull down import and ultimately both the balances are maintained at point E.

Let us consider the case of the imperfect capital market as presented in the right-side figure. The two balances are maintained at point E where IS and LM intersect and the flatter BP line also intersects them. There is neither unemployment nor inflation and neither BOP surplus nor deficit at point *E*. Now suppose there is a deviation from *E* to *H* which corresponds to the new internal economy equilibrium ($IS' = LM$) but BOP is in surplus meaning there is external imbalance. In a fixed exchange system, the surplus in BOP (i.e. surplus in foreign exchange) influences the central bank to purchase more foreign currency to peg the exchange rate at the fixed level. That means money supply in the domestic economy will increase which will lead to increase in *Y* and as a result import will rise which will pull down the BOP surplus into BOP balance. If there is a floating exchange system, then surplus in BOP will allow the home currency to appreciate which will push up import as it is cheaper now and pull down export as it is relatively costlier now and ultimately the BOP balance will be maintained.

Now suppose the new internal balance is maintained at *K* where IS intersects the new LM, *LM'*. We see that at *K*, there is BOP deficit. In a fixed exchange system, BOP deficit will induce the central bank to sell more foreign currency to meet the excess demand for foreign currency. As a result of that, money supply will fall, which will reduce *Y* which further reduces import demand and ultimately the BOP deficit may be cured and external balance will be maintained. On the other hand, if there is a floating exchange system then the BOP deficit at *K* will depreciate the home currency which will pull up export and pull down import and solves the BOP deficit problem and maintains the external balance.

One thing we must disclose here that we just concentrated on is restoring the external balance as one of the important policy objectives. But there should be additional adjustments in the internal economy as well by means of varying *Y* and *r*. In the following discussions we will highlight all these policy changes and their associated interactions to justify the effectiveness of two important policy prescriptions widely used in macroeconomic perspectives – the monetary and fiscal policies.

21.5 IS-LM model under open economy — the Mundell—Fleming model

We are now in a position to make an exhaustive analysis of the fiscal and monetary policies taken by the government and the monetary authority of the home country and their interactions with the external economy through the balance of payment channel. The combination of IS-LM-BP is thus the nomenclature widely used in open economy macroeconomics. It is an extension of the Hicks-Hansen IS-LM model, which was formulated by two economists, Robert Mundell and Marcus Fleming, who almost simultaneously made an analysis of open economies in the 1960s. Basically the Mundell–Fleming model is a version of the IS-LM model for an open economy. Even though both of them put their effort into the same topic, at about the same time, they have come up with different analyses. Mundell's work on *Capital Mobility and Stabilization Policy under Fixed and Flexible Exchange Rates* in 1963 analyses the case of perfect mobility of capital across the countries, while Fleming's model, illustrated in his article *Domestic Financial*

Policies under Fixed and under Floating Exchange Rates in 1962, was more realistic as it assumed imperfect capital mobility and thus made this one a more precise and comprehensive model. The present scenario of a high degree of international linkages has made Fleming's model the actual world situation as it has more resemblance with total capital mobility that fits better than Mundell's approach. Albeit the difference, both the models presumed the following:

i) A small open economy
ii) Tax rates patriotism are equal all over the place
iii) Depositors abroad do not tolerate political risk of default by overseas nationalism of overseas assets, limitations of shift of assets, or risk of non-payment by the overseas government.

The presumption of a small open economy entails that the economy can borrow or let others borrow as much as it likes in world financial markets devoid of affecting rate of interest. Therefore, for a small open economy, rate of interest is determined by the global interest rate. Capital is ideally movable globally when depositors can buy properties in any nation they select rapidly with low transaction costs and in unlimited amounts. No government imposes additional tax burdens upon the investors.

The Mundell Fleming model of a small open economy with ideal capital mobility can be explained by the succeeding equations for IS, LM, and BOP = 0 curves.

$$\text{IS equation: } Y = C_0 + C(Y - T_0) + I_0 + I(r) + G_0 + X(P,\ e) - m(Y,\ P,\ e) \qquad (21.6)$$

$$\text{LM equation: } M / P = L\ (Y,\ r) \qquad (21.7)$$

$$\text{BOP balance equation: } P \cdot f(P,\ e) - (P_f / e) \cdot f(Y,\ P,\ e) = F(r) \qquad (21.8)$$

where T_0 is the income tax. There are three equations with three unknowns, namely Y, r, and e. We can solve for these three unknowns with the help of the parameters set by Cramer's rule. We are not going into rigorous mathematics here in this book; the readers can attempt to solve for it. We rather concentrate on the intuitive aspects of the linkages among the three sectors; the first two are internal sectors and the last one is the external sector which we are already aware of. Point E in Figure 22.4 and Figure 22.5 depicts the initial state of equilibrium in both internal and external balances respectively for perfect and imperfect capital mobility. The equilibrium values corresponding to E are calculated from equation's 22.6, 22.7, and 22.8. We cover all the related discussions of policy effects in the following cases depending upon the exchange systems and degrees of capital mobility.

21.5.1 *Policy effects*

In the present section we will discuss the roles of expansionary fiscal and monetary policies to solve for the internal and external imbalances for fixed exchange and floating exchange systems under perfect capital mobility (Mundell's approach) and imperfect capital mobility (Fleming's approach). The following eight cases are considered for both the fiscal and monetary policies. We already know that expansionary fiscal policy will shift the IS function in an upward direction and result in increase in Y and r and an

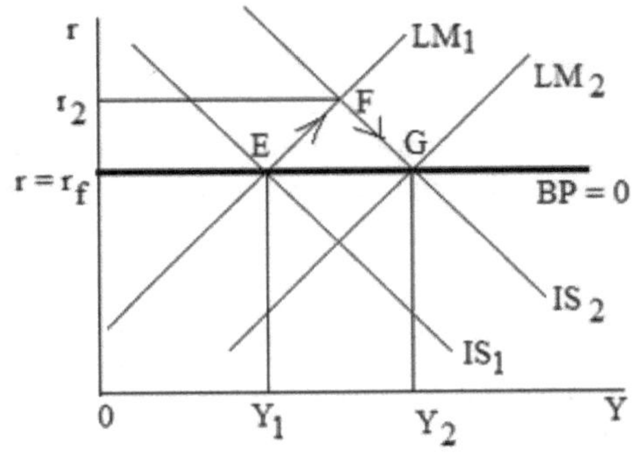

Figure 21.4 Fiscal policy effects under fixed exchange rate

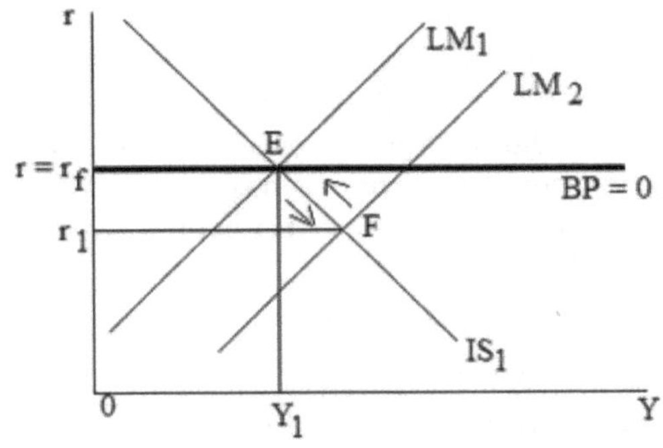

Figure 21.5 Monetary policy effects

expansionary monetary policy will shift the LM function rightward resulting in increase in Y and decrease in r. Our objective is to find the situations where either or both of the policies are effective to solve the internal and external problems.

21.5.1.1 *Case I – Fiscal policy effects under fixed exchange rate with perfect capital mobility*

An expansionary fiscal policy may work when government purchase of goods and services increases or tax burden decreases. Suppose E is the initial equilibrium where IS_1 and LM_1 intersect and meet the horizontal BP = 0 line because of perfect capital mobility leading to equalisation of r (home rate of interest) and r_f (foreign rate of interest) along the BP line. Figure 21.4 depicts the scenario.

An expansionary fiscal policy will shift the IS function from IS_1 to IS_2, with a given monetary sector's equilibrium and produce a new internal equilibrium at F where home interest rate rises to r_2 generating the BOP surplus. In a fixed exchange system, the surplus in BOP will induce the central bank to purchase the excess foreign currency to maintain the exchange rate at the pegged level. Purchase of foreign currency alternatively means more supply of home currency. That means the excess supply of money will cause rightward shifting of the LM function to LM_2 that pulls down the interest rate back to the r_f which bars capital inflow, and at the same time, increases in income to Y_2 will also increase import demand. Therefore, at new equilibrium point G, both the internal and external balances are restored but with an expanded level of national income. This concludes that fiscal policy is fully effective under a fixed exchange rate system with perfect capital mobility.

21.5.1.2 *Case II – monetary policy effects under fixed exchange rate with perfect capital mobility*

Let us suppose that the central bank of the country attempts an expansionary monetary policy corresponding to the initial point E (Figure 21.5). The LM function will shift to LM_2 which makes the equilibrium to shift from E to F. Since the new equilibrium lies below the BP curve there is BOP deficit since there is fall in domestic rate of interest to r_1 compared to the foreign rate r_f. Since the economy follows fixed exchange rates, government intervention is required to peg it at the stipulated rate on the presumption that the currency will depreciate. The central bank will sell foreign currency and accordingly purchase domestic currency which will drop the money supply and therefore shift the LM_2 curve to its original position which restores the equilibrium at *E*. This shows that the monetary policy has no effect on income under the circumstances of a fixed exchange system and perfect capital mobility.

21.5.1.3 *Case III – fiscal policy effects under flexible exchange rate with perfect capital mobility*

Let us consider the cases of policy shifting under the flexible exchange rate system. We know that in this system the central bank has nothing to manage – only the market has the automatic adjustment mechanism to settle the exchange rate. An expansionary fiscal policy, given the existing monetary base of the country, will shift the IS_1 curve to IS_2 which will move the equilibrium from point *E* to point *r* (Figure 21.6). The economy will therefore have a balance of payments surplus because high domestic interest rate will allow huge inflow through the capital account. The domestic currency this case of flexible exchange rate will appreciate, which will decrease net exports since the citizens' import demand for more goods and services rises with less money, while foreigners will import fewer of our products because of our appreciated domestic currency. This drop in net exports will shift the IS_2 curve back to its original position IS_1. The fiscal policy is no longer effective under the flexible exchange rate system.

21.5.1.4 *Case IV – monetary policy effects under flexible exchange rate with perfect capital mobility*

An expansionary monetary policy, given the existing fiscal position of the country, will shift the LM_1 curve to LM_2 which will move the equilibrium from point *E* to point *F* (Figure 21.7). The economy will therefore have a balance of payments deficit because low domestic interest rate will allow huge outflow through the capital account. The domestic currency in this case of flexible exchange rate will depreciate which will increase net exports since the citizens face costly import items now, while foreigners will import more of our products because they are relatively less costly than

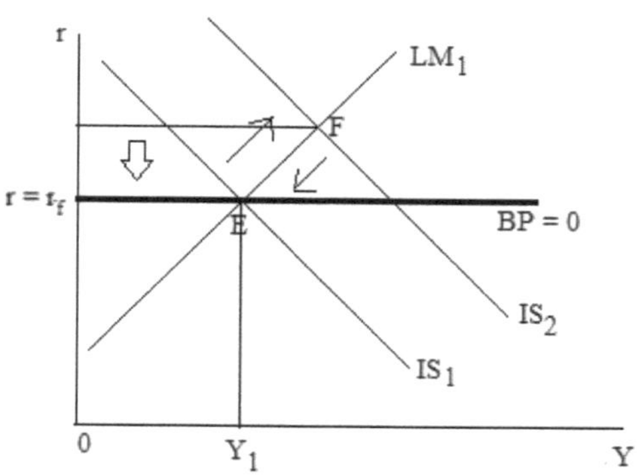

Figure 21.6 Fiscal policy effects

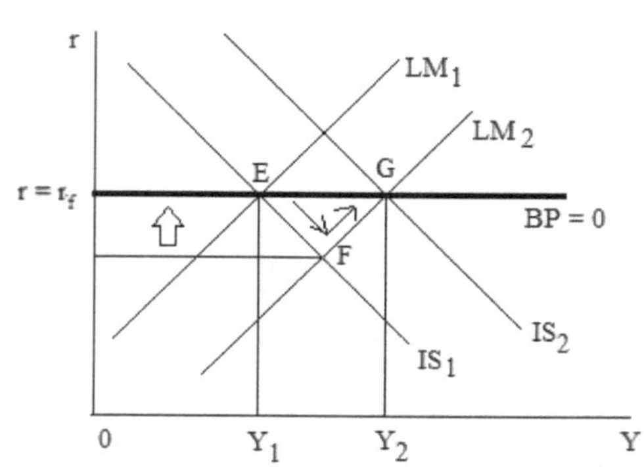

Figure 21.7 Monetary policy effects

the products of the home country. This boost in net exports will shift the IS_1 curve rightward to IS_2. The new internal as well as external equilibrium is maintained at point *G* where the interest rate differentials are neutralised and the economy faces expansion in income. Thus, under the flexible exchange rate system, the monetary policy is highly effective.

The corollary from the previous four cases is that fiscal policy is effective under the fixed exchange rate system but the monetary policy is effective in the case of flexible exchange rate and both occur under the condition of perfect capital mobility.

21.5.2 *The impossible trinity*

We came to know from the previous discussion that there are policy dilemmas in the case of effectiveness of the two policies under the situation of perfect capital mobility and a fixed exchange rate system. There is another dilemma that both perfect capital mobility and fixed exchange rate conditions do not comply with the independent and efficient monetary policy (which is also called sovereign monetary policy). Therefore, it arises that the three situations – perfect capital mobility, fixed exchange rates, and an independent and efficient monetary policy – can never exist simultaneously. Mundell termed it the impossible trinity (also known as the Trilemma or Unholy Trinity) since, under the perfect capital mobility assumption and in order to have an efficient monetary policy, exchange rates must be flexible or have fixed exchange rates but assume that monetary policy won't be efficient. Figure 21.8 sketches the trilemma.

In the figure, A, B, and C are three parts of the trilemma which show a pair of policy combinations. For example, "A" holds the pair of fixed exchange rate with efficient monetary system under sovereignty, "B" holds the pair of sovereign monetary system with perfect capital market, and "C" represents the pair of fixed exchange rate system with the perfect capital mobility. The authority of a country should adopt any two policies at a time, not the three at a time, since not all of them are perfectly compatible in producing economic results of the fiscal or monetary policies.

21.5.2.1 *Case V – fiscal policy effects under fixed exchange rate with imperfect capital mobility*

Let us allow the capital market to be imperfect in the sense that there is a difference between the home and foreign interest rates and there is no scope of equalisation of

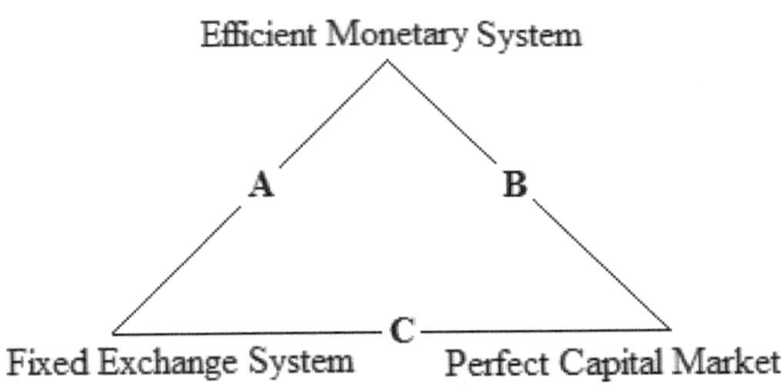

Figure 21.8 The impossible trinity

interest rates across the countries. The BOP balance line is upward sloping and usually flatter but in some cases may be steeper depending on the degrees of imperfections. Figure 21.9 presents the effect of expansionary fiscal policy under the fixed exchange system.

An increase in government expenditure will shift the IS function from IS_1 to IS_2 (arrow shows the direction). The equilibrium in the internal system will shift from *E* to *F*. At *F* there is surplus in the BOP which leads the central bank to purchase foreign currency and supply more money. As a result of that, the LM function shifts from LM_1 to LM_2 (assuming the BOP line is flatter than the LM line). Rate of interest will fall and income will rise which ultimately leads to more import and capital outflow making the BOP balanced at point *G*. We see that the expansionary fiscal policy is effective here since $Y_3 > Y_1$. On the other hand, if the BOP line would be steeper than the LM function, say $BP' = 0$, then the expansionary fiscal policy would lead to BOP deficit in place of surplus that would lead to a fall in money supply. The new LM function, as a result of that, would shift leftward to LM_0 and would still produce the income expansion effect corresponding to point *H*, although the magnitude of income expansion would be lesser than that under a flatter BOP line (i.e. $Y_1Y_2 < Y_1Y_3$).

21.5.2.2 *Case VI – monetary policy effects under fixed exchange rate with imperfect capital mobility*

Let us attempt the effect of expansionary monetary policy under the imperfect capital market with a fixed exchange system. The initial equilibrium point is *E* where both the internal and external balances are maintained. Here we have considered the flatter BOP = 0 line (Figure 21.10). As money supply is increased by the central bank of the home country, the LM function will shift to the right to LM_2. The new LM function makes internal balance at point *F* but there is BOP deficit since it lies below the BOP line. The deficit in BOP will force the central bank to sell more foreign currency which means purchase of money. That means money supply will fall and the process will continue until the LM_2 shifts back to LM_1 (the arrows show the direction) and restores the external balance. Thus, expansionary monetary policy under the imperfect capital market with a fixed exchange system does not produce any income effect. If the BOP

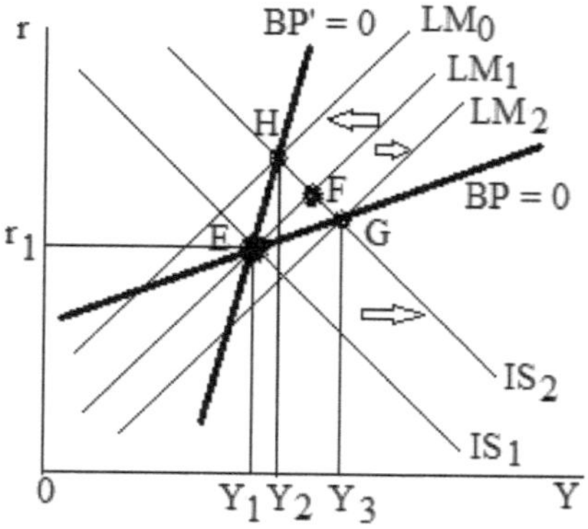

Figure 21.9 Fiscal policy effects

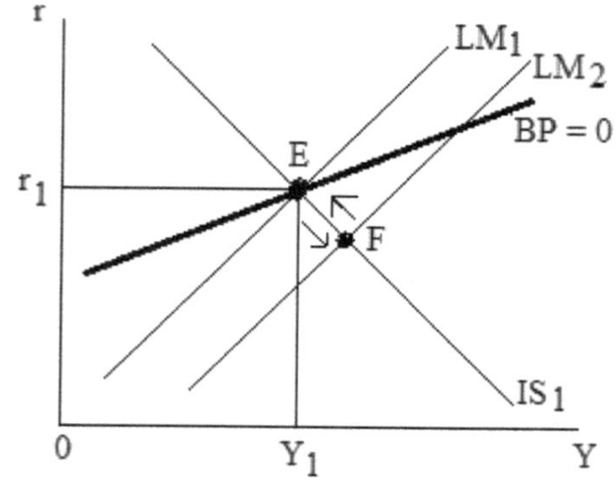

Figure 21.10 Monetary policy effects

line would be steeper than the LM then still there would be no income effect of the expansionary monetary policy. The readers can try it out diagrammatically like that of the earlier case.

21.5.2.3 *Case VII – fiscal policy effects under flexible exchange rate with imperfect capital mobility*

An expansionary fiscal policy under flexible exchange rate with imperfect capital mobility makes different types of adjustments since the foreign exchange is determined in a market system. As public expenditure increases, the IS function shifts upward to IS_2 and the new equilibrium shifts to *F* from the initial equilibrium point *E* resulting in BOP surplus, considering a flatter BOP line (Figure 21.11). The rate of interest in the home market will increase which will result in inflow of more capital. The home currency, as a result, will appreciate, leading to export items being costly and import items being cheap. That will further lead to a fall in net export which will pull back the shifted IS curve to its original position, IS_1. Thus, expansionary fiscal policy is not effective in the case of flexible exchange rate with imperfect capital mobility.

21.5.2.4 *Case VIII – monetary policy effects under flexible exchange rate with imperfect capital mobility*

An expansionary monetary policy under the conditions of flexible exchange rate with imperfect capital mobility will produce effective results unlike the fiscal policy. Let us see how. The initial internal and external balances coexist at point *E* with Y_1 level of output and EY_1 rate of interest (Figure 21.12). An expansionary monetary policy will shift the LM function to LM_2 where the home economy faces BOP deficit. The home currency will depreciate due to flexible exchange rate. As a result of this depreciation, export will increase and import will fall which ultimately leads to increase in net export. The IS function will shift to the right to IS_2 as a result of increase in net exports. Rate of interest will increase which will push up the capital inflow and reduce the BOP deficit. The new equilibrium is at *G* where the economy restores both the internal and external balance but with an increased value of income. Therefore, we say that under the condition of flexible exchange rate with imperfect capital mobility, the expansionary monetary policy

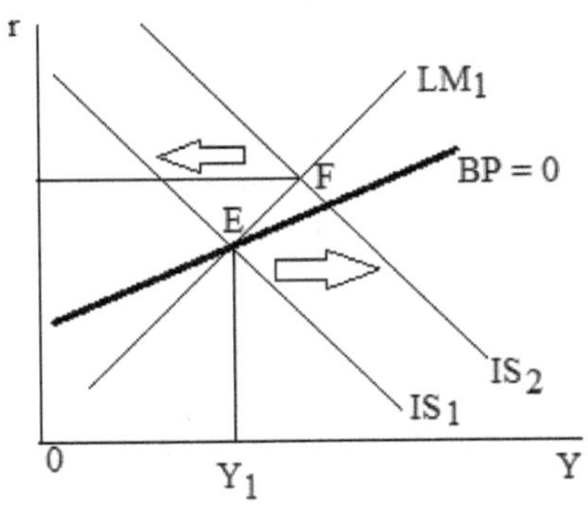

Figure 21.11 Fiscal policy effects

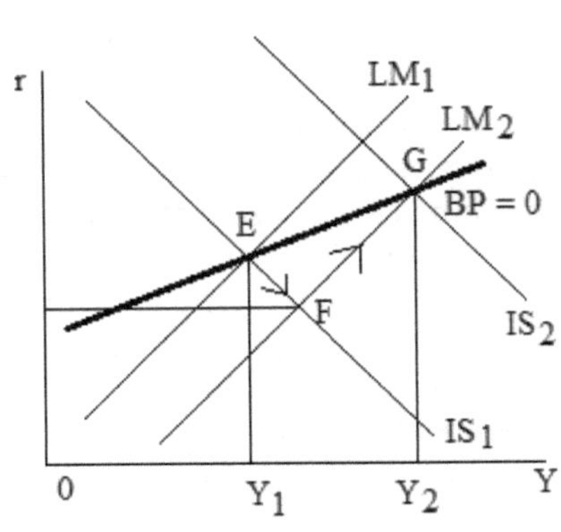

Figure 21.12 Monetary policy effects

will be effective. The readers can verify the conclusions obtained from Case VII and VIII with a relatively steeper BOP line.

We can now sum up the results obtained from all eight cases. Fiscal policy is effective under fixed exchange system with both perfect and imperfect capital mobility and monetary policy is effective under flexible exchange rate under both perfect and imperfect capital mobility conditions.

21.5.3 Consequences of policy-induced depreciation — the beggar-thy-neighbour policy and competitive depreciation

In the previous discussions we saw that expansionary monetary policy in a flexible exchange system caused the depreciation of the home currency whose ultimate result was increase in export and the home country's output and employment. The result is good from the home country's perspective but its consequence is costly or bad for the trading foreign country or countries. The grounds for this bad consequence is that the increase in home export and fall in import by the home country means the foreign countries are worse off in the sense that their output and employment levels get reduced by the progress of the home country. The home demand for foreign goods gets converted into the home goods or goods of the import competing industries. In other words, the money-supply-induced depreciation makes an export of unemployment to the trading countries and imports the foreign income to a large extent. The foreign countries are getting beggared and hence it is called the beggar-thy-neighbour policy by the home country.

If this beggar policy continues then the opponent countries will not stay unarmed. They will also apply the policy to depreciate their own currencies artificially and there will be competitive depreciation that may take all the countries back to their original exchange rates. The ultimate result will not be beneficial to all the countries. For instance, if the level of total world demand is deficient, then depreciation in exchange rate by various countries will affect only the distribution of given world demand among countries and will not help in increasing the level of world demand for goods and services. In other words, exchange rate adjustments by various countries experiencing recessionary conditions are merely policies of a beggar-thy-neighbour variety. It would be better if instead the countries would apply fiscal and monetary policies to boost home demand.

Box I Competitive devaluations after 2009 – some instances

Competitive devaluation is a trade policy strategy where countries seek to gain a trade advantage over other countries by inducing the home currency to fall in relation to the currencies of the other countries. It allows the devaluing country to extract a favourable balance of payments by means of increase in net exports. As a result, the output and employment in the home country get boosted and correspondingly the trading foreign country loses its national income and employment. It is alternatively called *currency war*. The first currency war broke out in the 1930s when countries abandoned the gold standard during the Great Depression and used currency devaluations in an attempt to stimulate their economies. Since this effectively pushes unemployment overseas, trading partners quickly retaliated with their own devaluation policies. The period is considered to have been an adverse situation for all concerned, as unpredictable changes in exchange rates reduced overall international trade.

In the recent past, Brazil's finance minister during September 2010 declared that an "international currency war" had broken out, with countries competitively trying to devalue their currency so as to boost exports. Brazil has been one of the few major economies lacking a reserve currency to abstain from significant currency intervention, with the home currency, the "real", rising by 25% against the dollar after January 2009. Some economists were apprehending the risks of tensions further escalating due to counter devaluation

Again, in January 2013, Japan's central bank, the Bank of Japan, signalled their intention to commence an open-ended bond buying programme which would likely devalue the yen through the excess supply channel of yen. This resulted in a short-lived but intense period of alarm about the risk of a possible fresh round of currency war. Numerous senior central bankers and finance ministers issued public warnings, the first being the deputy chairman of Russia's central bank, the Central Bank of Russia, and then the finance minister of South Korea, and the president of the Bundesbank of Germany. After that, in February of the same year, ECB president Mario Draghi hinted that the ECB might take action if the euro continued to appreciate, and this saw the value of the European currency fall considerably. The risks of currency war took a significant spot on the G7 agenda. In a mid-February statement, the G7 confirmed that the advanced economies were committed to avoiding currency war.

21.5.4 Devaluation-inflation-wage spiral

Devaluation, with its adverse consequences, has historically rarely been a preferred strategy. Richard Cooper (1971), in his work *Currency devaluation in developing countries*, stated that a substantial devaluation is one of the most dramatic, even traumatic, policies a government can adopt – it almost always resulted in cries of anger and demanded the government be replaced. Devaluation can lead to a reduction in citizens' standard of living as their purchasing power is reduced both when they buy unavoidable imports like equipment, raw materials for industrial use, etc. and when they travel abroad. If the devaluing country is largely dependent upon imports of intermediate goods for industrial uses, then the devaluation strategy may add to inflationary pressure. If the import cost rises, the producers of the goods intensively using the import items will add cost to their produced goods. That means the employees of the sectors along with those of the others will have to struggle to maintain their standards of living as their purchasing power gets reduced. To keep them in their earlier standard of living, the employees can demand a wage hike from the owners of the industries and other sectors. As a result of that, general inflation can again emerge. As general price level increases, the home country's export items become more costly (since $P > P_f$) which will pull down net export and current account as well as BOP face deficit. To get rid of such deficit, the central bank of the home country can again go for devaluation of the home currency. The inflation and wage hike situations will again prevail. Hence, there can be the situation of a devaluation-inflation-wage spiral.

21.5.5 *Does devaluation necessarily improve trade balance? The Marshall—Lerner condition*

In the preceding discussions on the effects of devaluation (or depreciation) we saw that in general the policies improve trade balance since it makes export cheaper for the foreigners and import costlier for the home customers. But technically this simple favourable effect may not work. That means a country with devaluation of the real exchange rate may not be capable of making its net export volume positive. Why? In line with the pure theory of international trade, we say that both the trading countries will gain from the trade if the export and import elasticities are sufficiently large and that is observed when two countries' offer curves make an intersection at their elastic zones so that the sum of the export and import elasticities with respect to exchange rate will be greater than unity in an absolute sense. This relation or condition is known as the Marshall–Lerner condition. Therefore, we can say that the benefit of devaluation will be obtained by the home country (the devaluing country) only if the Marshall–Lerner condition is satisfied. If export increase is sufficiently larger than the fall in imports then only the net export will be positive and this makes the home country better off.

Let us derive the Marshall–Lerner condition first. It is a mathematical task.

Using this definition, the trade balance denominated in domestic currency (with domestic and foreign prices normalised to one) is given by:

The net export (trade balance) is given as:

$$NX = X - M \tag{21.9}$$

$$NX = X - e \cdot m \tag{21.10}$$

where X denotes exports, and "m" is imports and "e" is defined as the price of one unit of foreign currency in terms of the domestic currency.

Differentiating with respect to "e" gives:

$$dNX / de = dX / de - e \cdot dm / de - m.$$

Dividing both sides by X, we get

$$(dNX / de) \cdot 1 / X = (dX / de) \cdot (1 / X) - (e / X) \cdot dm / de - m / X.$$

At equilibrium, $X = e.m$. Therefore,

$$(dNX / de) \cdot 1 / X = (dX / de) \cdot (1 / X) - (1 / m) \cdot dm / de - 1 / e.$$

Multiplying both sides by e we get

$$(dNX / de) \cdot \ e / X = (dX / de) \cdot (e / X) - (e / m) \cdot dm / de - 1.$$

The previous expression can be written as

$$(dNX / de) \cdot \ e / X = \varepsilon_x - \varepsilon_m - 1. \tag{21.11}$$

where ε_x and ε_m are the common notations for the elasticity of exports and imports with respect to the exchange rate respectively. We can alternatively define ε_x as the exchange rate elasticity of export which measures the degree of response of the quantity of export with 1% increase or decrease in the exchange rate. And ε_m is the exchange rate elasticity of import that measures the magnitude of import change due to 1% change in the exchange rate.

In order for a fall in the relative value of a country's currency (i.e. a rise in "*e*" using the previous definition) to have a positive effect on that country's trade balance, the left-hand side of the equation must be positive (i.e. for a rise in *e* to cause a rise in NX).

Therefore, we have

$$\varepsilon_x - \varepsilon_m - 1 > 0 . \qquad (21.12)$$

This can be written as

$$\varepsilon_x - \varepsilon_m > 1$$

$$\varepsilon_x + |\varepsilon_m| > 1 . \qquad (21.13)$$

The previous relation is the Marshall–Lerner condition. It is an important condition for which the trading countries gain from trade. It shows that the elasticity of export to the foreign country and import by the home country should be large enough to make both the countries better off after trade. It is the position where two countries' offer curves are relatively flatter and their intersection point (the trade equilibrium) occurs at these elastic zones. If goods exported are elastic to price, their quantity demanded will increase proportionately more than the decrease in price, and total export revenue will increase. Similarly, if goods imported are elastic, total import expenditure will decrease. Both will improve the trade balance. The effectiveness of devaluation (or depreciation) of the home currency on the trade balance is also governed by this relation. Empirically, it has been unearthed that trade in goods tends to be inelastic in the short term since it takes time to change consumption patterns and trade agreements. Thus, the Marshall–Lerner condition is not met in the short run, and devaluation is likely to worsen the trade balance initially. In the long term, consumers will adjust to the new prices, and trade balance will improve. This effect is called the J-curve effect.

Box II Example of effectiveness of devaluation

Exchange rate (e)	*Export* (X)	*Import* (M)	*Net Export* (NX = X – M)
\$1 = Rs. 30	1,000	1,200	1,000 – 1,200 = -200
\$1 = Rs. 35	If 10% ↑ = 1,100	If 5% ↓ = 1,140	1,100 – 1,140 = -40
\$1 = Rs. 35	If 20% ↑ = 1,200	If 5% ↓ = 1,140	1,200 – 1,140 = +60

The previous table presents an example on the effects of devaluation on the trade balance of a country, say India, vis-à-vis the USA. At the initial exchange rate of \$1 = Rs. 30, export is 1,000 and import is 1,200 and trade balance is – 200 meaning there is a deficit in trade balance. Suppose the Indian Rupee is devalued by the RBI to \$1 = Rs. 35 and also suppose that export rises by 10% but import falls by 5%. As a result of that, trade balance is improved to –40. Still, it is in deficit. That means insignificant increase in export may not expand export at the desired level. Now suppose export increases by 20% and import still falls by 5%, then the trade balance is +60 which a surplus position in the trade account. Hence, we can say that to have effective devaluation policy, the Marshall–Lerner condition is to be satisfied and that happens in the case of 20% increase in export. We can also try for more than 5% reduction in import that will also comply with the Marshall–Lerner condition.

21.5.5.1 The J-curve

In international trade theory, the *J-curve* explains the relationship between the exchange rate for currency of a country and its balance of trade position. The curve is so named because of its shape like the English letter, J. The shape of the curve has close links with the Marshall–Lerner condition which states that devaluation policy of the central bank of a country will have a positive effect upon the trade balance if the sum of elasticity of export and import with respect to price (exchange rate) exceeds unity. We know that devaluation of a currency makes export items cheaper and import items costly and thereby there is the possibility of it having a positive effect of devaluation upon trade balance. In the initial stage of trade relation or in the short term, devaluation cannot make export items cheaper in great magnitude and increase import price also in great magnitude because consumers and businesses take time to adjust with the international changes. Hence, in the early stage, devaluation cannot improve the trade balance situation and there are deficits in the phase. The export and import elasticity are low in this phase (i.e. violation of Marshall–Lerner condition). As the devaluation policy continues and the consumers and industrial sectors become accustomed to the changing dimensions then export demand by the foreigners will sufficiently increase and the import demand by the home citizens will fall significantly. That means the export and import elasticity are significantly large in the long run and thus devaluation will lead to a balance of trade surplus and it becomes larger and larger in magnitude as time goes on. Therefore, in the initial stage, the effect of devaluation creates negative trade balance (the falling part of J) and as time goes on it creates positive and increasing trade surpluses (the steep rising part of J). Figure 21.13 presents the J-curve.

21.6 India's foreign currency reserves and GDP trends

The external performance of a country is judged by, among other things, the reserve of foreign currency earned through the transactions in current and capital accounts. In a globalised world, a slump in the forex reserve in a country severely impacts the progress of the country because of the shortage of important raw materials, technology, equipment, crude oil, etc. that are imported from abroad. For example, India faced its severe BOP crisis in the late 80s and early 90s and the forex reserve was well below the 1976–1977 value. After facing the external crisis, along with internal crisis, the country moved towards liberalising the economy, and, within a half of a decade, it

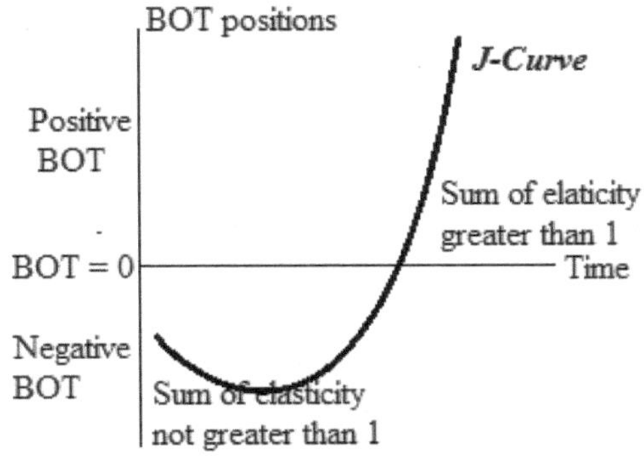

Figure 21.13 The J-curve

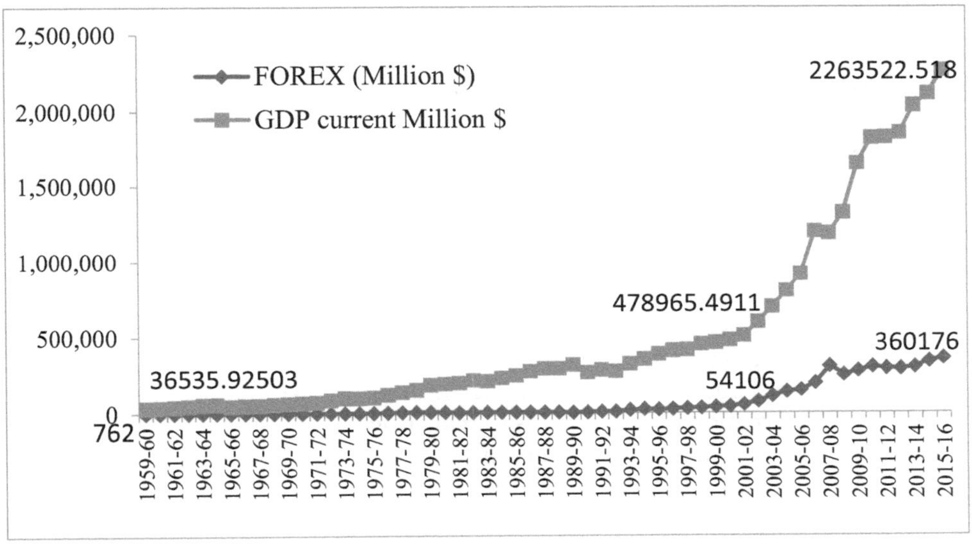

Figure 21.14 Trends of forex reserve and GDP for India for the period 1959–1960 to 2015–2016

managed to survive the forex crisis along with improving other macroeconomic indicators. Figure 21.14 shows the trends of forex reserve and GDP for India for the period 1959–1960 to 2015–2016 (borrowed from the RBI database).

We observe from the figure that India started with 762 million USD in forex reserve and maintained a steady rate over time with some fluctuations. The forex reserve makes a jump in 1976–1977 due to voluminous export increase and continues up to 1986–1987 and then starts dwindling and reaches its lowest figure of 3,962 million USD in 1989–1990. The liberalisation process brings recovery phases, and from 2001–2002 it jumped to a great height and the accelerated growth continues today. The figure in 2015–2016 stood at 36,0176 million USD. Here we also show the relation between the external performance in terms of forex reserve and the GDP of the country. We observe that the GDP is increasing over time and it from 1992–1993 it increased by leaps and bounds. The high growth phase started in 2001–2002 like that of the forex reserve. Both the trends have close linkages. The correlation between them is +0.98 which is very big and statistically significant. Hence, the external economy and internal economy are highly related in the case of India.

21.7 Pros and cons of international linkages

International linkages may be good or bad for the associated countries. Linking the sectors of an economy to the international markets in terms of exporting and importing of goods/services/financial assets offers the associated countries both gains and risks. Before studying the macroeconomic aspects of international linkages, we should know about the pros (the positive sides) and cons (the negative sides) of such openness available in the history of trade information and theoretical foundations.

The pros

i) International linkages open up the possibility for the exporting countries to achieve increased levels of growths of incomes which are not possible under autarky. As the boundaries are opened, more goods flow out of the country because of international demands for the goods of the domestic country which further expands the productive capacity of the existing firms. It finally leads to more employment and gross national product (not just the GDP) of the domestic country.
ii) Studies have shown that overseas trade works to increase financial performance and ultimately augment the returns on investment. As the investment opportunities across the foreign countries open up after international linkages, the firms have better options to choose among the better assets and thereby get the scopes to grasp high returns on investment.
iii) Considering the consistency of the size of the domestic market, opening up the economy to the international market leads to reduction of risk associated to the fixed-size domestic market. If the home market faces contraction in demands due to any reasons like fall in income, increase in price of the goods, turmoil in political conditions, etc. then the domestic market is relatively unsafe but the foreign market has enough scope to absorb the additional supply.
iv) Exposure to international markets makes the domestic firms more efficient as they can grasp the flavour of different technologies applied in their competing products. Also, the domestic firms make their products in greater varieties to be competitive in the international market; the domestic consumers can also reap the benefits from the utility of the greater variety of products imported from the foreign country.

There are more pros that can be added. The readers can think of them.

The cons

i) There may be risks from exchange rate fluctuations that could affect either the value of existing assets or liabilities denominated in foreign currency. If the domestic country is import dependent then there may be a crisis or shortage in the reserves of the leading foreign currencies or the foreign exchange reserves. The dwindling forex reserves may further make the domestic country more vulnerable to the international markets.

ii) The domestic country can face economic backwardness or growth retardation if there is any global meltdown like what happened in the Great Depression of the 30s, the East Asian Crisis of 1997–1998, the Global Financial Crisis of 2006–2008, or the Sovereign Debt Crisis of the major European Countries. Due to international linkages, all such crises spread around the major trade centres of the leading industrialised nations through the stock markets. India was able to keep itself away from the global shocks of the twentieth or twenty-first century not because of their shock-absorbing capacity but due to their low degree of trade openness.
iii) There may be political risks occurring in both home and foreign countries. Investing in different countries whose political regimes can change over time also poses a few risks since the governments of the countries could discriminatorily change laws, regulations, or contracts governing an investment. The firms engaged in international business thus use a combination of legal contracts, insurance, and trade in financial instruments to protect income streams for protection against policy risks. For example, the outbreak of the Gulf War in the early 1990s pushed up the price of petroleum products. The recent years' ISIS movements in Syria, Iraq, etc. also made fluctuations in the oil prices at the global market. The Brexit verdict also made the UK-based firms quit the country and hence the associated flow of goods and services though these companies affected the firms in the other countries. For example, the TATA Group wanted to pull off their business from the UK and the home concern in India also faced some bottlenecks in future policy prescriptions of their existing units in India. The frequent testing of the nuclear bomb by North Korea disturbs the border of South Korea, hence their trading relations with the countries like USA have been hampered.

You can add items into the list of *cons* as you gather knowledge over time.

21.8 Conclusion

The present chapter included a detailed discussion on the interactions among the goods sector, monetary sector, and external sector. The open economy IS function became steeper compared to its closed economy position. Different fiscal and monetary policy combinations were attempted to restore the internal as well as external balances under the conditions of perfect and imperfect capital movements across the borders. It was observed that fiscal policy was effective under a fixed exchange system with both perfect and imperfect capital mobility and monetary policy was effective under flexible exchange rate under both perfect and imperfect capital mobility conditions. It was also observed that the relation between exchange rate movements and the trade balance of countries usually took the shape of the English letter "J" – named the J-curve.

Summary

The whole discussion of the present chapter on the interactions among two internal sectors and one external sector can be summarised by the following points:

- The IS function under the open economy transactions is relatively steeper with no change in the position of the LM function.
- Fiscal policy is effective under a fixed exchange system with both perfect and imperfect capital mobility conditions.

- Monetary policy is effective under flexible exchange rate under both perfect and imperfect capital mobility conditions.
- Perfect capital mobility and fixed exchange rate conditions do not comply with the independent and efficient monetary policy. Mundell termed it the impossible trinity
- The relation between exchange rate movements and the trade balance of countries usually took the shape of English alphabet "J" – named the J-curve.
- Effectiveness of devaluation policy depends on the Marshall–Lerner conditions which say that the import elasticity plus export elasticity will be greater than unity
- India's *forex* reserves have been increasing over time with leaps and bounds.

Keywords

Product market
Money market
External sector
Fixed exchange rate
Flexible exchange rate
Fiscal policy
Monetary policy
Perfect capital mobility
Imperfect capital mobility
J curve

Multiple choice questions and answers

1. Entire external sector transactions include

   (a) Merchandise exports and imports of goods.
   (b) Export and imports of services.
   (c) Import and export of capitals.
   (d) All of the above.

2. The IS function in the open economy system vis-à-vis the closed economy relatively

   (a) Becomes flatter.
   (b) Becomes steeper.
   (c) Remains the same.
   (d) None of the above.

3. If there is perfect capital flow between the countries with fixed exchange regime, we will have the results –

   (a) Fiscal policy alone will be effective.
   (b) Monetary policy alone will be effective.
   (c) No policy is effective.
   (d) Both (a) and (b) are true.

4. If there is perfect capital flow between the countries with flexible exchange regime, we will have the results –

   (a) Fiscal policy alone will be effective.
   (b) Monetary policy alone will be effective.
   (c) No policy is effective.
   (d) Both (a) and (b) are true.

5. The relation between the exchange rate changes and the trade balances of countries usually take the form of English letter

    (a) U.
    (b) V.
    (c) J.
    (d) Inverted U.

Answers

1. (d); 2. (b); 3. (a); 4. (b); 5. (c)

Review questions

1. What is external economy transaction? Draw the IS function under open economic transactions and compare its slope with that of the closed economy.
2. Use the IS-LM-BP model (assuming perfect capital mobility) to show the following: i) Under fixed exchange rates, monetary policy does not work. ii) Under flexible exchange rates monetary policy is very effective.
3. Use the Mundell–Fleming model (assuming imperfect capital mobility) to show the following: i) under fixed exchange rates, monetary policy does not work. ii) Under flexible exchange rates monetary policy is very effective.
4. What is competitive depreciation of currency? Point out some historical instances of countries making competitive depreciations. Is it true that competitive depreciation makes a country transform its neighbour country into a losing position? Justify with arguments.
5. What is the Marshall–Lerner condition? Using the condition, prove that devaluation may not be always effective.
6. What is the J-curve effect? Explain the J-curve in a diagram. Point out the occurrence of this curve with the help of any country's trade balance data.
7. What should happen to the elasticity of demand for imports if the INR remains weak in the long run? How will this affect India's position on the J-curve?
8. Mention, with explanations, some advantages and disadvantages of international linkages to any national economy. Is India growing in terms of stock of foreign exchange reserves? Explain.

Additional readings

Fleming, J. M. (1962). "Domestic financial policies under fixed and floating exchange rates". *IMF Staff Papers*, 9, 369–379. http://doi.org/10.2307/3866091.

Mundell, R. A. (1963). "Capital mobility and stabilization policy under fixed and flexible exchange rates". *Canadian Journal of Economic and Political Science*, 29(4), 475–485.

Part VI

Economics of growth and convergence – the longer run models

22 Theories of economic growth – classical, Harrod and Domar

22.1 Introduction — meaning of economic growth

Economic growth, in the usual sense, means the percent change in the levels of nominal or real national income of a country in comparison to the level of income of the previous time period which may be termed as the base period's income. Suppose Y_t is the national income of a country in time "*t*" and Y_{t-1} is the national income at the previous time period, $t - 1$, then the growth rate of income – or simply the growth rate – is

$$g_t = \left[\left(Y_t - Y_{t-1}\right) / Y_{t-1}\right] * 100 = \left(dY / Y\right) * 100. \tag{22.1}$$

g_t may be positive, negative, or even zero depending on the conditions, whether $Y_t > Y_{t-1}$, $Y_t < Y_{t-1}$, or $Y_t = Y_{t-1}$. Although the occurrences of zero or negative growth rates seem absurd, they may happen depending on certain unusual conditions. An economy can have a declining value of income in the future period because of recession, bad climate, and wars, situations that may hinder the normal production and consumption activities within the domestic economic periphery. Suppose nominal income in the year 2015, $Y_{t-1=2015}$ is ₹100 and $Y_{t=2016}$ = ₹110, then growth rate g_t = [(110 – 100) / 100] * 100 = 10 %. This means the nominal income of the country rises by 10% in one year. The figure of 10% growth rate of income is universally accepted as very high growth rate which the presently growing economy, in China, had achieved a few years ago for a very small duration of a financial year. But it is also important to keep in mind that if the extra ₹10 is accompanied by an extra 5 unit increase of overall price level of the economy, then the real income virtually grows by 10% minus 5%, which is 5%. How?

Suppose P_t is the overall price level in period "*t*" and P_{t-1} is the price level at "$t - 1$", then over time price rise – or *inflation rate* – is

$$g_p = \left[\left(P_t - P_{t-1}\right) / P_{t-1}\right] * 100 = \left(dP / P\right) * 100. \tag{22.2}$$

Suppose $P_{t-1} = 10$, $P_t = 10.5$ then g_p = [10.5 – 10) / 10] * 100 = 5%. That means there is an inflation of 5%. Reducing the nominal income of 10% increase in the real income by dividing the nominal income growth by the rate of inflation, we get real income as Y / P (= y) or its growth rate $d(Y / P) / (Y / P) = d - Y / YdP / P = g_t - g_p$ = 10% – 5% = 5%. Hence, the real income growth rate is actually falling short of the nominal income growth rate because of overall price escalation.

Let us introduce another negative aspect of the nominal income growth besides the inflation rate, that is, the growth of population of the country. That means what matters

DOI: 10.4324/9781003501138-28

now is the per capita real income, which can be defined as the national income divided by the existing population of the country which consumes the national output. Suppose, besides the 5% growth rate of real income of the country, the national population at the same time increases by 2% per annum, then the per capita income, y, grows further by a lesser rate which is, like before, the difference between dy / y and dN / N where N is the total population of the country at a particular time period. Hence, the growth of per capita income is (5% – 2%), equal to only 3%, which is a meagre figure in comparison to 10% increase in the nominal income. Hence, the international standard is now to accept the growth rate in terms of per capita real income which reflects two broad indicators, the population and the price level.

22.2 Revisiting long run real income determination: classical vs. Keynesian thoughts

As addressed and discussed in detail in Chapters 9, 11, and 14 we here recall the process through which real income of a capitalistic economy is determined. The classical school of thought was heavily dependent on the free market competitive assumptions with money wage and price level flexibility and established that there was always self-adjusting equilibrium output and employment with no under use of existing production capacity. This is another way to say that there is always full employment equilibrium with zero excess supply. Hence, the government, like outside agencies, is strictly disallowed to interfere in the self-adjusting economic system. Entire forces of supply decide how much to employ and how much to produce; neglecting the role of aggregate demand for the same determination. Therefore, the classical output and employment bear the *long run* feature where the potential capacity of an economy becomes fully exhausted. Figure 22.1 (left side) highlights the determination of output and price level under the classical system.

The aggregate supply function (AS) is vertical signifying the full employment level of output. The aggregate demand function (AD) is negatively sloped which is based on the transaction demand function with a given quantity of money supply or velocity of money, discarding any source of demand from the government sector. E is the initial equilibrium in the aggregate economy that makes the AD bounded to be matched with AS generating y_f level of full capacity output and a corresponding price level of P_1. Allowing

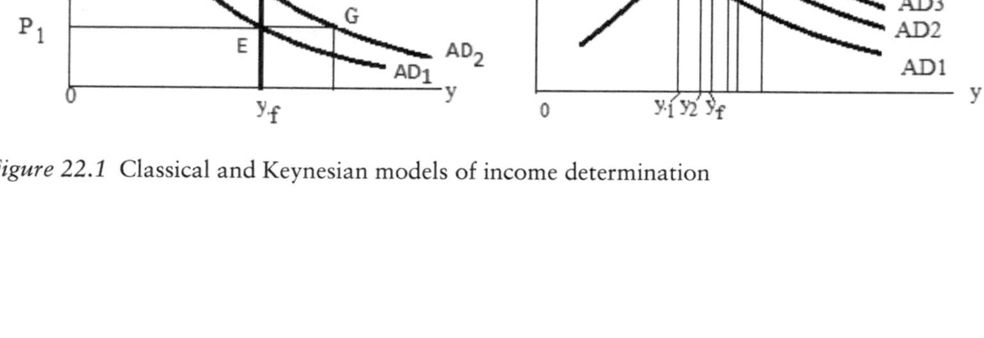

Figure 22.1 Classical and Keynesian models of income determination

increase in aggregate demand to AD_2 followed by increase in money supply or increase in velocity of money leads to full strength increase in price level to P_2 without having any real effect upon output and employment. The new equilibrium of the economy is reached at F, a vertical movement from E. This phenomenon is popularly known as *neutrality of money* or more generally, the *neutrality of aggregate demand* in the classical system. Equal magnitudes of changes in the price level vis-à-vis the change in aggregate demand nullify the impact upon the output and employment. Hence, the classical system gives the socially accepted output where all the active labour forces are absorbed into the existing production structure; no question of involuntary unemployment arises. All who are unemployed are voluntarily unemployed in nature and the economy has no compulsion to feed them.

Keynesian economics rejected such a superficial conclusion made by the classical economists which is far from reality. The perfect flexibility in the money wage rate and price level assumed by the classical system neglects the process by which the wage contracts are made by the labourers in an imperfect market with existing trade union movements and policies like governments' minimum wage laws. Hence, to Keynes, without treating the short run problem of the economy, classical economics has jumped into a long run conclusion. According to Keynes, money wage becomes *rigid or inflexible* around a specific value for the short run which gives rise to underemployment equilibrium where all the unemployed are involuntarily unemployed in the sense that the existing shortage of aggregate demand (one of the main causes of the Great Depression of the 1920s and 30s) cannot generate enough job opportunities for the unemployed. Hence, the output that is ultimately generated is not only decided by the aggregate supply side but by the aggregate demand as well. Hence, the aggregate supply curve is not vertical, rather it is positively sloped. Figure 22.1 (right side) highlights the equilibrium under the Keynesian framework. Point A is the initial equilibrium with output and price level respectively at y_1 and Ay_1. The output level y_1 is well short of the full employment output y_f, the classicists' only output solution. Hence, there is underemployment equilibrium in Keynes.

Keynes solved the short run involuntary unemployment problem of the economy by means of active public investment projects by direct interference of the government sector into the real activity of the economy. Increase in public investment will lead to a multiplier effect upon output and employment, and the private investors get confidence in the economy to further invest and contribute further to output and employment. These dynamics have been given in the diagram where primary equilibrium gets shifted from point A towards the right via upward shifting of aggregate demands to AD_3. The existing involuntary unemployment problem gets solved by increase in aggregate demand and the economy reaches y_f output and full employment of all the factors, leaving no labour force unemployed involuntarily. This is the convergence of Keynesian results into the long run results of the classicists. That means Keynes ultimately justifies the process by which an economy can reach the full employment production level. If the aggregate demand is further increased over AD_3 then only price level gets inflated with no real changes in output and employment. Hence, an economy should attempt first to reach this *long run* equilibrium.

Now, think of how an economy grows from such a background as depicted in both parts of Figure 22.1. It is now obvious that an economy will experience growth from the point E corresponding to an initial long run level of output, y_f. Again, to experience growth over time, an economy has to think of *longer runs*, not just long run static equilibrium like point E. As we know from the previous discussion, aggregate demand solves the short run unemployment problem of a depressed economy, but the long run problem needs to be addressed by the supply-side factors, which fix the position of the vertical aggregate supply function. The sustained growth of output would be possible if we could shift the vertical AS function rightward along the horizontal axis backed by the supply determining parameters given the potential demand of the economy. These supply-side parameters become the sources of economic growth.

22.3 Forces behind growth

An economy grows when its potential capacity is improved over time. Again, the potential capacity is changed when the primary, secondary, and other auxiliary resources of the economy are changed. There are three such forces which encapsulate the expansion of potential capacity as well as longer run output changes of an economy. They are:

- *Primary force* which includes *natural force* and *anthropogenic force*
- *Secondary force* which includes the supplies of produced means of production like all sorts of capital formation. For example, machineries, equipment, roads, and other infrastructures
- *Auxiliary force* which includes technology which further covers scientific inventions and innovations, managerial efficiencies, etc.

The natural force explaining the economic growth consists of natural capital, land, whose quantity of supply is fixed by nature (it is called a gift of nature). Land may be used in production in variety of ways. Its erosion and pollution degrade the environmental quality which ultimately affects the entire system of income generation on an economy in particular and the global economy in general. Anthropogenic force, on the other hand, constitutes the amount of labour supply in both quantitative and qualitative natures. Labour force, both skilled and unskilled (or human capital) is determined by the growth of the population of an economy and the amount of investment the households spend on educational developments or skill developments. In this sense, to quote the UN Secretary General Ban Ki Moon, the present 700 crore in the world is not a liability but an asset or human resource that can be used in production and growth-generating activities.

The secondary source mainly covers the magnitude of capital accumulation in an economy backed by generations of extra savings and investment. Besides, all capital (physical and environmental) has a natural depreciation while their uses start that has to be deducted from the gross investment. Hence, the term net investment is wise to account for investment and growth of income in place of gross investment.

The auxiliary force, unlike the primary and secondary force, is not tangible, but it is inherent of the two forces that enhance the quality of capital and labour as well as enhance the output level with a given state of capital and labour. This is obtained by scientific invention and innovations in production and managerial activities. Therefore the aggregate production function becomes

$$y = A.\, F\left(T,\ N,\ K\right) \tag{22.3}$$

where T is the total stock of natural resources, land and environment, N is the total population or labour force, K is the total stock of capital, and A is the level of technological progress. As the inputs of labour, capital, or natural resources rise, it is expected that output will increase, although at a diminishing rate. The role of technology, A, is to augment the productivity and hence efficiency of the inputs T, N and K where productivity refers to the ratio of output to the index of all the inputs. This is known as total factor productivity.

22.4 Measurement of technology effects on output — the concept of growth accounting

The concept of growth accounting captures contributions of different inputs and technology upon the growth rate of output. Based on the production function as given earlier, the total output growth is segregated into the growth or contributions of T, N, K, and A. That means:

Growth of Y in percent = Growth of T in percent + Growth of N in percent + Growth of K in percent + Growth of A in percent

Assuming constancy of natural resources and their limited variability, the effect of T change can be ignored. Hence,

$$dY/Y*100 = dN/N*100 + dK/K*100 + dA/A*100. \qquad (22.4)$$

The last term of the previous relation is known as technological progress (TP) which shifts the production function up, meaning more output with the same amount of the two variable inputs, N and K. The two variable factors need not contribute equally to the overall output. We can assume that three-fourths of total output is attributable to labour and the remaining one fourth is attributable to capital. Hence, the previous relation can be reframed as

$$dY/Y*100 = \tfrac{3}{4}*dN/N*100 + \tfrac{1}{4}*dK/K*100 + TP. \qquad (22.5)$$

Thus the effect of TP can now be expressed as a *residual* which is

$$TP = dY/Y*100 - \tfrac{3}{4}*dN/N*100 - \tfrac{1}{4}*dK/K*100. \qquad (22.6)$$

This is an important relation in the sense of which part of economic growth is due to high capital-labour ratio and what part is due to technological advances. For example, if output or income growth in an economy is 5% in a year, population or labour force grows by 2%, and capital formation grows by 3% then the contribution of TP is 0.05 – 3 /4 * .02 – 1 /4 * .03 = 2.75%.

The growth history of different countries and regions of the world can be viewed as resultant of the mixture of the four forces of production. Nineteenth-century England, post-world war USA, and then Japan, the late-twentieth-century South East Asian countries, and the twenty-first-century growth experience of two Asian giants, China and India, are examples of histories of growth across the nations and regions. The per capita income of the leading developed countries with a history of more than 50 years of development is far above that of countries like China, India, and the emerging countries from the Latin America and African zones. These highly developing countries from the Asian and other zones are growing at a higher speeds compared to the so-called developed nations to catch up with the latter ones. This is a crucial prediction from the growth theories that in the longer run the cross-country differences will be reduced and the poor countries will converge on the rich ones, and ultimately they will end up in a common *steady-state* level of growth of income where *growth of income will be fixed at the rate of capital formation and population growth.*

22.5 Cross-country evidence — what the data says

Let us view the scenario of the average growth of GDP as well as per capita GDP over the period from 1961–2015 in a gap of 10 years across some industrial nations with a history of development of around 150 years along with some newly developed countries from the east and highly emerging countries like China and India. Tables 22.1 and 22.2 and Figures 22.2 and 22.3 present the data borrowed from the World Bank data base. With respect to the average growth rates of GDP over all the decades except 1961–1970, it is observed that the figures for the so-called developed countries, USA, UK, France, Japan, and OECD members, show lower rates compared to the other countries who became developed later like Singapore, Hong Kong, and South Republic and the highly developing countries who are going to be developed, China and India. When we consider the initial decade, 1961–1970, we find Japan to be the most highly growing country, not developed, compared to the countries from the west.

There are steady declines of the average growth rates of GDP of all the countries except China and India. The difference is prominent since the beginning of the twenty-first century. China has maintained around 10% rates during 1981–1990, 1991–1900 and 2001–2010 which was comparable to the East Asian giants in the preceding two phases. The engines behind these high growth rates for the countries were *huge capital formation* backed by *high savings ration, low value of capital–output ratio* (that determines requirement of capital per unit of output) and the *large volume of manufacturing outputs.* India was trying to chase China during the last phase and superseded China during the 2015–2016 financial year (RBI data base). *But low growth rates of the so-called developed economies do not mean they are lagging behind China and India.* Despite the fact of low growth rates of the developed economies, the per capita GDP of these countries are well ahead of the other two countries. The figure for China is almost 60 times lower than that of the USA during 1981–1990 and 40 times lower than that of India. But the margin for China has gone down at a tremendous speed to around seven times lower during the last phase, while it is too slow for India.

Table 22.1 Average growth of GDP in different periods

Periods	*USA*	*UK*	*France*	*Japan*	*Singapore*	*Hong Kong*	*S Korea*	*China*	*India*	*OECD average*
1961–70	4.5107	3.0585	5.57008	9.2984	9.35449396	5.46911164	8.7146	4.98	4.032	5.399277
1971–80	3.1974	2.144	3.64007	4.495	9.08850608	9.09081552	9.0529	6.299	3.085	3.523139
1981–90	3.3591	2.9525	2.492	4.6439	7.79373848	6.7992102	9.7423	9.38	5.57	3.187418
1991–00	3.4494	2.4425	2.10204	1.1381	7.18561373	4.019346	6.6311	10.46	5.599	2.672935
2001–10	1.661	1.6203	1.22426	0.8021	5.91293898	4.12957175	4.4388	10.52	7.42	1.597062
2011–15	2.0338	2.0987	0.85072	0.6172	3.96429002	2.91241936	2.9647	7.817	6.742	1.566106

Source: World Bank.

Table 22.2 Average values of per capita GDP (USD current prices) in different periods

Periods	*USA*	*UK*	*France*	*Japan*	*Singapore*	*Hong Kong*	*S Korea*	*China*	*India*	*OECD average*
1961–70	4,054.4	1,839.87	2,139.7	1,108.13	607.1448	681.7458	156.92	90.04	103.77	1,963.324
1971–80	8650	4,970.55	7,147.84	5,622.42	2,647.265	2,927.593	940.2	161.3	178.53	5,496.131
1981–90	18,697	11,932	13,790.7	16,356.8	7,799.114	8,315.47	3,517.9	260.1	319.17	11,922.06
1991–00	29,858	22,644	24,262.7	35,134.3	21,552.86	22,864.34	10,333	628.7	383.27	21,472.34
2001–10	43,962	37,682.7	35,114.3	35,809.9	32,211.44	27,903.22	17,783	2,322	827.07	30,831.68
2011–15	52,822	42,924.5	41,202.3	40,022.1	54,411.71	38,570.6	25,964	6,869	1,502.9	37,552.33

Source: World Bank.

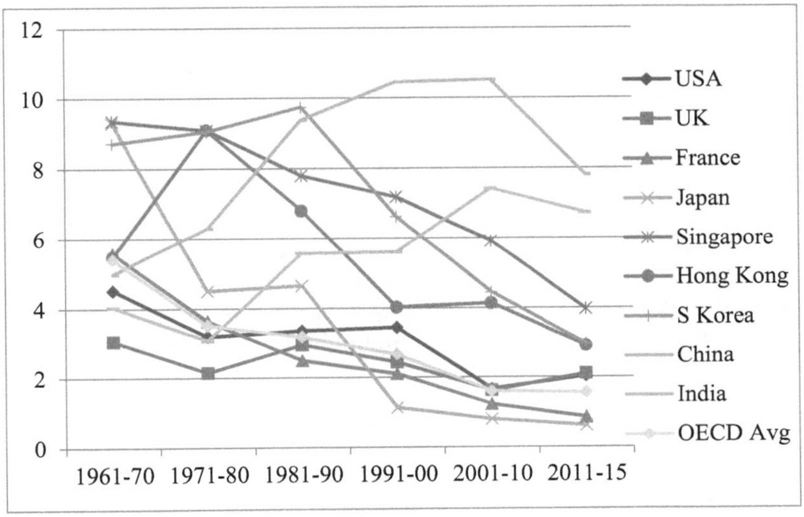

Figure 22.2 Average growth of GDP in different periods

There was a miraculous history of growth of per capita income for Japan, the worst-hit after the World War II. The country has recovered from this devastation in such a way that, within a very short span of time, it became widely believed to be possible that by immitating and innovating foreign technology, it would catch up with the richest country in the group, the USA. The per capita average values of income for Japan followed a steep path after 1971–1980 and superseded the USA during 1981–1990 and remained in the dominant position for a decade up to the year 2000. After that, the USA regained its lost glory and remained in the same position until Singapore overtook it in the phase 2011–2015.

Moreover, most of the countries were hit hard by the oil price shocks in the 70s and the global financial crisis for the phase 2001–2010. Most of the East Asian countries in the list like Hong Kong and South Korea were hit by the crisis during the phase 1991–2000. These crises reveal that no countries, even the highly developed countries of the world, have attained the path of the true long run, rather there are some short run problems which hindered the countries from reaching such a steady-state growth rate that helps in the true development of a country in all respects.

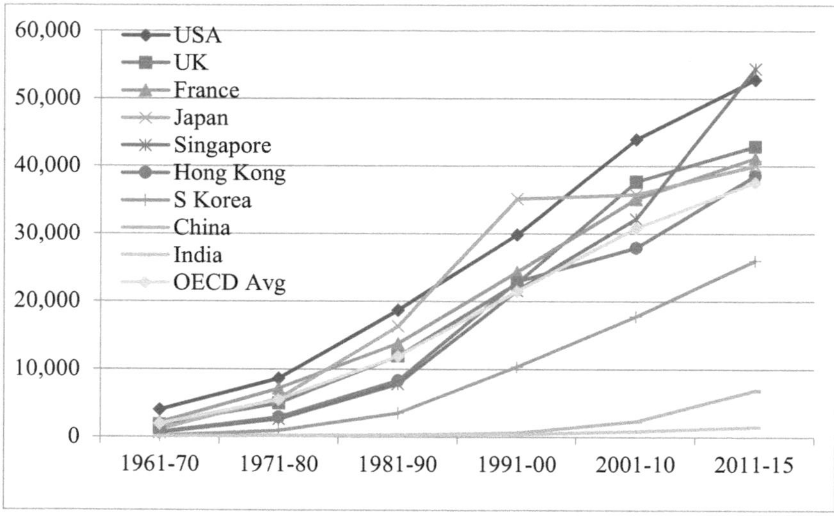

Figure 22.3 Average values of per capita GDP (USD current prices) in different periods

The cross-country differences in scenarios of GDP growth rates as well as the trends of per capita GDP become the inputs for the growth theoreticians. *Why such differences appeared and what the factors behind it are becomes the motto of studying growth economics.* In the following discussion we will highlight all of these issues one by one.

22.6 Models of economic growth — from classical to endogenous systems

Despite the theoretical and temporal differences among different schools of thoughts, especially between the classicists and the Keynesians, in determining output and employment of an economy, all are in favour of economic growth as it is the only panacea to the longer run process of developments. But there are strong disagreements among different models regarding how an economy can grow from its full employment equilibrium. The vintage growth models originate from Adam Smith and T. R. Malthus who predicted growth on the basis of stock of natural resources like land as sole determinant of growth. Later, the starting point for the modern growth theory was the classic article of Ramsey (1928). But economists did not widely adopt Ramsey's approach until the 1960s. Between Ramsey and the late 50s, the period immediately after the Great Depression, Harrod (1939) and Domar (1946) attempted to integrate Keynesian economics with different elements of economic growth. They used the production function with a low degree of substitutability among the factors to show that the capitalist system is inherently unstable. The next and more important contributions to economic growth were those of Solow (1956) and Swan (1956). The central aspect of the Solow–Swan model is the consideration of the neoclassical production function that incorporates constant returns to scale, diminishing returns to each of the factors, and some positive and smooth substitution among the inputs. Then the Ramsey model comes up with consideration of optimum savings derived from households' optimum consumption behaviour. But the major invention in the growth models comes out as the possible answer to the exogenous technological progress of the Solow model and it considers the technology to be endogenous by means of other economic and social factors. The endogenous growth theory starts from the classic work of Romer (1986) where the assumption of exogenous technological progress by the Solow model has been replaced by the endogenous technological progress backed by human capital which is further backed by research and development activities. Later the role of institutions and government came into the picture of growth theories after the crisis experiences of some of the leading countries in the world.

22.6.1 Classical models of growth

22.6.1.1 Smithian model – an optimistic approach

The classical model of growth originates from Adam Smith. In his handbook called *The Wealth of Nations* (1776), he emphasised the role of land more than all the other factors on growth of output of an economy. According to him, in the early stage of world economy, land was freely available and the existing population at that time had an endless quantity of land to use in production activity. As population increased there was equal increase in the quantities of production of all the goods leading to parallel and outward shifting of the production possibility frontier that indicated increase in growth of outputs. At the same time, as population increased, increase in national output was absorbed solely by labour, and real wage remained constant along all possible combinations of land and population. This concept of land-induced growth with constant real wage is a golden age according to Smith.

In spite of this golden feature, predictions of the Smithian model cannot persist for long because, as population continues to rise, a time will come when all the land will be possessed and the parallel shifting of the production possibility curve will not be possible. More labourers will begin to swarm into the full capacity land-use systems of production. Land will become scarce and rent will be imposed to control the use of land. Besides, as population rises, output now will increase at a diminishing rate because of the land-labour ration is going down which leads to decrease in real wage rate, not constant real wage over time. Malthus explained the dynamics in a different and advanced level.

22.6.1.2 Malthusian model – a pessimistic approach

Malthus thought that population pressure would lead the economy to a point where labourers were at the minimum level of subsistence wage. The reason was that when wage rate moved above this rate, people felt secure and happy and got married and so population would expand and when it was below the subsistence wage rate then the population would go down because of high mortality and uncertainty in lives. Under this situation, if the population figure was doubled, there would be nonparallel shifting of the production possibility frontier which indicated that there would be less than doubling of outputs. The effect of diminishing returns on land pulls down the per capita output and hence growth rates, and the real wage continues to fall.

The prediction of the Malthusian model did not carry weight since he disregarded the utility of capital accumulation and technological progress in the production system. If they are allowed to work, the operation of diminishing returns of land may subside.

22.6.2 Harrod model of growth — founded upon Keynesian economics

The Harrod model, named after Roy F. Harrod (1939), is an early post-Keynesian model of economic growth which is based on the experiences of advanced economies. They are primarily addressed to an advanced capitalist economy and attempt to analyse the requirements of steady growth in such an economy. The Harrod model is the direct outcome of projection of the short run Keynesian analysis into the long run. This model is based on the capital factor as the crucial factor of economic growth. It concentrates on the possibility of steady growth through adjustment of supply of demand for capital. The model is used in development economics to explain an economy's growth rate in terms of the level of *saving* and *productivity of capital* or the inverse of incremental *capital–output ratio*. It suggests that there is no natural reason for an economy to have balanced growth.

The model assumes substitution between capital and labour and a neutral technological progress in the sense that technological progress is neither saving nor absorbing labour or capital. Both the factors are used in the same proportion even when neutral technical progress takes place. The production indifference curve, hence, looks like right-angled and the production points lie along the diagonal points through the origin. Both Harrod and Domar assigned a dual role to capital accumulation in the process of growth. On the one hand, new investment generates new income through the multiplier effect, and on the other hand it increases productive capacity of the economy by expanding its capital stock.

One of the important aspects of the model is that the economy makes a knife-edge balance in the process of economic growth from the point of full employment where the warranted rate of growth is equal to actual and natural rates of growth. Once the economy slips up or down from this balance, the magnitudes of excess demand or explosion and magnitudes of excess supply or dampening will arise, which is criticised by the neoclassical economists as the knife-edge instability problem in the long run growth systems. The economy never comes back to this initial knife-edge balance. This is like the way by which our earth is maintaining its function in a rhythmic manner; the deviation from this creates devastation for its creatures.

22.6.2.1 *Important assumptions of the Harrod model*

i) The model is based on the assumption of a closed economy with no government interference in the functioning of the economy.
ii) The economic variables such as savings, investment, income, and expenditure are without lags in the sense that they adjust themselves completely within the same period of time.
iii) The consumption and saving functions are of long run or proportional type. That means the average propensity to save (APS) and marginal propensity to save (MPS) are equal to each other. Hence, $S / Y = dS / dY = s$.
iv) Both propensity to save (s) and capital–output ratio ($v = dK / dY$) are given constant. This amounts to assuming that the law of constant returns operates in the economy because of fixity of "v".
v) Income, investment, and savings are all defined in the net sense, which is, they are considered net of physical wear and tear of capital equipment.
vi) Saving and investment are equal in the ex-ante as well as in the ex post sense, which is, there is accounting as well as functional equality between saving and investment. Hence, $S = I$, which is, whatever is saved gets invested.
vii) The economy is already in a full employment position.

The growth model raised three issues

i) How can steady growth be achieved for an economy with fixed saving-income ratio and a fixed capital–output ratio?

ii) How can the steady growth rate be maintained?
iii) How do the natural factors limit the growth rate of the economy?

In order to discuss these issues, they adopted three different concepts of growth rates: i) the actual growth rate, g_A, ii) the warranted growth rate, g_w, and (*iii*) the natural growth rate, g_n.

The actual growth rate is the growth rate determined by the actual rate of savings and investment in the country.

Warranted growth refers to that growth rate of the economy when it is working at full capacity. It is also known as full-capacity growth rate. This growth rate denoted by g_w is interpreted as the rate of income growth required for full utilisation of a growing stock of capital, so that entrepreneurs would be satisfied with the amount of investment actually made.

g_n, the natural growth rate, is determined by natural conditions such as labour force, natural resources, capital equipment, technical knowledge, etc. These factors place a limit beyond which expansion of output is not feasible. This limit is called full-employment ceiling.

22.6.2.2 *The basic equations under the Harrod model – short run equilibrium condition*

Let us define aggregate saving function (or the abstention from consumption function) in period "*t*" as $S_t = sY_{t-1}$ which is ex ante as well as ex post and the investment function which is in addition to capital stock as $I_t = dK_t = K_t - K_{t-1}$. Because of the *acceleration principle*, capital stock is determined by aggregate output of the economy, which is $K_t = vY_t$ and $K_{t-1} = vY_{t-1}$, where v is the incremental capital–output ratio. Hence, $I_t = v(Y_t - Y_{t-1})$. The basic equation follows from Keynesian product market equilibrium as

$$S_t = I_t \tag{22.7}$$

$$or,\ sY_{t-1} = v(Y_t - Y_{t-1}) \tag{22.8}$$

$$or,\ (Y_t - Y_{t-1}) / Y_{t-1} = s / v \tag{22.9}$$

or $g_A = s / v$ = savings ratio / incremental capital – output ratio = savings behaviour / technological characteristics of production = savings propensity as a ratio to additional capital required to produce one unit of output. Figure 22.4 explains how the growth

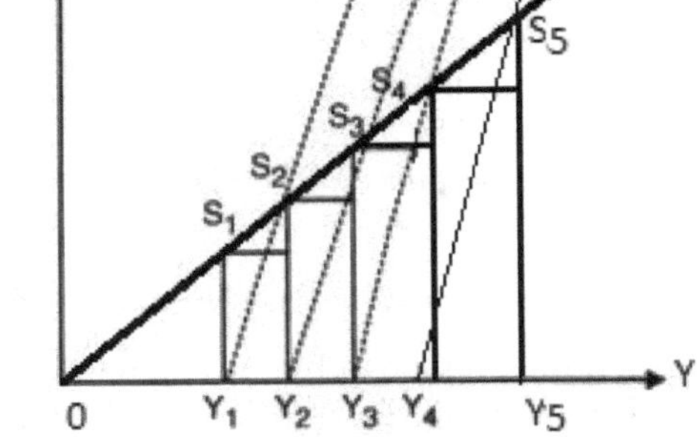

Figure 22.4 Process of growth in the H-D model

process is generated from the Keynesian system of equilibrium income determination. OS is the saving line presenting a long run relation between savings and income where average propensity to save is equal to marginal propensity to save (s). On the other hand, Y_1I_1, Y_2I_2 . . . lines represent the investment functions generated from savings whose slopes indicate incremental capital–output ratio (v).

At initial amount of savings, S_1Y_1, initial income is OY_1. Investing this amount of savings, income would rise by Y_1Y_2. At OY_2 level of income, savings would rise further to Y_2 S_2. This will further stimulate investment and, hence, income. Income would now increase to OY_3. At OY_3 level of income, saving would be S_3Y_3. Again, investing in the economy will further lead to rise in income. This growth process continues in this repetitive manner.

Let us recall the basic growth equation, $g_A = s / v$. Here, s / v is known as warranted rate of growth (g_w). It is so named because it is warranted to be achieved by the short run available resources of the economy, *S* and *I*; the savings plan of the households will always be matched with the investment plans of the business houses. So, in the short run growth process, economy, according to Harrod, should reach this condition where *actual rate of growth should be equal to the warranted rate of growth*. This is called the knife-edge balance in the Harrod model. For example, suppose savings rate $s = 0.3$ (i.e., 30% of income is saved in the economy) and $v = 3$ (i.e., 3 units of capital are required to increase output by one unit) then $g_w = 0.3 / 3 = 0.1$ or 10% growth rate. This means that 10% growth would be required to keep the potential and equilibrium output levels at equal values.

22.6.2.3 *Policy prescriptions*

It follows from the short run growth equation that $g_A = g_w = s / v$. g_w can be increased if "s" increases and/or "v" decreases. That means increased rate of savings makes an increase in the capital accumulation and hence investment (that increases the volume of demand in the economy) that ultimately helps in growth of output. *It is to note here that increase in savings rate here does not produce the paradox of thrift result that was common in the simple Keynesian demand-side economics because, in growth economics, the economy starts from the full employment position, not in the depressionary situation of the post 1930s Keynesian economics. There, saving was a leakage item, not like here as injection item.* And, with a given savings rate, if productivity of capital rises (i.e., v falls) then growth rate also increases. For example, suppose savings rate $s = 0.4$ (in place of $s = 0.3$ in the earlier example) and $v = 3$ (like the earlier example), then $g_w = 0.4 / 3 = 0.133$ or 13.3% growth rate. This means that extra 3.3% growth rate (13.3 > 10) is possible from extra 10% increase (0.4 > 0.3) in the savings rate with a constant v.

Now suppose "s" remains at 0.3 and "v" falls to 2 from 3, then $g_w = 0.3 / 2 = 0.15$ or 15% of growth is obtainable from one unit reduction in v. Hence, extra 5% growth can be obtained if v falls by one unit. The effect of increase in "s" and/or decrease in "v" produces *growth effects, not the level effects* in the Harrod model.

22.6.2.4 *The basic equations under the Harrod model – long run equilibrium condition*

The growth prospects in the short run system by the changes in savings ratio or capital–output ratio in the Harrod model cannot be sustained in the long run since, in the long run, population growth of the economy becomes a negative force to this growth effect since it swallows the extra generation of output. Hence, the basic equation maintaining the growth relation should be that the actual rate, warranted rate, and natural rates of growth should be equal. Natural rate of growth is that rate of growth which is bounded by the population growth rate. Suppose "n" is the rate of growth of population over time then the long run equation becomes

$$g_A = g_w = s / v = g_N = n\,. \tag{22.10}$$

How does this happen? We have now to link the product market condition (s / v) with the labour market to have growth of output. Let us assume that the labour market always clears and demand for labour is equal to total supply of labour at any point of time, i.e. $L^d_t = L^s_t$ and $L^d_{t+1} = L^s_{t+1}$. Therefore, $L^d_{t+1} - L^d_t = L^s_{t+1} - L^s_t$.

The origin of labour demand is from the firms who demand labour in any point of time on the basis of the realised output of the previous period. That means $L^d_t = mY_{t-1}$, where m is the constant labour-output ratio. The origin of labour supply, on the other hand, is the initial stock of population of the economy, say L_0. If population grows by the rate "n" then labour supply in period "t" becomes $L^s_t = L_0(1 + n)^t$ and at $t + 1$ period is $L^s_{t+1} = L_0(1 + n)^{t+1}$. Hence, the difference between two periods' labour supply is $L^s_{t+1} - L^s_t = L_0(1 + n)^t = nL^s_t$, since we have assumed that $L^s_t = L^d_t = aY_{t-1}$. Let us reconsider our previous relation as

$$L^d_{t+1} - L^d_t = L^s_{t+1} - L^s_t \tag{22.11}$$

$$\begin{aligned} &or,\ mY_t - mY_{t-1} = n\ mY_{t-1}\left(since\ L^d_t = L^s_t\right) \\ &or,\ \left(Y_t - Y_{t-1}\right) / Y_{t-1} = n. \end{aligned} \tag{22.12}$$

We already know that $(Y_t - Y_{t-1}) / Y_{t-1} = s / v$. Hence, the long run equilibrium growth equation becomes

$$g_A = \left(Y_t - Y_{t-1}\right) / Y_{t-1} = g_w = s / v = g_N = n\,. \tag{22.13}$$

22.6.2.4.1 IMPORTANT PROPOSITIONS

i) **Equilibrium theory or knife-edge balance:** once the warranted rate of growth (i.e. s / v) is achieved, it will be eternally maintained.
ii) **Instability in short run or knife-edge imbalance:** if there is any temporary deviation from this equilibrium, there will be continuous and amplified deviations over time with no signs of moving back to the original position.
iii) **Long run equilibrium with and without full employment:** population factor bars the rising growth trend observed from the short run systems of warranted growth but the equilibrium may have full employment or underemployment.

22.6.2.4.2 DISCUSSIONS ON THE PROPOSITIONS

22.6.2.4.2.1 Equilibrium theory or knife-edge balance The first proposition states that once the warranted rate of growth (i.e. s / v) is achieved, it will be eternally maintained. To justify this proposition we recall that if ex ante investment is equal to ex ante savings then growth rate of income in period $t + 1$ will be equal to the growth rate of income in period t. And if ex ante investment is more (or less) than the ex-ante savings then growth rate of income in period $t + 1$ will be more (or less) than the growth rate of income in period t. That means, if $I_t = S_t$ then $g_{t+1} = g_t$ and if $I_t > S_t$ (or $I_t < S_t$) then $g_{t+1} > g_t$ (or $g_{t+1} < g_t$). That means there is some unexplained part of growth arising out of whether $I_t > S_t$ or $I_t < S_t$. This unexplained part is known as random disturbance term, say U_t. If $U_t > 0$ then demand of aggregate output, I_t, is greater than supply of aggregate output S_t and if $U_t < 0$ then $I_t < S_t$. Hence, the magnitudes of excess demand or excess supply determine whether there will be perpetual growth rates or not.

$$\text{We have, } g_t = (Y_t - Y_{t-1}) / Y_{t-1} = s / v$$
$$\text{or } v(Y_t - Y_{t-1}) = sY_{t-1}$$

or $I_t = S_t$. That means there is zero disturbance term and there is neither unanticipated stocks nor clearance of inventories.

Let us move to another period in the future. If $U_t = 0$, then $I_{t+1} = S_{t+1}$ is maintained and $g_{t+1} = g_t = s / v$ is also maintained. For "n" number of future periods, the similar type of relation will be maintained such as $g_{t+n} = g_{t+(n-1)} = \ldots\ldots\ldots\ldots = g_{t+2} = g_{t+1} = g_t = s / v$ = warranted rate of growth. This is a perpetual balance over the edge of a knife or *knife-edge balance*.

22.6.2.4.2.2. *Instability in short run or knife-edge imbalance* If there is any temporary deviation arising out of any shock affecting the behaviour of households and firms, from this equilibrium happens, and there will be continuous and amplified deviations over time with no signs of moving back to the original position. This is known as the knife-edge instability problem of the model. Let us justify the proposition by the assumptions made in justifying the first proposition. Suppose $I_t > S_t$, then $U_t > 0$. This means additional demand (arising out of any positive business environment captured by a positive value of U_t), and there will be more and more growth rates of income in actual terms compared to the warranted rate of s / v and it will continue for all future periods without looking back to the original rate, s / v. This is one form of instability which is explosive in nature. That means if $I_t > S_t$, then

$$g_{t+n} > g_{t+(n-1)} > \ldots\ldots\ldots > g_{t+2} > g_{t+1} > g_t > s / v = g_w. \tag{22.14}$$

On the other hand, if $I_t < S_t$ then $U_t < 0$. This means additional supply (arising out of any negative business environment captured by a negative value of U_t) and there will be fewer and fewer growth rates of income in actual terms compared to the warranted rate of s / v in a continuous manner. That means, the situation of excess supply ($I_t < S_t$) leads to

$$g_{t+n} < g_{t+(n-1)} < \ldots\ldots\ldots < g_{t+2} < g_{t+1} < g_t < s / v = g_w. \tag{22.15}$$

The growth rates over time will be dampened, and dampening and is another form of instability. Another way to state this is that the warranted rate of growth is unstable. One important prediction from this growth theory is that the capitalistic development is on a knife-edge; any deviation from that position leads to a perpetual collapse or prosperity.

Let us explain Proposition I and II diagrammatically. Figure 22.5 explains this. In both the parts of the figure, actual growth rate ($g_A = g_t$) is equal to warranted growth rate (g_W)

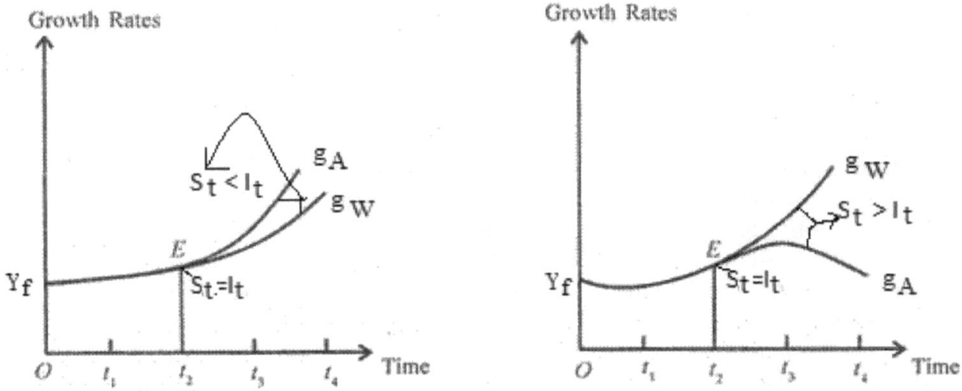

Figure 22.5 Interactions between warranted and actual growth rates

in period t_2, starting from the economy from with full employment output Y_f. The equilibrium point E maintains the knife-edge balance where $g_t = g_A = g_W = s / v$. That means Proposition I is satisfied up to point E. In the first part of the figure, after crossing the time point t_2, there arises the gap between g_A and g_W due to excess of ex ante investment over savings and aggregate production would fall short of aggregate demand. In subsequent periods, the deviation between the two becomes larger and larger. There would thus be explosive growth leading to chronic inflation.

In the second part of the figure, after time t_2 passes, the economy moves to the position of excess savings over desired investment which leads to a depressionary situation and the magnitudes of depressions become higher and higher as time goes on. Proposition II is satisfied in both the parts of the figure after point E. Hence, there is perpetual imbalance once the economy slips from E either in an upward or downward direction – a phenomenon of major crisis of the capitalistic developments.

22.6.2.4.2.3 Long run equilibrium with and without full employment

According to Harrod, an economy will grow in the long run in a natural way in the sense that the growth is barred or limited by the growth of population as well as labour force. Hence, besides the concepts of actual and warranted rates of growth, there is another concept of growth which is the natural rate of growth. The *natural growth rate* is the rate of output progress of the economy required to maintain full employment. It depends on the macro variables like population, technology, natural resources, and capital equipment. If the labour force grows at 2.5% per year, then to maintain full employment, the economy's annual growth rate must be 2.5% under the condition that there is no growth in productivity of the inputs. Hence, the growth equation in the long run system of the Harrod model is as follows

$$g_A = (Y_t - Y_{t-1}) / Y_{t-1} = g_w = s / v = g_N = n \qquad (22.16)$$

where g_A is actual rate of growth, s / v is warranted rate of growth, and "n" is the natural growth of the population. This is again a knife-edge balance in the long run model. Any deviation from this condition may lead to either unemployment of labourers or unemployment of capital. Suppose warranted rate of growth is less than natural rate of growth (i.e. $s / v < n$). It means warranted rate of growth can be achieved with an increasing rate of unemployment of labour. On the other hand, if $s / v > n$ then full employment of labour is achieved but with excess supply of capital or unemployment of capital. That means the economy can maintain full use of labour and capital if warranted rate of growth is equal to natural rate of growth ($s / v = n$). Figure 23.6 presents the long run balance and imbalance of the capitalistic economy. The additional function that has been inserted here is the g_N. All the three growth paths have met at Y_f level of (full employment) output and the point on the vertical axis of both the parts of the figure indicate long run growth equilibrium where the condition, $g_A = (Y_t - Y_{t-1}) / Y_{t-1} = g_w = s / v = g_N = n$, is being satisfied.

In the first part of the figure, as time starts running, natural growth lies below the warranted rate of growth (i.e. $s / v > n$); although there is balance in the savings and investment, up to E, there is an excess of capital goods due to a shortage of labour. The shortage of labour keeps the rate of increase in output to a level less than g_w. Capital becomes idle and there is excess capacity which further dampens investment, output, employment, and income. The reverse situation, i.e. $s / v <$ n, happens in the second part of the figure. There is a shortage of capital goods and labour is plentiful. Profits are high since desired investment is greater than realised investment and the businessmen have a tendency to increase their capital stock. This will lead to secular inflation and unemployment of labour. Hence, in the long run, if imbalances arise, there will be unemployment either of capital or of labour.

22.6.2.5 Steady state and scopes of further growth under the Harrod model

The *steady state* is a position where growth rate is constant or stationary. In other words, the variables deciding the growth rate of output grow at constant and equal rates. In the Harrod model, the steady-state condition is reached when $s / v = n$ which ensures that output, capital, and the level of population all grow at the same rate which further means that per capita output and the capital–labour ratio remain stationary. In other words, the condition leads to the following relation:

$$s / v - n = 0. \tag{22.17}$$

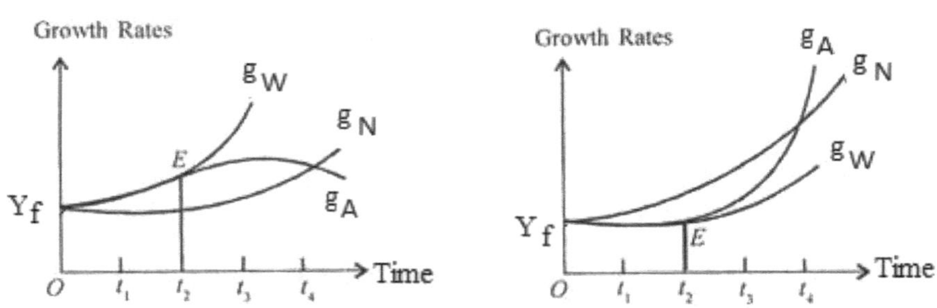

Figure 22.6 Long run balance and imbalance

An economy, according to the Harrod model, if one wants to improve the per capita income of its citizens, they can do it openly in three ways: increasing value of s and decreasing values of v and n separately or simultaneously.

Possibility 1 – increasing savings rate:increasing rate of savings with constant v and n means additional capital formation/accumulation which will help increase the growth rate of aggregate as well as per capita output. That means,

$$s_1 / v - n > s_0 / v - n \quad (22.18)$$
$$or,\ g_W > g_N \quad (22.19)$$

where new savings rate, $s_1 > s_0$ (old savings rate) or $s_1 / v - n > 0$ and new growth rate $g_W > g_N$. If we allow "v" and "n" to go down alongside increase in "s" then we still have $g_W > g_N$ if rate of increase in savings rate outweighs the rates of decrease in "v" and "n". See the example given in Policy Prescription.

Possibility 2 – decreasing capital–output ratio: decreasing value of incremental capital–output ratio with constant "s" and "n" means additional productivity of capital ($dY / dK > 0$) which will help in increasing the growth rate of aggregate as well as per capita output. That means,

$$s / v_1 - n > s / v_0 - n \quad (22.20)$$
$$or,\ g_W > g_N \quad (22.21)$$

where new capital–output ratio, $v_1 < v_0$ (old rate of v) or $s / v_1 - n > 0$ and new growth rate $g_W > g_N$. That means, once capital is more productive backed by technological developments, growth of output will increase with same rate of savings and population growth.

Possibility 3 – decreasing rate of population growth: decreasing rate of growth of population with unchanged rate of capital accumulation and productivity of capital can swallow a lesser amount of output and hence there is a surplus remaining that helps in growth of per capita income. That means

$$s / v - n_1 > s / v - n_0 \quad (22.22)$$
$$or,\ g_W > g_N \quad (22.23)$$

where $n_1 < n_0$.

22.6.2.6 *Important predictions under the Harrod model*

So far as the previous three possibilities are concerned, the important predictions of the H-D model are as follows:

i) It is possible to achieve permanent and continuous improvements in the per capita income by increasing savings rate, reducing capita–output ratio, or increasing productivity of capital by introducing new technology and reducing growth of population. Hence, the myth of increasing consumption expenditure by households and growth of population cannot improve the standard of living of the citizens of a country.
ii) If the two countries have the same equilibrium growth rates but one country's income is higher than that of the other, the absolute gap between countries will go on increasing over time.

iii) If the income of one country is greater than that of the other but the growth rate of the latter country is more than the former, then a time will come when the low-income country will catch up with the high-income country. Today's developing countries, thus, require growing at faster rates to converge on the developed countries.

22.6.2.7 *The Harrod model used in national planning*

Growth theory in advanced capitalistic economies has been associated with three principal components: the saving ratio, the capital–output ratio, (or the productivity of capital), and population growth rate. The Harrod model is primarily developed in order to elucidate secular stagnation that was threatening the advanced economies in the post-war period. According to Hirschman, the H-D model has proved to be remarkably multitalented in the sense that it allows us to show not only the rate at which the economy must grow if it is to make full use of the capacity created by new investment but, inversely, the required savings and the capital–output ratios if income is to attain a certain target growth rate. The application of these models has now been extended to the development problems of underdeveloped as well as developing economies.

Underdeveloped economies have low savings rates which produce very low rates of growth. At the same time, these economies also suffer from sophisticated capital goods that produce high capital–output ratio. History shows that today's developing countries also experience higher growth rates of population. All of these internal economic and demographic conditions have retarded their growth prospects and they have fallen into debt burden. The Harrod model ushers these economies to grow quickly by increasing their propensity to abstain from consumption and inflowing foreign technologies to improve productivity of capital. India has applied the growth model from its first five-year national plan in the early 1950s and has achieved sound economic progress with an increasing savings rate to over 30% presently. Along with that, the capital–output ratio has gone down and the growth rate of income in 2015–2016 is such that it has surpassed the highly growing economy of China even with the very high savings rate of the latter. India has remarkably improved its position in productivity of capital compared to China.

Although we have discussed the usefulness of the Harrod model in the economic growth of today's underdeveloped and developing economies, it should be kept in mind that it is not too easy to apply this model in a clean-cut way to these economies because the economies of these countries are running under complex conditions arising out of societal, political, and structural rigidities' aspects. Extra income gained is often spent on increased consumption rather than saved. Many countries suffer from a persistent domestic savings gap. Increased saving by households does not necessarily mean there will be greater funds available for firms to borrow to invest because of a lack of sound financial systems. Efficiency gains that reduce the capital–output ratio are difficult to achieve in developing countries due to weaknesses in human capital, causing capital to be used inefficiently. Economic growth, say by applying the Harrod model, cannot solve the structural problem of the economies; it requires the multidimensional factors to work in a simultaneous manner.

22.6.2.8 *Limitations of the Harrod model*

Although the Harrod model is a primary model of growth and created the opportunity for the economists of following schools of thought and established the three basic factors behind the short run and long run dynamic process of growth based on post Keynesian foundations, it has suffered from a series of limitations which are inherent to the simplistic assumptions it has considered. Some of them are highlighted here.

i) The savings rate and the capital–output ratio are assumed to be constant. In reality, they are likely to change in the long run and thus modify the requirements for steady-state growth. A steady rate of growth can, however, be maintained without this assumption. Other factors can play the same role other than these two. Although s, v, and n are constant, it would be a complete fluke to reach the condition of $s / v = n$. It is very unlikely that this condition will prevail. A marginal slip from this point leads to capitalistic crisis in terms of either inflation or depression.
ii) The assumption that labour and capital are used in fixed proportions is indefensible. Generally, in a production system, labour can be substituted for capital or the reverse and the economy can move more smoothly towards a path of steady growth.
iii) The constancy in the price levels and interest rates is a very restrictive assumption when the economy is not in extreme conditions like general excess supply.
iv) Although the model originated from Keynesian income determination, it did not consider the role of government in influencing the main determinants, s, v, and n.

Despite these limitations, the Harrod growth model is designed to indicate conditions of progressive equilibrium for an advanced economy. They are important because they represent a stimulating attempt to dynamize and secularise the Keynesian static short run saving and investment theory.

Box I Notes on actual, warranted, and natural rates of growth

In the Harrod model of growth the growth rate is defined from three different aspects, actual, warranted, and natural. Actual growth rate (g_A) is the real rate of increase in a country's GDP per year adjusted for inflation or deflation. If $Yt - 1$ is the GDP in time $t - 1$ and Yt is GDP in time t then actual growth rate is calculated as

$$g_A = [(Yt - Yt - 1) / Yt - 1] * 100$$

Short run actual economic growth is caused by an increase in aggregate demand and the long run economic growth is caused by increase in aggregate supply. Therefore, any change in the components of aggregate demand like consumer spending, investment, government spending, and net international trade will result in a change in economic growth. On the other hand, the supply-side factors are capital accumulation through savings, population growth, research and development, human capital, institution, etc.

The warranted rate of growth (g_W), according to Harrod, is the rate "at which producers will be content with what they are doing". It is the "entrepreneurial equilibrium; it is the line of advance which, if achieved, will satisfy profit takers that they have done the right thing". Thus, this growth rate is primarily related to the behaviour of businessmen. It follows the savings–investment equilibrium at any point of time.

$$S_t = I_t$$
$$or,\ sY_{t-1} = v(Y_t - Y_{t-1})$$
$$or,\ (Y_t - Y_{t-1})/Y_{t-1} = s/v$$
$$\text{or } g_W = s/v.$$

The natural rate of growth (g_N) is the rate of advance which the increase of population and technological improvements allow. The natural rate of growth depends on the macro variables like population, technology, natural resources, and capital equipment.

Now, for full-employment equilibrium growth, $g_A = g_w = g_N$ holds. But this is a knife-edge balance. For once, if there is a difference among natural, warranted, and actual rates of growth conditions of secular stagnation, inflation would be generated in the economy. If $g_A > g_w$, investment increases faster than saving and income rises faster than g_w. If $g_A < g_w$, saving increases faster than investment and rise of income is less than g_w. If $g_w < g_N$, the tendency is for secular inflation to develop in the economy. When g_w is less than g_N, there is a shortage of capital goods and labour is plentiful. Profits are high since desired investment is greater than realised investment and the businessmen have a tendency to increase their capital stock. This will lead to secular inflation.

22.7 Domar model of growth

Evsey Domar is probably the first who has clearly explained the fundamental relationship between capital accumulation and economic growth. He starts from the acknowledgement of Keynes that investment of today competes not only with the investment of yesterday but also with the investment of the tomorrow. It offers a new productive capacity of the system, which, if it is not sufficiently used, will disincentivise further investment tomorrow that will increase the surplus of idle capital, making the problem more complicated. In contrast to Keynes, Domar justified that there was nothing certain about this outcome. If the total demand of tomorrow were sufficiently higher than today's demand, the newly added productive capacity could be fully utilised and there would be further scope of investment tomorrow, and the process would continue. That is, for a state of equilibrium in the economy, it is required that total supply (or productive capacity) equals total demand (or income).

22.7.1 *Assumptions of the model*

i) There is the prevalence of the long run condition which is the full employment level of income.
ii) The marginal and average propensities to save are equal.
iii) The propensity to save and capital coefficient are considered constant.
iv) There are no lags in adjustment.

v) Depreciation is measured to the cost of replacement of depreciated asset by another one of the same productive capacity.
vi) There is an absence of government interference and foreign aids.
vii) The economic system is closed.

22.7.2 *Structure and explanation of the model*

The model is built upon the fundamental demand and supply sides. Investment has a dual character which provides the solution for steady growth.

Y_3 = level of productive capacity or supply at full employment level.
K = real capital
I = net investment which results in the increases of real capital which is ΔK.

The basic equation for the demand-side system of the Domar model is given as

$$Y_d = I / \alpha \ldots\ldots\ldots\ldots \qquad (22.24)$$

Where Y_d is the level of national income or level of effective demand at full employment, α is the marginal propensity to save (which is "s" in the Harrod model) which is a reciprocal of a multiplier ($dY / dI = 1 / \alpha$), and $1 - \alpha$ is the consumption propensity. The equation shows that the level of national income is directly proportional to the net investment. Any increase in the level of investment increases the national income and vice-versa. The effective demand is inversely proportional to marginal propensity to save. Any increase in marginal propensity to save will decrease the level of effective demand and vice-versa. This equation explains the demand side of investment.

On the other hand, the basic equation for the supply-side system of the Domar model is given as-

$$Y_s = \sigma K \ldots\ldots\ldots\ldots\ldots \qquad (22.25)$$

This equation explains that supply of output (Y_s) at full employment depends upon two factors: productive capacity of capital σ (which is "v" in the Harrod model) and amount of real capital (K). Any increase or decrease in either of these two factors will raise or reduce the supply of output. This is the supply side of investment.

For the equilibrium between the demand and supply sides we have the following relation:

$$Y_d = Y_s$$
$$\text{or } I / \alpha = \sigma K$$
$$\text{or } I = \alpha\,\sigma\,K \ldots\ldots\ldots\ldots\ldots\ldots \qquad (22.26)$$

The previous equation explains the condition for steady growth and it is possible only when investment equals the product of saving–income ratio, capital productivity, and capital stock. For this, we must give increments to the demand as well as to supply equation.

The demand and supply equations in incremental forms are as:

$$\Delta Y_d = \Delta I / \alpha \text{ and } \Delta Y_s = \sigma \Delta K$$

As the change in real capital stock is the net investment (i.e. $\Delta K = I$), we can write

$$\Delta Y_s = \sigma I \text{ . . . .} \tag{22.27}$$

Or, due to the conditions for steady growth, we have:

$$\Delta I / \alpha = \sigma I$$
$$\text{or } \Delta I / I = \sigma.\alpha \text{ . . . .} \tag{22.28}$$

This means that the growth rate of net investment must be equal to the product of marginal propensity to save and the productivity of capital. Well known economist Kenneth Kurihara writes in this respect,

> It is an increase in productive capacity (Y_s) due to increment of real capital (K) which must be matched by an equal increase in effective demand (ΔEd) due to an increment of investment (I), if a growing economy with an expanding stock of capital is to maintain continuous full-employment.
>
> Further, from the previous demand-side relation we have

$$\Delta Y / Y = \Delta I / I \text{ . . . .} \tag{22.29}$$

Therefore, the necessary condition to maintain steady growth of an economy is

$$\Delta Y / Y = \sigma\alpha \text{ . . . .} \tag{22.30}$$

Thus, the answer to the problem of what rate of growth is necessary to maintain a continuous state of full employment is that investment and real income must grow at a constant annual percentage rate equal to the product of the propensity to save and the average productivity of investment.

Let us explain the Domar model with the help of a diagram. Figure 22.7 explains the scenario when investment is fixed and any more increases in the capital stock do not influence investment to increase. Under such a situation, having the savings–investment equality as under the Keynesian set up, increase in savings (as shown in the first quadrant) will produce output of Y_0 corresponding to the fixed investment I_0. As savings increases, with the same fixed investment, there will be equal increase in capital stock by K_0 amount but it does not help in increasing investment as well as the productive capacity of the economy. Thus, the movement of the changes will not go along the 45-degree line (the equilibrium line), rather through the AB line, making excess capital accumulation, but its contribution adds nothing to income growth.

But, once investment is taken to be proportional to income, then it moves side by side with the savings, and more capital accumulation leads to more investment as well as capacity creation whose ultimate effects fall upon output growth (Figure 22.8). The movements of the equilibrium points then go along the 45-degree line.

The rate of increase of income depends upon the productivity of capital. In short, the Domar model has explained the technological relationship between the capital accumulation and full-employment growth rate of output. But, on the contrary, Harrod has shown

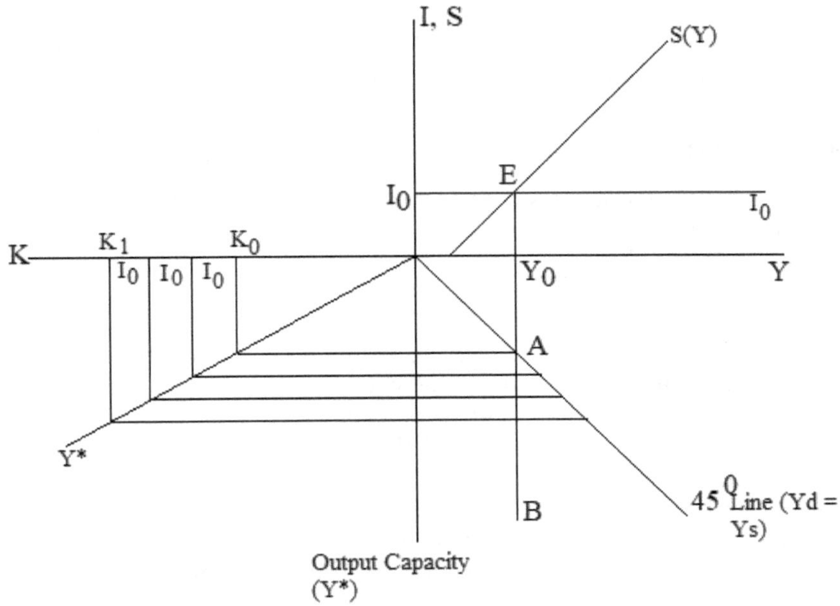

Figure 22.7 Domar model when investment is fixed

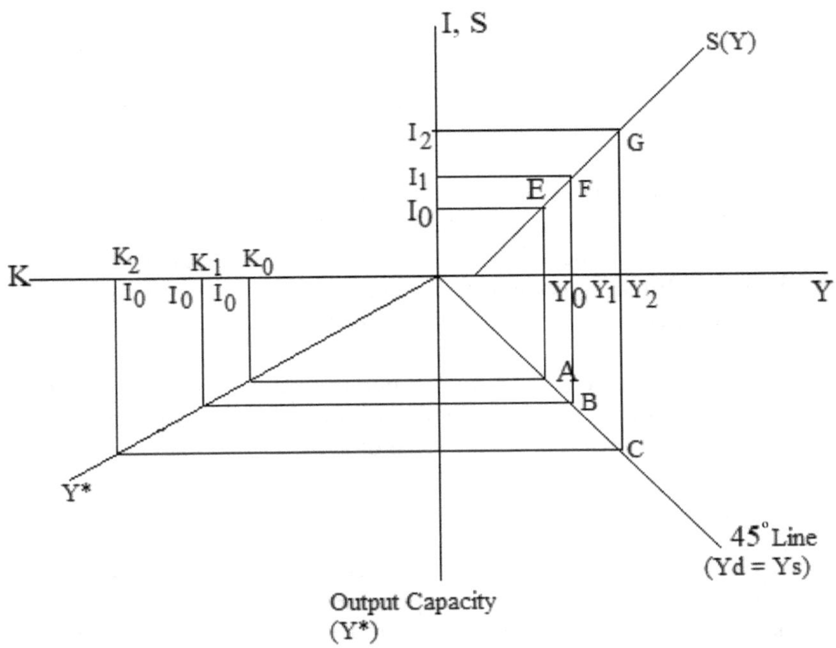

Figure 22.8 Domar model when investment is variable

the psychological relationship between capital accumulation and full capacity growth rate of output. Therefore, the Domar model suggests the role of planned investment in economic development, while the Harrod model stresses induced investment.

22.8 Harrod and Domar models of economic growth: a comparison

Comparison of the two models has two sides: congruence and conflicts. We discuss them in the following sections.

22.8.1 *Congruence*

- The two models are founded upon similar assumptions. They employ Keynesian saving–investment equality as a condition for steady growth.
- Harrod's warranted growth rate ($gw = s/v$) signifies the same thing as the product of the marginal propensity to save (α) and the productivity of capital (σ) in Domar's model. Both the models stress the "knife-edge equilibrium".
- Both the models have been built in the context of the developed economies, where capital is found in abundance, but they are hardly to be applied to the less-developed economies.
- As against the Keynes' macro-static theory, Harrod and Domar opine that a dynamic approach to growth should be introduced in the long run, not always the short run.

22.8.2 *Conflicts*

Although both the models have so many areas of congruence in explaining the process of economic growth, there are differences in the two models.

- In Domar's model, the concept of productivity of capital is represented by the output-capital ratio as always, while in Harrod's model the concept of capital–output ratio is used frequently.
- Though Harrod and Domar have employed the acceleration coefficient, there is a subtle difference between the two. Harrod's acceleration coefficient may be called psychological while that of Domar is technological. Harrod is of the opinion that when income increases, the producers' psychology would be to make a net investment. On the other hand, in Domar's accelerator principle, investment is the cause and output is the result, and so it depends on the nature of technology.

Although the two models have their own foundations, their insights are more-or-less similar. That is why many economists read the models not separately as Harrod and Domar but rather as the Harrod-Domar model of growth.

22.9 Conclusion

In the present chapter we covered the concepts of growth and different theories of growth belonging to the classical and Keynesian approaches. Smith and Malthus put emphasis on land and labour as the prime sources of economic growth. But in the Keynesian line of thought, the Harrod model is based on the demand-side factors behind growth, capital accumulation, as the crucial factors of economic growth. It concentrates on the possibility of steady growth through adjustment of supply of demand for capital. Specifically, the model is used in development economics to explain an economy's growth rate in terms of the level of *saving* and *productivity of capital* or the inverse of incremental *capital–output ratio*. At equilibrium, the actual growth rate will be equal to warranted rate of growth (s / v) and any deviation from it in the short run will generate instability in either an upward or downward direction. That particular feature is known as knife-edge instability. Under the Keynesian formulation like the Harrod model, the Domar model explains the fundamental relationship between capital accumulation and economic growth in a demand–supply model of income incorporating technological developments.

Summary

The extracts of the present chapter on classical and Keynesian growth models are:

- Income growth is defined as the percentage change in income from one period to the other with respect to the income of the base period.
- There are three forces of growth – *primary force* which includes *natural force* and *anthropogenic force*, *secondary force* which includes the supplies of produced means of production like all sorts of capital formation, and *auxiliary force* which includes technology which further covers scientific inventions and innovations, managerial efficiencies, etc.
- The classical model of growth is based on land and labour.
- The Harrod model is based on capital accumulation as the crucial factor of economic growth. It concentrates on the possibility of steady growth through adjustment of supply of demand for capital.
- The Harrod model is used in development economics to explain an economy's growth rate in terms of the level of saving and productivity of capital or the inverse of incremental capital–output ratio. At equilibrium, the actual growth rate will be equal to warranted rate of growth (s / v) and any deviation from it in the short run will generate instability in either an upward or downward direction. That particular feature is known as knife-edge instability.
- The Domar model explains the fundamental relationship between capital accumulation and economic growth starting from Keynes that the investment of today competes not only with the investment of the yesterday, but also with the investment of tomorrow.

Keywords

Economic growth
Classical growth model
Harrod model
Domar model
Steady state
Actual growth rate
Warranted growth rate
Savings ratio
Capital–output ratio
Knife-edge instability
Population growth rate
Natural growth rate

Multiple choice questions and answers

1. In the Harrod equation $g = s/v$, v is defined as
   (a) The value of the country's capital stock.
   (b) The ratio of the country's capital stock to its output.
   (c) The change in the country's capital stock.
   (d) None of the above.

2. According to the Harrod model, an increase in growth rates depends on
   (a) Increase in capital–output ratio.
   (b) Decrease in capital–output ratio.
   (c) Increase in marginal propensity to consume.
   (d) None of the above.
3. Growth of income can be calculated by the formula ("*d*" for change, *Y* for income)
   (a) $dY * 100$.
   (b) $1/dY * 100$.
   (c) $dY/Y * 100$.
   (d) $Y/dY * 100$.
4. Steady-state equilibrium is attained in the long run Harrod model when
   (a) $s/v = n = g$.
   (b) $s/v = g$.
   (c) $s/v = n$.
   (d) None of the above.
5. The knife-edge instability problem in the short run Harrod model arises when
   (a) $I_t = S_t$.
   (b) $I_t > S_t$.
   (c) $I_t < S_t$.
   (d) Both (b) and (c).

Answers

1. (b); 2. (b); 3. (c); 4. (a); 5. (d)

Review questions

1. Define growth rate of income. Calculate the growth rates of income over time from the following table and comment on the derived results

Time>>>	*2007*	*2008*	*2009*	*2010*	*2011*	*2012*	*2013*
Income	80	100	90	110	120	115	130
Growth rate	-						

2. What is a steady-state growth rate? Explain how the steady-state growth rate is derived under the Harrod model.
3. Define actual growth rate, warranted growth rate, and natural growth rate. Explain how the equilibrium growth of income is explained by the Harrod model in a diagram.
4. What is knife-edge instability? How does knife-edge instability arise in the Harrod model? On what factor does growth in labour force depend?
5. What are the major propositions of Harrod growth theory in both the short run and long run system? Explain them with proper justifications.
6. Explain how the interactions between warranted and actual growth rates are done in the Harrod model of growth. What are the major limitations of the model?

7. Explain the Harrod model in the long run system. Discuss how the full employment and underemployment conditions are inserted into the long run model of growth.
8. Mention major predictions under the Harrod model of growth. Discuss how the Indian economy had applied the Harrod model in their national planning in the 1950s.
9. Write a note on actual, warranted, and natural rates of growth. Discuss their relationships with respect to equilibrium and deviations from the equilibrium.
10. Discuss the Domar model of growth. Explain how the model has congruence and conflicts with the Harrod model.

Additional readings

Domar, E. (1946). "Capital expansion, rate of growth, and employment". *Econometrica*, 14(2): 137–147.

Harrod, R. F. (1939). "An essay in dynamic theory". *The Economic Journal*, 49(193), 14–33.

23 The neoclassical growth model

23.1 Introduction

The neoclassical growth model developed by Robert M. Solow (1956) and Trevor Swan (1956), popularly known as the Solow–Swan model, is a contested growth model over the classical and Harrod–Domar model. The Malthusian pessimistic approach did not recognise the technological inventions and innovations which can guard the workings of the law of diminishing returns from land. On the other hand, the H-D model predicted that increase in savings rate with a constant capital–output ratio can generate additional prosperity for the economy on a permanent basis and the economy faces a knife-edge imbalance from which no chance of moving back to the original balance is possible. The neoclassical growth model has criticised the restrictive assumptions like the fixed capital–labour ratio taken in the H-D model and has provided the smooth production function approach to the growth analysis by the exogenous technological progress. Both the labour and capital inputs are substitutes for each other and the associated isoquants are smooth and downward sloping in contrast to the right-angled shapes under the H-D model. The crucial factor which explains the foundation of Solow–Swan model is the law of diminishing returns to the factors, which makes the capital–output ratio, v, variable instead of fixed as supposed by the H-D model. Let us see intuitively how this happens.

According to the H-D model, an increase in capital accumulation supported by increase in savings rate over the growth of the labour force would increase the growth of per capita output on a permanent basis. Solow, on the other hand, criticised it in the way that this increase was temporary rather than permanent since, as savings rate increases, with constant v, the steady state condition became $s / v > n$, which means capital is growing faster than the rate of labour force leading to increase in capital–labour ratio. In the absence of any technological progress, this increase in capital-labour ratio leads to fall in the productivity of capital due to the working of the law of diminishing returns which in turn leads to increase in v (the inverse of productivity of capital). If this trend continues, s / v will be reset to n and the economy will move back to the steady state (or balanced growth position) with no progressive results from increase in savings rate. However, the period of transition over which the growth of per capita income remains higher than the rate of population growth may be quite substantial in length. Hence, the per capita income stops rising and the effect of rate of savings increase is temporary. On the other hand, Solow pointed out that the maximum increase of savings rate is 100% (i.e. zero unit of consumption) and so increase in savings rate cannot be a permanent solution.

A similar argument can be made if there is fall in population growth rate with s and v constant. As n decreases, capital–labour ratio rises which leads to decrease in productivity

DOI: 10.4324/9781003501138-29

of capital that makes an increase in v which ultimately brings the per capita output back to steady state with no permanent increase in per capita income in the long run; only a short run effect is present. Hence, the assumption of diminishing returns to capital does the trick in criticising the growth models prior to the neoclassical model. Only if savings rate is more than 100% (that means perpetual borrowing by the whole economy) and population growth is negative (that means birth rate is less than death rate always) can the working of diminishing returns be stopped and hence there can be permanent growth of per capita income. Since these two conditions are hard to find in reality, the workings of diminishing returns as well as permanent growth of income cannot be halted. So what is the beauty of the Solow–Swan model then?

According to the Solow–Swan model, the working of diminishing returns can be stopped and the increase in growth rates is perpetual if we introduce *technological progress* into the growth model. As technological progress begins, capital becomes more productive and the capital–output ratio falls, leading to increase in growth rates with fixed s and n. If the technological progress is continued, unlike "s" towards 100% and "n" towards negative values, then s / v would start rising over time and the effect would become perpetual or permanent. Hence, the neoclassical model gives the *level effect as well as growth effects* (we will come to this point later). Besides, the neoclassical model predicts that if all the countries of the world are identical in all respects except the initial level of aggregate or per capita output or capital–labour ratio, then the poor countries with low capital–labour ratios will catch up with the rich ones and all of them will converge into the common steady state because of the underlying assumption of diminishing returns to capital. Let us establish the Solow–Swan growth model in detail in the following section.

23.2 The descriptive Solow—Swan model of growth

The central aspect of the Solow–Swan model is the consideration of the neoclassical production function that incorporates constant returns to scale, diminishing returns to each of the factors, and some positive and smooth substitution among the inputs. This production function is combined primarily with a constant exogenous savings rate (s) and a constant rate of depreciation to capital (δ). After that the model incorporated constant population growth rate (n) and exogenous technological progress to find the steady-state or long run growth rate of the economy. The model shows how savings, population growth, and technological progress affect the level of an economy's output and its growth over time.

Suppose the production function is $Y = F(K,L)$ where Y is aggregate output and K is aggregate capital stock, which is a key determinant of the economy's output, but the capital stock can change over time, leading to change in economic growth. Specifically, two opposite forces influence capital stock: investment and depreciation. L is the total labour force in the economy. Because of constant returns to scale, the per capita production becomes

$$Y / L = F(K / L, 1) \tag{23.1}$$

$$or, \; y = f(K / L) \tag{23.2}$$

or $y = f(k)$ where k is the per capita quantity of capital and y is per capita output. The per capita production function is concave because of the assumption of diminishing marginal productivity of k. That is, $MPk = f'(k) > 0$ and $dMPk / dk = f''(k) < 0$.

Suppose the savings function is proportional to income, which is $S = sY$ where $s = S / Y = dS / dY$ and $0 < s < 1$. Also suppose that the capital depreciates at the rate δ per year and population rises at a constant rate n, then the Solow–Swan growth equation becomes

$$dk / dt = i - (n + d)k \tag{23.3}$$

where dk / dt is the change in capital stock per worker over time, i is the investment per worker ($= I / L$) and $(n + \delta)k$ is the break-even investment. Break-even investment has two components: to keep k constant, δk is needed to replace the depreciated capital and "nk" is necessary to provide capital for new workers added through growth of population. In equilibrium, per capita investment is equal to per capita savings. In other words

$$i = sf(k) = s.y \tag{23.4}$$

Therefore, after substitution of investment by savings, the growth equation becomes

$$dk / dt = sf(k) - (n + d)k = s.y - (n + d)k. \tag{24.5}$$

This is the basic equation of growth under the neoclassical model. The rate of increase in per capita capital, k, over time is determined by how much additional savings or capital accumulation is generated over the depreciation of capital and catering to the additional population added to work force. If capital deepens over time then the neoclassical model predicts uninterrupted growth of per capita output, y ($= Y / L$) given the assumption of diminishing returns and technological progress, which reduces the value of capital–output ratio, v. Let us present the per capita production function, per capita investment function, and the residual income as consumption and the capital–output ratio under the neoclassical model in Figure 23.1.

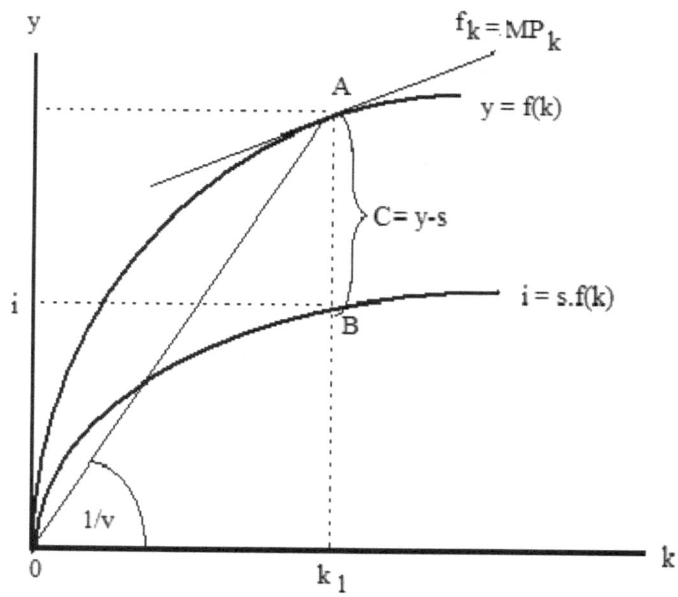

Figure 23.1 The production function, investment, and consumption

The per capita production function concave and the actual investment function, $i = s.f(k)$ lies below y because of $0 < s < 1$ and the magnitude of consumption is derived by scaling down the amount of per capita savings from the per capita output function. AB is the per capita consumption. The capital–output ratio, $v = K/Y = k/y$ (or $1/v = y/k$), is captured as the slope of a ray from the origin to production function. Thus, changing k will change the ray and thus v. So, unlike the Harrod-Domar model, v is *not* exogenously fixed. At any per capita capital, say at k_1, per capita income is Ak_1, savings is Bk_1 and AB is the per capita consumption and $dk / dy = 1 / v = Ak_1 / 0k_1$. As k increases, productivity of capital falls due to diminishing returns and v rises and $1 / v$ falls. The OA line becomes flatter or moves rightward. Inversely, as k falls, v falls and $1 / v$ rises.

23.2.1 *Steady state under the Solow—Swan model*

Steady state is a position of the economy when per capita capital remains fixed, which is $dk / dt = 0$. This means the following

$$sf(k) = (n + d)k \tag{23.6}$$

or actual investment $[s.f(k)]$ equals required investment $(n + \delta)k]$

Required investment means the amount of investment required to accommodate additional population, nk and replace depreciated capital, δk. By considering any specific production function following CRS, we can calculate the steady-state value of k, say k^*. Any amount of k below or above k^* will make the economy adjust its amount of k by either increasing or decreasing to maintain the equality between the actual and required rate of investment. Figure 23.2 presents the steady-state equilibrium with dynamics of the neoclassical growth model.

In the first part of the diagram, the steady-state growth of k has been explained. The function, $sf(k)$, represents the per capita actual investment which is increasing at a decreasing rate due to diminishing returns and the required per capita investment, $(n + \delta)k$, has been presented by the upward sloping line through the origin. At zero value of k, actual and required investment are also zero. As k rises, both of them rise but the actual

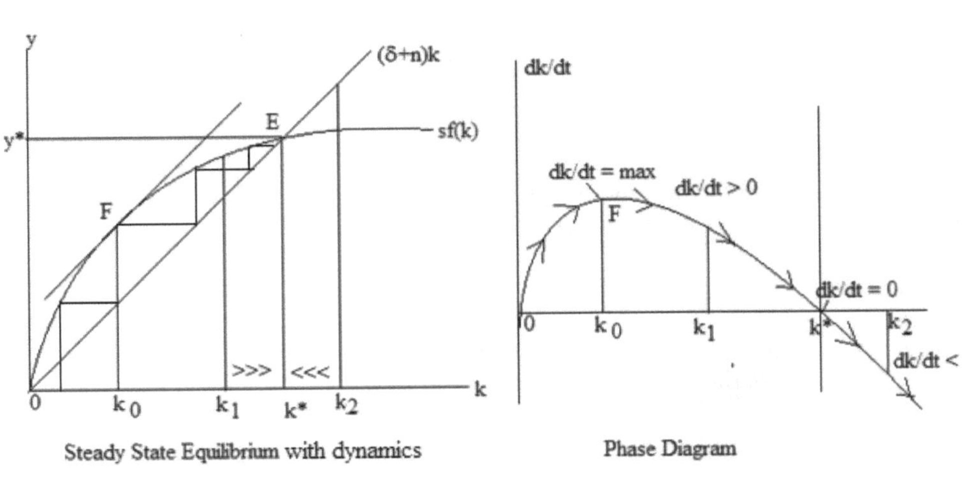

Figure 23.2 Steady-state equilibrium and phase diagram

one is at a higher but diminishing rate than the required one up to point E where both of them are equal and k reaches k^*. This means capital is actually growing faster than labour, so k will increase up to E through the zigzag process. Beyond E or k^*, the reverse happens, which means the required part is rising over the actual one meaning the rate of depreciation and population growth become more than the actual growth of investment. That means capital is actually growing more slowly than labour, so k will decrease and hence k will fall over time and is better back to E. Hence, E is the steady-state equilibrium or stable equilibrium where k^* is the steady-state capital stock per capita which maintains the balance between the actual and required investments and keeps k at constant or stationary state. The corresponding y is y^*.

In the second part of the diagram, we have shown the dynamics of k change or the phase diagram of the neoclassical model. The phase diagram looks like a concave function to the k axis. At k^* the trajectory meets the k axis, implying $dk / dt = 0$; before that $dk / dt > 0$ and after that $dk / dt < 0$. The point F on both the parts of the figure represents maximum value of k which is not steady state where the gap between the actual and required investment is maximum and growth of K over labour is maximum. The economy should not stay at that point since it is not in the position to exploit all the economic opportunities that lie within the production system. The vertical line drawn through k^* divides both sides of the steady-state equilibrium.

23.2.2 *Calculation of steady-state k by the Cobb—Douglas production function*

We can now compute the steady-state value of per capita capital stock with the help of a Cobb–Douglas production function depicting CRS and the phase diagram given earlier presenting the movement of dk / dt over the values of k as given by the equation

$$dk / dt = sf(k) - (n + d)k. \tag{23.7}$$

Let us assume the production function as

$$Y = L^{\alpha} K^{1-\alpha} \tag{23.8}$$

where $0 < \alpha < 1$ is the elasticity of output with respect to labour and $1 - \alpha$ is that with respect to capital. Reducing this function into per capita form we get

$$f(k) = y = k^{1-\alpha}. \tag{23.9}$$

The fundamental growth equation under the Solow–Swan model is thus a nonlinear differential equation in the following form:

$$dk / dt = sk^{1-\alpha} - (n + \delta)k. \tag{23.10}$$

To solve this, we can linearise it by setting a new term $x = k^{\alpha}$, which after differentiation with respect to t gives the following relation

$$dx / dt = \alpha(dk / dt) / k^{1-\alpha}. \tag{23.11}$$

Now, dividing the original growth equation by $k^{1-}\alpha$, we obtain:

$$(dk / dt) / k^{1-\alpha} = s - (n + \delta) k / k^{1-\alpha}. \tag{23.12}$$

In terms of the variable "x", we get the following

$$dx / dt = \alpha[s - (n + \delta) k^{\alpha}]. \tag{23.13}$$

Now, substituting $x = k\alpha$, this equation can be expressed as:

$$dx / dt = \alpha s - \alpha(n + \delta)x \tag{23.14}$$

which is a simple linear first-order differential equation in x. Its solution has two components; one is the particular or equilibrium solution and the other is the complimentary solution which is the deviation from equilibrium. The particular solution can be obtained by setting $dx/dt = 0$. Hence, we get the particular solution from the growth equation with respect to x as

$$\begin{aligned} &\alpha s - a(n + \delta)x = 0 \\ &or,\ x = s / (n + \delta) = x^* (say)\cdot \end{aligned} \tag{23.15}$$

For a complimentary solution we take $x = Ae^{mt}$ (A is any constant) as the trial solution which gives the solution as

$$x(t) = Ae^{-\alpha nt}. \tag{23.16}$$

Hence the total solution or equilibrium time path is

$$x(t) = Ae^{-\alpha nt} + s / (n + \delta). \tag{23.17}$$

To convert this to obtain the solution $k(t)$, we just re-transform it back, which is as $x = k^{\alpha}$, then $k = z^{1/}\alpha$. Hence, the time path of per capita capital (or the equation of the phase diagram) is as

$$k(t) = [Ae^{-\alpha nt} + s / (n + \delta)]^{1/\alpha}. \tag{23.18}$$

We can eliminate A by assuming initial condition as when $t = 0$, then the initial value of k, say $k(0) = k_0$. Thus

$$k(0) = [A + s / (n + \delta)\}^{1/\alpha} = k_0. \tag{23.19}$$

By rearranging we get

$$A = k_0^{\alpha} - s / (n + \delta). \tag{23.20}$$

Therefore, the solution to the Solow–Swan differential equation is:

$$k(t) = \{[k_0^{\alpha} - s / (n + \delta)]e^{-\alpha nt} + s / (n + \delta)\}^{1/\alpha}. \tag{23.21}$$

Now, as n, $\delta > 0$ and $0 < \alpha < 1$ by assumption, then the equation is stable in the sense that as $t \to \infty$, $[k_0^{\alpha} - s / (n + \delta)]e^{-\alpha n t} \to 0$, so that in the end, $k(t) \to k^*$, or actual capital stock matches with the steady state. Hence, the computed steady-state value of per capita capital is

$$k^* = \{s / (n + \delta)\}^{1/\alpha}. \tag{23.22}$$

And the steady-state per capita output (y^* in the figure) is

$$y^* = (k^*)^{1-\alpha} = [s / (n + \delta)\}^{1/\alpha}]^{1-\alpha} = [s / (n + \delta)\}(^{1-\alpha)/\alpha}]. \tag{23.23}$$

Suppose $s = 0.20$ (or 20%), $n = 0.02$ (or 2%), and depreciation is equal to zero, and $\alpha = 1 / 2$, then $k^* = \{0.2 / (0.02 + 0)\}^{1/1/2} = 10^2 = 100$ and $y^* = 10$.

23.2.3 *The golden rule of steady-state capital—labour ratio*

We have noticed that at steady-state gross capital stock grows at the rate of population, n, and the per capita capital stock remains constant. In terms of the gross capital stock, gross investment is $I = sY = (n + \delta)K$. Reaching steady-state in K does not necessarily mean aggregate consumption in the economy is maximum. The golden rule comes into the picture then. The *golden rule of steady state* is a position when the economy reaches maximum social welfare in the long run by maximising per capita consumption of the citizens. The consumption expenditure in aggregate is

$$C = Y - S = Y - (n + \delta)K \tag{23.24}$$

or, in per capita terms, it is

$$c = y - (n + \delta)k = f(k) - (n + \delta)k. \tag{23.25}$$

The previous equation shows that as steady state k gets changed then per capita output rises on one hand and raises the output per labour that must be used to medicate capital's wear and tear and growth of population, which is the term $(n + \delta)k$. We describe the golden rule of steady-state capital in Figure 23.2 whose clues have already been given in the first part of Figure 23.3.

The golden rule capital is derived by the level of k, say k_g, where sf(k) or total savings (= investment) line is parallel to the $(n + \delta)k$ line. In other words, $MP_k = (n + \delta)$. This implies that extra per capita output generated by additional per capita capital (or the reverse of incremental capital–output ratio) is equal just to the rate of population growth and depreciation rate. This happens at point F where the gap FG denotes the maximum consumption of per citizen of the country at the steady-state capital kg where k_g is the highest among all the possible steady states. What is the corresponding rate of savings which ensures k_g? It can be derived graphically at a point where the $sf(k)$ function intersects the $(n + \delta)k$ line (point G in the diagram). The steady-state savings rate at golden rule, say s_g, can derived from the previous equation by putting k as k_g in the way that the following relation holds

$$s_g f(k) = (n + \delta)k_g \tag{23.26}$$

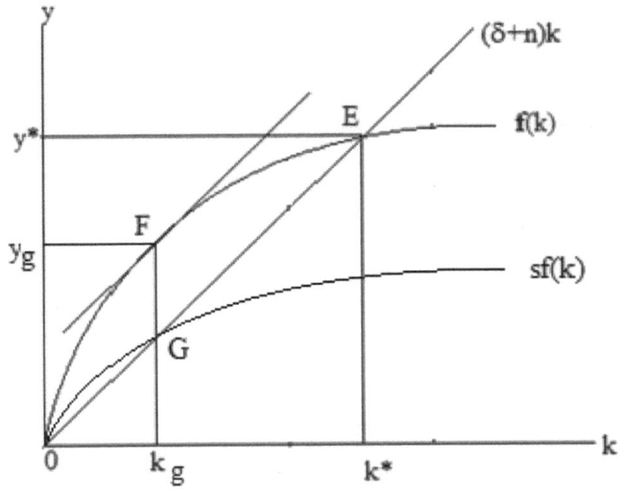

Figure 23.3 Golden Rule of capital per capita

$$or,\ s_g = (n+\delta)k_g / f(k) = (n+\delta)k_g / y. \tag{23.27}$$

The implication of the previous relation is that, as savings rate of any economy is more than s_g, then there is overaccumulation of capital, which creates low rate of consumption and hence worsens the welfare of the economy. On the other hand, if savings rate falls short of s_g, then the welfare of the economy increases as the people consume more.

23.2.4 *What about factor prices in the Solow—Swan model with capital accumulation?*

There should be a matter of discussion in the neoclassical model of growth regarding the possible impact of capital accumulation (i.e. capital deepening) on the factor prices in the absence of technological progress. In a system of two generalised factors, labour and capital, the factor prices are respectively the real wage and real rate of interest. Under the classical models, while the Smithian model claims that the real wage will be constant in the long run because of unlimited land supply leading to parallel increase in output due to increase in labour use, the Malthusian model, on the other hand, claims a falling real wage towards the subsistence level. We observed from the neoclassical model that, as capital accumulation continues with no technological progress, each labourer gets more and more capital to work with and the economy moves along the production function in an upward direction leading to increase in output per capita labour. Due to diminishing returns, the economy ultimately reaches the steady-state position where growth of per capita output becomes stationary. Now implications of factor prices come into the picture.

As capital accumulates more, the workings of diminishing returns to capital lead to a fall in rate of return on capital (or the marginal productivity of capital or inverse of capital–output ratio) and the real rate of interest falls. On the other hand, because each labourer gets more and more capital, their marginal productivities rise and consequently the real wages go up. The underlying market clearing assumption is that each of the

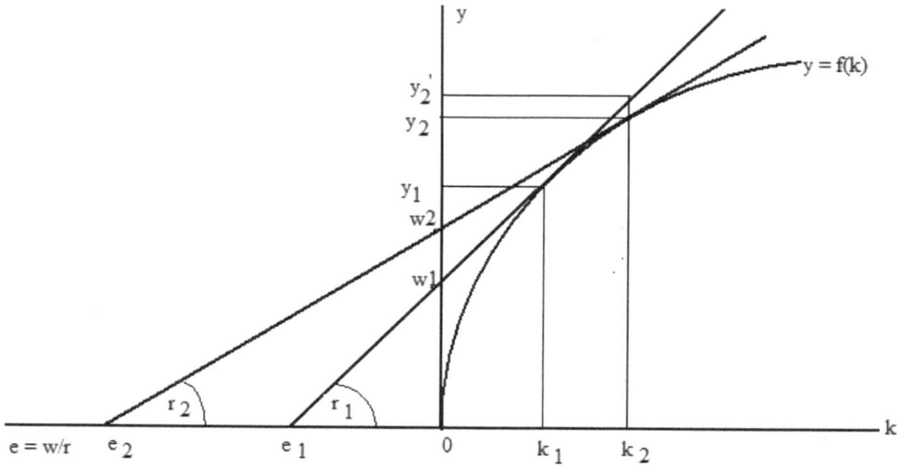

Figure 23.4 Effects of capital deepening on factor prices

factors is paid according to its marginal productivities. Hence, capital owners are hurt and the labour class benefits due to capital deepening. Figure 23.4 presents a possible description of the effect of capital accumulation on the factor prices.

For a constant return to scale, intensive production function, at any k, the slope of a tangent ray is $f_k = F_k = r$, the marginal product of capital, while the intercept of the tangent ray on the vertical axis is merely $y - f_k.k = F_L = w$, the marginal product of labour, where w and r are the per unit price of labour and capital respectively. As capital deepening rises from k_1 to k_2, the slope of the tangent (i.e. r) falls and the gap along the vertical axis (i.e. w) rises and, as a result, the factor price ratio rises from e_1 to e_2.

But in the long run, the economy will reach the steady-state position where capital accumulation stops rising (without technological progress) and real wage stops rising and the capital's return also stops falling. This is a different but relatively better outcome from the neoclassical model of growth over the classical model, specifically the pessimistic Malthusian model and the Harrod-Domar model. The corollary from the process of only capital deepening in the neoclassical model is that the standard of living of the citizens eventually stops rising. It can be improved, as the Solow–Swan model defends itself, if technological progress is allowed with capital accumulation.

23.2.5 *Parametric effects upon the steady state*

Let us see how the steady state k is affected by the parameters of the Solow–Swan model which are, namely, s, n, and δ. The steady-state value of k is given by the following relation:

$$s.y^* = (n+\delta)k^* \tag{23.28}$$

$$\text{or, } k^*/y^* = s/(n+\delta). \tag{23.29}$$

The neoclassical model predicts that the effects of the parameters are temporary, not permanent like the Harrod-Domar model, because of the working of diminishing returns. Hence, in the long run, as savings rate rises there are no changes in the growth of k or per capita income, but there is an increase in the level of income. The same effects of n and δ are also observed, of course in the reverse direction. Hence, all the parameters have level effects, not growth effects like the Harrod-Domar model. Let us see how.

From the previous relation, as "s" rises, ceteris paribus, the right-hand side increases, which requires the left-hand side, rather k, to increase. Logically, as "s" rises, new capital is added to the existing population, which increases the per capita capital and, because of diminishing returns, per capita k and y at a steady state should increase. Hence, per capita level of income rises by increase in savings rate. Figure 23.5 presents these parametric effects.

In the first part of the figure, the equilibrium moves from E to F due to increase in savings rate from s_1 to s_2. The steady-state k and y rise but the growth rate of k and y remain unchanged (that is, $dk / k = dy / y = 0$). It remains equal to the growth rate of population and depreciation, $(n + \delta)$. The second part of the figure presents the effect of increase in $(n + \delta)$ upon the steady states k and y. As $(n + \delta)$ (either n, δ, or both increase) increases, the $(n + \delta)k$ line rotates leftward leading to fall in the level of steady-state k and per capita income but with no effect upon their growth rates. This means, as n or δ or both rise, a part of this increase in y is swallowed by the additional population and replacement expenditure upon the worn-out capital, which means less capital per capita, and income ultimately appears as a result of increase in $(n + \delta)$. In fact, growth of population has both level as well as growth effects upon the per capita income because of increase in volume of demand for consumers goods.

23.2.6 *Effect of technological progress — growth accounting revisited*

In the introductory part of the chapter, we gave in a logical form the impact of technological progress upon factor productivity. We now present the details of the concept here. Solow assumed a very basic model of annual aggregate output over a year (t). He said that the output quantity would be governed by the amount of capital (for example, the infrastructure), the amount of labour (i.e., the number of people in the workforce), and the productivity of that labour. He thought that the productivity of labour was the factor

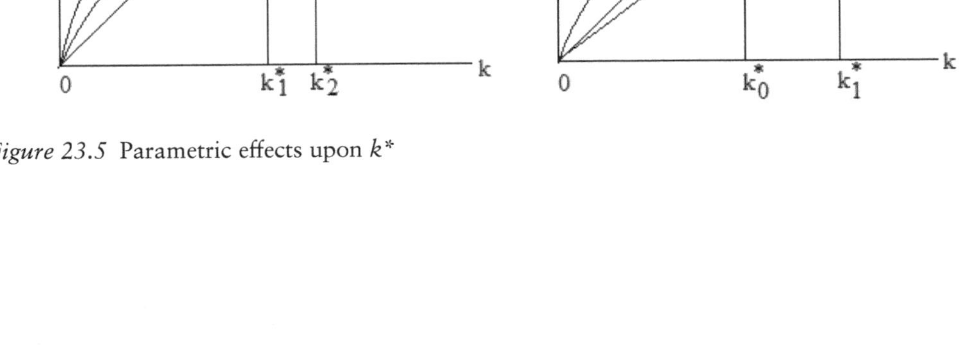

Figure 23.5 Parametric effects upon k^*

driving long run GDP increases. For example, the production function in an economic model of this form is given here as:

$$Y(t) = [K(t)]^{\alpha} [A(t)L(t)]^{(1-\alpha)}. \tag{23.30}$$

Where:

$Y(t)$ represents the total production in an economy (which may be the GDP) in any year, t.

$K(t)$ is capital in the productive economy – which might be measured through the combined value of all the companies in a capitalist or market economy.

$L(t)$ is labour which is simply the number of people in the existing workforce. Further, since growth models are long run models, they tend to ignore cyclical unemployment effects, assuming instead that the labour force is a constant fraction of an expanding population in an economy.

$A(t)$ represents multifactor productivity which is frequently generalised as "technology". The change in this figure from A for the year 1960 to A_1 for the year 1980, for instance, is the key source in estimating the growth in labour "efficiency" between 1960 and 1980. This is the Solow residual estimated in 1980 vis-à-vis 1960.

α represents the elasticity of output with respect to capital and $(1 - \alpha)$ represents the elasticity of output with respect to labour and technology. In a competitive market clearing system, these exponents represent the relative factor shares.

To measure the Solow residual or total factor productivity (or the effect of technological progress) or to predict the change in output within this model over the two periods, the previous equation is differentiated in time (t), giving a formula in partial derivatives of the relationships: labour-to-output, capital-to-output, and productivity-to-output, as shown:

$$\partial Y / \partial t = (\partial Y / \partial K)(\partial K / \partial t) + (\partial Y / \partial L)(\partial L / \partial t) + (\partial Y / \partial A)(\partial A / \partial t). \tag{23.31}$$

Using the previously mentioned production function, we see the following set of relations:

$$\partial Y / \partial K = \alpha [K(t)]^{(\alpha-1)} [A(t)L(t)]^{(1-\alpha)} = (\alpha Y) / K(t).$$

Similarly:

$$\partial Y / \partial L = [(1-\alpha)Y] / L(t) \tag{23.32}$$

$$\partial Y / \partial A = [(1-\alpha)Y] / A(t). \tag{23.33}$$

The previous three expressions show the correspondence between marginal productivities and average productivities of the related factors, K, L, and A.

Now we substitute these marginal expressions in the expression for $\partial Y / \partial t$ and obtain the following:

$$\partial Y / \partial t = (\alpha Y / K(t))(\partial K / \partial t) + [(1-\alpha) Y / L(t)](\partial L / \partial t) + [(1-\alpha) Y / A(t)](\partial A / \partial t). \tag{23.34}$$

The growth factor in the economy is a proportion of the output last year, which is given (assuming small changes year-on-year) by dividing both sides of this equation by the output, Y (= $[Y_t - Y_{t-1}) / Y_{t-1}]$):

$$[\partial Y / \partial t] / Y = \alpha(\partial K / \partial t) / K(t) + (1-\alpha)(\partial L / \partial t) / L(t) + (1-\alpha)(\partial A / \partial t) / A(t). \quad (23.35)$$

The first two terms on the right-hand side of this equation are the proportional changes in labour and capital year-on-year, and the left-hand side is the proportional output change. The remaining term on the right, giving the effect of productivity improvements on GDP, is defined as the Solow residual (SR):

$$SR(t) = [\partial Y / \partial t] / Y - \alpha(\partial K / \partial t) / K(t) - (1-\alpha)(\partial L / \partial t) / L(t) \quad (23.36)$$

or

$$SR(t) = Output\,Growth - K's\,share * Capital\,Growth - L's\,share * Labour\,Growth. \quad (23.37)$$

The residual, $SR(t)$, is that part of growth not explicable by measurable changes in the amount of capital, K and the number of workers, L. If output, capital, and labour all double every 20 years, the residual will be zero, but in general, it is higher than this: output goes up faster than growth in the input factors. The residual varies between periods and countries but is almost always positive in peacetime capitalist countries. For example, according to some estimates, the post-war US residual credited the country with a 3% productivity increase per annum until the early 1970s when productivity growth appeared to stagnate which led to phenomenal policy changes in the US economy.

But there is a real problem with the growth accounting process. Growth accounting requires data for the growth rates of labour, intermediaries, and physical capital. This is problematic, because these factors of production consist of heterogenous objects, which cannot be accurately compared to each other in a quantitative manner.

Application 1: suppose capital's share of output is 0.25, and labour's share is 0.75

i) Find the growth of total factor productivity ($\Delta A/A$) when the labour supply increases 1%, capital increases 4%, and output growth is 4%.
ii) Find the growth of TFP when the labour supply increases 3%, capital increases 3%, and output increases 4%.

Solution:

i) $\alpha = 0.25$, $(1 - \alpha) = 0.75$
$\Delta A / A = 0.04 - 0.25 * 0.04 - 0.75 * 0.01 = 0.0225 = 2.25\%$

ii) $\Delta A / A = 4\% - 3\% * 0.25 - 3\% * 0.75 = 1\%$

Application 2: let $Y = A\,K^{0.5}\,L^{0.5}$. Prove that equation for the steady-state capital–labour ratio is $k = A^2(s^2 / \delta^2)$ where s = saving rate and δ is depreciation rate.

Solution:

$Y = A\,K^{0.5}\,L^{0.5}$

Now, dividing both sides by L, we get $Y / L = A\ K^{0.5}\ L^{-0.5}$

$$\Rightarrow y = A\ (K / L)^{0.5} \Rightarrow y = A\ k^{0.5} \Rightarrow y = A\ \sqrt{k}$$

In steady state we know savings per worker equals depreciation of investment per worker.

i.e. $s\ y = \delta k$
i.e. $s\ A\sqrt{k} = \delta k$
i.e. $s\ A\sqrt{k} = \delta\sqrt{k}\ \sqrt{k}$
$\Rightarrow \delta\sqrt{k} = s\ A$
$\Rightarrow k = s^2\ A^2 / \delta^2 \Rightarrow k^* = A^2\ (s^2 / \delta^2)$

Although the model of capital accumulation or capital deepening is an initial path to understanding economic growth, there is enough unanswered in the model, recapitulating the essence of neoclassical growth model that says that the per capita income and real wages will be stagnant if the economy only depends upon capital accumulation to count for growth in the absence of technological progress. The history of the developed countries shows that the real wage has not fallen during the latter part of the twentieth century (Table 23.1 and Figure 23.6) and the trend of per capita income has also maintained an upward direction (refer to the preceding chapter).

Table 23.1 Real wage growth trends

Year	*USA*	*UK*	*France*	*Sweden*	*Finland*	*Japan*	*Australia*
1980	3.6	2.7	3.4	2	2.4	2.6	2.7
1990	4.4	3.3	3.4	2	2.6	2.8	2.7
2000	4.8	3.5	3.3	2.4	2.5	2.8	3.1
2013	5.4	3.7	3.2	2.4	2.5	2.9	3.6

Source: OECD Stat Extracts database.

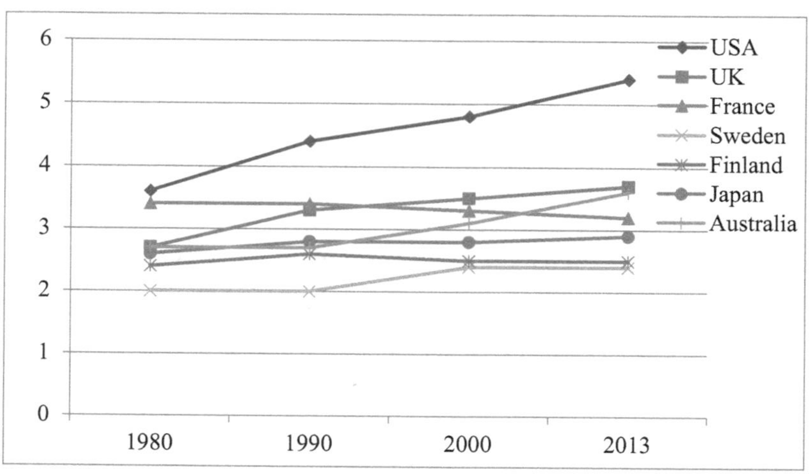

Figure 23.6 Real wage growth trends

What is the missing factor behind such a nonstatic growth of per capita income and real wages? The neoclassical model propounded that there have been tremendous developments in the technology of production across the nations during the twentieth century which improves the productivity or efficiency of the factors of production which again subsides the constant growth prediction of the capital accumulation model. If technological progress is continuously done, then there should be no end to the growth of per capita income and then the steady-state growth rate will be equal to the rate of technical progress plus growth rate of the population. The process is exhibited by the shifting of the production function in an upward direction, which creates increasing growth rates of per capita income by offsetting the effect of diminishing returns of capital, without leading it to stagnate.

To incorporate the efficiency effect of technological progress into the production function, we reorient the production function in terms of efficient labour units and capital as it is. Suppose "*e*" is the efficiency of labour after technical progress; then "*Le*" is the labour in efficiency unit. The efficient production function is then:

$$Y = F(Le,\ K). \tag{23.38}$$

With L and K constant, Y can be increased by an increase in efficiency which is supported by the advancement of technology. This is to say that $dY / de > 0$ with $L = L_0$ and $K = K_0$. The effect of technological progress is given by Figure 23.7. The steady-state capital is now given by the following equation:

$$dk = s.f(k) - (n + \delta + g)k \tag{23.39}$$

where "*g*" is the rate of technological progress which has been taken as exogenous by the neoclassical model. Here again, $(n + \delta + g)k$ is termed as *break even investment* which includes three components. To keep k ($= K / Le$) constant, nk ($= n.K / Le$) amount is needed to arrange capital for additional workers generated through extra population, δk is the amount needed to replace depreciated capital by new capital, and gk is needed to provide capital for newly effective workers generated through the progress of technology.

The first part of Figure 23.7 depicts that the rate of growth of per capita output is going to stagnate through only the capital deepening (the movement along the TP_1 curve from k_1 to k_2) and the effect of technological progress has been shown by the diagonal movement from TP_1 to TP_2 through the range of per capita capital $k_1 - k_2$. In the second

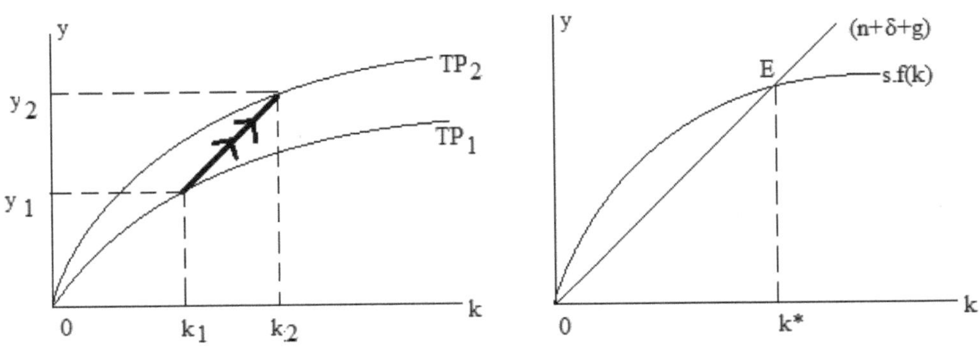

Figure 23.7 Effect of technological change and steady-state equilibrium

part of the figure, the steady-state equilibrium is given at E where $dk = 0$. That means k^* is the steady-state per capita capital which shows total investment of capital is distributed among population, depreciation, and technological progress. This means, if efficiency of labour improves due to uninterrupted progress of technology, then per capita output will grow continuously in the long run at the rate of $(n + g)$ but only at the rate of "g" in the longer runs since population ceases to grow in the longer runs; it is only technical progress which will determine the sustained growth rate of per capita income.

23.2.7 *The golden rule of capital after technological progress*

We have introduced the concept of the golden rule of capital in our discussion of the neoclassical growth model in the pretechnological progress system. The *golden rule of capital* is recalled as the steady-state capital which maximises the aggregate as well as per capita consumption from the point of view of a benevolent social planner. Let us reorient the concept after we incorporate the effect of technological progress into the Solow model of growth. The golden rule of capital is now the steady-state capital which maximises the *consumption per effective worker*. Like before, just incorporating the term "g" into Solow's basic equation, the golden rule of capital (k_g) maximises consumption by the amount which is given by the following relation:

$$c_g = y_g - (n + \delta + g)k_g . \qquad (23.40)$$

Steady-state consumption, c_g, can be maximised if $dc_g / dk_g = 0$. This requires the following

$$dy_g / dk_g - (n + \delta + g) = 0 \qquad (23.41)$$

$$\begin{aligned} &or, MPk_g = (n + \delta + g) \\ &or,\ MPk_g - \delta = (n + g). \end{aligned} \qquad (23.42)$$

This means the consumption maximising the golden rule of capital is such where the net marginal productivity of capital over rate of depreciation should be equal to the rate of growth of output $(n + g)$. The figure of this golden rule of capital may be drawn similarly to that of the pretechnological progress scenario (it is left for the readers to verify their knowledge accumulation so far).

23.3 Prediction of the Solow—Swan model — the cross-country convergence

In the neoclassical growth model, Solow and Swan incorporated the law of diminishing returns which made the incremental capital–output ratio variable in contrast to the Harrod-Domar model's fixed value on it and showed how capital accumulation makes the growth rate of income temporary, rather than permanent. Besides, the stagnancy of the growth of per capita income has been overcome by the introduction of technological progress in the neoclassical model. Although the Solow–Swan model was originally developed to focus on how an economy's growth of output behaves in the long run over the Harrod–Domar model, it has an important prediction that there can be cross-country comparisons and the countries will eventually *converge* to a single steady-state level of capita and output per capita.

There are two concepts of convergence as proposed by the Solow model; one is *absolute or unconditional convergence* which is a strong concept and the other is the *conditional convergence* which is a weak concept. Robert Barro Jr. has named the unconditional convergence as absolute β convergence because of the regression coefficient, β, depicting the notion as well as speed of convergence. We will use the term absolute β convergence as a replacement for the term unconditional convergence in the following discussion.

23.3.1 *Absolute β convergence*

Theory of absolute β convergence states that if all the regions of a geography have a unique steady-state level or they are homogeneous in all respects (for example, they have access to the same technology, same population growth rate, same savings propensity, etc.) except initial capital stocks, the poor regions with lower capital stocks will grow at a higher rate than that of the rich, and ultimately the poor regions will catch up with the richer ones in the long run. The underlying logic is given by the working of diminishing returns to capital. A country with a historical record of low level of capital stock (poor country) will grow at a faster rate and the country with a high stock of capital (rich country) in the same historical time period will grow at lesser speed so that a time will come when the low capital-possessing country will catch up with the high capital-possessing country in a common steady-state position. The concept of speed of convergence thus arises. To have a catch-up effect, the poor country should grow at a higher speed and the rich country at a lower speed. The Solow–Swan fundamental growth equation can show this.

We have

$$dk = sf(k) - (n+d)k\,. \tag{23.43}$$

The growth rate of per head capital is

$$g_k = dk/k = sf(k)/k - (n+d)\,. \tag{23.44}$$

Since f is concave ($f' < 0$), $f(k) / k$ will decrease as "k" rises. So g_k will decrease as "k" increases. An economy with a lower k will have a faster rate of growth. This implies that the growth rate and initial capital stock are inversely related. Figure 23.8 explains the

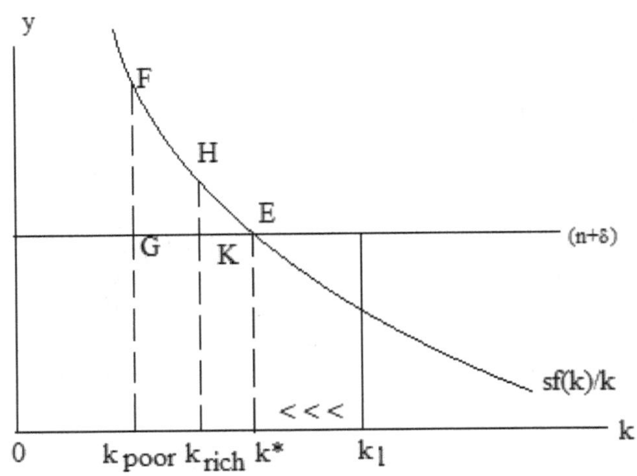

Figure 23.8 Absolute beta convergence

idea of unconditional convergence where the previous growth equation for k is expressed as the combination of a downward sloping function $sf(k) / k$ (it is downward since as k rises, $f(k)$ or per capita output rises at a decreasing rate because of diminishing returns) and a straight line function $(n + \delta)$ (which is a fixed per-unit requirement of k to cater to population growth and capital replacement cost).

Growth rate of per capita capital is measured by the vertical distance between the $sf(k) / k$ function and $(n + \delta)$. The steady-state growth of per capita capital is reached at a point (E) where $dk / k = 0$. This means $sf(k) / k = (n + \delta)$. k^* is the steady-state capital which is considered as common to all the countries under the unconditional convergence hypothesis.

Let us see how different categories of economies converge to this common steady-state position starting from different values of k. Suppose k_{poor} and k_{rich} are the respective per capita stocks of capital of poor and rich countries ($k_{poor} < k_{rich}$) and $(k^* - k_{poor}) > (k^* - k_{rich})$, which is the poor country is well below the position of k^* compared to the rich country. The common target of these two countries is to reach the steady state k^* in the long run and thereby the inter-country differences will die out. Left to k^*, $dk / k > 0$ $dk / k_{poor} > dk / k_{rich}$ (or $FG > HK$). Convergence in terms of k to k^* leads to convergence from y to y^* in the long run. Hence, the growth rate of k is inversely related to the initial or base period's value of k. The clue behind such a conclusion is the working of diminishing returns. This is probably the ultimate and holistic objective of the process of globalisation across all the countries of the world.

Let us think of the unconditional convergence hypothesis in terms of cross sectional regression with β as a coefficient, hence the hypothesis of absolute β convergence comes into play. Let us see how.

We can now derive the expression for β in the form of cross section regression. Let us suppose that there are n numbers of regions or countries within a geographical boundary with k_{it} being the capital per head of the ith country. Consider the following regression model:

$$log(k_{it}) = \alpha + (1 - \beta)\ log(k_{i,t-1}) + u_{it} \tag{23.45}$$

It can be rewritten as

$$log(k_{it} / k_{i,t-1}) = \alpha - \beta log(k_{i,t-1}) + u_{it} \tag{23.46}$$

where α and β are constants respectively for intercept and slope with $0 < \beta < 1$ and "u_{it}" is a regular disturbance term. In this equation a positive sign of β means absolute convergence. That is, growth rate of per capita capital [log $(k_{it} / k_{i,t-1})$] is inversely related to the initial per capita capital $(k_{i,t-1})$. It is also to note that β is nothing but the slope of the per capita capital growth function. In other words $\beta = -\text{dlog}(k_t /_{kt-1}) / \text{dlog}(k_{t-1})$. Here β also works as one of the parts of the notion of speed of convergence. Rassekh (1998) provides one possible derivation of computing speed of convergence with the help of the slope factor β. Since the rate or speed of convergence depends on the gap between the initial value and the steady-state value of the variable, it can be determined by the reorientation of the growth equation (Equation 24.38) in the following form:

$$1 / T\left[log(k_{it} /\ k_{i,t-1})\right] = \alpha - \left[(1 - e^{-\lambda t}) / T\right].log(k_{i,t-1}) + \varepsilon_{it} \tag{23.47}$$

where λ stands for the speed of convergence and T stands for total period of time under observation. According to the study, λ can be simplified by the following relation

$$\lambda = -log(1+\beta). \tag{23.48}$$

The estimated value of speed of convergence λ determines the time required for all countries to reach the steady-state point in the long run. Since the value of the variable at a steady state depends on so many parameters appearing in the future, sometimes it is estimated as the time to cross the half line of the steady-state value using the formula $e^{-\lambda t} = 1 / 2$ or $t = \log(2) / \lambda$.

23.3.2 *Conditional β convergence*

The hypothesis of absolute β convergence works well when the group of economies is homogeneous in character with similar values of the parameters. This condition is more likely to be satisfied for different regions of the same country or same geography. But under the heterogeneous nature of the regions there should be a difference in the steady-state levels. Each economy has a separate steady state of per capita capital, but the steady-state growth rate of the per worker output will be zero as the empirical evidence shows. This concept of convergence has been proposed by Robert J. Barro. The countries in Asia, Latin America, and Africa have failed to catch up with the so-called rich countries of the west.

We then have to modify the theory of absolute convergence to accommodate the concept of conditional convergence. Conditional β convergence can be presented by the following equation:

$$log(k_{it}) = \alpha + (1-\beta)\ log(k_{i,t-1}) + \gamma Z_t + u_{it} \tag{23.49}$$

where Z is the vector of other variables that affect capital stock such as infrastructure development, government policy, degree of trade openness, rate of inflation, etc. Conditional convergence occurs when the partial correlation between the growth rate and the initial level of capital per worker is negative. The essence of the conditional convergence is that an economy grows faster the further it is from its own steady-state values of the variables.

Figure 23.9 illustrates the concept of conditional convergence by taking two economies that are different in two respects. First, they have different initial capital stock per capita which is $k_{poor} < k_{rich}$ and second, they differ because of their difference in savings rates which is $s_{poor} < s_{rich}$. But the parameters like growth rate of population and rate of depreciation are the same for both the rich and poor countries. The diagram illustrates that the poor countries have less capital stock compared to the rich countries and have a lower steady-state k^*_{poor} and the rich have a higher steady state k^*_{rich}. Hence, per capita output in a steady state will be higher for the rich country. Income difference will persist even in the long run. In such a framework the rich economy can grow faster than the poor if the low savings rate of the poor economy offsets its higher average productivity of capital as a determinant of economic growth. The neoclassical model predicts the conditional convergence in the way that a lower starting value of a variable tends to generate a higher per capita growth rate once we control the determinants of the steady-state value. The two concepts of β convergence are identical if a group of countries or regions or states tends to converge to the same steady-state position.

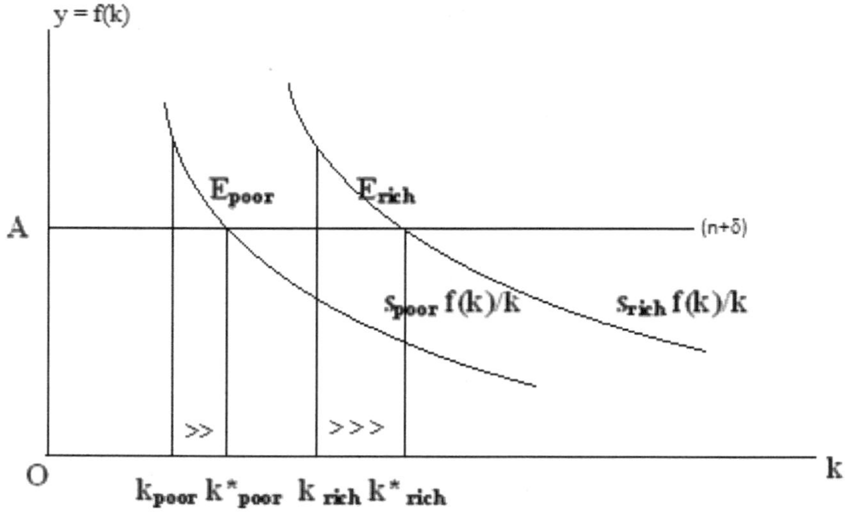

Figure 23.9 Conditional beta convergence

23.3.3 Sigma (σ) convergence

Workings of the condition of the absolute and conditional convergence do not necessarily mean that the dispersion of the distribution of the per capita income across the cross section of the economies will continuously fall over time. Differences in the per capita incomes across different groups of regions stand for the notion of inequality or divergence among the groups. The model of σ *convergence* states that the coefficients of variation of a variable across different regions should be declining over time. We can express the concept of σ convergence by means of the following regression equation

$$log(CV) = a + bt + u_t \tag{23.50}$$

where "*a*" is intercept constant, "*b*" is the slope constant or growth rate of CV over time, and *u* is the random disturbance term. If the sign of *b* is found to be negative and significant then we can say that the trend of CV is downward and that there is convergence among the regions or countries as far as the criterion of σ convergence is concerned.

Here is a natural question: with respect to the fact that a group of economies are converging in absolute terms by means of β convergence, will they be converging in terms of σ convergence definition? According to Barro and Sala-i-Martin (2004), the error term in the regression equation of absolute β convergence has a specific type of distribution with zero mean and constant variance. Also, to them, the dispersion of the concerned variable for studying convergence depends upon the variance of the error term. The dispersion of the error term in the initial period and the steady-state value of such variance determines whether absolute β convergence also leads to σ convergence. The relation among steady-state value of the dispersion of the concerned variable (D^*), β, and the variance of the error term (σ_u^2) is given by

$$D^* = \sigma_u^2 / [1 - (1 - \beta)]. \tag{23.51}$$

This relation shows that the steady-state dispersion is inversely related to speed of absolute convergence but rises with variance of the disturbance term. To show it in more detail, let us take the progress of the dispersion at time t as

$$D_t = D^* + (1-\beta)^{2t} \cdot (D_0 - D^*) \tag{23.52}$$

where D_0 is the dispersion of the concerned variable at initial period "0". The equation shows that D_t approaches its steady-state value D^* monotonically as time goes on since $0 < \beta < 1$. So, dispersion rises or falls even with absolute β convergence if D_0 begins below or above the steady-state rate D^*.

Nayyar (2008), in his work on economic growth and regional inequality in India, has pointed out that the concept of σ divergence is consistent with the concept of conditional β convergence and vice-versa. For example, a change in relevant parameters that leads the steady-state income levels of the rich away from the poor regions will lead to the state of σ divergence, in spite of the fact that each region may still be conditionally converging to a divergent steady-state path.

23.3.4 Gamma (γ) convergence

Quah (1993), on the other hand, suggests a methodological approach that is capable of capturing the full dynamics of developing cross-country distributions of per capita GDP. In their contribution, Boyle and McCarthy (1997) advocated for the use of the trend in rank concordance of per capita GDP in another context, in conjunction with the trend in the coefficient of variation which stands for σ convergence (Sala-i-Martin, 1995), as suggested by Friedman (1992), in a first pass at determining the nature and extent of the convergence process within and between countries. But there is a debate on which measure of convergence is sufficient. Both Sala-i-Martin (1995) and Quah (1993) point out that σ convergence is sufficient but not necessary for β convergence. The implication of this result is that the absence of β convergence cannot be taken as implying the absence of β convergence. Although σ convergence is considered as sufficient over the concept of β convergence, the former also suffers from lack in generalisation of testing in the latter. The approach of Boyle and McCarthy (1997), thus, seems an improved version of the former. They suggested that an index of rank concordance could be used in addition to β convergence in testing for β convergence. That particular measure can be referred to as the index of rank concordance which can be named γ convergence. It can be presented by the following formula:

$$\gamma = \left[Var\left(x_{ti} + x_{t0}\right) / \, Var\left(x_{t0}{}^{2}\right) \right] \tag{23.53}$$

where $Var(x)$ is the corresponding variance of the ranks of the variable X; ti refers to the time series from 0, 1, ..., n, and t_0 is the reference or base year. If the value of γ is close to unity then extreme inequality occurs, and if it tends to zero near egalitarian distribution of the concerned variable occurs.

This suggestion carries an important insight which means that in a situation where σ convergence is constant the researcher can use the proposed measure of γ convergence to ascertain whether β convergence exists.

Whatever be the hypothesis of convergence, there has been some common evidence on cross-country convergence or divergence. According to Jack Goldstone,

> in the twentieth century, the Great Divergence peaked before the First World War and continued until the early 1970s, then, after two decades of indeterminate fluctuations, in the late 1980s it was replaced by the Great Convergence as the majority of Third World countries reached economic growth rates significantly higher than those in most First World countries

thus the present-day convergence should be regarded as a continuation of the Great Divergence. In the 1960s and 1970s the East Asian Tigers rapidly converged with developed economies. These include Singapore, Hong Kong, South Korea, and Taiwan – all of which are today considered developed countries. In the post-war period (1945–1960) examples include West Germany, France, and Japan, which were able to quickly regain their prewar status by replacing capital that was lost during World War II.

23.3.5 *Graphical solution to convergence from empirical data*

If we plot the data of each region's growth rate and initial capital stock in log values in a scatter diagram and fit a linear trend through these points, then a downward trend will imply convergence of this region. This is the notion of absolute β convergence. On the contrary, if the fitted line is upward sloping then there is divergence, which means the richer zones become more and rich and the poorer zones become more and more poor. This is the notion of absolute β divergence. If we consider heterogeneity among the group of countries, then there may be conditional convergence where different control variables can be identified by cross-country regression of average growth rate of the variable (which is mostly per capita income and capital formation, households' consumption expenditure, etc.) upon the logarithm of base values and other control variables. If some of the control variables are observed to be significant along with the negative and significant value of β in statistical terms, then we can say that there are conditional convergences among the countries. In other words, each country is converging to their own steady states which are determined by their control variables which made then heterogeneous. Hence, the law of diminishing returns works in the case of absolute convergence but it does not work in the case of conditional convergence. This is a major drawback of the Solow model which considered only the homogeneity assumption across the countries.

23.4 Sample study report I: convergence analysis of households' consumption expenditure

Households' consumption expenditure becomes an important determinant of GDP of a country, particularly when the economy is struck by depression with low levels of private and public investments. So, maintaining growth of this head of expenditure over time becomes the crucial agenda of policymakers all over the world. The study by Das and Das (2016) tries to analyse whether the developing countries' levels of household consumption expenditure are converging to the ones in the developed countries during 1980–2013 in the sample of 40 countries based on the data developed by the world bank. The study reveals that there is no significant absolute β and γ convergence among either in the cross section or in pooling of the data during the given period. But population growth factor is making the countries significantly converge in a conditional sense. By separating the entirety of the data, we observe that, for the entire period, the developed countries are significantly converging in an absolute sense but the developing countries are not, although there are mixed results in σ convergence.

23.4.1 β convergence results

With the single year (i.e. 1980) data as a base value of per capita consumption expenditure and the annual average growth rates of the same determinant of the cross section of 40 countries over the entire period (i.e. 1980–2013), the plotted scattered diagram (Figure 23.10) depicts a negatively sloped trend line. This means there is a converging tendency in line with the absolute β convergence definition.

Whether the downward trend line is significant to justify the cross-country absolute convergence, the study has run regression as given in the discussion about the same in the preceding sections. It observes from the estimated results that there are insignificant absolute β convergences across the selected countries. The value of the β coefficient is (–)0.34 which is insignificant even at the 10% levels of significance.

23.4.2 σ convergence results

Let us see whether there is σ convergence in terms of the declining trend of the CV of the distribution of households' consumption expenditure of all 40 countries over the entire period 1980–2013, although there is insignificant absolute β convergence among the countries (that means the failure of the developing countries to catch up with the developed ones). The results are derived from Figure 23.11.

We observe that there is again insignificant σ divergence as the trend of CV takes a very light upward sloping function. Hence, we do not arrive at the conclusion that the countries are converging either in absolute β and σ convergence definitions when the entire period of study is considered for all the selected countries.

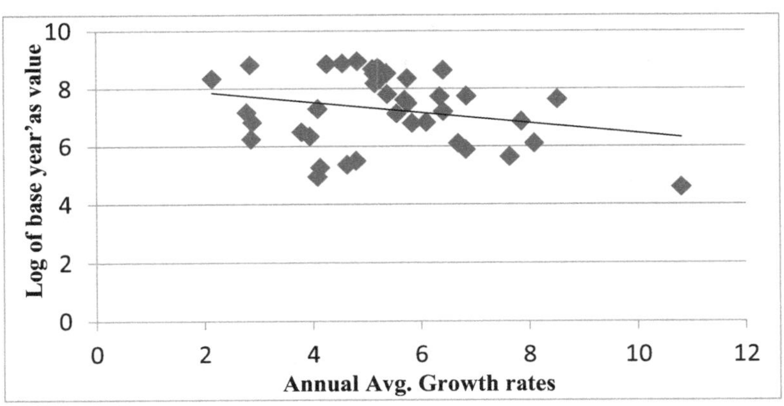

Figure 23.10 Absolute β convergence in per capita consumption expenditure (1980 as base value)

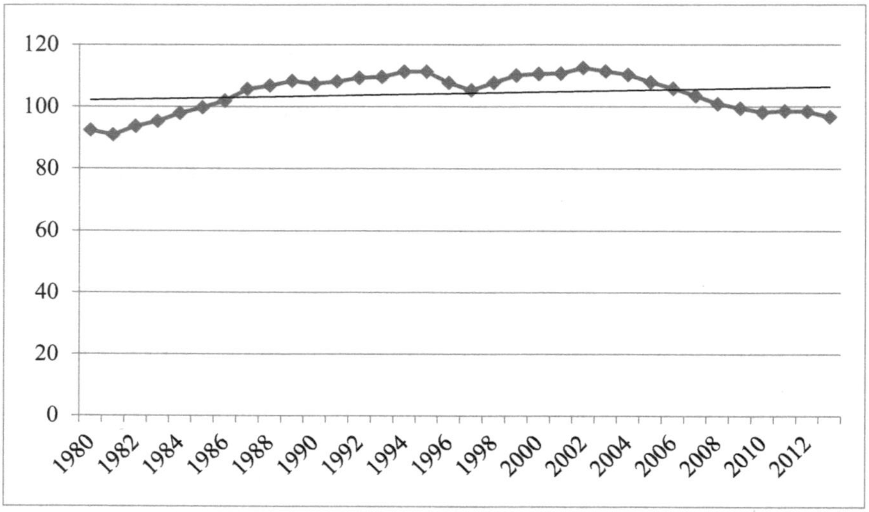

Figure 23.11 Trend of coefficient of variation (CV) of per capita consumption expenditure for 1980–2013

23.4.3 *Convergence analysis of developed countries only*

Sometimes it happens that, in a broad spectrum of selection of countries, the countries may not converge. But there may be convergence among sub groups or regional convergence. Having mixed results in absolute β convergence for all the countries in the entire period of study, the authors have gone through the same exercise across a near homogeneous nature of history of developments of the developed or high-income countries which are 17 in number. The scatter diagrams and the trend of CV are presented in Figures 23.12 and 23.13 respectively.

It is observed from the previous figure that out of the entire period of study there, the trend line passing through the scattered points is negatively sloped and relatively steeper, signifying the presence of significant absolute β convergence results. After estimating the growth equation like before, we find that the high-income countries are converging significantly with an estimated coefficient of –1.3 at the probability level of 0.06. The speed of convergence is calculated at 83% annually. This means the high-income countries belonging to the lower strata of the 17-country sample like Portugal, Russia, Greece, and South Korea are trying to catch up the countries lying in the upper strata of the sample like the USA, France, and Germany. This is not to say, like the previous discussion, that the catching up process will necessarily lead to falling dispersion across the countries or the presence of σ convergence among the high-income countries.

It is observed from the figure that the trend of CV is negatively sloped with a very low gradient. The quantification of the slope of the CV trend over time (which is –0.08) shows that there is insignificant σ convergence among the high-income countries.

23.4.4 *Convergence analysis of developing countries only*

Let us see the convergence/divergence analysis of another economic community which belongs to the middle- and low-income-generating developing countries which are 23 in

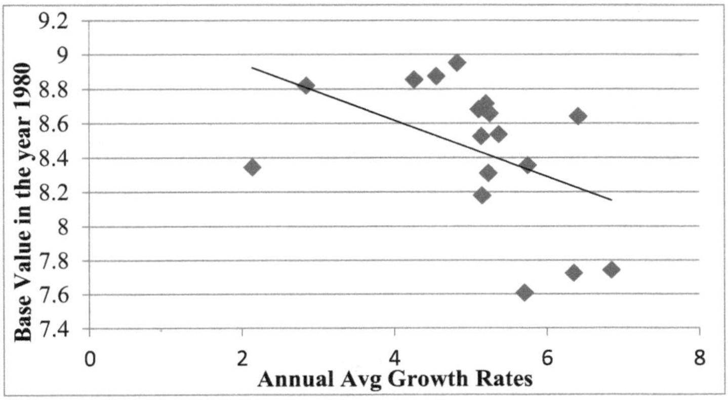

Figure 23.12 Absolute β convergence in per capita consumption expenditure of high-income countries (1980–2013)

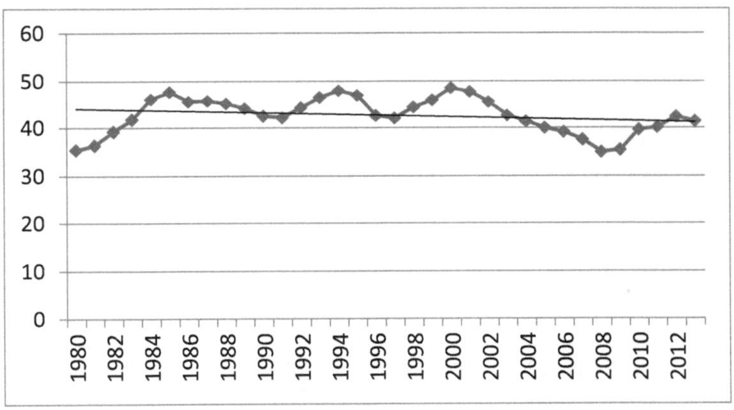

Figure 23.13 Trend of coefficient of variation (CV) of per capita consumption expenditure of high-income countries

number. Although they are near homogeneous in terms of the per capita GDP, they vary in line with the other economic and social factors. The scattered diagram and the trend of CV have been presented in Figures 23.14 and 23.15 respectively.

The study observed negative trend lines in both the diagrams but with very flat shapes for the entire period of study. The estimated regression results show highly insignificant absolute β convergence (–0.34 with probability of 0.09) and σ convergence (–0.09 with probability of 0.61). Both the definitions of convergence are consistent in this respect.

23.4.5 Conditional β convergence results

As we have already stated, under the conditional β convergence approach each country has separate steady-state value of the consumption expenditure in the long run and each country tries to catch up with its own steady states depending upon the differences in the

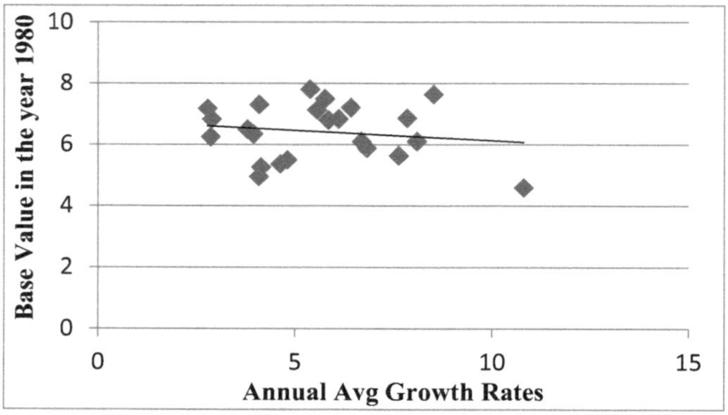

Figure 23.14 Absolute β convergence in per capita consumption expenditure of middle- and low-income countries (1980–2013)

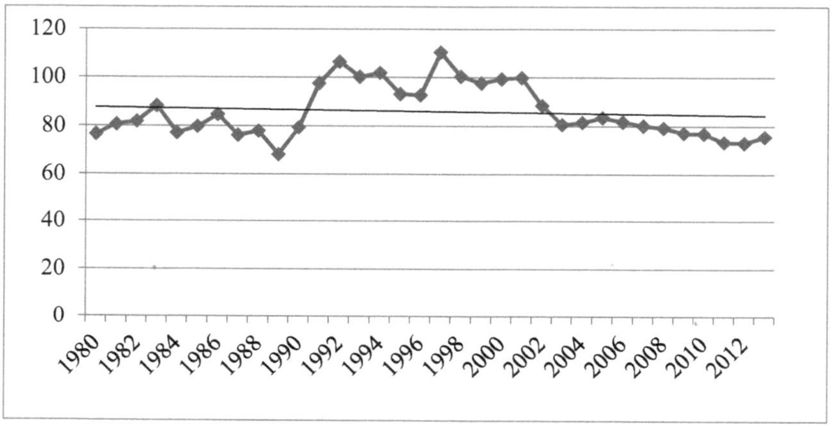

Figure 23.15 Trend of coefficient of variation (CV) of per capita consumption expenditure of middle- and low-income countries (1980–2013)

conditional structural variables. The conditional variables the study has considered for having impact upon consumption expenditure are per capita GDP, inflation rate, rate of interest, annual average population growth rates, and a regional dummy (which is 1 for developed and 0 for others) to capture differences in steady states.

Testing for conditional β convergence with respect to the selected additional explanatory variables, the study observes that no conditional variable except population growth rate works for cross-country convergence for the all country samples. The result is insignificant convergence although the population growth rate has an expected sign (–0.76 with probability of 0.03) with the significant role of the average growth rates to converge. Maybe the additional variables are correlated or there is a multicollinearity problem. Omitting the conditional variables other than the population growth rate from the list, the study has further run the same regression on the log value of the base year's consumption and population growth rates. We find a significant conditional β convergence result (–0.69 with probability of 0.01). This means a rise in population growth rates of the countries affects inversely the convergence among the countries.

23.5 Sample study report II: absolute β and σ convergence analysis of capital formation across countries

The study of Ray, Das, and Das (2016) has considered per capita gross capital formation (PCGCF) for exploring the convergence aspect across the selection of 37 countries (which constitute about 90% of world GCF) for the period 1980–2013 based on World Bank data. The scatter diagram has been presented in Figure 23.16.

The scatter diagram of pairs of observations of logarithm of values of per capita capital during the base year 1980 and the corresponding average annual growth rates of per capita capital from 1980 to 2013 of all 37 countries allows us to say that there is a strong evidence of neoclassical concept of absolute β convergence across the nations. The lower the value of per capita capital, the higher would be the average growth rate, signifying poor nations would catch up with the rich countries if all other things remained the same. In contrast, the rich nations in terms of relatively moderate values of per capita capital correspond to relatively lower values of average annual growth rates of per capita capital, despite the heterogeneous characters of the countries selected from different continents. The estimated regression coefficient has been derived as negative as desired and significant at a 5% level. This means the there is significant absolute β convergence among the selected countries. The estimated regression coefficient is 0.008 which may also stand for speed of convergence. It means the countries are converging at the rate of 0.8% annually which is weak in nature. Also, if the base level of per capita capital stock rises by \$1 USD then the average growth rate of the per capita capital stock will fall by 0.8 unit. So, β convergence is evident which may lead to a falling tendency of expected inequality of the distribution of per capita capital formation across the selected nations.

Since the value of common or individual steady state (to which to converge) is unknown and difficult to estimate, there is a natural question of how many years are required for

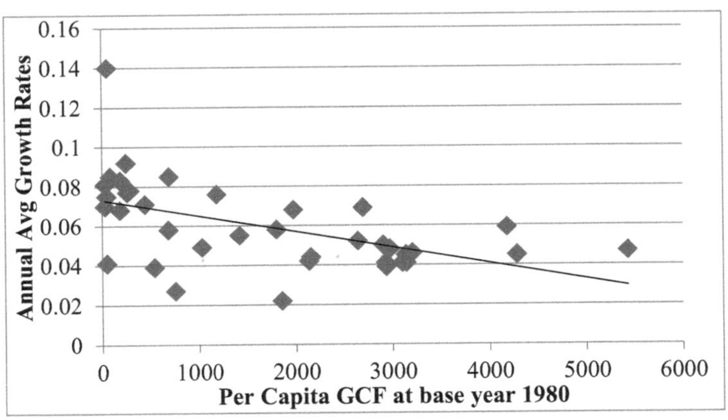

Figure 23.16 Scatter diagram of growth rates and base values of PCGCF

all the countries to converge to that common steady-state level of per capita gross capital formation. According to our convergence speed of 0.008 annually, the time required to cross the half line is about 86 years.

It is also understood from the theories of absolute β convergence that it is a narrow concept of convergence and its sufficiency may be assessed by the concept of σ convergence. The fluctuations of capital per person across the all 37 nations in cross sectional aspect are justified by the dispersions by means of coefficient of variations of the distribution. Accordingly, the declining trend of CV (Figure 23.17) justifies σ convergence. It is evident that CV is declining at the rate of 0.26 units on an average over time, construing significant evidence of σ convergence across the nations. It implies that the capital-gap between the nations will be declining in the future time horizon and it would have an impact on the global economy since 90% of global capital is incorporated in the present study. As per capita capital is taken as a proxy variable of per capita GDP, the convergence of wellbeing across the selected nations cannot be denied at a future time, as the present study shows.

We know that the Brazil, Russia, India, China, and South Africa (BRICS) group was formed out of the world's highly developing countries having the capability of catching up with the so-called developed countries. It has a history of about twenty years of establishment. As China and Russia are there in the group, it is a natural question whether the group members have maintained any sort of convergence among them. A recent study by Das and Nayak (2023) focuses on the dynamics of the four key indicators, per capita gross domestic product (PCGDP), savings, capital-output ratio, and population, for the BRICS group in order to analyse the convergence, divergence, or others in line with the neoclassical and stochastic convergence methods for 1991–2019. The cross-country regression results, as per the unconditional β convergence, show no signs of convergence or divergence in any of the four indicators, although there is sigma convergence in some of them. Further, the results of the stochastic convergence analysis do not show any sign of convergence in income in any pair of the countries. There is non-diverging catching

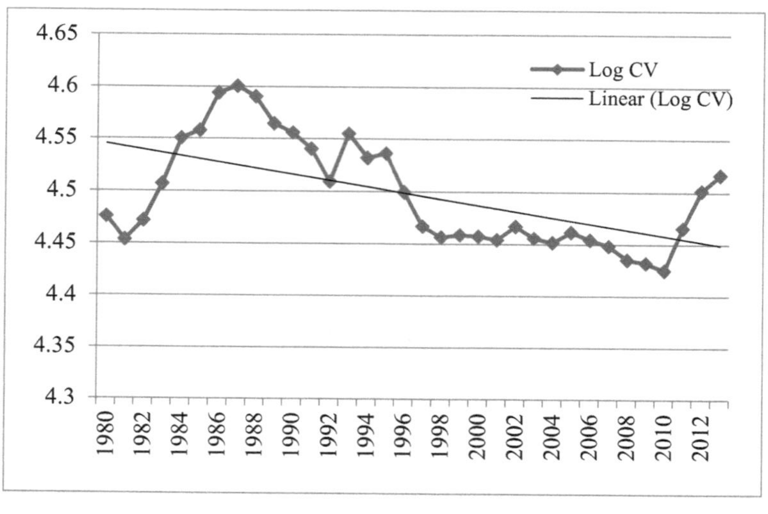

Figure 23.17 Trend of coefficients of variations

up in incomes per capita for two pairs of countries only, Brazil–China and Brazil–Russia, and divergence results in PCGDP for two other pairs, Brazil–India and India–Russia.

23.6 Some problems and solutions of the Solow model

1. Consider how unemployment would affect the Solow growth model. Suppose that output is produced according to the production function $Y = K\alpha[(1 - u)\ L]^{1\ -\ \alpha}$ where u is natural rate of unemployment. The national savings rate is s, the labour force grows at the rate n, and capital depreciates at rate δ.

   a. Express output per worker ($y = Y / L$) as a function of capital per worker ($k = K / L$) and the natural rate of unemployment.
   b. Illustrate the steady state graphically.
   c. Suppose that some change in government policy reduces the natural rate of unemployment. Describe how this change affects output both immediately and over time. Is the steady-state effect on output larger or smaller than the immediate effect? Explain.

Solution:

a. $Y = K\alpha[(1 - u)\ L]^{1\ -\ \alpha}$

   $\Rightarrow y = k^{a}[1 - u]^{1\ -\ \alpha}$. Clearly, unemployment reduces the amount of output per worker for any given capital–labour ratio because some of the workers are not producing anything.

   At the steady state, $sy = (\delta + n)k$

   $\Rightarrow k\alpha\ s\ [1 - u]^{1\ -\ \alpha} = (\delta + n)\ k$

   $\Rightarrow k^{1\ -\ \alpha} = s\ (1 - u)^{1\ -\ \alpha} / (\delta + n)$

   $\Rightarrow k^{*} = (1 - u)\ [s / (\delta + n)]^{1/1 - \alpha}$

   Unemployment lowers steady-state output for two reasons: i) for a given k unemployment lowers y, and ii) unemployment also lowers the steady-state value of k^{*}.

b. Unemployment lowers the marginal productivity of capital per worker and hence acts like a negative technological shock that reduces the amount of capital the economy can maintain at the steady-state level. Figure 23.18 shows that an increase in unemployment lowers the *sf*(*k*) line and the steady-state level of capital per worker.

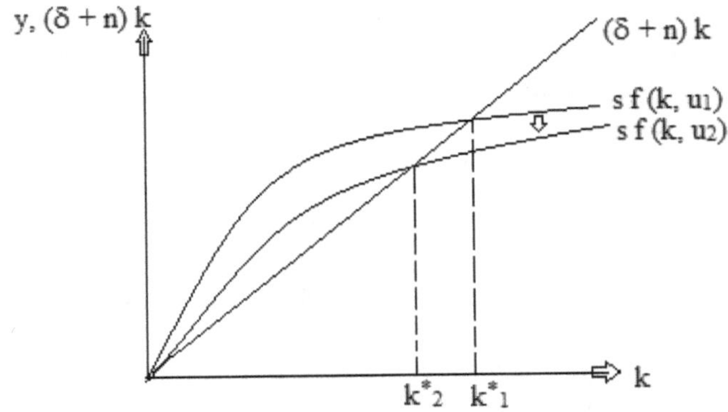

Figure 23.18 Steady-state equilibrium

c. As soon as u falls from u_1 to u_2 (opposite to this diagram) output jumps up from its initial steady-state values. The economy at that point has the same amount of capital (since it takes time to adjust capital stock), but this capital is combined with more workers. The economy begins its transition by accumulating more capital, raising output even further than the initial jump. Eventually the capital stock and output converge to their new higher steady-state level.

2. Consider the following data as $n = 1\%$, $g = 2\%$, $\Delta Y / Y = \Delta K / K = 3$, $\alpha = 0.3$.
   If you use the growth accounting equation to divide output growth rate into three sources, how much would you contribute to each source?

Solution:

We know $\Delta Y / Y = \alpha(\Delta K / K) + (1 - \alpha)(\Delta L / L) + \Delta A / A$
From the given information we can obtain $\alpha(\Delta K / K) = 0.9$ a d $(1 - \alpha)(\Delta L / L) = 0.7$
$\therefore \Delta A / A = 3 - 0.9 - 0.7 = 1.4$

23.7 Conclusion

The neoclassical model of growth developed by Solow and Swan is a major departure from the classical and Keynesian models of growth. According to the Solow–Swan model, the workings of diminishing returns can be stopped and the increase in growth rates is perpetual if we introduce *technological progress* into the growth model. As technological progress begins, capital becomes more productive and the capital–output ratio falls, leading to increase in growth rates with fixed s and n. A major prediction from the Solow model is that, if the diminishing productivity works, then the poor countries will converge to the rich countries in per capita income. This is popularly known as cross-country convergence. However, if there are marked differences between a poor and a rich country in several aspects, there will be conditional convergence in the sense that the rich country will converge to its new and better level.

Summary

The neoclassical theory of growth, mainly through the initiatives of Robert Solow, was a strong counterargument against the classical and Keynesian models of growth. Assuming diminishing returns to capital, the increase in growth rates can be made everlasting if technological progress is introduced into the growth model. As technological progress begins, capital becomes more productive and the capital–output ratio falls, leading to increase in growth rates even with a fixed savings ratio and growth of population. The salient features of the present chapter are:

- Technological progress is the cause of perpetual growth rates of an economy.
- Steady-state capital stock per capita is attained at a point where actual investment $[s.f(k)]$ is equal to required investment $(n + \delta)k]$
- The aggregate production function follows constant returns to scale which means that at whatever rate the factor quantity is increased, per capita income will increase by the same rate.
- The golden rule steady state is attained at a point of capital accumulation where the economy reaches maximum social welfare in the long run by maximising per capita consumption of the citizens.
- An important prediction of the Solow growth model is the cross-country convergence which says that the countries starting with low capital stock will grow faster than

the countries who possess relatively more stock of capital at the initial period. This is known as absolute β convergence. The reason behind this result is the working of diminishing returns to capital.

- If there are marked differences between a poor and a rich country in several aspects, there will be conditional convergence in the sense that the rich country will converge to its new and better level.
- σ convergence states that the countries will converge in a true sense if the cross-country coefficient of variations declines over time.

Multiple choice questions and answers

1. According to the neoclassical growth model, an increase in growth rates depends on

   (a) Increase in capital–output ratio.
   (b) Decrease in capital–output ratio.
   (c) Increase in marginal propensity to consume.
   (d) None of the above.

2. According to the neoclassical growth model, an increase in growth rates depends on

   (a) Increase in savings ratio.
   (b) Decrease in savings ratio.
   (c) Increase in marginal propensity to consume.
   (d) None of the above.

3. The Solow growth model predicts that

   (a) Rich nations will grow faster than poor nations.
   (b) The rich will get richer and the poor will get poorer.
   (c) The rich will get poorer and the poor will get richer.
   (d) Poor nations will grow faster than rich nations.

4. If the central prediction of the Solow growth model is valid,

   (a) Per capita real GDP differences among nations will increase.
   (b) Per capita real GDP differences among nations will diminish.
   (c) Economic freedom as measured by the Heritage Foundation Index will decrease.
   (d) Population growth rates in rich countries will increase.

5. By absolute β convergence, the Solow model means the countries starting from a low value of income at the base period will

   (a) Grow at lesser rate compared to the country with high value of income at base period.
   (b) Grow at faster rate compared to the country with high value of income at base period.
   (c) Be absolutely unchanged.
   (d) None of the above.

6. By σ convergence, it is meant that the coefficients of variation of income across different regions should be

   (a) Increasing over time.
   (b) Remaining the same over time.
   (c) Declining over time.
   (d) All of the above.

7. The golden rule steady state is a position when the economy reaches maximum social welfare in the long run by maximising

   (a) Per capita consumption of the citizens.
   (b) Per capita savings of the citizens.
   (c) Per capita consumption of gold.
   (d) Per capita savings of gold.

Answers

1. (b); 2. (a); 3. (d); 4. (b); 5. (b); 6. (c); 7. (a)

Review questions

1. What are major departures between the Harrod-Domar model of growth and the neoclassical model of growth? Discuss the Solow model of growth with appropriate diagrams.
2. What is growth accounting? Can you illustrate the accounting process of growth with an example? Explain.
3. In the Solow model, how does the saving rate affect the steady-state rate of growth? What is the golden rule of capital? Explain what will happen to the golden rule of capital if technological progress is allowed.
4. Might a policymaker choose a steady state with i) golden rule level of capital, ii) more capital than in the golden rule steady-state and iii) less capital than in the golden rule steady state? Explain your answers.
5. In the Solow model, how does the rate of population growth affect the steady-state level of income? How does it affect the steady-state rate of growth?
6. What is Solow residual? Why is Solow residual often used as a measure of technological progress?
7. An economy has the per capita production function $y = k^{1/2}$. Find the balanced growth value of k, given that the saving rate is 16%, depreciation rate is 10%, and population growth rate is zero.

   a. Express output per worker as a function of capital per worker and the natural rate of unemployment. Describe the steady state of this economy.
   b. Suppose that some change in government policy reduces the natural rate of unemployment. Describe how this change affects output both immediately and over time. Is the steady-state effect on output larger or smaller than the immediate effect? Explain.

8. Prove each of the following statements about the steady state with population growth and technological progress.

   a. The capital–output ratio is constant.
   b. Capital and labour each earn a constant share of an economy's income.
   c. Total capital income and total labour income both grow at the rate of population growth plus the rate of technological progress, $n + g$.
   d. The rental price of capital is constant, and the real wage grows at the rate of technological progress g.

9. Labour productivity is defined as Y / L. Start with the growth accounting equation and show that the growth in labour productivity depends on growth in TFP and growth in K / L ratio. In particular, show that $\Delta(Y / L) / (Y / L) = \Delta A / A + \alpha\Delta(K / L) / K / L$.

10. What major prediction can be made from the neoclassical theory of growth? Differentiate absolute β convergence from conditional β convergence and absolute β convergence from σ convergence.
11. Give a brief note on γ convergence. Using a cross-country data on income, calculate the values of the Gamma Convergence Index.
12. Explain how the poor countries catch up with the rich countries in the world with the help of the tools used in the Solow model of growth. Will the results differ if two countries of concern significantly differ in the indicator considered? Discuss.

Additional readings

Das, R. C. & Das, A. (2016). *Convergence Analysis of Households' Consumption Expenditure: A Cross Country Study*. Pennsylvania: IGI Global.

Das, R. C. & Nayak, A. (2023). "Bi-polar convergence analysis of income and related factors in the BRICS nations: A stochastic convergence approach". *Global Business Review*. https://doi.org/10.1177/09721509221139689

Ray, K., Das, R. C. & Das, U. (2016). *Convergence Aspect of Capital Formation: A Study on Major Countries*. Pennsylvania: IGI Global.

Solow, R. M. (1956). "A contribution to the theory of economic growth". *Quarterly Journal of Economics*, 70(1), 65–94.

24 Endogenous growth theories – the modern growth approach

24.1 Introduction

In the preceding chapter, we discussed in detail the neoclassical growth model developed by Professor Solow and Professor Swan. The model was well developed compared to the classical and Harrod–Domar models in the way it introduced the working of the diminishing returns to capital and showed that the exogenous savings rate cannot create permanent growth in income as claimed by the H-D model. The neoclassical model, hence, introduced the effect of technological progress as exogenous which was capable of combating diminishing returns to capital so that growth rate of income can be maintained in the longer run with the rate of growth of income rising by the growth of technological progress. But the central feature of the failure of the neoclassical model was that it could not explain why the so-called developed countries of the world had experienced tremendous growth of output in the post-world-war phase with such exogenous technological progress. Was the technological progress really exogenous, or something different from the claim of the neoclassical model? The theoreticians who pointed out this lacuna of the neoclassical model in explaining the growth performances of the leading countries in the last few decades are the proponents of endogenous growth literatures where the effect of technological progress is determined by the system itself, not by outside factors. Endogenous growth is long run economic growth at a rate determined by forces that are internal to the economic system, particularly those forces governing the opportunities and incentives to create technological knowledge. Endogenous growth theories predict increasing returns to scale in technology, which translate into long-term knowledge-based growth. The endogenous growth theory primarily holds that the long run growth rate of an economy depends on policy measures. For example, subsidies for research and development or education increase the growth rate in some endogenous growth models by increasing the incentive for innovation.

The first one to study this endogenous theory is the Ramsey model which endogenises the savings rate by households' optimum consumption behaviour over intertemporal choices, and the others are the Arrow, Lucas, Romer, and Barro where endogenous technological progress is explained by introducing human capital, research and development activity, and introduction of government as institutional supports. These factors create returns to capital that are increasing, rather than diminishing. We will discuss the salient features of the endogenous growth theories in the following sections one by one.

24.2 Growth under consumption optimisation — the Ramsey model

One primary model to tackle the flaw in the neoclassical model was established by Ramsey in the year 1928 which was later sophisticated by Cass and Koopmans in 1965. The

DOI: 10.4324/9781003501138-30

neoclassical model considered the savings and consumption behaviour of the households as exogenous and showed that the long run steady-state growth of per capita income became zero. The Ramsey model considers optimal consumption and savings behaviour of the households in an intertemporal model where the factors affecting consumption and savings are endogenous. By not allowing endogenous households' behaviour, the neoclassical model did not account for how incentives such as tax reductions, subsidy provisions, increased interest rates, etc. affected the overall economic performance. Hence, the inefficient oversavings or undersavings in the neoclassical model can be precluded by the endogenous households' behaviour. The Ramsey model considers households to be immortal and choose their consumption and savings to maximise total family utility subject to the intertemporal budget functions. We want to establish the same long run steady-state solution in the Ramsey model like the neoclassical model but from the perspective of a social planner who makes synchronisation of households and firms' behaviour in a decentralised system.

The Ramsey model is one of the basic workhorse models of macroeconomics. It can be seen as placed at one end of a line, with another workhorse model placed at the other end, namely Diamond's overlapping generations model. In the Diamond model there is an infinite number of agents (since in every new period a new generation enters the economy) and these have a finite time horizon. In the Ramsey model there is a finite number of agents with an infinite time horizon; further, these agents are completely alike. The Ramsey model is thus a representative agent model, whereas the Diamond model has heterogeneous agents (young and old) interacting in every period. These differences in the basic setup turn out to have important implications for the conclusions. Along the line of the two frameworks as polar cases, fewer abstract models are scattered, some being closer to Ramsey's pole, others closer to Diamond's. For example, in Barro's model, with parental altruism, when the bequest motive is operative, the Barro model coincides with a Ramsey model (in discrete time); again, when the bequest motive is not operative, the Barro model coincides with a Diamond OLG model.

24.2.1 *The formal model — the decentralised problem*

There are two sectors acting independently, households and firms, and the other sector is the market which creates association/interactions between these two distinct sectors. On the demand side, the households' objective is to maximise utility subject to their intertemporal budget constraints, and on the supply side, firms maximise profits subject to the factor accumulation constraint. Then supply equals demand in the equilibrium in real terms.

24.2.1.1 *First, the households' problem*

The Ramsey model makes some important assumptions to solve the utility maximisation problem. They are as follows:

- i) Households have infinite lives and they maximise intertemporal utility.
- ii) The households receive wage income in exchange for their labour supplies and interest incomes for their accumulated assets.
- iii) The incomes are used in purchasing goods for consumption and savings for the accumulation of additional assets.
- iv) Population grows at the constant rate, n. At initial time $t = 0$, there is only one individual in the economy (i.e. $L0 = 1$), so that the total population at any time t is given by $Lt = ent$.

v) All households' behaviour is identical.
vi) Households cannot borrow unlimited amounts to finance their arbitrarily high levels of consumption. Hence, households' debt cannot increase at a rate asymptotically higher than the interest rate.
ii) The present value of current and future assets must be asymptotically nonnegative.

Let us first consider the budget (M) constraint which shows the change in assets at time "t" as equal to the sum of labour and interest incomes minus consumption. It can be written as

$$dM / dt = w_t L_t + r_t M_t - C_t \tag{24.1}$$

where w_t is the wage rate, r_t is the rate of interest, and C_t is the consumption expenditure at time t. Dividing both sides by the population figure we get budget constraint in per capita terms (all the lowercase letters denote per capita values) which is as follows:

$$dm / dt = w_t + r_t m_t - n m_t - c_t \,. \tag{24.2}$$

The per capita budget constraint takes the population term as a residual component.

Since households' debt cannot increase at a rate asymptotically higher than the interest rate, the following expression will hold. A household can borrow to finance current consumption and then use future borrowings for rolling the principal and paying all the streams of interest rates. That is

$$Lt_{t \to \infty} (m_t e^{\int_0^t (r_q - n) dq}) \geq 0 \,. \tag{24.3}$$

This previous expression stands for the credit market constraint. It addresses that, in the long run, borrowing per capita or the negative values of m_t cannot grow at the rate of r_q – n (that is, interest rates minus population growth rate).

Now consider the intertemporal utility function of each of the households where they want to maximise overall utility. The aggregate utility (U) function is thus the integral value of the utility of each household (u) associated with the size of population in the family (L_t) and rate of time preference, ρ, which represents whether the household prefers current consumption over the future depending upon its values.

$$U = \int_0^t u(c_t).L_t.e^{-\rho t}.dt \tag{24.4}$$

$$U = \int_0^t u(c_t).e^{nt}.e^{-\rho t}.dt \tag{24.5}$$

$$U = \int_0^t u(c_t).e^{-(\rho - n)t}.dt \tag{24.6}$$

where c_t represents consumption per person. A positive value of ρ means the household prefers the current period over the future period. That means they discount the future; the future generation is given lower importance by the households. It may be called selfishness of the parents. It is also assumed that $\rho > n$ which implies that utility is bounded by constant c_t over time. When $\rho = 0$, the households put equal importance on all the periods.

The utility function $u(c_t)$ follows two properties. One, it is increasing ($du / dc > 0$) and concave ($d^2u / dc^2 < 0$), and two it satisfies the Inada conditions, i.e. marginal utility from consumption du / dc is infinity when c tends to zero and it is zero when c tends to infinity.

Now consider the problem of the household who wants to maximise intertemporal utility subject to the lifetime budget constraint. Since it is a dynamic problem, not a static problem, we apply the present value Hamiltonian approach (like the Lagrangian function in the static consumer's optimisation problem) to solve the dynamic optimisation problem of the household. The present value of the Hamiltonian expression is thus

$$H = u(c_t) . e^{-(\rho-n)\,t} + \beta_t[w_t + r_t m_t - nm_t - c_t] \tag{24.7}$$

where suffix t stands for function of time. β_t means the rate of change of the utility with respect to marginal relaxation of the budget function. This may be called the marginal utility of budget or the shadow price, which depends also on time like utility, asset, consumption, and factor incomes.

The first-order conditions for maximum utility are given by following equations:

$$\delta H / \delta c = 0 => \delta u / \delta c\ .e^{-(\rho-n)\,t} - \beta = 0 \tag{24.8}$$

$$or,\ \delta u / \delta c\ .e^{-(\rho\,-\,n)\,t} = \beta$$

$$\delta H / \delta m = -\delta\beta / \delta t => \delta\beta / \delta t = -\beta.(r-n). \tag{24.9}$$

Taking the derivative of (25.9) with respect to time, we get

$$\delta^2 u / \delta c^2 .\partial c / \partial t.e^{-(\rho-n)t} = \partial\beta / \partial t = -\beta(r-n) \tag{24.10}$$

The transversality condition is,

$$Lt_{t\to\infty} = [\beta_t .m_t] = 0. \tag{24.11}$$

That means the value of the representative household's assets must approach zero as time approaches infinity. Individuals thus do not prefer to hold assets for indefinite periods, or if they do these assets should have no value in terms of the objective function.

The condition for optimum consumption can be derived from the first-order conditions by differentiating the first condition with respect to time and substituting β and $\delta\beta / \delta t$ from the second condition. Formally it is known as *Euler's condition* which is as follows:

$$\delta^2 u / \delta c^2 .\partial c / \partial t.e^{-(\rho-n)\,t} = \partial\beta / \partial t.$$

Now,

$$\delta^2 u / \delta c^2 .\partial c / \partial t.e^{-(\rho-n)t} = \partial\beta / \partial t = -\beta(r-n).$$

From (25.9) we get . . .

$$\delta^2 u / \delta c^2 . \partial c / \partial t . e^{-(\rho - n)\, t} = -\delta\ u / \delta c . e^{-(\rho - n)\, t} .(r - n).$$

Taking $n = \rho$

$$r = \rho - \left\{\left[\left(\delta^2 u / \delta c^2\right). c\right] / \left[\delta u / \delta c\right]\right\}. \left\{\left(\delta c / \delta t\right) / c\right\}. \tag{24.12}$$

This means, $r = \rho - [\delta(\delta u / \delta c) / (\delta u / \delta c)] . \{(\delta c / \delta t) / c\}$. It is known as *Euler's condition.*

or $r = \rho -$ [Marginal of $(\delta u / \delta c)$ / Average of $(\delta u / \delta c)$] . $\{(\delta c / \delta t) / c\}$
or $r = \rho - \sigma. \{(\delta c / \delta t) / c\}$

where σ gives the elasticity of marginal utility of consumption at different time periods.

Households choose consumption so as to equate the rate of return to savings, r, to the "rate of return" to consumption. In other words, the return on future consumption is equal to the return on current consumption. The higher the rate of return on savings, the more willing households are to save and shift their consumption to the future periods or to prefer the future generations in place of themselves. On the other hand, the higher the rate of return to consumption is (that is, low value of r), the more willing households are to sacrifice future consumption for more current consumption and thereby less current savings. Finally, when r is equal to rate of time preference, ρ, then households are indifferent between consumption (current period) and saving (future periods). The equality condition also points out that (from Euler's condition) $(\delta c / \delta t) / c = 0$. That means the rate of growth of per person consumption becomes zero or a flat consumption pattern over the years. Therefore the relation between r and ρ determines whether to choose a pattern of per capita consumption that may rise, fall, or remain constant over time.

24.2.1.2 *Second, firms' problem*

The basic function of a firm is to be involved in production activity of goods using the factor services supplied by the households in terms of payments of wages, w and interest rates, r. The ultimate objective of involvement in the production activity is to maximise profit. The Ramsey model assumes the following in establishing firms' behaviour in a decentralised economy:

i) the economy consists of an large number of identical firms producing a homogeneous consumption good, say, Y
ii) Each firm uses a production technology I = $F(K,L)$ that satisfies the neoclassical properties (i.e. smooth, rising, and concave), and pays wages and rent in exchange for labour and capital services respectively. Here K is the capital input in terms of commodity units and L is the labour input in person-per-hour unit and technology is taken as fixed like in the neoclassical model.
iii) Capital stock depreciates at the rate δ; the net rate of return to a household owning capital is $R\ \delta$. At the same time, households receive r for lending capital to other households and, due to perfect substitutability between these two types of capital, the rates of return should be equal. That is $R - \delta = r$ or $R = r + \delta$.

The objective function or the profit function of a representative firm (i) is given by the following expression

$$\pi(K, L) = F(K, L) = (r + \delta).\ K - w.\ L. \qquad (24.13)$$

The first order conditions for profit maximisation are:

$$\delta\pi / \delta K = 0 => f_k = (r + \delta) \qquad (24.14)$$

$$\delta\pi / \delta L = 0 => f - k.f_k = w \qquad (24.15)$$

where $k = K / L$ and $f - k.\ f_k$ = marginal productivity of labour. The previous results show that the marginal product of each input equals its associated cost.

24.2.1.3 *Equilibrium analysis of the Ramsey model in a decentralised problem*

Let us group the households' behaviour with the firms' behaviour that we discussed in previous sections to analyse the structure of competitive market equilibrium. In equilibrium, the stock of per capita assets equals the stock of capital per worker, i.e. $m = k$ since the economy is closed and all the debts in the economy will be cancelled out in an overall sense. On the other hand, inclusion of international transactions into the model may lead to nonzero foreign debt.

In equilibrium, there should be equality between the stock of per capita assets and the stock of per capita capital (combining the results of the households' and firms' problems). That is $m = k$.

This implies rate of growth of per capita capital is the per capita output net of population growth, depreciation, and per capita volume of consumption expenditure. They are to be linked to Euler's equation in the households' problem.

That is, on one hand,

$$dk / dt = f(k) - (n + \delta)k - c \qquad (24.16)$$

and on the other hand,

$$\left[(dc / dt) / c\right] = 1 / \sigma[f_k - \delta - \rho] \qquad (24.17)$$

$$\left[\dot{c} / c\right] = 1 / \sigma\left[f_k - (\rho + \delta)\right]$$

where σ is the (absolute) elasticity of marginal utility and indicates how much the consumer wishes to smooth consumption over time. The inverse of $\sigma(ct)$ is the elasticity of intertemporal substitution in consumption. It measures the willingness to incur variation in consumption over time in response to a change in the interest rate. Further, $1 / \sigma$ reflects the individuals' willingness to accept deviations from a uniform pattern of consumption over time. The lower σ, the slower the decline of the marginal utility in response to consumption growth, and therefore the more willing individuals are to accept variations in their consumption. This is a system of two differential equations of first degree that yield the market equilibrium time paths of consumption and capital per capita.

24.2.1.4 *Steady-state solution under Ramsey model*

Let us see how the per capita capital and consumption grow in the long run steady-state position. Recall that, under the neoclassical model, the per capita output and capital do not grow or they remain constant. Let us see what happens to the per capita capital and consumption under the Ramsey model.

In the steady state, growth rates of per capita consumption and the capital stock per worker equal zero. That is, $dk / dt = dc / dt = 0$. From the equilibrium condition under the Ramsey model, we have

$$dk / dt = f(k) - (n+\delta)k - c. \tag{24.18}$$

Putting $dk / dt = 0$ at steady state, we get

$$\begin{aligned} &f(k) - (n+\delta)k - c = 0 \\ &or,\ c = f(k) - (n+\delta)k. \end{aligned} \tag{24.19}$$

Taking the derivative with respect to time on both sides we get

$$dc / dt = f_k - (n+\delta). \tag{24.20}$$

Putting $dc / dt = 0$, we get

$$or,\ f_k = \delta + \rho. \tag{24.21}$$

Hence, in the absence of technological progress, the Ramsey model predicts zero growth as in the simple Solow–Swan model and the level variables grow at the rate of n. If we allow technology to grow at the rate g then the level variables grow at $n + g$ in the steady state and the per capita variables do not grow at all. The results of the Ramsey model and neoclassical models, thus, produce identical results in the steady state but the difference between the two is that the former model endogenises the households' consumption and savings behaviour whereas the latter considers the exogenous savings rate with no explanation.

24.2.2 *The formal model — the social planner problem*

Let us analyse the Ramsey model from the perspective of a benevolent social planner who wants to optimise the overall objective of a group or economy. We want to see, particularly, whether the decentralised equilibrium of the economy is the first-best outcome or Pareto optimal.

Now set the social planner aim as maximising households' intertemporal utility subject to the aggregate budget constraint, which shows how the economy's output is allocated to different uses. In a two-sector closed economy without government, the aggregate outcome can be used for consumption and investment in physical capital: That is

$$Y = C + I \tag{24.22}$$

We know investment is the change in capital stock, dK / dt, plus amount of funds devoted to depreciation adjustment, δK. Hence,

$$Y = C + dK / dt + \delta K. \tag{24.23}$$

In per capita terms,

$$dk / dt = f(k) - (n + \delta)k - c. \tag{24.24}$$

Considering the utility function as a constant intertemporal elasticity of substitution (σ), the relevant Hamiltonian for utility maximisation of a social planner is

$$H(c, k) = \left(c^{1-\sigma} / 1 - \sigma\right). e^{(n-\rho)t} + \beta \left[f(k) - (n + \delta)k - c\right]. \tag{24.25}$$

The first-order conditions with respect to consumption and capital are the following:

$$\partial H / \partial c = 0 => c^{-\sigma}.e^{(n-\rho)t} = \beta \tag{24.26}$$

$$Or,\ \beta = c^{-\sigma}.e^{(n-\rho)t} \tag{24.27}$$

$$\partial H / \partial k = -\ \partial \beta / \partial t => \partial \beta / \partial t = \beta\ [(n + \delta) - f_k]. \tag{24.28}$$

Taking the derivative of the first equation with respect to t we get

$$\partial \beta / \partial t = -\sigma.\ c^{-\sigma-1}.\ \partial c / \partial t.e^{(n-\rho)t} \tag{24.29}$$

$$Or, \partial \beta / \partial t = -\sigma.\ c^{-\sigma}.\ \left[(\partial c / \partial t) / c\right].e^{(n-\rho)t}. \tag{24.30}$$

Now comparing the previous result with the second condition of the Hamiltonian we get

$$-\sigma.\ c^{-\sigma}.\ \left[(\partial c / \partial t) / c\right]\ .e^{(n-\rho)t} = \beta\ [(n + \delta) - f_k].$$

Again from (25.27) we replace the value of β

$$\left[(\partial c / \partial t) / c\right]\ .e^{(n-\rho)t} = [(n + \delta) - f_k]$$

$$\left[\dot{c} / c\right] = 1 / \sigma \left[f_k - (\rho + \delta)\right]. \tag{24.31}$$

This expression is like the result obtained under the decentralised individual agent's problem.

Since, $\partial c / \partial t = \partial k / \partial t = 0$ in the steady state, we get k^* as the steady-state capital per capita and the corresponding consumption per capita is $c^* = f(k^*) - (n + \delta)\ k^*$ and the marginal output of per capita capital is $f_{k^*} = \rho + \delta$. These two steady-state values are same as under the decentralised problem and hence the Ramsey model produces the Pareto optimal allocation of resources under the competitive market equilibrium.

24.2.3 *Transitional dynamics in the Ramsey model*

Like the neoclassical growth model with constant saving ratio (s), the Ramsey model with optimum "s" has transitional dynamics but in a different manner. The Ramsey

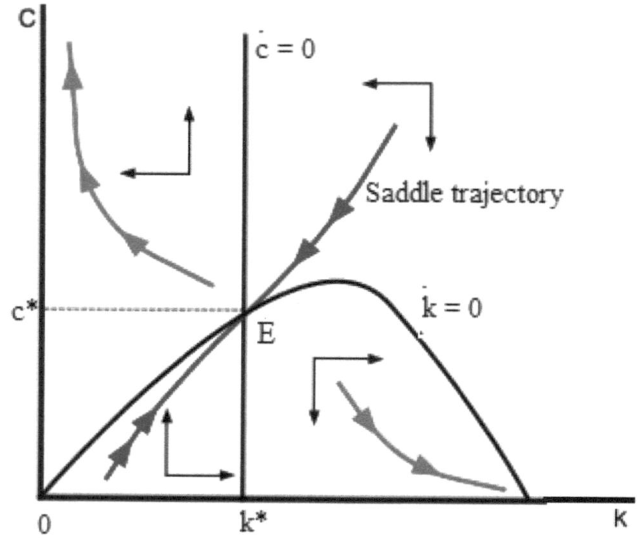

Figure 24.1 Transitional dynamics in Ramsey model

model has a saddle or optimum dynamic path of the economy in which all the constraints present in the model are satisfied. It is required to find the saddle trajectory or the optimum trajectory in the Ramsey model incorporating the optimum combination of (k, c). Figure 24.1 explains the same.

Any optimal trajectory must follow the dynamical system. However, since the variable "c" is a control variable, at each capital intensity k, to find its corresponding optimal trajectory, we still need to find its starting consumption rate $c(0)$. As it turns out, the optimal trajectory is the unique one that converges to the interior equilibrium point. Any other trajectory either converges to the all-saving equilibrium with $k^* > 0$, $c^* = 0$ or diverges to k tending to zero and c tending to infinity, which means that the economy expends all its capital in finite time. Both achieve a lower overall utility than the trajectory towards the interior equilibrium point. In the figure, the blue line represents the dynamic adjustment (or saddle) path of the economy in which all the constraints present in the model are satisfied. It is a stable path of the dynamic system. The red lines represent dynamic paths which are ruled out by the transversality condition.

A steady state (k^*, c^*) for the system is found by setting $(dk / dt) / k = 0$ and $(dc / dt) / c = 0$. There are three solutions:

$$f_k(k^*) = \rho + \delta,\ c^* = f(k^*) - (n + \delta)k^* \text{ and } f(k^*) = (n + \delta)k^* \text{ with } k^*>0 \text{ and } c^* = 0.$$

The first is the only solution in the interior of the upper quadrant. It is a saddle point (as shown later). The second is a repelling point. The third is a degenerate stable equilibrium. Though the results look like that of the neoclassical growth model, the Ramsey model produces the Pareto optimal allocation of resources under the competitive market equilibrium as the two steady-state values are same as under the decentralised problem.

24.3 Endogenous technology and growth theory

Endogenous growth theory attempts to make the steady-state growth rate endogenous, in place of the neoclassical proposed exogenous growth rates that explained technological progress depending upon non-economic factors. There are lot of good reasons, however, to believe that technological change depends on economic decisions, because it comes from industrial innovations made by profit-seeking firms and depends on the funding of science, the accumulation of human capital, and other such economic activities. Technology is thus an endogenous variable, determined within the economic system. There are two basic ways of endogenising the steady-state growth rate. First, if there are constant returns to factors of production that can be accumulated, then the steady-state growth rate will be affected by the rate at which the factors are accumulated. The working of diminishing returns then will vanish and the growth rate of per capita variables will not be fixed but rather will be changeable. This can be explained by the simplest production function of $Y = AK$, where A stands for the marginal productivity of capital which is not diminishing, rather constant. Second, the rate of technological progress can be made endogenous.

Incorporating endogenous technology into the growth theory forces us to deal with the difficult phenomenon of increasing returns to scale. More specifically, people must be given an incentive to improve technology. But because the aggregate production function F exhibits constant returns in K and L alone, Euler's theorem tells us that it will take all of the economy's output to pay capital and labour their marginal products in producing final output, leaving nothing to pay for the resources used in improving technology. Therefore, a growth theory of endogenous technology cannot be based on the usual theory of competitive equilibrium, which requires that all factors be paid their marginal products.

The proponents of the endogenous growth theory pronounce that the investment in generating human capital, learning by doing, expenditure in R&D activities, government's intervention into economic activities, etc. can facilitate the working of increasing returns to scale in the overall production system that will ultimately enable both the level as well as per capita variables to grow and there should be no end to the growth process, hence the neoclassical prediction of cross-country convergence will not appear. There will be a significant difference between the countries with high levels of endogenous growth factors, which are the developed ones, compared to the developing ones, and there should be conditional convergence in place of absolute convergence across the economies.

24.3.1 The model under AK technology

The AK model was developed by Rebelo (1991) which is able to predict endogenous and persistently positive growth rates even in the absence of any technological progress. It assumes that when people accumulate capital, learning by doing generates a technological progress that tends to raise the marginal product of capital, thus offsetting the tendency for the marginal product to diminish when technology is unchanged. The model results in a production function of the form $Y = AK$, in which the marginal product of capital is equal to the constant A. The AK model predicts that a country's long run growth rate will depend on economic factors such as thrift and the efficiency of resource allocation. The production function of $Y = AK$ is a very simple function which provides proportional relation between output and capital at level values with labour force assumed to be fixed. The production function follows CRS and the marginal product of capital is constant which prohibits the working of diminishing marginal returns to the factors. $MP_K = AP_K = A > 0$ and $dMP_K / dK = 0$, not ≤ 0. Since L is fixed, per capita growth of income, y ($y = Ak$) will be equal to growth of level income, Y. Note the production function does not allow technological progress. The equilibrium growth rate in the long run can be determined by some basic relations that we had considered under the neoclassical framework. They are as follows:

$$S = sY \tag{24.32}$$
$$dK = I - (n + \delta)K. \tag{24.33}$$

$S = I$ at equilibrium in a simple economic system without public sector and international flow of goods and services.

Making necessary substitutions we get the following-

$$dK = sY - (n + \delta)K \tag{24.34}$$

$$or,\ dK = sAK - (n + \delta)K \tag{24.35}$$

$$or,\ dK / K = sA - (n + \delta). \tag{24.36}$$

On the other hand, in per capita terms, the growth equation becomes

$$dk / k = sA - (n + \delta). \tag{24.37}$$

Hence, there is no difference in considering the steady-state growth rates of level variable and per capita variable. It is also of note that $dK / k = dY / Y = sA - (n + \delta)$. Hence, as long as $sA > (n + \delta)$ there will be perpetual growth of all the variables, either in level or per capita terms, in the long run, which is a strong claim of the endogenous growth theoreticians against the neoclassical growth model. Figure 24.2 shows the AK model and its growth phenomenon.

The figure shows that the positive difference between sA and $(n + \delta)$ can be maintained even when there is no technological progress. Hence, the AK type production function allows the growth to be endogenous instead of exogenous.

We can analyse the parametric effects of savings rate, level of technological progress, population growth rate, and depreciation. Unlike the Solow–Swan model, an increase in the savings rate in the AK-type production function has permanent growth effect upon

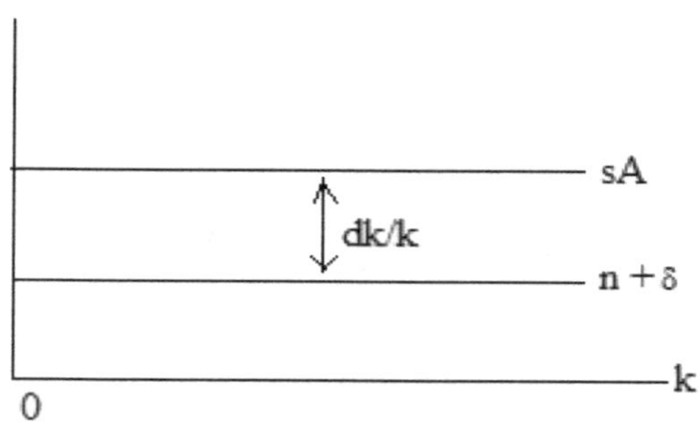

Figure 24.2 The AK model

per capita growth rate and the over savings in this model is not inefficient. Similarly, improvement of technology can create positive growth rates of per capita income. On the other hand, increase in population growth rate and depreciation make permanent decrease in the growth rates of per capita income and the reverse happens for decrease in population growth supported by effective population policy and maintenance of capital to avoid depreciation.

As the effects of parameters are permanent and the working of diminishing returns to capital is absent in AK-type production function, the prediction of the neoclassical model with regard to absolute convergence across the economies does not make sense; rather there may be convergence in conditional sense.

24.3.1.1 *Can there be transitional dynamics in the AK model?*

Due to its relative simplicity, the AK model (Rebelo, 1991) has gained an important place within the new growth theory. By assuming that the marginal and average products of capital are always constant, this theory is able to predict endogenous and persistently positive growth rates even in the absence of any technological progress. The main drawback of the AK approach to economic growth, however, resides in the fact that it cannot explain convergence: per capita variables always grow at the same constant rate (the model does not exhibit any transitional dynamics). Unlike the neoclassical growth model, the standard AK formulation also predicts that growth rates do not exhibit any tendency towards (absolute or conditional) convergence. In other words, the model has no transitional dynamics (per capita variables always grow at the same constant rate). But recent works such as of Bucci and Guerrini (2008), Gomez (2008), etc. have proposed a different way (alternative to other possible solutions proposed till now by economic literature) to get back transitional dynamics in the AK model with an exogenous savings rate. The idea consists of introducing a logistic-type population growth law in an otherwise standard neoclassical model with linear aggregate technology. As is well known, the main problem behind the assumption of constant population growth is that, as time goes to infinity, population size goes to infinity as well, which is clearly unrealistic. Using the logistic, as opposed to the exponential, population growth hypothesis (Verhulst, 1838) has the advantage that population size tends towards a finite saturation level in the very long run. We have shown that under this hypothesis the standard AK model is able to generate transitional dynamics. More generally, we can conclude that the dynamic of the Solow–Swan model with AK production function and logistic population growth is richer than the one with exponential population growth.

24.3.1.2 *Can there be cross-country convergence under AK model?*

The neoclassical model of growth criticises the AK model as it cannot explain cross-country convergence. But a recent attempt at saving the AK model from the criticism that it cannot explain convergence as developed by Acemoglu and Ventura (2002), henceforth AV, which links to international trade and the notion of terms of trade. The idea is to show that, if we take into account that countries are tied together by international trade, even AK models can exhibit convergence in growth rates. We can explain it intuitively. In an open economy the term "A" will depend on the country's terms of trade, and if it keeps growing faster than the rest of the world, the supply of its goods on world markets will keep growing relative to the supply of foreign goods, which will drive down their relative price – the terms of trade will fall, lowering A and therefore lowering the country's growth rate until it converges to the growth rate of the rest of the world. In such a world each country will look like an AK model for given terms of trade and yet it will converge not because of a diminishing physical marginal product of capital but because of a diminishing value of the marginal product of capital. The argument is clever and logically tight, even though one may object to it on empirical grounds. The readers cum researchers can attempt empirical investigations of the claim.

24.4 Growth under endogenous technological progress

This is the second possibility, as we have already mentioned in the preceding section, of making the growth rates endogenous. Given diminishing returns of the factors, an economy can grow in the long run uninterruptedly if the technological progress is continuously done in an endogenous way. There has been a wide literature on various possibilities of making technological progress endogenous. They are of Arrow's (1962) *learning by doing* or *experience* factor, in taking investment or production decisions. Later Romer (1986) used this concept and reoriented the effect into knowledge capital which has a spill over effect across the firms and economies and allows the working of increasing returns to factor (i.e. external economies of scale) that guards the diminishing returns and allows permanent growth of per capita capital and output. Lucas (1988) introduced the concept of human capital into the production function and there is no end to improving the quality of humans; there is the possibility of endless growth rates in the long run. Barro (1990), on the other development of the growth theory, captured the effect of government as institution in assisting the rest of the economy to grow in an indefinite term. In the following discussion we will highlight the basic structures of two models of endogenous growth one by one as of Romer and Barro.

24.4.1 Romer model — role of research and development in economic growth

Paul Romer includes the level of knowledge in firms' stock of capital. The knowledge part of the stock of capital is essentially a public good (as it has been shown with the term A in the Solow model). This knowledge or information shifts over to the other firms rapidly in the form of a jumping shift. In the model, larger markets induce more research and faster growth. Another relevant feature that emerges from the analysis of the model is that the growth rate is increasing in the stock of human capital. However, it does not depend on the size of the labour force or population. Romer took three key elements in his model, namely externalities, increasing returns in the production of output and diminishing returns in the production of new knowledge. According to him, it is spill overs from research efforts by a firm that lead to the creation of new knowledge by other firms and become the source of positive growth in the per capita income. Here the important content is the process of "learning by investing" which follows from Arrow's concept of "learning by doing". Neither Solow nor those of the past managed to explain how technological progress could be accelerated. The work of Romer, however, resolves this problem by demonstrating that internal factors can indeed influence the willingness of governments and companies to invest in innovation, which in turn drives economic growth in the longer runs too.

Important assumptions under the Arrow and Romer model of growth are as follows:

i) There are many firms in a market.
ii) Knowledge or technological advance is a non-rival good.
iii) There are increasing returns to scale to all factors taken together and constant returns to a single factor, at least for one.
iv) Technological advance comes from things people do. This means that technological advance is based on the creation of new ideas.
v) Many individuals and firms have market power and earn profits from their discoveries. This assumption arises from increasing returns to scale in production that lead to imperfect competition.

Romer, in his seminal work on endogenous growth in 1986, presented a variant on Arrow's model which is known as learning by investment. He assumes creation of knowledge as a side product of investment. Romer took three key elements in his model, namely externalities, increasing returns in the production of output, and diminishing returns in the production of new knowledge. According to Romer, it is spill overs from research efforts by a firm that lead to the creation of new knowledge by other firms. In other words, new research technology by a firm spills over instantly across the entire economy, or knowledge is public property with non excludability and non rivalry. In his model, new knowledge is the ultimate determinant of long run growth which is determined by investment in research technology. Research technology exhibits diminishing returns which means that investments in research technology will not double knowledge.

Let us discuss the formal model of Romer in line with Arrow's learning-by-doing factor.

Suppose the production function of the ith firm is

$$Y_i = AK_i^{\alpha} L_i^{1-\alpha} \tag{24.38}$$

where A is the level of technology which determines the total factor productivity (TFP) which depends on stock of capital. The higher the capital stock, the more the economy is able to use new technologies. Thus the progress of technology under the Romer model is determined by the accumulation of capital. The capital-to-technology transformation may be given by the following relation:

$$A = BK^{1-\alpha} \tag{24.39}$$

where K is the aggregate level of capital stock and B is the learning-by-doing factor which generates the positive externality effect to others. That means $dA / dK = B.(1 - \alpha) / K\alpha > 0$ for $0 < \alpha < 1$. Assuming symmetry across firms and substituting this relation into the production function, we get the aggregate production function as follows:

$$Y = BKL^{1-\alpha} \tag{24.40}$$

Further assuming that labour force, L, as equivalent to population is constant and normalised into 1, we get the aggregate production function as

$$Y = BK. \tag{24.41}$$

This production function is characterised by constant return to scale and looks like the AK type production function. This means marginal productivity of capital is constant and equal to the average productivity of capital and is equal to B ($dY / dK = Y / K = B$).

The basic rule of capital accumulation is recalled as

$$dK = s.Y - \delta K \tag{24.42}$$

$$or,\ dK = s.\ BK - \delta K \tag{24.43}$$

where δ is the rate of depreciation of capital. The growth of population is zero as $L = 1$. Hence the growth rate of capital can be written as

$$dK / K = s.B - \delta \tag{24.44}$$

This is the basic growth equation in the Romer model. Rate of growth of capital (dK / K) will be positive in the long run as long as $s.B > \delta$. Hence, $dK / K = dY / Y = B$. That means, given the value of s and δ, positive growth of capital and output is possible under a positive accumulation of knowledge driven by learning by doing.

Now the rate of growth of technology under the Romer model is given by (follows from the equation $A = BK^{1-}\alpha$)

$$dA / A = (1 - \alpha).\ dK / K = (1 - \alpha).\ (s.B. - \delta). \tag{24.45}$$

The expression gives that the rate of growth of technology depends on the rate of growth of capital. At the same time, technology affects capital. This means growth is an endogenous process without any transitional dynamics.

24.4.1.1 *What is the rate of growth of output?*

We have the output function as:

$$Y = BK$$

Now, $dY = KdB + BdK$

$$\text{Or } dY / Y = (KdB + BdK) = (KdB) / Y + (BdK) / Y = (KdB) / BK + (BdK) / BK$$

$$\text{Or } dY / Y = dB / B + dK/K \ldots\ldots\ldots\ldots\ldots\ldots\ldots\ldots \tag{24.46}$$

We have

$$dA / A = dB / B + (1 - \alpha).\ dK / K$$

$$\text{or } dK / K = (1 / 1 - \alpha) . dA / A - (1 /1 - \alpha) . dB / B \ldots\ldots\ldots\ldots \tag{24.47}$$

Now, substituting the previous expression into the expression for dY / Y we get

$$dY / Y = dB / B + dK / K$$

$$\text{or } dY / Y = dB / B + (1 /1 - \alpha) . dA / A - (1/1 - \alpha) . dB / B$$

$$\text{or } dY / Y = (1 / 1 - \alpha) . dA / A - (\alpha / 1 - \alpha) . dB / B \ldots\ldots\ldots\ldots\ldots\ldots \tag{24.48}$$

This is the net growth of income or net value of addition the learning-by-doing factor does for the technological advancement.

24.4.1.2 *Effect of savings*

This further establishes that an increase in savings leads to increase the growth rate of per capita capital and income permanently. This is a strong departure from the neoclassical model's conclusion of temporary growth of per capita income because of exogenous technological progress and savings rate. The effect of diminishing returns to the factors under the Solow–Swan model gets replaced by constant returns to the variable factor in a system of increasing returns to scale in a total production system.

24.4.2 *Lucas model — role of human capital in economic growth — basic structure*

We mentioned that one interpretation of the $Y = AK$ model is that capital should be viewed broadly to include physical and human capital. The Lucas model is such a model which includes both types of capital to justify the endogenous technological progress, one form of explaining "A". Lucas presents an economic growth model where homogeneous individuals maximise their lifetime utility by choosing an optimal consumption path as well as the optimal allocation of their available time in education (human capital accumulation) and production. The model explains how economic growth, in the long term, is attributed to the accumulation of human capital. In order to produce human capital, education should be used. Therefore, the model assumes that human capital is the only input element in the education sector.

For the detailed discussion on the model, we follow the approach of Barro and Sala-i-Martin (2004). Suppose the capitals are K (physical capital) and H (human capital), labour being constant under the normalisation condition. The production function becomes:

$$Y = f(K, H)$$

Where the production function has standard neoclassical properties with CRS but there are no diminishing returns to scale in K and H.

In intensive form the production function becomes:

$y = aY = f(aK, aH)$ where "a" is scale change.
Assuming $a = 1 / K$
$Y / K = f(1, H / K)$
Or, $Y = K. f(1, H / K)$
Or, $Y = K. f(H / K)$

Where $f' = df / d(H / K) > 0$. This means more human capital per physical capital leads to more output.

Output (Y) can be used on a one-for-one basis for consumption, physical capital formation, and human capital formation like investment in education, training, and the health sector.

Suppose both forms of capital depreciate respectively at the rates δ and μ. Further assume that population (L) is constant. This means increase in H leads to increase in human capital without being exploited by L.

Now suppose Rk and Rh are the rental prices of per unit physical capital and human capital. Having competitive structure in both of the two capital markets, the long run profit by the firms using these two capitals will be zero, which means marginal productivity of K and H will be equal to Rk and Rh.

We have our production function:

$$Y = K.\, f(H/K) \ldots\ldots\ldots\ldots\ldots\ldots\ldots\ldots \qquad (24.49)$$
$$MPK = f(H/K) - K.\, f'(H/K).\,(-H/K^2)$$
$$\text{or } MPK = f(H/K) - (H/K).\, f'(H/K) = Rk$$
$$\text{Again, } MPH = K.\, f'(H/K).1/K = Rh$$
$$\text{or } MPH = f'(H/K) = Rh. \qquad (24.50)$$

After deducting the depreciation rates from the rental prices of each of the capitals, we get net rental prices. These prices are $(Rk - \delta)$ and $(Rh - \mu)$. Hence, the previous two marginal conditions will be rewritten as:

$$MPK = f(H/K) - (H/K).\, f'(H/K) = Rk - \delta \qquad (24.51)$$
$$\text{and } MPH = f'(H/K) = Rh - \mu. \qquad (24.52)$$

These two net rental prices will ultimately be equal to the market rate of interest (r), which means $Rk = Rh = r$. That leads to:

$$MPK = f(H/K) - (H/K).\, f'(H/K) = r - \delta$$
$$\text{and } MPH = f'(H/K) = r - \mu$$
$$\text{Which means } MPK = MPH = r$$
$$f(H/K) - (H/K).\, f'(H/K) + \delta = r$$
$$\text{and } f'(H/K) + \mu = r$$
$$\text{or } f(H/K) - (H/K).\, f'(H/K) + \delta = f'(H/K) + \mu$$
$$\text{or } f(H/K) - (H/K).\, f'(H/K) - f'(H/K) = \mu - \delta$$
$$\text{Or, } f(H/K) - [1 + (H/K)].\, f'(H/K) = \mu - \delta. \qquad (24.53)$$

The left-hand side is monotonically increasing in H/K which means there exists a unique and constant value of H/K. Figure 24.3 explains this.

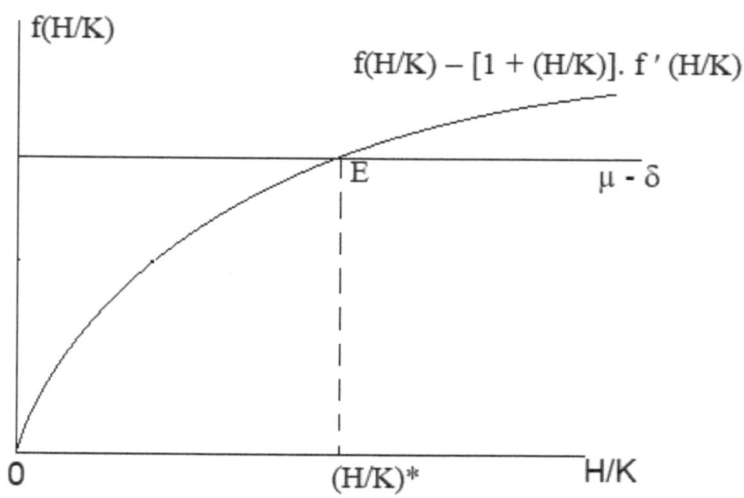

Figure 24.3 The optimum *H–K* ratio in the Lucas model

If we define $A = f(H / K)$ [so $f'(H / K)\, dA / d(H/K) = 0$ and then $f(H / K) = \mu - \delta =$ constant] then the production function as given in Equation (24.49) will look like:

$$Y = K.\ A = AK$$

This means the model with two types of capital (K and H) is essentially the same as the AK model. Which means MPk is not diminishing and it is guarded by the human capital term, H.

Hence, the presence of human capital in a production system makes the productivity of K constant and allows the growth rate of income, K and C, to be non-zero in the long run. Converting into per capita terms, as L is constant, there will be no change in the growth rates of the per capita variables as well. The ultimate rate of growth of all the variables are at the rate at which the H / K (per unit human capital to physical capital) is growing.

Box I Human capital vs. knowledge capital

Human capital means acquired characteristics that make workers more productive. Although it includes such characteristics as health, strength, and stamina, the most commonly analysed sources of human capital are the education, training, and experience that a worker embodies. Since education and training involve the transmission of knowledge, it might seem like human capital is the same as the knowledge capital that we have studied in the R&D model of Romer. However, there is a crucial difference. Knowledge capital is potentially a public good whereas human capital is not. An easy way of distinguishing between them is to think about the two major roles that most professors play in their classrooms and research laboratories. Professors are most often in the classroom, where they are imparting existing knowledge to students. This increases the students' human capital but does not create new knowledge for society. When they are not in the classroom, they are likely to be engaged in research activities. If successful, this research leads to new knowledge capital that everyone can potentially share on a nonrival basis. Thus, simply put, society's knowledge capital is everything that is known by someone in the society; your human capital includes your personal familiarity with and ability to use part of that knowledge. Your human capital is personal to you, holding a private good property – the fact that one has obtained knowledge may make him more productive but it does not usually raise anyone else's productivity. Thus, human capital does not have the public-good characteristics of knowledge capital.

24.4.2.1 *Lucas model with human capital formation – descriptive structure*

24.4.2.1.1 ONE-SECTOR MODEL

In this model it is assumed that physical capital and human capital (through education) are generated by the same production system. Education, which makes human capital, is not considered as a separate system of production unit.

Here, in this descriptive model, we will recall the structure of the Ramsey model where households, firms, and social planners' objective maximisations are taken into account to justify the role of human capital to form an AK-type production function without transitional dynamics.

Let us consider a C-D-type production function with physical capital (K) and human capital (H):

$$Y = AK^{\alpha}H^{1-\alpha}. \tag{24.54}$$

We can think of H as the number of physical workers (L) multiplied by quality of labour ($h = H / L$) which means $H = h \,.\, L \,.\, = (H / K) \,.\, L$.

It is assumed that, as a fixed quantity of H is required, there should be perfect substitutability between physical labour, L and quality of labour, h. This further means doubling of K and H with L constant will lead to doubling of Y.

Output (Y) can be used for consumption or investment in physical capital or human capital. Suppose both forms of capital depreciate at the rate of δ. The depreciation of H includes losses from mortality, skill deterioration, and net of benefits from new experience.

The resource constraint of the economy is:

$$Y = AK^{\alpha}H^{1-\alpha} = C + I_K + I_H \tag{24.55}$$

Where I_K and I_H are gross investments in physical and human capital. The changes of two capital are:

$$dK / dt = \dot{K} = I_K - \delta \text{ and } dH / dt = \dot{H} = I_H - \delta. \tag{24.56}$$

Recall that households and producers may be different units, or households may also play the role of producer. This assumption will not hamper us in reaching our conclusions.

Assuming no growth of population ($n = 0$), the households' utility function becomes

$$\int_0^{\infty} u(C).\, e^{-\rho t} dt \,.$$

Subject to the two constraints $\dot{K} = I_K - \delta$ and $\dot{H} = I_H - \delta$ and also subject the economy-wide resource constraint, $AK^{\alpha}H^{1-\alpha} = C + I_K + I_H$

The Hamiltonian expression is

$$H(C, I_K, I_H, K, H) = u(C)\,.e^{-\rho t} + \upsilon\,(I_K - \delta) + \mu\,(I_H - \delta) + \omega\,(AK^{\alpha}H^{1-\alpha} - C - I_K - I_H). \tag{24.57}$$

Suppose the utility function is $u = (C^{1-\sigma} - 1) / (1 - \sigma)$ where σ is elasticity of substitution. So, the Hamiltonian becomes

$$H\,(C, I_K, I_H, K, H) = \left(C^{1-\sigma} - 1\right) / \left(1 - \sigma\right).\, e^{-\rho t} + \upsilon\,(I_K - \delta K) + \mu\,(I_H - \delta H) + \omega\,(AK^{\alpha}H^{1-\alpha} - C - I_K - I_H)$$

The FOCs are:

$$\text{i)}\ \frac{\partial H}{\partial C} = 0, >> C^{-\sigma}.e^{-\rho t} = \omega \ldots\ldots\ldots\ldots\ldots\ldots\ldots \tag{24.58}$$

$$\text{ii)}\ \frac{\partial H}{\partial IK} = 0, >> \upsilon - \omega = 0 \ldots\ldots\ldots\ldots\ldots\ldots\ldots\ldots \tag{24.59}$$

iii) $\dfrac{\partial H}{\partial IH} = 0$, >> $\mu - \omega = 0$ . . . . (24.60)

iv) $\dfrac{\partial H}{\partial K} = -\dot{v}$ >> $-\delta v + \omega \, . \, A \, . \alpha \, . \, K^{\alpha-1} \, . \, H^{1-\alpha} = -\dot{v}$ . . . . (24.61)

v) $\dfrac{\partial H}{\partial H} = -\dot{\mu}$ >> $-\delta \mu + \omega . \, A \, . \, (1 - \alpha) \, . \, K^{\alpha} . \, H^{-\alpha} = -\dot{\mu}$ . . . . (24.62)

vi) $\dfrac{\partial H}{\partial \omega} = 0$ >> $AK^{\alpha}H^{1-\alpha} = C + I_K + I_H$ . . . . (24.63)

And transversality conditions.

From (24.59) and (24.60) we have $v = \omega = \mu$ which means all the shadow prices are identical.

Now taking the derivative of (24.58) *w.r.t* time and using all the expressions (24.58 to 24.63), we get the rate of growth of *C* as (following the Ramsey model)

$$\frac{\dot{c}}{c} = 1/\sigma\left[f_k - n - \delta\right]$$

or

$$\frac{\dot{c}}{c} = 1/\sigma\left[MP_k - n - \delta\right] \quad (24.64)$$

Using the expression for *MPK* we have $MPK = A\,\alpha. \, (K/H)^{-(1-\alpha)}$.

Hence,

$$\frac{\dot{c}}{c} = 1/\sigma\left[\mathrm{A}\ \alpha.\ (\mathrm{K}/\mathrm{H})^{-(1-\alpha)} - n - \delta\right]. \quad (24.65)$$

This means the rate of consumption growth will be on par with the rate of *K / H*.

Since, we have $v = \mu$,

the net rate of return from *K* = net rate of return from *H*

This means $A\,\alpha. \, (K/H)^{-(1-\alpha)} - \delta = A\,(1-\alpha). \, (K/H)^{\alpha} - \delta$

or $K/H = \alpha/(1-\alpha)$ = constant

This means diminishing *MPk* does not work. This is capable of generating positive growth of *C*, *Y*, and *K* in per capita terms.

Or,

$$\frac{\dot{c}}{c} = 1/\sigma\left[\mathrm{A}\ \alpha.\ (\alpha/(1-\alpha))^{-(1-\alpha)} - n - \delta\right] > 0. \quad (24.66)$$

Putting *MPk* in the original production function we get

$Y = AK\,[\alpha/(1-\alpha)]^{-(1-\alpha)} = AK$ type

The previous expression shows that the derived expression of the production function under the Lucas model is basically an AK-type production function. The expression for growth of per capita consumption shows that it can be positive over the long run as long as the *MPk*, $A\,\alpha. \, (\alpha/(1-\alpha))^{-(1-a)}$ is greater than the effective depreciation part $(n + \delta)$.

24.4.2.1.2 WHETHER THE LUCAS THEORY WORKS FOR INDIA

The Lucas model has been empirically tested by many researchers. One such work was done recently by Sasmal and Sasmal (2023) which investigates the effect of social expenditure of the government on economic growth via its effect on human capital formation using the theoretical framework of Lucas in some modified forms and analysing the empirical results on the theoretical arguments in the Indian context. The Lucas model has been modified to incorporate the role of public expenditure in human capital formation. The theoretical results suggest that the growth rate will be higher if production elasticity of human capital is higher and social expenditure has significant impact on human capital formation. The empirical results using the time series analysis based on Indian data at the national level show that social expenditure has significant positive effect on GDP along with other factors like physical capital and economic expenditure of the government. Further, the investigation across the states in India through the panel regressions considering literacy rate as a proxy for human capital show that higher social expenditure results in higher literacy rate and literacy rate has a significant positive effect on per capita income. Thus, the Lucas theory works in highly developing countries like India.

24.4.3 The Barro model — the role of the public institution in economic growth

Like the learning-by-doing approach or knowledge spill over model, Barro (1990) developed increasing returns to scale in the overall production system by introducing the public sector that is capable of endogenising the technological progress and thereby explaining the increasing growth of capital and output per capita in the long run. In the Barro model, public spending goes for public investment (infrastructures, schools, sanitation, institutional facilities, good governance, etc.). Public investments, which are financed through income taxes, complement private investments so that there are crowding-in effects of this public investment thereby promoting growth of output. Since public investments raise the productivity of private investments, higher taxes can be associated with an increase or a decrease in overall growth. If government expenditure is kept fixed and there are constant returns to scale in L and K, then the working of diminishing returns to the factors cannot be barred. If we allow government expenditure as a variable in accumulation of capital, then the working of diminishing returns will no longer be there and the economy is capable of producing endogenous growth like the simple AK-type model.

The model of Barro adds public spending to the AK model. Suppose the production function is like the following:

$$Y = AL^{1-\alpha}.\, K^{\alpha}.\, G^{1-\alpha} \tag{24.67}$$

where G stands for the public expenditure on goods and services. The production function exhibits increasing returns to scale (IRS). Suppose increase of all the factors by λ proportion, then new output is

$$A.(\lambda L)^{1-\alpha}.\,(\lambda K)^{\alpha}.\,(\lambda G)^{1-\alpha} = \lambda^{2-\alpha}.\, AL^{1-\alpha}.\, K^{\alpha}.\, G^{1-\alpha} = \lambda^{2-\alpha}.\, Y. \tag{24.68}$$

Since $0 < \alpha < 1$, $2 - \alpha > 1$, new output after introduction of the government sector is greater than the scale effect. Hence, IRS is working and there is a possibility of making increasing growth rates of income over time.

Suppose the production function in the Barro model is

$$Y = BK^{1-\alpha}G^{\alpha} \tag{24.69}$$

where $BK^{1-\alpha}$ is technological progress, A, determined by the accumulation of capital. Public expenditure, G, depends on the amount of revenue generated through income tax, $\upsilon.Y$, where "υ" represents rate of income tax with $0 < \upsilon < 1$. Hence the public expenditure function is

$$G = \upsilon.Y\,. \tag{24.70}$$

To determine the long run growth rate of capital and income, we first determine the value of B. To get this let us substitute the government expenditure function into the production function which gives the following:

$$\begin{aligned} Y &= BK^{1-\alpha}\left(\upsilon.Y\right)^{\alpha} && (24.71)\\ Or,\; Y^{1-\alpha} &= B\upsilon^{\alpha}.K^{1-\alpha} \\ Or,\; Y &= B^{1/1-\alpha}.\upsilon^{\alpha/1-\alpha}.K \\ Or,\; Y &= D.K && (24.72) \end{aligned}$$

where $D = B^{1/1-\alpha}.\upsilon^{\alpha/1-\alpha}$

The marginal productivity of capital with given government expenditure and population is $dY / dK = D$ = constant, not diminishing. Hence, there is the possibility of scale effect and getting output growth to be positive.

Now recall the rule of capital which is as follows:

$$dK = I - \delta K \tag{24.73}$$
$$or,\; dK = s.\left(1-\upsilon\right).Y - \delta K\,. \tag{24.74}$$

After substitution of the expression of Y from earlier we get

$$\begin{aligned} dK &= s.\left(1-\upsilon\right).D.K - \delta K \\ or,\; dK &= s.\left(1-\upsilon\right).B^{1/1-\alpha}.\upsilon^{\alpha/1-\alpha}.K - \delta K \\ or,\; dK / K &= s.\left(1-\upsilon\right).B^{1/1-\alpha}.\upsilon^{\alpha/1-\alpha} - \delta \\ or,\; dK / K &= s.\left(1-\upsilon\right).D - \delta\,. && (24.75) \end{aligned}$$

Now the rate of growth will be positive as long as $s.(1 - \upsilon).D > \delta$. Therefore, introduction of public expenditure in developmental projects creates the positive growth of income and consumption in place of zero growth results under the neoclassical growth model. Hence, the public sector makes the technological progress endogenous.

24.4.3.1 Barro model of growth – detailed analysis

We saw in the $Y = AK$ model that anything that changed the level of baseline technology, A, affected the per capita K and income in the long run that broke the chain of diminishing marginal productivity of K.

In the models of Arrow and Romer we saw the roles of knowledge creation and spill overs (through learning by doing and learning by investments) to justify A (or to break diminishing MPk) and in the Lucas model we saw the role of human capital formation, besides physical capital formation, K) proved the role of A and justified MPk as constant. In all these models we established the existence of positive growth of per capita income in the long run framework which was an unlikely event in the Solow model.

In the Barro model, the replacement of "A" is done by government intervention where the government provides public services like internal security, food security, and public infrastructure (like education, health, defence, etc.) which are nonrival and nonexcludable in nature. Hence, public goods or public services without variable tax and congestion and corruption are another source of the AK form of production function of an economy. Here, the government's choices about public services determine the coefficient "A" and thereby affect the long run growth rate of the economy. We can have both a decentralised and social planner's solution like the Ramsey model.

24.4.3.1.1 THE MODEL FOR DECENTRALISED OBJECTIVES BY HOUSEHOLDS AND FIRMS

The original form of the model is followed from the model of Ramsey. Suppose there is G as the additional input (to represent public services or public input) with L and K (as private inputs). The Cobb Douglas production function for firm "i" is

$$Y_i = AL_i^{1-\alpha}.\ K_i^{\alpha}.\ G^{1-\alpha} \tag{24.76}$$

where $0 < \alpha < 1$.

The production function for each firm shows the working of CRS in private inputs, L and K (as the sum of their powers is 1) and the inclusion of G as another factor of production that leads the total production system to IRS (as the sum of their powers is greater than 1).

Assume that aggregate labour force is constant. In that case, if G is constant, the returns from private capital (K) will diminish since the production function will then be

$$Y_i = AL^*.\ K_i^{\alpha}.\ G^* = AL^*G^*.\ K_i^{\alpha} = A^*.\ K_i^{\alpha} \tag{24.77}$$

$$\text{Here } dY_i / dK_i = A^*.\ \alpha.\ K_i^{1-\alpha} \tag{24.78}$$

and $d^2Y_i / dK_i^2 = -A^*.\ \alpha.(1 - \alpha)\ K_i^{\alpha-2} < 0$ (as in the Solow and Ramsey models). Since $\alpha < 1$, $\alpha - 1$ and $\alpha - 2 < 0$, and as a result d^2Y_i / dK_i^2 is negative. Thus, as K increases, dY_i / dK_i decreases and vice-versa.

On the other hand, if G increases along with K (that means both private and public capitals move in positive directions simultaneously like crowding-in effects), then diminishing MPk will not arise. Here public capital is complementary to K and L and increase in G leads to increase in the MPL and MPk (this is the source of endogenous growth).

This means the production function will exhibit CRS in K and G with a constant labour force L^*. For this reason, the economy will be capable of generating endogenous growth as in AK-type production function.

Suppose the government finances its purchase of goods and services with lump-sum tax, not by any variable tax.

For given G, each profit maximising firm will optimise the use of K where the equilibrium condition will be satisfied. The equilibrium condition is MPk = rental price = $r + \delta$.

We have the production function as

$$Y_i = AL_i^{1-\alpha}.\ K_i^{\alpha}.\ G^{1-\alpha}$$

In per capita terms

$$y_i = Y_i / L_i = (AL_i^{1-\alpha}.\ K_i^{\alpha}.\ G^{1-\alpha}) / L_i = A.\ L_i^{-\alpha}.\ K_i^{\alpha}.\ G^{1-\alpha}$$
$$\text{or } y_i = A.\ (K_i^{\alpha} / L_i^{\alpha}).\ G^{1-\alpha} = A.\ (K_i / L_i)^{\alpha}.\ G^{1-\alpha} = A.\ (k_i)\alpha.\ G^{1-\alpha}$$
$$\text{Hence, } MP_k = \alpha.A.\ (k_i)^{\alpha-1}.\ G^{1-\alpha} = r + \delta. \quad (24.79)$$

If this marginal condition holds for all the firms, then each firm will choose the same $k_i = k$. Hence the aggregate production function will be

$$\Sigma y_i = y_i{}^*L = Y = AL.\ k^{\alpha}.\ G^{1-\alpha} = AL.\ k^{\alpha}.\ (G / G^{\alpha})$$
$$\text{or } G^{\alpha} = (AL.\ k^{\alpha}.\ G) / Y = AL.\ k^{\alpha}.\ (G / Y)$$
$$\text{or } G = (G / Y)^{1/\alpha}.\ (AL)^{1/\alpha}.\ K. \quad (24.80)$$

Now the firms' equilibrium condition becomes (putting the value of G in MPk):

$$r + \delta = MP_k = \alpha.A.\ (k)^{\alpha-1}.\ [(G / Y)^{1/\alpha}.\ (AL)^{1/\alpha}.\ k]^{\ 1-\alpha}$$
$$\text{or } r + \delta = \alpha.A.\ (k)^{\alpha-1}.\ k^{1-\alpha}\ (G / Y)^{\ 1-\alpha\ /\alpha}.\ A^{1-\alpha\ /\alpha}\ L^{1-\alpha\ /\alpha}$$

or $r + \delta = \alpha.A^{1/\alpha}.\ (G / Y)^{\ 1-\alpha\ /\alpha}.\ L^{1-\alpha\ /\alpha} \neq f(k)$ since (G / Y) is usually kept constant.

Usually governments of all the economies want to maintain a constant ratio of G / Y (= government expenditure / GDP). If G / Y is constant, then MP_k (or $r + \delta$) is invariant to per capita capital, k. It is observed from the previous equilibrium condition that there is no "k" term in this relation. So, MP_k cannot diminish as "k" increases due to the presence of public good or services. Hence, positive growth of per capita GDP can be possible under the Barro model.

Further, it is seen that as L increases MP_k also increases. This is the scale effect which was similar to that of the Romer and Lucas model. With the constant magnitude of government intervention as population size increases, there is the scope of additional growth rates of per capita income and consumption as good institutional quality leads to good-quality population through the interaction effects.

24.4.3.1.2 COMPARISON WITH THE AK MODEL

This constant MP_k parallels the conclusion made by the AK model. The constant MP_k plays the same role in the growth process that the constant A played in the AK model. Hence, there are no transitional dynamics in the Barro model (as MPk is constant).

Thus, the growth rates of per capita consumption (c), per capita capital (k), and per capita income (y) grow at the same constant rate.

Now we can determine that common growth from the consumption growth expression. We had the consumption growth expression from Ramsey model that –

$$\frac{\dot{c}}{c} = 1 / \sigma\left[f_k - n - \delta\right]$$

or the rate of growth of "c" $= 1 / \sigma[\alpha.A^{1/}\alpha.\ (G / Y)^{\ 1-}\alpha\,{}^{/}\alpha.\ L^{1-}\alpha\,{}^{/}\alpha - n - \delta]$. (24.81)

This result shows that rate of growth of consumption is positively related to G / Y since the public services were not financed by non-distorting income tax. In addition, with the same (G / Y) ratio, if stock of labour force increases, the per capita consumption increases.

24.4.3.1.3 SOCIAL PLANNER'S PROBLEM UNDER LUMP-SUM TAX

In the previous analysis we considered the decentralised behaviour of households and firms under the structure of lump-sum tax. "G" was financed from other sources in place of any variable taxes.

The production function is as before: $y = A. (k_i)^{\alpha}. G^{1-\alpha} = A. k\alpha. G^{1-\alpha}$

The common budget constraint faced by the planner is:

$$dk / dt = dm / dt = \dot{m} = y - c - \delta k - G / L. \tag{24.82}$$

(G / L = per capita consumption of public goods/services). Here "m" is the state variable.

Like in the Ramsey model we set the Hamiltonian function for utility maximisation with respect to c, G, and k. Here "c" and "G" are the control variables and k is the state variable.

$$H = u(c_t) . e^{-(\rho - n) t} + \beta_t [y - c - \delta k - G / L]$$

Here β_t is the co-state variable. Assuming $n = 0$ (since L is constant) and the constant elasticity of substitution utility function:

$$\text{or } H(c, G, k) = (c^{1-\sigma} / 1- \sigma) . e^{-\rho t} + \beta_t[y - c - \delta k - G / L]$$
$$\text{or } H(c, G, k) = (c^{1-\sigma} / 1 - \sigma) . e^{-\rho t} + \beta_t[A . k^{\alpha} . G^{1-\alpha} - c - \delta k - G / L]$$

Here β is a co-state variable.

The FOCs are

i) $\delta H / \delta c = 0, >> c^{-\sigma}. (1 - \sigma) / (1 - \sigma). e^{-\rho t} = \beta \ldots\ldots\ldots$ (24.83)

ii) $\delta H / \delta G = 0, >> (1 - \alpha) . \beta . A . k^{\alpha}. G^{-\alpha} - \beta / L = 0$

or, $(1 - \alpha) . A . k^{\alpha}. G^{-\alpha} = 1 / L \ldots\ldots\ldots\ldots\ldots\ldots$ (24.84)

iii) $\delta H / \delta k = -\delta\beta / \delta t >> \beta . \alpha . A. k^{\alpha-1}. G^{1-\alpha} - \beta \delta = -\delta\beta / \delta t \ldots\ldots\ldots\ldots$ (24.85)

And the transversality condition $\underset{t \to \pm}{Lt} = [^2{}_t \cdot m_t] = 0$

Now take the derivative of β *w.r.t* time from (24.83) and substitute it into (24.85).

We get from (24.83) $-\sigma . c^{-\sigma-1}. \delta c / \delta t. e^{-\rho t} = \delta\beta / \delta t$

or $-\sigma . c^{-\sigma}. [(\delta c / \delta t) / c] . e^{-\rho t} = \delta\beta / \delta t$

After substitution to (24.85) we get

$$\beta (\alpha. A. k^{\alpha-1}. G^{1-\alpha} - \delta) = -(-) . \sigma . c^{-\sigma}. [(\delta c / \delta t) / c]. e^{-\rho t}$$

Now putting the value of β from (1) into the previous relation

$$c^{-\sigma}. (1 - \sigma)/(1- \sigma). e^{-\rho t} . (\alpha . A . k^{\alpha-1} . G^{1-\alpha} - \delta) = \sigma . c^{-\sigma}. [(\delta c / \delta t) / c] . e^{-\rho t}$$

or $\alpha.\ A.\ k^{\alpha-1}.\ G^{1-\alpha} - \delta = \sigma.\ [(\delta c / \delta t) / c]$
or $[(\delta c / \delta t) / c] = 1 / \sigma\ [\alpha.\ A.\ k^{\alpha-1}.\ G^{1-\alpha} - \delta]$ . . . . (24.86)

Now from (24.84) we have

$(1 - \alpha).\ A.\ k^{\alpha}.\ G^{-\alpha} = 1 / L$
or $(1 - \alpha).\ A.\ k^{\alpha}.\ G^{-\alpha}.\ G = G / L$
or $(1 - \alpha).\ A.\ k^{\alpha}.\ G^{1-\alpha} = 1 / L$
or $(1 - \alpha).\ A.\ L.\ k^{\alpha}.\ G^{1-\alpha} = 1$
or $(1 - \alpha).\ Y = G$
or $G / Y = (1 - \alpha)$. (24.87)

This means government expenditure to GDP ratio (= G / Y) is constant. In other words, the optimal condition of the government is to maintain a constant G / Y in the model with lump-sum tax.

Now recall that we have the expression for G as derived in the case of a decentralised model which is:

$$G = (G / Y)^{1/\alpha}.\ (AL)^{1/\alpha}.\ K.$$

Now put the previous expression of G in (24.86) and obtain the following expression for the optimum growth of consumption per capita as

$(\delta c / \delta t) / c = 1 / \sigma\ [\alpha.\ A.\ k^{\alpha-1}.\ G^{1-\alpha} - \delta]$
Or, $(\delta c/\delta t)/c] = 1/ \sigma\ [\alpha.\ A.\ k^{\alpha-1}.\ \{(G/Y)^{1/\alpha}.\ (AL)^{1/\alpha}.\ k\}^{1-\alpha} - \delta]$
Or, $(\delta c/\delta t)/c] = 1/ \sigma\ [\alpha.\ A.\ k^{\alpha-1}.\ \{(1-\alpha)^{1-\alpha/\alpha}.\ (AL)^{1-\alpha/\alpha}.\ k^{1-\alpha} - \delta]$
Or, $(\delta c/\delta t)/c] = 1/ \sigma\ [\alpha.\ A^{1/\alpha}.\ (1-\alpha)^{1-\alpha/\alpha}.\ L^{1-\alpha/\alpha} - \delta]$ (24.88)

Therefore, the social planner's optimum solution is identical to that under the decentralised system under the lump-sum tax assumption.

The optimal rate of growth of k, y, and c will be at the rate of

$$\frac{\dot{c}}{c} = 1 / \sigma\left[f_k - n - \delta\right]$$

$\dot{c} / c = 1 / \sigma[\alpha.A^{1/\alpha}.\ (G / Y)^{1-\alpha/\alpha}.\ L^{1-\alpha/\alpha} - n - \delta]$
$= 1 / \sigma\ [\alpha.A^{1/\alpha}.\ (1 - \alpha)^{1-\alpha/\alpha}.\ L^{1-\alpha/\alpha} - n - \delta]$. (24.89)

Hence, as scale factor, L, increases, MPk increases, breaks its diminishing productivity nature of capital, and ultimately $\dot{c} / c$ increases. This is the prevalence of positive per capita growth of consumption and income due to the incorporation of the public good model or of the good institutional quality

24.4.3.2 Introduction of income tax on households' wage and asset income, consumption tax, and firms' profit tax

As we know, one constituent of endogenous-growth models assumes constant returns to a broad concept of capital, not diminishing. Robert Barro extends these models to include tax-financed government services that affect production or utility. Growth and saving rates fall with an increase in utility-type expenditures; the two rates rise primarily with productive government expenditures but afterward decrease.

Let us recall the Ramsey model with the government sector. The government spends G and make transfer payments V in a lump-sum amount. Hence, the total amount of government expenditure is $G + V$. The government finances this expenditure by means of taxes upon households' wage and asset income, consumption tax, and firms' profit tax.

Suppose "Tw" is tax rate on wage income, "Ta" is the rate on asset income, "Tc" is on consumption, and "Tf" is on firms' income. Wage income after tax will now be $wL-Tw.wL = (1 - Tw).wL$. Similarly for asset income, it will be $(1 - Ta)r.M$, for consumption, $(1 - Tc).C$.

So, the government's balanced budget equation is-

$$G + V = Tw \,.\, w \,.\, L + Ta \,.\, r \,.\, M + Tc \,.\, C + Tf \,.\, F \tag{24.90}$$

24.4.3.2.1 HOUSEHOLD'S POST-TAX PROBLEM

The households' budget constraint says that change of per head asset (m) over time will be the difference between sum of wage and asset income net of tax and consumption tax and population growth factor plus transfer amount per capita. This is:

$$dm \,/\, dt = \dot{m} = (1 - Tw) \,.\, w + (1 - Ta) \,.\, r \,.\, m - (1 + Tc) \,.\, C - n \,.\, m + v \tag{24.91}$$

where $v = V \,/\, L$

Now with the household's utility function, $u(c) = (c^{1-\sigma}-1 \,/\, 1 - \sigma)$, the consumption growth rate is given as

$$\dot{c} \,/\, c = 1 \,/\, \sigma \,[(1 - Ta)\, r - n]. \tag{24.92}$$

That means the household's decision to defer consumption depends on the after-tax returns on asset $(1 - Ta)r$. The tax rate on consumption does not get entered to the growth of consumption expression because it is constant over time.

24.4.3.2.2 FIRM'S POST-TAX PROBLEM

$Y = F(K, L)$, and $R = r + \delta$
Profit before tax $= F(K,L) - wL - RK$
Profit after tax $=\Pi = (1 - Tf)\, [F(K,L) - wL - \delta\, K] - r.K$
FOC: $d\Pi \,/\, dk = (1 - Tf)\, [fk - \delta] - r = 0$
or $fk = r \,/\, (1 - Tf) + \delta.$ (24.93)

This means a higher Tf raises the required MPk. Further, as r and δ increase, the required fk increases.

24.4.3.2.3 SOCIAL PLANNER'S PROBLEM

Here we form the Hamiltonian under this variable tax regime and calculate the following consumption growth expression from the first-order conditions like before. The current value Hamiltonian for the post-tax scenario is thus:

$$H = u(c_t).\, e^{-(\rho - n)t} + \beta_t\, [\dot{m}]$$

Or $H = u(c_t).\, e^{-(\rho - n)\, t} + \beta_t[(1 - Tw).\, w + (1 - Ta).\, r.\, m - (1 + Tc).\, C - n.\, m + v]$

Now taking the household's constant elasticity utility function as before, the growth rate of consumption per capita is rewritten as

$$\dot{c} / c = 1 / \sigma\, [(1 - Tw)\,(1 - Tf).\, \alpha.A^{1/\alpha}.\, (G / Y)^{1-\alpha/\alpha}.\, L^{1-\alpha/\alpha} - n - \delta]. \tag{24.94}$$

The underlined term in the previous expression indicates the after-tax *MPk*. It shows that the post-tax *MPk* is smaller than pre-tax *MPk* as $Tw > 0$ and $Tf > 0$. Now the impact of increase in (G / Y) may not unambiguously affect $\dot{c} / c$, $\dot{y} / y$ or $\dot{k} / k$ because now the financing of G is done by variable or distorting income taxes, not by non-distorting lump-sum tax.

Therefore, as G / Y increases, $\dot{c} / c$ will increase if the effect of G on $\dot{c} / c$ is not offset by "*Tw*" or "*Tf*". The relation between G / Y and $\dot{c} / c$ will then be nonmonotonic-first rising (when tax effect is not dominant) and subsequently falling (when tax effect is dominant).

24.4.3.3 The Ricardo–Barro effect: meaning, arguments against, evidence

We found in the Barro growth model that the effects of government spending in terms of public good creation would lead to a positive rate of growth of per capita income under no tax or with some lump-sum taxes, but the results differed when there were taxes upon assets, firms' incomes, and households' consumption. Governments can finance their expenditures by creating new money, by levying taxes, or by issuing bonds. Since bonds are loans, they must eventually be repaid – presumably by raising taxes in the future. The choice is therefore "tax now or tax later". Suppose that the government finances some extra spending through deficits, which is it chooses to tax later. According to the hypothesis, taxpayers will anticipate that they will have to pay higher taxes in the future. As a result, they will save, rather than spend, the extra disposable income from the initial tax cut, leaving demand and output unchanged.

David Ricardo was the first to propose this possibility in the early nineteenth century; however, he was unconvinced of its empirical relevance. Robert J. Barro took the question up independently in the 1970s, in an attempt to give the proposition a firm theoretical foundation. The theory stipulates that a person's consumption is determined by the lifetime present value of his after-tax income – their intertemporal budget constraint. The Ricardo–Barro effect, also known as Ricardian equivalence, is an economic theory that suggests that when a government tries to stimulate an economy by increasing debt-financed government spending, demand remains unchanged, because the public increases their saving to pay for expected future tax increases that will be used to pay off the debt.

So the government cannot stimulate consumer spending since people assume that whatever is gained now will be offset by higher taxes due in the future. It also implies that no matter how a government chooses to increase spending by borrowing or raising taxes, demand will remain unchanged, because debt-financed public spending will "crowd out" private spending. Figure 24.4 explains the Ricardo–Barro effect.

Ricardian equivalence has been the subject of extensive empirical inquiry. According to Gabriella (2005), it reviews the theoretical and empirical literature that has investigated the conditions under which a contractionary fiscal policy is effective in reducing debt and deficit but does not have a negative effect on growth. The study concludes that the

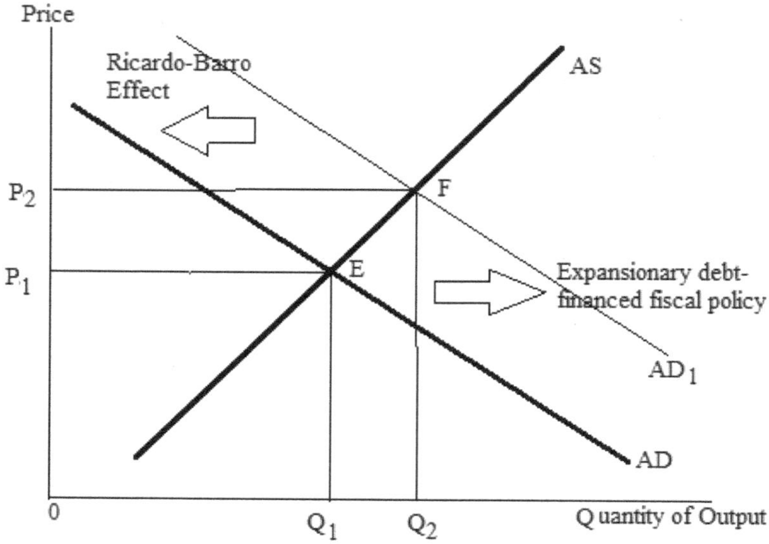

Figure 24.4 The Ricardo–Barro effect

theoretical impact of fiscal policy on aggregate demand and economic activity depends largely on the conceptual framework considered and its assumptions about the world. Empirical studies based on macro-econometric model simulations find evidence that fiscal consolidations lead initially to production losses, while they can result in a higher output in the medium term. Barro himself found some confirmation in post WWI years.

24.4.3.3.1 ARGUMENTS AGAINST THE RICARDO–BARRO EFFECT

The major arguments against the Ricardo–Barro effect are due to what are perceived as the unrealistic assumptions on which the theory is based. These assumptions include the existence of perfect capital markets and the ability for individuals to borrow and save whenever they want. Additionally, there is the assumption that individuals are willing to save for a future tax increase, which they may not see in their lifetime.

There is no evidence that the Ricardo–Barro effect changed saving when the Reagan administration cut taxes and hiked military spending between 1981–1986. The US government had a historically large budget deficit due to the Reagan administration tax cuts and increases in military spending. During 1976–1980, government revenue was 10.01% of potential GNP, and it declined to 8.86% during 1981–1985. The ratio of the US government's budget deficit to its potential GNP did not exceed 4% from World War II until 1981, and it exceeded 4% after 1981. In fact, net private savings as a percentage of GNP fell to 3.3% in Q4 of 1986 from 8.6% in Q3 of 1981. This also does not ring true today, when the US personal saving rate has fallen to multi-decade lows, even as US government borrowing soars. If the Ricardian equivalence hypothesis is true, the rational consumers of the economy, who expect the government to raise taxes, try to reduce their consumption and increase their saving. The reality was that the net private saving as a percentage of GNP was 8.55 in the 1976–1980 period, and it decreased to 7.47% in the 1981–1986 period. The ratio of consumption to GNP was 62.96% in the 1976–1980 period and slightly increased to 64.72% in the 1981–1986 period. People just didn't seem to behave in a way that is consistent with Ricardian equivalence.

The Eurozone financial crisis has provided some evidence to support Ricardian equivalence. Based on data from 2007, there is a strong correlation between government debt burdens and changes in households' financial assets for 12 of the 15 countries within the union.

24.5 Conclusion

The present chapter highlighted different sources that are capable of making the exogenous technology of the neoclassical model endogenous to ensure the result that growth can be perpetual, not limited. The endogenous factors make possible the production function to transform from the constant returns to scale to increasing returns to scale that can ensure positive growth rates relentlessly. We started with the Ramsey model where endogenous savings, not exogenous behaviour, is justified by optimising behaviour of the households. The steady-state growth results, thus, are derived using the households' utility maximisation problem. To make the technology endogenous, primarily the AK model is discussed, which shows that there is a permanent gap between the savings rate and the effective rate of depreciation. The Romer model used the learning-by-doing or knowledge expansion through experience to make technology endogenous. Then the Lucas model of human capital formation and its impacts upon growth of income and consumption are discussed. Finally, Barro introduced active government intervention that can influence the growth of per capita income endlessly.

Summary

The summary results that we derived from the discussion on endogenous technological progress are given as follows:

- Factors like optimising households' behaviour and experience, education, and government intervention can create an endless growth process.
- Optimising households make rational decisions on savings and consumption and hence growth rate can be increased by means of increasing optimum savings rate.
- The AK technology offers the conclusion that a continuous gap between savings and effective depreciation will make the steady-state growth rate positive, in place of zero.
- The Romer's instrument of gathering experience through a learning-by-doing process, a source of increasing returns to scale, is capable of explaining endogenous technology which can offer an eternal growth rate.
- Human capital as a source of perpetual growth of per capita income is explained in the Lucas model.
- Barro introduced government expenditure into the production function which establishes increasing returns to scale condition and hence endogenous technology to explain endless growth rate.
- Whether public spending leads to aggregate demand as well as economic output changes depends upon the Ricardo-equivalence theory.

Keywords

Growth rate
Savings rate
Endogenous technology
Steady state
Ramsey model
AK model
Increasing returns to scale
Romer model
Lucas model
Barro model

Multiple choice questions and answers

1. In the endogenous growth theory, the sources of increasing returns to scale are
   - (a) Investment in education.
   - (b) Learning by doing.
   - (c) Active government participation.
   - (d) All of the above.
2. Lack of investment in strong education and health care systems
   - (a) Causes a deterioration in human capital and a decline in labour productivity.
   - (b) Causes a deterioration in human capital and an increase in physical capital.
   - (c) Increases human capital and a causes a decline in labour productivity.
   - (d) Causes a decline in physical capital and a decline in labour productivity.
3. In which model of endogenous growth theory is there a perpetual constant gap between savings and effective depreciation?
   - (a) Barro model.
   - (b) Ramsey model.
   - (c) AK model.
   - (d) Romer model.
4. The fundamental difference between the neoclassical model and Ramsey model is that
   - (a) The Ramsey model endogenises the households' savings behaviour whereas the neoclassical model considers the exogenous savings rate.
   - (b) The Ramsey model endogenises the households' consumption behaviour whereas the neoclassical model considers the exogenous savings rate.
   - (c) Either (a) or (b) or both.
   - (d) All of the above.
5. Imposition of different taxation upon the households and firms in the endogenous growth model will lead to
   - (a) The increase in the steady-state growth rate.
   - (b) The decrease in the steady-state growth rate.
   - (c) No change in the steady-state growth rate.
   - (d) None of the above.

Answers

1. (d); 2. (a); 3. (c); 4. (d); 5. (b)

Review questions

1. Why is the growth called endogenous? Mention different sources of endogenous growth. Explain on what grounds the endogenous growth theory is treated as an improved version of growth theory compared to the neoclassical model.
2. What is the basic difference between the savings behaviour of the households under the neoclassical model and the Ramsey model? Explain in detail the Ramsey model of growth from the point of view of optimisations made by private agent and social agent. Give a brief note on the steady-state growth level in the model.
3. Determine the returns to scale in the AK technology model. Prove that perpetual growth rate can be maintained if the economy uses the AK-type technology in its production system.
4. Explain whether phase dynamics can be in the AK model. Can you intuitively explain how the AK model explains cross-country convergence?
5. What are the sources of endogenous technological progress under the Romer model? Describe the Romer model and calculate the steady-state growth level of the economy.
6. Define physical capital and human capital. Discuss how perpetual growth in the per capita consumption and income can be obtained through human capital formation.
7. Explain how the optimum ratio of human capital to physical capital is determined in the Lucas model of growth. Try to compare the production function under the Lucas model with the AK model.
8. Make basic differences between the Ramsey model and overlapping generations model. Discuss phase diagram in the former model to derive optimum trajectory of growth.
9. What is the Barro model called in the IRS model? Explain how the introduction of public expenditure on different sectors creates a perpetual growth process under the Barro model. Calculate steady-state value of capital with a production function of your own choice.
10. Define steady-state growth rate. Suppose the production function is $Y = 1{,}000K$ and consumption function is $C = C(Y)$ and savings function $S = S(Y)$ with $0 < C_y, S_y < 1$. Determine the steady-state growth rate and show that it is perpetual.
11. What is Ricardian equivalence? Explain the theory using a diagram. Point out some of the limitations of the theory.
12. Make comparisons between the Cobb-Douglas production function and an AK-type production function in terms of returns to scale, returns to factors, and output elasticity of capital.

Additional readings

Acemoglu, D. & Ventura, J. (2002). "The world income distribution". *The Quarterly Journal of Economics*, 117(2), 659–694.

Barro, R. J. (1990). "Government spending in a simple model of endogenous growth". *The Journal of Political Economy*, 98(5), 103–125.

Barro, R. J. & Sala-i-Martin, X. I. (2004). *Economic Growth*, 2nd ed. New Delhi: Prentice Hall of India.

Bucci, A. & Guerrini, L. (2008). *Transitional Dynamics in the Solow-Swan Growth Model with AK Technology and Logistic Population Change.* www.york.ac.uk/media/economics/documents/seminars/Bucci_Guerrini.pdf

Gabriella, B. M. (2005). "Economic reactions to public finance consolidation: A survey of the literature". European Central Bank Occasional Paper. No. 38.

Gomez, M. A. (2008). "Convergence speed in the AK endogenous growth model with habit formation". *Economics Letters*, 100(1), 16–21.
Ramsey, F. P. (1928). "A mathematical theory of saving". *Economic Journal*, 38(152), 543–559.
Rebelo, S. (1991). "Long-run policy analysis and long-run growth". *Journal of Political Economy*, 99(3), 500–521.
Romer, P. M. (1994). "The origins of endogenous growth". *The Journal of Economic Perspectives*, 8(1), 3–22.
Verhulst, P. F. (1838). "Notice on the law that the population follows in its growth". *Mathematical and Physical Correspondence*, 10, 113–121.

Part VII

Sustainable development and green macroeconomics

25 Sustainable development

25.1 Introduction

So far, we have gathered knowledge about green accounting of national output and the interactions of aggregate demand components with the environmental constraints. Also we have seen how different public policies and trade policies worked in generating effective income effects under the presence of environmental constraints. We will try now to relate the green output growth with the new concept of development which is in some ways different from the traditional concept of development. That particular type of development is called sustainable development, a concept which has been emerging for the last two decades derived mostly from the United Nations World Commission on Environment and Development, 1987, popularly known as the Brundtland Commission's Report. *Sustainable development* is a principle for satisfying human development goals at the same time as sustaining the capacity of natural systems to provide the natural resources and ecosystem services upon which the economy and society depend. Simply, we can term sustainable development as the process by which economic activities are on par with nature's capacity so that the future generations get the same package of natural environment like the present generation.

Box I Sustainable development as per the Brundtland report, 1987

"Sustainable development is development that meets the needs of the present without compromising the ability of future generations to meet their own needs. It contains within it two key concepts:

The concept of 'needs', in particular, the essential needs of the world's poor, to which overriding priority should be given; and the idea of limitations imposed by the state of technology and social organization on the environment's ability to meet present and future needs".

25.1.1 Sustainable development goals

Taking into account the severity of the increasing levels of environmental degradation in all aspects and the outputs of the series of environmental conferences all over the world recommended by the concerned experts, the United Nations General Assembly formally

DOI: 10.4324/9781003501138-32

adopted the "universal, integrated and transformative" 2030 Agenda for Sustainable Development in September 2015. It is a set of 17 Sustainable Development Goals (SDGs) consisting of 169 targets among them in different sectors, including the environment, which are to be implemented and achieved in every country from the year 2016 to 2030 without fail. The goals are as follows:

Goal 1: *No Poverty*
Goal 2: *Zero Hunger*
Goal 3: *Good Health and Wellbeing*
Goal 4: *Quality Education*
Goal 5: *Gender Equality*
Goal 6: *Clean Water and Sanitation*
Goal 7: *Affordable and Clean Energy*
Goal 8: *Decent Work and Economic Growth*
Goal 9: *Industry, Innovation, and Infrastructure*
Goal 10: *Reduced Inequalities*
Goal 11: *Sustainable Cities and Communities*
Goal 12: *Responsible Consumption and Production*
Goal 13: *Climate Action*
Goal 14: *Life Below Water*
Goal 15: *Life on Land*
Goal 16: *Peace, Justice, and Strong Institutions*
Goal 17: *Partnerships for the Goals*

This list of goals shows the range of fulfilling the basic needs to a perfect world in all dimensions. There are year marks of 2030 in the targets for poverty reduction and zero hunger, good health, education, etc., although some agencies like the International Food Policy Research Institute criticised it on the grounds that they should be fulfilled by 2025. The countries have started implementing the targets, although it may not be assumed that all the countries have equal capability to fulfil the targets. There is a long list of goals with respect to natural resources and the environment. The targets are very difficult to achieve as the countries from the lower- and middle-income strata face a trade-off between environmental degradation and growth of the countries. Hence, there are enormous hurdles to satisfy the all-inclusive development at the world level.

25.2 Conservation capital

In the preceding discussion we have seen the effectiveness of the fiscal and monetary policies upon output of the economy in the presence of investment upon green capital formation towards conservation capital to maintain environmental sustainability. It is now thus required to focus upon the discussion of conservation capital in several aspects to have a better idea of it and to use it in future economic planning of the countries who have discharged huge volumes of economic waste into the environment.

25.2.1 Defining conservation capital

The world economy is growing in terms of income at a spectacular rate and the highly promising economies are those of the developing nations. Whatever we earn in terms of the growth of total or per capita incomes is from using physical capital or manmade capital, labour force, and fossil fuel in particular as the other input. We are losing the reserve of the natural resources, underground, atmospheric, water, soil, forestry, etc. and taking away from the future generation the use of the resources like what we have today. It is thus an issue of inter-generational inequity which makes the high growth and development of these countries unsustainable.

The term "capital" is generally used by the economist to describe a stock of whatsoever has the capacity to generate a flow in the economic system, that benefits and is valued by the people. The capital stock takes different identifiable forms. The five capitals, Human, Social, Financial, Manufactured, and Natural capital, are defined from where we derive goods and services for our lives and livelihoods. Each form of capital generates services, either independently or in combination with other capital stocks, used to convert and augment human welfare in the society (Costanga and Daly, 1992). The Organization for Economic Co-operation and Development (OECD) in its report in the year 2005 defines Natural Capital as "Natural assets in their role of providing natural resource inputs and environmental services for economic production". Similarly, the World Forum on Natural Capital in its report in the year 2015 states that natural capital is a "stock of natural assets which include geology, soil, air, water, and all living things". Pearce and Atkinson (1996) define natural capital as the stock of renewable and non-renewable natural assets (e.g. air, water, minerals, plants, animals, and soil) that combine to yield a flow of benefits to people and businesses in the economy in particular and society in general.

But there is a long debate on the use of the environmental or natural capital. While one view maintains that environmental regulations are needed to protect the environment, others suggest that technological change induced by market forces can protect the environment even in the absence of regulation (Ayres and Ayres, 1996; Green et al, 2000). Additionally, while some argue that environmental regulations impede economic growth, proponents of environmental regulation stress that it can stimulate technological innovation which increases input productivity and the efficiency of resource use and can lead to higher rates of economic growth.

To ensure sustainability in growth and development, the countries need to invest in developing green capital or natural capital to conserve or preserve nature. The investment which is made for ensuring sustainable development is called conservation capital.

25.2.2 *Differences between physical capital and conservation capital*

In the production system in economics, we use mainly physical capital so far as the earlier version of the production function is concerned. But in the modern era after the advent of the SDGs the importance of natural or conservation capital increases. The physical capital (or manmade capital or manufactured capital) comprises material goods or fixed assets which contribute to the production process rather than being the output itself – for example tools, machines, and buildings. It is basically the produced means of production. It contains a dirty component in the sense that its uses lead to environmental pollution.

On the other hand, Natural Capital is any stock or flow of energy and material that produces goods and services. It includes:

- Resources – renewable and non-renewable materials
- Sinks – that absorb, neutralise or recycle wastes
- Processes – such as climate regulation

Natural capital is the basis not only of production but of life itself! We are facing a sustainability crisis because we are consuming our stocks of natural, human, and social capital faster than they are being produced. Unless we control the rate of this consumption, we cannot sustain these vital stocks in the long term and will not be able to protect the human civilisation on the earth. We believe that by maintaining and trying to increase stocks of these capital assets, we can live off the income without reducing the capital itself. But for this to happen, it is the responsibility of every organisation, business or otherwise, to manage these capital assets sustainably. The roles of corporate social responsibility should matter much in this respect.

25.2.3 *Why does natural capital matter?*

In 1972, the book titled *Limits to Growth* was published that tell us that, by end of the twenty-first century, if we continued to grow at the same rate in terms of natural resource usage, the world might be on a collision course with calamity. Further, in 1998, the Centre for Science and Environment (CSE) conducted a study with the help of Anil Agarwal and titled the report "Slow Murder – The Deadly Story of Vehicular Pollution in India" which has explained how the vehicular pollution in India has grown side-by-side with the growth of its economic outputs. In an edited book, Das (2023) covered a wide variety of studies on the economic, health, and environmental consequences of conservation capital in the world economies. It tackles the oft ignored role of conservation capital in mainstream discussions in maintaining sustainable development of a country in particular and the world economy in general. A continuous increase in global temperature trends, climate change, and other related factors has compelled academicians from natural as well as social sciences to reorient classical thought from high growth through high resource extraction to sustainable growth through lower extraction. This leads one to the important roles of generation of conservation capital to satisfy long-term growth and development objectives of economies. Therefore, taking nature for granted can have grave consequences. We all rely on natural capital: oceans, minerals ecosystems, and atmosphere. We also heavily depend on the services natural capital provides like fuel, food, natural medicines, and services like water filtration, erosion control, and climate regulation. However, most of these services provided by nature are unpriced or economically invisible. These invisible dependences on natural capital possess significant unmanaged risks and stability of businesses.

In recent times the emergence of conservation capital reflects the recognition that the environmental system plays a vital role in outlining human wellbeing and economic output. It is considered as the foundation of economics, businesses, and agriculture in particular. The flow of benefits provided by natural capital comes in the form of ecosystem services and these services provide basic conditions for human existence like food production, water, climate regulation, etc. Therefore, natural capital is the most vital of the core forms of capital which are social, manufactured, financial, and human. According to the Nature Conservancy and Corporate EcoForum, 2012 report, nature provides an estimated $72 trillion of free goods and services. In the long term the rate at which natural capital is depleted needs to match the rate at which it can regenerate, otherwise the life support systems that we need from nature will run out. The SDGs were developed on the basis that we can achieve a sustainable rate of natural capital usage.

25.2.4 *What have corporate bodies done so far?*

Biodiversity-related financial risks are not yet fully appreciated by most investors. Investors have "limited awareness" of the issue, and there are very few commitments or policies in place to address it. But momentum is congregating. According to Hannah Simons,

> there are efforts underway by the World Bank and global investors to establish collaborative engagement along similar lines to the Climate Action 100+. The so-called Nature Action 100+ would seek to drive change at the top 100 companies having the biggest negative impact on nature.

Simons further points out that work has begun on a Taskforce for Nature-related Financial Disclosures with a plan to create a framework, similar to the Taskforce for Climate-related Financial Disclosures, for firms to disclose their exposure to nature-related financial risks by the end of 2023 in which the science-based targets for nature are in the early stages of development. These targets are a route by which businesses can bring into line their individual sustainability action with globally settled environmental goals.

25.2.5 *Advantages of investment upon conservation capital*

According to the World Economic Forum (2020) more than half of the world's total gross domestic product, or $44 trillion, involves activities that are moderately or highly dependent on nature. Thus, nature should be protected to have the following benefits:

- It ensures long run growth of the economies to have sustainable development features.
- It saves the degradation of natural capital, including the loss of biodiversity and depletion of renewable stocks and reduces real risk for businesses, their earnings, and investors.
- It leads to lowering insurance risks, higher costs of capital, and a loss of investment opportunities to the business, banks, and investors.
- It reduces health cost, both private and public, leading to higher budgetary allocations to the education sector leading to high human capital formation and high growth.
- It reduces inter-generational inequality in the sense that future generations get the opportunity to avail the same quantity and quality of natural resources that we have today.
- It ensures global peace and happiness. It preserves the biodiversity and raises the carrying capacity of the earth.

25.2.6 *Scenario of government expenditure on conservation capital — a case in India*

In order to offer good environmental quality to the world's citizens, the governments can or should make a difference by supporting small local producers who, unlike large factory firms, employ sustainable practices, care about land restoration, benefit nearby communities, and make animals and crops more resilient to climate change. Here are some scenarios of the world's highly growing economy in India on her moves towards sustainable global environment.

25.2.6.1 *Allocation in central budget*

In the financial year 2019–2020, expense on environmental protection accounted for nearly 0.1% of the total government expenditure in India. In comparison to the last few fiscal years, more funds were earmarked for environmental stability in that year. In 2021–2022, the Ministry of Environment, Forests, and Climate Change has been allocated Rs. 2,870 crore, which is an annual increase of 6% over the actual expenditure in 2019–2020. The allocation to the ministry is 0.1% of the estimated expenditure of the union government for 2021–2022.

25.2.7 *Major policies to protect nature by the countries*

The governments of the countries in their commitments to the global community in respect to containing climate changes are required to make a list of policies as mentioned in the following sections:

25.2.7.1 *Protecting and restoring key ecosystems*

Governments must protect ecosystems key to the fight against climate change: rivers, wetlands, oceans, forests, and mangroves absorb large quantities of carbon, slowing warming. Mangroves also serve as a barrier against tropical storms, and wetlands absorb excess water from floods, both extreme weather events exacerbated by climate change. In terms of conservation and restoration, the people are in a race against time, and we are already beginning to witness alarming natural phenomena, like forests so degraded they are losing their ability to absorb carbon.

25.2.7.2 *Supporting small agricultural producers*

According to the FAO (2013), the meat industry is responsible for 15 to 18% of all greenhouse gas emissions in the world, exceeding even those of the transportation sector. In addition, it is the most significant source of water use and contamination in the world. Today, 80% of all agricultural production goes towards feeding animals, not people. The expansion of land for livestock – and the crops to feed them – is one of the most significant causes of deforestation in the Amazon area. The governments can make a difference by supporting small local producers who, unlike large factory farms, **employ sustainable practices, care about land restoration, benefit nearby communities, and make animals and crops more resilient** to climate change.

25.2.7.3 *Promoting green energy*

According to the Environmental Protection Agency (EPA), about 35% of all global emissions come from energy production. But as countries bet on more development, they are also betting on more energy production. While thermoelectric and hydroelectric energies were long considered the cheapest options, technological developments have allowed us to find better, cheaper, more efficient alternatives. **We thus must give absolute priority to the protection of nature**. Every action, public policy, or strategy should be analysed with nature in mind, and the production of energy is a good starting point.

25.2.7.4 *Combating short-lived climate pollutants*

Carbon dioxide (CO2) is the most infamous greenhouse gas. Since it remains in the atmosphere for centuries (even millennia), even if we stopped all its emissions sources today, the effects of climate change would continue. The good news is that other contaminants exist that contribute to climate change and only last a few days or years in the atmosphere. They are known as short-lived climate pollutants, and they're responsible for 30 to 45% of the emissions that cause global warming. These pollutants include black carbon (soot), methane, ozone, and the hydro fluorocarbons found in refrigerants. Their effective control, through national policies and regulations, could accelerate the fight against climate change in the short term, directly benefitting human health.

25.2.7.5 Gamble on adaptation, not just mitigation

In the fight against climate change, work aimed at reducing emissions, stopping their effects, and diminishing future consequences is known as mitigation. However, some communities are already experiencing tragic consequences due to changes in climate over a short period of time. So we also must act to prevent catastrophes, increase resilience, and reduce vulnerability, which is known as adaptation. Projects to mitigate emissions are more attractive financially than those designed for adaptation, which are generally focused on the most vulnerable communities. But it is important to give adaptation the significance it deserves in recognition of the fact that the impacts of climate change are already a grave reality for many.

25.3 The new development on sustainability — the circular economy approach

For about a decade environmental scientists have practiced a new mechanism to provide a long-term and quick solution to unsustainable use of natural capital, climate change, and global warming problems. It is unlike the traditional linear economy where the use of environmental resources leads to production and consumption of goods and environmental pollution as a by-product. A circular economy approach does the reverse in the sense that it recycles the waste products in all spheres of production and consumption activities and adds to the existing inputs of production and reduces pollution leading to sustainable development. The three principles required for the transformation to a circular economy are: designing out waste and pollution, keeping products and materials in use, and regenerating natural systems.

25.3.1 Linear economy vs. circular economy

In a linear economy, natural resources are turned into products that are ultimately intended to become waste because of the way they have been designed and manufactured. This process is often summarised as "take, make, waste". The current linear economic model focuses on products, which are produced, used, and then thrown away as waste. By contrast, a circular economy aims to transition from a "take-make-waste" approach to a more restorative and regenerative system. It employs reuse, sharing, repair, restoration, re-manufacturing, and recycling to create a closed-loop system, reducing the use of resource inputs and the creation of waste, pollution, and carbon emissions. The linear economy focuses on profitability and utility, irrespective of the product life cycle, whereas the circular economy targets sustainability. In a circular economy, waste is the new raw material. There is no longer the line: produce, consume, and then throw it away. This saves raw materials and the environment and reduces CO_2 emissions. It stimulates innovation, new business activity, and employment.

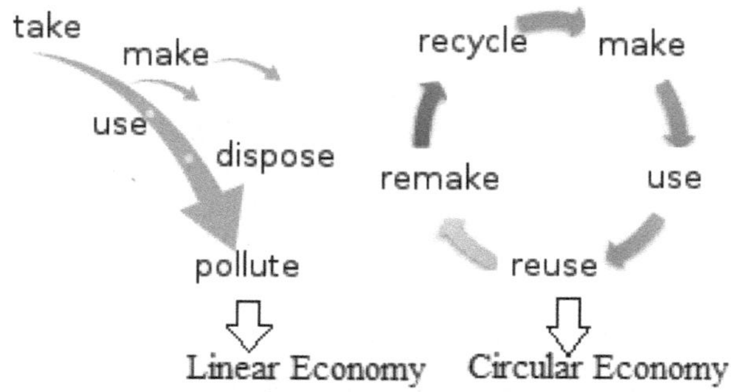

Figure 25.1 Linear economy and circular economy

Figure 25.1 explains the two economy concepts. The left-hand side of the diagram shows the linear economy where the "take-make-use-pollute" chain works, leading to unsustainable growth and development while on the right-hand side the circular economy concept presented as the "make-use-reuse-recycle" chain is operates, leading to sustainable use of the economic and environmental resources.

There so many examples of the circular economy concept operating at the global level. The Danish deposit and return system for recycling drink cans and bottles, the solid waste management in Europe, and Denmark's first circular social housing project are some examples.

25.3.2 *Circular economy in business*

Circular development is a model of economic, social, and environmental production and consumption that aims to build an autonomous and sustainable society in tune with the issue of environmental resources. In a circular economy, business models play a crucial role in enabling the shift from linear to circular processes. Various business models have been identified that support circularity, including product-as-a-service, sharing platforms, and product life extension models, among others. These models aim to optimise resource utilisation, reduce waste, and create value for businesses and customers alike, while contributing to the overall goals of the circular economy. For example, industrial symbiosis is a strategy where waste from one industry becomes an input for another, creating a network of resource exchange and reducing waste, pollution, and resource consumption. Similarly, circular cities aim to integrate circular principles into urban planning and development, fostering local resource loops and promoting sustainable lifestyles among their citizens. According to Bank, European Investment (May 26, 2023) less than 10% of economic activity worldwide in 2022 and 2023 has been circular; mostly the developed countries and regions take part in this green initiative. Hence, there are miles to go to reap its full benefit in terms of sustainable development.

25.3.3 *Circular economy and sustainable development*

The circular economy concept has been developed in order to mitigate the issues of climate change and global warming that hinder achieving sustainable development. The circular economy aims to change the paradigm in relation to the linear economy by limiting the environmental impact and waste of resources, as well as increasing efficiency at all stages of the production and consumption economy. The global policymakers and the environmental scientists have given warnings recently about how waste pollution and the limits of natural resources are encouraging the development of a circular economy. Circular economy is a new production and consumption model that guarantees sustainable growth over time. With the circular economy, the optimisation of resources reducing the consumption of raw materials can be derived, and the waste can be recovered by recycling or giving it a second life as a new product. It contributes to economic sustainability, environmental sustainability, and social sustainability which are as the following:

Economic: the circular economy provides sustainable benefits to the economy in the way that it stimulates innovation and boosts economic growth and could in the long run enhance the competitiveness of national companies. It tries to capture the value of existing products and materials and decreases the use of primary materials in industries and enhances sustainable growth in order to benefit the future generations via the current generation.

Environmental: the environmental contribution of a circular economy is the protection of the environment, reducing waste and the emissions of greenhouse gases, systematising recycling, and ending planned obsolescence. In addition, the circular economy allows decrease of the dependence on importation of resources like raw materials, water, energy, etc. This model involves reusing, recycling, and repurposing materials to minimise the depletion of natural resources, reduce pollution, and achieve sustainability in economic growth.

Social: the circular economy creates jobs and enables people to save money, reducing unemployment and poverty as well as reducing the social impacts of pollution and climate change. It helps in recovery of waste resources, saves energy, and generates surplus in food and non-food items, leading to reducing poverty and food insecurity and develops social capital through good social bonding.

Therefore, sustainability is a driver of the circular economy and is mediated by innovation. Sustainability's three main pillars represent the environment, social responsibility, and economics. These pillars are also informally referred to as people, planet, purpose, and profits. Circular economy, so far as its trends of progress are concerned, has the potential to achieve sustainable development in all types of economies in the world.

25.4 Conclusion

We addressed the concept of sustainable development by means of the UN's 17-point agenda on a broad-spectrum basis and the scenarios of the countries in mitigating environmental pollution. The most important way to ensure environmental quality for future generations is the investment in conservation capital by both the private and public sectors. The investment helps the economy through the endogenous growth process without hampering the environment. The development of a new concept, the circular economy, has the potential to reinstate the nature's capacity for a better and more sustainable developmental position of nature.

Summary

The prominent results we observed from the whole chapter can be addressed by the following summary results:

- The United Nations offered 17-point goals for attaining sustainable development for all types of economies of the world and the moves by the countries on mitigating climate change are discussed.
- Conservation capital formation is a type of capital, green capital, which is used to control environmental pollution and to achieve sustainable development.
- Circular economy is a new development in the sustainable practices of economic and environmental resources.

Keywords

Green national income
Sustainable development
Circular economy
Environmental sustainability
Conservation capital

Review questions

1. Define sustainable development. Discuss the 17-point agenda of sustainable development as forwarded by the United Nations.
2. Define a circular economy. Note the differences between it and a linear economy. Write down the key benefits of a circular economy in terms of sustainability.
3. Define conservation capital. Explain how it helps in increasing economic growth without distorting environmental quality.
4. Discuss corporate social responsibility in relation to environmental protection. Portray some efforts taken up by different companies in India and abroad in mitigating environmental pollution via corporate social responsibility.
5. Elucidate theoretically the major policies taken up by the countries regarding nature. Do you think the developing countries like India have dominated in the area of nature's conservation? Explain.
6. Write a note on the pros and cons of the investment upon conservation capital.
7. Discuss major components of the sustainable development goal which are related to environmental protection. Justify how far they can be achieved within the target period of 2030.

26 Green macroeconomics

26.1 Introduction

Till now whatever we have discussed was accounted for in market transactions and the fiscal and monetary policies undertaken upon them were producing the best outcome out of the available market information. No items which were out of market transaction were taken as nonexistent and there were no externality effects of production, consumption, and above all the gross national products or gross domestic products. The only erosion from the flow of the income stream was the physical wear and tear of the fixed capital that was termed as "depreciation". Depreciation was the erosion of fixed capital which was produced and used by human activities; no natural sources of resources like reserves of coal, oil, forest, clean air, water, land, etc. were taken into account in the economic activities as the market did not work for them (it was popularly known as *market failure*). The natural sources of capital related to resources and environment work as the externality factor to the accounting of national incomes of countries, the inclusion of which create the inefficiency of market operations. Exclusion of all these externality factors from the accounting of national income and the effectiveness of the related fiscal and monetary policies upon the income, employment, rate of interest, and general price levels like important macroeconomic determinants disproves the gross national product (GNP) as the measure of welfare. This, in other words, means that the earlier version of GNP is unsustainable. The inclusion of all the natural resource factors into the economic activities gives rise to the concept of green macroeconomics or sustainable macroeconomics. Further, the inclusion of environmental sustainability or stability factors into the interactions of commodity and money sectors will authenticate the genuineness of all the macroeconomic indicators.

In the following sections we will address first the flaws of GNP as a deserving indicator of welfare or overall development and determine optimum resource extraction and pollution and internalisation of pollution, policies to control pollution, trade-off between pollution and growth, green accounting of national income, and rebuilding the effectiveness of fiscal and monetary policy combinations with and without the presence of international transactions.

26.1.1 Flaws of GNP as the sole indicator of development

An important distinction is often made by the development economists between growth and development of a country. Economic growth is defined as the percentage increase

DOI: 10.4324/9781003501138-33

in the gross income or per capita income of a country over time; no other indicators are taken into consideration. It is hence a narrow definition of progress of a country. The accounting of GNP cannot take into account different indicators and issues in generating the growth rate. GNP is the sole factor in addressing the issue of growth of a country. The concept of development, on the other hand, is a broader version of progress of a country since it takes into account all the related factors of society, economy, environment, etc. in its calculations. No doubt, GNP is a major part of the developmental index. In this sense, it is often said that development means growth but growth may not reflect development. A country can earn higher and higher incomes in a gross sense but may not improve in education, health, sanitation, and gender-related areas. A wealthier person may not be educated or have good health conditions. India and China have been the countries with gigantic growth rates of their incomes, but the disparity between the rich and poor sections of the countries has been widened which is a bad symptom of development.

It is further important to mention that GNP takes into account the final values of all goods and services which are exchanged in market mechanisms. It does not take into account the items of non-market transactions like self-produced goods, owner occupied houses, the services of housewives, self-driven vehicles, etc. The organisations of computing national income prescribe imputing alternative prices (which are called shadow prices) to all the non-market transacted items by their alternative market prices to avoid underestimation of national output and income.

Suppose, for the sake of simplicity, the income computing agencies (for example, the Central Statistical Organization in India) became able to account for all the non-marketed goods and services by proper imputations and the country also became very efficient in controlling overall inequality across different classes, then can we be sure to take into account the flow of GNP as sustainable? Definitely not, since economic activities do not only use private capital or manmade capital in production and consumption, but also use, rather destroy, the natural sources of capital like resources and ambient environment. Hence, we need to incorporate the costs/depreciation of extractions of natural resources and pollution of the environment into the valuation of national income to make the GNP sustainable. Sustainable GNP means the existing stock of natural resources and quality of the ambient environment can be used equally for the present as well as future generations so that inter-generational equities can be maintained. Private producers and consumers make use of natural resources and ambient environment, although they do not possess the right to do so and do not incorporate the costs of such damage of natural resources into the cost of the goods produced and consumed. That means the products' prices do not incorporate the effect of positive externality into them and, hence, there will always be overexploitation of the natural resources. But effects of pollution and shortage of natural resources are the components of negative externality which need to be internalised in terms of public policies like taxation, subsidies, command and control, etc. Of course all volumes of pollution and resource extractions are the real threats to the earth since the environment has its own power to assimilate a part of the anthropogenic source of pollution (this is called carrying capacity of the earth) and some resources have a renewability property that can regenerate the loss of resources. When the magnitude of manmade pollution exceeds the carrying capacity of the earth and the renewability power falls short of the magnitudes of extractions, only then are pollution and resource extraction real threat to the earth.

26.2 Social cost of environmental pollution

Since the effects of negative externalities are not incorporated into the determination of market prices of the goods, therefore, it induces the producers or generators of the negative externalities to produce more than the society or nature has the ability to absorb. The effect of pollution, once created, affects all the persons in the locality or even outside the locality and no one can get rid of its adverse effects. This means environmental pollution has the public bad (not good) character.

Suppose there is a thermal power plant in a locality owned and managed by a private firm. The production of power needs coal as the principal raw material and the ambient environment. The combustion of coal leads to exhaustion of fly ash that mixes with the ambient environment and as a result the environment gets polluted. The residents within the locality and outside the locality face health hazards in terms of respiratory problems. So, there is an additional cost of production which is known as the cost of pollution or the marginal externality cost (MEC). Therefore, the total cost faced by the owner of the thermal power is the marginal cost of thermal power (MC) and the society faces the social marginal cost (SMC) which is the sum of MC and MEC. The extent of MEC is alternatively named as the marginal cost of damage (MDC) that includes the health cost, unpleasantness, erosion of soils and beauty of the environmental amenities, etc. As the quantity of power production rises, the quantity of smoke emission rises so the marginal social cost also rises. Therefore, like the private cost of production, the SMC is also upward rising and convex to the output axis and it lies above the MC. At the same time, the producer of energy gets private marginal benefit (MNPB) from extra production of power. Suppose the firm faces perfect competition in the power market, then the price of power will be constant and the MNPB or the demand function of power is a horizontal line. The equilibrium of the private firm exists at point *E* where MNPB is equal to MC (Figure 26.1).

The equilibrium private profit maximising output is x_1 at the price P_1. But the society reaches equilibrium at point *F* where it is desirable by the society to produce less power since less power generation means lesser magnitudes of pollution. The social equilibrium

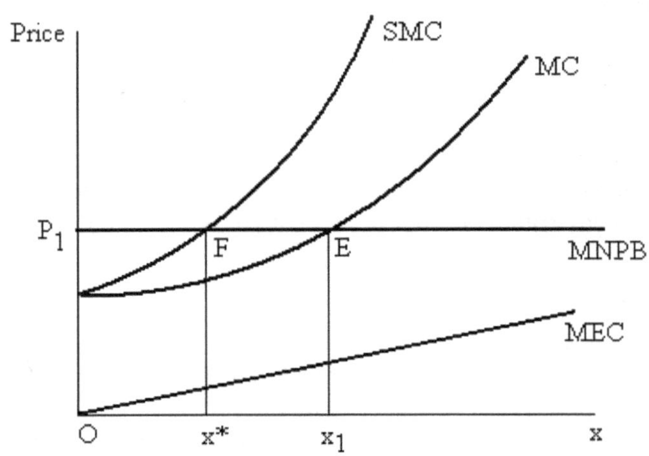

Figure 26.1 Private and social optimum of production

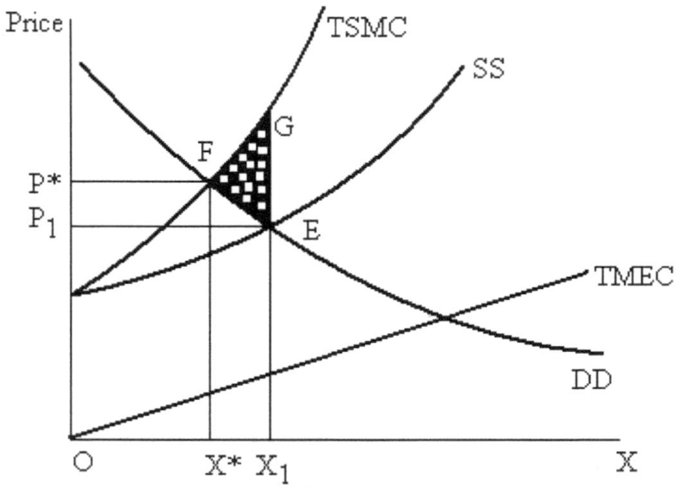

Figure 26.2 Optimum production under many private firms

condition is MNPB = SMC and the optimum level of output is x^* ($x^* < x_1$). This means the exclusion of pollution effect (or the effect of negative externality) from the private production cost overproduces the quantity of power but the society does not like that much power.

If there are many power-producing firms in the economy, each with the similar marginal cost functions, the supply function of power will be the horizontal sum of all marginal cost functions which is shown by $SS = \Sigma MC_i$ (Figure 26.2). Also suppose that each firm generates similar quantities of smoke and so the aggregate social marginal cost is TSMC which lies above SS. The industry demand curve is negatively sloped which is the sum of all firms' marginal benefit curves (*DD*). The industry equilibrium is attained at *E* which is net of SMC where the aggregate production of power is Q_1 but inclusion of environmental cost leads to lower industrial output X^* ($X^* < X_1$).

The extra price ($P^* - P_1$) is to be charged to combat the pollution. But the market price net of SMC is P_1 which is lower than P^*. The shaded area EFG is the social (or inefficiency) cost of environmental pollution (or negative externality) which is a source of social cost. Unless this magnitude of social cost is controlled or internalised by the producers in the market prices of the goods, a day will come when we will have no natural resources and the environment will be fully polluted. The future generations will have to bear all the costs of environmental pollution created by their predecessors.

26.3 Internalisation of externality

In the present context we concentrate on the problem of negative externality in the form of environmental pollution only. Pollution, in its many forms, as a by-product of economic activities, is widely regarded as our major threat to the ambient environment, like the coal as the commodity which is used for the production of power has a price. The production of power will be stopped if no smoke is allowed to emit through the chimneys or exhaust pipes. Therefore, smoke emission – or the environment – is also an economic resource for which the producers should make a payment to protect against its depletion. In other words, the case of pollution should be treated as a commodity (this is called commodification of pollution or externality) and its price should be fixed by the demand–supply mechanism. The process of treating environment as commodity is called *internalisation of pollution or externality*. Prof. A. C. Pigou was perhaps the first economist to suggest the incorporation of pollution as an instance of externality in the framework of economic theory. The role of government in this context is a necessary precondition to settle the pricing of pollution, provided individual negotiation fails to achieve this. We present here the microeconomic foundation of internalisation of negative externalities like pollution.

Methods of internalisation vary along with the types of externalities. If the externality is depletable in the sense that the consumption of that externality by one individual excludes other individuals from its consumption (that means it has a private good property), then a market mechanism will fully internalise it. No outside agencies like the government are required in this context. Private bargaining between the polluter and the victims will solve or internalise the problem. On the other hand, if the externality is non-depletable, then it will have public property. No private bargaining will solve the problem; government intervention is a necessary alternative in this context. The government can apply different public policy instruments which can vary from direct control (which is called command and control) to indirect controls. Under the command and control (CAC) policy, the government directly intervenes by its administrative instruments to shut down or regulate the source of pollution. But the problem with this CAC technique is that, in doing the operation, the government has to bear a huge administrative cost and the implementation of different guidelines to the sources is very difficult to achieve. In the following sections we highlight the indirect method of controlling pollution by means of market-based principles.

26.3.1 Indirect unit pollution tax

The alternative market-related control instruments for internalisation of externalities is the per unit tax on pollution. This is prescribed by Prof. Pigou. The polluters are subject to the effluent tax and so the policy is called *polluter pays principle*. According to Pigou, if the social marginal damage of pollution or the marginal externality cost is clearly valued in monetary units, then a per unit tax equal to marginal damage cost or marginal externality cost (MEC) will fully internalise the negative externality that will bring the *Pareto optimal solution* to society. Therefore, the equilibrium rate of pollution tax will be

$$t^* = MEC \tag{26.1}$$

Referring to Figure 26.2, t^* equal to GE will internalise the entire pollution problem. The price of the commodity will now be $P = MC + t^*$ which automatically leads to a cut in production of power from X_1 to X^*.

A positive feature of indirect pollution tax is that it can encourage the polluters to install pollution abatement devices that require additional cost of production. Suppose TAC is the total abatement cost of installing a device recommended by the controlling authority. The marginal abatement cost (MAC) is the extra cost that is required to fight against extra pollution. As the level of pollution rises, the cost of abatement will be lower. So the MAC function is negatively sloped.

The optimum level of pollution will be attained at a point where extra cost of pollution is equal to the extra cost of abatement. Therefore, the equilibrium tax t^* will be such that it makes equality between MAC and MEC. So tax at equilibrium is

$$t^* = MAC = MEC \tag{26.2}$$

This is obtained at point E in Figure 26.3 where the magnitude of emissions is s^* and tax rate is Es^*. The amount Es^* covers all the cost of pollution. Although the mechanism of an indirect pollution tax looks good, it has certain negative aspects. In measuring the MEC it requires an improved technology which requires a huge cost. At the same time it has cost of compliances to implement.

26.3.2 *Marketable pollution permits (MPP)*

Since a unit tax on effluents generates high compliance as well as administrative costs, another technique is proposed by J. H. Dales. This is a quantity-based marketable or tradable pollution permit system. By setting a standard on the permissible level of pollution, the authority issues permits on par with the quantity of emission. However, whereas the standard setting ends there, the pollution permits are tradable in the sense that any firm can pollute below the level of permit and sells the excess permit to the other firms who pollute more than the standard level. The system allows the construction of a permit market where the right to pollute the environment is traded. Whether a particular polluting unit will be interested in trading or not would depend on the comparative cost of abatement of pollution and the revenue earned through trading of a surplus amount of permit by producing less. If there are two firms, one with high marginal abatement cost and another with low marginal cost of abatement, then instead of trying to abate pollution the former would be interested in buying permits and thereby exceeding the initial assigned permit, whereas the latter would actually abate and sell the surplus permits to the former. The trading equilibrium will be attained by equating the marginal abatement costs of all the firms. The price of permit per unit will be equal to the marginal abatement cost of any firm.

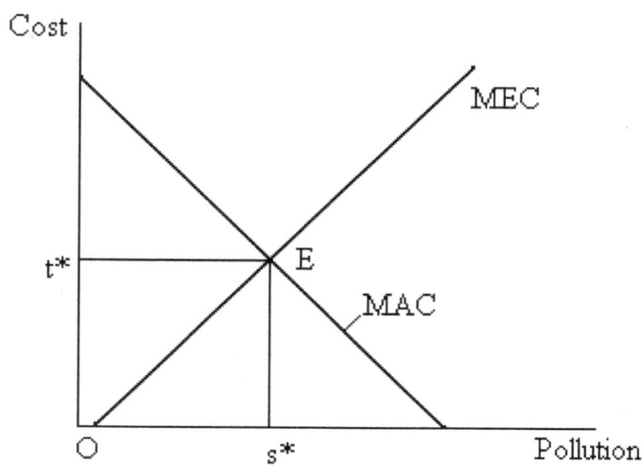

Figure 26.3 A pollution tax

Let s_i be the total emissions by an individual firm. x_i is the total quantity of pollution abated. Therefore, the unit of permit required by the *i*th firm is $(s_i - x_i)$. Suppose $C(x_i)$ is the total cost of abatement. Let *P* be the price of permit per unit. The decision of the firm is to minimise the cost of abatement and permit. The total cost function of the ith firm is

$$TC = C(x_i) + P(s_i - x_i). \tag{26.3}$$

TC will be the minimum, when $dTC / dx_i = 0$.

This means

$$dC / dx_i - P = 0$$
$$Or,\ P = MAC_i. \tag{26.4}$$

This price of permit works as an alternative instrument of pollution control that gives another efficient result so far as objective of social welfare is concerned. It is also of note that the traded zones of permits may not have identical assimilative capacities of nature. If there are differences in nature's assimilative capacities of pollution then the trading of permit should be weighted by a transfer coefficient "d_{ij}" from zone *i* to *j*. Therefore, the efficient allocation of permits will be made when $\Sigma d_{ij} \, . \, P = MAC_i$.

26.4 Trade-off between pollution and growth — the environmental Kuznets curve

The country-specific historical data on the relation between the growth of income (or of per capita income) and interclass inequality shows that, in the early stage of development, as industrialisation process starts, rural labour migrates to the urban (industrial) areas and, as income grows, the gap between the earnings of the rural labour and the industrialists (or entrepreneurs) increases and reaches a maximum limit. After that, the continuation of growth process allows all the other remaining sectors like education, health, empowerment, etc. to improve and as a result of that the magnitude of inequality goes down. This is the inverted-U hypothesis of Simon Kuznets, developed in the 1950s and 1960s. It is popularly known as the Kuznets curve in development economic literature.

Further, Kuznets, in the early 1990s, discovered that the process of industrialisation at the cost of damaging environmental resources also generated increasing cost to society in terms of increasing magnitudes of pollution in the early stage and until it reaches the maximum limit, after that, it continues to go down because of improved technological innovations, increase in awareness of the world population, enactment of international environmental laws, etc. This is again an inverted-U-shaped curve which is popularly known as the environmental Kuznets curve (EKC). Although the subject of continuing debate, some empirical evidence defends the claim that environmental health indicators, such as water and air pollution, show the inverted-U-shaped curve and that this trend occurs on the level of many of the environmental pollutants like nitrogen oxide, sulphur dioxide, chlorofluorocarbons, etc. Figure 26.4 describes the EKC.

Up to y^* level of income, the level of pollution grows with income, and beyond y^* it falls down continuously. The declining part of the EKC may start rising if the technology inventions and innovations stop. *E* is the critical point corresponding to y^* level of income which divides the bad phase from the good phase. Hence, below y^*, there is a

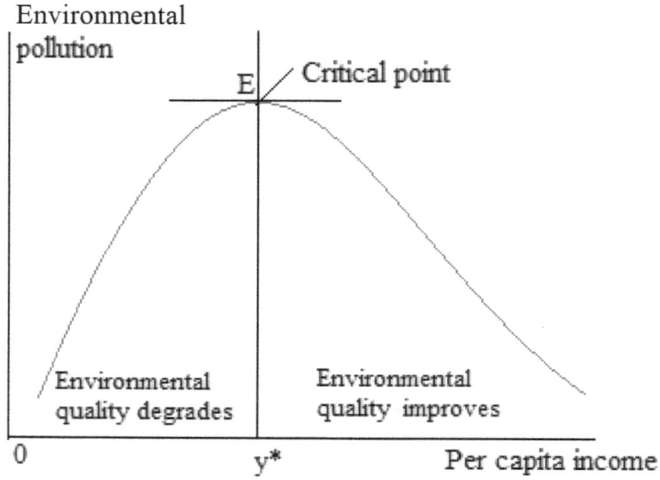

Figure 26.4 Environmental Kuznets curve

trade-off between growth/development and environmental pollution. The countries in the preindustrialisation stage belong to the initial part of the upward rising portion of the EKC and the countries with matured industrialisation also depend upon the service sector-led developments belonging to the last part of the downward sloping portion of the EKC. The industrialised countries in their midterms belong to the periphery of the critical point, *E*.

There are two arguments on the shape of the EKC. In one argument, the EKC suggests that the solution to pollution can be achieved through more economic growth, and contrastingly, pollution is seen as a regrettable output that should be reduced when the benefits brought by its production are exceeded by the costs it imposes in externalities like health decrements and loss of ecosystem services.

26.4.1 Limitations of EKC

The EKC, although a new idea, has many limitations. We point out a few of them here.

i) The empirical evidence does not fully support the prevalence of the EKC. There is no guarantee that economic growth will see a decline in pollutants always.
ii) The EKC relates growth or development with pollution but pollution is not only a function of income; many factors are there to explain pollution. For example, the effectiveness of government regulation, the development of the economy, population levels, etc. play a role in deciding the magnitudes of pollution and hence position of the economy.
iii) Some economists claim that there is a range within which the degree of reduced environmental degradation is will be observed during the post-industrialisation phase. But, if the economy continues to expand, then inevitably some resources will continue to be used in greater measure. Along with that there will be constraints to technological progress. There is no guarantee that long-term levels of environmental degradation will continue to fall. We can then find a N-shaped EKC.

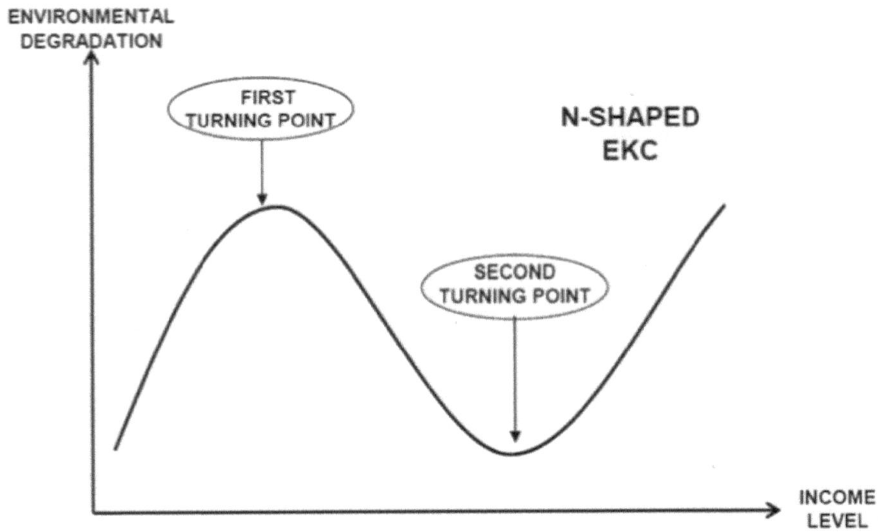

Figure 26.5 The N-shaped environmental Kuznets curve

26.4.2 *The N-shaped environmental Kuznets curve*

The N-shaped EKC suggests that the original EKC hypothesis will not hold in the long run. Instead, beyond a certain income level, increased income might once again lead to a positive relationship between economic growth and environmental degradation. The relationship becomes N-shaped when technological change arises (Figure 26.5). The strength of the relationship is based on a reduced scale and scope to better classify industrial sectors.

Torras and Boyce (1998) suggest that the N-shaped relationship occurs when the scale effect overcomes the composition and technical effects. This might be the consequence of reduced possibilities to further improve distribution of industries or because of diminishing returns on technological changes.

26.5 Green accounting of national output

Environmental degradation in terms of different types of pollution and extraction of resources affects economic output and welfare since the environmental services are considered as part and parcel of human civilisation. Producers use environmental resources to generate economic output but its degradation in the current period will inevitably affect the future generation in terms of cost of living, loss of aesthetic values of environment, etc. Hence, the current economic system should account for this cost of degradation in the current period. The statistical division of the United Nations has developed the System of Environmental Economic Accounting (SEEA) to incorporate the environmental factors into the System of National Accounts (SNA). A new system of sustainable accounting, known as Green Accounting, has thus emerged. Green Accounting permits the computation of income for a nation by taking into account the economic damage and depletion in the natural resource base of an economy. It is a measure of sustainable income level that can be secured without decreasing the stock of natural assets.

The concept of Green National Accounting can be viewed as an extension of the original concept of national economic accounts formalised in the SNA framework.

The basic form of the national accounts as developed in SNA can be summarised as follows:

$$NNP = C + I - D + X - M \tag{26.5}$$

where *NNP* is net national product, *C* is consumption, *I* is investment, *D* is depreciation, *X* is exports, and *M* is imports. Thus, the NNP of an open economy consists of consumption plus net investment (investment minus depreciation) plus net exports (exports minus imports). The theoretical basis for the framework is Keynesian, in that it was developed to be used for the Keynesian macroeconomic analysis and stabilisation policy.

With respect to the valuation of natural resources and environment, SNA has three main flaws. It does not take into account

- The depletion of natural capital such as forests, fishing stock, minerals, etc.
- Defensive or preventive expenditures which the society incurs in facing the external effects of environmental degradation
- Environmental degradation mainly from pollution

To incorporate all the aforementioned issues, the UN's System of Environmental-Economic Accounting (SEEA) (https://unstats.un.org/unsd/envaccounting/seea.asp) is a noble idea of accounting of national output. SEEA's accounting framework is a path towards sustainable development which is a principle for meeting human development goals while at the same time sustaining the ability of natural systems to provide the natural resources and ecosystem services upon which the economy and society depend. The revised national output is thus called the *sustainable NNP (SNNP) or green NNP (GNNP) or environmental domestic product (EDP)*. We will use the terms interchangeably in our following discussions. GNNP includes the economic cost of degrading natural resources which are required to produce goods and services directly and indirectly besides physical wear and tear of physical manmade capital. To compute GNNP, we have to replace net capital accumulation (*I*) with net capital accumulation of produced and non-produced economic assets minus net accumulation of non-produced natural assets. The revised national output identity becomes

$$GNNP = C + NAPEA + (NANPEA - NANPNA) + (X - M) \tag{26.6}$$

where

EDP = Environmental domestic product.
C = Capital accumulation
NAPEA = Net accumulation of produced economic assets.
NANPEA = Net accumulation of non-produced economic assets
NANPNA = Net accumulation of non-produced natural assets
(X – M) = Exports – Imports

26.5.1 Basic structure of SEEA

The United Nations' Statistics Division has structured the Green Accounting System in the form of a matrix containing stocks and flows accounts. There are six columns (flows) and eight rows (stocks) in the structure. There are three broad heads of flow accounts – economic activities, economic assets, and environmental activities under which there are six heads like production, final consumption, produced economic assets, non-produced economic assets, non-produced natural assets, and the rest of the world (X – M). In the stock items, which are the rows, the eight heads are opening stock of the assets, total supply, economic uses, consumption of fixed capital, net national product (NNP), uses of non-produced natural assets, accumulation of non-produced natural assets, and environmentally adjusted aggregates in monetary environmental accounting. Table 26.1 presents the structure of SEEA.

The last row, that is Row 8, gives out to the environmental national product and satisfies the identity as given in the previous equation. The flow chart makes segregation of all stocks and flows of assets related to environment that helps in the estimation of the total expenditure for the protection of the environment. Also it allows the estimating agencies to identify that part of the gross domestic product that reflects the costs necessary to compensate for the negative impacts of economic growth, that is, the preventive expenditures from environmental costs.

26.5.1.1 Some examples of green GDP estimates

There are some examples on the attempts for measuring green GDP in countries and groups. The USA has developed a comprehensive system of environmental-economic accounts that provide various indicators of the interactions between the economy and the environment, environmental expenditures, and environmental taxes. However, the USA does not produce a single measure of green GDP. The US has environmental-economic accounts but no green GDP measure. The EU requires member states to compile accounts covering emissions, taxes, materials, and protection expenditure, which can be used to derive green GDP or adjusted domestic product. Green GDP is not officially measured or reported in India, but some attempts by various researchers and institutions have been made to estimate it. According to a paper published by the Reserve Bank of India in October 2022, researchers estimated the green GDP of India to be somewhere around Rs. 167 trillion for 2019. This implies a reduction of about 10% from the conventional GDP of Rs. 185.8 trillion for the same year.

26.6 Interactions of IS-LM and environmental constraint without conservation capital investment and pollution permit market

Environmental degradation is treated as the by-product of aggregate economic activity comprising consumption, investment, production, etc. which are grouped under aggregate demand side (product and money market) and aggregate supply side in the macroeconomic theory. The traditional macroeconomic theories overlooked the importance of introducing the environmental factor into the construction of economic models. Recently, the development of enormous literature on overall environmental crisis starting from the unearthing of the World Development Report (1992) has motivated the economists and policymakers to accommodate environmental factors in the mainstream economic system. A vast literature has been developed on environmental economics on the basis of

Table 26.1 Structure of SEEA

	Economic activities			*Economic assets*		*Environment*
	(1) Production	*(2) Final Consumption*	*(3) Rest of the World*	*(4) Produced Economic Assets*	*(5) Non-produced Economic Assets*	*(6) Non-produced Natural Assets*
1. Opening Stock of Assets	—	—	—	Opening Stock of Produced Economic Assets	Opening Stock of Non-produced Economic Assets	—
2. Supply	Production	—	Imports	—	—	—
3. Economic Uses	Intermediate Consumption	Final Consumption	Exports	Gross Capital Formation	—	—
4. Consumption of Fixed Capital	Consumption of Fixed Capital	—	—	Negative of Consumption of Fixed Capital	—	—
5. NNP	NNP	Final Consumption	Net Exports	Net Capital Accumulation (= Investment or I)	—	—
6. Uses of Non-produced Natural Assets	Uses of Non-produced Natural Assets in Production System	—	—	—	Negative of Uses of Non-produced Economic Natural Assets	Degradation of Non-economic Natural Assets
7. Accumulation of Non-produced Natural Assets	—	—	—	—	Change in the Stock of Non-produced Economic Assets	Decrease in Natural Assets other than Economic Assets
8. Environmentally adjusted aggregates in monetary environmental accounting	GNNP	Final Consumption	Net Exports (X – M)	Net Accumulation of Produced Economic Assets (NAPEA)	Net Accumulation of Non-produced Economic Assets (NANPEA)	Net Accumulation of Non-produced Natural Assets (NANPNA)

pure micro foundations. The work of Anthony Heyes (2000) is probably the first that tried to directly superimpose the environmental constraints into the traditional macroeconomic where the well-known Keynesian aggregate demand-side equilibrium (IS-LM model) has been analysed in the presence of environmental sustainability in the long run.

In his commentary note, Prof. Heyes attempted to establish the environmental macroeconomic equilibrium with the assumption that environmental sensitivity with respect to rate of interest dominates the sensitivity of investment with respect to the rate of interest and hence the combination of fiscal-monetary policies necessary to maintain environmental sustainability was discussed. In the following sections we will first build up the IS-LM model and an environment constraint function and re-establish the aggregate economy's equilibrium in the presence of the environmental constraint function. Then we focus all the policy implications made by Prof. Heyes and will add other policies under different conditions of physical as well as environmental capital's sensitivity to rate of interest.

26.6.1 *The basic model*

To exhibit the model, we adopt the basic Keynesian product and money market equilibrium with standard notations. The standard equation of IS curve is given by

$$y = C(y - T) + I(r) + G \tag{26.7}$$

and equation of LM curve is given by

$$M_0 = L(y, r) \tag{26.8}$$

Here P, being the general price level, is taken as fixed and so the corresponding product supply curve is perfectly elastic.

The slope of the IS curve is

$$dr / dy = (1 - c_y) / I_r < 0$$

The slope of IS curve is as usual negative since $I_r < 0$ and $0 < c_y < 1$. The slope of the LM curve is

$$dr / dy = -\ L_y / L_r > 0.$$

The slope of LM curve is positive as usual since $L_y > 0$ and $L_r < 0$.

Any point outside the curves represents dis-equilibrium in either of the markets and the intersection between them generates the only output and interest level where both the markets are in equilibrium. But such equilibrium values of "*y*" and "*r*" are free from any sort of environmental bottlenecks.

26.6.2 *Introduction of the environmental constraint*

Earlier we have mentioned that economic activity generates environmental pollution as a by-product; alternatively economic activity requires environment (*E*) as an additional input for the accommodation of production residues like smoke, solid waste, noise, etc. Again ambient environment has its own assimilative or renewable capacity which is termed as the carrying capacity of the environment. Hence aggregate economic activity will be viable only when total use of environment is identical to its total regenerative capacity.

Let "e" be the environment intensity of the economic activity which is treated as one type of factor intensity and it can be determined by aggregate choice of techniques. Environment, being the natural capital, has substitution possibility with the physical capital or investment such that $I_r < 0$ leads to $e_r > 0$ i.e. when physical capital is costlier, the producer will go for less pollution abatement activity and use more natural capital and vice-versa. Again "*e*" can be induced by the institutional factor "Δ" which captures environmental regulation. For example, to control environmental degradation, the authority can apply per-unit tax on the polluter, or it can impose a pollution quota on the sources, etc. Therefore, the range of Δ will be $0 \leq \Delta \leq 1$ and the factor intensity function will be $e = e(r, \Delta)$ where $e_r > 0$, $e_\Delta < 0$, and $e_{r,}\ \Delta < 0$. The environment intensity economic activity is increasing in the cost of capital and decreasing in the extent to which environmental costs are internal to the user. Total employment of environmental services by the economy is, therefore, $e(r, \Delta)\ y$.

Let *Et* be the physical stock of environment as capital at the time "*t*" and it is assumed that it self-renews by the amount $s.E_t$, where "*s*" is the rate of renewal. So the total environmental degradation is expressed as

$$-(dE / dt) = e(r,\ \Delta)\ .\ y - s\ .\ E. \tag{26.9}$$

The steady-state environment or the long run environmental stability requires

$$(dE / dt) = 0 \tag{26.10}$$

$$Or,\ e(r,\ \Delta)\ .\ y = s\ .\ E. \tag{26.11}$$

Therefore, the steady-state environment curve (*EE*) depends upon "*y*" and "*r*" like IS-LM. The slope of the environmental constraint function under the steady-state condition can be derived in the following way. Taking total differentiation to the previous equation we get

$$(\partial e / \partial r) dr\ .\ y + e(r,\ \Delta)\ .\ dy = 0$$
$$Or,\ e_r\ .\ dr\ .\ y + e(r,\ \Delta)\ .\ dy = 0^{\cdot}$$

Now the slope of the *EE* curve under steady-state condition is

$$dr / dy = -\ e\ (r,\ \Delta) / e_r\ .\ y < 0 \tag{26.12}$$

The slope of the EE curve is negative since $e_r > 0$. Along the *EE* curve, there is a steady-state condition prevailing in the nature's system in the sense that total use of environmental services by economic activity is just equal to the renewal of the environmental services by the natural process (or $dE / dt = 0$). Outside the *EE* curve there is disequilibrium in the environmental services. To the right of the *EE* curve is degradation of environment (or $dE / dt < 0$) and to the left of it is environmental upgradation (or $dE / dt > 0$). Hence, economic activities should match with any point on the *EE* curve. We will now have to group the IS, LM and the *EE* curve into a single diagram to establish the commodity and money market equilibrium under the presence of environmental constraint given by the negatively sloped *EE* curve. Just as Mundell and Fleming superimposed the balance of payment (BOP) line into the IS-LM framework and divided the area outside the BOP line as deficit or surplus in the open economy trade (refer to Chapter 21), Prof. Heyes introduced the *EE* curve indicating environment degradation and enhancement for the rightward and leftward areas respectively.

It is seen that both IS and EE curves are of the same sign in their slopes. In the work of Heyes, it is considered that *EE* is steeper than IS which is the sensitivity of investment to "r" is higher than sensitivity of environment to "*r*". But the reverse case may arise and that has been considered sincerely in the following discussions.

26.6.3 Environmental macroeconomic equilibrium

The aggregate economic activity will be sustainable in terms of long run condition of the environmental capacity when all three curves (IS, LM and EE) intersect with each other (associating Equation 26.7, 26.8, and 26.11). Figures 26.6 and 26.7 present the equilibrium.

We have drawn two *EE* curves; one is relatively steeper and the other is relatively flatter than the IS function. The flatter *EE* curve is shown by the dotted marks. *E* is the point where there are balances in commodity market, money market, and sustainability in the environment. This point is called the IS-LM-EE equilibrium which generated y^* and r^* levels of income and rate of interest respectively. Any activity beyond the ecological carrying capacity creates environmental degradation and reduces the long run sustainable development potential of the economy.

The aggregate economic activity will be sustainable in terms of long run condition of the environmental capacity when all three curves (IS, LM, and EE) intersect each other. The equilibrium output y^* is supposed to correspond to the full employment level. Any activity beyond the ecological carrying capacity creates environmental degradation and reduces the long run sustainable development potential of the economy.

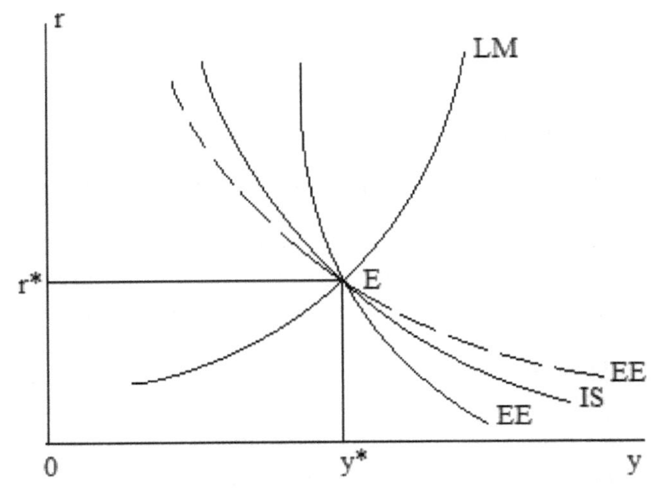

Figure 26.6 IS-LM-EE equilibrium

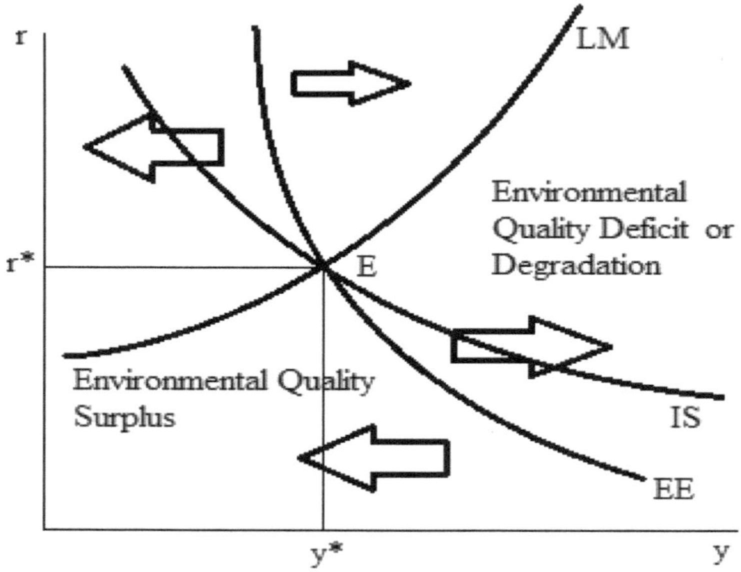

Figure 26.7 The IS-LM-EE equilibrium with manifestations of environmental quality

Right to the EE curve with either of the same *y* or *r*, the increase in any of the two leads to environmental degradation. For example, if y^* is fixed and rate of interest increases, to the right of *EE*, investment for physical capital decreases, and due to substitute relationships, the use of natural capital will increase, leading to environmental degradation. On the other hand, with the same *r* at r^*, as income increases to the right of *EE*, rate of interest will increase due to increase in demand for money. Hence, physical investment will go down and natural capital use will go up, leading to environmental degradation. The reverse scenario, that is environmental surplus or conservation or environmental quality improvement, will occur when the economy stays to the left of the *EE*.

26.6.4 *Comparative static analysis*

The comparative static analysis in the presence of environmental constraint is done in line with that of textbook macroeconomics. Here the analysis is done with respect to fiscal-monetary policy combinations, export promotion, and monetary policy combinations under the same specification regarding sensitivity with respect to "*r*" as we have stated earlier. For each of the policy combinations, we have considered two sub-cases on the basis of the differences in sensitivities of physical and natural capital to rate of interest. The differences in sensitivities will make the *EE* curve either steeper or flatter than the IS function.

26.6.4.1 *Case I:* combination of fiscal and monetary policies

The two sub-cases to this previous case are as follows.

26.6.4.1.1 SENSITIVITY OF INVESTMENT TO "*R*" OUTWEIGHS THE SENSITIVITY OF ENVIRONMENT TO "*R*"

This is the case when slope of the *IS* curve is less than the slope of the *EE* curve. Suppose expansionary fiscal policy (FP) is introduced. The increase in government spending leads the economy to demand more output $y_1 > y^*$ (Figure 26.8) which creates environmental damage since new IS-LM equilibrium exists to the right of the *EE* curve. If long run sustainability of the environment is to be maintained, then the economy should be contracted through tight monetary policy (MP) which further leads the economy to generate less output $y_0 < y^* < y_1$. Therefore, to maintain the environmental stability, expansionary fiscal policy should be combined with the contractionary monetary policy.

Again, if the monetary expansion is initially introduced, the result will be the generation of more demand-side output $y_1 > y^*$ (Figure 26.9) and it creates environmental degradation. To control such degradation, the product market should be contracted through tight fiscal policy by means of increase in tax rates, which will lead the economy to the new equilibrium *F* and produce less output $y_2 < y_1$, but the sustainable output in this situation which is y_2 is more than the output prior to the comparative static analysis. But in the first case, which is starting with the fiscal policy first, the sustainable output (y_1) was less than that of the initial point *E*.

26.6.4.1.2 SENSITIVITY OF ENVIRONMENT TO "*R*" OUTWEIGHS THE SENSITIVITY OF INVESTMENT TO "*R*"

This is the situation when slope of IS is greater than the slope of *EE* curve. We have presented the fiscal and monetary policy effects in Figures 26.10 and 26.11. In both the figures, the relatively steeper *EE* curve intersects IS-LM at point *E* and produces y^* level of income and r^* level of rate of interest. Let us first introduce the expansionary FP. The aggregative output will rise from y^* to y_1 (Figure 26.9) and the new aggregative demand-side equilibrium (*F*) generates environmental degradation since *F* is to the right of the *EE* curve. To control such damage, expansionary MP is necessary, leading to further rise in output to y_2. Here it is observed that both the policies are to be expansionary in nature.

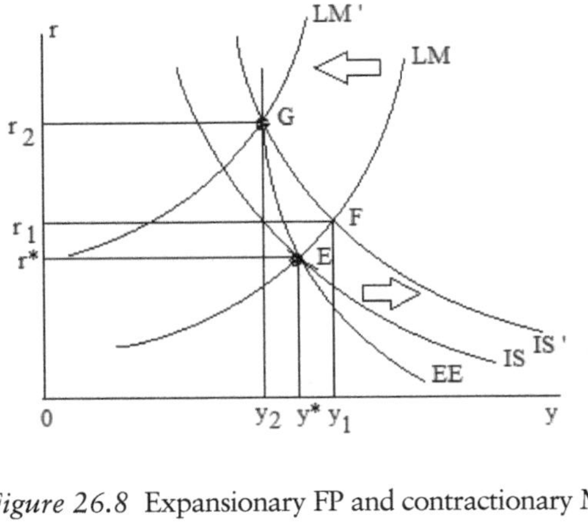

Figure 26.8 Expansionary FP and contractionary MP

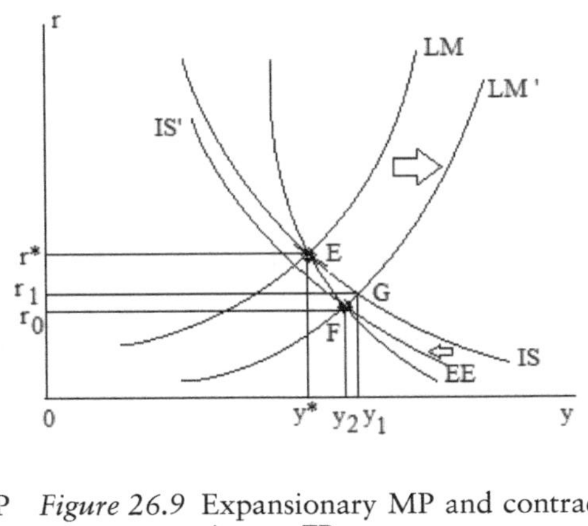

Figure 26.9 Expansionary MP and contractionary FP

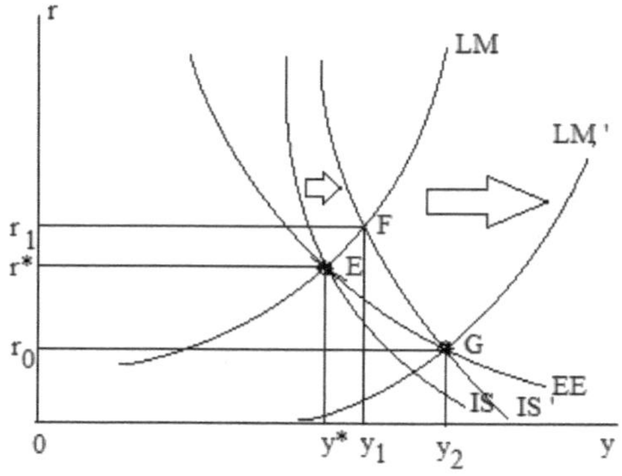

Figure 26.10 Expansionary FP and expansionary MP

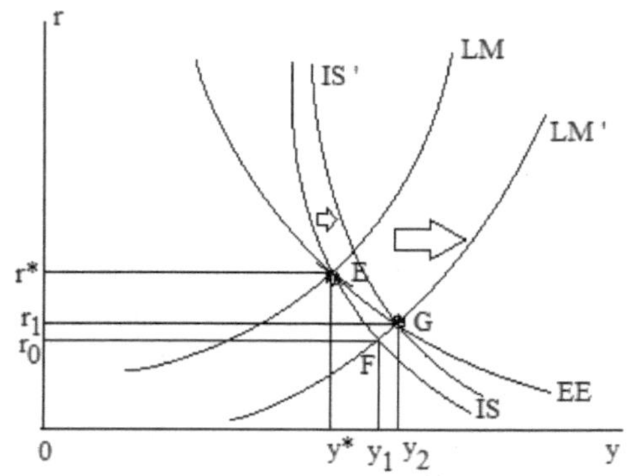

Figure 26.11 Expansionary MP and expansionary FP

Alternatively, if the expansionary MP is initially attempted, then the policy will raise output to $y_1 > y^*$ (Figure 26.11), leading to environmental betterment. If environmental betterment is to be maintained (i.e. pollution-free environment) then no FP is required. But, if the objective is to maintain the steady-state growth of environmental services, then expansionary FP can be taken, which will further raise output to y_2. So, expansionary MP is accompanied by a conditional expansionary FP.

26.6.4.2 *Case II: export promotion or import substitution*

Incorporation of foreign transaction into the autarkic product market equilibrium will design the IS-equation as $Y = C(y - T) + I(r) + G_0 + [X_0 - M(y)]$ where X_0 is autonomous export and M is induced import demand. The slope of IS in the open economy case (which we have already established in the open economy macroeconomics chapter) is

$$dr\,/\,dy = \left(1 - c_y - M_y\right) /\, I_r < 0$$

since $I_r < 0$ and $0 < c_y < 1$, $M_y > 0$ and $c_y + My < 1$.

M_y is the propensity to import. So the IS curve is still negatively sloped but relatively flatter under the open economy framework since $M_y > 0$ has been deducted from the numerator.

26.6.4.2.1 SLOPE OF IS CURVE IS LESS THAN THAT OF THE EE CURVE

A policy of export promotion (EP) or import substitution (MS) (to make favourable balance of payments) leads the IS curve to shift rightward from IS to IS′, producing demand-side output $y_2 > y^*$ at point F (Figure 26.12). There is degradation of environment at the new equilibrium point. The management of such degradation may be done either by internal arrangements or by external pressure (like restricting the production of dirty goods). The proper policy will now be the tight monetary policy to maintain steady-state environment and thereby generating lower output $y_1 < y^*$. If Y_1 is taken to be full-employment level of output, then even under external pressure the economy will try to compromise the environmental loss.

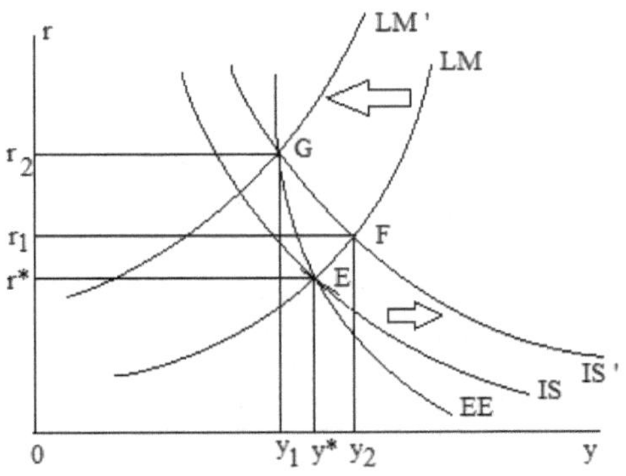

Figure 26.12 EP and contractionary MP

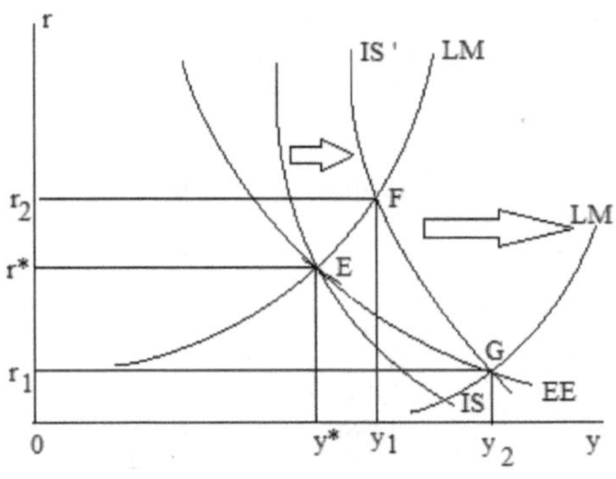

Figure 26.13 EP and expansionary MP

26.6.4.2.2 SLOPE OF IS CURVE IS GREATER THAN THAT OF THE EE CURVE

Here, as the economy goes for export promotion, output will rise to y_1 with environmental degradation (Point F in Figure 26.13). To maintain sustainability of environment, expansionary monetary policy will be required which will further raise output to y_2. Therefore, export promotion (or import substitution) will be accompanied by expansionary monetary policy. The readers may try out other policy packages like export-competitiveness, the change in "Δ" etc. and their corresponding effects on the aggregate output and environment.

Therefore, so far as our analysis in concerned, it is seen that if the sensitivity of investment to rate of interest is more than that of the environment as substitute to physical capital, among both the policies, if one being expansionary then other will be contractionary in nature. But under the reverse case, that is, when the relative sensitivity changes, both the policies will be expansionary in nature simultaneously.

Box II Case study for China, the USA, and India (world's three largest emitters of CO_2), in computing sensitivity of I and E with respect to rate of interest (r) i.e. for *dI / dr* and *dE / dr*

Year	*Sensitivity of I with respect to* r			*Sensitivity of E with respect to* r		
	China	*USA*	*India*	*China*	*USA*	*India*
1980	0	0	0	0	0	0
1981	-0.44	0.55	0	0.0135	0.0031	0
1982	0	-0.04	0	0	0.0023	0
1983	0	2.28	0	0	-0.0069	0
1984	6.64	0.43	0	-0.0883	0.0035	0
1985	-132.28	0.28	0	5.1711	0.0034	0
1986	0	0.93	0	0	0.0129	0
1987	1.64	-0.71	0	-0.0472	-0.0028	0

Year	*Sensitivity of I with respect to* r			*Sensitivity of E with respect to* r		
	China	*USA*	*India*	*China*	*USA*	*India*
1988	−0.86	−0.20	0	−0.0279	−0.0036	0
1989	1.60	1.14	0	0.0079	0.0021	0
1990	−1.57	0.92	−3.38	0.0117	0.0023	0.0376
1991	0	0.01	1.31	0	0.0014	−0.0007
1992	1.88	−1.26	0.35	0.0065	0.0091	−0.0062
1993	0	0.78	−1.86	0	−0.0028	0.0171
1994	−1.17	0.00	0.85	−0.0823	−0.0015	−0.0119
1995	0.66	−0.77	−3.50	0.0252	0.0027	−0.0031
1996	1.41	4.14	−0.98	0.0274	−0.0187	0.0017
1997	0.29	−6.27	5.15	0.0168	0.034	−0.0053
1998	1.32	−1.28	−2.67	0.0362	0.0081	0.0047
1999	0	0.21	10.43	0	−0.0016	−0.0118
2000	0	0.65	0.10	0	0.0012	0.0315
2001	−1.21	0.21	−3.34	−0.0026	0.0006	0.0602
2002	0	−0.06	−4.99	0	0.0038	0.0526
2003	8.38	4.21	−12.15	−0.0223	−0.0106	0.0339
2004	0	0.39	−11.93	0	−0.0016	0.0847
2005	−0.85	0.09	1.88	−0.0384	−0.0018	−0.0223
2006	0.41	−10.23	1.65	−0.0286	−0.0144	−0.0132
2007	−0.84	0.50	−13.99	0.0152	0.0007	0.0503
2008	0	1.80	−2.01		0.0012	0.0004
2009	2.40	0	−0.03	−0.025	0	0.0071
2010	0.14	0	−0.34	−0.0205	0	−0.0016
2011	0.76	0	−2.84	0.0204	0	0.0203
2012		0	13.84	0	0	0.003
2013	0.91	0	−5.87	0.0207	0	−0.0158
2014	1.28	−28.64	8.90	0.0047	0.2039	-8E-05
2015	0	−2.62	5.67	0	−0.0281	0.0048
2016	0	0.46	−4.44	0	−0.013	0.0073
2017	0	0.43	−6.77	0	−0.0094	0.0252
Average	**−4.76**	**−0.99**	**−1.11**	**0.22**	**0.01**	**0.01**

Note: the blank cells show zero values as there were no changes in interest rates in these years. The values of $dE / dr > 0$ and $dI / dr < 0$, and the absolute values of dE / dr are smaller than dI / dr which means EE curves are steeper than the IS curves of the countries.

Source: the computation was done by the authors using the World Bank data on CO_2 and rate of interest.

26.7 Interactions of IS-LM and environmental constraint with conservation capital investment and pollution permit market

With an advancement over earlier works, mainly of Heyes (2000), Lawn (2003a, b) and Sim (2006) have attempted to make the IS-LM-EE framework to add more policies besides the fiscal and monetary ones. Lawn (2003a, b) has used the same IS-LM-EE model adding the technological progress and pollution permit factors. Lawn has used IS-LM-EE and illustrated that monetary policy of either form in response to expansionary fiscal policy may not be required to maintain sustainability of the economic and environmental activities if continuous progress is made in favour of greener technologies. Unlike Lawn (2003a, b), Sim (2006) has proposed a model of IS-LM with EE to derive a socially optimum solution. In fact, Sim (2006) has showed that fiscal or monetary shocks are required to reach the simultaneous intersection of all three schedules reached through a naturally adjusting process. Moreover, Sim (2006) has shown that the expansionary fiscal policy may lead to poor environmental quality and lower planned expenditure. Under such circumstances Sim (2006) has proposed strict environmental regulatory standards to reach higher output levels in the long run. Decker and Wohar (2012) have assumed that physical capital and natural resources are complements to each other and find a positively sloped EE schedule. The new EE schedule gives new results following fiscal and monetary policies. In the recent past, Zhang and Lee (2017) have also considered complementarity between physical capital and natural capital under the IS-LM-EE structure to justify the stability and policy significance of the equilibrium point. Here we present the approach considered by Lawn (2003).

26.7.1 *Lawn's approach: introducing technological progress and permit market*

To present Lawn's approach we modify the energy intensity function and the environmental sustainability function of Heyes by introducing the technological factor and the pollution permit price. Let "e" be the environment intensity of the economic activity (e.g. emission/GDP) which is treated as one type of factor intensity and it can be determined by aggregate choice of techniques. The environment, being the natural capital, has substitution possibility with the physical capital or investment, such that $I_r < 0$ leads to $e_r > 0$, which is, when physical capital is costlier, the producer will go for a decreased pollution abatement activity and use more natural capital. Again "e" can be induced by the institutional factor "Δ" which captures environmental regulation (Heyes, 2000) and by the technological progress factor, β (Lawn, 2003a, b), for generating low pollution and energy saving production inputs. To control environmental degradation, the authority can apply unit tax on the polluters, or it can impose a pollution quota on the sources, etc. Therefore, the range of Δ will be $0 \le \Delta \le 10$. Further, as the value of β increases, "e" falls, and as a result Y increases. Hence, the factor intensity function will be $e = e(r, \Delta, \beta)$, where $e_r > 0$, $e_\Delta < 0$ and $e_{r,\Delta} < 0$ and $e_\beta < 0$. The environment intensity economic activity is increasing in the cost of capital (r) and decreasing in the extent to which environmental costs are internal to the user and technological progress. Total employment of environmental services by the economy is, therefore, $e(r, \Delta, \beta)Y$.

Δ, β

Let "E" be the physical stock of environment as capital at the time "t" and let us assume that it self-renews by the amount sE, where "s" is the rate of renewal. So, the total environmental degradation is expressed as

$$-(dE/dt) = -\dot{E} = e(r, \Delta, \beta) . Y - s . E. \qquad (26.13)$$

The steady-state environment or the long run environmental stability requires $\dot{E} = 0$

$$Or, \ e(r, \Delta, \beta) . Y = s . E. \qquad (26.14)$$

Under Lawn's approach, $e = e(r, \Delta, \beta)$ where β stands for technological progress towards greener capital with $de / d\beta < 0$. According to Lawn, there is a maximum limit of β and for that reason, output expansion sticks to *Ymax*. And there is a pollution permit market which runs when there is disequilibrium in EE. Permit price (PMC) has close association with the general price level (*P*), which is $P = f(PMC)$ and $dP / dPMC > 0$. If there is environmental degradation (to the right of EE) then there is additional demand for permit which pushes the price of permit up, which further leads to increase in *P* and reduces the real money balance (M / P) leading to endogenous monetary contraction due to expansionary FP unlike exogenous monetary contraction as in Heyes. And reversely, to the left of EE, permit price goes down, M / P increases and there is endogenous monetary expansion due to contractionary FP.

26.7.1.1 *Effects of expansionary fiscal policy*

Figure 26.14 presents the expansionary FP effects. There are different positions of the EE curve depending on the level of technological progress measured by the values of the parameter, β. As the value of β increases the EE curve shifts rightward, generating more output in the long run and becoming inelastic. Y_{max} is the vertical line depicting maximum output that can be obtained by using all of the technological progress endowed with the economy. This is the limit to technological progress with the available scientific knowledge. *E* is the initial sustainable equilibrium with IS1 and LM1. Adopting exogenous expansionary increase in public expenses with unchanged monetary instruments, the new equilibrium of the goods and money sector becomes F, which generates more output. However, that extra output is not sustainable as there is environmental degradation through high entropy generation. Such an environmental degradation will require demand for pollution permits, which will push up the cost of production and general price level through inflationary effects. As a result, real money balance (M / P)

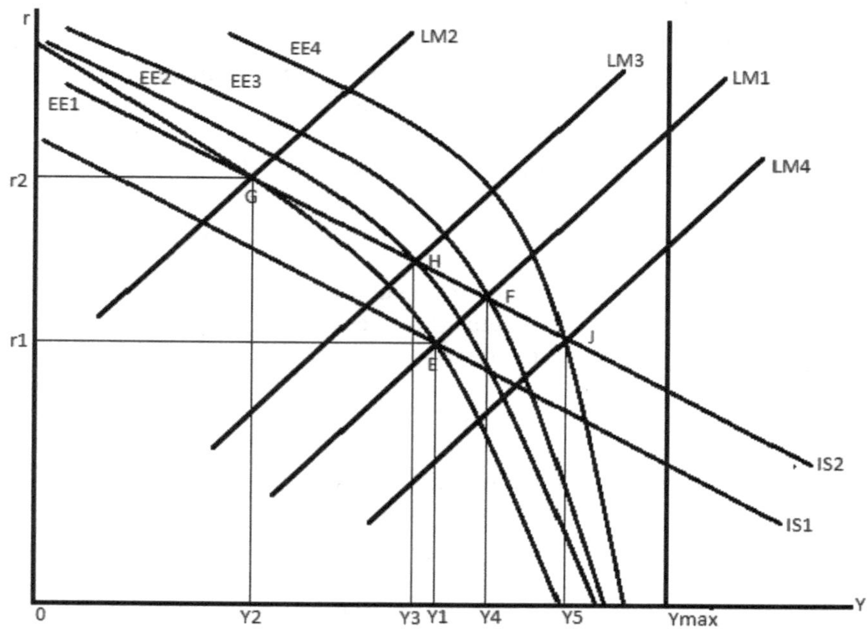

Figure 26.14 Effects of expansionary fiscal policy

will go down, leading to leftward shifting of LM to LM2, where sustainable equilibrium is reached at G, but this is accompanied by a low level of output. Lawn then proposed that technological progress in favour of green technology, in place of paying permit costs, would reduce the cost of production and price of the goods. This, in turn, would increase real balance and result in LM shifting rightward to LM3, LM4 . . . . depending on the level of technological progress. Once it may reach that the price level goes down below the initial value as represented through LM1.

Hence, exogenous expansionary FP will be accommodated first by contractionary endogenous monetary policy and then by expansionary endogenous monetary policy until *Ymax* is reached. There is no limit to this expansion till *Ymax*.

26.7.1.2 Effects of expansionary monetary policy

Figure 26.15 explains Lawn's approach on the effect of an exogenous monetary expansion through an increase in money supply with an unchanged fiscal policy. Initial equilibrium of the goods sector, monetary sector, and environmental sustainability is attained at E with the combination of IS1-LM1-EE1. (*Y1* and *r1*) is the combination of income and rate of interest. An expansionary MP creates a new demand-side equilibrium at F, where there is more output and less rate of interest. As the expansionary monetary policy is undertaken, the new equilibrium shifts to F which is accompanied with high permit cost and high goods price (P) which pushes back LM to LM1 with a low *y*. Hence, monetary policy is not effective. Heyes argued for contractionary FP to increase output.

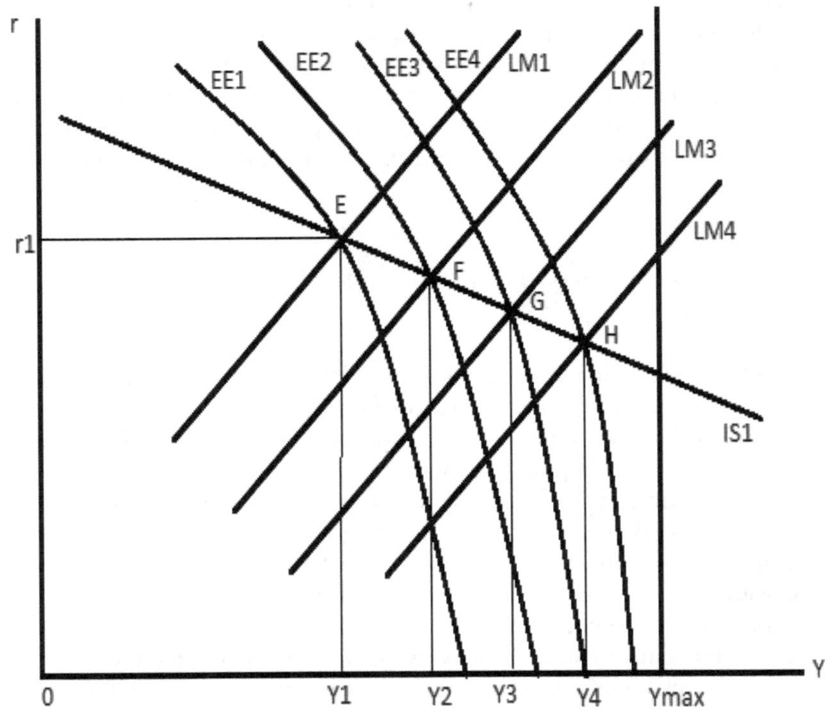

Figure 26.15 Effects of an exogenous monetary expansion

To avoid output loss, according to Lawn, technological progress might help *P* to go down leading the rightward shift of LM until *Ymax*. With technological progress in favour of the environment, Lawn suggested that prices will go down and LM will shift rightward along new EE curves (EE2, EE3, EE4 . . .). Output will increase continuously with technological progress until *Ymax* is reached, which Lawn recommended. Hence, LM will freely move along the initial IS with technological progress.

To conclude, the literature on the effectiveness of the fiscal and monetary policies in a green macroeconomic equilibrium starts with the combinations of one's expansionary and other's contractionary effects under Heyes. Then Lawn introduced the impact of permit cost and technological progress and concluded that expansionary FP is accommodated with endogenous monetary policy and the technological effects bring price level down, leading to continuous rightward shifting of the LM curve until *Ymax* is reached. On the other hand, the exogenous expansionary monetary policy effects lead to first monetary contraction due to permit cost and then the technological progress make rightward shift until *Ymax* is reached.

26.8 Conclusion

We got a new idea about macroeconomics subject as Green Macroeconomics by incorporating the environmental costs into determination of principal variable, national income. We did it through micro foundations where optimum level of pollution was determined. To control pollution, there were the policies like taxation, tradable pollution permits to internalise all the costs of environmental pollution. In computing national income after the inclusion of environmental factors, which is known as green national income, the traditional SNA has been replaced by UN's concept SEEA. In addition to that the inclusion of environmental sustainability function has been inserted upon the traditional IS-LM model to determine the optimum income and rate of interest and accordingly the policies like expansionary fiscal and monetary policy, and export promotion are attempted and a set of mixed results are obtained on equilibrium income and rate of interest.

Summary

The prominent results we observed from the whole chapter can be addressed by the following summary results:

- Optimum level of pollution can be maintained at a point where the marginal benefit from pollution is equal to the social marginal cost.
- Environmental pollution can be solved or internalised into the product price by means of pollution tax or tradable pollution permits.
- The SNA of estimating national income has been replaced by SEEA of UN to incorporate the environmental cost into the estimation procedure
- Introduction of environmental sustainability curve into the IS-LM model provides new dimension to the demand-side macroeconomics. Different policy combinations are prescribed under the conditions that interest sensitivity of physical investment is greater or smaller than the interest sensitivity of the environmental capital.
- When physical investment's sensitivity to rate of interest is more than that of the environment, then expansionary fiscal policy is accompanied by contractionary monetary policy and if the condition gets reversed then both the policies are expansionary in nature to maintain environmental sustainability.

- Lawn introduced the impact of permit cost and technological progress and concluded that expansionary FP is accommodated with endogenous monetary policy and the technological effects make price level down leading to continuous rightward shifting of the LM curve until *Ymax* is reached. On the other hand, the exogenous expansionary monetary policy effects lead to first monetary contraction due to permit cost and then the technological progress make a rightward shift until *Ymax* is reached.

Keywords

Environmental pollution
Environmental cost
Pollution tax
Green national income
Environmental sustainability
Fiscal policy
Monetary policy
Export promotion

Multiple choice questions and answers

1. Environment is a public good since

   (a) It is equally available for all.
   (b) It is controlled by the government.
   (c) It is a national asset.
   (d) None of the above.

2. Optimum pollution is attained when

   (a) Marginal net private benefit = Marginal social cost.
   (b) Marginal net social benefit = Marginal social cost.
   (c) Marginal net private benefit = Marginal private cost.
   (d) All of the above.

3. Environmental pollution can be fully internalised, as prescribed by Pigou, when

   (a) Per unit tax = Marginal externality cost.
   (b) Per unit tax = Marginal externality cost = Marginal cost of abatement.
   (c) Per unit tax = Marginal private cost.
   (d) (a) or (b) or both.

4. Green national income accounting takes into account the

   (a) Depreciation of physical capital.
   (b) Depreciation of physical as well as natural capital.
   (c) Pollution tax.
   (d) None of the above.

5. When physical investment's sensitivity of rate of interest outweighs the environmental sensitivity of rate of interest, then policy combination for maintaining environmental stability will be

   (a) Expansionary fiscal and monetary policy.
   (b) Contractionary fiscal and monetary policy.
   (c) Expansionary fiscal policy and contractionary monetary policy.
   (d) None of the above.

Answers

1. (a); 2. (a); 3. (d); 4. (b); 5. (c)

Review questions

1. Define public good. Is environment a public good? Explain with proper arguments.
2. Why is pollution an externality? Can market rule work when there is externality in production or consumption? Explain.
3. What is optimum pollution? Explain how optimum pollution is determined in a cost–benefit framework.
4. What is known as internalisation of externality? Explain how pollution tax and tradable pollution permits internalise the effect of pollution into commodity prices to control pollution.
5. Define Green NNP and write down its expression. Discuss how welfare is affected by the inclusion of green accounting in GDP of a country.
6. What is green accounting in national income? Discuss the method of accounting national income in the presence of environmental factors as per the United Nation's methodology.
7. Write down the equation of the sustainability of environment. Mention the condition when steady state or equilibrium in the use of natural capital is attained.
8. Derive the slope of the EE curve. Explain the shapes of EE curve when environment is fully sensitive or not at all sensitive to the rate of interest.
9. Explain the effectiveness of fiscal and monetary policies upon sustainable income and rate of interest under the conditions of no pollution permit system and no investment upon conservation capital.
10. What is the meaning of the sensitivity of natural capital to rate of interest? Explain in this context the substitutability and complementarity between physical and natural capital. How will the shapes and slopes of the EE curve differ under the substitutability and complementarity relationships? Explain.
11. What is environmental sustainability? Explain how different policy combinations become effective in restoring environmental sustainability when environment is sensitive to rate of interest like physical investment.
12. Explain how the pollution permit market works and how it is related to general price level of an economy. Discuss the role of technological progress towards natural capital formation upon the positions of the EE curve.
13. Explain the effectiveness of fiscal and monetary policies upon sustainable income and rate of interest under the presence of the conditions of pollution permit system and investment upon conservation capital.
14. A question on the mental ability test: do you think "capacity utilisation" may play a role in countering the model of Lawn (2003) regarding the effectiveness of fiscal and monetary policies? Try to answer intuitively.

Additional readings

Ayres, R. & Ayres, L. (1996). *Industrial Ecology: Towards Closing the Materials Cycle*. Cheltenham, UK: Edward Elgar.

Centre for Science & Environment. (1998). *Slow Murder – The Deadly Story of Vehicular Pollution in India*. New Delhi: Jain Book Agency. www.jainbookagency.com/newdetails.aspx?id=7611

Costanza, R. & Daly, H. E. (1992). "Natural capital and sustainable development". *Conservation Biology*, 6, 37–46. http://doi.org/10.1046/j.1523-1739.1992.610037.x

Das, R. C. (ed) (2023). *Economic, Environmental and Health Consequences of Conservation Capital: A Global Perspective*. Singapore: Springer Nature.

Decker, S. & Wohar, M. E. (2012). "Substitutability or complementarity? Re-visiting Heyes' IS-LM-EE model". *Ecological Economics*, 74, 3–7.

FAO. (2013). *Tackling Climate Change through Livestock: A Global Assessment of Emissions and Mitigation Opportunities*. Rome. www.fao.org/3/i3437e/i3437e.pdf

Green, K., Morton, B. & New, S. (2000). "Greening organizations: Purchasing, consumption, and innovation". *Organization & Environment*, 13(2). https://doi.org/10.1177/1086026600132003

Hayes, A. (2000). "A proposal for the greening of textbook macroeconomics: IS-LM-EE". *Ecological Economics*, 32(1), 1–8.

Lawn, P. A. (2003a). "On Heyes' IS-LM – EE proposal to establish an environmental macroeconomics". *Environment and Development Economics*, 8, 31–56, Cambridge University Press.

Lawn, P. A. (2003b). "Environmental macroeconomics: Extending the IS-LM model to include an 'environmental equilibrium' curve". *Australian Economic Papers*, 42(1), 118–134.

Nature Conservancy and Corporate EcoForum. (2012). *Failing to Protect Nature's Capital Could Cost Businesses Trillions*. www.iucn.org/content/failing-protect-natures-capital-could-cost-businesses-trillions

Pearce, D. H. K. & Atkinson, G. (1996). "Measuring sustainable development: Progress on indicators". *Environment and Development Economics*, 1(1), 85–101.

Sim, N. C. S. (2006). "Environmental Keynesian macroeconomics: Some further discussion". *Ecological Economics*, 59(4), 401–405.

Torras, M. & Boyce, J. K. (1998). "Income, inequality, and pollution: A reassessment of the environmental Kuznets curve". *Ecological Economics*, 25(2), 147–160.

World Economic Forum. (2020). *Half of World's GDP Moderately or Highly Dependent on Nature, Davos, Switzerland*. www.weforum.org/press/2020/01

Zhang, M. R. & Lee, C. M. (2017). "Economic policy of sustainable development based on IS-LM-EE model". *Applied Ecology and Environmental Research*, 15(3), 785–795.

Index

FSC
www.fsc.org
MIX
Papier | Fördert
gute Waldnutzung
FSC® C083411

Kolibri 360 GmbH
Ferdinand-Jühlke-Straße 7
99095 Erfurt, Deutschland
produktsicherheit@kolibri360.de